OSWAL – GURUKUL

CBSE CLASS XII

36 SAMPLE QUESTION PAPERS

2021 EXAMINATION

SCIENCE STREAM (PCB)

English Core, Physical Education, Physics, Chemistry, Biology

New Sample Question Paper Released by CBSE in Sept 2021 (Fully Solved)

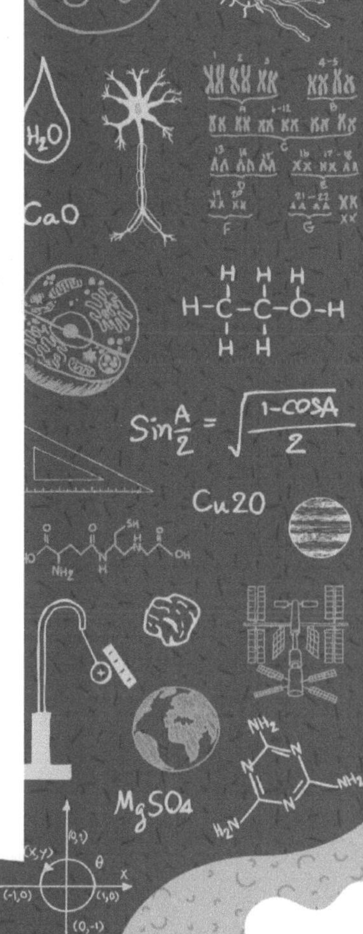

BY
PANEL OF AUTHORS

DISCLAIMER

With the ambition of providing standard academic resources, we have exercised extreme care in publishing the content. In case of any discrepancies in the matter, we request readers to excuse the unintentional lapse and not hold us liable for the same. Suggestions are always welcome.

EDITION : 2021

ISBN : 978-93-91184-96-4

PRICE : ₹ 625.00

PRINTED AT : Upkar Printing Unit, Agra

PUBLISHED BY

 **OSWAL PUBLISHERS**

Head Office: 1/12, Sahitya Kunj, M.G. Road, Agra - 282002

Phone   : (0562) 2527771-4, +91 7534077222

E-mail   : info@oswalpublishers.in

Website   : www.oswalpublishers.com

The cover of this book has been designed using resources from Freepik.com

Preface

Based on the [CBSE/DIR (ACAD)/2021] Circular No. Acad-75/2021, issued by the Board.

We at Oswal-Gurukul believe that preparation in the right direction is the key to avoid stress, and perform well in one's board exams. Therefore, in order to excel in exams we have compiled CBSE 36 Sample Question Papers for TERM I Examination of class XII. To provide best matter to students, subject-matter experts and the experienced teachers from across the country have collaborated to bring together this book.

This book comprises detailed solved Sample Question Paper by CBSE of each subject and sample papers of English Core, Physical Education, Physics, Chemistry and Biology according to the new SQP, explained in detail for better understanding of the concepts. We have made every attempt to cover as much ground as possible from the entire syllabus and to keep the language of the book lucid and crisp for easy grasping.

We sincerely hope that this book will prove to be a tool for effective time-management, as well as enable smart-study practices.

—The Publisher

⊕oswal.io

create your own exam sample papers in 2 mins

Prepare a chapter, take practice test & get —— evaluated to perform better ——

Create unlimited tests based on the latest board paper pattern once you are done practicing the book questions

Scan the **QR code** and get instant access to **oswal.io** for **free**. Just register & get started!

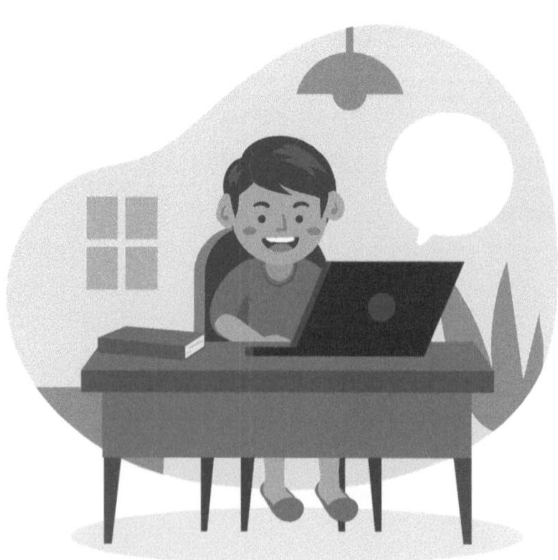

A winning effort begins with daily practice of tests

Easy steps to follow :

Step 1 - In a few clicks, you can completely customize your test

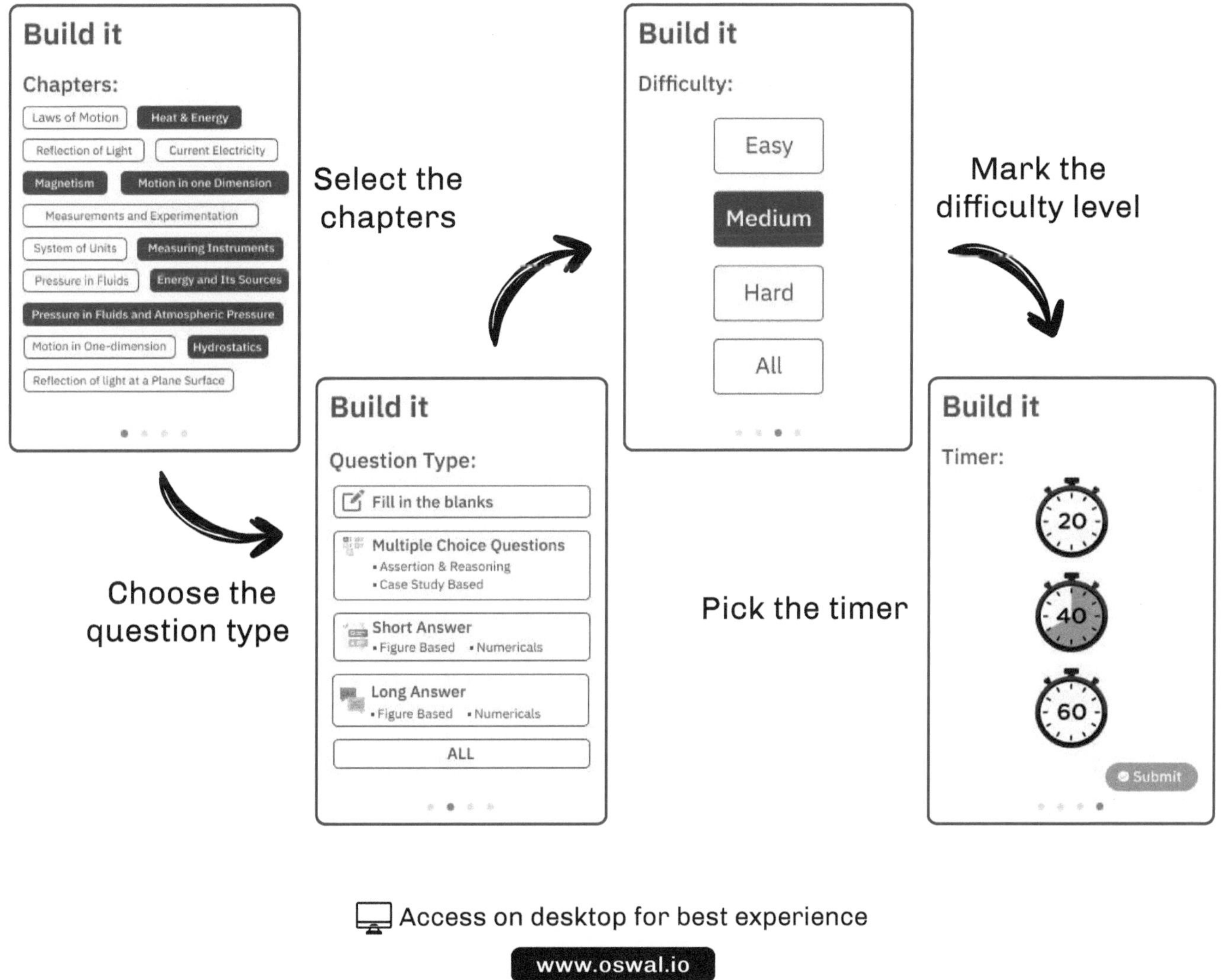

Step 2 - Test is based on the selected question type, chapters, difficulty, time

Step 3 - Click on start and type your answers in the given space

Step 4 - Use insert $\TeX$ equation editor to quickly & accurately insert the difficult math/physics/chem formulas

Step 5 - Skip any question if not sure, proceed to next & submit

Step 6 - You will get your result emailed right away

Contents

केन्द्रीय माध्यमिक शिक्षा बोर्ड

(शिक्षा मंत्रालय, भारत सरकार के अधीन एक स्वायत्त संगठन)

CENTRAL BOARD OF SECONDARY EDUCATION

(An Autonomous Organisation under the Ministry of Education, Govt. of India)

CBSE/DIR (ACAD)/2021

Date: 02-09-2021
Circular No. Acad-75/2021

All the Heads of Schools Affiliated to CBSE

**Subject: Sample Question Papers of Classes X and XII
for Term 1 Exams 2021-22**

Dear Principal,

The Sample Question Papers for classes X and XII Term 1 Exams 2021-22 are now available at CBSE website www.cbseacademic.nic.in at the link given below:

Sample Papers Class X:
http://cbseacademic.nic.in/SQP_CLASSX_2021-22.html

Sample Papers Class XII:
http://cbseacademic.nic.in/SQP_CLASSXII_2021-22.html

Dr. Joseph Emmanuel
Director (Academics)

 'शिक्षा सदन' ,17 राऊज़ एवेन्यू ,इंस्टीट्शनल एरिया, नई दिल्ली—110002
'Shiksha Sadan', 17, Rouse Avenue, Institutional Area, New Delhi - 110002

फ़ोन/Telephone: 011-23212603,23233227 वेबसाइट/Website :http://www.cbseacademic.nic.in ई-मेल/e-mail: mailto:directoracad.cbse@nic.in.

NOTICE

Important Points for Sample Question Papers

The following points are to be noted while studying/referring to the Sample Papers for Classes X & XII Term 1 for the academic session 2021-22:

1. The Multiple Choice Questions given in the sample papers are not of one mark each for all papers.

2. In the SQPs of Mathematics and all languages except English, each question carries one mark.

3. For other subjects, each question carries equal marks viz.-a-viz. the total marks given i.e. 40 or 35 or 25 or 15 and the weight age of marks per question will be as follows:-

Max. Marks	No. of Questions to be attempted	Marks per Question
40	50	0.80
35	50	0.70
40	45	0.88
35	45	0.77
25	40	0.625
15	25	0.60

4. If total marks scored by a candidate is in fraction, then the same will be rounded off to the next higher numerical number, for example, if the child gets 16.1marks then the total marks will be rounded off to 17 and so on.

English Core

Sample Question Paper

English Core [Code (301)]

Term - I

Time : 90 Minutes   Max. Marks : 40

General Instructions :

1. The Question Paper contains THREE sections.
2. Section A–READING has 18 questions. Attempt a total of 14 questions, as per specific instructions for each question.
3. Section B–WRITING SKILLS has 12 questions. Attempt a total of 10 questions, as per specific instructions for each question.
4. Section C–LITERATURE has 30 questions. Attempt 26 questions, as per specific instructions for each question.
5. All questions carry equal marks.
6. There is no negative marking.

READING

I. Read the passage given below.

 I. I got posted in Srinagar in the 1980s. Its rugged mountains, gushing rivers and vast meadows reminded me of the landscapes of my native place – the Jibhi Valley in Himachal Pradesh. Unlike Srinagar that saw numerous tourists, Jibhi Valley remained clouded in anonymity. That's when the seed of starting tourism in Jibhi was planted. I decided to leave my service in the Indian Army and follow the urge to return home.

 II. We had two houses – a family house and a traditional house, which we often rented out. I pleaded with my father to ask the tenant to vacate the house so that I could convert it into a guesthouse. When my family finally relented, I renovated the house keeping its originality intact, just adding windows for sunlight.

 III. I still remember the summer of 1992 when I put a signboard outside my first guesthouse in Jibhi Valley! The village residents, however, were sceptical about my success. My business kept growing but it took years for tourism to take off in Jibhi Valley. Things changed significantly after 2008 when the government launched a homestay scheme. People built homestays and with rapid tourism growth, the region changed rapidly. Villages turned into towns with many concrete buildings. Local businesses and tourists continued putting a burden on nature.

 IV. Then, with the 2020-21 pandemic and lockdown, tourism came to a complete standstill in Jibhi Valley. Local people, who were employed at over a hundred homestays and guesthouses, returned to their villages. Some went back to farming; some took up pottery and some got involved in government work schemes. Now, all ardently hope that normalcy and tourism will return to the valley soon. In a way, the pandemic has given us an opportunity to introspect, go back to our roots and look for sustainable solutions.

 V. For me, tourism has been my greatest teacher. It brought people from many countries and all states of India to my guesthouse. It gave me exposure to different cultures and countless opportunities to learn new things. Most people who stayed at my guesthouse became my repeat clients and good friends. When I look back, I feel proud, yet humbled at the thought that I was not only able to fulfil my dream despite all the challenges, but also play a role in establishing tourism in the beautiful valley that I call home. (394 words)

Source: *https://www.outlookindia.com/outlooktraveller/explore/story/71458/how-one-mansconviction-put-jibhi-valley-on-the-world-tourism-map*

Based on your understanding of the passage, answer <u>any eight</u> out of the ten questions by choosing the correct option

Q.1. The scenic beauty of Srinagar makes the writer feel

    A. awestruck   B. nostalgic   C. cheerful   D. confused

Ans. B. nostalgic

Q.2. A collocation is a group of words that often occur together.

The writer says that Jibhi valley remained <u>clouded in anonymity</u>.

Select the word from the options that correctly collocates with *clouded in*.

    A. disgust   B. anger   C. doubt   D. terror

Ans. C. doubt

Q.3. Select the option that suitably completes the given dialogue as per the context in paragraph II.

Father: Are you sure that your plan would work?

Writer: I can't say (1) ....

Father: That's a lot of uncertainty, isn't it?

Writer: (2) .... , father. Please let's do this.

    A. (1) that I would be able to deal with the funding (2) Well begun is half done

    B. (1) anything along those lines, as the competition is tough (2) Think before you leap

    C. (1) that, because it's a question of profit and loss (2) All's well that ends well

    D. (1) I'm sure, but I can say that I believe in myself (2) Nothing venture nothing win

Ans. D. (1) I'm sure, but I can say that I believe in myself (2) Nothing venture nothing win

Q.4. Which signboard would the writer have chosen for his 1992 undertaking, in Jibhi Valley?

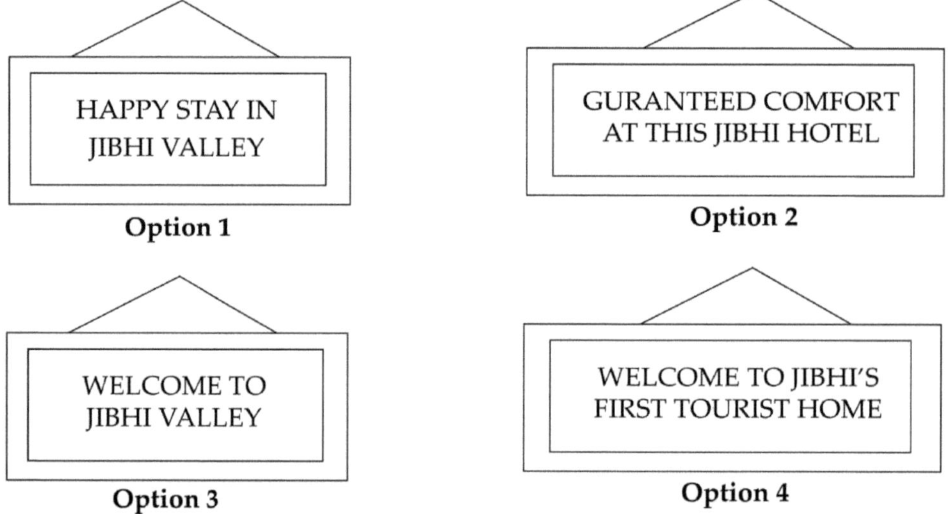

    A. option 1   B. option 2

    C. option 3   D. option 4

Ans. D. option 4

Q.5. Select the option that clearly indicates the situation before and after 2008, in Jibhi Valley.

A.

Before 2008	After 2008
picturesque landscapes	construction sites and commerce

B.

Before 2008	After 2008
zero tourism in the valley	sceptical villagers

C.

Before 2008	After 2008
buildings and hotels	profitable ventures

D.

Before 2008	After 2008
scenic surroundings	zero tourism in the valley

Ans. A.

Before 2008	After 2008
picturesque landscapes	construction sites and commerce

Q.6. What is the relationship between (1) and (2)?
- (1)   …tourism came to a complete standstill in Jibhi Valley.
- (2)   … tourism has been my greatest teacher.

A.	(2) is the cause for (1).	B.	(1) repeats the situation described in (2).
C.	(2) elaborates the problem described in (1).	D.	(1) sets the stage for (2).

Ans. D.   (1) sets the stage for (2).

Q.7. The writer mentions looking for sustainable solutions. He refers to the need for sustainable solutions because he realises that
- A.   even though all natural ecosystems are essential pillars of resilience, we need to focus on using their resources to address the economic needs of mankind, as a priority.
- B.   the exposures to pandemics are a reality and a big threat to the countries across the world.
- C.   for an economic recovery to be durable and resilient, a return to 'business as usual' and environmentally destructive investment patterns and activities must be avoided.
- D.   there is an increasing urgency in the climate movement and the need for collaborative action for the future.

Ans. C.   for an economic recovery to be durable and resilient, a return to 'business as usual' and environmentally destructive investment patterns and activities must be avoided.

Q.8. Select the option that lists the customer review for the writer's project.
- A.   Beautiful accommodation in the lap of nature. Luxurious cottage with indoor pool and garden.
- B.   Comfortable and peaceful. Neat room with ample sunlight. Pleasant and warm host.
- C.   Enjoyed the sprawling suite on the fifth floor. Great view. Professional service.
- D.   Remote locale, good food and clean room. Would have loved more natural light, though.

Ans. B.   Comfortable and peaceful. Neat room with ample sunlight. Pleasant and warm host.

Q.9. Which quote summarises the writer's feelings about the pace of growth of tourism in Jibhi Valley?
- A.   We kill all the caterpillars, then complain there are no butterflies.   *– John Marsden*
- B.   Nature will give you the best example of life lessons, just open your eyes and see.   *– Kate Smith*
- C.   We do not see nature with our eyes, but with our understanding and our hearts.   *– William Hazlett*
- D.   I'd rather be in the mountains thinking of God than in church thinking of the mountains.
  – John Muir

Ans. A.   We kill all the caterpillars, then complain there are no butterflies.   *– John Marsden*

Q.10. Select the option that lists what we can conclude from the text.
- (1)   people of Jibhi Valley practiced sustainable tourism.
- (2)   the people of Jibhi Valley gradually embraced tourism.
- (3)   tourists never revisited Jibhi Valley.
- (4)   the writer was an enterprising person.

A.	(1) and (2) are true.	B.	(2), (3) and (4) are true.
C.	(2) and (4) are true.	D.	(1), (3) and (4) are true.

Ans. C.   (2) and (4) are true.

II. Read the passage given below.

I.   Over the last five years, more companies have been actively looking for intern profiles, according to a 2018-19 survey by an online internship and training platform. This survey reveals that India had 80% more internship applications — with 2.2 million applications received in 2018 compared to 1.27 million in the year before. The trend was partly due to more industries looking to have fresh minds and ideas on existing projects for better productivity. What was originally seen as a western concept, getting an internship before plunging into the job market, is fast gaining momentum at Indian workplaces.

II.   According to the survey data, India's National Capital Region has been the top provider of internships, with a total of 35% internship opportunities, followed by Mumbai and Bengaluru at 20% and 15%, respectively. This includes opportunities in startups, MNCs and even government entities. The survey also revealed popular fields to find internships in (Fig 1). There has been growing awareness among the students about the intern profiles sought by hiring companies that often look for people with real-time experience in management than B- school masters.

Internship Trends 2018
Popular fields to find internships in

Source: Internshala

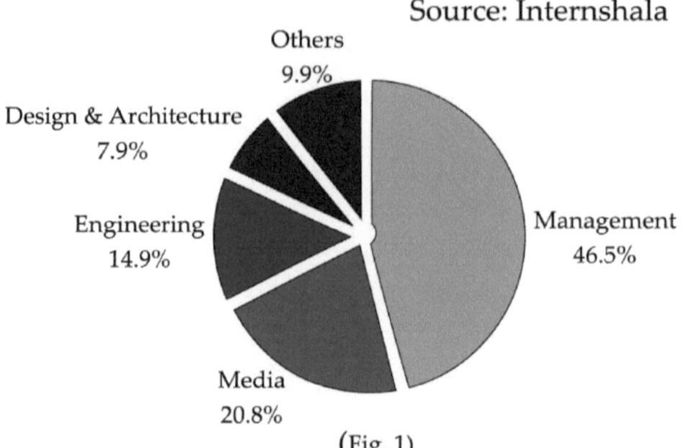

(Fig. 1)

III. The stipend has been an important factor influencing the choice of internships. The survey data reveals that the average stipend offered to interns was recorded as ₹7000 while the maximum stipend went up to ₹85,000. According to statistics, a greater number of people considered virtual internships than in-office internships. Virtual internships got three times more applications than in-office, since a large chunk of students were the ones already enrolled in various courses, or preferred working from home.

IV. Internship portals have sprung up in the last three to four years and many of them already report healthy traffic per month. Reports suggest that on an average, an internship portal company has around 200,000-plus students and some 8,000 companies registered on it. It gets around two lakh visits online every month. The Managing Director of a leading executive search firm says that though these web platforms are working as an effective bridge between the industry and students, most established companies are still reluctant to take too many interns on board for obvious reasons. (355 words)

Source:

(1) *https://www.businessinsider.in/internships-in-india-on-the-rise-with-startups-leading-theway/articleshow/67655265.cms*

(2) *https://www.businesstoday.in/magazine/features/story/online-portals-helping-collegestudents-paid-internships-46215-2014-06-03*

Based on your understanding of the passage, answer <u>any six</u> out of the eight questions by choosing the correct option.

Q.11. Select the correct inference with reference to the following:

Over the last five years, more companies have been actively looking for intern profiles…

A. The past five years have seen active applications by interns to several companies.

B. The activity for intern profiling by the companies has reached a gradual downslide over the past five years.

C. There were lesser companies searching for intern profiles earlier, as compared to those in the recent five years.

D. Several companies have initiated intern profiling five times a year in the recent past.

Ans. C. There were lesser companies searching for intern profiles earlier, as compared to those in the recent five years.

Q.12. Select the central idea of the paragraph likely to precede paragraph I.

A. Process of registering for internships   B. Knowing more about internships

C. Dos and Don'ts for an internship interview   D. Startups and internships

Ans. B. Knowing more about internships

Q.13. Select the option that displays the true statement with reference to Fig 1.

A. Internships for Engineering and Management are the top two favourites.

B. Design & Architecture internships are significantly more popular than Others.

C. Internships for Media and Others have nearly equal popularity percentage.

    D.   Management internships' popularity is more than twice that for Media.

Ans. D.   Management internships' popularity is more than twice that for Media.

Q.14. Based on your reading of paragraphs II-III, select the appropriate counter- argument to the given argument.

    Argument: I don't think you'll be considered for an internship just because you've been the student editor and Head of Student Council.

    A.   I think I have a fair chance because I'm applying for a virtual position than an inoffice one.

    B.   I have real-time experience in managing a team and many companies consider it more meritorious than a degree in Management.

    C.   I know that my stipend might be on the lower side but I think that it's a good 'earn while you learn' opportunity.

    D.   Lot of metro-cities have a good percentage of positions open and I think I should definitely take a chance.

Ans. B.   I have real-time experience in managing a team and many companies consider it more meritorious than a degree in Management.

Q.15. Select the option that displays the correct cause-effect relationship.

A.

cause	effect
Several students had academic courses to complete	Students applied for online internship

B.

cause	effect
A large chunk of students preferred in-office internships	Applications were three times more than for virtual internships

C.

cause	effect
A greater number of students wanted to work from home	Several students had courses to complete

D.

cause	effect
Students applied for online internship	An equal number of students applied for work-from-home

Ans.

A.

cause	effect
Several students had academic courses to complete	Students applied for online internship

Q.16. The survey statistics mention the average stipend, indicating that

    A.   50% interns were offered ₹85,000.

    B.   ₹7,000 was the lowest and ₹85,000 was the highest.

    C.   most interns were offered around ₹7,000.

    D.   No intern was offered more than ₹7,000.

Ans. C.   most interns were offered around ₹7,000.

Q.17. The phrase 'healthy traffic' refers to the

    A.   updates from portals about health and road safety.

    B.   statistics about adherence to traffic rules by the portals.

    C.   sizeable number of visitors to the portal per month.

    D.   monthly data about the health of internship applicants.

Ans. C.   sizeable number of visitors to the portal per month.

Q.18. Read the two statements given below and select the option that suitably explains them.

    (1)   Established companies are reluctant to take too many interns on board.

    (2)   Probability of interns leaving the company for a variety of reasons, is high.

    A.   (1) is the problem and (2) is the solution for (1).

    B.   (1) is false but (2) correctly explains (1).

    C.   (1) summarises (2).

    D.   (1) is true and (2) is the reason for (1).

Ans. D.   (1) is true and (2) is the reason for (1).

WRITING

III. **Answer <u>any four</u> out of the five questions given, with reference to the context below.**

The President of R.W.A. Chelavoor Heights, Kozhikode, has to put up a notice to inform residents about a power-cut for their residential area.

Q.19. Select the appropriate title for the notice.

    A.   Choosing Own Power Cuts

    B.   Scheduled Power Cut

    C.   The Need to Save Power

    D.   Power and Resident Safety

Ans. B.   Scheduled Power Cut

Q.20. Select the option that lists the most accurate opening for this notice.

    A.   Greetings and attention please, to one and all in Chelavoor Heights.

    B.   This notice is written to share some news with you all about…

    C.   This is to inform all the residents of Chelavoor Heights about…

    D.   I wish to share with all officials of R.W.A. Chelavoor Heights that…

Ans. C.   This is to inform all the residents of Chelavoor Heights about…

Q.21. Select the option with the information points to be included in the body of the notice.

    (1)   Opinion about regular power cuts

    (2)   Resolution for power cuts

    (3)   Reason for the power cut

    (4)   Timings of the power cut

    (5)   Complaint against regular power cuts

    (6)   Date of the power cut

    A.   (1) and (4)   B. (2), (3) and (5)

    C.   (2) and (6)   D. (3), (4) and (6)

Ans. D.   (3), (4) and (6)

Q.22. Would this notice reflect the name of the R.W.A?

    A.   Yes, because it is the issuing body.

    B.   No, because it is understood through the signature.

    C.   Yes, because it makes it informal.

    D.   No, because the title makes it clear.

Ans. A.   Yes, because it is the issuing body.

Q.23. Select the appropriate conclusion for this notice.

    A.   Stay informed.   B. Collaboration solicited.

    C.   Stay prepared.   D. Inconvenience regretted.

Ans. D.   Inconvenience regretted.

IV. **Answer <u>any six</u> of the seven questions given, with reference to the context below.**

Venu is a member of Co-existence, a school club that actively promotes animal rights and care. He has to write an article emphasising the need for prevention of cruelty to animals and peaceful coexistence between animals and human beings.

Q.24. Select the option that lists an appropriate title for Venu's article.

    A.   Man and Animal-A Struggle to Co-exist

    B.   The Rehabilitation and Conservation of Species

    C.   Remodelling the Future by Peaceful Co-existence

    D.   Smart Moves- Survival of the Fittest

Ans. C.   Remodelling the Future by Peaceful Co-existence

Q.25. Which option (1-4), should Venu choose to elaborate on reasons for cruelty to animals?

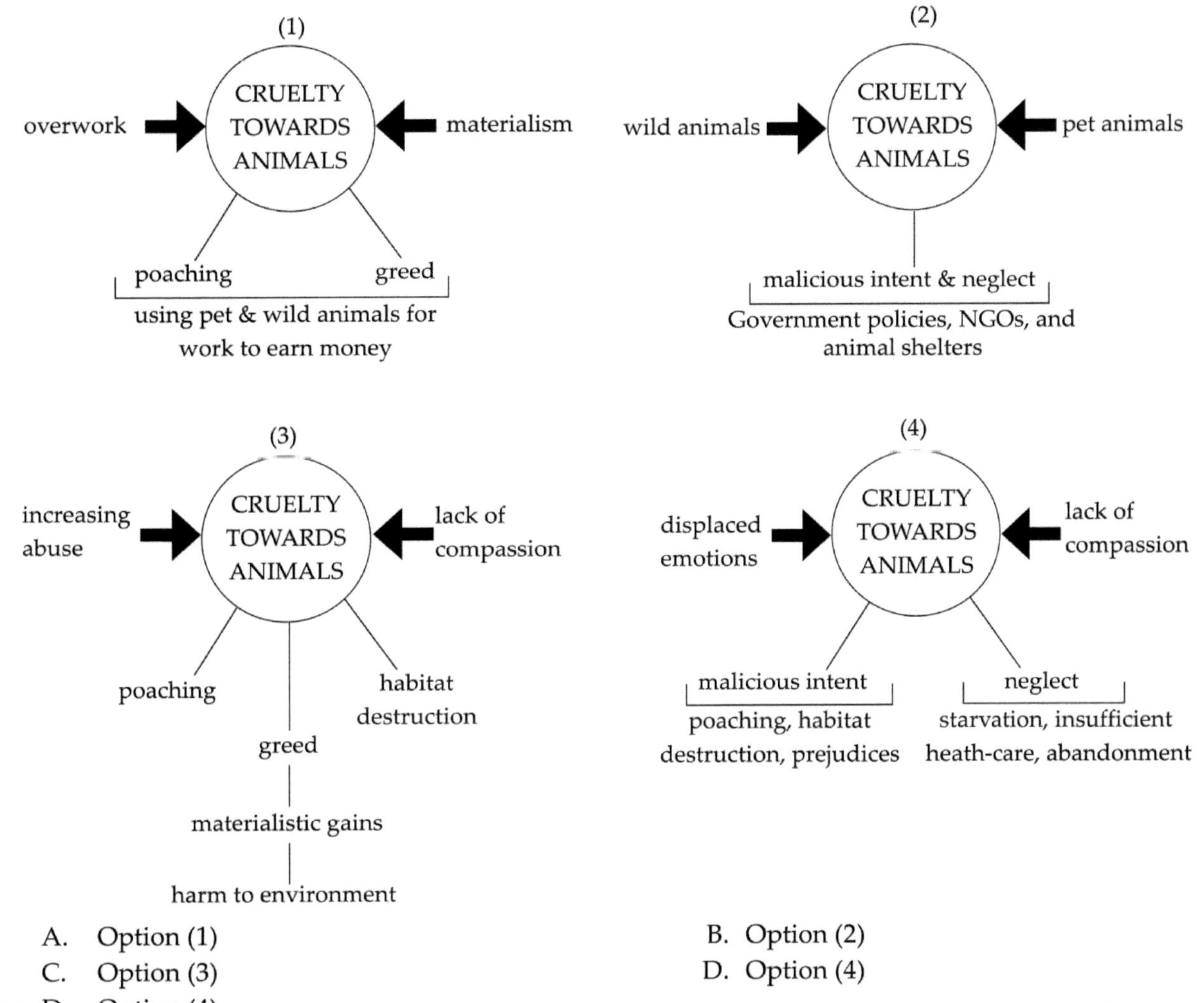

  A. Option (1)   B. Option (2)

  C. Option (3)   D. Option (4)

Ans. D. Option (4)

Q.26. Which option would help Venu with the appropriate organisation of relevant ideas for this article?

  A. Expressing concern about several cases of cruelty to animals—Exploring the reasons—Stating the effects—Providing suggestions for peaceful co-existence— Presenting a conclusive outlook

  B. Stating the effects of cruelty to animals— Presenting a concluding viewpoint—Providing suggestions for peaceful co-existence—Expressing concern for animal cruelty— Exploring the reasons for cruelty to animals

  C. Introducing the purpose of the article—Information about policies and laws for animal protection—Exploring the reasons for the laws— Providing suggestions for peaceful co-existence —Presenting a pledge for awareness

  D. Exploring the laws for animal protection—Questioning the efficacy of the laws—Providing suggestions for improvements in the behaviour towards animals— Introducing the purpose of the article—Appeal for joining Co-Existence

Ans. A. Expressing concern about several cases of cruelty to animals—Exploring the reasons—Stating the effects—Providing suggestions for peaceful co-existence— Presenting a conclusive outlook

Q.27. Which suggestions, from those given below, would be appropriate for Venu's article?

  A. reducing human-wildlife conflict, banning habitat destruction, creating more wildlife sanctuaries

  B. protecting the environment, penalising poachers

  C. strengthening execution of animal rights' laws, increasing awareness, reducing human-wildlife conflict

  D. creation of more wildlife sanctuaries and promotion of research on animals.

Ans. C. strengthening execution of animal rights' laws, increasing awareness, reducing human-wildlife conflict

Q.28. Read a sentence from Venu's article draft and help him complete it by selecting the most appropriate option.

As animals find their natural habitat shrinking daily, their interactions with humans keep rising, often to the (i)_________ of the humans and with (ii)_________ for the animals.

    A.   (i) joy (ii) dangerous outcomes   B.   (i) thrill (ii) lethal consequences

    C.   (i) irritation (ii) minimal effects   D.   (i) fear (ii) disastrous results

Ans. D.   (i) fear (ii) disastrous results

Q.29. Which quote should Venu use to summarise the central idea of his article?

    A.   "Animals are such agreeable friends—they ask no questions; they pass no criticisms."

– George Eliot

    B.   "The greatness of a nation and its moral progress can be judged by the way its animals are treated."

– Mahatma Gandhi

    C.   A tiger may pray, "O Lord, how wicked are these men who do not come and place themselves before me to be eaten; they are breaking Your law."   *– Swami Vivekananda*

    D.   "Clearly, animals know more than we think, and think a great deal more than we know."

– Irene M. Pepperberg

Ans. B.   "The greatness of a nation and its moral progress can be judged by the way its animals are treated."

– Mahatma Gandhi

Q.30. Read the following options for the self-checklist for this article and select the option that includes the most appropriate self-checklist for this article.

(1)

MY ARTICLE CONTAINS	☑	☒
1. first person address to the audience as title		
2. content that lists the topical points		
3. opinions of stakeholders as by-line		
4. personal observations		
5. designation and date at the end		

(2)

MY ARTICLE CONTAINS	☑	☒
1. an eye-catching title that is thematically related		
2. content that offers a balanced view of the issue		
3. input for the cause-effect & suggestions		
4. a conclusion including personal observations		
5. a by-line		

(3)

MY ARTICLE CONTAINS	☑	☒
1. a thoughtful quote as title		
2. content that analyses pros and cons		
3. address of the writer		
4. a conclusion including published evidence		
5. expression of gratitude by-line		

(4)

MY ARTICLE CONTAINS	☑	☒
1. relevant data & by-line as title		
2. content that offers a balanced view of the issue		
3. name of the publishing body		
4. a conclusion including personal observations		
5. designation and date at the end		

    A.   Option (1)   B.   Option (2)

    C.   Option (3)   D.   Option (4)

Ans. B.   Option (2)

LITERATURE

This section has sub-sections: V, VI, VII, VIII, IX. There are a total of 30 questions in the section. Attempt any 26 questions from the sub-sections V to IX.

V.   **Read the given extract to attempt questions that follow:**

"I have nothing else to do," he mutters, looking away. "Go to school," I say glibly, realising immediately how hollow the advice must sound.

"There is no school in my neighbourhood. When they build one, I will go."

"If I start a school, will you come?" I ask, half-joking. "Yes," he says, smiling broadly.

A few days later I see him running up to me. "Is your school ready?"

"It takes longer to build a school," I say, embarrassed at having made a promise that was not meant. But promises like mine abound in every corner of his bleak world.

Q.31. Saheb's muttering and 'looking away' suggests his

    A.   anger   B. shyness   C. embarrassment   D. anxiety

Ans. C.   embarrassment

Q.32. Of the four meanings of 'glibly', select the option that matches in meaning with its usage in the extract.

    A.   showing a degree of informality   B. lacking depth and substance

    C.   being insincere and deceitful   D. speaking with fluency

Ans. B.   lacking depth and substance

Q.33. Who do you think Saheb is referring to as 'they', in the given sentence?

"When they build one, I will go"

    A.   The officials   B. The inhabitants

    C.   The teachers   D. The journalists

Ans. A.   The officials

Q.34. Select the option that lists the feelings and attitudes corresponding to the following:

    1.   *I ask half-joking*

    2.   *...he says, smiling broadly*

A.

(1)	part arrogance, part seriousness
(2)	hesitation

B.

(1)	part amusement, part irritation
(2)	submissiveness

C.

(1)	part concern, part hurt
(2)	pride

D.

(1)	part humour, part earnestness
(2)	self-belief

Ans.

D.

(1)	part humour, part earnestness
(2)	self-belief

Q.35. Select the option that lists reasons why Saheb's world has been called 'bleak'.

    (1) The absence of parental presence   (2) The poor socio-economic conditions

    (3) His inability to address problems   (4) His lack of life-skills

    (5) The denied opportunities of schooling

    A.   (1) and (4)   B. (2) and (5)

    C.   (3) and (5)   D. (2) and (4)

Ans. B.   (2) and (5)

VI.   **Read the given extract to attempt questions that follow:**

Tiny vestiges of the old terror would return. But now I could frown and say to that terror, "Trying to scare me, eh? Well, here's to you! Look!" And off I'd go for another length of the pool. This went on until July. But I was still not satisfied. I was not sure that all the terror had left. So, I went to Lake Wentworth in New Hampshire, dived off a dock at Triggs Island, and swam two miles across the lake to Stamp Act Island. I swam the crawl, breast stroke, side stroke, and back stroke. Only once did the terror return. When I was in the middle of the lake, I put my face under and saw nothing but bottomless water. The old sensation returned in miniature.

Q.36. Why did Douglas go to swim at Lake Wentworth?

    A.   To showcase his skills for all who had doubted him.

    B.   To honour the efforts of his swimming instructor.

    C.   To build on his ability of swimming in a natural water body.

    D.   To know for sure that he had overcome his fear of drowning in water.

Ans. D.   To know for sure that he had overcome his fear of drowning in water.

Q.37. Select the option that lists the correct inference based on the information in the extract.
- A.   Triggs Island and Stamp Act Island are both located in Lake Wentworth.
- B.   Lake Wentworth is a part of Triggs Island.
- C.   Stamp Act Island is two miles away from New Hampshire.
- D.   Lake Wentworth is connected via docks to New Hampshire.

Ans. A.   Triggs Island and Stamp Act Island are both located in Lake Wentworth.

Q.38. What was the reason for the 'return' of terror?
- A.   Superstitions about the dock at Triggs Islands
- B.   Recent reports about drowning incidents
- C.   Prior drowning experiences
- D.   Warnings by experienced swimmers

Ans. C.   Prior drowning experiences

Q.39. Douglas mentions that the *old sensation returned in miniature.*
He means that he felt the familiar feeling of fear ....
- A.   at irregular intervals.
- B.   on a small scale.
- C.   repeatedly.
- D.   without notice.

Ans. B.   on a small scale.

Q.40. How did Douglas handle the 'old sensation'?
- A.   Addressed it.
- B.   Avoided it.
- C.   Submitted to it.
- D.   Stayed indifferent to it.

Ans. A.   Addressed it.

VII.   **Read the given extract to attempt questions that follow:**
The tall girl with her weighed-down head. The paperseeming
boy, with rat's eyes. The stunted, unlucky heir
Of twisted bones, reciting a father's gnarled disease,
His lesson, from his desk. At back of the dim class
One unnoted, sweet and young. His eyes live in a dream…

Q.41. The poet draws attention to the problem of __________ while describing the boy as *paper-seeming.*
- A.   malnutrition
- B.   untidiness
- C.   isolation
- D.   abandonment

Ans. A.   malnutrition

Q.42. Which option has the underlined phrase that applies the poetic device used for 'rat's eyes'?
- A.   He shut up <u>like a clam</u> when interrogated.
- B.   She runs <u>as swift as a gazelle</u>.
- C.   He is considered the <u>black sheep</u> of the family.
- D.   She ran away <u>chattering with fear</u>.

Ans. C.   He is considered the <u>black sheep</u> of the family.

Q.43. Select the correct option to fill the blank.
The tall girl's head is weighed down due to the __________ .
- A.   effect of diseases
- B.   need for concentration
- C.   desire to remain unnoticed
- D.   burdens of poverty

Ans. D.   burdens of poverty

Q.44. The literal meaning of 'reciting' refers to delivering the lesson aloud. What does its figurative meaning refer to?
- A.   Showing extra interest in the lesson.
- B.   Carrying his father's disease.
- C.   Resigning to his disease and condition.
- D.   Voicing the poor conditions, he lives in.

Ans. B.   Carrying his father's disease.

Q.45. How does the 'unnoted' pupil present a contrast to others?
- A.   He appears to be in a world of dreams.
- B.   He struggles with the fulfilment of dreams.
- C.   He seems taller than most.
- D.   He sits in the dimmest part of the classroom.

Ans. A.   He appears to be in a world of dreams.

VII.   **Read the given extract to attempt questions that follow:**
He said I was unhappy. That made my wife kind of mad, but he explained that he meant the modern world is full
of insecurity, fear, war, worry and all the rest of it, and that I just want to escape. Well, who doesn't? Everybody

I know wants to escape, but they don't wander down into any third level at Grand Central Station. But that's the reason, he said, and my friends all agreed. Everything points to it, they claimed.

My stamp collecting, for example; that's a 'temporary refuge from reality.' Well, maybe, but my grandfather didn't need any refuge from reality.

Q.46. Why did Sam's verdict make Charley's wife 'mad'?

    A.   It made it difficult for her to accept that Charley would consult a psychiatrist.

    B.   It seemed to suggest to her that she was the cause of Charley's unhappiness.

    C.   It made her aware of Charley's delicate state of mind.

    D.   It offended her that Charley and Sam collectively accused her.

Ans. B.   It seemed to suggest to her that she was the cause of Charley's unhappiness.

Q.47. Sam's explanation to the reaction of Charley's wife was ____________ in nat

    A.   critical   B. aggressive   C. clarifying   D. accusatory

Ans. C.   clarifying

Q.48. Select the option that signifies the condition of people of the 'modern world' mentioned in the extract.

    (1)   unsure   (2)   lazy

    (3)   offensive   (4)   anxious

    (5)   afraid

    A.   (1) and (3)   B. (2) and (5)

    C.   (2), (3) and (4)   D. (1), (4) and (5)

Ans. D.   (1), (4) and (5)

Q.49. Select the option that displays a cause-effect set.

A.

Cause	Effect
Charley's stamp collecting	Wandering into the third level

B.

Cause	Effect
Everybody wants to escape	Modern world full of insecurity

C.

Cause	Effect
Charley's wandering into the third level	Charley's stamp collecting

D.

Cause	Effect
Modern world full of insecurity	Everybody wants to escape

Ans.

D.

Cause	Effect
Modern world full of insecurity	Everybody wants to escape

Q.50. Why didn't Charley's grandfather need refuge from reality?

    A.   He was too busy to bother.   B. He had chosen to deny his reality.

    C.   He lived in peaceful times.   D. He was a very secure person.

Ans. C.   He lived in peaceful times.

IX.   **Attempt the following.**

Q.51. In 'Keeping Quiet' the poet does not want the reader to confuse his advice for _________ with total inactivity.

    A.   experimentation   B. relaxation

    C.   isolation   D. introspection

Ans. D.   introspection

Q.52. On his way to school, Franz says that he had the *strength to resist* and chose to hurry off to school. The underlined phrase suggests that Franz was

    A.   hesitant.   B. threatened.

    C.   tempted.   D. repentant.

Ans. C.   tempted.

Q.53. Select the suitable option for the given statements, based on your reading of *Lost Spring*.

    (1)   The writer notices that Saheb has lost his carefree look.

    (2)   Saheb has had to surrender his freedom for ₹800 per month.

A. (1) is false but (2) is true.   B. Both (1) and (2) are true.

C. (2) is a fact but unrelated to (1).   D. (1) is the cause for (2).

Ans. B.   Both (1) and (2) are true.

Q.54. Select the option that lists the qualities of Douglas' trainer.

(1) adventurous   (2) generous

(3) patient   (4) methodical

(5) encouraging   (6) courageous

A. (1) and (6)   B. (3), (4) and (5)

C. (2) and (5)   D. (1), (4) and (6)

Ans. B.   (3), (4) and (5)

Q.55. The metaphor 'lead sky', is used by Stephen Spender to bring out

A. the image of sky-high constructions in the slum.

B. a response to death and destruction.

C. the strong dreams and aspirations of the children.

D. a sense of hopelessness and despair.

Ans. D.   a sense of hopelessness and despair.

Q.56. Sadao's servants leave his house, but none of them betrays the secret of the American P.O.W. Select the option that explains this.

A. The servants truly believed that they must not be a part of the household which sheltered a prisoner of war, but their love and loyalty to Sadao made them keep the secret safe.

B. The servants knew that any information about the P.O.W would result in punishment for them and their families which is why they revealed nothing.

C. The servants were superstitious and scared with a white man on the premises and consequently, chose to remove themselves and stay silent about the situation.

D. The servants did not want to incur the wrath of Dr. Sadao and lose their jobs, therefore they chose to exit instead, and return later.

Ans. A.   The servants truly believed that they must not be a part of the household which sheltered a prisoner of war, but their love and loyalty to Sadao made them keep the secret safe.

Q.57. Classify (1) to (4) as fact (F) or opinion (O), based on your reading of *The Third Level*.

(1) First day covers are never opened.   (2) Grand Central is growing like a tree.

(3) President Roosevelt collected stamps.   (4) Sam was Charley's psychiatrist.

A. F-1,3,4; O-2   B. F-2, 3; O-1,4

C. F-2; O-1,3,4   D. F-3,4; O-1,2

Ans. A.   F-1,3,4; O-2

Q.58. Identify the tone of Pablo Neruda in the following line:

Perhaps the Earth can teach us....

A. Confident and clear about the future events.

B. Dramatic about the prediction he made.

C. Convinced about the sequence of events to follow.

D. Uncertain, yet hopeful about the possibility.

Ans. D.   Uncertain, yet hopeful about the possibility.

Q.59. Dr. Sadao mutters the word 'my friend' while treating the American P.O.W. in the light of the circumstances, we can say that this was

A. humourous.   B. climactic.   C. ironical.   D. ominous.

Ans. C.   ironical.

Q.60. The sight of young trees and merry children, on the way to Cochin, is ________ the poet's aging mother.

A. like a divine assurance for   B. in sharp contrast to

C. a distraction from pain for   D. the bridge between the poet and

Ans. B.   in sharp contrast to

❏❏

Sample Paper 1

English Core

READING

I. Read the passage given below.

I. A bookshop is not something you find in every street or area these days. Books, which were once a permanent accompaniment for youngsters in their formative years, are fading out of their list of engagements.

II. Ask any youngster which is the latest book he has read and he will be baffled. Apart from a few consistent readers, others just befool themselves with a bookseller's name or lament the curriculum load for justifying themselves, like this seventeen-year-old school-goer who says, 'I just read my Physics book.'

III. Television has been blamed for this calamitous situation, which is producing square-faced people and a bookless society. Furthermore, today's children are under pressure to be smart and popular and to succeed on a social level. Parties, dancing and hanging out at different places begin early. Moreover, computers, video games, the Internet, swimming lessons, cricket and a youngster's passion for an hour-long tete-a-tete on the telephone with friends eat up all their leisure time.

IV. A child who is constantly under pressure to live up to his parents' expectations, which are at times unreasonable, does not like to throw himself into another set of books after the laborious school work, unless he comes from a family of readers where the engrossing work of Shakespeare and Dickens are just a matter of pulling them out from the shelves.

V. Many parents also believe that today's children have become more aware and demand logical reasoning for everything. They can no longer be fooled by fairy tales or animal stories, as they have not seen any fairies or animals except for those old and tired ones in the city zoo. This has made them more interested in movies or TV serials than a turtle talking to a rabbit or a frog changing into a prince.

VI. But a visit to the capital's leading bookstores presents a contrasting picture of youngsters' reading habits. These bookshops claim they are doing healthy business and have many regular buyers from this age group.

VII. Though the works of Shakespeare, Charles Dickens, Jane Austen and Mark Twain no longer interest teenagers, bestsellers from Daniel Steele, Sidney Sheldon and Jeffery Archer are on the list of all reading teens. Self-help books, such as those on personality development or relationship management, are also picked up by many of them.

VIII. Mystery books like Nancy Drew and Hardy Boys are popular with kids and Mills and Boons and other romance novels with their fairly predictable formula with teenage girls. For parents of children below ten, volumes of Panchatantra Stories, Amar Chitra Katha and other bedtime stories are worthy purchases as these teach the child what is wrong in their own special way. What seems to be the case is that parents have surrendered to others what was their most precious right—that of making their children what they should become. With the old techniques of child rearing losing ground, modern parents must consciously spend time with their children. Taste and enthusiasm for literature can be communicated artfully to children by reading bedtime stories to them, encouraging them to play historical characters and giving books as birthday gifts.

IX. The family reading which was once popular in the West could well be adopted here. Reading aloud the works of great men by parents to their children not only forms a warm bond between them but also attracts young minds to the world of books which gives them a chance to explore the sea of life.

Based on your understanding of the passage, answer <u>any eight</u> out of the ten questions by choosing the correct option.

Q.1. Choose the CORRECT option that takes away the teenagers from reading good books.

A.	Cinema	B.	Television
C.	Dance shows	D.	Music programs

Q.2. Select the option that would suitably complete the given dialogue between the parents and the child as per the context in paragraph 5.

Parents: Why don't read the books that we bought you? All you do is to look at the television the entire day!

Child: I don't (1) ....

Parents: And does the television provide you any logic to what you see?

Child: Yes! (2) .... I enjoy it.

A. (1) want to read the books (2) they do.

B. (1) understand the logics behind those fairy tales (2) the stories are realistic and well described through animations.

C. (1) want to exhaust my mind thinking about the logic in them (2) totally.

D. (1) like to read (2) it makes my imagination vivid.

Q.3. The passage uses a French word *'tete-a-tete'*. This refers to:

A. making group calls

B. bad-mouthing people behind them

C. having an argument

D. having a private conversation between two people

Q.4. Select the CORRECT image of the activity that was once popular in the West.

A.	Option 1	B.	Option 2
C.	Option 3	D.	Option 4

Q.5. Select the correct hobby that youngsters use to posses before and the one they posses today.

Before	Today		Before	Today		Before	Today		Before	Today
Watching television	Reading books		Reading poetry	Reading novels		Reading books	Watching television		Watching movies on television	Watching movies online
A.			B.			C.			D.	

Q.6. What is the relationship between (1) and (2).

(1) children have become more logic-demanding

(2) children prefer watching television to reading fairy tales

A.	(1) is the cause of (2)	B.	(2) elaborates the affirmation of (1)
C.	(2) is the reason behind (1)	D.	(1) is the advice for (2)

Q.7. Based on information given in the passage, select the option that describes the cause of children ignoring books.

A.	They find them uninteresting	B.	They are more addicted to online entertainment
C.	They lament the curriculum load	D.	They don't have patience to read books

Q.8. Select the option that lists the importance of reading for writer.

A. warms the bond between parents and children, attracts young minds to the world of books, a chance to explore the sea of life.

B. bring harmony among people, create calm, keep people busy.

C.   makes people look trendy, learn something new, a chance to revive self.

D.   creates a huge burden on young minds, makes them anxious, an intense mind activity.

Q.9.   Which quote summarizes the importance of the books as given in the last paragraph of the passage?

A.   *"You can swim all day in the Sea of Knowledge and still come out completely dry. Most people do."*
— Norton Juster

B.   *Sleep is good, he said, and books are better.*   *-George R.R. Martin*

C.   *If you don't like to read, you haven't found the right book.*   *-J.K. Rowling*

D.   *Books should go where they will be most appreciated, and not sit unread, gathering dust on a forgotten shelf, don't you agree?*   *-Christopher Paolini*

Q.10. Select the option that can be concluded from the text.

(1)   Youngsters are no longer interested in reading books

(2)   The number of Bookshops is increasing due to the increase in demand of the books

(3)   Shakespeare is the most beloved writer among the youngsters

(4)   Children desire logical content

A.   (1), (2) and (3) are true (4) is false   B.   (1) and (3) are true (2) and (4) are false

C.   (1) and (4) are true, (2) and (3) are false   D.   all are false

II. Read the passage given below.

I.   The passenger pigeon (Ectopistesmigratorius) was once found in huge numbers in North America. Records tell of passing flocks that darkened the skies for several days at a time. The species may have peaked at five billion individuals. A more conservative estimate is three billion.

II.   Within a short time, the species disappeared completely.

"Given the huge size of the population, it's simply amazing that the species disappeared so quickly," says Tom Gilbert. Gilbert is a professor at the University of Copenhagen's Centre for GeoGenetics, but he also has a part-time position as an adjunct professor at the Norwegian University of Science and Technology (NTNU).

III.   The history of the passenger pigeon is interesting, partly because it can tell us something about how and why species become extinct. Native Americans also relied on passenger pigeons for food. But at least in parts of the passenger pigeons' range, people had learned to harvest the species at a sustainable level that didn't threaten to eradicate it. It was common in some parts of North America to only eat young pigeons that were hunted at night, since this did not seem to scare away the adult birds or prevent them from re-nesting.

IV.   But starting around 1500, a more aggressive variant of humans came to the continent with the arrival of Europeans. The hunt for passenger pigeons grew and culminated in a massive hunt for the species throughout the 1800s, before the species finally collapsed and disappeared. In 2014, a study in published in the scientific journal PNAS strongly suggested that humans were simply the final straw in destroying a species that was already vulnerable and headed to oblivion.

The cladogram below follows the 2012 DNA study showing the position of the passenger pigeon among its closest relatives:

Macropygia (cuckoo-doves)

Reinwardtoena

Turacoena

Columba (Old World pigeons)

Streptopelia (turtle doves and collared doves)

Patagioenas (New World pigeons)

Ectopistes (passenger pigeon)

V. The researchers asserted that despite their enormous numbers, the passenger pigeons were already in trouble. The population of the species varied greatly, similar to lemmings, but over a longer period of time. When the Europeans arrived, the species was already in a strong decline. The population was plummeting long before Europeans arrived, and perhaps Europeans even contributed to a short-term increase in numbers.

VI. Studies of the genetic variation of the species using an investigative method called PSMC formed the background for these assertions. And now we have to concentrate a bit. The PSMC method can use the information in the genes of a single individual of a species to map the history of the species.

VII. You should therefore be able to see how the species developed over many generations, and estimate how many individuals there were at any given time, all based on a single genome. Using this method, researchers found that the number of passenger pigeons was in free fall even before the arrival of the Europeans.

Although the species might not have become extinct, it would have shrunk significantly in any case, maybe to only a few hundred thousand individuals.

Based on your understanding of the passage, answer <u>any six</u> out of the eight questions by choosing the correct option.

Q.11. Select the correct inference with reference to the following.

"Records tell of passing flocks that darkened the skies for several days at a time."

    A.   The innumerable individual passenger pigeons flocked the skies of North America.

    B.   The black pigeons together turned the blue sky dark.

    C.   When the pigeons passed through the skies of North America, the sky was covered with black clouds.

    D.   The pigeons carried bad omens with them which were visible through the sky getting dark.

Q.12. According to cladogram 2012 DNA study in fig-1, the species that was famous among Old World pigeons were:

    A.   Reinwardtoena   B.   Columba

    C.   Patagioenas   D.   Turacoena

Q.13. Choose the correct cause and effect relationship from the given options.

Cause	Effect
The hunt for passenger pigeons grew and culminated in a massive hunt for the species throughout the 1800s.	The species finally collapsed and disappeared.

A.

Cause	Effect
The history of the passenger pigeon is interesting.	It can tell us something about how and why species become extinct

B.

Cause	Effect
The PSMC method can use the information in the genes of a single individual of a species.	Mapping the history of the species.

C.

Cause	Effect
Studies of the genetic variation of the species is using an investigative method called PSMC.	It formed the background for these assertions.

D.

Q.14. Select the central message in paragraph – II according to Tom Gilbert's study about Passenger pigeon.

It conclude that

    A.   It's simply astonishing that the species found in large number, disappeared so quickly.

    B.   It's pathetic that passenger pigeons were disliked by Europeans.

    C.   It's incredible that the species flourished quickly.

    D.   It's unbelievable that the species suddenly migrated.

Q.15. Based on your reading of paragraph III, select the appropriate counter- argument to the given argument.

Argument : The North Americans ate young pigeons that were hunted at night, since this did not seem to scare away the adult birds or prevent them from re-nesting.

A. I think the North Americans could have eaten the birds at day too as it won't make any difference.

B. I don't think that eating young birds at night wouldn't scare the adult birds. After all, they can sense fear and it is just an assumption of the North Americans.

C. I feel that hunting adult birds could have been better because the young birds wouldn't have been able to judge the scene.

D. I don't feel that what North Americans did was right.

Q.16. The phrase "The population was plummeting long before Europeans arrived" refers to:

A. The number of migrating passenger pigeons was decreasing slowly.

B. There was a rapid decrease in the population of passenger pigeons.

C. The species of passenger pigeons were extinct.

D. There was a rapid increase in the population of passenger pigeons.

Q.17. Based on the reading of the passage, choose the fact that the researchers find about the number of passenger pigeons.

A. It's number started deteriorating with the arrival of Europeans.

B. It was in free fall even before the arrival of the Europeans.

C. It became extinct after the arrival of Europeans.

D. It's species began to multiply with the arrival of Europeans.

Q.18. Read the two statements given below and select the option that explains them.

(1) PSMC method uses the information in the genes of a single individual of a species.

(2) It is important to map the history of the species to know more.

A. (1) is the result of (2)

B. (2) is the requirement for (1)

C. (1) is true, (2) is false

D. (2) is the research through (1)

WRITING

III. **Answer <u>any four</u> out of the five questions given, with reference to the context below.**

Deepak Kumar, the Police Commissioner of Kanpur wants to write a notice advising the residents to drive carefully and use fog lights to prevent accidents

Q.19. Select the appropriate title for the notice.

A. The Dense Fog

B. Traffic Advisory

C. Prevent accidents

D. Be vigilant on roads

Q.20. Select the option that lists the most accurate opening for this notice.

A. Greetings and attention please, to one and all….

B. This notice is written to share some news with you all about…

C. This is to notify that in view of …

D. I wish to share this notice that ……

Q.21. Select the option with the information points to be included in the body of this notice.

(1) Opinion about the weather

(2) Resolution for accidents due to the fog

(3) Reasons for the fog

(4) Importance of fog lights for vehicles

(5) Complaint against people without fog lights

A. (2) and (4)

B. (1), (3) and (5)

C. (3) and (5)

D. (2) and (3)

Q.22. What is the purpose of writing this notice?

A. to threaten people

B. to praise people

C. to demean people

D. to warn people

Q.23. Select the appropriate conclusion for this notice.

A. Stay safe

B. Don't panic

C. Stay humble

D. Inconvenience regretted

IV.   **Answer <u>any six</u> of the seven questions given, with reference to the context below.**

You are Megha, a resident of Lodhi road, New Delhi. You have to write a letter to the editor bringing the issue of daylight robbery in your neighborhood into the view of concerned authorities.

Q.24. Choose the CORRECT start for the letter.

A.   Please look at the daylight robbery in our area

B.   Through the columns of your esteemed newspaper, I want to draw your kind attention towards the daylight robbery in our area

C.   With your newspaper I want to open the eyes of the concerned authorities to the daylight robbery of the area

D.   I want to complaint about the daylight robbery

Q.25. Pick the CORRECT tone in which this letter to the editor shall be ended.

"I hope that the concerned authorities may look into the matter at the earliest."

A.   friendly and warm   B.   cool and polite

C.   polite and formal   D.   rude and strict

Q.26. Choose the CORRECT option for the following.

"________________: Need to take a strict action against the daylight robberies"

A.   Subject   B.   Topic

C.   Salutation   D.   Title

Q.27. Choose the option that shows what the letter to the editor would NOT do for Megha.

A.   Bring changes in conditions

B.   Take actions against the issue

C.   Make her area safer to live

D.   Getting a reward for her to bring it to the notice of concerned authorities

Q.28. Writing a letter to the editor will help Megha to ________________.

A.	B.	C.	D.
• vent out her frustration • Demean the police department	• look superior than other locals • Come out as a brave girl	• remove undeserving policeman from their job • Get hired instead	• Solve the robbery issues in the area by highlighting it in a newspaper • Make the area safe for people

Q.29. Megha shares some suggestions in her letter, to address the issue.

Select the option that helps her complete these suggestions, appropriately.

Much of this problem will be dealt if(i)________________at the colony entrance. It will be so kind if the concerned authorities could provide at least two policemen to look around the area during the morning and the evening hours.

A.   security guards are posted   B.   arms are provided to the gatekeeper

C.   restriction is made   D.   there is a lock

Q.30. Which of the following approach is most appropriate for drafting a letter on the above subject?

A.   Suggesting improvement methods—Introducing problem faced by the people—Conclusion.

B.   Introducing problems faced by the people—Suggesting improvement methods—Conclusion.

C.   Suggesting improvement methods—Conclusion—Introducing problems faced by the people.

D.   Conclusion—Introducing problems faced by the people—Suggesting improvement methods

LITERATURE

This section has sub-sections: V, VI, VII, VIII, IX. There are a total of 30 questions in the section. Attempt any 26 questions from the sub-sections V to IX.

V.   **Read the given extract to attempt questions that follow:**

Poor man! It was in honour of this last lesson that he had put on his fine Sunday clothes, and now I understood why the old men of the village were sitting there in the back of the room. It was because they were sorry, too, that they had not gone to school more. It was their way of thanking our master for his forty years of faithful service and of showing their respect for the country that was theirs no more.

Q.31. The narrator referred to M. Hamel as 'Poor man!' because he:

   A.   empathised with M. Hamel as he had to leave the village.

   B.   believed that M. Hamel's "fine Sunday clothes" clearly reflected that he was not rich.

   C.   felt sorry for M. Hamel as it was his last French lesson.

   D.   thought that M. Hamel's patriotism and sense of duty resulted in his poverty.

Q.32. Choose the CORRECT idiom that describes the villagers' act of attending the last lesson most accurately.

   A.   'Too good to miss'   B.   'Too little, too late'

   C.   'Too many cooks spoil the broth'   D.   'Too cool for school'

Q.33. Choose the option that might raise a question about M. Hamel's "faithful service".

   A.   When Franz came late, M. Hamel told him that he was about to begin class without him.

   B.   Franz mentioned how cranky M. Hamel was and his "great ruler rapping on the table".

   C.   M. Hamel often sent students to water his flowers, and gave a holiday when he wanted to go fishing.

   D.   M. Hamel permitted villagers put their children "to work on a farm or at the mills" for some extra money.

Q.34. Select the option that most appropriately fills in the blanks, for the following description of the given extract.

The villagers and their children sat in class, forging with their old master a (i) ___ togetherness. In that moment, the class room stood (ii)___. It was France itself, and the last French lesson a desperate hope to (iii) ___to the remnants of what they had known and taken for granted. Their own (iv) ___.

   A.   (i) graceful; (ii) still; (iii) hang on; (iv) country

   B.   (i) bygone; (ii) up; (iii) keep on; (iv) education

   C.   (i) beautiful; (ii) mesmerised; (iii) carry on; (iv) unity

   D.   (i) forgotten; (ii) transformed; (iii) hold on; (iv) identity

Q.35. Identify the villagers' emotions from the extract.

   A.   happiness   B.   desperation

   C.   depression   D.   regret

VI.   **Read the given extract to attempt questions that follow:**

"I will learn to drive a car," he answers, looking straight into my eyes. His dream looms like a mirage amidst the dust of streets that fill his town Firozabad, famous for its bangles. Every other family in Firozabad is engaged in making bangles. It is the centre of India's glass-blowing industry where families have spent generations working around furnaces, wielding glass, making bangles for all the women in the land it seems.

Mukesh's family is among them. None of them know that it is illegal for children like him to work in the glass furnaces with high temperatures, in dingy cells without air and light; that the law, if enforced, could get him and all those 20,000 children out of the hot furnaces where they slog their daylight hours, often losing the brightness of their eyes. Mukesh's eyes beam as he volunteers to take me home, which he proudly says is being rebuilt.

Q.36. The phrase *'Dream looms like a mirage amidst the dust of streets'* signifies that

   A.   his dream was a reality, yet seemed distant.   B.   his dream was lost in the sea of dust.

   C.   his dream was illusionary and indistinct.   D.   his dream was hanging in the dusty air.

Q.37. Identify the emotions of Mukesh from the phrase: *'I will learn to drive a car'*.

   (1)   arrogant   (2)   hopeful

   (3)   sad   (4)   ambitious

   (5)   sneaky

   A.   1 and 5   B.   2 and 4

   C.   2 and 5   D.   3 and 6

Q.38. Which of the following statements is NOT TRUE with reference to the extract?

   A.   Children work in badly lit and poorly ventilated furnaces.

   B.   The children are unaware that it is forbidden by law to work in the furnaces.

    C.   Children toil in the furnaces for hours which affect their eyesight.

    D.   Firozabad has emerged as a nascent producer of bangles in the country.

Q.39. *"Every other family in Firozabad is engaged in making bangles"*. What does this line highlight?

    A.   bangle making is the only industry that flourishes in Firozabad.

    B.   the entire population of Firozabad is involved in bangle making.

    C.   majority of the population in Firozabad is involved in bangle making.

    D.   bangle making is the most loved occupation in Firozabad.

Q.40. *"Mukesh's eyes beam as he volunteers to take me home."* This indicates that Mukesh was:

    A.   happy   B.   sad

    C.   gloomy   D.   dreamy

VII.   **Read the given extract to attempt questions that follow:**

Driving from my parent's home to Cochin last Friday

morning, I saw my mother, beside me,

doze, open mouthed, her face ashen like that

of a corpse and realised with pain

that she was as old as she looked but soon

put that thought away,…

Q.41. Which of the following options best applies to the given extract?

    (1)   a conversation   (2)   an argument

    (3)   a piece of advice   (4)   a strategy

    (5)   a recollection   (6)   a suggestion

    A.   (1), (3) and (6)   B.   (2), (4) and (5)

    C.   Only (5)   D.   Only (1)

Q.42. Select the book title that perfectly describes the condition of the poet's mother.

Title 1	Title 2	Title 3	Title 4
You're Only Old Once! by *Dr. Seuss*	The Gift of Years by *Joan Chittister*	Somewhere Towards the End by *Diana Athill*	The Book You Wish Your Parents Had Read by *Philippa Perry*

    A.   Title 1   B.   Title 2

    C.   Title 3   D.   Title 4

Q.43. Choose the option that applies correctly to the two statements given below.

    Assertion: The poet wards off the thought of her mother getting old quickly.

    Reason: The poet didn't want to confront the inevitability of fate that was to dawn upon her mother.

    A.   Assertion can be inferred but the Reason cannot be inferred.

    B.   Assertion cannot be inferred but the Reason can be inferred.

    C.   Both Assertion and Reason can be inferred.

    D.   Both Assertion and Reason cannot be inferred.

Q.44. Choose the option that displays the same literary device as in the given lines of the extract.

her face

ashen like that

of a corpse…

    A.   Just as I had this thought, she appeared and…

    B.   My thoughts were as heavy as lead that evening when …

    C.   I think like everyone else who…

    D.   I like to think aloud when …

Q.45. Her face *'ashen like a corpse'*. The phrase here means:

    A.   there was ashes of smoke on her face

    B.   her face was full of dirt and dust

C.   her face was lifeless and dull like that of a dead person

D.   the wrinkles on her face made her looked ashen

VII.   Read the given extract to attempt questions that follow:

He was very light, like a fowl that had been half-starved for a long time until it is only feathers and skeleton. So, his arms hanging, they carried him up the steps and into the side door of the house. This door opened into a passage, and down the passage they carried the man towards an empty bedroom. It had been the bedroom of Sadao's father, and since his death it had not been used. They laid the man on the deeply matted floor. Everything here had been Japanese to please the old man, who would never in his own home sit on a chair or sleep in a foreign bed. Hana went to the wall cupboards and slid back a door and took out a soft quilt. She hesitated. The quilt was covered with flowered silk and the lining was pure white silk.

Q.46. The description of Sadao's father in the extract demonstrates that he was a ______________ person.

A.   witty

B.   modern

C.   traditional

D.   wacky

Q.47. 'She hesitated' means that Hana

A.   didn't want to carry the soldier as he had a limp in his leg

B.   didn't want to use her silk as he was their guest

C.   didn't want to use her white silk as the soldier was bleeding

D.   didn't like to share her stuff

Q.48. *"his arms hanging"* indicated the state of the soldier. Pick the option that correctly tells his state.

(1)   unconscious

(2)   weak

(3)   strong

(4)   rebellious

(5)   calm

(6)   conscious

A.   (1) and (2)

B.   (1) and (3)

C.   (5) and (6)

D.   (4) and (5)

Q.49. They avoided bringing the person home as he was

A.   foreigner, white, enemy

B.   enemy, soldier, Japanese

C.   Japanese, soldier, friend

D.   foreigner, friend, bleeding

Q.50. Select the option that displays a cause-effect set.

A.

Cause	Effect
Hana didn't want to use her beloved quilt for the American soldier.	She hesitated while taking it out.

B.

Cause	Effect
She hesitated while taking out quilt.	Hana didn't want to use her beloved quilt for an American soldier.

C.

Cause	Effect
Sadao's father was a traditional man.	He liked modern furniture in the house.

D.

Cause	Effect
He was not a true patriot.	Sadao was ready to treat the enemy.

IX.   Attempt the following.

Q.51. When M. Hamel addressed Franz saying, *"I've plenty of time, I'll learn"*, what does this imply?

A.   Self-realization

B.   Astonishment

C.   Lethargic responsibilities

D.   Evading responsibilities

Q.52. Which of the following profession is prevalent in Seemapuri?

A.   bangle making

B.   iron making

C.   rag picking

D.   pick pocketing

Q.53. *"Hi, Skinny! How'd you like to be ducked?"* This line shows that the speaker was a:

A.   trainer

B.   bully

C.   teacher

D.   swimmer

Q.54. The poetic device in the line *"wan, pale as a late winter's moon"* is:

    A.   hyperbole   B.   irony

    C.   simile   D.   metaphor

Q.55. The children's faces are compared to 'rootless weeds'. This means they are _______________.

    A.   insecure   B.   ill-fed

    C.   wasters   D.   dumb

Q.56. Select the suitable option for the given statements, based on your reading of *The Third Level*.

    (1)   Charley's wife Louisa was always worried for her husband's distrainment.

    (2)   Charley wanted to escape his depressing reality of life through the third level.

    A.   (1) is false but (2) is true.   B.   Both (1) and (2) are false.

    C.   (2) is a fact but unrelated to (1)   D.   (1) is the cause for (2).

Q.57. Dr. Sadao decided to help the man, irrespective of :

    A.   not knowing the cure   B.   being an American

    C.   the fear of being caught   D.   being a patriot

Q.58. Which of the following option does the poet NOT mean when he talks about 'keeping quiet'?

    A.   total inactivity   B.   contemplating

    C.   self introspection   D.   being calm

Q.59. Identify the tone of Kamala Das in the following line:

    I saw my mother, beside me, doze, open mouthed….

    A.   elated and excited   B.   heartbroken and despaired

    C.   scared and anxious   D.   serene and satisfied

Q.60. Dr. Sadao didn't further his feelings for Hana before ensuring that she was a Japanese. This shows that Dr. Sadao was:

    A.   fake   B.   selfish

    C.   confused   D.   ethical

❑❑

Sample Paper 2

English Core

READING

I. Read the passage given below.

I. The Titanic, in its watery grave, is a great museum of human history and is at risk of being lost forever because of curious voyagers and treasure hunters, fears Bob Ballard, who first discovered the remains of the iconic ship in 1985. Famous for discovering the great ship, Ballard is a former US Navy Officer and a professor of oceanography.

II. "Titanic is a museum of human history without door and guard. I am deeply concerned about not only the Titanic but all the ancient history that is now at risk. If we cannot save this iconic ship, then there is a very little hope we can save ancient ships. The world should realize that you don't have to go down and take everything and you do not have to do a treasure hunt. This is a common heritage of all of us and if we really want to take steps to preserve human history in the ocean, we need to start with Titanic," Ballard said in a telephonic interview from London.

III. Ballard, as part of a tie-up, is presenting a documentary called "Save the Titanic" on the 100th anniversary of the sinking of the great ship – April 15, 1912. The ship and her fate continue to fascinate, largely because of the horror that took place that night, with 1,522 passengers and crew losing their lives.

IV. Ballard says that despite being on the ocean floor for 100 years, the ship is full of human footprints. "You will find pairs of shoes everywhere. The sea and the life below has claimed everything but they do not know what to do with shoes so you will find a pair of mother's shoes next to her little daughter and that's their grave-stone. At her wreckage, we almost felt that we were surrounded by the lifeboats of all the people that were in the water at that spot".

V. Ballard says that the fate of Titanic continues to fascinate so many years after it sank because it is "irony personified in history". "The story has all the ingredients to make it timelessly fascinating. You have this revolutionary ship that's unsinkable and carrying a cross-section of people in society. And then, it goes and hits an iceberg and sinks on its maiden journey. It's an irony personified in history".

VI. Talking about his discovery, which came after great research and 75 years later, Ballard, says it was a somber moment went they first spotted the boiler of the Titanic. "In the 90s, advanced technology gave us double diving capabilities in the Atlantic Ocean. I knew that the Titanic was sitting at almost 12,000 feet. What led me to her discovery was a simple technique that I followed. We decided to look for the debris trail instead of the ship".

VII. Ballard says the ship, if preserved well and not subjected to constant submarine journeys, will last for a long time on the Atlantic floor. "The deep sea, because of its darkness, its cold temperatures and its great pressure, creates a high state of preservation. With a little caution, we can protect the Titanic for future generations to visit."

VIII. Ballard has also connected to the people of Belfast, who refused to talk about the tragedy. "The ship's construction took place at Belfast. After the tragedy, families of the workers refused to talk about it because of the shame and sadness in the loss of life involved".

(**Source:** archive.indianexpress.com)

Based on your understanding of the passage, answer <u>any eight</u> out of the ten questions by choosing the correct option.

Q.1. The vandalism on the remains of the Titanic ship by divers makes the writer feel:

A. shocked   B. concerned

C. awestruck   D. annoyed

Q.2. Euphemism is a word or phrase used to avoid saying an unpleasant or offensive word.

The writer says that the titanic is in its <u>watery grave</u>.

Select the word from the options that correctly translates to the euphemism presented here.

A.	sunk	B.	saved
C.	stopped	D.	sifted

Q.3. Select the option that suitably completes the given dialogue as per the context in paragraph VIII.

Writer: Are you related to the workers who made the Titanic?

Man from Belfast: Yes, but (1)...........................

Writer: I just wanted to know about the incident.

Man from Belfast: I am sorry but (2)...........................

A.   (1) it wasn't me who made it (2) I am willing to tell you only if you pay me.

B.   (1) I cannot recognize you (2) we don't disclose such confidential affairs.

C.   (1) only distantly (2) you don't look like you care enough.

D.   (1) why do you ask? (2) I would rather not talk about that unfortunate tragedy.

Q.4. What could've been the news headline when the writer first discovered the remains of the Titanic ship in 1985?

1. Titanic the unsinkable now in ruins.

2. Headed to the port, now in the ocean.

3. Titanic found preserved in its watery grave.

4. Positive news for voyagers, Titanic found.

A.	option 1	B.	option 2
C.	option 3	D.	option 4

Q.5. Select the option that clearly indicates the situation before and after Titanic was discovered in 1985.

	Before 1985	After 1985
A.	Ruins preserved in cold dark ocean.	Hunters and voyagers exploiting the ruins.
B.	Ruins sinking deeper into the ocean.	Hunters and voyagers bringing the entire ship out.
C.	Ruins remaining intact.	Ruins preserved untouched.
D.	Ship getting lost to sea creatures.	Conservationists saving the remains.

Q.6. What is the relationship between (1) and (2)?

(1) ....In the 90s, advanced technology gave us double diving capabilities in the Atlantic Ocean.

(2) ....We decided to look for the debris trail instead of the ship.

A.   (2) is the cause of (1).   B.   (1) and (2) were independent of each other.

C.   (2) did not cause (1).   D.   (1) is the cause of (2).

Q.7. The writer mentions the Titanic as a great museum of human history. He says so because he realises that:

A.   No matter what may come, we should protect the Titanic as it is the only reminder of the greatest ship that sunk into the ocean.

B.   Titanic contains hidden treasures from the century old rich passengers that boarded the ship.

C.   The deep dark and cold conditions of the ocean has well preserved a century old specimen of human endeavour and failure which is an irony personified in history.

D.   Titanic has been claimed by the sea life below so there's no point now in trying to salvage it from further disintegration.

Q.8. Select the option that lists the eulogy for the Titanic's passengers by the ship-makers from Belfast.

A.   We are all grieving today for the greatest loss to mankind in recent history. We have failed all those on board by not building them a strong enough Titanic.

B.   Loss to human life is the most miserable one can imagine, but remember it was the fury of nature that took it down, and nothing more.

    C.   Grieve we must yes! But life goes on for us unfortunates who are still alive and have to live with the horrors of this tragedy.

    D.   Titanic and its human companions are resting in the depths of the ocean. The tragedy has immortalized them all forever.

Q.9. Which quote summarises the writer's feelings about the conservation of Titanic as a cultural icon for human history?

    A.   The object of war is victory; that of victory is conquest; and that of conquest preservation.

—Montesquieu

    B.   The people without the knowledge of their past history, origin and culture is like a tree without roots.   *—Marcus Garvey*

    C.   Until the moment she actually sinks, the Titanic is unsinkable.   *—Julia Hughes*

    D.   Government has no other end, but the preservation of property.   *—John Locke*

Q.10. Select the option that lists what we can conclude from the text.

    (1) The writer has unrealistic expectations of protecting Titanic from degradation.

    (2) The writer is addressing all of us to be responsible in preserving our heritage.

    (3) The technologies haven't advanced much since the 90s to help save the ruins of the ship.

    (4) Before going for deep sea treasure hunting, one must understand the cultural impact of their actions.

    A.   (2) and (3) are true   B.   (2), (3) and (4) are true

    C.   (1) and (4) are true   D.   (2) and (4) are true

II. Read the passage given below.

    I.   NSYNC singer Lance Bass can't afford the $20 million price tag for a ride into space now, he should try again, in say, a decade. But within a decade or so, even some of Bass's fans could afford a quick and safe trip to the suborbital edge of space, roughly 50-60 miles above earth, says Frank Seitzen, President of the Space Transport Association.

    II.   "I think you're may be 10 or 12 years away from having companies that are reliable and that can go through that process for $5,000 or $10,000," Seitzen said. There's a hungry demand from would be space tourists and a $10 million prize is inspiring designers. The Prize, created in 1994 to spur the development of new space travel technologies, has attracted at least 21 space vehicle designs from people in five countries. The non-profit X Prize Foundation, founded by a group of donors inspired by the $25,000 Orteig Prize that Charles Lindbergh won in 1927, will give the prize.

    III.   Each design team is hoping to develop the first reusable rocket capable of blasting a pilot and two to five passengers to a height of 62 miles. NASA awards astronaut status for flights above 50 miles. Some design contestants boast that such trips will be available by 2005, although the first few travellers will face $100,000 bills until the market matures.

    IV.   Despite steep prices and lagging technology, Seitzen and others are convinced that a lucrative travel business awaits. Space Adventures, a travel agency that helped coordinate the first tourist trip to the International Space Station last year by US businessman Dennis Tito, claims it has collected $2 million in deposits from more than 120 would-be suborbital tourists. For client Wally Funk, who has paid her deposit, suborbital travel is a disappointing, yet feasible, alternative to decades of trying to reach space. Funk, a retired aviation safety investigator says, "I would do (a space station trip) in a heartbeat, but I can't because I'm not a millionaire."

    V.   Compared to Tito's groundbreaking effort last year, future suborbital flights look easy. Tito was subjected to rigid medical requirements and a gruelling six-month training course in Russia. But suborbital travellers will need only a few days of training and pending FAA approval, would have to pass a much lower bar for medical standards."We always say that if you can safely ride a roller coaster, then you are fit for a suborbital flight," says Space Adventures spokeswoman Tereza Predescu.

    VI.   Four commercial spaceports, which launch rockets into space like airports launch planes, are already licensed to operate by the FAA in Virginia, California, Alaska and Florida, and they are eager to welcome extra business from space tourists, negating the need to catch a ride to Russia. For those reasons, suborbital travel may represent a $1 billion in a year market, according to Space Adventures President and CEO Eric Anderson, that's 10,000 travellers paying $100,000 each during the first few years of adventure space travel.

(Source: auto.economictimes.indiatimes.com)

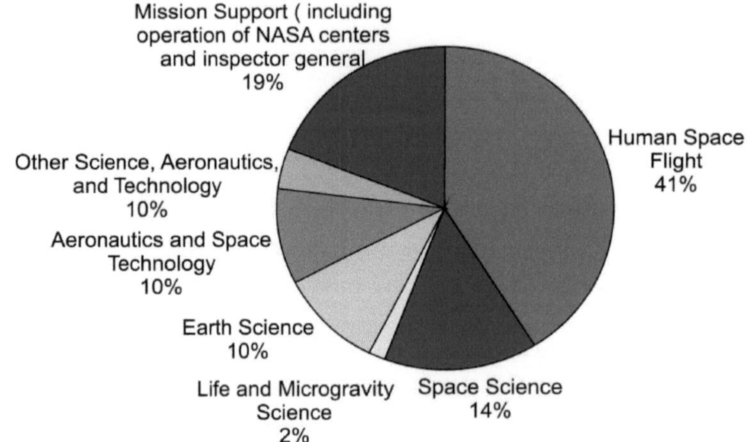

NASA budget for science-related programs and activities, FY 1997 (constant FY 1995 dollars)

Based on your understanding of the passage, answer <u>any six</u> out of the eight questions by choosing the correct option.

Q.11. Select the correct inference with reference to the following:

There's a hungry demand from would be space tourists and a $10 million prize is inspiring designers......

   A.   Space tourists have collectively bet a $10 million prize to anyone who can take them for a space trip.

   B.   Space tourists are demanding for restaurants in space to satiate a hungry stomach.

   C.   There's a potential for space tourism market but unfortunately no one is tapping into it.

   D.   Spacecraft designers are competing to bring the quickest and most affordable options for space tourism.

Q.12. Select the central idea of the paragraph I.

   A.   Space tourism may not be feasible as of now but next decade may prove more promising.

   B.   Space tourism is only for the super-rich, be it at present or in the next decade.

   C.   Space tourism is a wasteful venture of resources and fuels.

   D.   Space tourism is going to be accessible only through NASA.

Q.13. Select the option that displays the true statement with reference to the figure given.

   A.   NASA's budget lays more emphasis on the study of Life and Microgravity science.

   B.   NASA's budget for Human Space Flight and Mission Support are in the priority.

   C.   It is not possible to correctly tell NASA's preferences as everything is for science at the end.

   D.   Space Science and Earth Science are the highest funded NASA programs.

Q.14. Based on your reading of paragraphs IV-V, select the appropriate counter- argument to the given argument.

Argument: Space trips are an egotistical way to flaunt your wealth to the poor and middle class, because at the end of the day you're contributing nothing to science and advancement.

   A.   The wealthy have collected about $ 2 million for space travel, so they all are working together setting their egos aside.

   B.   It is not for us to judge what others are doing as long as they are aware of the carbon footprints they are going to leave behind.

   C.   History holds testimony that the rich has always had unrealistic tastes, earlier it was precious stones and ivory, now it is space travel.

   D.   The wealthiest are willing to fund for research and development in space science, so even if it is for their ego, it will still be a way for advancement in faster and cheaper technologies.

Q.15. Select the option that displays the correct cause-effect relationship.

	Cause	Effect
A.	$10 million prize for spacecraft designers.	Faster development of cost-effective space trips.
B.	Rising interest in space tourism.	Decrease in space science studies.
C.	Lower budget constraints for researchers.	Lesser productivity and slow advancements.
D.	Faster development of cost-effective space trips.	$10 million prize for spacecraft designers.

Q.16. The survey statistics mention the speculated average space flight budget, indicating that:

    A.   The ticket price can be either of $100,000 or $5,000.

    B.   The demand and development lack the potential to lower ticket price from $100,000 to $5,000.

    C.   The demand for a space flight is now saturating.

    D.   The demand and development have the potential to lower ticket price from $10,000 to $5,000.

Q.17. The phrase 'blasting a pilot' refers to the:

    A.   bombing the pilot into shreds.

    B.   launching a pilot into space.

    C.   shooting a pilot into space.

    D.   hurling a pilot into space.

Q.18. Read the two statements given below and select the option that suitably explains them.

    (1) Each design team is hoping to develop the first reusable rocket.

    (2) Suborbital travel may represent a $1 billion in a year market.

    A.   (2) is false but (1) is true.

    B.   (1) is true and (2) is the reason of (1).

    C.   (1) and (2) are false.

    D.   (2) and (1) are true but independent of each other.

WRITING

III.   Answer <u>any four</u> out of the five questions given, with reference to the context below.

General Manager of Digimart Infotech, New Delhi needs a marketing executive for the organisation.

Q.19. Which of the following title is suitable for this classified advertisement?

    A.   Bumper Vacancy

    B.   Want a job in a reputed Delhi based marketing company?

    C.   Position Vacant

    D.   Get your dream job.

Q.20. Which of the following details must be included in this advertisement?

    1.   Requirement

    2.   Eligibility

    3.   Daily roles and responsibilities.

    A.   1 only   B.   2 only

    C.   1 and 2 only   D.   2 and 3 only

Q.21. Which of the following is the most suitable starting line for this advertisement?

    A.   Wanted marketing executive for a reputed Delhi based organisation...

    B.   Want to become a part of a reputed Delhi based organisation?

    C.   Your dream job is calling you...

    D.   Make the most of this golden opportunity....

Q.22. Which of the following is not required in the above advertisement?

    A.   Address of the General Manager   B.   Eligibility criteria for applicants

    C.   Contact details   D.   Title of the advertisement

Q.23. Which of the following can't be skipped in the above advertisement?

    A.   UID details of the General Manager

    B.   Revenue earned by the company on yearly basis

    C.   Title of the advertisement

    D.   Address of the General Manager

IV.   Answer <u>any six</u> of the seven questions given, with reference to the context below.

Ravi is the member of Meghdhanush, a school club that actively promote mental health awareness. He has to write an article emphasizing need to consider mental health as essential part of our lives and stop stigmatizing the mental health patients.

Q.24. Select the most suitable title for the above article.

    A.   Subjective well-being   B.   Depression is lethal

    C.   Mental health – your greatest wealth   D.   Light at the end of the tunnel

Q.25. Which option (1-4), should Ravi choose to elaborate what mental health is?

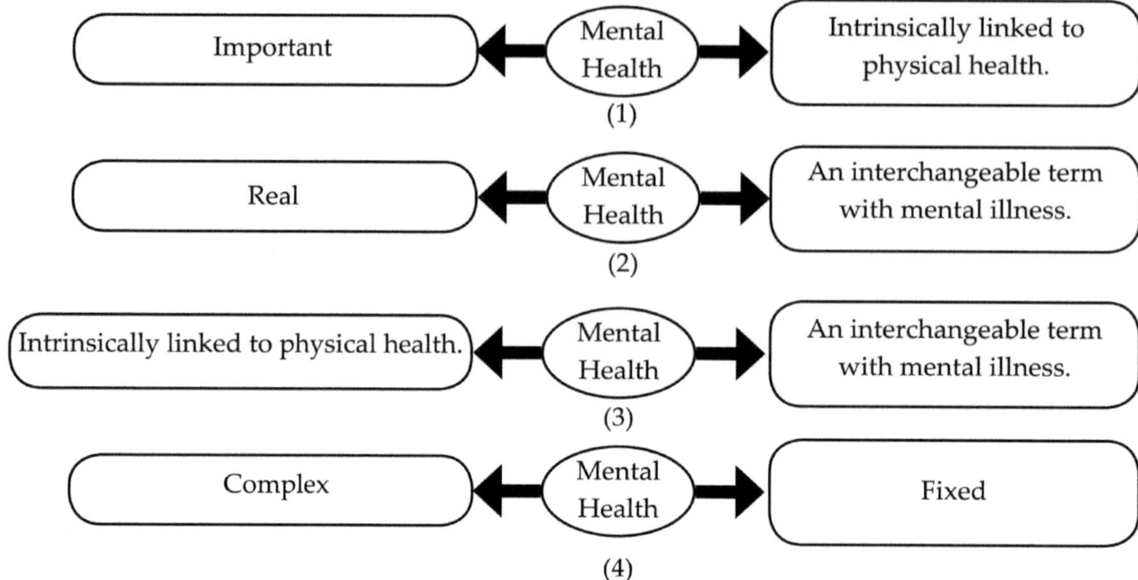

    A.   option 1   B.   option 2

    C.   option 3   D.   option 4

Q.26. Which option would help Ravi with appropriate organisation of relevant ideas for this article?

    A.   Expressing concern about several cases of suicide due to depression- exploring the reasons with factual support – stating the effects – providing the suggestion to create mental health awareness – presenting a conclusive outlook.

    B.   Exploring the reasons - Expressing concern about several cases of suicide due to depression - Providing the suggestion to create mental health awareness - Stating the effects - presenting a conclusive outlook.

    C.   Exploring the reasons - Stating the effects - Providing the suggestion to create mental health awareness - presenting a conclusive outlook.

    D.   Presenting a conclusive outlook - Stating the effects - Exploring the reasons - Providing the suggestion to create mental health awareness.

Q.27. Which of the following suggestion would be appropriate for Ravi's article?

    A.   Open more mental asylums.

    B.   Government should make budgetary allocations every year for dealing with mental health.

    C.   There should be compulsory mental health check up every year.

    D.   Individuals should understand the importance of mental health and society should be more sensitive towards such causes.

Q.28. Read the following sentence from Ravi's article draft and help him complete it by selecting the most appropriate term.

Reducing the _______ associated with mental health may enable more individuals to _______ from mental illness.

    A.   Medicines, infect   B.   Treatment, recover

    C.   Stigma, Recover   D.   Medicines, recover

Q.29. Which quote should be used to summarize the central idea of the article?

    A.   "It's okay to not to be okay"

    B.   "Mental health treatment is a science of uncertainty and art of possibility"

    C.   "There is no such problem like mental health; everything is simple made-up issue in mind."

    D.   "Unresolved issues lead to mental health"

Q.30. Select the most appropriate checklist for the above article.

A.   My article contains -

> 1. An eye-catching title
> 2. A by-line
> 3. Proper set of causes and effects for mental illness
> 4. Well deliberated suggestions
> 5. A quote to enhance the quality of the article
> 6. Factual information to support argument

B.   My article contains -

> 1. Quote as title
> 2. Opinion of experts
> 3. Aggressive arguments against those who stigmatize mental health.
> 4. Fact sheet to convince readers.
> 5. Free hand drawing at the end to make your article more eye catching
> 6. Date

C.   My article contains -

> 1. An eye-catching title
> 2. Opinion of doctors
> 3. Opinions of general public
> 4. Opinions of Mental health patients
> 5. Quote at the end
> 6. Date

D.   My article contains -

> 1. Causes for negligence of mental health
> 2. Suggestion to improve the condition
> 3. Three to four quotes.
> 4. By line
> 5. Date
> 6. Opinion of experts

LITERATURE

This section has sub-sections: V, VI, VII, VIII, IX. There are a total of 30 questions in the section. Attempt any 26 questions from the sub-sections V to IX.

V.   Read the given extract to attempt questions that follow:

Then all effort ceased. I relaxed. Even my legs felt limp; and a blackness swept over my brain. It wiped out fear; it wiped out terror. There was no more panic. It was quiet and peaceful. Nothing to be afraid of. This is nice... to be drowsy... to go to sleep... no need to jump... too tired to jump... it's nice to be carried gently... to float along in space... tender arms around me... tender arms like Mother's... now I must go to sleep... I crossed to oblivion, and the curtain of life fell.

Q.31. Choose the correct option with reference to the two statements given below.

Statement 1: The author tried his best to jump out of water.

Statement 2: After a while, the author was not anxious in water.

A.   If Statement 1 is the cause, Statement 2 is the effect.

B.   If Statement 1 is the effect, Statement 2 is the cause.

C.   Both the statements are the effects of a common cause.

D.   Both the statements are the effects of independent causes.

Q.32. The *'curtain (of life) fell'* corresponds to an aspect of:

A.   Geometry   B.   History

C.   Sports   D.   Drama

Q.33. The purpose of using "..." in the above passage is to:

A.   show omission   B.   indicate pauses

C.   shorten a dialogue   D.   replace an idea

Q.34. Which option indicates that the poet lost consciousness?

A.   *'It was quiet and peaceful.*   B.   *'I crossed to oblivion.'*

C.   *'Tender arms like Mother's.'*   D.   *'It wiped out fear.'*

Q.35. Why did a blackness swept over Douglas' brain?

1. He felt paralysed   2.   He felt drowsy

3. The water deep inside was black   4.   He began losing his memory

A.	1 and 3	B.	2 and 3
C.	3 and 4	D.	1 and 2

VI. **Read the given extract to attempt questions that follow:**

Thirty years later I visited his town and the temple, which was now drowned in an air of desolation. In the backyard, where lived the new priest, there were red and white plastic chairs. A young boy dressed in a grey uniform, wearing socks and shoes, arrived panting and threw his school bag on a folding bed. Looking at the boy, I remembered the prayer another boy had made to the goddess when he had finally got a pair of shoes, "Let me never lose them." The goddess had granted his prayer. Young boys like the son of the priest now wore shoes. But many others like the ragpickers in my neighbourhood remain shoeless.

Q.36. *"But many others like the ragpickers in my neighbourhood remain shoeless."* What does this line suggests about the author?

   A. He is stating facts.

   B. He is concerned about many others like the ragpickers.

   C. He is indifferent towards it.

   D. He is angry that the priest's son has got new shoes but ragpickers hadn't.

Q.37. Of the four meanings of 'desolation', select the option that matches in meaning with its usage in the extract.

A.	encouragement	B.	isolation
C.	wilderness	D.	joy

Q.38. Who do you think the author is referring to as 'his', in the given sentence?

   "Thirty years later I visited his town and the temple"

A.	Saheb	B.	A man from Udipi
C.	His friend	D.	His Colleague

Q.39. Select the option that lists the feelings and attitudes corresponding to the following:

   (1) *"Let me never lose them."*

   (2) *"arrived panting and threw his school bag on a folding bed"*

A.	(1)	self-belief	B.	(1)	pride
	(2)	arrogant and indifferent		(2)	pride and arrogant

C.	(1)	hope	D.	(1)	seriousness
	(2)	tired and oblivious		(2)	tired and exhausted

Q.40. Select the option that lists reasons why the temple has been called *'drowned in an air of desolation'*.

   1. Become old and dilapidated.

   2. Has become more crowded.

   3. People of all types visit there.

   4. It has renovated a lot and attracts lot of tourists.

   5. People no longer go to it.

A.	1 and 2	B.	1 and 5
C.	2 and 3	D.	1 and 4

VII. **Read the given extract to attempt questions that follow:**

And yet, for these

Children, these windows, not this map, their world,

Where all their future's painted with a fog,

A narrow street sealed in with a lead sky

Far far from rivers, capes and stars of words."

Q.41. Why are the windows of the classroom called the world of the children?

   A. School going children have a bright future which can be seen through the windows

   B. Their world is confined to the classroom windows full of poverty and diseases

   C. These windows are full of hopes and aspirations for children

   D. The world of the poor children living in slum is full of bounties

Q.42. How is the world of the slum children in contrast with the world of common people?

    A.   With a bright prospect   B.   Dull and unpleasant

    C.   Vibrant future   D.   Overall functioning

Q.43. Select the correct option to fill in the blank.

A lead sky here suggests ____________.

    A.   Dull and grey colour of the sky   B.   Sky which is loaded with clouds

    C.   The dull life of the slum children   D.   Pollution in the sky

Q.44. Which option has the underlined phrase that applies the poetic device used for in *'Far far from rivers'*?

    A.   She was <u>as red as a rose</u>   B.   He was <u>lion in the battle</u>

    C.   The <u>Pied Piper of Hamelin</u>   D.   He was <u>swift like a Cheetah</u>

Q.45. The literal meaning of 'fog' refers to an atmospheric condition where visibility is reduced. What does its figurative meaning refer to?

    A.   Future of the slum children is grey and not colourful

    B.   Future of the slum children is unclear and uncertain

    C.   Future of the slum children is blissful but cold

    D.   Their future is clearly visible

VIII. **Read the given extract to attempt questions that follow:**

Have you ever been there? It's a wonderful town still, with big old frame houses, huge lawns, and tremendous trees whose branches meet overhead and roof the streets. And in 1894, summer evenings were twice as long, and people sat out on their lawns, the men smoking cigars and talking quietly, the women waving palm-leaf fans, with the fire-flies all around, in a peaceful world. To be back there with the First World War still twenty years off, and World War II over forty years in the future... I wanted two tickets for that.

Q.46. What do you think who is 'you' in the given sentence?

'Have you ever been there?'

    A.   Charley's psychiatrist, Sam Weiner   B.   Charley's wife, Louisa

    C.   The reader   D.   Nobody in particular

Q.47. Choose the option that best describes the society represented in the above extract.

    A.   content, peace-loving   B.   leisurely, sentimental

    C.   orthodox, upper class   D.   comfortable, ancient

Q.48. Imagine that the city of Galesburg is hosting a series of conferences and workshops. In which of the following conferences or workshops are you least likely to find the description of Galesburg given in the above extract?

    A.   Gorgeous Galesburg: Archiving a Tourist Paradise

    B.   Welcome to the home you deserve: Galesburg Realtors

    C.   Re-imagining a Warless Future: Technology for Peace

    D.   The Woman Question: The world of women at home

Q.49. *"Tremendous trees whose branches meet overhead and roof the streets"* is NOT an example of:

1. imagery
2. metaphor
3. alliteration
4. anachronism

    A.   option (1) and (2)   B.   option (1) and (3)

    C.   option (2) and (3)   D.   option (2) and (4)

Q.50. Select the option that displays a cause-effect set.

	Cause	Effect
A.	The speaker wanted two tickets.	The World War was far off.
B.	The World War was far off.	The speaker wanted two tickets.
C.	The speaker wanted to be in a peaceful world.	He wanted two tickets to go there.
D.	He wanted two tickets to go there.	The speaker wanted to be in a peaceful world.

IX. Attempt the following.

Q.51. Repetition of the same word *'smile'* in the last line by Kamala Das implies that:

  A. poetess was feeling happy
  B. was hiding her feelings of fear
  C. poetess was grinning from ear to ear
  D. poetess was amused at what was happening

Q.52. *'They looked like little flags floating.'* What are referred to as flags by Alphonse?

  A. copies of resignation letters
  B. copies of written notes
  C. notices on bulletin boards
  D. flags of honour

Q.53. Which option has the underlined phrase that applies the poetic device that Stephen Spender used for *'stars of words'*?

  A. He shut up like a clam when interrogated
  B. She runs as swift as a gazelle.
  C. He is considered the black sheep of the family.
  D. She ran away chattering with fear.

Q.54. *"It's nice to be carried gently"*. What was carrying Douglas gently?

  A. Water at Y.M.C.A swimming pool
  B. Water at Lake Wentworth
  C. Water at Tieton
  D. Water at Maine lakes

Q.55. The poem *My Mother at Sixty-six* does not have full stop. What effect does this have?

  A. a lucid flow of emotions
  B. rhythmic flow
  C. ambiguity of ideas
  D. a sense of confusion

Q.56. Read the statements given below carefully. Choose the option that best describes these statements, with reference to the poem.

Statement-I: The poem *Keeping Quiet* calls for change as much in the individual as human society at large.

Statement-II: The poem *Keeping Quiet* implies that individual change will lead to bigger societal change.

Statement-III: Neruda believes that when people come together as a community, they will be able to bring a transformation in each person.

  A. Statement I is True, Statement II is False, and Statement III cannot be inferred.
  B. Statement I and II cannot be inferred, Statement III is True.
  C. Statement I is True, Statements II and III cannot be inferred.
  D. Statement I cannot be inferred, Statement II cannot be inferred, Statement III is False.

Q.57. Anees Jung says, *'But promises like mine abound in every corner of his bleak world'*. This suggests that:

  A. there is no dearth of promises which remain unfulfilled.
  B. there is a scarcity of people promising things for betterment.
  C. people make a lot of promises which are often fulfilled.
  D. promises made, live up to the expectations of people.

Q.58. *The Third Level* refers to the third level at the Grand Central Station. As a metaphor, which of the following would NOT be an appropriate explanation of the title?

  A. The convergence of reality and fantasy.
  B. The bridge between the past and the present.
  C. The oppressive monotony of modern life.
  D. The need for an alternate plane of understanding.

Q.59. How would you describe Charley's vision of his grandfather's life and times?

  A. wistful escapism
  B. idealized sentimentality
  C. nostalgic simplicity
  D. dreamy perfection

Q.60. *"Those scars,"* she murmured, lifting her eyes to Sadao.

The 'scars' DO NOT indicate:

  A. torture perpetrated on prisoners of war.
  B. superiority of Japan over America.
  C. the quest for supremacy in war.
  D. the rumours of torture often heard.

Sample Paper 3

English Core

READING

I. Read the passage given below.

I. No student of a foreign language needs to be told that grammar is complex. By changing word sequences and by adding a range of auxiliary verbs and suffixes, we are able to communicate tiny variations in meaning. We can turn a statement into a question, state whether an action has taken place or is soon to take place, and perform many other word tricks to convey subtle differences in meaning. Nor is this complexity inherent to the English language. All languages, even those of so-called 'primitive' tribes have clever grammatical components. The Cherokee pronoun system, for example, can distinguish between 'you and I', 'several other people and I' and 'you, another person and I'. In English, all these meanings are summed up in the one, crude pronoun 'We'. Grammar is universal and plays a part in every language, no matter how widespread it is. So, the question which has baffled many linguists is—who created grammar?

II. At first, it would appear that this question is impossible to answer. To find out how grammar is created, someone needs to be present at the time of a language's creation, documenting its emergence. Many historical linguists are able to trace modern complex languages back to earlier languages, but in order to answer the question of how complex languages are actually formed, the researcher needs to observe how languages started from scratch. Amazingly, however, this is possible.

III. Some of the most recent languages evolved due to the Atlantic slave trade. At that time, slaves from a number of different ethnicities were forced to work together under colonizer's rule. Since, they had no opportunity to learn each other's languages, they developed a make-shift language called a pidgin. Pidgins are strings of words copied from the language of the landowner. They have little in the way of grammar, and in many cases it is difficult for a listener to deduce when an event happened, and who did what to whom. Speakers need to use circumlocution in order to make their meaning understood. Interestingly, however, all it takes for a pidgin to become a complex language is for a group of children to be exposed to it at the time when they learn their mother tongue. Slave children did not simply copy the strings of words uttered by their elders, they adapted their words to create a new, expressive language. Complex grammar systems which emerge from pidgins are termed creoles and they are invented by children.

IV. Further evidence of this can be seen in studying sign languages for the deaf. Sign languages are not simply a series of gestures; they utilise the same grammatical machinery that is found in spoken languages. Moreover, there are many different languages used worldwide. The creation of one such language was documented quite recently in Nicaragua. Previously, all deaf people were isolated from each other, but in 1979 a new government introduced schools for the deaf. Although children were taught speech and lip reading in the classroom, in the playgrounds they began to invent their own sign system, using the gestures that they used at home. It was basically a pidgin. Each child used the signs differently, and there was no consistent grammar. However, children who joined the school later, when this inventive sign system was already around, developed a quite different sign language. Although it was based on the signs of the older children, the younger children's language was more fluid and compact, and it utilised a large range of grammatical devices to clarify meaning. What is more, all the children used the signs in the same way? A new creole was born.

V. Some linguists believe that many of the world's most established languages were creoles at first. The English past tense –ed ending may have evolved from the verb 'do'. 'It ended' may once have been 'It end-did'. Therefore, it would appear that even the most widespread languages were partly created by children. Children appear to have innate grammatical machinery in their brains, which springs to life when they are first trying to make sense of the world around them. Their minds can serve to create logical, complex structures, even when there is no grammar present for them to copy.

Based on your understanding of the passage, answer <u>any eight</u> out of the ten questions by choosing the correct option.

Q.1. The linguists are ……….. at the complexity of grammar.

A.	annoyed	B.	bewildered
C.	indifferent	D.	confident

Q.2. Circumlocution is the use of a large number of words to express an idea or thing.

The writer says that Sign languages are not simply a series of gestures.

Select from the options that is correctly circumlocutory for the word *gestures*.

A. systematic form of expressions by leg movements.

B. random actions performed to deliver messages.

C. expressing through different emojis.

D. systematic form of expressions by hand movements.

Q.3. Select the option that suitably completes the given dialogue as per the context in paragraph V.

Student: It is sometimes hardtop make sense how children can learn something as complex as grammar when even adults have a hard time getting it.

Professor: You mustn't underestimate a (1)……………………………

Student: How come a child sensibly understands grammar then?

Professor: (2)……………..………………… in their brains!

A. (1) child's capability to learn new things (2) The whole magic lies

B. (1) human being like that even if it's a child (2) They have complex neurological connections

C. (1) child who wants to learn new things (2) They can have unlimited power

D. (1) child's ability to make sense of this world (2) They have an innate grammatical machinery

Q.4. Which signboard can be chosen for the government school for deaf in Nicaragua?

1. Government school for deaf, Nicaragua	2. Public school for Nicaraguan studies.	3. Government school for sign language, Nicaragua	4. Sign language school for deaf and dumb, Nicaragua

A.	option 1	B.	option 2
C.	option 3	D.	option 4

Q.5. Select the option that clearly indicates the situation before and after slave children were exposed to pidgin.

	Before exposure to pidgin	After exposure to pidgin
A.	Little complexity to the grammar.	Adapting new words to create a fresh expressive language.
B.	Grammar existent and full of big words.	Grammar became less expressive.
C.	Difficulty in understanding the language.	Language becomes more difficult and complex.
D.	Lack of words and inconvenience for landowners.	New words added for the sake of landowners.

Q.6. What is the relationship between (1) and (2)?

(1) …… the researcher needs to observe how languages started from scratch.

(2) ……. Complex grammar systems which emerge from pidgins are termed creoles.

A.	(2) explains the question described in (1).	B.	(1) repeats the question in (2).
C.	(1) is not the cause for (2).	D.	(1) and (2) are unrelated.

Q.7. The writer mentions looking at Atlantic slave trade for a better understanding of languages because he realises that:

A.   Atlantic slave trade was filled with teachers who were well versed in linguistics.

B.   It is the most effective way to check the linguistic development which requires no books.

C.   It is the most recent and well documented form of linguistic study in how grammar is created.

D.   Atlantic slave trade was a blotch in human history and should not be forgotten.

Q.8. Select the option that lists a linguist's review for the Nicaraguan sign language.

A.   Children are not that silly when it comes to bringing up names or new words after all.

B.   Interesting how something like the sign language made by children can be so inventive and fluid.

C.   Needless to say that the children have done what their teachers couldn't have expected.

D.   Each child was using the signs differently, and there was no consistent grammar.

Q.9. Which quote summarises the unmatched ingenuity of children?

A.   "If a cluttered desk is a sign of a cluttered mind, of what, then, is an empty desk a sign?"
- Albert Einstein

B.   "It is easier to build strong children than to repair broken adults."   *- F. Douglas*

C.   "Children have real understanding only of that which they invent themselves."   *- Jean Piaget*

D.   "By education I mean an all-round drawing out of the best in the child and man; body, mind and spirit."   *- Mahatma Gandhi*

Q.10. Select the option that lists what we can conclude from the text.

(1)   Grammar develops over a generation gradually.

(2)   Children are credited with new inventive forms of transforming languages.

(3)   English grammar derives a lot from French and Germanic languages.

(4)   Creole is a mix of different language forms.

A.   (1), (2) and (3) are true.   B.   (1), (2) and (4) are true.

C.   (1) and (2) are true.   D.   (3) and (4) are true.

II. Read the passage given below.

I.   When plastic waste is burnt, a complex weave of toxic chemicals is released. Breaking down Poly Vinyl Chloride (PVC) used for packaging, toys and coating electrical wires. It produces dioxin, an organochlorine which belongs to the family of Persistent Organic Pollutants (POPs). A recent Dioxin Assessment Report brought out by the United States Environment Protection Agency (USEPA) says the risk of getting cancer from dioxin is ten times higher than reported by the agency in 1994.

II.   Yet the Delhi government is giving the green signal to a gasification project which will convert garbage into energy without removing plastic waste. Former transport minister Rajendra Gupta, the promoter of this project, says this is not necessary.

He claims no air pollution will be caused and that the ash produced can be used as manure. An earlier waste-to-energy project set-up in Timarpur failed. The new one, built with Australian assistance, will cost ₹ 200 crore. It will generate 25 megawatts of power and gobble 1,000 tonnes of garbage everyday.

III.   "Technologies like gasification are a form of incineration," says Madhumita Dutta, central coordinator with Toxics Link, New Delhi. Incineration merely transfers hazardous waste from a solid form to air, water and ash, she points out. Toxins produced during incineration include acidic gases, heavy metals as well as dioxins and furans. "The 'manure' will be hazardous and a problem to dispose," says Dutta.

IV.   Municipal solid waste contains a mix of plastics. Breaking down this waste emits hydrochloric acid which attacks the respiratory system, skin and eyes, resulting in coughing, vomiting and nausea.

Polyethylene generates volatile compounds like formaldehyde and acetaldehyde, both suspected carcinogenic. Breathing styrene from polystyrene can cause leukaemia. Polyurethane is associated with asthma. Dioxin released by PVC is a powerful hormone disrupter and causes birth defects and reproductive problems. There is no threshold dose to prevent it and our bodies have no defence against it.

V.   "Even the best run incinerators in the world have to deal with stringent norms, apart from contaminated filters and ash, making them hugely expensive to operate," says Dutta. In Germany, air pollution devices accounted for two-thirds the cost of incineration. Despite such efforts, the European Dioxin Inventory noted that the input of dioxin into the atmosphere was the highest from incineration.

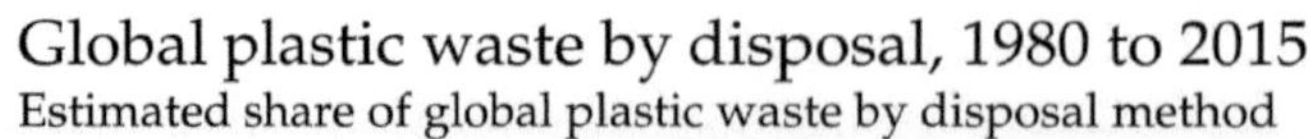

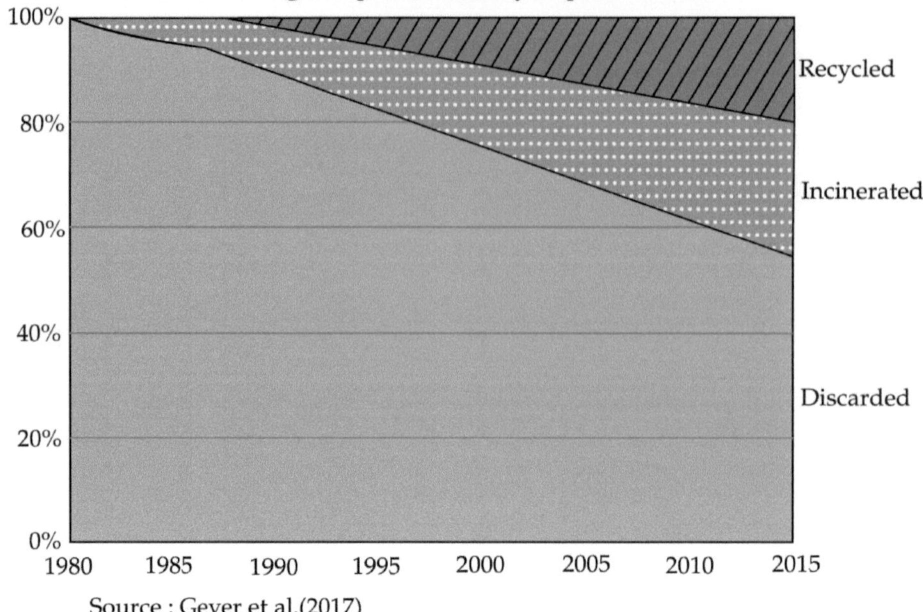

Source : Geyer et al.(2017)

VI. How has global plastic waste disposal method changed over time? In the chart, we see the share of global plastic waste that is discarded, recycled or incinerated from 1980 through to 2015. Prior to 1980, recycling and incineration of plastic was negligible; 100 percent was therefore discarded. From 1980 for incineration and 1990 for recycling, rates increased on average by about 0.7 percent per year. In 2015, an estimated 55 percent of global plastic waste was discarded, 25 percent was incinerated and 20 percent recycled.

VII. "India does not have the facility to test dioxin and the cost of setting one up is prohibitively expensive," says Dutta.Besides, Indian garbage has a low calorific content of about 800 cal/kg, since it has high moisture and requires additional fuel to burn. Toxics link calculates that the electricity generated from such technology will cost between ₹5-7 per unit, which is six times higher than conventional energy. India has chosen a dioxin preventive route and burning of chlorinated plastics is prohibited under Municipal Solid Waste and Biomedical Rules.

Nearly 80 percent of Indian garbage is recyclable or compostable. Resident associations, the informal sector and the municipal corporation can make Delhi's garbage disappear in a sustainable manner. "Instead, the government promotes end of pipeline solutions," says Dutta.

Based on your understanding of the passage, answer <u>any six</u> out of the eight questions by choosing the correct option.

Q.11. Select the correct inference with reference to the following:

Instead, the government promotes end of pipeline solutions.

    A.   Government is promoting solutions which can end the supply of garbage.

    B.   Government is planning to promote effective measures for waste disposal.

    C.   Government is planning to connect garbage disposal pipelines.

    D.   Government is promoting last stage actions instead of tackling the problem in initial steps.

Q.12. Select the central idea of the paragraph III.

    A.   Incineration is only going to bring more pollutants in the air.

    B.   Incineration will control the air quality index of Delhi.

    C.   Delhi air quality isn't improving anyway, so incineration will have little to no effect.

    D.   The benefits of incineration outweigh the risks in Delhi.

Q.13. Select the option that displays the true statement with reference to the given figure.

    A.   Incineration of plastic waste has stabilized since 1995.

    B.   Awareness towards recycling of plastic is reflected in recent years.

C.   The trend of discarding garbage hasn't changed much since 1980.

D.   Incineration of waste now is almost double that of discarded garbage.

Q.14. Based on your reading of paragraphs IV-V, select the appropriate counter- argument to the given argument.

Argument: Incineration is the quickest way of waste disposal, and even if it generates harmful toxins, proper measures can ensure that they don't escape in the environment.

A.   Recycling and reducing waste consumption are better options.

B.   Regulations are not enough to contain the toxic carcinogens it will generate along with a huge cost of operating it.

C.   Incinerators are a form of infrastructure development that is going to generate jobs.

D.   They are expensive to operate and do not generate enough electrical output.

Q.15. Select the option that displays the correct cause-effect relationship.

	Cause	**Effect**
A.	Burning of polyurethane.	Leukaemia.
B.	Emission of hydrochloric acid from wastes.	Birth defects and reproductive problems.
C.	Burning of polyethylene.	Release of formaldehyde and acetaldehyde.
D.	Wasteful consumption of products.	Dissatisfaction by the consumers.

Q.16. The survey statistics mention the global plastic waste disposal methods, indicating that:

A.   Prior to 1980, recycling and incineration of plastic was negligible.

B.   In 1990, recycling rates increased on average by about 7 per cent.

C.   In 2015, an estimated 55 percent of global plastic waste was recycled.

D.   100 per cent of garbage was incinerated in 1980.

Q.17. The phrase 'low calorific content' refers to the:

A.   lower calories for a healthy consumption   B.   lower content to remove all the moisture

C.   lower spectrum of behaving as toxin   D.   lower quality to burn as a fuel on its own

Q.18. Read the two statements given below and select the option that suitably explains them.

(1)   India has chosen a dioxin preventive route.

(2)   USEPA says the risk of getting cancer from dioxin is ten times higher than reported by the agency in 1994.

A.   (1) is the problem and (2) is the solution.   B.   (1) and (2) don't relate.

C.   (1) is true and (2) correctly explains it.   D.   (2) is false but (1) is true.

WRITING

III.   **Answer <u>any four</u> out of the five questions given, with reference to the context below.**

The Secretary of Panchsheel Apartments is supposed to publish a notice for the residents of society, about the electric power cut scheduled for tomorrow.

Q.19. Which of the following is the most suitable title for the notice?

A.   Summer, heat, and electric power cut

B.   This is the notice to inform about the scheduled power cut for maintenance

C.   Scheduled Power Cut

D.   The electricity will remain shut because of the maintenance related power cut

Q.20. Which of the following points must be necessarily included in this notice?

(1)   Time of power cut

(2)   Date of power cut

(3)   Reason for power cut

(4)   Technical details of maintenance work

A.   1 only   B.   1 and 2

C.   1,2 and 3   D.   1,2,3 and 4

Q.21. Which of the following is the most suitable opening line for this notice?

    A.   All society members are hereby informed about the scheduled power cut...

    B.   It is quite heart breaking to inform you all that ....

    C.   I, the secretary of Panchsheel society, feel privileged to inform....

    D.   Get ready to sweat dear society members as tomorrow there is a power cut...

Q.22. Should the notice contain the name of Panchsheel Apartments?

    A.   The notice must not have the name of publishing authority.

    B.   Can be published but not mandatory.

    C.   If Signature of publisher is given, then name of authority is not required.

    D.   Name of publishing authority must be given.

Q.23. Select the appropriate conclusion for this notice.

    A.   Pack your bags and plan a trip to some amusement spot nearby.

    B.   Residents are requested to be prepared for this problem.

    C.   Inconvenience regretted

    D.   Be informed

IV.   **Answer <u>any six</u> of the seven questions given, with reference to the context below.**

You are Aadarsh, Chairman of "Vidyamandir" an NGO that works for the upliftment of status of education in society. You are supposed to draft a letter to the editor of Navbharat Jansatta stating opinion on infrastructure requirements for learning and education in these changing COVID times.

Q.24. Which of the following can be the appropriate opening line for the above letter?

    A.   The world is changing so rapidly and the context that our schools confront is so dynamic that we, as educators....

    B.   As an editor of such a big media agency you should be aware that the teachers are distressed.

    C.   I hope you and other family members are doing fine.

    D.   I am extremely delightful to express my opinion on the matter...

Q.25. Which of the following is the most appropriate subject for the above letter?

    A.   Deterioration of the quality of education with COVID

    B.   How Corona ruined education and economy

    C.   Education infrastructure and its requirement in COVID era

    D.   Teachers are not to be taken for granted

Q.26. Which of the following approach is most appropriate for drafting a letter on the above subject?

    A.   Analysing change in education system—Suggesting Improvements in the system—Introducing problem faced by teachers—Conclusion

    B.   Introducing problems faced by teachers—Analysing change in education system—Suggesting improvements in the system—Conclusion

    C.   Analysing change in education system—Suggesting improvements in the system – Conclusion—Introducing problems faced by teachers

    D.   Conclusion—Introduction - Analysing change in education system—Suggesting improvements in the system.

Q.27. Complete the following phrase with the most appropriate terms.

Education system must _______ the change and ______ accordingly

    A.   Discard, be rigid   B.   Discard, Adjust

    C.   Accept, Adjust   D.   Accept, be rigid

Q.28. Which of the following is the most appropriate closing signature:

    A.   Your Loving subscriber   B.   Your Dearest Subscriber

        Aadarsh   Aadarsh

    C.   Yours Sincerely   D.   Forever Yours

        Aadarsh   Aadarsh

Q.29. Study the fragment of following draft and find out the error.

Teachers often feel they are not in power and yet in a position of great responsibility. The world is changing so rapidly and the context that our schools confront is so dynamic that we, as educators, must embrace change and make adjustments or potentially lose the franchise for preparing the next generation. Also, I strongly believe that Government should act proactively in this matter to facilitate teacher's fraternity.

Yours Sincerely
Aadarsh

A.	Complementary closure is too formal	B.	Closing signature must be on right
C.	Closing signature is too formal	D.	Language is too formal

Q.30. What is the type of the letter, which Aadarsh is about to draft?

A.	Informal Letter	B.	Technical Letter
C.	Letter stating opinion on public interest	D.	Letter of Resignations

LITERATURE

This section has sub-sections: V, VI, VII, VIII, IX. There are a total of 30 questions in the section. Attempt any 26 questions from the sub-sections V to IX.

V. **Read the given extract to attempt questions that follow:**

Then, as I hurried by as fast as I could go, the blacksmith, Wachter, who was there, with his apprentice, reading the bulletin, called after me, "Don't go so fast, bub; you'll get to your school in plenty of time!" I thought he was making fun of me and reached M. Hamel's little garden all out of breath. Usually, when school began, there was a great bustle, which could be heard out in the street, the opening and closing of desks, lessons repeated in unison, very loud, with our hands over our ears to understand better, and the teacher's great ruler rapping on the table.

Q.31. Franz's hurriedly walking towards the school suggests his ……………

A.	Fright	B.	Diligence
C.	Anxiety	D.	Stress

Q.32. Which bulletin do you think blacksmith, Wachter had been reading?

A.	School journal	B.	Local news
C.	Announcement from Berlin	D.	Sports Day notice

Q.33. Select the option that lists the feelings and attitudes corresponding to the following:

(1) ………… *Don't go so fast*
(2) ………… *reached M. Hamel's little garden all out of breath.*

A.	(1)	Sarcastic	B.	(1)	Humorous
	(2)	Carelessly		(2)	Meticulous

C.	(1)	Concern	D.	(1)	Cheerful
	(2)	Seriousness		(2)	Miserable

Q.34. Select the option that tells the reason why Franz thought that the blacksmith was making fun of him?

(1) Franz's manner of running
(2) Blacksmith's practice of making fun of him
(3) Due to his frivolousness about studies
(4) Franz habit of being customarily late

A.	1 and 3	B.	2 and 3
C.	3 and 4	D.	1 and 4

Q.35. Of the four meanings of the phrase *'out of breath'*, select the option that matches in the meaning with its usage in the extract.

A.	gasping for air	B.	breathing fast with difficulty
C.	without any breath	D.	breathing effortlessly but awkwardly

VI. **Read the given extract to attempt questions that follow:**

My breath was gone. I was frightened. Father laughed, but there was terror in my heart at the overpowering force of the waves. My introduction to the Y.M.CA. swimming pool revived unpleasant memories and stirred childish fears. But in a little while I gathered confidence. I paddled with my new water wings, watching the other boys and trying to learn by aping them. I did this two or three times on different days and was just beginning to feel at ease in the water when the misadventure happened.

Q.36. Choose the correct option with reference to the two statements given below.

Statement 1: The author's father laughed to mock his son's inability to swim.

Statement 2: The author wanted to swim just to prove to his father that he can swim.

    A.   Statement 1 is true but Statement 2 is false.

    B.   Statement 1 is false but Statement 2 is true.

    C.   Both Statement 1 and Statement 2 cannot be inferred.

    D.   Both Statement 1 and Statement 2 can be inferred.

Q.37. *"My introduction to the Y.M.CA. swimming pool revived unpleasant memories and stirred childish fears."* It can be inferred that this was a clear case of __________.

    A.   suppression   B.   oppression

    C.   depression   D.   repression

Q.38. The misadventure that took place right after the author felt comfortable was that:

    A.   the author slipped and fell into the swimming pool.

    B.   a bully tossed him into the pool for the sake of fun.

    C.   his coach forgot to teach him how to handle deep water.

    D.   his father couldn't help him from drowning into the water.

Q.39. Why is the fear "childish"?

    A.   because it is from childhood   B.   because it was expected to go by now

    C.   because it was not such a big fear   D.   because it was fear of a child

Q.40. What is the tone of the author?

    A.   expository   B.   narrative

    C.   ominous   D.   conservative

VII. **Read the given extract to attempt questions that follow:**

"If we were not so single-minded

about keeping our lives moving,

and for once could do nothing,

perhaps a huge silence

might interrupt this sadness

of never understanding ourselves

and of threatening ourselves with death"

Q.41. The main focus of the poet is towards __________.

    A.   Peace, responsiveness, brotherhood   B.   Peace, humanity and brotherhood

    C.   Brotherhood, desertion and fondness   D.   Humanity, isolation and brotherhood

Q.42. The literal meaning of *'do nothing'* refers to remain inactive. What does its figurative meaning refer to?

    A.   Complete state of relaxation   B.   Experience the independence

    C.   Enjoy the freedom   D.   Scrutinize our activities

Q.43. Which sadness is the poet referring to?

    (1)   The sadness of remaining alone

    (2)   The sadness that has made man self-absorbed

    (3)   The sadness that has caused threat to man's own destruction

    (4)   The sadness of not speaking to anyone

    A.   1 and 3   B.   2 and 3

    C.   3 and 4   D.   1 and 2

Q.44. Select the correct option to fill in the blank.

A huge silence can help in __________.

    A.   reconciliation   B.   reuniting with friends

    C.   dealing with threats   D.   achieving goals of life

Q.45. What is the man *'single-minded'* about?

    A.   His own well-being and progress

    B.   Mindful of the destruction caused by human activities

    C.   Conscious about nature's advancement

    D.   Problems of the society and nation

VII. **Read the given extract to attempt questions that follow:**

It was at this moment that both of them saw something black come out of the mists. It was a man. He was flung up out of the ocean .... flung, it seemed, to his feet by a breaker. He staggered a few steps, his body outlined against the mist, his arms above his head. Then the curled mists hid him again.

Q.46. Why did the figure of the man appear black?

    A.   Due to mist in the air   B.   Because he was wounded

    C.   Because of the dark night   D.   Because it was dark

Q.47. How would they have felt when they saw something black come out of the mists'?

    A.   terrified   B.   shocked

    C.   happy   D.   ignorant

Q.48. Select the option that signifies the walking style of the figure.

    A.   Elegant   B.   Offensive

    C.   Stranded   D.   Defensive

Q.49. Select the option that displays a cause-effect set.

A.

Cause	Effect
He was a prisoner.	Arms above head.

B.

Cause	Effect
Arms above head.	He was a prisoner.

C.

Cause	Effect
He flung out of the ocean.	He staggered.

D.

Cause	Effect
He staggered.	He flung out of the ocean.

Q.50. Pick the quote that best describes the theme of the story.

    A.   World belongs to humanity, not this leader, that leader or that king or prince or religious leader. World belongs to humanity.

    B.   You must not lose faith in humanity. Humanity is an ocean; if a few drops of the ocean are dirty, the ocean does not become dirt.

    C.   The purpose of human life is to serve, and to show compassion and the will to help others.

    D.   To deny people their human rights is to challenge their very humanity.

IX. **Attempt the following.**

Q.51. *I looked again at her, wan, pale*

as a late winter's moon and felt that old

What is the literary device used in the lines?

    A.   metaphor   B.   personification

    C.   anaphora   D.   simile

Q.52. Why does Hamilton refer to prison in his speech?

    A.   to show knowing one's language is escape from exploitation

    B.   to argue in favour of liberal ways

    C.   to prove submission is the key to comfortable living

    D.   none of the above

Q.53. Identify the figure of speech used in the sentence *"Garbage to them is gold"*.

    A.   hyperbole   B.   simile

    C.   synecdoche   D.   personification

Q.54. *Keeping Quiet* uses fishermen to symbolize man's:

    A.   persistent pollution of the natural environment.

    B.   rapid degradation of human values.

C.　limitless exploitation of natural resources.

D.　constant participation in acts of terror.

Q.55. Spender's use of imagery in *"His eyes live in a dream, of squirrel game, in tree room, other than this"*, brings out:

A.　the similarity between the frail bodies of a squirrel and the children in the classroom.

B.　the contrast between studying in the dreary classroom and playing outside freely.

C.　the comparison of the dingy home of the squirrel and the dreary classroom.

D.　the difference between the games of the squirrel and those of the children.

Q.56. Choose the statement that is NOT TRUE with reference to Douglas.

A.　Douglas's fear kept him away from leisurely activities in water.

B.　The fall in the pool at YMCA taught Douglas a life lesson.

C.　The fear of drowning was the source of Douglas's anxiety and terror.

D.　Douglas decided to practice relentlessly to overcome his fear.

Q.57. The expression, *"Shakespeare's head"* in the poem *An Elementary School Classroom in a Slum* is an example of:

A.　pun.　　　　　　　　　　　　　　　B.　satire.

C.　parody.　　　　　　　　　　　　　D.　irony.

Q.58. *"He was very light, like a fowl that had been half-starved for a long time."* Which figure of speech is used by Buck in the given line?

A.　simile　　　　　　　　　　　　　B.　metaphor

C.　comparison　　　　　　　　　　D.　paradox

Q.59. *He was taking out the packing now, and the blood began to* <u>*flow more quickly.*</u>

The underlined phrase suggests that the blood was:

A.　passive　　　　　　　　　　　　B.　vigorous

C.　oozing　　　　　　　　　　　　　D.　dribbling

Q.60. Select the suitable option for the given statements, based on your reading of *The Third Level*.

(1)　Sam had a grain business.

(2)　Sam went back to his work to Galesburg, Illinois.

A.　1 is false but 2 is true.　　　　B.　Both 1 and 2 are false.

C.　2 is a fact but unrelated to 1.　　D.　1 is the cause for 2.

❑❑

Sample Paper 4

English Core

READING

I. Read the passage given below.

I. A bookshop is not something you find in every street or area these days. Books, which were once a permanent accompaniment for youngsters in their formative years, are fading out of their list of engagements.

II. Ask any youngster which is the latest book he has read and he will be baffled. Apart from a few consistent readers, others just befool themselves with a bookseller's name or lament the curriculum load for justifying themselves, like this seventeen-year-old school-goer who says, 'I just read my Physics book.'

III. Television has been blamed for this calamitous situation, which is producing square-faced people and a bookless society. Furthermore, today's children are under pressure to be smart and to succeed on a social level. Parties, dancing and hanging out at different places begin early. Moreover, computers, video games, the internet, swimming lessons, cricket and a youngster's passion for an hour-long tete-a-tete on the telephone with friends eat up all their leisure time.

IV. A child who is constantly under pressure to live up to his parents' expectations, which are at times unreasonable, does not like to throw himself into another set of books after the laborious school work, unless he comes from a family of readers where the engrossing work of Shakespeare and Dickens are just a matter of pulling them out from the shelves.

V. Many parents also believe that today's children have become more aware and demand logical reasoning for everything. They can no longer be fooled by fairy tales or animal stories, as they have not seen any fairies or animals except for those old and tired ones in the city zoo. This has made them more interested in movies or TV serials than a turtle talking to a rabbit or a frog changing into a prince.

VI. But a visit to the capital's leading bookstores presents a contrasting picture of youngsters' reading habits. These bookshops claim they are doing healthy business and have many regular buyers from this age group.

VII. Though the works of Shakespeare, Charles Dickens, Jane Austen and Mark Twain no longer interest teenagers, bestsellers from Daniel Steele, Sidney Sheldon and Jeffery Archer are on the list of all reading teens. Self-help books, such as those on personality development or relationship management, are also picked up by many of them.

VIII. Mystery books like Nancy Drew and Hardy Boys are popular with kids and Mills, Boons and other romance novels with their fairly predictable formula with teenage girls. For parents of children below ten, volumes of Panchatantra Stories, Amar Chitra Katha and other bedtime stories are worthy purchases as these teach the child what is wrong in their own special way. What seems to be the case is that parents have surrendered to others what was their most precious right, that of making their children what they should become. With the old techniques of child rearing losing ground, modern parents must consciously spend time with their children. Taste and enthusiasm for literature can be communicated artfully to children by reading bedtime stories to them, encouraging them to play historical characters and giving books as birthday gifts.

IX. The family reading which was once popular in the West could well be adopted here. Reading aloud the works of great men by parents to their children not only forms a warm bond between them but also attracts young minds to the world of books which gives them a chance to explore the sea of life.

Based on your understanding of the passage, answer <u>any eight</u> out of the ten questions by choosing the correct option.

Q.1. Society demands smart and successful people at present, which makes the children feel

A. relieved

B. pressured

C. left out

D. passionate

Q.2. Hyperbole is an exaggerated statement or emphasized claim, not meant to be taken literally.

The writer says that young people not reading books is a <u>calamitous situation</u>.

Select the word from the options that correctly replaces *calamitous situation*.

A. crisis

B. misfortune

C. pandemic

D. godsend

Q.3. Select the option that suitably completes the given dialogue as per the context in paragraph IV.

Parent: I've seen you spending your free time sleeping all the day. Why not do something productive?

Child: The school is laborious enough for me to (1)..............

Parent: That's not an excuse! How about reading some good novels to freshen up your mind?

Child: (2)................... I don't think I have the mental capacity to read more books.

A. (1) be active all the day (2) As if the school books weren't enough for me

B. (1) be a jack of all trades (2) You should understand that

C. (1) be a productive student (2) I am now a part of school's book club

D. (1) drain all my energy, I don't have time for additional activities. (2) I am already reading books in school

Q.4. Which signboard would the writer have chosen for his bookstore to attract young crowd?

1. Limited edition Jeffrey Archer, John Green and many more!	2. Shakespeare's classics now available!	3. Romantic novels from Jane Austin now in sale!	4. Best sellers from Charles Dickens for this season!

A. option 1

B. option 2

C. option 3

D. option 4

Q.5. Select the option that clearly indicates the situation before and after the introduction of television.

	Before television	After television
A.	Parents never felt the need to force kids to read books.	Parents are now pressuring kids to be smart and athletic.
B.	Family reading culture was popular in west.	Family reading culture is popular in east.
C.	Reading books was the usual hobby.	Reading books has become a rarity.
D.	Novels were not digitally printed.	Printing press is fully automated.

Q.6. What is the relationship between (1) and (2)?

(1).......... parents must consciously spend time with their children.

(2).......... children have become more aware and demand logical reasoning for everything.

A. (1) is the problem for (2).

B. (2) sets the stage for (1).

C. (1) repeats what is said in (2).

D. (1) and (2) are both independent.

Q.7. The writer mentions reading aloud the works of great authors by parents to their children, because he realises that

A. it not only forms a warm bond between them but also attracts young minds to the world of books which gives them a chance to explore the sea of life.

B. enthusiasm for literature can be communicated artfully to children by reading bedtime stories to them.

C. today's children are under pressure to be smart and to succeed on a social level.

D. it not only forms a warm bond between them but also attracts young minds to the world of possibilities which gives them a chance to excel in career.

Q.8. Select the option that lists the young reader's feedback for the writer's book awareness campaign.

A. I was surprisingly engrossed in the novel that I started to read, it isn't that boring or geeky as it sounds.

B. I just wanted to score some brownie points by being here, it reflects good on my CV.

C. I'm still indifferent to that fact that books can be interesting, I got bored after one page.

D. I don't get the need to read books when every information is at fingertips with internet.

Q.9. Which quote summarises the writer's feelings about the necessity of reading books?

A. "Fairy tales are more than true: not because they tell us that dragons exist, but because they tell us that dragons can be beaten." — *Neil Gaiman*

B. "Outside of a dog, a book is man's best friend. Inside of a dog it's too dark to read." — *Groucho Marx*

C. "I have always imagined that Paradise will be a kind of library." — *Jorge Luis Borges*

D. "If you read a book, you will unlock unknown doors of your soul. And who knows; you can find a treasure inside…" — *George Spyrou, Roxanne*

Q.10. Select the option that lists what we can conclude from the text.

(1) Children should not be swayed by any means if they are not into reading books.

(2) demand or classic authors is on an all-time high.

(3) contrary to popular belief, youngsters love reading.

(4) parents must add some efforts to raise a habit of reading in children.

A. (1), (2) and (3) are true.   B. (3) and (4) are true.

C. (1) and (2) are true.   D. (2), (3) and (4) are true.

II. Read the passage given below.

I. The passenger pigeon (*Ectopistes migratorius*) was once found in huge numbers in North America. Records tell of passing flocks that darkened the skies for several days at a time. The species may have peaked at five billion individuals. A more conservative estimate is three billion.

II. Within a short time, the species disappeared completely. "Given the huge size of the population, it's simply amazing that the species disappeared so quickly," says Tom Gilbert. Gilbert is a professor at the University of Copenhagen's Centre for GeoGenetics, but he also has a part-time position as an adjunct professor at the Norwegian University of Science and Technology (NTNU).

III. The history of the passenger pigeon is interesting, partly because it can tell us something about how and why species become extinct. Native Americans also relied on passenger pigeons for food. But at least in parts of the passenger pigeons' range, people had learned to harvest the species at a sustainable level that didn't threaten to eradicate it. It was common in some parts of North America to only eat young pigeons that were hunted at night, since this did not seem to scare away the adult birds or prevent them from re-nesting.

The cladogram below follows the 2012 DNA study showing the position of the passenger pigeon among its closest relatives:

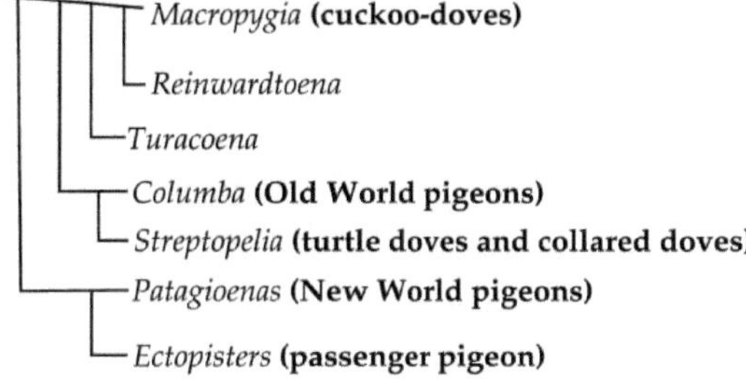

IV. But starting around 1500, a more aggressive variant of humans came to the continent with the arrival of Europeans. The hunt for passenger pigeons grew and culminated in a massive hunt for the species throughout the 1800s, before the species finally collapsed and disappeared. In 2014, a study published in the scientific journal PNAS strongly suggested that humans were simply the final straw in destroying a species that was already vulnerable and headed to oblivion.

The cladogram follows the 2012 DNA study showing the position of the passenger pigeon among its closest relatives:

V. The researchers asserted that despite their enormous numbers, the passenger pigeons were already in trouble. The population of the species varied greatly, similar to lemmings, but over a longer period of time. When the Europeans arrived, the species was already in a strong decline. The population was plummeting long before Europeans arrived, and perhaps Europeans even contributed to a short-term increase in numbers.

VI. Studies of the genetic variation of the species using an investigative method called PSMC formed the background for these assertions. And now we have to concentrate a bit. The PSMC method can use the information in the genes of a single individual of a species to map the history of the species.

VII. You should therefore be able to see how the species developed over many generations, and estimate how many individuals there were at any given time, all based on a single genome. Using this method, researchers found that the number of passenger pigeons was in free fall even before the arrival of the Europeans.

Although the species might not have become extinct, it would have shrunk significantly in any case, maybe to only a few hundred thousand individuals.

Based on your understanding of the passage, answer <u>any six</u> out of the eight questions by choosing the correct option.

Q.11. Select the correct inference with reference to the following:

The population was plummeting long before Europeans arrived.

A. the population of passenger pigeons was at a rise way before Europeans arrived.

B. passenger pigeons were thriving abundantly even before the arrival of the Europeans.

C. the number of passenger pigeons was in free fall even before the arrival of the Europeans.

D. Europeans killed the passenger pigeons and brought their population down.

Q.12. Select the central idea of the paragraph III.

A. Native Americans practiced sustainable hunting, thus cannot be blamed for passenger pigeon extinction.

B. Passenger pigeon extinction started during the times of Native American hunting.

C. Passenger pigeons may have peaked at five billion individuals.

D. Native Americans hunted passenger pigeons for their sport and thus, have a fair share of blame for their extinction.

Q.13. Select the option that displays the true statement with reference to the given figure.

A. Turtle doves and Old world pigeons are from very different genetic branches.

B. Cuckoo-doves and Old world pigeons are from similar branch.

C. New world pigeons and Passenger pigeons had the closest DNA.

D. Old world pigeons and New world pigeons share same DNA.

Q.14. Based on your reading of paragraphs VI-VII, select the appropriate counter- argument to the given argument.

Argument: The PSMC method proves the innocence of the Europeans that they had nothing to do with the decline in the population of passenger pigeons who were already doomed towards extinction.

A. PSMC method does not tells the exact number of individuals left, it only gives an idea based on vague evidences, so it were actually the Europeans who drove them to extinction.

B. It is not possible to see how the species developed over many generations, and estimate how many individuals there were at any given time.

C. PSMC is a very recent technique that relies on assumption, so it is unfair to judge something that had already happened in the past based on it.

D. There were still a few hundred thousand individuals left from the passenger pigeon population, which could've been easily saved by conservation programs, yet the Europeans hunted them all.

Q.15. Select the option that displays the correct cause-effect relationship.

	Cause	Effect
A.	PSMC method uses the genetic information of a single individual.	PSMC method can map the history of the species.
B.	Native Americans only hunted young pigeons.	Old pigeons died without raising any offspring.
C.	Passenger pigeons had an increase in number.	Passenger pigeons became extinct.
D.	Europeans relied on passenger pigeons for food.	There was a food shortage for Native Americans.

Q.16. The cladogram indicates that:

A.   new world pigeons is just another term for passenger pigeons.

B.   collared-doves are more closely related to old world pigeons, than they are to cuckoo-doves.

C.   passenger pigeons may have aroused independently from rest of the pigeons.

D.   turtle doves and collared-doves are totally different species.

Q.17. The phrase 'final straw' refers to the

A.   last of the event in the series of unfortunate trail of passenger pigeons.

B.   second last event before extinction of the passenger pigeons.

C.   final passenger pigeon that survived and kept the species alive.

D.   the last straw of food that the passenger pigeon ate before going extinct.

Q.18. Read the two statements given below and select the option that suitably explains them.

(1)   The hunt for passenger pigeons grew massively throughout the 1800s.

(2)   PSMC method formed the background for these assertions.

A.   (1) is false and (2) is the reason.   B.   (2) summarises (1).

C.   (1) is true and (2) explains it.   D.   (2) is false and (1) explains it.

WRITING

III.   Answer <u>any four</u> out of the five questions given, with reference to the context below.

You are Ranjan/Ragini of Navi Mumbai. You wish to sell your ancestral property lying unattended in the locality nearby.

Q.19. Which of the following details must be included in this advertisement?

I.   Location of Property

II.   General layout/ rooms in house

III.   History of people lived in that house.

A.   I only   B.   II only

C.   I and II   D.   I, II and III

Q.20. Which of the following language is suitable for drafting the above advertisement?

A.   Sale, Sale, Sale, we present a golden opportunity to buy a house...

B.   Always dreamed of purchasing your own house? Your dream has come true...

C.   Available for sale a three room flat in ...

D.   Your sacred space is where you find yourself again and again. Make your sacred three-room space near Navi Mumbai.

Q.21. Which of the following is the most suitable title for this advertisement?

A.   Golden opportunity to buy a property   B.   Get your dream house

C.   Give your loved ones a gift for lifetime   D.   Sale and Purchase

Q.22. Which of the following is not required in the above advertisement?

A.   Address of Ranjan/Ragini   B.   Description of property

C.   Contact details   D.   Title of the advertisement

Q.23. Which of the following can't be skipped in the above advertisement?

A.   UID details of the Ranjan/Ragini   B.   Income earned by Ranjan/Ragini's family

C.   Title of the advertisement   D.   Address of the Ranjan/Ragini

IV.   Answer <u>any six</u> of the seven questions given, with reference to the context below.

Sonam is a member of "Antheen" a college club that actively promote water conservation awareness. She has to write an article emphasizing the need to consider water conservation as essential part of our lives and promote domestic rainwater harvesting to increase ground water levels.

Q.24. Select the most suitable title for the above article.

A.   Water conservation   B.   Conserve water - No water no life

C.   Deserted Earth is not a good place to live   D.   Water helps human to survive

Q.25. Which option (1-4), should Sonam choose to elaborate on reasons for promoting domestic rainwater harvesting?

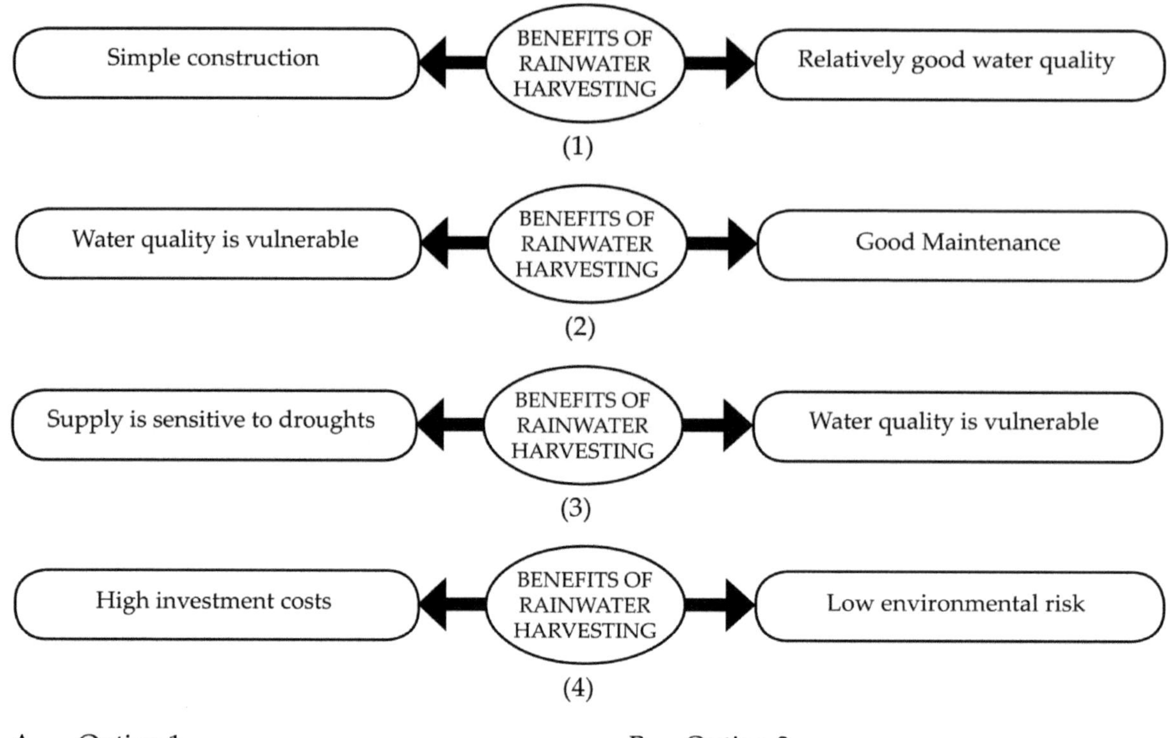

A.   Option 1   B.   Option 2
C.   Option 3   D.   Option 4

Q.26. Which option would help Sonam with appropriate organisation of relevant ideas for this article?

A.   Expressing concern about several cases of land water depletion- exploring the reasons with factual support – stating the effects – providing the suggestion to create water conservation awareness–presenting a conclusive outlook.

B.   Exploring the reasons - Expressing concern about several cases of land water depletion - providing the suggestion to create water conservation - Stating the effects - presenting a conclusive outlook.

C.   Exploring the reasons - Stating the effects - providing the suggestion to create water conservation - presenting a conclusive outlook - Expressing concern about several cases of land water depletion.

D.   Presenting a conclusive outlook - Stating the effects - Exploring the reasons - providing the suggestion to create water conservation.

Q.27. Which of the following suggestion would be appropriate for Sonam's article?

A.   Everyone should have water wells in their houses
B.   Submersible water pumps must be banned.
C.   People wasting water should be sentenced to rigorous imprisonment.
D.   Individuals should understand the importance of water conservation and do the needful.

Q.28. Read the following sentence from Sonam's article draft and help her complete it by selecting the most appropriate term.

There should be mass _______ about ways and means to __________ water.

A.   Conscience, deplete   B.   Conscience, Conserve
C.   Awareness, deplete   D.   Awareness, Conserve

Q.29. Which quote should be used to summarize the central idea of the article?

A.   You never know the worth of water until the well runs dry.
B.   I only feel angry when I see wastage of water
C.   Time spent among tree is never a time wasted.
D.   Environment is no one's property to destroy.

Q.30. Select the most appropriate checklist for the above article.

A. My article contains -

My article contains -
1. An eye-catching title
2. A by-line
3. Proper set of causes and effects for water wastage
4. Well deliberated suggestions on water conservation
5. A quote to enhance the quality of the article
6. Factual information to support argument

B. My article contains -

My article contains -
1. Quote as title
2. Opinion of experts
3. Aggressive arguments against those who waste water.
4. Fact sheet to convince readers.
5. Free hand drawing at the end to make your article more eye catching
6. Date

C. My article contains -

My article contains -
1. An eye-catching title
2. Opinion of Geologists
3. Opinions of general public
4. Opinions of Government officials
5. Quote at the end
6. Date

D. My article contains -

My article contains -
1. Causes for negligence of water wastage
2. Suggestion to improve the condition
3. Three to four quotes.
4. By line
5. Date
6. Opinion of experts

LITERATURE

This section has sub-sections: V, VI, VII, VIII, IX. There are a total of 30 questions in the section. Attempt any 26 questions from the sub-sections V to IX.

V.   Read the given extract to attempt questions that follow:

She still has bangles on her wrist, but no light in her eyes. "Ek waqt ser bhar khana bhi nahin khaya." she says, in a voice drained of joy. She has not enjoyed even one full meal in her entire lifetime-that's what she has reaped! Her husband, an old man with a flowing beard says, "I know nothing except bangles. All I have done is made a house for the family to live in." Hearing him one wonders if he has achieved what many have failed in their lifetime. He has a roof over his head! The cry of not having money to do anything except carry on the business of making bangles, not even enough to eat, rings in every home. The young men echo the lament of the elders. Little has moved with time, it seems in Firozabad, years of mind-numbing toil have killed all initiative and the ability to dream.

Q.31. *'She still has bangles on her wrist, but no light in her eyes.'* This implies that:

A.   she is married but has lost the charm in her eyes.

B.   she is a married woman who has lost her grace and beauty.

C.   though she is married, her eyes are devoid of happiness.

D.   she is a married woman who has lost her eyesight.

Q.32. *'He has a roof over his head!'* The tone of the author is:

A.   pessimistic   B.   empathetic

C.   sympathetic   D.   optimistic

Q.33. Choose the term which best matches the statement *'The young men echo the lament of their elders.'*

A.   acceptance   B.   reflection

C.   reiteration   D.   doubtfulness

Q.34. *'Years of mind-numbing toil have killed all initiative and the ability to dream'.* This shows that:

A.   the bangle makers are exhausted yet they are enterprising and have dreams.

B.   the drudgery of work has destroyed their willingness to improve their lot.

C.   the daily grind has stolen the dreams of the bangle makers and made them dull.

D.   the bangle makers have been working so hard that there's no time to dream.

Q.35. Select the option that lists the meaning of expression *'Little has moved with time'.*

A.   The speed of the bangle making has gradually zoomed up.

B.   Nothing has changed at all.

C.   There is a steady change in the condition of the bangle makers.

D.   The state of bangle makers has changed completely.

VI.   Read the given extract to attempt questions that follow:

It was three months before the tension began to slack. Then he taught me to put my face under water and exhale, and to raise my nose and inhale. I repeated the exercise hundreds of times. Bit by bit I shed part of the panic that seized me when my head went under water.

Next he held me at the side of the pool and had me kick with my legs. For weeks I did just that. At first my legs refused to work. But they gradually relaxed; and finally I could command them.

Q.36. Of the four options given below, which one suits best to the explanation of *'I shed part of the panic'* in the extract?

A.   The terror completely left   B.   Somewhat terror still left

C.   Little fear was gone   D.   Major part of panic returned

Q.37. Select the option that lists the correct inference based on the information in the extract.

A.   It took Douglas three months to get rid of his terror.

B.   Three months ago, Douglas's tension began to reduce.

C.   After three months of practice, Douglas got rid of his terror.

D.   Within three months, Douglas was able to get over his fear.

Q.38. The qualities imbibed in the instructor helped Douglas turn into a good swimmer. What are these? Choose the correct options.

I.   Practical   II.   Uncouth

III. Motivating   IV.   Punitive

A.   I and II   B.   I and IV

C.   II and III   D.   I and III

Q.39. Select the option that displays a cause-effect set.

A.

Cause	Effect
Douglas commanded over swimming skills.	The instructor taught Douglas.

B.

Cause	Effect
The instructor taught Douglas.	Douglas commanded over swimming skills.

C.

Cause	Effect
Douglas was completely dependent on instructor.	Douglas shed panic gradually.

D.

Cause	Effect
Douglas shed panic gradually.	Douglas was completely dependent on instructor.

Q.40. Choose the option which tells why Douglas had been under terror?

A.   Once he was ducked by a big boy into deep water

B.   His mother had terrorized him

C.   No training by an instructor

D.   Heard several drowning incidents

VII.   Read the given extract to attempt questions that follow:

but after the airport's

security check, standing a few yards away, I looked again at her, wan, pale

as a late winter's moon and felt that old

familiar ache, my childhood's fear, but all I said was, see you soon,

Amma,

all I did was smile and smile and

smile.....

Q.41. *"all I did was smile and smile and smile"* -pick out from the following options the actual reason for the smile:

A.   she was happy to board the plane   B.   hiding her fear from mother

C.   was grinning with mirth   D.   was reassuring her mother

Q.42. The smile on the author's face at the end can be described as

    A.   all knowing   B.   enigmatic

    C.   open and frank   D.   untinged with sorrow

Q.43. How is the comparison of winter moon and face of mother appropriate here?

    A.   mother's face as round as moon's face   B.   silvery hair matched with silver moon

    C.   lack of strength and colour   D.   both are shining

Q.44. Kamala Das uses technique of the running over of a sentence from one poetic line to another- this is called __________.

    A.   functional break   B.   clear jump

    C.   enjambment   D.   juxtaposition

Q.45. *"smile and smile and smile"* is a rhetoric device called:

    A.   onomatopoeia   B.   alliteration

    C.   simile   D.   repetition

VII. **Read the given extract to attempt questions that follow:**

The man moaned with pain in his stupor but he did not awaken. "The best thing that we could do would be to put him back in the sea," Sadao said, answering himself. Now that the bleeding was stopped for the moment he stood up and dusted the sand from his hands. "Yes, undoubtedly that would be best," Hana said steadily. But she continued to stare down at the motionless man. "If we sheltered a white man in our house we should be arrested and if we turned him over as a prisoner, he would certainly die," Sadao said. "The kindest thing would be to put him back into the sea," Hana said. But neither of them moved. They were staring with curious repulsion upon the inert figure.

Q.46. In which of the following options can the underlined words NOT be replaced with 'stupor'?

    A.   She hung up the phone feeling as though she had woken up from a <u>slumber</u>.

    B.   The manager complained about the employee's <u>sluggishness</u>.

    C.   He seemed to be in a <u>trance</u> when the doctor called upon him last week.

    D.   Seeing him in a <u>daze,</u> the lawyer decided not to place him in the witness box.

Q.47. Pick the option that best describes Sadao and Hana in the passage.

    A.   Sadao: scrupulous Hana: wary   B.   Sadao: daring Hana: prudent

    C.   Sadao: prudent Hana: suspicious   D.   Sadao: wary Hana: daring

Q.48. Pick the idiom that best describes the situation in which Sadao and Hana were in.

    A.   to be like a fish out of water   B.   like water off a duck's back

    C.   to be dead in the water   D.   to be in hot water

Q.49. Choose the correct option with reference to the two statements given below.

Statement 1: Sadao and Hana cared about the soldier but were worried about the consequences of being considerate.

Statement 2: Sadao and Hana wanted to shirk their responsibilities of looking after an injured soldier, who could be an American.

    A.   Statement 1 is true but Statement 2 is false.

    B.   Statement 1 is false but Statement 2 is true.

    C.   Both Statement 1 and Statement 2 are true.

    D.   Both Statement 1 and Statement 2 are false.

Q.50. Select the option that signifies the state of mind of Hana when she said *"If we sheltered a white man in our house we should be arrested…….."* in the extract.

    I.   anxious   II.   compassionate

    III.   vigilant   IV.   satisfied

    A.   I and III   B.   II and IV

    C.   II and III   D.   I and IV

IX. **Attempt the following.**

Q.51. Hamilton uses two words to define two beautiful linguistic characteristics of French . What are they?

    A.   Musical and rhythmic   B.   Clear and logical

    C.   Lyrical and poetic   D.   Prosaic and mundane

Q.52. The words *"sprinting and spilling"* are used to show:

    A.   life and enthusiasm   B.   speed and tranquillity

    C.   life and death   D.   surplus energy

Q.53. There is a difference in the fear of separation felt in the past and the present moment by Kamala Das. Which expressions bring out this in the best manner?

    A.   Childish insecurity and knowledge born of maturity

    B.   peevishness of a child left alone

    C.   fear of getting neglected by her mother

    D.   fear of temporary separation and permanent one.

Q.54. From the chapter *Lost Spring*, it is evident that the author has an attitude of:

    A.   sympathy   B.   apathy

    C.   empathy   D.   bewilderment

Q.55. Pick the quote that highlights the contrasting image portrayed in the poem *An Elementary School Classroom in a Slum*.

    A.   'The worst form of inequality is to try and make unequal things equal.'

    B.   'An imbalance between the rich and poor is the oldest and most fatal ailment of all republics.'

    C.   'We must work together to ensure equitable distribution of wealth, opportunity and power in our society.'

    D.   'No amount of artificial reinforcement can offset the natural inequalities of human individual.'

Q.56. Charley decided not to tell his psychiatrist friend about his idea. Choose the option that reflects the reaction Charley anticipated from his friend.

    A.   "That's such a lovely comparison. Why don't you become a writer, Charley?"

    B.   "Oh Charley. It is so sad to see your desperation to run away! So very sad."

    C.   "Maybe that's how you entered the third level. Who would have thought?!"

    D.   "You need help, my raving friend. You are way too invested in this crazy thought!"

Q.57. The chap that threw me in was saying, *"But I was only fooling."* Choose the option mentioning the personality traits of this 'chap'.

    1.   persuasive   2.   irresponsible

    3.   domineering   4.   manipulative

    5.   callous

    A.   1, 2, 4   B.   2, 4, 5

    C.   2, 3, 5   D.   1, 3, 5

Q.58. *"Now I'll count up to twelve and you keep quiet and I will go."* Why does the poet wish to go at the end of the poem?

    A.   The poet does not believe people will be quiet.

    B.   The poet has already invested enough time.

    C.   The poet will move on and seek to inspire others.

    D.   The poet is marking the end of the poem by leaving.

Q.59. What does "blood" in the story *The Enemy* symbolise?

    A.   racism   B.   prejudice

    C.   unity   D.   nationalistic pride

Q.60. The fierce look of resistance upon Yumi's face was due to _________

    A.   the thought of being declared as a traitor

    B.   her willingness to turn over the prisoner to the officials

    C.   the thought of her master's well being

    D.   love and respect for her country

Sample Paper 5

English Core

READING

I. Read the passage given below.

I. The youth is a dynamo, an ocean, an inexhaustible reservoir of energy. But this energy cannot be kept caged in prison. Its basic nature is to flow, to express itself. The youth energy on the basis of the nature of its expression can be divided into four categories.

II. The vast majority of the youth today is with the establishment, whose formula of life is learn, earn, burn and enjoy. It means learn to operate the modern devices and employ them to earn the maximum amount of wealth to the point of burning the natural resources of the earth, as well as yourself out, and then enjoy your own funeral. This category of youth is intelligent, skillful and hardworking but it lacks insight and foresight. They are self-indulgent and any sense of moral code of conduct is alien to their nature. Neither are they able to see in depth, to find out whether there is a deeper meaning and purpose to their human life, nor have they the capacity to look beyond the tips of their nose to find out the consequences of their way and approach, where it is leading them to. They are the ends into themselves and enjoyment is the motto of their life.

III. The second category of youth in nature and approach is the same but as it is less privileged and less qualified and skilled; it has lesser opportunities for earning and enjoying. Such youth may be incited to be against the establishment. This opposition takes various forms. When it is well-organised and systemic it may take the form of political opposition and even go to the extent of expressing itself in unjust ways. When the opposition is not so intense and organised, it remains contended with giving verbal expression to its resentment periodically. The youth of the above two categories need to be shown the right path to positively channelise their energy.

IV. The third section of youth is a sober and thoughtful class of people, which objectively observes and studies the phenomenon of development of the world. These youth find that man in his insatiable thirst for consumption has become blind and lost the sense of distinction between milk and blood. Today man in his mad rush for exploitation is sucking the blood of Mother Earth; leading to their destruction and is thereby digging his own grave. This responsible category of young people is looking for an alternative mode of development based on co-operation between man and man. This development based on mutual love, friendship and harmony is not only sustainable but leading to endless prosperity mutually. To bring about his natural revolution from death-movement to life-movement is the aim of this group.

V. The fourth and most vital group of youth which is going to steer humanity into the third millennium and act as the pioneer for the future development of planetary life is engaged in evolving a new way of life and releasing a new principle of global consciousness through a fundamental research in the science of life. The science of life is a new branch of knowledge which takes the whole man into account without dividing him into subjective and objective halves of spirituality and physicality and does not treat him either as a refined (thinking) animal or an ethereal entity, having its base in some other non-physical world. It rather, recognises man as a basic unit of conscious life which has got immense, practically inexhaustible, possibilities and potentialities for evolution, development and growth.

As per the Vedic formula, man is the micro-cosmos and his fullest flowering and enfoldment lies in his identification with the cosmos.

Based on your understanding of the passage, answer <u>any eight</u> out of the ten questions by choosing the correct option.

Q.1. The writer feels that the youth's energy needs to be

   A.   expressed   B.   harnessed

   C.   reserved   D.   preserved

Q.2. Oxymoron is self-contradicting word or group of words.

The writer says that the vast majority of the youth today indulges to '<u>enjoy your own funeral</u>'.

Select from the options that correctly explains this oxymoron.

   A.   there is no deeper meaning and purpose to the human life.

   B.   formula of life is learn, earn, burn and enjoy.

   C.   self-indulgent people usually die alone and lonely.

   D.   The vast majority of the youth today lacks insight and foresight.

Q.3. Select the option that suitably completes the given dialogue as per the context in paragraph III.

Writer: So you're organizing a political rally today as I see. Any particular agenda that you're running for?

Youth leader: We are voicing our opinions (1)................................

Writer: Well that sounds a bit extreme and unnecessary, don't you think?

Youth leader: (2)..............................., we are doing what we feel is right.

   A.   (1) on the lack of proper garbage disposal bins in the city (2) Being conscious about climate change is good

   B.   (1) for building a new yoga center (2) a little bit of violence is ok if it is done for good

   C.   (1) against the promotion of only topper students (2) It is important that every child qualifies

   D.   (1) against unemployment, and we will barge into the DM office if need be (2) It is the only way the authorities will listen to us

Q.4. Which signboard would the writer have chosen for his description of the third section of youth?

1. Sober, sensitive and thoughtful youngsters.	2. Sober, selfish and thoughtful youngsters.	3. Drunk in power and self-indulgent youngsters.	4. Sensitive, grounded and delusional youngsters.

   A.   option 1   B.   option 2

   C.   option 3   D.   option 4

Q.5. Select the option that clearly indicates the comparison between first and fourth group of the youth.

	First group	**Fourth group**
A.	intelligent, skillful and insightful.	Mindful, intelligent and conscious.
B.	Sensitive, thoughtful and productive.	Immoral, unjust and self-indulgent.
C.	Self-absorbed, lacks insight and shallow.	Deep, insightful and thinking way ahead for the future.
D.	Rude, fast-paced and always in a hurry.	Pretentious, show-off and wannabe.

Q.6. What is the relationship between (1) and (2)?

(1)   .... but it lacks insight and foresight.

(2)   .... whose formula of life is learn, earn, burn and enjoy.

   A.   (2) is the cause for (1).   B.   (1) is the cause for (2).

   C.   (2) sets the stage for (1).   D.   (1) cannot describe (2).

Q.7. The writer mentions that man is the micro-cosmos and his fullest flowering and enfoldment lies in his identification with the cosmos, because he realises that:

   A.   Man is a basic unit of conscious life which has got immense potentialities for evolution, development and growth.

   B.   The youth needs to be shown the right path to positively channelise their energy.

   C.   The science of life is a new branch of knowledge which studies the development of planetary life.

   D.   Man should be divided into subjective and objective halves of spirituality and physicality.

Q.8. Select the option that lists the review for the writer's views on the second group of youth.

   A.   The writer clearly hates this group of youth the most as is clear with his choice of words for them.

   B.   The writer empathizes with this less privileged group and sees good potential in them if they are shown the right path.

C.   The writer mocks them for being less qualified and skilled, and sees them as a potential threat to the society.

D.   The writer is not much hopeful for this group of youth because they lack proper emotional intelligence.

Q.9. Which quote summarises the writer's feelings about the youth?

A.   "Youth offers the promise of happiness, but life offers the realities of grief."   *— Nicholas Sparks*

B.   "Older men declare war. But it is youth that must fight and die."   *— Herbert Hoover*

C.   "What should young people do with their lives today? Many things, obviously. But the most daring thing is to create stable communities in which the terrible disease of loneliness can be cured."

— Kurt Vonnegut

D.   "Youth is wasted on the young."   *— George Bernard Shaw*

Q.10. Select the option that lists what we can conclude from the text.

(1)   The youth is an inexhaustible reservoir of energy.

(2)   The second category of youth is a sober and thoughtful class of people.

(3)   The third section of youth may be incited to be against the establishment.

(4)   The fourth group of youth is going to steer humanity into the third millennium.

A.   (1) and (3) are true.   B.   (2), (3) and (4) are true.

C.   (1), (2) and (4) are true.   D.   (1) and (4) are true.

II. Read the passage given below.

I.   Over 100 persons have died in the floods in Assam so far while another 147 were killed in lightning strikes in Bihar last month. But with the monsoon season less than half way through, more loss of lives and property are expected if the trend in the past five years is anything to go by.

II.   Take for instance human lives lost. In 2015, a little less than 1,000 persons died of flood and rain-related incidents, but in 2019, nearly 2,500 persons had lost their lives, according to government data. The loss of cattle also increased. While in 2015, less than 30,000 cattle died, in 2019, it was nearly 72,000.(See graphic 1)

III.   To sum up the flood and its impact in the past five years, over 8,700 people were killed, over 2 lakh cattle died and more than 36 lakh houses were destroyed in floods. The cost of damage to property has also shot up in these five years. While in 2015, the damage suffered totalled ₹33,257 crore, in 2018, the last year for which data is available, it went up to ₹95,736 crore. The cost of damage is likely to be more in 2019 as over a dozen states, including Bihar, Assam, Himachal Pradesh, Kerala and Maharashtra, witnessed large-scale devastation.

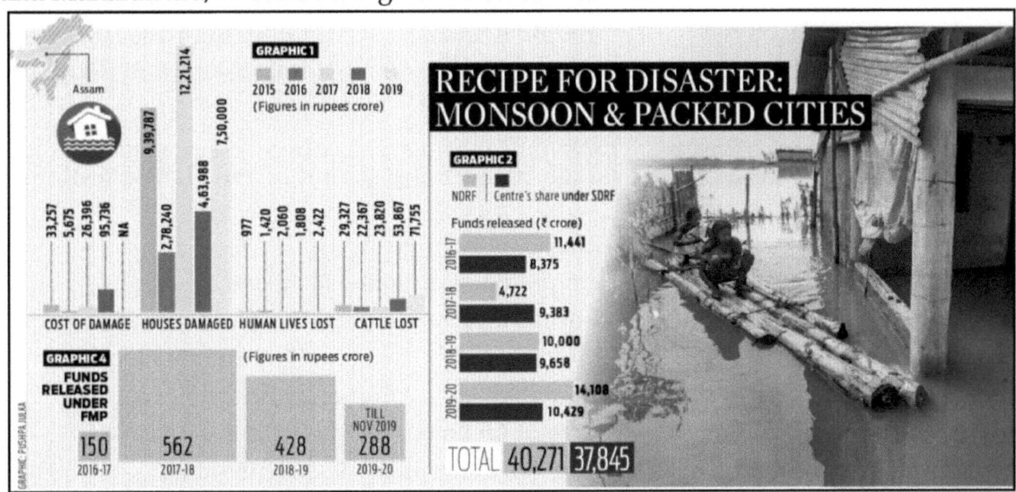

IV.   Besides the rising damages, the cost to the exchequer towards relief work has also increased. In 2016-17, the Centre released ₹11,441 cr under the National Disaster Relief Fund while its share under the State Disaster Relief Fund was ₹8,375 crore. This increased to ₹14,108 cr and ₹10,429 cr respectively in 2019-20. (See graphic 2)

V.   The flood's increasing loss of lives and property appears to make a mockery of all the expert committees, task forces and commissions the government has formed. In 1972, the Ganga Flood

Control Commission was set-up in Patna to address the flood problem and erosion in the Ganga basin states. In 1980, the Brahmaputra Board came into existence to address the flood erosion problem in the northeastern states and Sikkim. (See table)

VI. The government also launched a Flood Management Programme in the Eleventh Plan (2007-12) for providing financial assistance to state governments to undertake work related to river management, flood control, anti-erosion, drainage development, flood proofing, among others. The FMP was continued for three years under the Twelfth Plan from 2017-18 to 2019-20. It has subsequently been included as a component of the Flood Management and Border Areas Programme in the Ministry of Jal Shakti. But all these appear to have come to a naught as the government's approach is more reactive than proactive, according to experts. Instead of focusing on the real problem, it was only concerned about relief measures, they said.

VII. They pointed out that the area affected by floods has doubled since 1950. "The flood-affected area in 1950 was 25 million hectare, now it has doubled to nearly 50 million hectare. But, what is surprising is that nobody looks concerned about the real issues. Earlier, only villages used to be affected but now cities are also getting flooded. Chennai and Patna are just examples. I had written to the government in 2015, highlighting the poor drainage system in cities," said former IIT professor Dinesh Kumar Mishra.

Himanshu Thakkar, the coordinator of the South Asia Network of Dams, Rivers and People, said effective management of dams could bring down the damage caused by floods. "We have over 5,000 dams. Every dam can help moderate floods in the downstream area but only if it is operated properly," Thakkar said.

Committees & commissions	Aim	Work
Ganga Flood Control Commission	Flood, erosion in Ganga basin states.	Prepared 23 comprehensive master plans.
Rashtriya Barh Aayog	To evolve coordinated, integrated approach for flood control.	Submitted report in 1980 recommending measures Brahmaputra Board.
Brahmaputra Board	Flood, erosion problems in northeastern states.	Prepared 57 master plans for implementation.
Task Force-2004	Flood management and erosion control.	Submitted report in December 2004, recommending short, long-term measures.
Flood Management Programme	To provide financial assistance for river management, flood control, erosion.	Other than allocating financial aid, it is involved in flood forecasting.

Based on your understanding of the passage, answer <u>any six</u> out of the eight questions by choosing the correct option.

Q.11. Select the correct inference with reference to the following:

The government's approach is more reactive than proactive, according to experts.

A. Instead of focusing on the relief measures, the government is only concerned about real problem.

B. The government focuses more after damage rather than handling the root cause of the problem.

C. The government reacts in a proactive way which is commended by the experts.

D. The government focuses on the Ministry of Jal Shakti for such natural disasters.

Q.12. Select the central idea from the given table on the Committees & commissions.

A. These committees and commissions are only for North Indian rivers.

B. These committees and commissions are involved in flood forecasting.

C. These committees and commissions have a severe lack of infrastructure.

D. These committees are solely dedicated for flood and erosion relief with their financial aids.

Q.13. Select the option that displays the true statement with reference to figure given.

A. The cost of house damages was the highest in 2017.

B.   Cattle loss was highest in the flood of 2016.

C.   NDRF released the lowest funds for the year 2019-2020.

D.   Funds released under FMP were the highest for the year 2016-2017.

Q.14. Based on your reading of paragraphs III-IV, select the appropriate counter- argument to the given argument.

Argument: The damage relief fund costs are rising because of inflation. However, the overall loss of life and livestock is consistent.

A.   The rising costs are in no way related to inflation because Indian economy does not rely on global market for its currency value.

B.   Damage to property is greater as compared to loss of lives and livestock.

C.   Center isn't giving more relief funds for loss of life, so people have stopped reporting the dead.

D.   It is very clear that the rising damage costs are only because life and livestock damage have increased, because they are the indicator of fund prices.

Q.15. Select the option that displays the correct cause-effect relationship.

	Cause	Effect
A.	Cities are also getting flooded.	Poor drainage system in cities.
B.	Monsoon season caused flood in Brahmaputra valley.	Over 147 people die in Bihar last month.
C.	Flood and erosion in Ganga basin states.	Ganga Flood Control Commission prepared 23 comprehensive master plans.
D.	Government task forces are a mockery of all the expert committees.	More than 36 lakh houses were destroyed in floods.

Q.16. The survey statistics mention the funds released under NDRF, indicating that:

A.   The center's share under SDRF is always more than NDRF.

B.   The center's share under SDRF was more than NDRF in 2017-2018.

C.   The center's share under SDRF is almost similar to NDRF.

D.   The center's share under SDRF was more than NDRF in 2019-2020.

Q.17. The phrase 'exchequer' refers to the:

A.   former staff of bank who handles cheques.   B.   cheques that are given to victims.

C.   relief funds from NGOs.   D.   national government treasury.

Q.18. Read the two statements given below and select the option that suitably explains them.

(1)   Every dam can help moderate floods in the downstream area but only if it is operated properly.

(2)   Chennai and Patna have poor drainage systems.

A.   (2) is the problem and (1) is the solution for (2).

B.   (1) and (2) are both false.

C.   (1) is true but (2) is not the reason for (1).

D.   (2) is false and (1) explains it.

WRITING

III.   Answer <u>any four</u> out of the five questions given, with reference to the context below.

The Sports Secretary of St. George's School, Hyderabad, has to draft a notice for your school notice board informing the students about the sale of old sports goods of your school.

Q.19. Select the appropriate title for this notice.

A.   Sale of Old Sports Goods

B.   The Need to Sell Sports Goods

C.   Sports and More

D.   Good Quality Sports Goods at discounted price

Q.20. Select the option listing the most appropriate opening for this notice.

A.   Attention, students of all classes...

B.   We are writing this notice to inform you all that....

    C.   Students are hereby informed that...

    D.   I hereby wish to share with you all that...

Q.21. Select the option with the information points to be included in the body of this notice.

    (1)   Information about the kind of goods   (2)   General opinion about old sports goods

    (3)   Date of the sale   (4)   Reason for selling the old sports goods

    (5)   Outcome of the sale   (6)   The place where the sale would be organised

    A.   1 and 3   B.   1, 2 and 3

    C.   5 and 6   D.   1, 3 and 6

Q.22. Should this notice include the name of the Sports Secretary?

    A.   Yes, because he is the one issuing the notice

    B.   No, because signature says it all

    C.   No, as the title itself is self-explanatory

    D.   Yes, because it makes it informal

Q.23. Select the appropriate conclusion for this notice.

    A.   All are welcome

    B.   Interested students are requested to visit during recess time

    C.   Collaboration solicited

    D.   Persuade your friends to attend to come forward

IV.   **Answer <u>any six</u> of the seven questions given, with reference to the context below.**

While returning from school you happened to see plastic bottles being flung into the middle of the road from a speeding car. This made you think how people can be so devoid of civic sense. Write an article in 125-150 words on the lack of civic sense in our country and how civic sense can be inculcated in children at a very young age. You are Shiva/Shivani.

Q.24. Which suggestions would be appropriate for Shiva/Shivani's article?

    A.   We should inculcate civic sense right from childhood

    B.   Parents should ask children to take responsibility

    C.   Every demand of the child should not be met

    D.   Children should be encouraged to save money

Q.25. Select an appropriate title for this article.

    A.   Lack of Civic Sense   B.   Save Environment

    C.   Ban Plastic   D.   Let's Come Together

Q.26. Which option should the writer choose to elaborate on the reasons why use of plastic has risen?

1.

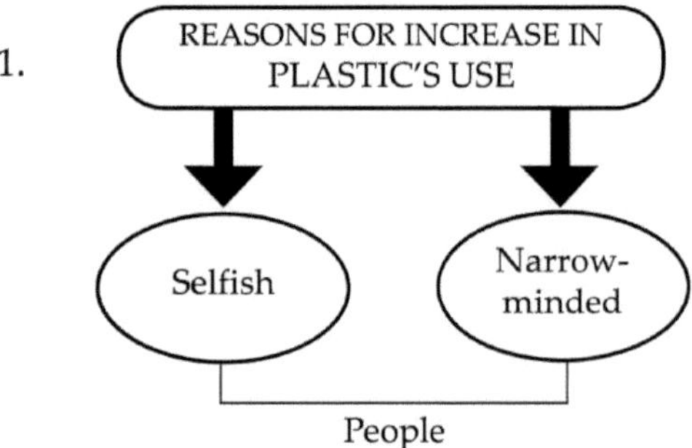

2.

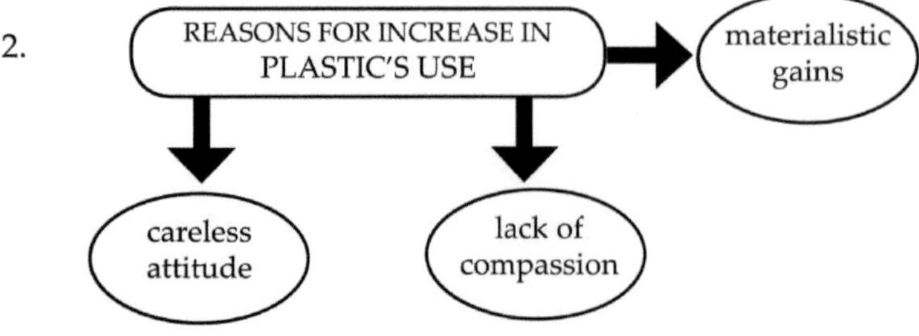

3.

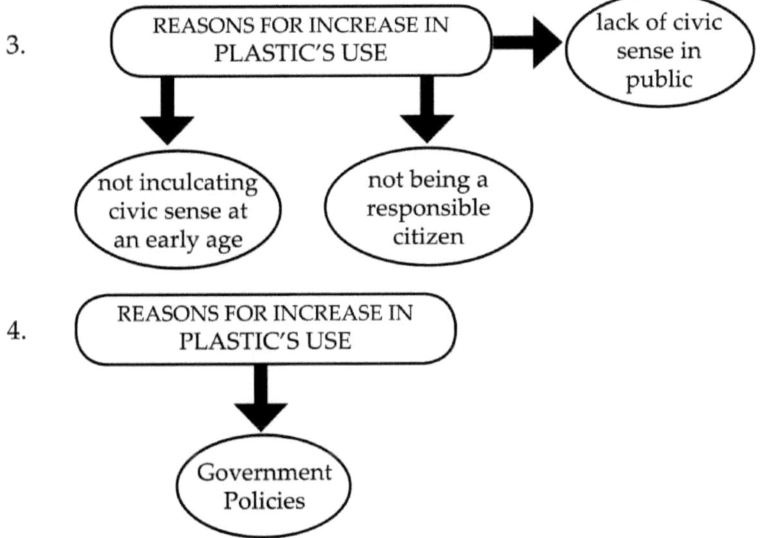

4.

A. Option 1	B. Option 2
C. Option 3	D. Option 4

Q.27. Which option would help Shiva/Shivani with the appropriate organisation of relevant ideas for this article?

A. Expressing concern about rise in use of plastic - looking at the reasons - presenting a concluding viewpoint - effects of the rise in use of plastic

B. Stating the effects of lack of civic sense - information about policies and laws - providing suggestions for saving the environment

C. Introducing the purpose of the article - presenting a pledge of saving environment - exploring the reasons for the laws - questioning the efficacy of laws

D. Showing the lack of civic sense in public - providing suggestions for improvements in the behaviour of people - talking about government policies - presenting a pledge for awareness

Q.28. Read a sentence from the article draft and complete it by selecting the most appropriate option.

Parents must (i) ____________ their children to keep their surroundings clean. All these things must be taught at (ii) ________.

A. (i) help (ii) school	B. (i) encourage (ii) at an early age
C. (i) ask (ii) childhood	D. (i) inculcate (ii) home

Q.29. Which quote summarises the central idea of the article?

A. Civic engagement is very important. We all live here together and we need to look out for one another. —*Elizabeth Goreham*

B. Civic education and civic responsibility should be taught in elementary school. —*Donna Brazile*

C. It seems to me that we are in danger of losing sight of certain basic civic values in society by allowing the growth of a whole generation of people who really have no sense of attachment to society. —*Alexander McCall Smith*

D. Without a sense of caring, there can be no sense of community. —*Anthony J D' Angelo*

Q.30. Read the options and select the option that includes the most appropriate self-checklist of the article.

A. My article contains -	B. My article contains -
1. First person address to the audience as title 2. Text that contains the topical points 3. Other people observation 4. Personal observations 5. Designation and date at the end	1. An eye-catching thematically related title 2. Content that offers a balanced view of the issue 3. Writer's opinion 4. Solution to the issue 5. A by-line

<table>
<tr><td>

C. My article contains -

1. A quote as title
2. Date
3. A conclusion including published evidence
4. Expression of gratitude
5. A by-line

</td><td>

D. My article contains

1. A content that analyses the pros and cons
2. Content that offers a balanced view
3. Input for the cause effect and suggestion
4. Name of the publishing body
5. Conclusion including personal observations

</td></tr>
</table>

LITERATURE

This section has sub-sections: V, VI, VII, VIII, IX. There are a total of 30 questions in the section. Attempt any 26 questions from the sub-sections V to IX.

V.   **Read the given extract to attempt questions that follow:**

"Will they make them sing in German, even the pigeons?" Whenever I looked up from my writing I saw M. Hamel sitting motionless in his chair and gazing first at one thing, then at another, as if he wanted to fix in his mind just how everything looked in that little school-room. Fancy! For forty years he had been there in the same place, with his garden outside the window and his class in front of him,.."

Q.31. What does the tone of Franz's question suggest?

A.   sarcasm   B.   satire

C.   cynicism   D.   caustic criticism

Q.32. Cooing is natural to pigeons. Similarly, what according to the context is as important to humans?

A.   own language   B.   music

C.   dreaming   D.   musing

Q.33. Mention the reason why Hamilton is sitting motionless in the chair.

A.   He was memorising the lessons to be taught.

B.   A recent development in his career came as a jolt from the blue.

C.   He was trying to think what best lesson he should teach so that everyone remembers him.

D.   He was worried about packing his things.

Q.34. Hamilton, in terms of his career, can be described as-

A.   a novice   B.   a pioneer

C.   a veteran   D.   a stickler

Q.35. Which of the following captions suits the theme of the story?

A.   Mother tongue is to ordinary people what notes are to musicians

B.   What is a Nation without mother tongue?

C.   Rhythm is our universal mother tongue

D.   Hearts can be ruled by imposing linguistic restrictions

VI.   **Read the given extract to attempt questions that follow:**

My acquaintance with the barefoot ragpickers leads me to Seemapuri, a place on periphery of Delhi yet miles away from it, metaphorically. Those who live here are squatters who came from Bangladesh back in 1971. Saheb's family is among them. Seemapuri was then a wilderness. It still is, but it is no longer empty. In structures of mud, with roofs of tin and tarpaulin, devoid of sewage, drainage or running water, live 10,000 ragpickers.

Q.36. The author used the word *'metaphorically'* for the location of Seemapuri. What does this suggest about the condition of the place?

A.   Well located   B.   Lacking basic amenities

C.   Advanced   D.   Retrograde

Q.37. Of the four meanings of 'wilderness', select the option that matches in meaning with its usage in the extract.

A.   situated in woods   B.   located in a secluded area

C.   full of wild animals   D.   occupied by tribal

Q.38. The author mentions that *'Those who live here are squatters who came from Bangladesh'*.

She means that the people are ___________ of Bangladesh.

    A.   Ration card holders   B.   Trespassers
    C.   Unlawful residents   D.   Native

Q.39. Select the option that lists the feelings and attitudes corresponding to the following:

(1)   .... *barefoot rag pickers*

(2)   .... *a place on periphery of Delhi yet miles away from it*

A.	(1) mocking	B.	(1) sympathetic
	(2) figurative		(2) sarcastic

C.	(1) remorseful	D.	(1) sympathetic
	(2) sarcastic		(2) rhetorical

Q.40. Select the option that lists reasons why rag pickers live in structures of mud, devoid of sewage, drainage or running water?

I.   no other option

II.   habitual of the atmosphere

III.   like to live in such places as it would help in their livelihood

IV.   denied the opportunity to live in clean places

    A.   I and III   B.   II and IV
    C.   II and III   D.   I and IV

VII. **Read the given extract to attempt questions that follow:**

For once on the face of the Earth
let's not speak in any language,
let's stop for one second,
and not move our arms so much.
It would be an exotic moment
without rush, without engines,
we would all be together
in a sudden strangeness.

Q.41. The poet uses the word "let's" to ________.

    A.   initiate a conversation between the poet and the readers.

    B.   invite readers as part of the poem's larger call to humanity.

    C.   welcome readers into the world of the poem and its subject.

    D.   address readers as fellow members of the human race.

Q.42. Margaret Atwood said, *"Language divides us into fragments, I wanted to be whole."*

Choose the option that correctly comments on the relationship between Margaret Atwood's words and the line from the above extract – *"let's not speak in any language"*

    A.   Atwood endorses Neruda's call to not speak in any language.

    B.   Atwood justifies Neruda's request to not engage in any speaking.

    C.   Atwood undermines Neruda's intent to stop and not speak in any language.

    D.   Atwood surrenders to Neruda's desire for silence and not speak in any language.

Q.43. Why do you think the poet employs words like "exotic" and "strangeness"?

    A.   To highlight the importance of everyone being together suddenly for once.

    B.   To emphasize the frenetic activity and chaos that usually envelops human life.

    C.   To indicate the unfamiliarity of a sudden moment without rush or without engine.

    D.   To direct us towards keeping quiet and how we all would be together in that silence.

Q.44. Which option has the underlined phrase that applies the poetic device used for in 'sudden strangeness'?

    A.   I had a <u>sleepless night</u>.   B.   The <u>trees whispered</u> their discontent.

    C.   The <u>crazy lady was very lazy</u>.   D.   The <u>gentle giant jumped</u> with joy.

Q.45. The literal meaning of 'and not move our arms' refers to a condition when one sits without any movement of hands. What does its figurative meaning refer to?

A.	exhibiting discipline	B.	not use weapons to harm others
C.	showing some kind of mourning	D.	remain still in punishment

VII. Read the given extract to attempt questions that follow:

I turned into Grand Central from Vanderbilt Avenue, and went down the steps to the first level, where you take trains like the Twentieth Century. Then I walked down another flight to the second level, where the suburban trains leave from, ducked into an arched doorway heading for the subway and got lost! That's easy to do. I've been in and out of Grand Central hundreds of times, but I'm always bumping into new doorways and stairs and corridors. Once I got into a tunnel about a mile long and came out in the lobby of the Roosevelt Hotel. Another time I came up in an office building on Forty-sixth Street, three blocks away.

Q.46. The expression *'where you take trains like the Twentieth Century'* shows that the narrator...................

- A. has confused state of mind
- B. has habit of living in past
- C. wants to deviate from the present situation
- D. has been living in some unknown constant fear

Q.47. Select the option that lists the correct inference based on the information in the extract.

- A. At the first level, suburban trains depart to subway.
- B. First level and second level are connected by suburban trains.
- C. Second level ends at subway.
- D. For reaching second level, one must take a flight from first level.

Q.48. Select the correct option to fill in the blanks.

Charley's always bumping into new doorways and stairs and corridors suggest that _______.

- A. it was the effect of his wife's behaviour towards him
- B. he was becoming forgetful due to stress
- C. Sam's behaviour had made him insane
- D. he was under the impression that he had reached the third level

Q.49. Why did Charley come out in the lobby of a Hotel when he got into a mile long tunnel?

- A. For a business meeting
- B. He had lost his way
- C. He was finding a refuge there
- D. It was the only exit point where he could go

Q.50. Select the option that displays a cause-effect set.

A.

Cause	Effect
The narrator ducked into an arched doorway	He got lost

B.

Cause	Effect
The narrator got lost	He ducked into an arched doorway

C.

Cause	Effect
The narrator walked down another flight to the second level	The suburban trains leave from there

D.

Cause	Effect
The suburban trains leave from there	The narrator walked down another flight to the second level

IX. Attempt the following.

Q.51. The all-pervasive mood of the poem *My Mother at Sixty-six* can be best described as:

- A. melancholic and cynical
- B. nostalgic and enthusiastic
- C. optimistic but tinged with fear
- D. cynical and optimistic

Q.52. The style of *The Last Lesson* is

- A. Descriptive
- B. Narrative
- C. Colloquial
- D. Melodramatic

Q.53. Sadao was not able to kill the American prisoner or get him arrested. What could be the possible reason for this?

- A. For the fear of getting arrested.
- B. He recalled the courtesy of the American when he was in US.
- C. It was against his profession.
- D. The Americans might take revenge and declare war.

Q.54. Select the option that tells about the feelings which developed in Douglas' mind after being thrown away in the pool by a big boy?
   I.   Aversion from water
   II.   Liking for swimming
   III. Lost confidence forever
   IV.   Terror seized him for a long time
   A.   I and II
   B.   I and IV
   C.   II and III
   D.   I and III

Q.55. *'Awarding the world its world'*, expression used by Stephen Spender illustrate that:
   A.   the world belongs to all equally
   B.   the world belongs to rich and influential
   C.   the world should be bestowed with bounties
   D.   the world should be reciprocated its resources

Q.56. Classify (1) to (4) as fact (F) or opinion (O), based on your reading of *The Third Level*.
   1.   Charley's three hundred dollars bought less than two hundred old style bills.
   2.   Charley was back on the second level.
   3.   I turned into Grand Central from Vanderbilt Avenue.
   4.   Charley never told his psychiatrist friend about his idea.
   A.   F-1, 3, 4; O-2
   B.   F-1, 2, 3; O-4
   C.   F-3, 4; O-1, 2
   D.   F-2; O-1, 3, 4

Q.57. Select the suitable option for the given statements, based on your reading of *Lost Spring*.
   1.   Many storms swept away Saheb's fields and homes.
   2.   Saheb didn't wear chappals.
   A.   (1) is false but (2) is true.
   B.   Both (1) and (2) are false
   C.   (2) is a fact but unrelated to (1).
   D.   (1) is the cause for (2).

Q.58. In 'Keeping Quiet' the poet induces a symbol in order to appeal that there can be life even without action. Which symbol is this?
   A.   water
   B.   earth
   C.   air
   D.   fire

Q.59. Inspite of complete defiance from the servants, Hana still helped Dr. Sadao in treating and serving POW. What does this reflect about her character?
   A.   Professionalism
   B.   Humanitarianism
   C.   Selfishness
   D.   Compulsion

Q.60. What could be the remedy of prevailing violence according to Pablo Neruda?
   A.   Refined and set language
   B.   Speech therapy
   C.   Rehearsing silence
   D.   Thorough wisdom

❑❑

Answers

READING

Q.1. B. Television

Q.2. B. (1) understand the logics behind those fairy tales (2) the stories are realistic and well described through animations.

Q.3. D. having a private conversation between two people

Q.4. C. Option 3

Q.5.

	Before	Today
C.	Reading books	Watching television

Q.6. A. (1) is the cause of (2)

Q.7. A. They find them uninteresting

Q.8. A. warms the bond between parents and children, attracts young minds to the world of books, a chance to explore the sea of life.

Q.9. D. *Books should go where they will be most appreciated, and not sit unread, gathering dust on a forgotten shelf, don't you agree?*
-Christopher Paolini

Q.10. C. (1) and (4) are true, (2) and (3) are false

Q.11. A. The innumerable individual passenger pigeons flocked the skies of North America.

Q.12. B. Columba

Q.13.

	Cause	Effect
A.	The hunt for passenger pigeons grew and culminated in a massive hunt for the species throughout the 1800s.	The species finally collapsed and disappeared.

Q.14. A. It's simply astonishing that the species found in large number, disappeared so quickly.

Q.15. B. I don't think that eating young birds at night wouldn't scare the adult birds. After all, they can sense fear and it is just an assumption of the North Americans.

Q.16. B. There was a rapid decrease in the population of passenger pigeons.

Q.17. B. It was in free fall even before the arrival of the Europeans.

Q.18. D. (2) is the research through (1)

WRITING

Q.19. B. Traffic Advisory

Q.20. C. This is to notify that in view of …

Q.21. A. (2) and (4)

Q.22. D. to warn people

Q.23. A. Stay safe.

Q.24. B. Through the columns of your esteemed newspaper, I want to draw your kind attention towards the daylight robbery in our area

Q.25. C. polite and formal

Q.26. A. Subject

Q.27. D. Getting a reward for her to bring it to the notice of concerned authorities

Q.28. D.

> • Solve the robbery issues in the area by highlighting it in a newspaper
> • Make the area safe for people

Q.29. A.　security guards are posted

Q.30. B.　Introducing problems faced by the people—Suggesting improvement methods—Conclusion.

LITERATURE

Q.31. C.　felt sorry for M. Hamel as it was his last French lesson.

Q.32. B.　'Too little, too late'

Q.33. C.　M. Hamel often sent students to water his flowers, and gave a holiday when he wanted to go fishing.

Q.34. D.　(i) forgotten; (ii) transformed; (iii) hold on; (iv) identity

Q.35. D.　regret

Q.36. C.　his dream was illusionary and indistinct.

Q.37. B.　2 and 4

Q.38. D.　Firozabad has emerged as a nascent producer of bangles in the country.

Q.39. C.　majority of the population in Firozabad is involved in bangle-making.

Q.40. A.　happy

Q.41. C.　Only (5)

Q.42. B.　Title 2

Q.43. C.　Both Assertion and Reason can be inferred.

Q.44. B.　My thoughts were as heavy as lead that evening when …

Q.45. C.　her face was lifeless and dull like that of a dead person

Q.46. C.　traditional

Q.47. C.　didn't want to use her white silk as the soldier was bleeding

Q.48. C.　(a) 1 and 2

Q.49. A.　foreigner, white, enemy

Q.50.

	Cause	Effect
A.	Hana didn't want to use her beloved quilt for the American soldier.	She hesitated while taking it out.

Q.51. A.　Self-realization

Q.52. C.　rag picking

Q.53. B.　bully

Q.54. C.　simile

Q.55. B.　ill-fed

Q.56. A.　(1) is false but (2) is true.

Q.57. C.　the fear of being caught

Q.58. A.　total inactivity

Q.59. B.　heartbroken and despaired

Q.60. D.　ethical

Sample Paper 2

READING

Q.1. B.   concerned

Q.2. A.   sunk

Q.3. D.   (1) why do you ask? (2) I would rather not talk about that unfortunate tragedy.

Q.4. C.   option 3

Q.5.

	Before 1985	After 1985
A.	Ruins preserved in cold dark ocean.	Hunters and voyagers exploiting the ruins.

Q.6. D.   (1) is the cause of (2).

Q.7. C.   The deep dark and cold conditions of the ocean has well preserved a century old specimen of human endeavour and failure which is an irony personified in history.

Q.8. A.   We are all grieving today for the greatest loss to mankind in recent history. We have failed all those on board by not building them a strong enough Titanic.

Q.9. B.   The people without the knowledge of their past history, origin and culture is like a tree without roots.
—Marcus Garvey

Q.10. D.   (2) and (4) are true

Q.11. D.   Spacecraft designers are competing to bring the quickest and most affordable options for space tourism.

Q.12. A.   Space tourism may not be feasible as of now but next decade may prove more promising.

Q.13. B.   NASA's budget for Human Space Flight and Mission Support are in the priority.

Q.14. D.   The wealthiest are willing to fund for research and development in space science, so even if it is for their ego, it will still be a way for advancement in faster and cheaper technologies.

Q.15.

	Cause	Effect
A.	$10 million prize for spacecraft designers.	Faster development of cost-effective space trips.

Q.16. D.   The demand and development have the potential to lower ticket price from $10,000 to $5,000.

Q.17. B.   launching a pilot into space.

Q.18. B.   (1) is true and (2) is the reason of (1).

WRITING

Q.19. C.   Position Vacant

Q.20. C.   1 and 2 only

Q.21. A.   Wanted marketing executive for a reputed Delhi based organization...

Q.22. A.   Address of the General Manager

Q.23. C.   Title of the advertisement

Q.24. C.   Mental health – your greatest wealth

Q.25. A.   option 1

Q.26. A.   Expressing concern about several cases of suicide due to depression- exploring the reasons with factual support – stating the effects – providing the suggestion to create mental health awareness – presenting a conclusive outlook.

Q.27. D.   Individuals should understand the importance of mental health and society should be more sensitive towards such causes.

Q.28. C.   Stigma, Recover

Q.29. A.   "It's okay to not to be okay"

Q.30. A. My article contains -

> 1. An eye-catching title
> 2. A by-line
> 3. Proper set of causes and effects for mental illness
> 4. Well deliberated suggestions
> 5. A quote to enhance the quality of the article
> 6. Factual information to support argument

LITERATURE

Q.31. A. If Statement 1 is the cause, Statement 2 is the effect.

Q.32. D. Drama

Q.33. B. indicate pauses

Q.34. B. 'I crossed to oblivion.'

Q.35. D. 1 and 2

Q.36. B. He is concerned about many others like the ragpickers

Q.37. B. isolation

Q.38. B. A man from Udipi

Q.39. C.

(1)	hope
(2)	tired and oblivious

Q.40. B. 1 and 5

Q.41. B. Their world is confined to the classroom windows full of poverty and diseases

Q.42. B. Dull and unpleasant

Q.43. C. The dull life of the slum children

Q.44. C. The Pied Piper of Hamelin

Q.45. B. Future of the slum children is unclear and uncertain

Q.46. D. Nobody in particular

Q.47. C. orthodox and upper class.

Q.48. C. Re-imagining a Warless Future: Technology for Peace

Q.49. D. option (2) and (4)

Q.50.

	Cause	Effect
C.	The speaker wanted to be in a peaceful world.	He wanted two tickets to go there.

Q.51. B. was hiding her feelings of fear

Q.52. B. copies of written notes

Q.53. C. He is considered the black sheep of the family.

Q.54. A. Water at Y.M.C.A. swimming pool

Q.55. A. a lucid flow of emotions

Q.56. A. Statement I is True, Statement II is False, and Statement III cannot be inferred.

Q.57. A. there is no dearth of promises which remain unfulfilled.

Q.58. C. The oppressive monotony of modern life.

Q.59. B. idealized sentimentality

Q.60. B. superiority of Japan over America.

Sample Paper 3

READING

Q.1. B. bewildered

Q.2. D. systematic form of expressions by hand movements.

Q.3. D. (1) child's ability to make sense of this world (2) They have an innate grammatical machinery

Q.4. C. option 3

Q.5.

	Before exposure to pidgin	After exposure to pidgin
A.	Little complexity to the grammar.	Adapting new words to create a fresh expressive language.

Q.6. A. (2) explains the question described in (1).

Q.7. C. It is the most recent and well documented form of linguistic study in how grammar is created.

Q.8. B. Interesting how something like the sign language made by children can be so inventive and fluid.

Q.9. C. "Children have real understanding only of that which they invent themselves." – *Jean Piaget*

Q.10. B. (1), (2) and (4) are true.

Q.11. D. Government is promoting last stage actions instead of tackling the problem in initial steps.

Q.12. A. Incineration is only going to bring more pollutants in the air.

Q.13. B. Awareness towards recycling of plastic is reflected in recent years.

Q.14. B. Regulations are not enough to contain the toxic carcinogens it will generate along with a huge cost of operating it.

Q.15.

	Cause	Effect
C.	Burning of polyethylene.	Release of formaldehyde and acetaldehyde.

Q.16. A. Prior to 1980, recycling and incineration of plastic was negligible.

Q.17. D. lower quality to burn as a fuel on its own.

Q.18. C. (1) is true and (2) correctly explains it.

WRITING

Q.19. C. Scheduled Power Cut

Q.20. C. 1,2 and 3

Q.21. A. All society members are hereby informed about the scheduled power cut…

Q.22. D. Name of publishing authority must be given.

Q.23. C. Inconvenience regretted

Q.24. A. The world is changing so rapidly and the context that our schools confront is so dynamic that we, as educators….

Q.25. C. Education infrastructure and its requirement in COVID era

Q.26. B. Introducing problems faced by teachers – Analysing change in education system – Suggesting improvements in the system – Conclusion

Q.27. C. Accept, Adjust

Q.28. C. Yours Sincerely
Aadarsh

Q.29. B. Closing signature must be on right

Q.30. C. Letter stating opinion on public interest.

LITERATURE

Q.31. A. Fright

Q.32. C. Announcement from Berlin

Q.33. C.

(1)	Concern
(2)	Seriousness

Q.34. C. 3 and 4
Q.35. B. breathing fast with difficulty
Q.36. C. Both Statement 1 and Statement 2 cannot be inferred.
Q.37. D. repression
Q.38. B. a bully tossed him into the pool for the sake of fun.
Q.39. B. because it was expected to go by now
Q.40. B. narrative
Q.41. B. Peace, humanity and brotherhood
Q.42. D. Scrutinize our activities
Q.43. B. 2 and 3
Q.44. A. reconciliation
Q.45. A. His own well-being and progress
Q.46. A. Due to mist in the air
Q.47. A. terrified
Q.48. C. Stranded
Q.49.

	Cause	Effect
A.	He was a prisoner	Arms above head

Q.50. C. The purpose of human life is to serve, and to show compassion and the will to help others.
Q.51. D. simile
Q.52. A. to show knowing one's language is escape from exploitation
Q.53. A. hyperbole
Q.54. C. limitless exploitation of natural resources.
Q.55. B. the contrast between studying in the dreary classroom and playing outside freely.
Q.56. D. Douglas decided to practice relentlessly to overcome his fear.
Q.57. D. irony.
Q.58. A. simile
Q.59. B. vigorous
Q.60. B. Both 1 and 2 are false.

Sample Paper 4

READING

Q.1. B. pressured
Q.2. A. crisis
Q.3. D. (1) drain all my energy, I don't have time for additional activities. (2) I am already reading books in school
Q.4. A. option 1
Q.5.

	Before television	After television
C.	Reading books was the usual hobby.	Reading books has become a rarity.

Q.6. B. (2) sets the stage for (1).
Q.7. A. it not only forms a warm bond between them but also attracts young minds to the world of books which gives them a chance to explore the sea of life.
Q.8. A. I was surprisingly engrossed in the novel that I started to read, it isn't that boring or geeky as it sounds.
Q.9. D. "If you read a book, you will unlock unknown doors of your soul. And who knows; you can find a treasure inside…"
— *George Spyrou, Roxanne*
Q.10. B. (3) and (4) are true.
Q.11. C. the number of passenger pigeons was in free fall even before the arrival of the Europeans.
Q.12. A. Native Americans practiced sustainable hunting, thus cannot be blamed for passenger pigeon extinction.

Q.13. C.   New world pigeons and Passenger pigeons had the closest DNA.

Q.14. D.   There were still a few hundred thousand individuals left from the passenger pigeon population, which could've been easily saved by conservation programs, yet the Europeans hunted them all.

Q.15.

	Cause	Effect
A.	PSMC method uses the genetic information of a single individual.	PSMC method can map the history of the species.

Q.16. B.   collared-doves are more closely related to old world pigeons, than they are to cuckoo-doves.

Q.17. A.   last of the event in the series of unfortunate trail of passenger pigeons.

Q.18. C.   (1) is true and (2) explains it.

WRITING

Q.19. C.   I and II only

Q.20. C.   Available for sale a three room flat in ...

Q.21. D.   Sale and Purchase

Q.22. A.   Address of Ranjan/Ragini

Q.23. C.   Title of the advertisement

Q.24. B.   Conserve water - No water no life

Q.25. A.   Option 1

Q.26. A.   Expressing concern about several cases of land water depletion- exploring the reasons with factual support – stating the effects – providing the suggestion to create water conservation awareness– presenting a conclusive outlook.

Q.27. D.   Individuals should understand the importance of water conservation and do the needful.

Q.28. D.   Awareness, Conserve

Q.29. A.   You never know the worth of water until the well runs dry.

Q.30. A.   My article contains -

> 1. An eye-catching title
> 2. A by-line
> 3. Proper set of causes and effects for water wastage
> 4. Well deliberated suggestions on water conservation
> 5. A quote to enhance the quality of the article
> 6. Factual information to support argument

LITERATURE

Q.31. C.   though she is married, her eyes are devoid of happiness.

Q.32. D.   optimistic

Q.33. C.   reiteration

Q.34. B.   the drudgery of work has destroyed their willingness to improve their lot.

Q.35. C.   There is a steady change in the condition of the bangle makers.

Q.36. C.   Little fear was gone

Q.37. C.   After three months of practice, Douglas got rid of his terror.

Q.38. D.   I and III

Q.39.

	Cause	Effect
B.	The instructor taught Douglas	Douglas commanded over swimming skills

Q.40. A.   Once he was ducked by a big boy into deep water

Q.41. B.   hiding her fear from mother

Q.42. B.   enigmatic

Q.43. C.   lack of strength and colour

Q.44. C. enjambment
Q.45. D. repetition
Q.46. B. The manager complained about the employee's <u>sluggishness</u>.
Q.47. C. Sadao: prudent Hana: suspicious
Q.48. D. to be in hot water
Q.49. A. Statement 1 is true but Statement 2 is false.
Q.50. A. I and III
Q.51. B. Clear and logical
Q.52. A. life and enthusiasm
Q.53. D. fear of temporary separation and permanent one.
Q.54. A. sympathy
Q.55. B. 'An imbalance between the rich and poor is the oldest and most fatal ailment of all republics.'
Q.56. D. "You need help, my raving friend. You are way too invested in this crazy thought!"
Q.57. C. 2, 3, 5
Q.58. C. The poet will move on and seek to inspire others.
Q.59. C. unity
Q.60. B. her willingness to turn over the prisoner to the officials

Sample Paper 5

READING

Q.1. A. expressed
Q.2. C. self-indulgent people usually die alone and lonely.
Q.3. D. (1) against unemployment, and we will barge into the DM office if need be (2) It is the only way the authorities will listen to us
Q.4. A. option 1

Q.5.

	First group	Fourth group
C.	Self-absorbed, lacks insight and shallow.	Deep, insightful and thinking way ahead for the future.

Q.6. B. (1) is the cause for (2).
Q.7. A. Man is a basic unit of conscious life which has got immense potentialities for evolution, development and growth.
Q.8. B. The writer empathizes with this less privileged group and sees good potential in them if they are shown the right path.
Q.9. C. "What should young people do with their lives today? Many things, obviously. But the most daring thing is to create stable communities in which the terrible disease of loneliness can be cured."
—*Kurt Vonnegut*
Q.10. D. (1) and (4) are true.
Q.11. B. The government focuses more after damage rather than handling the root cause of the problem.
Q.12. D. These committees are solely dedicated for flood and erosion relief with their financial aids.
Q.13. A. The cost of house damages was the highest in 2017.
Q.14. D. It is very clear that the rising damage costs are only because life and livestock damage have increased, because they are the indicator of fund prices.

Q.15.

	Cause	Effect
C.	Flood and erosion in Ganga basin states.	Ganga Flood Control Commission prepared 23 comprehensive master plans.

Q.16. B. The center's share under SDRF was more than NDRF in 2017-2018.
Q.17. D. national government treasury.
Q.18. C. (1) is true but (2) is not the reason for (1).

WRITING

Q.19. A.   Sale of Old Sports Goods
Q.20. C.   Students are hereby informed that...
Q.21. D.   1, 3 and 6
Q.22. A.   Yes, because he is the one issuing the notice
Q.23. B.   Interested students are requested to visit during recess time
Q.24. A.   We should inculcate civic sense right from childhood
Q.25. A.   Lack of Civic Sense
Q.26. C.   Option 3
Q.27. D.   Showing the lack of civic sense in public - providing suggestions for improvements in the behaviour of people - talking about government policies - presenting a pledge for awareness
Q.28. B.   (i) encourage (ii) at an early age
Q.29. B.   Civic education and civic responsibility should be taught in elementary school.   —*Donna Brazile*
Q.30. B.   My article contains -

1. An eye-catching thematically related title
2. Content that offers a balanced view of the issue
3. Writer's opinion
4. Solution to the issue
5. A by-line

LITERATURE

Q.31. A.   sarcasm
Q.32. A.   own language
Q.33. B.   A recent development in his career came as a jolt from the blue.
Q.34. C.   a veteran
Q.35. B.   What is a Nation without mother tongue?   **Q.36.** B.   Lacking basic amenities
Q.37. B.   located in a secluded area   **Q.38.** C.   Unlawful residents

Q.39. D.

(1)	sympathetic
(2)	rhetorical

Q.40. D.   I and IV
Q.41. B.   invite readers as part of the poem's larger call to humanity.
Q.42. A.   Atwood endorses Neruda's call to not speak in any language.
Q.43. B.   To emphasize the frenetic activity and chaos that usually envelops human life.
Q.44. D.   The gentle giant jumped with joy.
Q.45. B.   not use weapons to harm others
Q.46. C.   wants to deviate from the present situation
Q.47. D.   For reaching second level, one must take a flight from first level.
Q.48. D.   he was under the impression that he had reached the third level
Q.49. B.   He had lost his way

Q.50.

	Cause	Effect
D.	The suburban trains leave from there	The narrator walked down another flight to the second level

Q.51. C.   optimistic but tinged with fear   **Q.52.** B.   Narrative
Q.53. C.   It was against his profession.   **Q.54.** B.   I and IV
Q.55. B.   the world belongs to rich and influential   **Q.56.** A.   F-1, 3, 4 ; O-2
Q.57. C.   (2) is a fact but unrelated to (1)   **Q.58.** B.   earth
Q.59. B.   Humanitarianism   **Q.60.** C.   Rehearsing silence

❑❑

Physical Education

Sample Question Paper

Physical Education [Code (048)]

Term - I

Time : 1 hr 30 Minutes   Max. Marks : 35

General Instructions :

1. There are three sections in the questions paper namely Section A, Section B and Section C.
2. Section A consists 24 questions amongst which 20 questions have to be attempted.
3. Section B consists 24 questions amongst which 20 questions have to be attempted.
4. Section C consists 12 questions amongst which 10 questions have to be attempted.

Section - A

(KNOWLEDGE AND UNDERSTANDING)

1. What is the other name for Vitamin B_2?
   - (a) Niacin
   - (b) Thiamin
   - (c) Folic Acid
   - (d) Riboflavin

Ans. (d) Riboflavin

2. What is the formula to divide an odd number of teams in the upper half for a knockout fixture?
   - (a) N+1/2
   - (b) N–1/2
   - (c) N(N–1)/2
   - (d) N(N+1)/2

Ans. (a) N+1/2

3. Which test is developed to test fitness in senior citizens?
   - (a) Harvard step
   - (b) Rikli and Jones
   - (c) AAHPER
   - (d) Rockport

Ans. (b) Rikli and Jones

4. 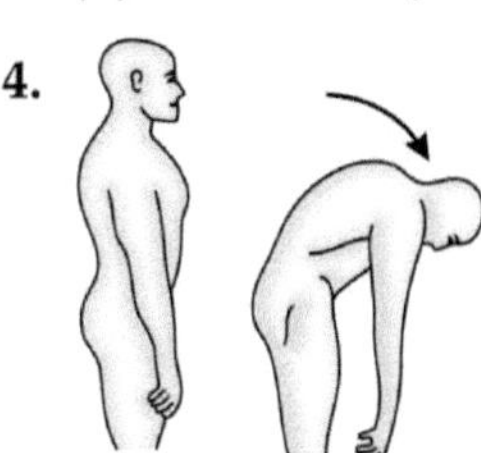

   Which action is shown in the illustration?
   - (a) Flexion
   - (b) Extension
   - (c) Adduction
   - (d) Abduction

Ans. (a) Flexion

5. Gliding movement occurs at which joint?
   - (a) Knee
   - (b) Hip
   - (c) Wrist
   - (d) Elbow

Ans. (c) Wrist

6. Consolation tournaments are a part of which type of fixture?
   - (a) Knockout
   - (b) league
   - (c) combination
   - (d) none of these

Ans. (a) Knockout

7. Which amongst these is not a macro mineral?
   - (a) Calcium
   - (b) Potassium
   - (c) Phosphorus
   - (d) Iodine

Ans. (d) Iodine

8. Who discovered Vitamin A?
   - (a) Dr. Mc Collum
   - (b) Dr. Coubertin
   - (c) Dr. J.B.Nash
   - (d) Dr. Harvard

Ans. (a) Dr. Mc Collum

9. Formula for determining the number of bye in the lower half of a knockout fixture when number of byes are odd?
   (a) nb+1/2   (b) nb–1/2   (c) nb/2   (d) nb+1

Ans. (a) nb+1/2

10. What is the name of the postural deformity caused due to increase in the curve at the lumbar region?
    (a) Knock knees   (b) Bow legs   (c) Kyphosis   (d) Lordosis

Ans. (d) Lordosis

11. Which test is used to test the functional ability amongst senior citizens?
    (a) Rockport one mile test   (b) Harvard step test
    (c) Rikli and Jones test   (d) Fitness Index score

Ans. (c) Rikli and Jones test

12. What is the test duration for the Arm curl test?
    (a) 1min   (b) 2 min
    (c) 30sec   (d) Number of repetitions

Ans. (c) 30sec

13. Which postural deformity has Convexities right or left?
    (a) Flat foot   (b) Knock knees   (c) Kyphosis   (d) Scoliosis

Ans. (d) Scoliosis

14. Which motor skill is involved in Smashing volleyball?
    (a) Gross motor skills   (b) Fine motor skills   (c) Cross motor skills   (d) Open skills

Ans. (b) Fine motor skills

15. Who gave Laws of motion?
    (a) Galileo   (b) Pascal   (c) Newton   (d) Darwin

Ans. (c) Newton

16. Harvard step is performed to check which kind of fitness?
    (a) Cardiovascular   (b) Explosive strength
    (c) Muscular strength   (d) Reaction ability

Ans. (a) Cardiovascular

17. Which fixture is also known as 'Berger system '?
    (a) Knockout fixture   (b) Round robin fixture
    (c) Combination fixture   (d) Challenge tournament

Ans. (b) Round robin fixture

18. Which of the following is not a spinal curvature deformity?
    (a) Kyphosis   (b) Scoliosis   (c) Lordosis   (d) Flatfoot

Ans. (d) Flatfoot

19. What according to you is the main cause for night blindness?
    (a) Deficiency of Vit. E   (b) Deficiency of Vit. C
    (c) Deficiency of Vit. A   (d) Deficiency of Vit. D

Ans. (c) Deficiency of Vit. A

20. Which law amongst the given ones is known as the First law of motion?
    (a) Law of inertia   (b) Law of reaction
    (c) Law of momentum   (d) Law of acceleration

Ans. (a) Law of inertia

21. What is the Ratio of carbon,hydrogen and oxygen in carbohydrates?
    (a) $1:2:1$ (b) $2:2:1$ (c) $2:1:1$ (d) $1:2:2$

Ans. (a) $1:2:1$

22. The formula for determining the number of rounds in a single league fixture when the number of teams is even?
    (a) N   (b) N–1/2   (c) N–1   (d) N(N–1)/2

Ans. (c) N–1

23. Which postural deformity is related to Posterior curve of the spine?

(a) Scoliosis   (b) Kyphosis   (c) Lordosis   (d) Knock knees

Ans. (b) Kyphosis

24. Which movement is caused by Moving a body part away from the medial line of the body?

(a) Flexion   (b) Extension   (c) Adduction   (d) Abduction

Ans. (d) Abduction

Section - B

(APPLICATION + HOTS)

25. Name the component which is measured by this test?

(a) Endurance   (b) Speed

(c) Flexibility   (d) coordinative ability

Ans. (c) Flexibility

26. Which exercise should be done to cure this deformity?

(a) Skipping   (b) Walking on heels

(c) Both (a) and (b)   (d) Hanging on horizontal bar

Ans. (c) Both (a) and (b)

27. Identify the component of fitness which is tested through this exercise

(a) Maximum strength   (b) Explosive strength

(c) Strength endurance   (d) Static strength

Ans. (b) Explosive strength

28. How many matches will be played if there are 22 teams for the knockout fixture?

(a) 10   (b) 21   (c) 12   (d) 32

Ans. (b) 21

29. How many byes will be given if there are 8 teams in the league tournament?

(a) 7   (b) 5   (c) 4   (d) 0

Ans. (d) 0

30. Halasana is used for curing which of the following deformities?

(a) Kyphosis   (b) Scoliosis   (c) Lordosis   (d) Flatfoot

Ans. (c) Lordosis

31. Match the following:

1.	Vitamin B12	A. Thiamin
2.	Vitamin B3	B. Biotin
3.	Vitamin B7	C. Cobalamin
4.	Vitamin B1	D. Niacin

Choose the correct option from the following:

(a) 4 3 1 2

(b) 2 3 4 1

(c) 1 2 3 4

(d) 3 4 2 1

Ans. (a) 4 3 1 2

32. Match the following:

1.		A. lower body strength
2.		B. lower body flexibility
3.		C. upper body strength
4.		D. abdominal strength

(a) 3 1 4 2

(b) 4 1 3 2

(c) 3 2 4 1

(d) 4 2 3 1

Ans. (b) 4 1 3 2

33. Match the postural deformities with their remedial activity:

1.		A.
2.		B.

(a) 1 3 2 4 (b) 1 4 3 2
(c) 1 3 4 2 (d) 4 2 3 1

Ans. (c) 1 3 4 2

34. Match the following:

1.		A. Flexion	
2.		B. Adduction	
3.		C. Extension	
4.		D. Abduction	

(a) 3 2 1 4 (b) 2 3 1 4
(c) 4 2 3 1 (d) 4 1 3 2

Ans. (d) 4 1 3 2

35. Which statement is not true about protein?

(a) Protein forms new tissues
(b) Protein regulates the balance of water and acids
(c) Protein helps in production of hormones
(d) Protein makes antibodies.

Ans. (c) Protein helps in production of hormones.

36. How many rounds will be played if the number of teams are 29 in the knockout fixture?

(a) 5 (b) 6
(c) 7 (d) 3

Ans. (a) 5

37. Identify the odd one.

1.  2. 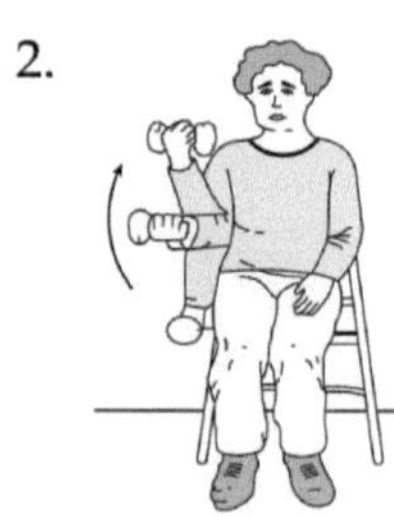 3.  4. 

(a) 4 (b) 3 (c) 2 (d) 1

Ans. (a) 4

38. **Assertion (A):** UNICEF says that water is not included in macro nutrients but USDA includes it as part of macronutrients.

Reason (R): Water must be taken in large quantities therefore it can be considered a macronutrient.

(a) Both (A) and (R) are true, but (R) is not the correct explanation of (A)

(b) (A) is true, but (R) is false

(c) Both (A) and (R) are true and (R) is the correct explanation of (A)

(d) (A) is false, but (R) is true

Ans. (c) Both (A) and (R) are true and (R) is the correct explanation of (A)

39. **Assertion (A):** Physical activities as corrective measure are very effective in functional deformity in comparison to structural deformity.

Reason (R): Muscles and ligaments are affected in functional deformity

(a) Both (A) and (R) are true, but (R) is not the correct explanation of (A)

(b) Both (A) and (R) are true and (R) is the correct explanation of (A)

(c) (A) is true, but (R) is false

(d) (A) is false, but (R) is true

Ans. (b) Both (A) and (R) are true and (R) is the correct explanation of (A)

40. Identify the movement

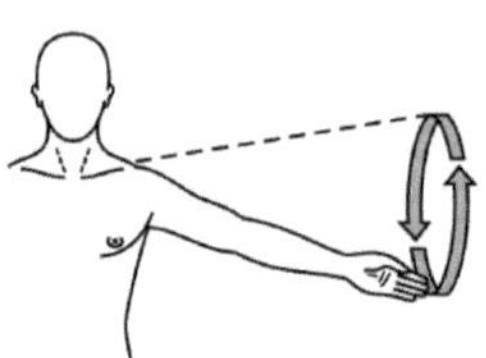

(a) Rotation (b) Circumduction (c) Flexion (d) Extension

Ans. (b) Circumduction

41. What will be the fitness index score of a girl if the test duration was 300sec and the pulse count(1min-1.5min) was 80.

(a) 73.2 (b) 62.8 (c) 68.1 (d) 85.3

Ans. (c) 68.1

42. Match the following

(a)	Technical committee	(i) To provide shifting facility
(b)	Finance committee	(ii) To resolve dispute
(c)	Transport committee	(iii) To deals with money and expenditure
(d)	First aid committee	(iv) To provide medical facilities.

(a) a–ii, b–iii, c–i, d–iv (b) a–iii, b–ii, c–i, d–iv

(c) a–ii, b–iii, c–iv, d–i (d) a–iv, b–iii, c–i, d–ii

Ans. (a) a–ii, b–iii, c–i, d–iv

43. Match the following vitamin with the disease caused due to their deficiency

1.	Vitamin A	A. Rickets
2.	Vitamin B	B. Night blindness
3.	Vitamin C	C. Beri beri
4.	Vitamin D	D. Scurvy

(a) 4 3 2 1   (b) 4 1 2 3

(c) 3 2 4 1   (d) 3 4 1 2

Ans. (b) 4 1 2 3

44. Starting a throwing event in athletics is an example of which law of motion.

 (a) First law of motion   (b) Second law of motion

 (c) Third law of motion   (d) First and third law of motion

Ans. (a) First law of motion

45. Assertion (A): "A change in the acceleration of an object is directly proportional to the force producing it and inversely proportional to its mass"

Reason (R): Lighter mass will travel at a faster speed

 (a) Both (A) and (R) are true, but (R) is not the correct explanation of (A)

 (b) Both (A) and (R) are true and (R) is the correct explanation of (A)

 (c) (A) is true, but (R) is false

 (d) (A) is false, but (R) is true

Ans. (b) Both (A) and (R) are true and (R) is the correct explanation of (A)

46. Identify which one of these is not the objective of Planning?

 (a) Enhance creativity   (b) Increase efficiency

 (c) Reduce chances of mistake   (d) Facilitates poor coordination

Ans. (d) Facilitates poor coordination

47.

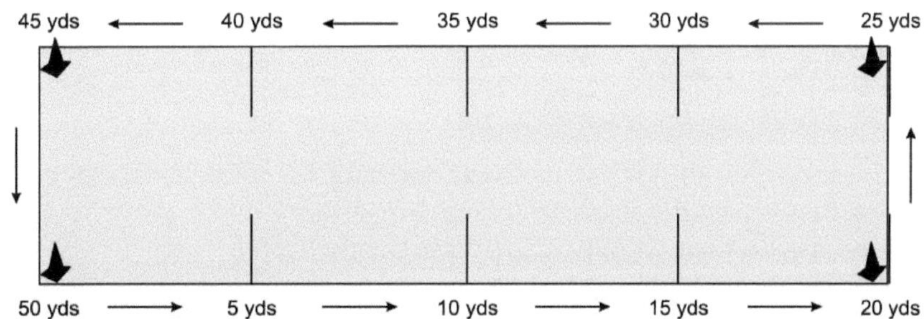

Identify the test for which this pattern is followed

 (a) 600 mtr   (b) 50 yard dash   (c) 400 mtr   (d) 6 min walk

Ans. (d) 6min walk

48. Calculate the BMI of a girl and identify the category if her weight is 68 kg and height is 161 cm.

 (a) Underweight   (b) Normal weight   (c) Overweight   (d) Obesity class I

Ans. (c) Overweight

Section - C

(CASE STUDIES)

49. Below given is the BMI data of a school's health check-up

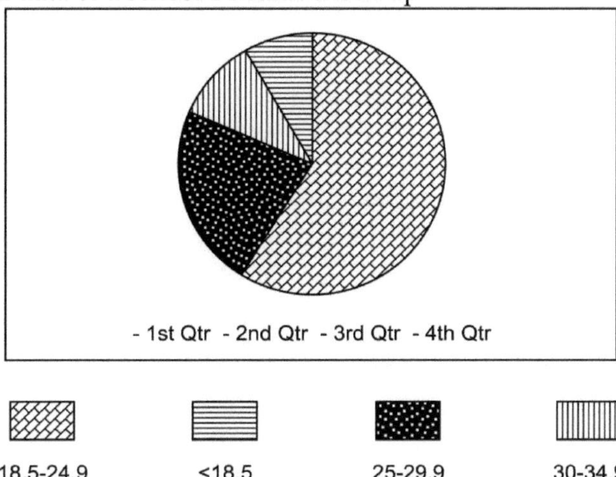

In which category does the major student population fall into?
(a) Obese

(b) Normal weight
(c) Underweight

(d) Overweight

Ans. (b) Normal weight

50. Mr. Lakshman, aged 65 years worked as a civil engineer in a construction company .He had to walk and climb a lot as part of his job. After retirement, he settled with his son and spent time with his grandchildren. Nowadays he is experiencing difficulty in doing certain chores which involve physical movement.

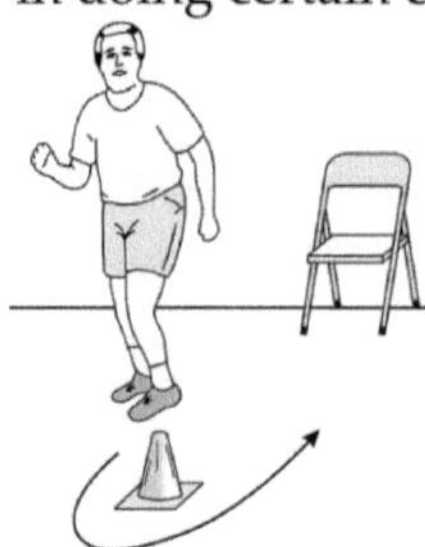

The test shown in the picture is performed to assess which component?
(a) agility   (b) endurance   (c) speed   (d) strength

Ans. (a) agility

51. 

Physical education teacher of ABC school was teaching the students about Newton's Laws of Motion. While explaining he showed the students this picture and tried to explain how there is a difference in the speed of an object due to their weight. Can you name the Law?
(a) Newton's First Law of Motion

(b) Newton's Second Law of Motion
(c) Newton's Third Law of Motion

(d) Action Reaction

Ans. (b) Newton's Second Law of Motion

52. Jatin is a weightlifter in the 96 kg category. He has to participate in a weightlifting competition next week for which he is taking good care of his practice and diet. He has included all the essential nutrients in his diet. Based on this case, answer the following questions.

What do you think would be the most important component of Jatin's diet?
(a) Proteins   (b) Carbohydrates   (c) Vitamins   (d) Minerals

Ans. (a) Proteins

53. Rohan and Satish organized a Volleyball tournament on Knock out basis. They found that the spectators were losing interest in the tournament because two good teams were out of the tournament as they were defeated in the beginning.

Which provision could have avoided this kind of situation?
(a) Bye   (b) Seeding   (c) Pools   (d) Halves

Ans. (b) Seeding

54. Sandy is diagnosed with postural adaptation of the spine in lateral direction. The curve is identified as convexity right. It happened due to Sandy's underdeveloped legs and carrying heavy loads on one side only.

What kind of postural deformity doctors found in Sandy?
(a) Scoliosis   (b) Kyphosis   (c) Bow Legs   (d) Flatfoot

Ans. (a) Scoliosis

55. Motor devlopment only happens when the child is biologically and mentally ready for it. Motor development refers to the development of movement and various motor abilities from birth till death. It is the ability to move around and manipulate his/her environment. The first stage is marked by extremely rapid growth and development, as is the second stage. By the age of 2 years, this development has begun to level out somewhat. The final stage does not have any marked new development; rather it is characterized by the mastering and development of the skills achieved in the first two stages.

Which Factor affecting motor development
(a) Biological,environmental,nutrition,opportunity
(b) Obesity, postural deformities, physical activities
(c) Both (a) and (b)
(d) Technique, skill and style

Ans. (b) Both (a) and (b)

56. Harvard step test is also called the Aerobic Fitness Test. It was developed by Brouha and others in1943. It is used to measure aerobic fitness by checking the recovery rate.

Few students were asked to conduct Harvard step test for their classmates and they were asked to note down the complete details of their aerobic capacity. For conducting tests they required a bench separate for boys 20 inches and girls 16 inches with one stop watch to note down the timing and their recovery rate.

How many times is the reading taken for calculating a long term fitness index?

(a) 5   (b) 3   (c) 2   (d) 4

Ans. (b) 3

57. Rishi who was studying in class XII is a science stream student. During his Physical Education class, he got confused how Newton's laws of Motion are useful in sports and how they can be applied in sports. But his teacher explained these laws with help of examples from sports which proved to be very helpful for him

Swimming is the best example of which law of motion?

(a) Law of inertia   (b) Law of acceleration   (c) Law of reaction   (d) Both (a) and (c)

Ans. (d) Both (a) and (c)

58. Posture plays a very significant role in our daily activities. Correct posture means the balancing of the body in an accurate and proper manner. Various types of postural deformities can be identified in individuals.

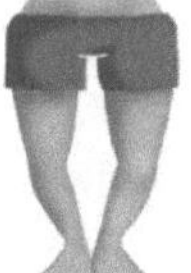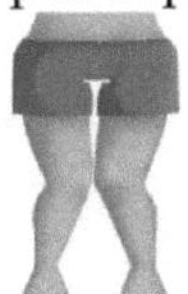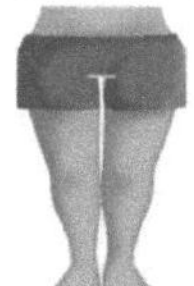

From the above given picture, the deformities seen on the left most is caused due to deficiency of which nutrient?

(a) Iron   (b) Calcium   (c) Vit D   (d) Both (b) and (c)

Ans. (d) Both (b) and (c)

59. Sohan, a new student in the school, was very much interested in sports and while learning various biomechanical aspects of the game including various movements he became curious to understand movements used in different games.

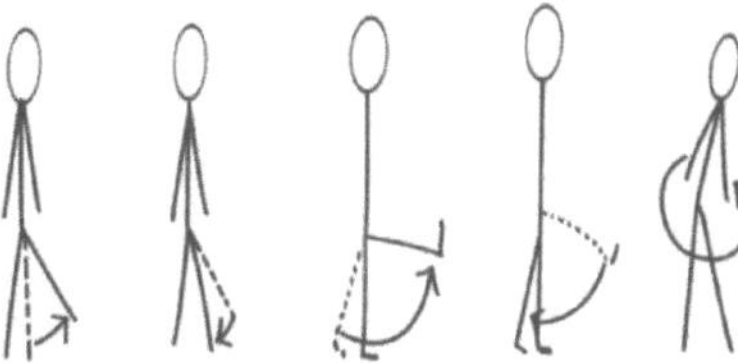

Flexion and extension comes under which movement.

(a) gliding   (b) angular   (c) rotation   (d) Circumduction

Ans. (b) angular

60. ABC School is one of the reputed schools in their location for the number of sports facilities it provides to its stake holders.Keeping that in consideration CBSE Sports cell has given them the responsibility of conducting CBSE Football cluster.35 teams have sent their entry for participation in the tournament.

A. Due to the large number of teams willing to participate the school should conduct the competition by which fixture?

(a) League   (b) Knock out   (c) Staircase   (d) Challenge

Ans. (b) Knock out

❏❏

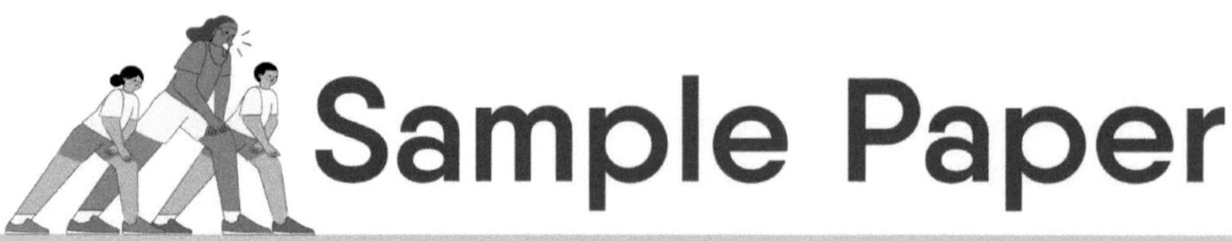

Sample Paper 1

Physical Education

Section – A

(KNOWLEDGE AND UNDERSTANDING)

1. What is Bye?
    (a) It's a method of drawing fixture.
    (b) Point system for team games.
    (c) Advantage given to a team to not play in initial round.
    (d) Placing of teams according to previous performance.

2. Which of the following food helps in sustaining prolonged routine of exercise?
    (a) Fats
    (b) Proteins
    (c) Vitamins
    (d) Carbohydrates

3. On average, how long does the statutory assessment process take?
    (a) Up to 26 weeks
    (b) Up to 12 weeks
    (c) Up to 8 weeks
    (d) Up to 52 weeks

4. Acceleration of an object will increase as the net force increases depending upon its:
    (a) Density
    (b) Mass
    (c) Shape
    (d) Volume

5. Which of the following treatments can be used to improve the processes underpinning motor skills?
    (a) Sensory integration therapy
    (b) Mathematic remediation programming
    (c) Exposure and operant conditioning
    (d) None of them

6. Vitamin E deficiency causes:
    (a) Anaemia
    (b) Weakness in heart and muscle
    (c) Both (a) and (b)
    (d) None of them

7. In normal walking at a person's preferred speed, the ratio of the durations of the stance and swing phases is roughly:
    (a) 1-1
    (b) 2-3
    (c) 2-1
    (d) 3-2

8. Partial curl up is to test.
    (a) agility and speed
    (b) leg strength and endurance
    (c) abdominal strength and endurance
    (d) upper body strength and endurance

9. Which of these are not gross motor skills?
    (a) Throwing a ball
    (b) Jumping
    (c) Balancing on one foot
    (d) Standing

10. A tournament where every team plays with every other team once and the number of matches is determined with the help of N(N-1) is called as:
    (a) Single league tournament
    (b) Double league tournament
    (c) Knock-out tournament
    (d) None of them

11. Vitamin E contributes to the production of __________, making our __________ system strong.
    (a) Strength, digestive
    (b) Antibodies, immunity
    (c) Both (a) and (b)
    (d) Hormones, muscular

12. Ramesh has to prepare formats of registration forms and batches for the participants. Which committee is Ramesh planning about?
    (a) Accommodation
    (b) Registration
    (c) Finance
    (d) Logistics

13. __________ Vitamin is a group of 8 water soluble vitamin which are important for cellular metabolism.
    (a) E   (b) B Complex   (c) C   (d) D

14. Which of the following players is associated with badminton?
    (a) Sania Mizra   (b) Saina Nehwal   (c) Karanam   (d) P.T.Usha

15. Which among the following is the next most important duty after planning
    (a) Feedback   (b) Organizing
    (c) Managing   (d) Planning

16. Rikli Jones test is conducted on:
    (a) Children   (b) Adults   (c) Adolescent   (d) Senior Citizens

17. Which method should he follow to improve the jump?
    (a) Flexibility   (b) Explosive power   (c) Push-ups   (d) Shuttle run

18. Which is the last function during an event organisation?
    (a) Organizing   (b) Planning   (c) Managing   (d) Feedback

19. Which of the following represents the smooth running of the event?
    (a) Managing   (b) Feedback   (c) Organizing   (d) Planning

20. Name the objective of planning shown in the figure given below:

    (a) Reduced mistakes   (b) Planning
    (c) Decision making   (d) None of them

21. Schedules fixed for the matches to be played their time, place, date and court, etc. known as:
    (a) bye   (b) fixture
    (c) advantage   (d) seeding

22. Allotment of bye is on basis of:
    (a) performance   (b) random draws
    (c) first come first serve   (d) pre-decided sequence

23. Select the correct development during infancy state.
    (a) Moral values   (b) Various senses
    (c) Fine motor skills   (d) Writing skills

24. The age of infancy is:
    (a) 0 to 1   (b) 0 to 2   (c) 0 to 3   (d) 0 to 4

Section – B

(APPLICATION + HOTS)

25. Which type of tournament is shown by the picture given?

    (a) League tournament   (b) Knock out tournament
    (c) Round robin tournament   (d) None of these

26. List the role of the following nutrients in the human body

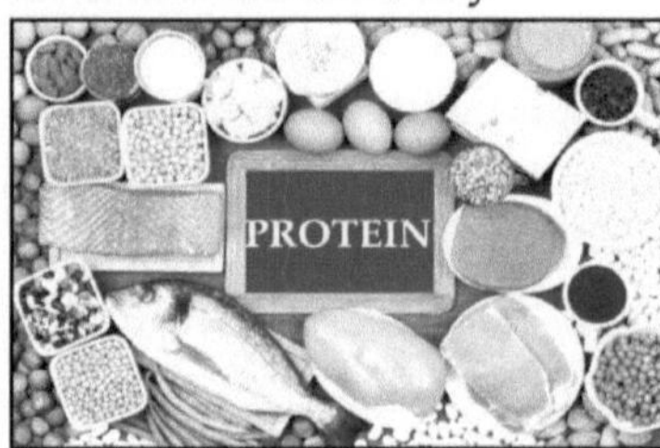

    (a) Instant source of energy   (b) Muscle repair
    (c) Insulate the body   (d) None of them

27. Which of the following is an example of Lordosis?

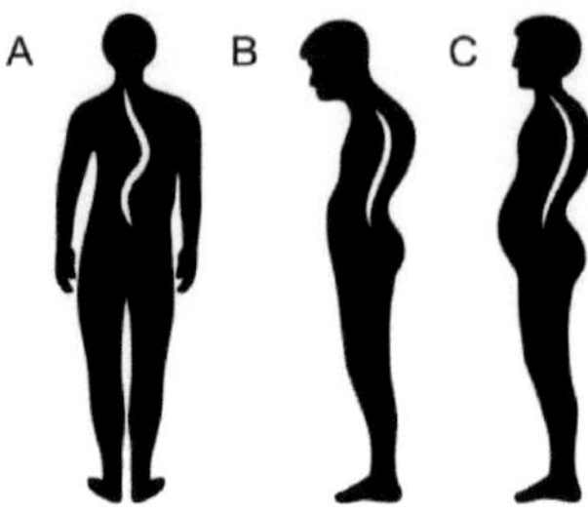

    (a) A   (b) B
    (c) C   (d) None of these

28. First step in sports management is :
    (a) planning   (b) organising
    (c) execution   (d) coordination

29. A __________ diet contains all the essential food constituents necessary for growth and maintenance of our body.
    (a) strict   (b) balanced
    (c) prescribed   (d) consistent

30. Fine motor development is involved in:
    (a) sitting   (b) walking
    (c) standing   (d) catching a ball

31. Match the following:

S. No.	LIST-I	LIST-II
1.	Abrasion	A. Joint Injuries
2.	Green stick fractures	B. Soft tissue injuries
3.	Shoulder Dislocation	C. Cause of sport injuries
4.	Lack of fitness	D. Bone injuries

Choose the correct option from the following:
    (a) 1–D, 2–A, 3–C, 4–B   (b) 1–B, 2–A, 3–C, 4–D
    (c) 1–B, 2–D, 3–A, 4–C   (d) 1–A, 2–D, 3–B, 4–C.

32. Match the following:

S. No.	LIST-I	LIST-II
1.	Technical committee	A. to provide shifting facility
2.	Finance committee	B. to resolve dispute
3.	Transport committee	C. to deals with money and expenditure
4.	First and committee	D. to provide medical facility

    (a) 1–B, 2–C, 3–A, 4–D   (b) 1–C, 2–B, 3–A, 4–D
    (c) 1–B, 2–C, 3–D, 4–A   (d) 1–D, 2–C, 3–A, 4–B.

33. Match the movements:

S. No.	LIST-I	LIST-II
1.		A. Adduction
2.		B. Flexion
3.		C. Abduction

(a) 1–A, 2–B, 3–C
(b) 1–B, 2–C, 3–A
(c) 1–C, 2–A, 3–B
(d) 1–A, 2–C, 3–B

34. Match the movements:

S. No.	LIST-I	LIST-II
1.		A. Flexion
2.		B. Extension
3.		C. Abduction

(a) 1–A, 2–B, 3–C
(b) 1–C, 2–A, 3–B
(c) 1–B, 2–A, 3–C
(d) 1–A, 2–C, 3–B

35. Motor fitness test is a set of __________ tests.

(a) six   (b) seven   (c) eight   (d) nine

36. The study of human body and various forces acting on it is:

(a) biology
(b) biomechanics
(c) physiology
(d) anatomy

37. Which of the following is not a cause of flat foot deformity?

(a) Body heaviness
(b) Standing for a long time
(c) Lack of vitamin D and calcium
(d) Faulty posture

38. **Assertion (A):** Physical Education is an elective discipline.

Reason (R): Physical Education borrows principles from other allied fields.

(a) Both (A) and (R) are true, but (R) is not the correct explanation of (A)
(b) (A) is true, but (R) is false
(c) Both (A) and (R) are true and (R) is the correct explanation of (A)
(d) (A) is false, but (R) is true

39. **Assertion (A):** The antibodies are created by the proteins in our body.
    Reason (R): Proteins are very important for the maintenance of our health.
    (a) Both (A) and (R) are true, but (R) is not the correct explanation of (A)
    (b) Both (A) and (R) are true and (R) is the correct explanation of (A)
    (c) (A) is true, but (R) is false
    (d) (A) is false, but (R) is true

40. Identify the following test:

    (a) Harvard step test
    (b) Sit and reach
    (c) Partial curl up
    (d) Chair stand test

41. Modified push ups are designed for:
    (a) volleyball player
    (b) boys
    (c) cricket player
    (d) girls

42. Match the following:

S. No.	LIST-I	LIST-II
1.	600 m run/walk	A. Flexibility
2.	Sit and reach	B. Upper muscular strength
3.	Push ups (boys)	C. Agility
4.	4 × 10 m shuttle run	D. Aerobic capacity

    (a) 1–C, 2–B, 3–D, 4–A
    (b) 1–D, 2–A, 3–B, 4–C
    (c) 1–B, 2–C, 3–D, 4–A
    (d) 1–B, 2–A, 3–C, 4–D.

43. Match the movements and select the correct answer from the codes given below:

S. No.	LIST-I	LIST-II
1.	Extension	A. lifting the upper limb horizontally to form a right angle with the side of the body.
2.	Abduction	B. returning the upper limb from horizontal position to the side of the body.
3.	Adduction	C. bending the lower limb at the knee.
4.	Flexion	D. straightening the lower limb at knee.

    (a) 1–D, 2–C, 3–A, 4–B
    (b) 1–C, 2–B, 3–A, 4–D
    (c) 1–D, 2–A, 3–B, 4–C
    (d) 1–C, 2–A, 3–B, 4–D.

44. Which of the following methods helps best in maintaining a healthy body weight?
    (a) Leading an active lifestyle
    (b) Missing at least one meal every day
    (c) Eating snacks frequently but no meals
    (d) Reducing calories drastically in food eaten

45. **Assertion (A):** Test protocol is the correct procedure for carrying out a test.
    Reason (R): If a test is done incorrectly, it might affect the results.
    (a) Both (A) and (R) are true, but (R) is not the correct explanation of (A)
    (b) Both (A) and (R) are true and (R) is the correct explanation of (A)
    (c) (A) is true, but (R) is false
    (d) (A) is false, but (R) is true

46. The age group of middle childhood is ___________ .
    (a) 6-10 years
    (b) 5-10 years
    (c) 7-12 years
    (d) 9-13 years

47. What are the two types of motor development of muscles in the body?

    (a) Gross and fine   (b) Gross and net

    (c) Coarse and fine   (d) Gross and measured

48. Purpose of the test is measured through:

    (a) reliability   (b) validity

    (c) objectivity   (d) split half method

Section - C

(CASE STUDIES)

49. Given below is the graphical presentation of an event organization:

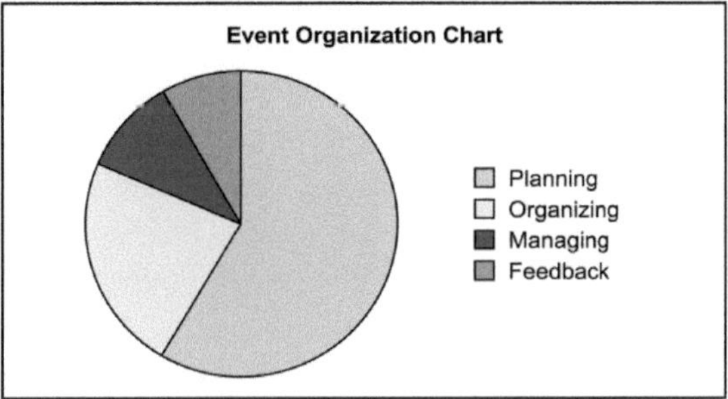

From the above diagram which of the following plays a major role in organizing an event?

    (a) Feedback   (b) Organizing   (c) Planning   (d) Managing

50. Ramesh is part of an event organizing team. He is appointed in the planning committee. Ramesh has to finalize a venue for the event. Which of the following points he must take into consideration?

    (a) Availability of the venue   (b) Capacity of the venue

    (c) Public access to the venue   (d) All of the above

51. XYZ event company's organizer Riya has to look after the finances of the event. Which of the following committee will she have to consult?

    (a) Finance and Budgeting   (b) Accommodation

    (c) Registration   (d) Transportation

52. Sports Minister, Mr. Kiren Rijuju has launched many sports schemes in India. Among these, one of the best schemes is Khelo India. Mr. Kannan, father of Kartik approached the PE teacher and enquired about the fitness levels of the students. PE teacher replied that Khelo India consisted of physical fitness tests for school children and they were analysing students' fitness through these tests.

To measure Lower body flexibility fitness, which one of the following is best?

    (a) Harvard Step test   (b) Sit and reach test

    (c) Barrow fitness test   (d) General fitness test

53. Below given is the Details of Different types of vitamins required for our body

The vitamins, minerals, and water collectively called as __________ food.

    (a) Body Building   (b) Defensive   (c) Energy Yielding   (d) Facilitating

54. Padma, a student of class XII, used to read books in the school library. One day she was studying the history of women participation in Indian Sports and felt that more girls and women must be encouraged to actively participate in sports. She believed that impossible things can be achieved through participating in sports. In which year did women first participated in Olympics?
    (a) 2000   (b) 1900   (c) 2012   (d) 1947

55. Rashmi is working on a project to collect data for assessing physical fitness amongst senior citizens at her residential complex. He plans to administer test for assessing upper body strength and upper body flexibility. Which of the following test should be conducted for assessing upper body flexibility?
    (a) Chair stand test   (b) Arm curl test
    (c) Chair sit and reach test   (d) Back scratch test

56. Mr. Sunder is a Physical Education teacher in a government school. Ramesh, a student is a long jumper but his landing is improper. So he could not win the event on sports day in the school. So Ramesh approached Mr. Sunder to seek his help to improve his performance. Mr. Sunder explained to Ramesh the proper technique to be followed so as to have the correct body posture while landing. Mr. Sunder also motivated Ramesh to constantly practise this technique to perfect it. After the one year of training, Ramesh won the gold medal in the Inter Zonal Athletic Meet. What was the problem faced by Ramesh?
    (a) Improper landing in long jump event   (b) Not winning any medal
    (c) Improper performance   (d) Incorrect body posture

57. Many children suffer from postural deformities. These can be corrected if recognised early and treated properly. Mahesh had a deformity in his spine which caused him to bend forward and his knees touched each other while he stood straight. What was the possible deformity Mahesh had?
    (a) Kyphosis   (b) Scoliosis
    (c) Lordosis   (d) Flat food

58. Sanaya got admission in Class XII in a reputed school. School is taking all the children on a picnic to Ramoji Film City. Sanaya suffered from a severe stomach ache on her journey. Immediately the class teacher consulted a Doctor who diagnosed the problem and told her that Sanaya had difficulty digesting a particular food. This can lead to symptoms such as intestinal gas, abdominal pain or diarrhoea. It is sometimes confused with or mislabelled as a food allergy. Food intolerance can cause:
    (a) Diarrhoea   (b) Anaemia
    (c) Fatigue   (d) Loss of Appetite

59. Kumar of XI-A is a great athlete. After the lockdown he went to see his Physical Education Teacher. Mr. Murugan, the PE teacher is shocked to see kumar, because Kumar has gained lot of weight. He also observed may other students have also gained weight. The PE teacher decided to conduct an 'Inter House Tournament' in the campus. Kumar requested PE teacher to conduct the tournament on league basis. Kumar feels that league method is best one for Inter house tournament. Why?
    (a) Less period required   (b) Limited official
    (c) True winner   (d) Players would be less tired

60. Below given is the tournament fixture procedure of a CBSE Volleyball National Competition.

```
1—2
1—3  2—3
1—4  2—4  3—4
1—5  2—5  3—5  4—5
1—6  2—6  3—6  4—6  5—6
```

The formula for calculating number of matches in Round robin tournament are where 'N' is number of team is __________ .
    (a) $N(N-1)/2$ (b) N   (c) $(N-1)$ (d) $(N+1)$

Sample Paper 2

Physical Education

Section – A

(KNOWLEDGE AND UNDERSTANDING)

1. In plantar flexion of the foot about the ankle joint:
    (a) The foot moves upwards towards the front of the calf
    (b) The foot moves upwards towards the rear of the calf
    (c) The foot moves sideways
    (d) None the above

2. The test duration for the Harvard fitness test is.
    (a) 3 minutes
    (b) 4 minutes
    (c) 5 minutes
    (d) 6 minutes

3. There are how many stages of motor development in children?
    (a) 3
    (b) 2
    (c) 4
    (d) 5

4. Which of the following is an example of food supplement?
    (a) Vitamins
    (b) Fatty acids
    (c) Both (a) and (b)
    (d) None of them.

5. A team which is defeated automatically gets eliminated from the tournament. It is known as:
    (a) League tournament
    (b) Knock-out tournament
    (c) Combination tournament
    (d) None of them

6. Before running a marathon, the trainer asked the athlete to monitor her vitamin and mineral levels to fight against free radicals which :
    (a) Damages cell
    (b) Limit conversion of proteins in ATP
    (c) Reduce effectiveness of electrolytes
    (d) Destroy stored glucose

7. Which is not an item of Barrow motor ability test?
    (a) Medicine Ball Put
    (b) Zig Zag Run
    (c) Standing Broad Jump
    (d) Push-ups

8. Development of a child's bone, muscles and ability to move around and manipulate their movement is referred to as:
    (a) Motor development
    (b) Physical activity
    (c) Both (a) and (b)
    (d) None of them

9. A league tournament is otherwise known as :
    (a) Round Robin tournament
    (b) Knock-out tournament
    (c) Combination tournament
    (d) None of them

10. Which of the following is a form of Fixtures?
    (a) Round Robin
    (b) League
    (c) Knock Out
    (d) All of the Above

11. Classes 8-12 should have exercises which help them in muscle training atleast:
    (a) 30 mins, twice a week
    (b) 60 mins, once a week
    (c) 60-120 mins, 3 days a week
    (d) 30 mins, 4 times a week

12. For Classes Nursery- Class 2, the PT period should have which of the following activities:
    (a) Endurance building, disciplined exercise
    (b) Running etc along with periodic completions
    (c) Movement based exercises coupled with recreative methods
    (d) None of these.
13. Ram is the seeded player, he played the next round and was eliminated. Which type of fixture were made for the tournament?
    (a) Knock Out
    (b) League
    (c) Round Robin
    (d) None of the above
14. Seema is a seeded player and she did not play the first round. Which of the following would be the reason?
    (a) She was not well
    (b) She had a bye
    (c) She was a champion in the previous season
    (d) She did not feel like playing
15. It is recommended to drink __________ of water daily.
    (a) 1-2 litres
    (b) 2-3 litres
    (c) 1-1.5 litres
    (d) 2-4 litres
16. Vitamins are called
    (a) Protective food
    (b) Body Building food
    (c) Energy giving food
    (d) Strong bones
17. In League tournaments the winner is decided by
    (a) British method
    (b) American Method
    (c) No of Matches won
    (d) Both (a) and (b)
18. Which of the following is Not a League Fixture Procedure?
    (a) Ladder method
    (b) Stair method
    (c) Cyclic method
    (d) Tabular method
19. What is the relationship between Mass and force?
    (a) Directly proportional
    (b) No relationship
    (c) Inversely proportional
    (d) Both (a) and (c)
20. Newton's second law is also known as
    (a) The law of reaction
    (b) The law of inertia
    (c) The law of acceleration
    (d) None of these
21. Name the objective of planning shown in the figure given below:

    (a) Reduced mistakes
    (b) Planning
    (c) Decision making
    (d) None of these
22. Which committee selects various officials such as refress, judges, etc. in tournament?
    (a) Committee for publicity
    (b) Reception committee
    (c) Committee for officials
    (d) Transport committee
23. A balanced diet is complete, when it will be:
    (a) complex carbohydrates
    (b) according to the needs of the person
    (c) animal fat rich
    (d) 4 to 5 litter water
24. Out of them which is not the work of organising committee?
    (a) To draw fixture
    (b) To decorate the tournament venue
    (c) To select referee panel for match
    (d) To conduct the matches

Section - B

(APPLICATION + HOTS)

25. Which type of tournament is shown by the picture given?

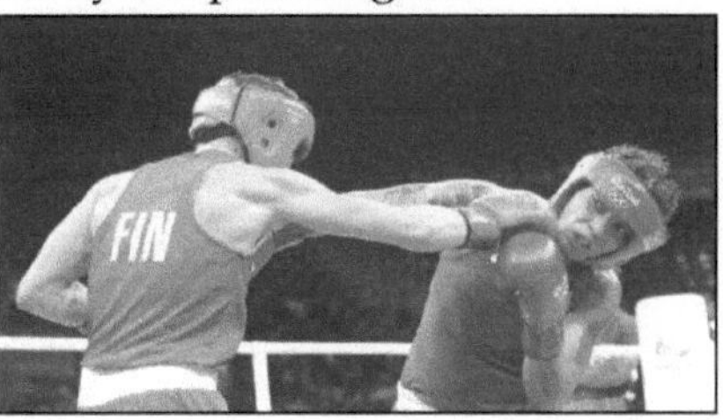

    (a) League tournament   (b) Knock out tournament

    (c) Round robin tournament   (d) None of these

26. List the role of the following nutrients in the human body

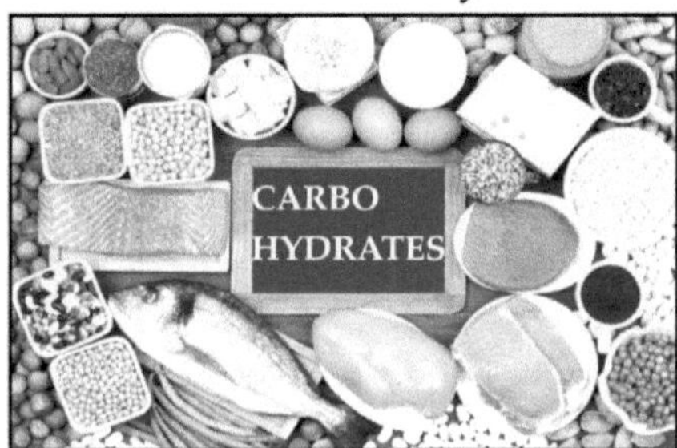

    (a) Intant source of energy   (b) Muscle repair

    (c) Insulate the body   (d) None of them

27. Identify the following test:

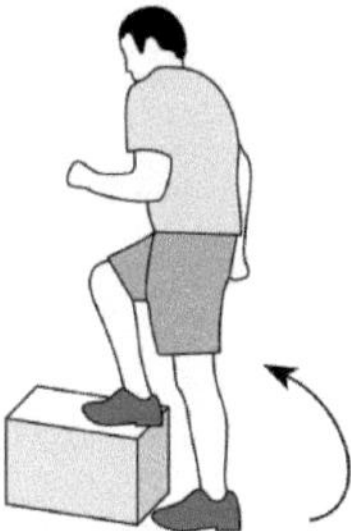

    (a) Zig-zag run   (b) Harvard step test

    (c) Standing broad jump   (d) None of these

28. Unit of energy that indicates the amount of energy contained in food.

    (a) Label   (b) Food guide pyramid

    (c) Calorie   (d) Basket

29. Which of the following is not a minerals?

    (a) Fluorine   (b) Niacin   (c) Sodium   (d) Phosphorus

30. Obesity is a condition in which excess only body __________ has accumulated to the extent that it may have a negative effect on health.

    (a) Carbohydrates   (b) Proteins   (c) Fats   (d) Minerals

31. Match the following:

S. No.	LIST-I	LIST-II
1.	Staffing	A. process of creating a comprehensive action
2.	Planning	B. all the processes that leaders create to monitor success
3.	Organizing	C. identifying key staff positions
4.	Controlling	D. distributing resources and organizing personnel

Choose the correct option from the following:

(a) 1–A, 2–B, 3–D, 4–C   (b) 1–C, 2–D, 3–A, 4–B

(c) 1–A, 2–D, 3–C, 4–B   (d) 1–D, 2–C, 3–B, 4–A

32. Match the following:

S. No.	LIST-I	LIST-II
1.	Arm curl test	A. Agility
2.	Eight foot up and go test	B. Upper body flexibility
3.	Chair Stand test	C. Upper body strength
4.	Back Scratch test	D. Lower body strength

(a) 1–C, 2–A, 3–B, 4–D   (b) 1–A, 2–B, 3–D, 4–C

(c) 1–B, 2–D, 3–A, 4–C   (d) 1–C, 2–A, 3–D, 4–B

33. Match the tests:

S. No.	LIST-I	LIST-II
1.	600 m run/walk	A. Cardiovascular fitness test
2.	Harvard step test	B. Rikli and Jones test
3.	Six minute walk test	C. Motor fitness test

(a) 1–C, 2–A, 3–B   (b) 1–A, 2–B, 3–C

(c) 1–C, 2–B, 3–A   (d) 1–B, 2–A, 3–C

34. Match the movements:

S. No.	LIST-I	LIST-II
1.	Abduction	A. Decreasing in Angle
2.	Newton's 2nd law	B. Frictional force
3.	Force that opposes	C. Away from midline movement
4.	Flexion	D. Law of Acceleration

(a) 1–C, 2–D, 3–B, 4–A   (b) 1–D, 2–C, 3–B, 4–A

(c) 1–D, 2–C, 3–A, 4–B   (d) 1–B, 2–D, 3–C, 4–A

35. What is Scoliosis?

(a) A heart disorder   (b) An ankle sprain

(c) Lateral curve in the spine   (d) Dislocated spine

36. __________ exercises are designed to correct the rotatory curvature of the spine.

(a) Kyphosis   (b) Scoliosis

(c) Lordosis   (d) Knock Knees

37. Which of the following is not a corrective measure for the postural deformity of knock knee?

(a) Keeping a pillow between the knees as much as possible

(b) Not standing for a long time

(c) Performing Padmasana and Gomukhasana

(d) Regular horse riding

38. **Assertion (A):** Testing motor fitness consists of measuring of all components of motor fitness.

Reason (R): Motor fitness test provides to the student a score regarding the level of fitness, effectiveness of any training programme.

(a) Both (A) and (R) are true, but (R) is not the correct explanation of (A)

(b) (A) is true, but (R) is false

(c) Both (A) and (R) are true and (R) is the correct explanation of (A)

(d) (A) is false, but (R) is true

39. **Assertion (A):** Sports biomechanics is a quantitative based study and analysis of professional athletes/sports persons and sports activities in general.

Reason (R): In simple terms, it may be described as the physics of sports.

(a) Both (A) and (R) are true, but (R) is not the correct explanation of (A)
(b) Both (A) and (R) are true and (R) is the correct explanation of (A)
(c) (A) is true, but (R) is false
(d) (A) is false, but (R) is true

40. This is a side-to-side curvature of the spine.

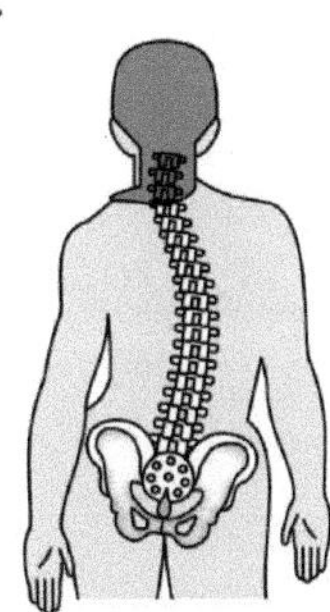

(a) Lordosis   (b) Kyphosis   (c) Scoliosis   (d) Myosis

41. Modified push are designed for:
(a) volleyball player   (b) boys   (c) cricket player   (d) girls

42. Match List-I with List-II:

S. No.	LIST-I	LIST-II
1.	Knock knees	A. Lack of exercise
2.	Lordosis	B. Lack of Vitamin D
3.	Flat foot	C. Heredity defects
4.	Scoliosis	D. Faulty posture

(a) 1–B, 2–A, 3–C, 4–D
(b) 1–B, 2–A, 3–D, 4–C
(c) 1–D, 2–C, 3–B, 4–A
(d) 1–D, 2–A, 3–C, 4–B

43. Match the following deformities with their respective symptoms:

S. No.	LIST-I	LIST-II
1.	Mechanical friction	A. Increased in angle
2.	Law of Inertia	B. Object are solid comes in contract
3.	Take off high jump	C. 3rd low of motion
4.	Extension	D. Things Remain in its position

(a) 1–B, 2–D, 3–C, 4–B
(b) 1–D, 2–B, 3–C, 4–A
(c) 1–D, 2–B, 3–A, 4–C
(d) 1–C, 2–B, 3–A, 4–D

44. Scoliosis deformity can be corrected by practicing.
(a) Trikonasana and Ardh Chakrasana
(b) Halasana and paschimotanasana
(c) Dhanurasana and Chakrasana
(d) Bhujangasana and Usthrasana

45. **Assertion (A):** Flat foot is a type of physical deformity.
Reason (R): It occurs in athletes.
(a) Both (A) and (R) are true, but (R) is not the correct explanation of (A)
(b) Both (A) and (R) are true and (R) is the correct explanation of (A)
(c) (A) is true, but (R) is false
(d) (A) is false, but (R) is true

46. The vitamin necessary for coagulation of blood is:
(a) Vitamin B
(b) Vitamin C
(c) Vitamin K
(d) Vitamin E

47. Food passes through the stomach directly by:
(a) the large intestine
(b) the small intestine
(c) the heart
(d) the pancreas

48. Which food contains the most fat?

(a) Graham crackers

(b) Brownies

(c) Pudding

(d) Angle food cake

Section - C

(CASE STUDIES)

49. Data of number of students falling in different age groups was collected from ABC School in Agra. The PT teacher wants to design exercises for different age groups.

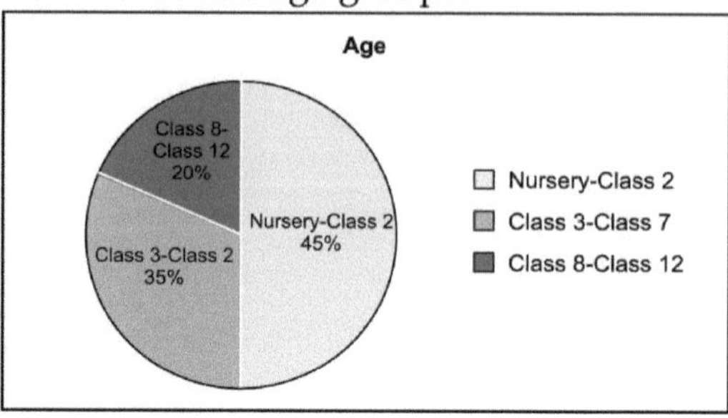

Nursery- Class 2 has children of the Age Group 3-7 years

Class 3-7 has children of age group 8-12 years

Class 8-12 has children of age group 13-18 years

Exercises like running, swimming, etc, which build agility, coordination and balance would be the most suitable for which age group?

(a) Nursery- Class

(b) Class 3- Class 7

(c) Class 8-Class 12

(d) Both (b) and (c)

50. Seema is a seeded player. But as per fixtures she did not play the first round while as she played the next round her opponent was eliminated. As she qualified to the 7th round she lost and she too was eliminated. The opponent was eliminated. What could be the reason?

(a) Opponent Lost

(b) She did not want to play

(c) Opponent was injured

(d) The referee gave a time out

51. The Ganga school teams have started the practice for Basketball Cluster Tournament. One day the school secretary visited the playground and watched the practice session. He felt that the players were weak. After discussion with the coach, he arranged a dietician to rectify the players' requirements. Which types of the nutrients are advisable for the player?

(a) Proteins

(b) Minerals

(c) Vitamins

(d) Carbohydrates

52. Below given is the Tournament fixture procedure of a CBSE Volley ball National competition

```
1—2
1—3 2—3
1—4 2—4 3—4
1—5 2—5 3—5 4—5
1—6 2—6 3—6 4—6 5—6
```

The formula for calculating number of matches in Round Robin tournament are where 'N' is number of teams is________

(a) N(N − 1)/2

(b) N

(c) (N − 1)

(d) (N + 1)

53. During the physical education class Newton's Laws of motion were discussed and their practical application in sports events was explained to students. These laws are most relevant in sports as most of the actions in sports are related to these laws. Newton's First law of motion is also known as:

(a) Law of inertia

(b) Law of Momentum

(c) Law of reaction

(d) Law of acceleration

54. Gopichand, a student of class XII, has recently joined a gym near his house to get a toned and muscular body. He consults the gym trainer regarding his diet and is advised to increase the intake of protein in his diet. Proteins are also known as:
   (a) nitrogenous food
   (b) body building food
   (c) fatty food
   (d) both (a) and (b)

55. Sheethal spent her weekned checking the health status of all the security guards of her huge gates community as a part of project work assigned by PE teachers. She found out that more than half of them have shown a significant deformity in the upper part of their vertebral column. The term used to define this deformity is ____________ .
   (a) lordosis
   (b) scoliosis
   (c) kyphosis
   (d) both (a) and (b)

56. On the basis of given figures, answer the following questions:

   Both the test shown in the picture are conducted to check __________ fitness.
   (a) muscular
   (b) skeletal
   (c) cardiovascular
   (d) respiratory

57. Abhishek, the Class 12 monitor, was asked to speak on different types of movements possible in human body and their importance. He talked about four basic movements namely flexion, extension, abduction and adduction. Rest of the movements at different joints are combinations of these four basic movements. He also demonstrated about dorsiflexion and planter flexion movements. What movement that he demonstrated were possible at the shoulder joint?
   (a) Gliding
   (b) Angular
   (c) Circumduction
   (d) Rotation

58. ABC School is one of the reputed school in their location for the number of sports facilities it provides to its stakeholders. Keeping that in consideration CBSE Sports cell has given them the responsibility of conducting CBSE Football cluster. 35 teams have sent their entre for participation in the tournaments.
   Due to large number of terms willing to participate, the school is conducting the competition by ________ fixture.
   (a) league
   (b) knock-out
   (c) staircase
   (d) challenge

59. Your school has received an invitation for participation in a Badminton competition being organised by XYZ School. There is a entry fee for the competition due to which very few students have shown their willingness to participate. What is the disadvantage of using this particular fixture?
   (a) More time consuming
   (b) Less expenditure
   (c) More opportunities
   (d) Both (b) and (c)

60. Vikas, a state level wrestler has been advised by his coach to take adequate amounts of simple carbohydrates, vitamins, minerals and proteins in his diet along with the training schedule. He has also been advised to follow the diet plan and be aware of the drawbacks of unsupervised dieting. Glucose, Fructose, Lactose are __________ .
   (a) simple carbohydrates
   (b) complex carbohydrates
   (c) minerals
   (d) fats

❑❑

Sample Paper 3

Physical Education

Section – A

(KNOWLEDGE AND UNDERSTANDING)

1. What is the primary nutrient that contributes to bone health ?
   (a) Iron   (b) Potassium   (c) Calcium   (d) Phosphorus

2. Seeding method refers to :
   (a) Pairing of all weak teams together   (b) Pairing of all strong teams together
   (c) Strong teams paired with weak or all strong teams grouped in upper half or lower half.
   (d) None of them

3. What is the weight of Medicine ball for boys in medicine ball put?
   (a) 1 kg   (b) 2 kg   (c) 3 kg   (d) 4kg

4. Gross motor development skills, head control, and sitting are the exercise guidelines for children belonging to the age group of :
   (a) 1-2 years   (b) 3-7 years   (c) 8-12 years   (d) None of them

5. Flexion and extension are:
   (a) Movements in the frontal plane about the sagittal axis
   (b) Movements in the sagittal plane about the frontal axis
   (c) Movements in the horizontal plane about the vertical axis
   (d) None of the above.

6. Writing, Holding, Catching, and Smashing are examples of:
   (a) Gross Motor Development   (b) Fine Motor Development
   (c) Both (a) and (b)   (d) None of them

7. The test duration for the Harvard fitness test is:
   (a) 3 minutes   (b) 4 minutes   (c) 5 minutes   (d) 6 minutes

8. Internal and external rotation are movements in which anatomical plane ?
   (a) Sagittal   (b) Frontal   (c) Horizontal   (d) None of these

9. A weight lifter should include _____________ in his/her diet.
   (a) Carbohydrate   (b) Protein
   (c) Fat   (d) Vitamins and minerals

10. In special seeding, the seeded players participate directly in the:
    (a) Finals   (b) Semi-finals
    (c) Quarter-final or semi-final   (d) None of them

11. Which of the following category of people are likely to live a healthy life style:
    (a) Under weight   (b) Normal weight
    (c) Obese   (d) Over Weight

12. Which category is related to underweight?
    (a) Obese   (b) Over weight
    (c) Normal weight   (d) Under weight

13. Which of the following is largely consumed but not neglected?
    (a) Minerals and Vitamins   (b) Carbohydrates
    (c) Fats   (d) Proteins

14. The acceleration of an object depends directly upon the net force acting upon the object and inversely upon the object's:

   (a) Weight   (b) Mass   (c) Height   (d) Density

15. The study of human body and various forces acting on it is:

   (a) Biology   (b) Biomechanics   (c) Physiology   (d) Anatomy

16. A high jumper can jump higher off a solid surface because it opposes his or her body with as much force as he or she is able to generate. This example refers to:

   (a) Law of conservation   (b) Law of inertia

   (c) Law of action and reaction   (d) Law of gravity

17. What could be the probable cause of this problem:

   (a) Weak muscles   (b) Sudden rise in body weight

   (c) Deficiency of Calcium, Vitamin D   (d) Only (a) and (b)

18. To rectify the problem of pain, which Yogasana would prove to be the most fruitful?

   (a) Gomukhasana   (b) Chakrasana

   (c) Halasana   (d) Vajrasana

19. Major portion of individuals diet constitute __________ nutrients

   (a) macro   (b) micro   (c) water   (d) roughage

20. Fat soluble vitamins are __________.

   (a) Vitamin A and D   (b) Vitamin A and K

   (c) Vitamin E and D   (d) Vitamin A, D, E and K

21. The body building nutrient is__________.

   (a) fat   (b) vitamin   (c) protein   (d) mineral

22. Ghee, Butter, Cheese and curds are rich sources of __________.

   (a) vitamins   (b) fats   (c) minerals   (d) proteins

23. Announcement of venue, date and events is done by ____________

   (a) Publicity committee   (b) Transportation committee

   (c) Ground committee   (d) Committee for officials

24. Name the objective of planning shown in the figure given below:

   (a) Reduced mistakes   (b) Planning

   (c) Decision making   (d) Goal oriented

Section – B

(APPLICATION + HOTS)

25. Which type of tournament is shown by the picture given?

    (a) League tournament   (b) Knock out tournament
    (c) Round robin tournament   (d) None of these

26. List the role of the following nutrients in the human body

    (a) Instant source of energy   (b) Muscle repair
    (c) Insulate the body   (d) None of them

27. This is humpback, abnormal outward curvature of thoracic spine.

    (a) Lordosis   (b) Kyphosis
    (c) Scoliosis   (d) Myosis

28. Organising and conducting of sports events involve ____________.
    (a) planning   (b) Forming committees
    (c) both (a) and (b)   (d) only delegation

29. Complete responsibility for success of competition is taken by __________.
    (a) Announcement committee   (b) Administrative director
    (c) First aid committee   (d) Committee for officials

30. To prepare a proper score sheet for record is ________ responsibility.
    (a) pre tournament   (b) during tournament
    (c) Post tournament   (d) all of the above

31. Match the following:

S. No.	LIST-I	LIST-II
	Vitamin	Disease
1.	Vitamin A	A. Pyorrhea
2.	Vitamin B	B. Rickets
3.	Vitamin C	C. Beriberi
4.	Vitamin D	D. Night Blindness

    (a) 1–D, 2–C, 3–A, 4–B   (b) 1–A, 2–B, 3–C, 4–D
    (c) 1–C, 2–A, 3–B, 4–D   (d) 1–D, 2–A, 3–C, 4–B

32. Match the following:

S. No.	LIST-I	LIST-II
1.	Motor fitness test	A. Chair stand test
2.	Rikli and Jones test	B. 4 × 10 m shuttle run
3.	Cardiovascular fitness test	C. Rockport one mile test

(a)   1–A, 2–B, 3–C
(b)   1–C, 2–B, 3–A
(c)   1–B, 2–A, 3–C
(d)   1–B, 2–C, 3–A

33. Match the following;

S. No.	LIST-I	LIST-II
1.	Iron	A. Nervous system
2.	Sodium	B. Haemoglobin
3.	Fluorine	C. Strong bone
4.	Phosphorus	D. Enamel

(a)   1–C, 2–D, 3–B, 4–A
(b)   1–D, 2–A, 3–C, 4–B
(c)   1–A, 2–C, 3–B, 4–D
(d)   1–B, 2–A, 3–D, 4–C

34. Match the Diseases with their causes:

S. No.	LIST-I	LIST-II
1.	Dryness	A. Deficiency of calcium
2.	Anaemia	B. Deficiency vitamin A
3.	Decreased bone density	C. Lack of water during dieting
4.	Night blindness	D. Deficiency iron

(a)   1–D, 2–C, 3–A, 4–B
(b)   1–C, 2–D, 3–A, 4–B
(c)   1–A, 2–B, 3–C, 4–D
(d)   1–D, 2–C, 3–B, 4–A

35. Partial or complete absence of the enzymes accountable for breaking down or absorbing the food elements causes __________ .

(a)   food intolerance
(b)   bulimia
(c)   ADHD
(d)   dieting

36. In which category BMI comes in 30 BMI?

(a)   Obesity II
(b)   Over lead
(c)   Obesity I
(d)   Healthy weight

37. Karan wishes to serve his country by qualifying NDA, he clears all rounds but he is unable to qualify for the medical test. He was asked to run 100 metres and the examiner noticed he was unable to run properly and has knock knees. What precautions can be taken up at an early age to ensure that children do not develop this problem at a later stage in their lives:

(a)   Balanced diet should be taken
(b)   Babies and children shouldn't be forced to walk at an early age
(c)   One should avoid sitting and walking in bent position
(d)   Only (a) and (b)

38. **Assertion (A):** Sports biomechanics is limited to the study of those individuals who are involved in exercise or sports or any physical activity.

Reason (R): Performance enhancement is one of the area of the study in sports biomechanics.

(a)   Both (A) and (R) are true, but (R) is not the correct explanation of (A)
(b)   (A) is true, but (R) is false
(c)   Both (A) and (R) are true and (R) is the correct explanation of (A)
(d)   (A) is false, but (R) is true

39. **Assertion (A):** Knock Knee is the physical deformity.

Reason (R): Yogic exercise which help in treatment of knock knee are Padmasana (Lotus posture), Vatayanasan (Horse face posture), and Bhadrasana.

(a)   Both (A) and (R) are true, but (R) is not the correct explanation of (A)
(b)   Both (A) and (R) are true and (R) is the correct explanation of (A)
(c)   (A) is true, but (R) is false
(d)   (A) is false, but (R) is true

40. This is swayback, abnormal inward curvature of the lumbar spine.

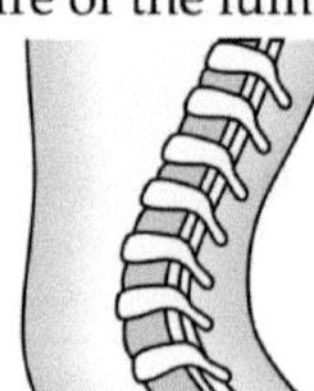

   (a) Lordosis   (b) Kyphosis

   (c) Scoliosis   (d) Myosis

41. Who is most likely to develop Scoliosis?

   (a) 30 year old woman   (b) 9 year old boy

   (c) 12 year old girl   (d) 20 year old man

42. Match the following:

S. No.	LIST-I	LIST-II
1.	Cyclic	A. Resolve dispute
2.	Technical committee	B. Arranging team
3.	Fixture	C. To avoid to meet in 1st round
4.	Seeding	D. League tournament

   (a) 1–C, 2–B, 3–A, 4–D   (b) 1–B, 2–C, 3–A, 4–D

   (c) 1–D, 2–A, 3–B, 4–C   (d) 1–D, 2–C, 3–B, 4–A

43. Match the following committee with their functions:

S. No.	LIST-I (Committee)	LIST-II (Function)
1.	Boarding and Lodging	A. Welcoming the chief guest
2.	Publicity	B. Making several announcements during the game
3.	Announcement	C. Providing accommodation and serving meals
4.	Reception	D. Announcement of date, venue to the public

   (a) 1–C, 2–A, 3–D, 4–B   (b) 1–B, 2–D, 3–A, 4–C

   (c) 1–C, 2–D, 3–B, 4–A   (d) 1–D, 2–A, 3–C, 4–B

44. How many byes will be given if 21 teams are participating in a knock-out tournament?

   (a) 11   (b) 12

   (c) 10   (d) 13

45. **Assertion (A):** To determine running speed and acceleration of a student.

   Reason (R): There will be distance of 50 meters between two straight lines.

   (a) Both (A) and (R) are true, but (R) is not the correct explanation of (A)

   (b) Both (A) and (R) are true and (R) is the correct explanation of (A)

   (c) (A) is true, but (R) is false

   (d) (A) is false, but (R) is true

46. If 8 teams are participating, the number of Knock-out matches will be:

   (a) 16   (b) 8

   (c) 7   (d) 9

47. In which tournament, strong teams may have the possibility to be eliminated in the preliminary round?

   (a) League tournament   (b) Knock-out tournament

   (c) Challenge tournament   (d) League cum league tournament

48. By which method the winner of a single league tournament is decided?

   (a) Percentage of matches won and drawn   (b) Number of matches won

   (c) Percentage of matches won   (d) All of these

Section – C

(CASE STUDIES)

49. Below given is the BMI data of general population's health check-up for the months of EBC (Economic Backward Class), Youth, Senior Citizens and Athletes:

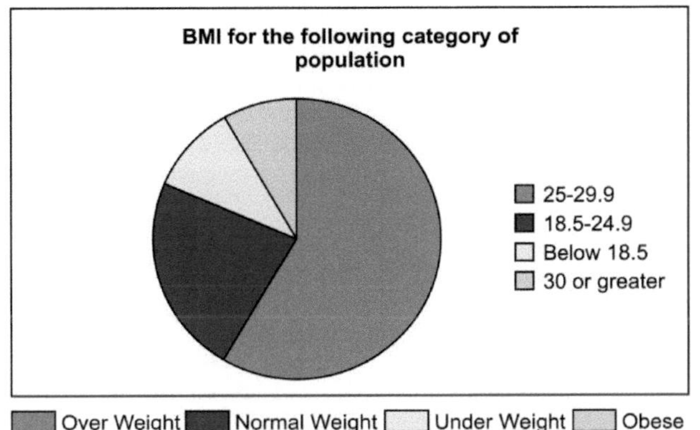

Which of the following category does most of the population fall into:

(a) Obese   (b) Normal weight   (c) Over weight   (d) Under weight

50. The teachers as well as coaches always make their best efforts to improve the performance of their students in various competitive games and sports. They can help to improve the performance of students if they have adequate knowledge of biomechanics.

The more force one exerts on the downward bounce, the higher the ball bounces into the air. Which law is this statement being referred to?

(a) Newton's 1st law   (b) Newton's 2nd law

(c) Newton's 3rd law   (d) Law of gravitation

51. Suresh is extremely fond of Cricket as a sport, and wants to take it up as a profession. However, he always had pain whenever he would run and would sometimes also complain of pain after prolonged standing.

Suresh dipped his feet in water and then walked on the floor, he did not obtain an arch, so he most likely has which one of the following problems

(a) Knock Knee   (b) Scoliosis

(c) Flat foot   (d) Bow Legs

52. Food is the basic requirement of every individual to fulfill the energy needs and to meet the development of the body. The nutritious diet directly affects the health of an individual. It contains various types of nutrients in it.

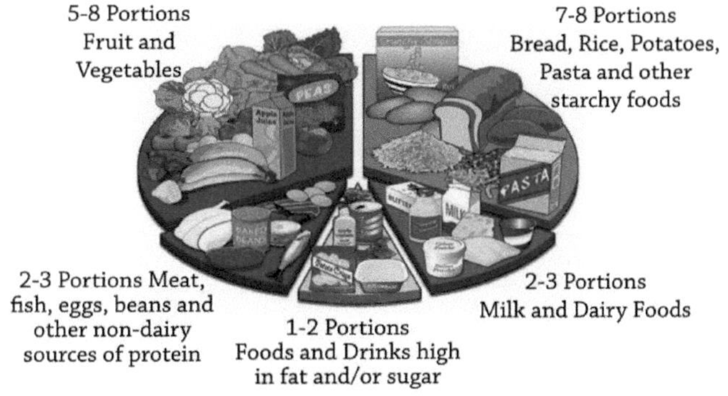

The bottom most part of the food pyramid is occupied by __________, indicating large quantities of intake.

(a) carbohydrates   (b) vitamins   (c) minerals   (d) fats

53. While organizing sports events for the Annual Sports Day, Arjun and Ravi being the captain and vice captain of sports, formed various committees as shown below.

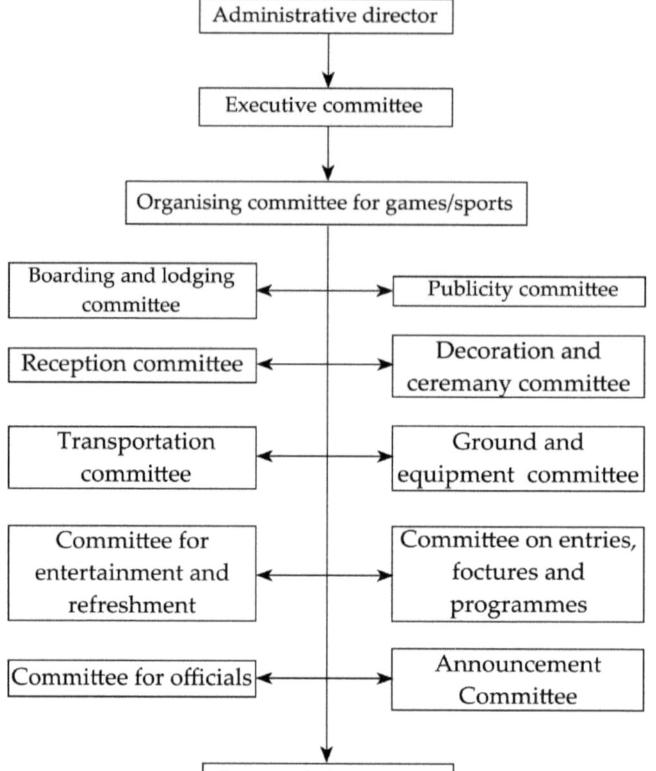

The members of this committee are responsible for welcoming guests and spectators

(a) Decoration committee   (b) Reception committee

(c) Publicity committee   (d) Transportation committee

54. Your school has been given the responsibility to conduct Zonal basketball competition. As the Head boy/ Head girl of the student council you have been asked to make various teams of students to help teacher in changes for smooth conduct of the tournament. To help the terms to know about the food and stay arrangements a group of students will be assigned __________ committee.

(a) transport   (b) registration

(c) boarding and lodging   (d) decoration

55. Below given is the details of different types of vitamins required for our body:

The vitamins, minerals and water are collectively called as __________ food.

(a) body building   (b) defensive

(c) energy yielding   (d) facilitating

56. With the aim of promoting physical fitness and healthy lifestyle amongst students the Physical Education Teacher at XYZ School plans to organise intranural competitions at school. For conducting the event he has given this assignment to the students of class XII who have taken up Physical Education subject so that they can get first had experience of organising events.

    The work committees is divided into ____________ .

    (a) pre, during and post   (b) pre and post

    (c) pre and during   (d) during and post

57. A balanced diet refers to the intake of food constituting all the necessary nutrients. Ram shares his knowledge of 'food and nutrition' with neighbours while visiting his grandparents in a village. Ram notices that few people living in that village are suffering with goitre and severe anaemia. Minerals are placed under __________ nutrient category on the basis of required quantity.

    (a) micro   (b) macro

    (c) roughage   (d) non-nutritive

58. Mahesh, Physical Education teacher at XYZ School observed that Raju a student of class VI has outward curve of vertebral column at Thoracic region. He suggested some exercises to rectify this problem. What is this deformity know as?

    (a) Scoliosis   (b) Kyphosis

    (c) Lordosis   (d) Flat foot

59. During an athletic meet in stadium, eight women were on the starting line ready for the 100 metres race. With the sound of the pistal, all these woman started running.

    Hardly had they covered 15 metres, when accidently one woman slipped and fell, spraining her ankle, Due to pain the woman started crying. As soon as the other women heard her cry, all of them stopped running, stood for while, turned back, and ran towards her. They pacified her, joined their hands together, lifted her and walked together to reach the finishing line together. The officials were shocked to see such a demonstration of unity. Many eyes were filled with tears. What happened to one woman after she had covered a distance of 15 metres?

    (a) She started running

    (b) She started crying

    (c) She accidentally slipped and fell spraining her ankle

    (d) She fell down and broke her legs

60. Thomas went to and old age home on the occasion of his birthday. At that time all the inmates in the home were assembled in one place. When he enquired, they replied that they have as physical fitness test. Give any one standard physical fitness test for senior citizen.

    (a) Push ups   (b) Standing broad jump

    (c) Zig-zag run   (d) Chair sit and reach test

□□

Answers

Section - A

(KNOWLEDGE AND UNDERSTANDING)

1. (c) Advantage given to a team to not play in initial round.
2. (a) Fats
3. (a) Up to 26 weeks
4. (b) Mass
5. (a) Sensory integration therapy
6. (b) Weakness in heart and muscle
7. (d) 3-2
8. (c) Abdominal strength and endurance
9. (d) Standing
10. (a) Single league tournament
11. (b) Antibodies, immunity
12. (b) Registration
13. (b) B Complex
14. (b) Saina Nehwal
15. (b) Organizing
16. (d) Senior Citizens
17. (b) Explosive power
18. (d) Feedback
19. (a) Managing
20. (a) Reduced mistakes
21. (b) fixture
22. (b) random draws
23. (c) Fine motor skills
24. (b) 0 to 2

Section - B

(APPLICATION + HOTS)

25. (a) League tournament
26. (b) Muscle repair
27. (c) C
28. (a) planning
29. (b) balanced
30. (d) catching a ball
31. (c) 1–B, 2–D, 3–A, 4–C
32. (a) 1–B, 2–C, 3–A, 4–D
33. (b) 1–B, 2–C, 3–A

34. (c) 1–B, 2–A, 3–C
35. (c) eight
36. (b) biomechanics
37. (c) Lack of vitamin D and calcium
38. (c) Both (A) and (R) are true and (R) is the correct explanation of (A)
39. (a) Both (A) and (R) are true, but (R) is not the correct explanation of (A)
40. (c) Partial curl up
41. (d) girls
42. (b) 1–D, 2–A, 3–B, 4–C
43. (c) 1–D, 2–A, 3–B, 4–C
44. (a) Leading an active lifestyle
45. (a) Both (A) and (R) are true, but (R) is not the correct explanation of (A)
46. (c) 7-12 years
47. (a) Gross and fine
48. (b) validity

Section - C

(CASE STUDIES)

49. (c) Planning
50. (d) All of the above
51. (a) Finance and Budgeting
52. (b) Sit and reach test
53. (b) Defensive
54. (b) 1900
55. (d) Back scratch test
56. (a) Improper landing in long jump event
57. (a) Kyphosis
58. (a) Diarrhoea
59. (c) True winner
60. (a) N (N – 1)/2

Sample Paper 2

Section - A

(KNOWLEDGE AND UNDERSTANDING)

1. (b) The foot moves upwards towards the rear of the calf
2. (b) flexibility
3. (c) 4
4. (c) Both (a) and (b)
5. (b) Knock-out tournament
6. (a) Damages cell
7. (b) Zig Zag Run
8. (a) Motor development
9. (a) Round Robin tournament
10. (d) All of the Above
11. (c) 60-120 mins, 3 days a week
12. (c) Movement based exercises coupled with recreative methods
13. (a) Knock out
14. (b) She had a bye
15. (b) 2-3 litres

16. (a) Protective food
17. (a) British method
18. (a) Ladder method
19. (a) Directly proportional
20. (c) The law of acceleration
21. (c) Decision making
22. (c) Committee for officials
23. (b) according to the needs of the person
24. (b) To decorate the tournament venue

Section - B

(APPLICATION + HOTS)

25. (b) Knock out tournament
26. (a) Intant source of energy
27. (b) Harvard step test
28. (c) Calorie
29. (b) Niacin
30. (c) Fats
31. (c) 1–A, 2–D, 3–C, 4–B
32. (d) 1–C, 2–A, 3–D, 4–B.
33. (d) 1–B, 2–A, 3–C
34. (a) 1–C, 2–D, 3–B, 4–A
35. (c) Lateral curve in the spine
36. (b) Scoliosis
37. (b) Not standing for a long time
38. (a) Both (A) and (R) are true, but (R) is not the correct explanation of (A)
39. (b) Both (A) and (R) are true and (R) is the correct explanation of (A)
40. (c) Scoliosis
41. (d) girls
42. (b) 1–B, 2–A, 3–D, 4–C
43. (b) 1–D, 2–B, 3–C, 4–A
44. (a) Trikonasana and Ardh Chakrasana
45. (a) Both (A) and (R) are true, but (R) is not the correct explanation of (A)
46. (c) Vitamin K
47. (b) the small intestine
48. (b) Brownies

Section - C

(CASE STUDIES)

49. (d) Both (b) and (c)
50. (a) Opponent lost
51. (d) Carbohydrates
52. (a) N (N – 1)/2
53. (a) Law of inertia
54. (d) both (a) and (b)
55. (c) kyphosis
56. (c) cardiovascular
57. (c) Circumduction
58. (b) knock-out
59. (a) More time consuming
60. (a) simple carbohydrates

Sample Paper 3

Section – A

(KNOWLEDGE AND UNDERSTANDING)

1. (c) Calcium
2. (c) Strong teams paired with weak or all strong teams grouped in upper half or lower half.
3. (c) 3 kg
4. (a) 1-2 years
5. (b) Movements in the sagittal plane about the frontal axis
6. (b) Fine Motor Development
7. (c) 5 minutes
8. (c) Horizontal
9. (b) Protein
10. (c) Quarter-final or semi-final
11. (b) Normal weight
12. (a) Obese
13. (d) Proteins
14. (b) Mass
15. (b) Biomechanics
16. (c) Law of action and reaction
17. (d) Only (a) and (b)
18. (d) Vajrasana
19. (a) macro
20. (d) Vit A, D, E and K
21. (c) protein
22. (b) fats
23. (a) Publicity committee
24. (d) Goal oriented

Section – B

(APPLICATION + HOTS)

25. (a) League tournament
26. (c) Insulate the body
27. (b) Kyphosis
28. (c) both (a) and (b)
29. (b) Administrative director
30. (b) during tournament
31. (a) 1–D, 2–C, 3–A, 4–B
32. (d) 1–B, 2–C, 3–A
33. (d) 1–B, 2–A, 3–D, 4–C
34. (b) 1–C, 2–D, 3–A, 4–B
35. (a) food intolerance
36. (c) Obesity I

37. (d) Only (a) and (b
38. (a) Both (A) and (R) are true, but (R) is not the correct explanation of (A)
39. (b) Both (A) and (R) are true and (R) is the correct explanation of (A)
40. (a) Lordosis
41. (c) 12 year old girl
42. (a) 1–C, 2–B, 3–A, 4–D
43. (c) 1–C, 2–D, 3–B, 4–A
44. (a) 11
45. (a) Both (A) and (R) are true, but (R) is not the correct explanation of (A)
46. (c) 7
47. (b) Knock-out tournament
48. (d) All of the above

Section – C

(CASE STUDIES)

49. (c) Over weight
50. (c) Newton's 3rd law
51. (c) Flat foot
52. (a) carbohydrates
53. (b) Reception committee
54. (c) boarding and lodging
55. (b) defensive
56. (a) pre, during and post
57. (a) micro
58. (b) Kyphosis
59. (c) She accidentally slipped and fell spraining her ankle
60. (b) Chair sit and reach test

Physics

Sample Question Paper

Physics (042)

Term – I

Time : 90 Minutes   Max. Marks : 35

General Instructions :

1. The Question Paper contains three sections.
2. Section A has 25 questions. Attempt any 20 questions.
3. Section B has 24 questions. Attempt any 20 questions.
4. Section C has 6 questions. Attempt any 5 questions.
5. All questions carry equal marks.
6. There is no negative marking.

Section – A

This section consists of 25 multiple choice questions with overall choice to attempt any 20 questions. In case more than desirable number of questions are attempted, ONLY first 20 will be considered for evaluation.

1. Which of the following is NOT the property of equipotential surface ?
    (a) They do not cross each other.
    (b) The rate of change of potential with distance on them is zero.
    (c) For a uniform electric field they are concentric spheres.
    (d) They can be imaginary spheres.

Ans. (c) For a uniform electric field they are concentric spheres.

> **Explanation:** In uniform electric field equipotential surfaces are never concentric spheres but are plane perpendicular to Electric field lines.

2. Two point charges $+8q$ and $-2q$ are located at $x = 0$ and $x = L$ respectively. The point on x axis at which net electric field is zero due to these charges is:

    (a) 8 L   (b) 4 L   (c) 2 L   (d) L

Ans. (c) 2L

> **Explanation:** Let P is the observation point at a distance r from $-2q$ and at $(L + r)$ from $+8q$.
>
> Given Now, Net Electric field intensity at $P = 0$
>
> $\therefore \qquad \overrightarrow{E_1}$ = Electric field intensity at P due to $+8q$
>
> $\qquad\qquad \overrightarrow{E_2}$ = Electric field intensity at P due to $-2q$
>
> $$\left|\overrightarrow{E_1}\right| = \left|\overrightarrow{E_2}\right|$$
>
> $\therefore \qquad \dfrac{k(8q)}{(L+r)^2} = \dfrac{k(2q)}{r^2}$
>
> $\therefore \qquad \dfrac{4}{(L+r)^2} = \dfrac{1}{(r)^2}$

$$4r^2 = (L + r)^2$$
$$2r = L + r$$
$$r = L$$

$\therefore$ P is at $\qquad x = L + L = 2L$ from origin

3. An electric dipole of moment p is placed parallel to the uniform electric field. The amount of work done in rotating the dipole by 90° is:

(a) $2pE$ (b) pE (c) $\dfrac{pE}{2}$ (d) Zero

Ans. (b) pE

Explanation: We know that,
$$W = pE \, (\cos \theta_1 - \cos \theta_2)$$
$$\theta_1 = 0°$$
$$\theta_2 = 90°$$
$$W = pE \, (\cos 0° - \cos 90°)$$
$$= pE \, (1 - 0) = pE$$

4. Three capacitors 2 μF, 3 μF and 6 μF are joined in series with each other. The equivalent capacitance is:

(a) $\dfrac{1}{2} \propto$F   (b) 1 μF   (c) 2 μF   (d) 11 μF

Ans. (b) 1 μF

Explanation: Given,
$$C_1 = 2 \ \mu F$$
$$C_2 = 3 \ \mu F$$
$$C_3 = 6 \ \mu F$$

and we know that combination in series is
$$\frac{1}{C_{series}} = \frac{1}{C_1} + \frac{1}{C_2} + \frac{1}{C_3}$$
$$\frac{1}{C_{series}} = \frac{1}{2} + \frac{1}{3} + \frac{1}{6}$$
$$= \frac{3 + 2 + 1}{6}$$
$$= \frac{6}{6}$$
$$C_{series} = 1 \ \mu F$$

5. Two point charges placed in a medium of dielectric constant 5 are at a distance r between them, experience an electrostatic force 'F'. The electrostatic force between them in vacuum at the same distance r will be:

(a) 5F   (b) F   (c) $\dfrac{F}{2}$ (d) $\dfrac{F}{5}$

Ans. (a) 5 F

Explanation: $\underset{r}{\overset{Q_1 \qquad\qquad Q_2}{\rule{3cm}{0.4pt}}}$ $K = 5$

$$F = \frac{1}{4\pi\varepsilon_0 k} \frac{Q_1 Q_2}{r^2}$$

$\underset{}{\overset{Q_1 \qquad\qquad Q_2}{\rule{3cm}{0.4pt}}}$ Force in the charges in the air is

$$F^- = \frac{1}{4\pi\varepsilon_0} \frac{Q_1 Q_2}{r^2}$$
$$= KF$$
$$= 5 \ F$$

6. Which statement is true for Gauss law?
   (a) All the charges whether inside or outside the gaussian surface contribute to the electric flux.
   (b) Electric flux depends upon the geometry of the gaussian surface.
   (c) Gauss theorem can be applied to non-uniform electric field.
   (d) The electric field over the gaussian surface remains continuous and uniform at every point.

Ans. (d) The electric field over the Gaussian surface remains continuous and uniform at every point.

> **Explanation:** From Gauss' law of electrostatics. We know that only charges contain within the Gaussian surface contribute to the flux. Also, we know that electric flux depends only on total charge and nature of medium and has nothing to do with geometry. Furthermore Gauss theorem is applicable to the case of uniform electric field as that will allow the formation of a symmetrical Gauss surface. Hence options (a), (b) and (c) are false. It turns out that electric field remains continuous at every point over a Gauss surface.

7. A capacitor plates are charged by a battery with 'V' volts. After charging battery is disconnected and a dielectric slab with dielectric constant 'K' is inserted between its plates, the potential across the plates of a capacitor will become:

   (a) Zero   (b) $\dfrac{V}{2}$ (c) $\dfrac{V}{K}$ (d) KV

Ans. (c) $\dfrac{V}{K}$

> **Explanation:**
>
> 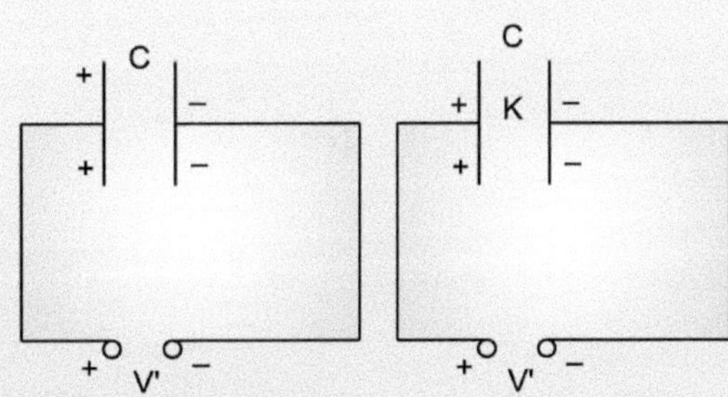
>
>
> when battery is disconnected its charge remains constant.
>
> $$Q = \text{Charge remains constant}$$
> $$C' = KC$$
> $$Q' = C'V'$$
> $$Q = C'V'$$
> $$Q = KCV'$$
> $$V' = \frac{Q}{KC} = \frac{V}{K}$$

8. The best instrument for accurate measurement of EMF of a cell is:
   (a) Potentiometer   (b) meter bridge
   (c) Voltmeter   (d) ammeter and voltmeter

Ans. (a) Potentiometer

> **Explanation:** Voltmeter draws some current from circuit, it cannot give accurate reading. But during measurement by potentiometer no current flows through it.
> Hence, potentiometer is the best instrument to measure EMF of cell.

9. An electric current is passed through a circuit containing two wires of same material, connected in parallel. If the lengths and radii of the wires are in the ratio of 3 : 2 and 2 : 3, then the ratio of the current passing through the wire will be:
   (a) 2 : 3   (b) 3 : 2   (c) 8 : 27   (d) 27 : 8

Ans. (c) 8 : 27

Explanation:

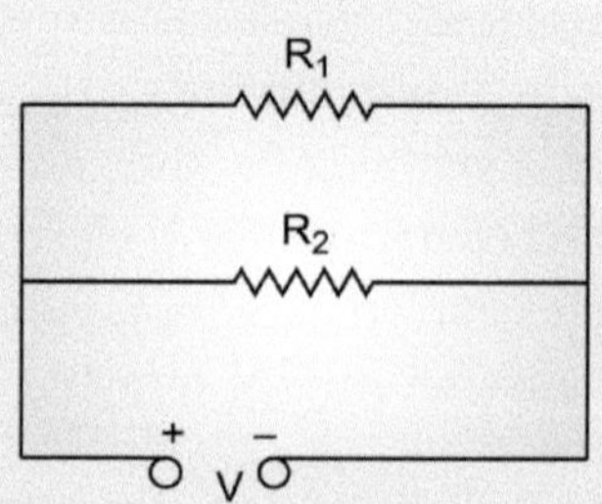

$$l_1 : l_2 = 3 : 2$$
$$r_1 : r_2 = 2 : 3$$
$$I_1 : I_2 = ?$$

$$R_1 = \rho \frac{l_1}{\pi r_1^2}$$

$$R_2 = \rho \frac{l_2}{\pi r_2^2}$$

$$\frac{R_1}{R_2} = \frac{l_1}{l_2} \frac{\pi r_2^2}{\pi r_1^2} = \frac{l_1}{l_2} \times \frac{r_2^2}{r_1^2}$$

$$= \frac{3}{2} \times \left(\frac{3}{2}\right)^2 = \frac{(3)^2}{(2)^3} = \frac{27}{8}$$

$$\therefore \quad \frac{I_1}{I_2} = \frac{\dfrac{V}{R_1}}{\dfrac{V}{R_2}} = \frac{R_2}{R_1}$$

$$= \frac{8}{27} = 8 : 27$$

10. By increasing the temperature, the specific resistance of a conductor and a semiconductor:

    (a) increases for both

    (b) decreases for both

    (c) increases for a conductor and decreases for a semiconductor

    (d) decreases for a conductor and increases for a semiconductor

Ans. (c) increases for a conductor and decreases for a semiconductor.

Explanation: We know that:

$\rho_T = \rho_0 (1 + \alpha \Delta T)$ where α is the temperature coefficient of resistivity.

Specific resistance of a conductor increases and for a semiconductor decreases with increase in temperature because for a conductor temperature coefficient of resistivity $\alpha = +\, ve$ and for a semiconductor, $\alpha = -ve$.

11. We use alloys for making standard resistors because they have:

    (a) low temperature coefficient of resistivity and high specific resistance

    (b) high temperature coefficient of resistivity and low specific resistance

    (c) low temperature coefficient of resistivity and low specific resistance

    (d) high temperature coefficient of resistivity and high specific resistance

Ans. (a) low temperature coefficient of resistivity and high specific resistance.

Explanation: Alloys have low temperature coefficient of resistivity and high specific resistance. If α = low, the value of 'R' with temperature will not change much and specific resistance is high then required length of the wire will be less.

12. A constant voltage is applied between the two ends of a uniform metallic wire, heat 'H' is developed in it. If another wire of the same material, double the radius and twice the length as compared to original wire is used then the heat developed in it will be:

(a) $\dfrac{H}{2}$ (b) H   (c) 2H   (d) 4H

Ans. (c) 2H

Explanation:

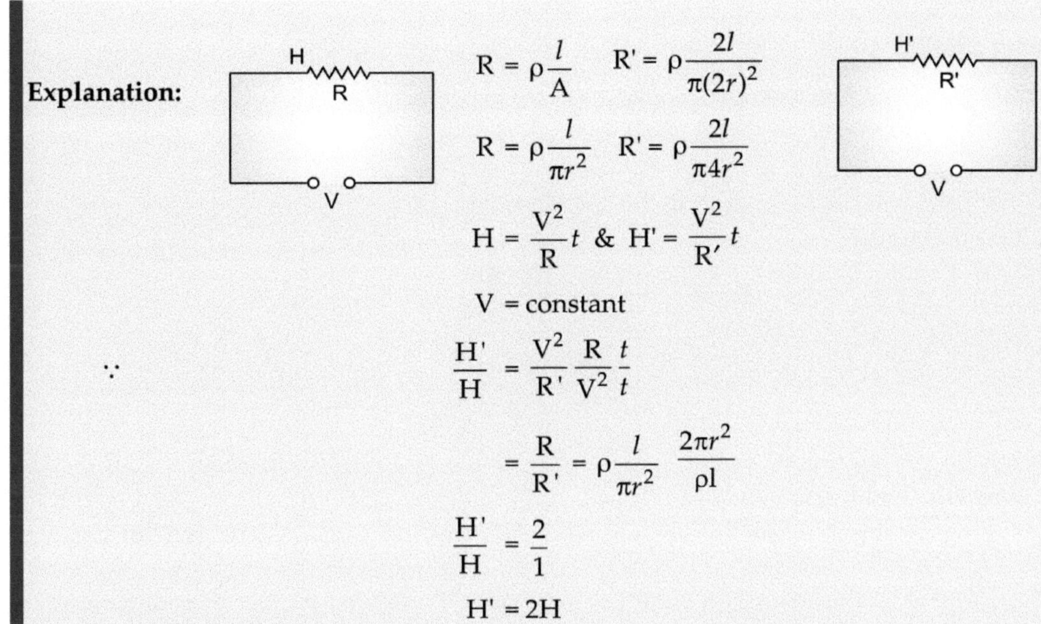

$$R = \rho\dfrac{l}{A} \qquad R' = \rho\dfrac{2l}{\pi(2r)^2}$$

$$R = \rho\dfrac{l}{\pi r^2} \qquad R' = \rho\dfrac{2l}{\pi 4r^2}$$

$$H = \dfrac{V^2}{R}t \ \&\ H' = \dfrac{V^2}{R'}t$$

$$V = \text{constant}$$

$$\therefore \quad \dfrac{H'}{H} = \dfrac{V^2}{R'}\dfrac{R}{V^2}\dfrac{t}{t}$$

$$= \dfrac{R}{R'} = \rho\dfrac{l}{\pi r^2}\ \dfrac{2\pi r^2}{\rho l}$$

$$\dfrac{H'}{H} = \dfrac{2}{1}$$

$$H' = 2H$$

13. If the potential difference V applied across a conductor is increased to 2 V with its temperature kept constant, the drift velocity of the free electrons in a conductor:

(a) remain the same   (b) become half of its previous value

(c) be double of its initial value   (d) become zero

Ans. (b) become half of its previous value.

Explanation: Drift velocity is given by:

$$v_d = \dfrac{-e\vec{E}}{m}\vec{\tau}$$

Since,

$$E = \dfrac{v}{d}$$

$$\therefore \quad v_d = \dfrac{-e\vec{V}\vec{\tau}}{md}$$

Hence, if potential difference 'v' is doubled to '$2v$' then:

$$v'_d = \dfrac{-e(2v)}{md} = 2v_d$$

14. The equivalent resistance between A and B is:

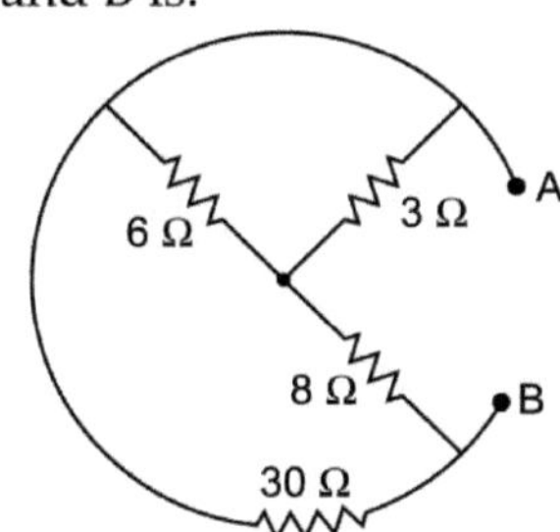

(a) 3 ohms   (b) 5.5 ohms   (c) 7.5 ohms   (d) 9.5 ohms

Ans. (c) $7.5\ \Omega$

Explanation: Redrawing the circuit, we get

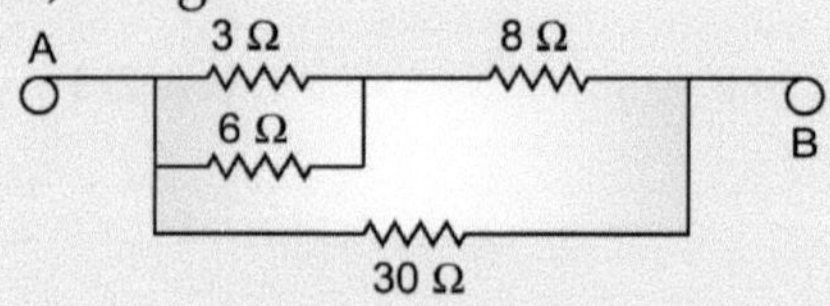

$3\ \Omega$ & $6\ \Omega$ are in parallel.

$\therefore \qquad R_1 = \dfrac{3 \times 6}{3+6} = \dfrac{18}{9} = 2\ \Omega$

Now R_1 and $8\ \Omega$ in series

$\therefore \qquad R_2 = R_1 + 8 = 2 + 8 = 10\ \Omega$

Now R_2 and $30\ \Omega$ in parallel

$$R_{eq} = \dfrac{R_2 \times 30}{R_2 + 30} = \dfrac{10 \times 30}{10 + 30}$$

$$= \dfrac{300}{40} = \dfrac{30}{4} = \dfrac{15}{2}$$

$$= 7.5\ \Omega$$

15. The SI unit of magnetic field intensity is:

(a) AmN^{-1} 　　(b) $NA^{-1}m^{-1}$ 　　(c) $NA^{-2}m^{-2}$ 　　(d) $NA^{-1}m^{-2}$

Ans. (b) $NA^{-1}m^{-1}$

Explanation: We know

$$B = \dfrac{F}{Il\sin\theta}$$

SI Unit of $\qquad B = \dfrac{N}{Am} = NA^{-1}m^{-1}$

16. The coil of a moving coil galvanometer is wound over a metal frame in order to:

(a) reduce hysteresis

(b) increase sensitivity

(c) increase moment of inertia

(d) provide electromagnetic damping

Ans. (d) provide electromagnetic damping.

Explanation: The coil of a moving coil galvanometer is wound over metallic frame to provide electromagnetic damping so it becomes dead beat galvanometer.

17. Two wires of the same length are shaped into a square of side 'a' and a circle with radius 'r'. If they carry same current, the ratio of their magnetic moment is:

(a) $2 : \pi$ 　　(b) $\pi : 2$ 　　(c) $\pi : 4$ 　　(d) $4 : \pi$

Ans. (c) $\pi : 4$

Explanation: 　　　　　　l = length of wire

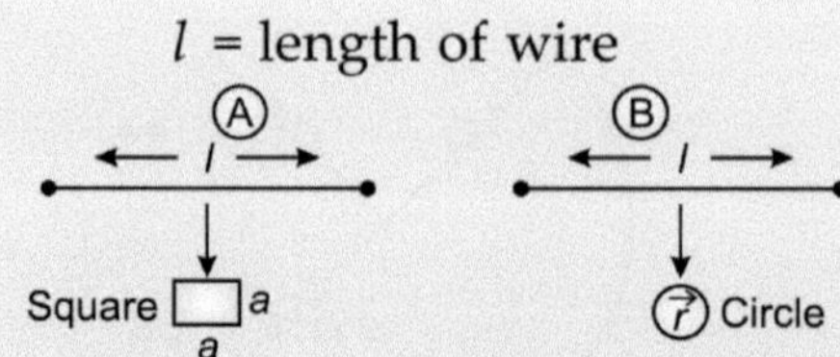

Area of a Square	Area of a Circle
$= a^2$	$= \pi r^2$
Also here, $l = 4a$	Also here, $2\pi r = l$
$a = \dfrac{l}{4}$	$r = \dfrac{l}{2\pi}$
$\therefore$ Area $= \dfrac{l^2}{16}$	Now Area $= \pi\left(\dfrac{l}{2\pi}\right)^2$
$A_1 = \dfrac{l^2}{16}$	$A_2 = \dfrac{l^2}{4\pi}$

Now,   Magnetic moment $= IA$

$\therefore$ $M_1 = IA_1$, & $M_2 = IA_2$

Since current is same in both

$\therefore$

$$\frac{M_1}{M_2} = \frac{A_1}{A_2} = \frac{l^2}{16} \times \frac{4\pi}{l^2} = \frac{\pi}{4}$$

$$M_1 : M_2 = \pi : 4$$

18. The horizontal component of earth's magnetic field at a place is $\sqrt{3}$ times the vertical component. The angle of dip at that place is:

(a) $\dfrac{\pi}{6}$ (b) $\dfrac{\pi}{3}$ (c) $\dfrac{\pi}{4}$ (d) 0

Ans. (a) $\dfrac{\pi}{6}$

Explanation: Tangent law $B_V = B_H \tan\delta$

$$\tan\delta = \frac{B_V}{B_H}$$

Given, $$B_H = \sqrt{3}\ B_V$$

$$\tan\delta = \frac{B_V}{\sqrt{3}\ B_V} = \frac{1}{\sqrt{3}}$$

$$\delta = 30° \text{ or } \frac{\pi}{6} \text{ radians.}$$

19. The small angle between magnetic axis and geographic axis at a place is:
(a) Magnetic meridian
(b) Geographic meridian
(c) Magnetic inclination
(d) Magnetic Declination

Ans. (d) Magnetic declination.

Explanation: Magnetic declination is the small angle between magnetic axis and geographical axis.

20. Two coils are placed close to each other. The mutual inductance of the pair of coils depends upon the:
(a) rate at which current change in the two coils
(b) relative position and orientation of the coils
(c) rate at which voltage induced across two coils
(d) currents in the two coils

Ans. (b) relative position and orientation of the coils.

Explanation: Mutual inductance of a pair of two coils depends on the relative position and orientation of two coils.

21. A conducting square loop of side 'L' and resistance 'R' moves in its plane with the uniform velocity 'v' perpendicular to one of its sides. A magnetic induction 'B' constant in time and space pointing perpendicular and into the plane of the loop exists everywhere as shown in the figure. The current induced in the loop is:

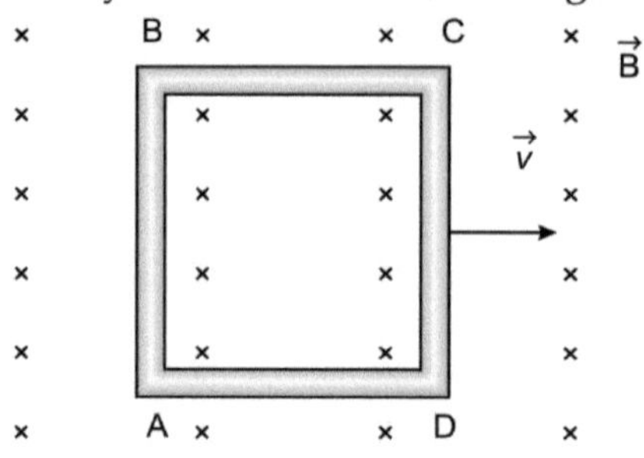

(a) $\dfrac{Blv}{R}$ Clockwise

(b) $\dfrac{Blv}{R}$ Anticlockwise

(c) $\dfrac{2Blv}{R}$ Anticlockwise

(d) Zero

Ans. (d) zero.

Explanation: The change in magnetic flux associated with the loop is zero as B is uniform everywhere. As there is no change in flux, induced EMF is zero and therefore no current induced.

22. The magnetic flux linked with the coil (in Weber) is given by the equation:
$$\phi = 5t^2 + 3t + 16$$
The induced EMF in the coil at time, $t = 4$ will be:

(a) –27 V (b) –43 V (c) –108 V (d) 210 V

Ans. (b) –43 V

Explanation: Given,
$$\phi = 5t^2 + 3t + 16$$
$$|e| = \frac{d\phi}{dt}$$
$$= \frac{d}{dt}[5t^2 + 3t + 16]$$
$$= 10t + 3$$
$$|e|_{t=4} = 10(4) + 3 = 43 \text{ V}$$
$$e = -43 \text{ Volts.}$$

23. Which of the following graphs represent the variation of current(I) with frequency (f) in an AC circuit containing a pure capacitor?

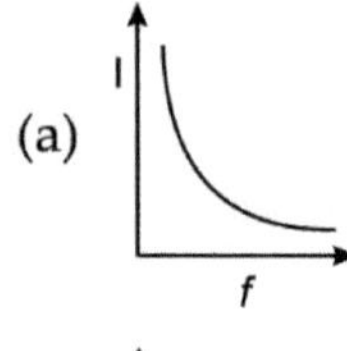

(a)

(b)

(c)

(d)

Ans. (c)

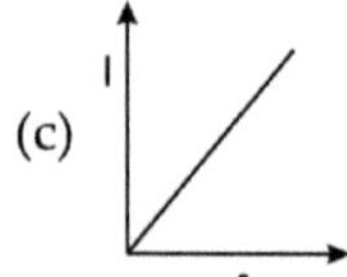
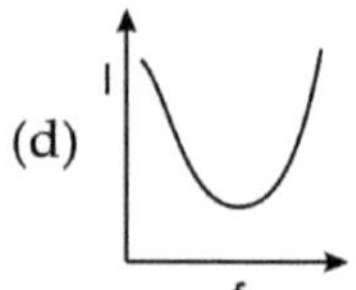

Explanation:

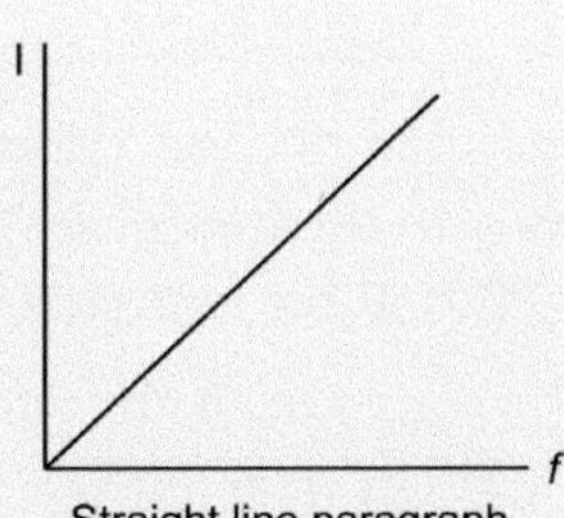

Straight line paragraph

$$I = \frac{V}{X_c} \text{ in Pure Capacitor}$$

$$= \frac{V}{\frac{1}{2\pi fc}} = V\,2\pi fc$$

$$\Rightarrow \qquad I \propto f$$

other parameters kept constant.

24. A 20 volt AC is applied to a circuit consisting of a resistance and a coil with negligible resistance. If the voltage across the resistance is 12 volt, the voltage across the coil is:

(a) 16 V   (b) 10 V   (c) 8 V   (d) 6 V

Ans. (a) 16 V

Explanation:

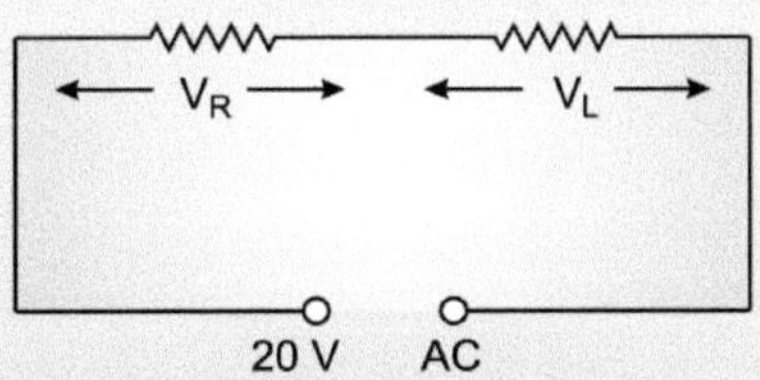

$$\therefore$$

$V_R = \text{Effective Voltage across R}$

$V_R = I_{eff}\,R$

$V_L = \text{Effective Voltage across L}$

$V_L = I_{eff} \times L$

$$\text{Net } V = \sqrt{V_R^2 + V_L^2}$$

$$= \sqrt{I_{eff}^{\,2} R^2 + I_{eff}^{\,2} \times L^2}$$

$$20 = \sqrt{(12)^2 + V_L^2}$$

$$(20)^2 = (12)^2 + V_L^{\,2}$$

$$400 = 144 + V_L^{\,2}$$

$$V_L = \sqrt{400 - 144} = \sqrt{256} = 16 \text{ Volts.}$$

25. The instantaneous values of emf and the current in a series ac circuit are:

$E = E_o \, \text{Sin } \omega t$ and $I = I_o \sin\left(\omega t + \frac{\pi}{3}\right)$ respectively, then it is

(a) Necessarily a RL circuit   (b) Necessarily a RC circuit

(c) Necessarily a LCR circuit   (d) Can be RC or LCR circuit

Ans. (d) Can be RC or LCR circuit.

Explanation:

$$E = E_0 \sin \omega t$$

$$I = I_0 \sin\left(\omega t + \frac{\pi}{3}\right)$$

as I can lead the Voltage in RC and LCR circuit, so it can be RC or LCR circuit.

Section – B

This section consists of 24 multiple choice questions with overall choice to attempt any 20 questions. In case more than desirable number of questions are attempted, ONLY first 20 will be considered for evaluation

26. A cylinder of radius r and length l is placed in an uniform electric field parallel to the axis of the cylinder. The total flux for the surface of the cylinder is given by:

    (a) zero   (b) πr^2 (c) $E\pi r^2$ (d) $2E\pi r^2$

Ans. (a) Zero.

Explanation:

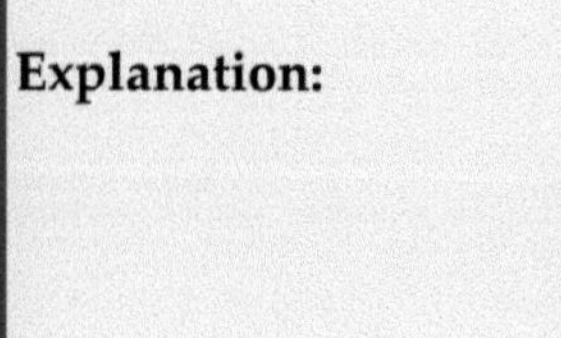
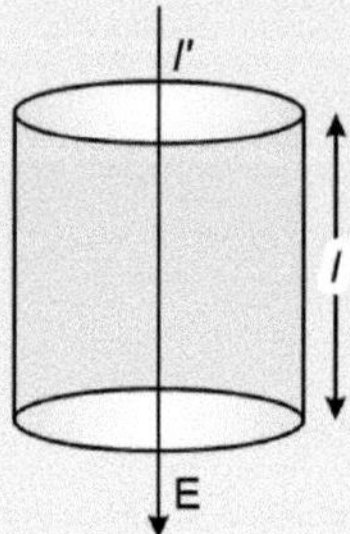

Since, the electric flux into the cylinder is the same as that going out of it hence net flux = 0

27. Two parallel large thin metal sheets have equal surface densities 26.4×10^{-12} C/m^2 of opposite signs. The electric field between these sheets is:

    (a) 1.5 N/C   (b) 1.5×10^{-16} N/C
    (c) 3×10^{-10} N/C   (d) 3 N/C

Ans. (d) $3\dfrac{N}{C}$.

Explanation:

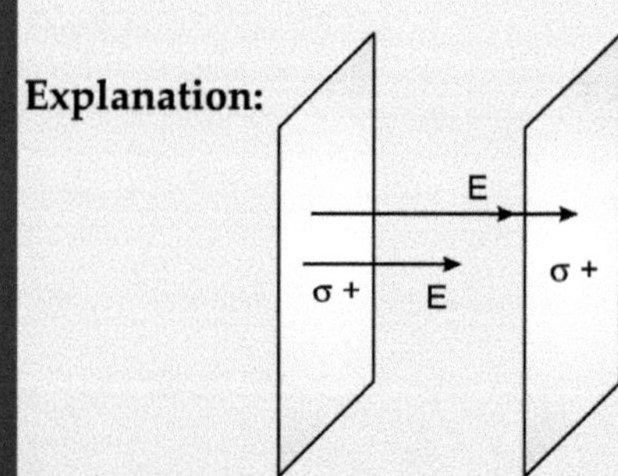

Surface Charge density,

$$\sigma = 26.4 \times 10^{-12}\ \frac{C}{m^2}$$

$$E = \frac{\sigma}{2\varepsilon_0} + \frac{\sigma}{2\varepsilon_0}$$

$$= \frac{2\sigma}{2\varepsilon_0} = \frac{\sigma}{\varepsilon_0}$$

$$= \frac{26.4 \times 10^{-12}}{8.85 \times 10^{-12}}\ \frac{N}{C}$$

$$= 3\frac{N}{C}$$

28. Consider an uncharged conducting sphere. A positive point charge is placed outside the sphere. The net charge on the sphere is then:

(a) negative and uniformly distributed over the surface of sphere

(b) positive and uniformly distributed over the surface of sphere

(c) negative and appears at a point the surface of sphere closest to point charge

(d) Zero

Ans. (d) zero.

> **Explanation:**
>
> 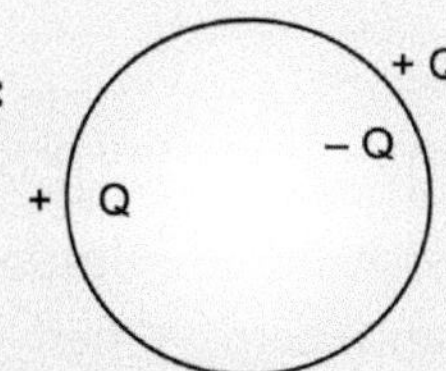
>
>
> Equal and Opposite charges appear on the nearby conductor due to induction, but still net charge on the conductor is zero.

29. Three Charges $2q$, $-q$ and $-q$ lie at vertices of a triangle. The value of E and V at centroid of triangle will be:

(a) $E \neq 0$ and $V \neq 0$

(b) $E = 0$ and $V = 0$

(c) $E \neq 0$ and $V = 0$

(d) $E = 0$ and $V \neq 0$

Ans. (c) $E \neq 0$ and $V = 0$.

> **Explanation:**
>
> 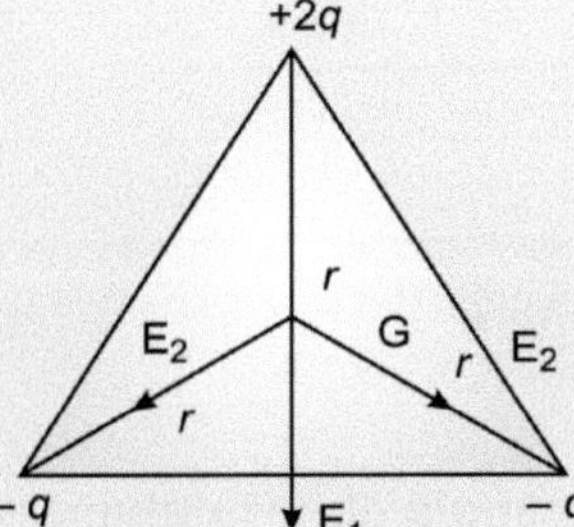
>
>
> As can be seen from the diagram the net electric field is non-zero. Potential at the centroid depends on the net charge which is zero and hence, potential is zero.

30. Two parallel plate capacitors X and Y, have the same area of plates and same separation between plates. X has air and Y with dielectric of constant 2 , between its plates. They are connected in series to a battery of 12 V. The ratio of electrostatic energy stored in X and Y is:

(a) $4: 1$ (b) $1: 4$ (c) $2: 1$ (d) $1: 2$

Ans. (c) $2: 1$.

> **Explanation:**
>
> 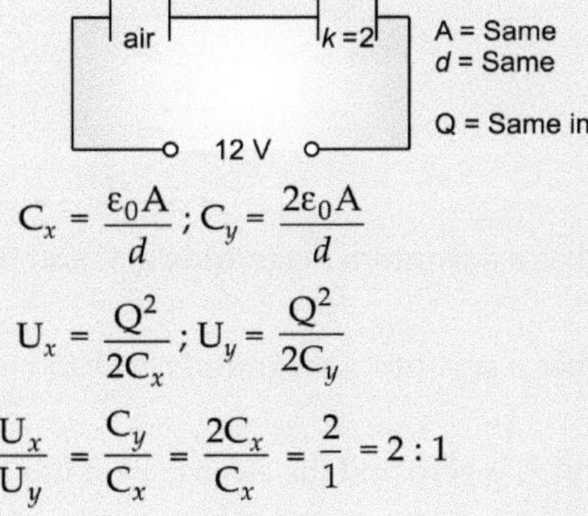
>
>
> $$C_x = \frac{\varepsilon_0 A}{d} \; ; C_y = \frac{2\varepsilon_0 A}{d}$$
>
> $$U_x = \frac{Q^2}{2C_x} \; ; U_y = \frac{Q^2}{2C_y}$$
>
> $$\therefore \quad \frac{U_x}{U_y} = \frac{C_y}{C_x} = \frac{2C_x}{C_x} = \frac{2}{1} = 2 : 1$$

31. Which among the following, is not a cause for power loss in a transformer:

(a) Eddy currents are produced in the soft iron core of a transformer.

(b) Electric Flux sharing is not properly done in primary and secondary coils.

(c) Humming sound produced in the transformers due to magnetostriction.

(d) Primary coil is made up of a very thick copper wire.

Ans. (d) Primary coil is made up of a very thick copper wire.

Explanation: Primary coil made of Thick copper wire has very less R. Therefore negligible power loss.

32. An alternating voltage source of variable angular frequency 'ω' and fixed amplitude 'V' is connected in series with a capacitance C and electric bulb of resistance R (inductance zero). When 'ω' is increased:

(a) The bulb glows dimmer.

(b) The bulb glows brighter.

(c) Net impedance of the circuit remains unchanged.

(d) Total impedance of the circuit increases.

Ans. (b) The bulb glows brighter.

Explanation:

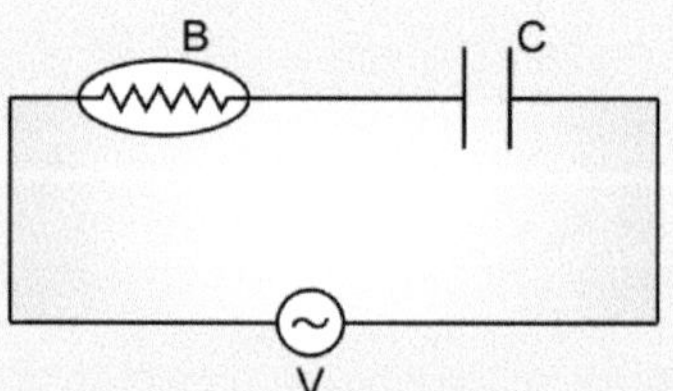

$\omega \uparrow$

$$X_C = \frac{1}{2\pi fc} = \frac{1}{\omega c} \downarrow \; i.e. \; X_C \downarrow$$

$I \uparrow \therefore$ Brightness of the bulb will $\uparrow$

Hence, $I \propto \omega$ which means increase of ω will increase I hence bulb glow brighter.

33. A solid spherical conductor has charge +Q and radius R. It is surrounded by a solid spherical shell with charge –Q, inner radius 2R, and outer radius 3R. Which of the following statements is true?

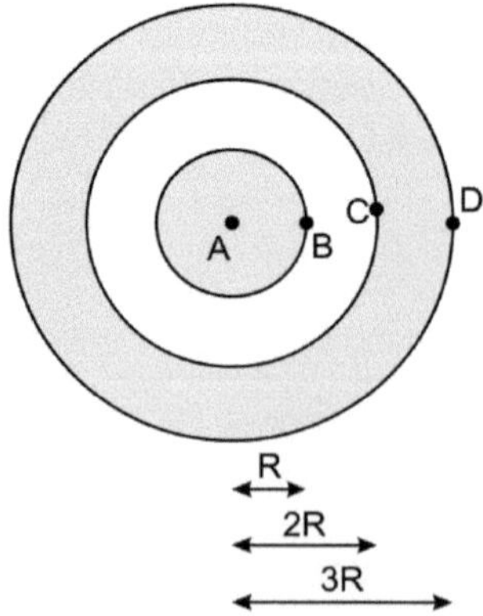

(a) The electric potential has a maximum magnitude at C and the electric field has a maximum magnitude at A.

(b) The electric potential has a maximum magnitude at D and the electric field has a maximum magnitude at B.

(c) The electric potential at A is zero and the electric field has a maximum magnitude at D.

(d) Both the electric potential and electric field achieve a maximum magnitude at B.

Ans. (d) Both the electric potential and electric field achieve a maximum magnitude at B.

Explanation: The electric field in the interior of conductors is zero. The charge of $+Q$ is on the surface of radius R and all of the charge $-Q$ of the solid spherical shell is on the inner surface of radius 2R. There is no electric field from 2R to infinity and from O to R. Hence, the electric field only exists between R and 2R with the field strongest at B.

$$E_B = \frac{kQ}{R^2} + \frac{kQ}{R^2} = 2\frac{kQ}{R^2}$$

The electric potential is zero at all points from infinity to C, at which point the magnitude increases up to point B. From zero to R, there is no electric field and hence no change in potential.

$$V_B = \frac{kQ}{R} - \frac{KQ}{2R}$$

Thus, the electric potential and electric field achieve a maximum magnitude at point B.

34. A battery is connected to the conductor of non-uniform cross–section area. The quantities or quantity which remains constant is:
    (a) electric field only
    (b) drift speed and electric field
    (c) electric field and current
    (d) current only

Ans. (d) Current only.

Explanation: Quantity which remains only is current only. Rest all quantities change with area of cross-section of a conductor.

35. Three resistors having values R_1, R_2, and R_3 are connected in series to a battery. Suppose R_1 carries a current of 2.0 A, R_2 has a resistance of 3.0 ohms, and R_3 dissipates 6.0 watts of power. Then the voltage across R_3 is:
    (a) 1 V
    (b) 2 V
    (c) 3 V
    (d) 4 V

Ans. (c) 3 V.

Explanation: Given,

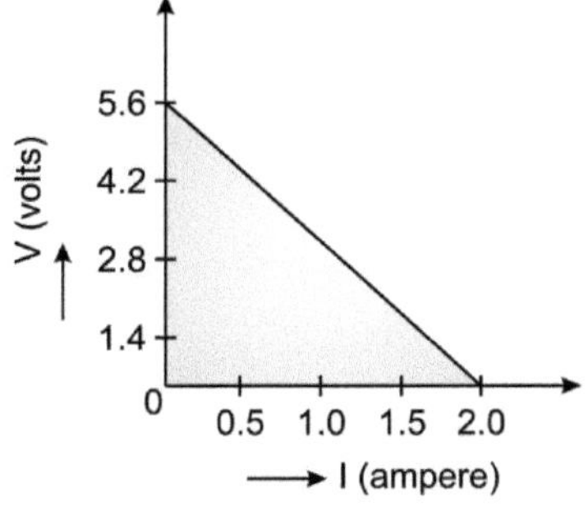

$$1 = 2\text{ A}, R_2 = 3\ \Omega, P_3 = 6\text{ W}$$

Power across

$$R_3 = V_3 1$$
$$6W = 1^2 R_3$$
$$\frac{6}{4} = R_3 = \frac{3}{2} = 1.5\ \Omega$$
$$V_3 = 1R_3 = 2(1.5) = 3\text{ V}$$

36. A straight line plot showing the terminal potential difference (V) of a cell as a function of current (I) drawn from it, is shown in the figure. The internal resistance of the cell would be then:

    (a) 2.8 ohms
    (b) 1.4 ohms
    (c) 1.2 ohms
    (d) zero

Ans. (a) 2.8 Ω

> **Explanation:**
> $$l = O, V = E, \therefore E = 5.6 \text{ V}$$
> $$r = \frac{E}{I} = \frac{5.6}{2.0} = 2.8 \ \Omega$$

37. A 10 m long wire of uniform cross-section and 20 Ω resistance is used in a potentiometer. The wire is connected in series with a battery of 5 V along with an external resistance of 480 Ω balanced at 6.0 m length of the wire, then the value of unknown emf is:

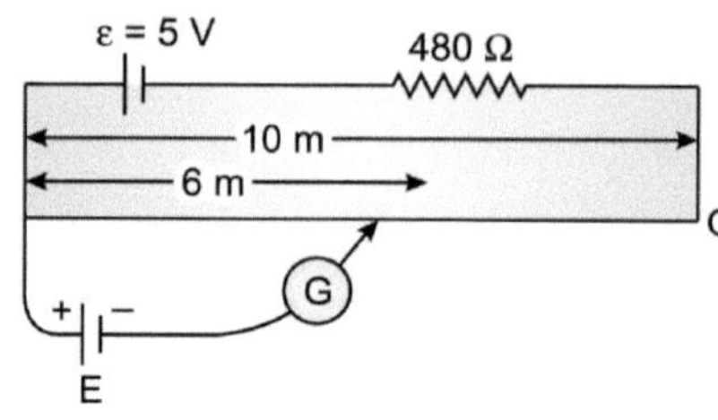

(a) 1.2 V　　　　(b) 1.02 V　　　　(c) 0.2 V　　　　(d) 0.12 V

Ans. (d) 0.12 V.

> **Explanation:** Let PQ is a potentiometer wire of length 10 m.
>
> $$1 = \frac{E}{R+R'} = \frac{5}{480+20} = \frac{5}{500}$$
> $$= \frac{1}{100} = 0.01 \text{ A}$$
> $$V_{PQ} = IR_{PQ} = 0.01 \times 20$$
> $$= 0.2 \text{ V}$$
>
> If 10 m potentiometer wire balances = 0.2 V
>
> Then 1 m potentiometer wire balance = $\dfrac{0.2}{10}$ V
>
> Then 6 m potentiometer wire balance = $\dfrac{0.2}{10} \times 6$ V
>
> $$= \frac{1.2}{10} = 0.12 \text{ V}$$

38. The current sensitivity of a galvanometer increases by 20%. If its resistance also increases by 25%, the voltage sensitivity will:

(a) decrease by 1%　　(b) increased by 5%　　(c) increased by 10%　　(d) decrease by 4%

Ans. (d) decreases by 4%.

> **Explanation:**
> $$I'_g = I_g + \frac{20}{100} I_g$$
> $$= \frac{120}{100} I_g = 1.2 I_g$$
> $$R' = R + \frac{25}{100} R = \frac{125}{100} R$$
> $$= 1.25 \text{ R}$$
> $$V'_g = ?$$
> $$V'_g = \frac{I'_g}{R'} = \frac{1.2 I_g}{1.25 R}$$

$$= \frac{120}{125}V_g = \frac{25}{25}V_g$$

$$\text{\% change} = \frac{V_g' - V_g}{V_g} \times 100$$

$$= \frac{\left(\dfrac{24}{25}V_g - V_g\right)}{V_g} \times 100$$

$$= \frac{(24 - 25)}{25} \times 100$$

$$= -\frac{1}{25} \times 100 = 4\%$$

Decrease by 4%.

39. Three infinitely long parallel straight current carrying wires A, B and C are kept at equal distance from each other as shown in the figure. The wire C experiences net force F. The net force on wire C, when the current in wire A is reversed will be:

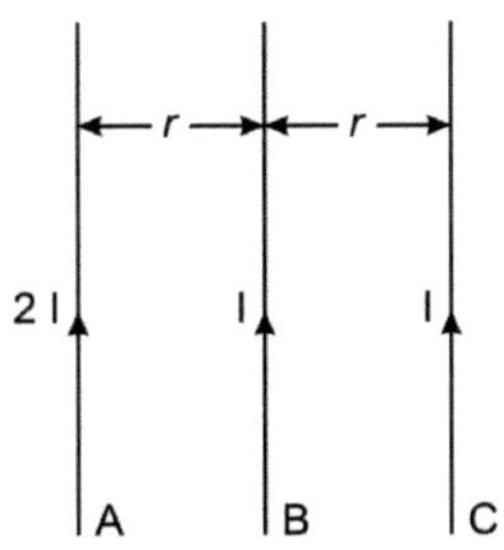

(a) Zero   (b) $\dfrac{F}{2}$ (c) F   (d) 2F

Ans. (d) zero.

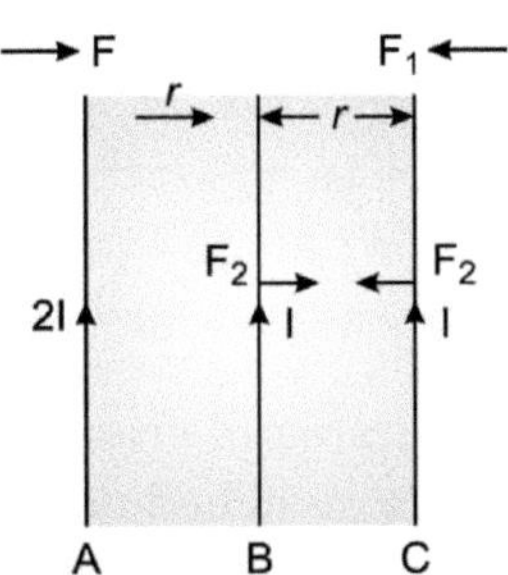

Explanation: Let F_1 is force per unit, length between A & C

i.e.
$$F_1 = \frac{\mu_0}{4\pi} \frac{2I \times I}{2r}$$

And F_2 is force per unit, length between B & C
$$F_2 = \frac{\mu_0}{4\pi} \frac{I \times I}{r}$$

Now net force on 'C' is per unit length
$$F_1 + F_2 = \frac{\mu}{4\pi} \frac{I^2}{r}(1+1)$$

$$= \frac{2\mu_0}{4\pi} \frac{I^2}{r} = F \text{ (given)}$$

Now

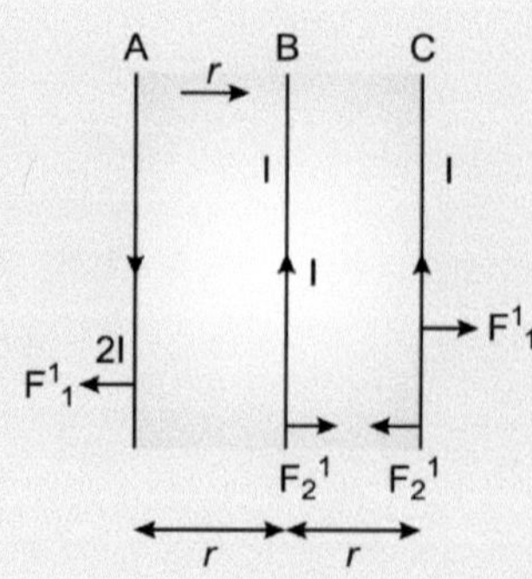

F_1' = Repulsive force between A & C

$$= \frac{\mu_0}{4\pi}\frac{2I^2}{2r}$$

$F_2' = F_2$ = A reactive force between B & C

∴ Net force on `C' $F_1' - F_2' = 0$

∵ $F_1' = F_2' = \frac{\mu}{4\pi}\frac{2I^2}{2r}$

∴ Net Force on `C' is zero.

40. In a hydrogen atom the electron moves in an orbit of radius 0.5 Å making 10 revolutions per second, the magnetic moment associated with the orbital motion of the electron will be:

(a) 2.512×10^{-38} Am^2 (b) 1.256×10^{-38} Am^2 (c) 0.628×10^{-38} Am^2 (d) zero

Ans. (b) 1.256×10^{-38} Am^2.

Explanation:

$R = 0.5$ Å

$\omega = 10$ rps $= 10 \times 2\pi$ rad/s

$\nu = 10$ Hz

$M = IA = e\nu\,\pi\,r^2$

$= 1.6 \times 10^{-19} \times 10 \times 3.14 \times 0.5 \times 0.5 \times 10^{-10} \times 10^{-10}$

$= 1.256 \times 10^{-38}$ Am^2.

41. An air-cored solenoid with length 30 cm, area of cross-section 25 cm^2 and number of turns 800, carries a current of 2.5 A. The current is suddenly switched off in a brief time of 10^{-3} s. Ignoring the variation in magnetic field near the ends of the solenoid, the average back emf induced across the ends of the open switch in the circuit would be:

(a) zero   (b) 3.125 volts   (c) 6.54 volts   (d) 16.74 volts

Ans. (d) 16.74 Volts.

Explanation: Magnetic field inside a solenoid.

$$B = \mu_0 \frac{N}{l} I'$$

Flux linked with `N' turns

Initial flux $\phi_1 = NBA = N\mu_0 \frac{N}{l} IA$

$$= \mu_0 \frac{N^2}{l} IA$$

$$= \frac{4\pi \times 10^{-7} \times 800 \times 800 \times 2.5 \times 2.5 \times 10^{-4}}{0.30}$$

$$= 16.74 \times 10^{-3} \text{ Wb}$$

Final flux ϕ_2 $\qquad = 0$

Average back emf $\qquad |e| = \dfrac{d\phi}{dt} = \dfrac{16.74 \times 10^{-3} - 0}{10^{-3}}$

$$= 16.74 \text{ V}$$

42. A sinusoidal voltage of peak value 283 V and frequency 50 Hz is applied to a series LCR circuit in which R = 3 Ω, L = 25.48 mH, and C = 796 μF, then the power dissipated at the resonant condition will be:

(a) 39.70 kW (b) 26.70 kW (c) 13.35 kW (d)Zero

Ans. (c) 13.35 kW.

Explanation:

$$V_0 = 283 \text{ V}, f = 50 \text{ Hz}$$
$$R = 3 \, \Omega, L = 25.48 \text{ mH}$$
$$C = 796 \, \mu\text{F}$$

Power dissipated $\qquad P|_{\text{at reasonance}} = ?$

$$P = I^2 R$$

$$I = \frac{I_0}{\sqrt{2}} = \frac{1}{\sqrt{2}}\left(\frac{283}{3}\right)$$

$$= 66.7 \text{ A}$$

$$P = I^2 A$$

$$= (66.7)^2 \, 3$$

$$= 13.35 \text{ kW}$$

43. A circular loop of radius 0.3 cm lies parallel to much bigger circular of radius 20 cm. The centre of the small loop is on the axis of the bigger loop. The distance between their centres is 15 cm. If a current of 2.0 A flows through the smaller loop, then the flux linked with the bigger loop is:

(a) 3.3×10^{-11} weber (b) 6×10^{-11} weber (c) 6.6×10^{-9} weber (d) 9.1×10^{-11} weber

Ans. (d) 9.1×10^{-11} weber.

Explanation: Let flux linked with smaller loop is ϕ_1 and with bigger loop is ϕ_2.

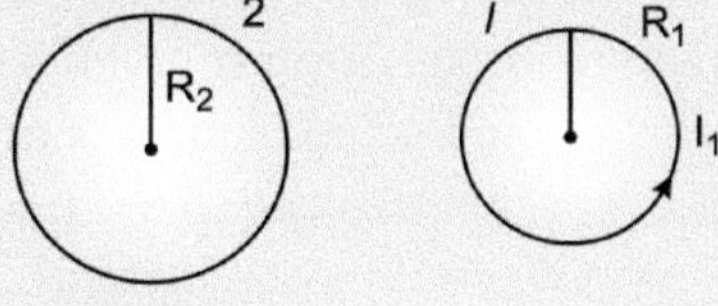

Given, $\qquad R_2 = 0.2 \text{ m}$
$$R_1 = 0.003 \text{ m}$$
$$x = 15 \text{ cm} = 0.15 \text{ cm}$$

Now $\qquad \phi_1 = B_2 A_1$

$$= \frac{\mu_0}{4\pi}\left[\frac{2\pi R_2^2 I_2}{(R_2^2 + x^2)^{3/2}}\right]\pi R_1^2$$

$$M = \frac{\phi_1}{I_2} = \frac{\mu_0}{4\pi}\left[\frac{2\pi R_2^2 \, \pi R_1^2}{(R_2^2 + x^2)^{3/2}}\right]$$

Now
$$\phi_2 = Ml_1$$
$$= \frac{\mu_0}{4\pi} \frac{2\pi R_2^2 \, \pi R_1^2}{(R_2^2 + x^2)^{3/2}} . I_1$$
$$= 9.1 \times 10^{-11} \text{ Weber}$$

44. If both the number of turns and core length of an inductor is doubled keeping other factors constant, then its self-inductance will be:

   (a) Unaffected   (b) doubled   (c) halved   (d) quadrupled

Ans. (b) doubled.

Explanation:
$$L = \mu_0 \frac{N^2}{l} A$$
$$L' = \mu_0 \frac{(2N)^2}{2l} A$$
$$= 2\mu_0 \frac{N^2}{l} A = 2L$$

45. Given below are two statements labelled as Assertion (A) and Reason (R)

Assertion (A): To increase the range of an ammeter, we must connect a suitable high resistance in series to it.

Reason (R): The ammeter with increased range should have high resistance.

Select the most appropriate answer from the options given below:

   (a) Both A and R are true and R is the correct explanation of A.

   (b) Both A and R are true but R is not the correct explanation of A.

   (c) A is true but R is false.

   (d) A is false and R is also false.

Ans. (d) A is False and R is also False.

Explanation: To increase the range of an ammeter, suitable low R (or shunt) should be connected in parallel to it. The ammeter with increased range has low resistance.

46. Given below are two statements labelled as Assertion (A) and Reason (R)

Assertion (A): An electron has a high potential energy when it is at a location associated with a more negative value of potential, and a low potential energy when at a location associated with a more positive potential.

Reason (R): Electrons move from a region of higher potential to region of lower potential.

Select the most appropriate answer from the options given below:

   (a) Both A and R are true and R is the correct explanation of A.

   (b) Both A and R are true but R is not the correct explanation of A.

   (c) A is true but R is false.

   (d) A is false and R is also false.

Ans. (c) A is true but R is also false.

Explanation: Assertion is correct but reason is wrong because electrons move a region of low potential to high potential.

47. Given below are two statements labelled as Assertion (A) and Reason (R)

Assertion (A): A magnetic needle free to rotate in a vertical plane, orients itself (with its axis) vertical at the poles of the earth.

Reason (R): At the poles of the earth the horizontal component of earth's magnetic field will be zero.

Select the most appropriate answer from the options given below:

(a) Both A and R are true and R is the correct explanation of A.

(b) Both A and R are true but R is not the correct explanation of A.

(c) A is true but R is false.

(d) A is false and R is also false.

Ans. (a) Both A and R are true and R is the correct explanation of A.

> **Explanation:** At poles, magnetic needle orients itself vertically because horizontal components of earth's field is zero there.

48. Given below are two statements labelled as Assertion (A) and Reason (R)

    Assertion (A): A proton and an electron, with same momenta, enter in a magnetic field in a direction at right angles to the lines of the force. The radius of the paths followed by them will be same.

    Reason (R): Electron has less mass than the proton.

    Select the most appropriate answer from the options given below:

    (a) Both A and R are true and R is the correct explanation of A.

    (b) Both A and R are true but R is not the correct explanation of A.

    (c) A is true but R is false.

    (d) A is false and R is also false.

Ans. (b) Both A and R are true but R is not the correct explanation of A.

> **Explanation:** We know $\dfrac{mv^2}{r}$ $Bqv \sin\theta = Bqv \sin\theta$
>
> Centripetal force = magnetic Lorentz force
>
> $\sin\theta = \sin 90° = 1$ (angle between $\vec{V}$ & $\vec{B} = 90°$)
>
> $$\frac{mv^2}{r} = Bqv$$
>
> $$\frac{mv}{r} = Bq$$
>
> $$r = \frac{mv}{Bq} = \frac{p}{Bq} = \frac{\text{linear momentum}}{Bq}$$
>
> Since $\qquad\qquad r = \dfrac{p}{Bq}$
>
> Given p, B are same
>
> Also q for proton & electron is same except its sign
>
> $\therefore$ Radius is same. So statement is correct but reason is not the correct explanation of the given assertion.

49. Given below are two statements labelled as Assertion (A) and Reason (R)

    Assertion (A): On Increasing the current sensitivity of a galvanometer by increasing the number of turns, may not necessarily increase its voltage sensitivity.

    Reason (R): The resistance of the coil of the galvanometer increases on increasing the number of turns.

    Select the most appropriate answer from the options given below:

    (a) Both A and R are true and R is the correct explanation of A.

    (b) Both A and R are true but R is not the correct explanation of A.

    (c) A is true but R is false.

    (d) A is false and R is also false.

Ans. (a) Both A and R are true and R is the correct explanation of A.

> **Explanation:** When we increase current sensitivity by increasing no. of turns, then resistance of coil also increases. So increasing current sensitivity does not necessarily imply that voltage sensitivity will increase because $V_g = \dfrac{I_g}{R}$
>
> $\therefore$ if I_g increases and R increases by different amounts, then V_g may increase or decrease.

Section - C

This section consists of 6 multiple choice questions with an overall choice to attempt any 5. In case more than desirable number of questions are attempted, ONLY first 5 will be considered for evaluation

50. A small object with charge q and weight mg is attached to one end of a string of length 'L' attached to a stationary support. The system is placed in a uniform horizontal electric field 'E', as shown in the accompanying figure. In the presence of the field, the string makes a constant angle θ with the vertical. The sign and magnitude of q:

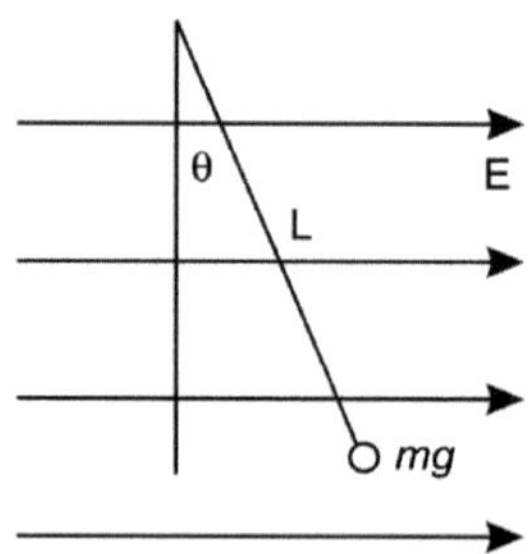

(a) positive with magnitude $\dfrac{mg}{E}$

(b) positive with magnitude $\dfrac{mg}{E}\tan\theta$

(c) negative with magnitude $\dfrac{mg}{E}\tan\theta$

(d) positive with magnitude $\dfrac{E\tan\theta}{mg}$

Ans. (b) positive with magnitude $\left(\dfrac{mg}{E}\right)\tan\theta$.

> **Explanation:**
>
> $$F_e = mg\tan\theta$$
> $$qE = mg\tan\theta$$
> $$q = \left(\dfrac{mg}{E}\right)\tan\theta$$
> $$\tan\theta = \dfrac{F_e}{mg}$$

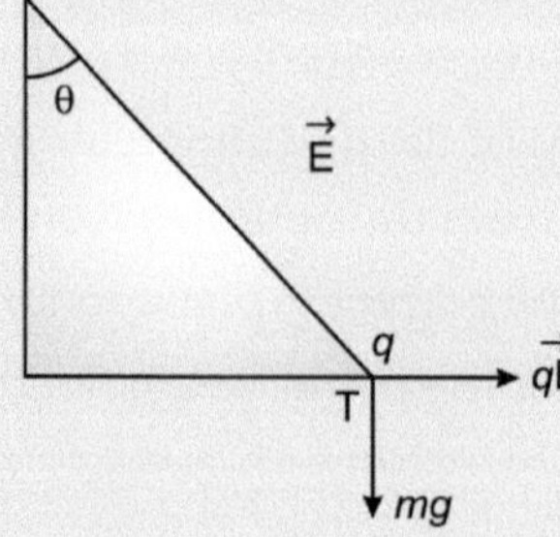

51. A free electron and a free proton are placed between two oppositely charged parallel plates. Both are closer to the positive plate than the negative plate.

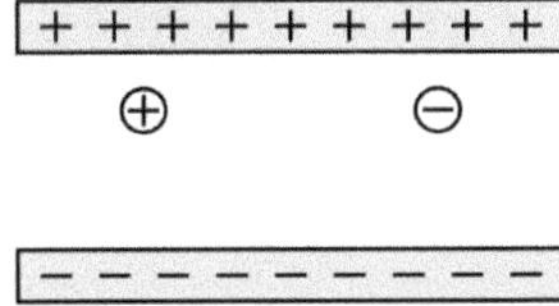

Which of the following statements is true ?

(I) The force on the proton is greater than the force on the electron.

(II) The potential energy of the proton is greater than that of the electron.

(III) The potential energy of the proton and the electron is the same.

(a) (I) only

(b) (II) only

(c) (III) and I only

(d) (II) and (I) only

Ans. (b) (II) only.

Explanation: $\because$ $\quad F_p = F_e$

$\therefore$ $\quad F = qE$

$E = $ same

$`q' = $ same

Now, $\quad P.\varepsilon = q\,V(r)$

$(P, \varepsilon)_p > (P, \varepsilon)_e$

Case study:

Read the following paragraph and answer the questions:

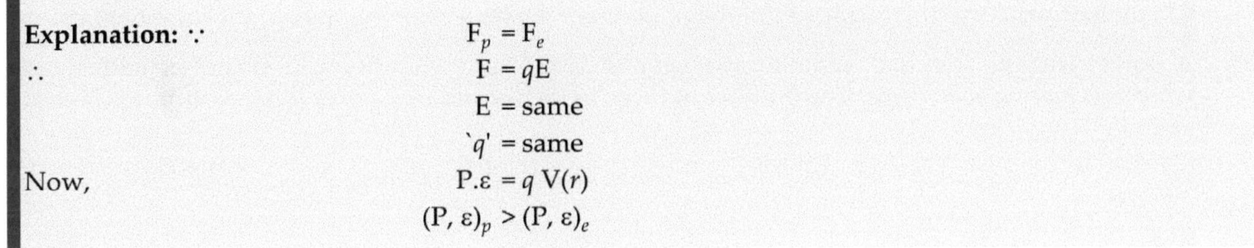

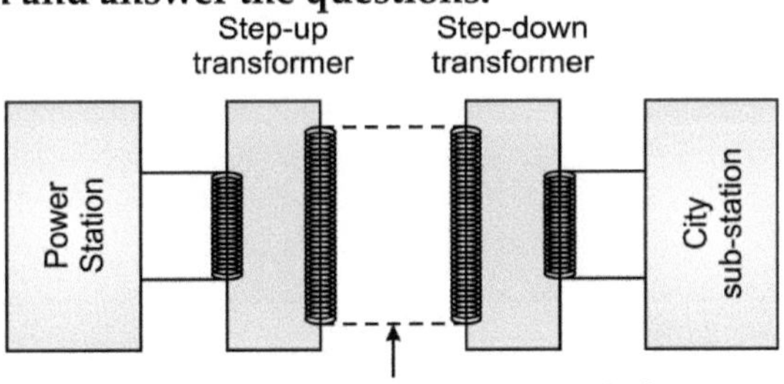

Figure: Long distance power transmission

The large-scale transmission and distribution of electrical energy over long distances is done with the use of transformers. The voltage output of the generator is stepped-up. It is then transmitted over long distances to an area sub-station near the consumers. There the voltage is stepped down. It is further stepped down at distributing sub-stations and utility poles before a power supply of 240 V reaches our homes.

52. Which of the following statement is true?

(a) Energy is created when a transformer steps up the voltage

(b) A transformer is designed to convert an AC voltage to DC voltage

(c) Step–up transformer increases the power for transmission

(d) Step–down transformer decreases the AC voltage

Ans. (d) step down transformer decreases the ac voltage.

Explanation: A transformer steps up (increases) or steps down (decreases) the AC voltage.

53. If the secondary coil has a greater number of turns than the primary:

(a) the voltage is stepped-up ($V_s > V_p$) and arrangement is called a step-up transformer

(b) the voltage is stepped-down ($V_s < V_p$) and arrangement is called a step-down transformer

(c) the current is stepped-up ($I_s > I_p$) and arrangement is called a step-up transformer

(d) the current is stepped-down ($I_s < I_p$) and arrangement is called a step-down transformer

Ans. (a) the voltage is stepped up ($V_s > U_p$) and arrangement is called a step-up transformer.

Explanation: *i.e.*
$$\frac{N_s}{N_p} = \frac{E_s}{E_p}$$

i.e. if no. of turns in secondary coil are more than no. of turns in primary, then voltage is increased or stepped up in secondary, so called step up transformer.

54. We need to step-up the voltage for power transmission, so that:
    (a) the current is reduced and consequently, the I^2R loss is cut down
    (b) the voltage is increased , the power losses are also increased
    (c) the power is increased before transmission is done
    (d) the voltage is decreased so $\dfrac{V^2}{R}$ losses are reduced

Ans. (a) the current is reduced and consequently, the I^2R loss is cut down.

Explanation: Current is reduced if voltage is stepped - up so corresponding I^2R losses are cut down.

55. A power transmission line feeds input power at 2300 V to a step down transformer with its primary windings having 4000 turns. The number of turns in the secondary in order to get output power at 230 V are:
    (a) 4   (b) 40   (c) 400   (d) 4000

Ans. (c) 400.

Explanation: Given,
$$E_i = 2300 \text{ V}$$
$$E_0 = 230 \text{ V}$$
$$N_p = 4000$$
$$N_s = ?$$
$$\frac{E_i}{E_o} = \frac{E_p}{E_s}$$
$$\frac{2300}{230} = \frac{4000}{x}$$
$$x = 400 = N_s = \text{No. of turns in secondary coil.}$$

Sample Paper 1

Section – A

This section consists of 25 multiple choice questions with overall choice to attempt any 20 questions. In case more than desirable number of questions are attempted, ONLY first 20 will be considered for evaluation.

1. The electric potential inside a conducting sphere:
   - (a) increases from centre to surface
   - (b) decreases from centre to surface
   - (c) remains constant from centre to surface
   - (d) is zero at every point inside

2. A charge Q is enclosed by a Gaussian spherical surface of radius R. If the radius is doubled then the outward electric flux will:
   - (a) be doubled
   - (b) increases four times
   - (c) be reduced to half
   - (d) remains the same

3. A body has a positive charge of 8×10^{-19} C. It has:
   - (a) an excess of 5 electrons
   - (b) a deficiency of 5 electrons
   - (c) an excess of 8 electrons
   - (d) a deficiency of 8 electrons

4. A hemisphere is uniformly charged positively. The electric field at a point on a diameter away from the centre is directed:
   - (a) perpendicular to the diameter
   - (b) parallel to the diameter
   - (c) at an angle tilted towards the diameter
   - (d) at an angle tilted away from the diameter

5. What will happen if the plates of a charged capacitor are suddenly connected by metallic wire ?
   - (a) It will start discharge
   - (b) It will remain same
   - (c) Either discharge or May remain same
   - (d) None of them

6. What will be the effect on the radius of a soap bubble on giving it a negative charge ?
   - (a) It will increase
   - (b) It will decrease
   - (c) First increase than decrease
   - (d) None of them

7. Two capacitors of capacitances C_1 and C_2 are connected in parallel. If a charge Q is given to the combination, the ratio of the charge on the capacitor C_2 to the charge on C_2 will be:
   - (a) $\dfrac{C_1}{C_2}$
   - (b) $\sqrt{\dfrac{C_1}{C_2}}$
   - (c) $\sqrt{\dfrac{C_2}{C_1}}$
   - (d) $\dfrac{C_2}{C_1}$

8. The Kirchhoff's first law ($\Sigma i = 0$) and second law ($\Sigma iR = 0$), where the symbols have their usual meanings, are respectively based on:
   - (a) Conservation of charge, conservation of momentum
   - (b) Conservation of energy, conservation of charge
   - (c) Conservation of momentum, conservation of charge
   - (d) Conservation of charge, conservation of energy

9. Consider a current carrying wire (current I) in the shape of a circle. Note that as the current progresses along the wire, the direction of J (current density) changes in an exact manner, while the current I remain unaffected. The agent that is essentially responsible is:
   - (a) source of emf
   - (b) electric field produced by charges accumulated on the surface of wire.
   - (c) the charges just behind a given segment of wire which push them just the right way by repulsion.
   - (d) the charges ahead.

10. Conventional current flows from:
    (a) point of higher potential to lower potential
    (b) point of lower potential to higher potential
    (c) point of lower potential to lower potential
    (d) All of them

11. A metallic hollow spherical surface of radius 5 cm is charged such that the potential on its surface is 10 V. The potential at the centre is:
    (a) zero
    (b) 10 V
    (c) same as at a point 5 cm away from the surface
    (d) same as at a point 25 cm away from the surface

12. A metal wire is subjected to a constant potential difference. When the temperature of the metal wire increases, then the drift velocity of the electron in it:
    (a) increases and thermal velocity of the electron decreases
    (b) decreases and thermal velocity of the electron decreases
    (c) increases and thermal velocity of the electron increases
    (d) decreases and thermal velocity of the electron increases

13. The element of a heater is rated (P, V). If it is connected across a source of voltage $\dfrac{V}{2}$, then the power consumed by it will be :
    (a) P
    (b) 2P
    (c) $\dfrac{P}{2}$
    (d) $\dfrac{P}{4}$

14. The plot represents the flow of current through a wire at three different times.

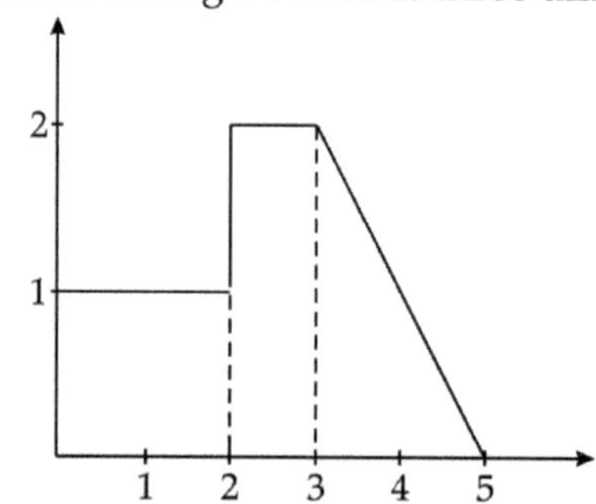

    (a) $2:1:2$
    (b) $1:3:3$
    (c) $1:1:1$
    (d) $2:3:4$

15. Biot-savart law indicates that the moving electrons (with velocity v) produce a magnetic field B such that:
    (a) $B \perp v$
    (b) $B \parallel v$
    (c) it obeys inverse cube law
    (d) it is along the line joining the electron and point of observation.

16. A current flow along the length of an infinitely long, straight thin-walled pipe. Then:
    (a) the magnetic field at all points inside the pipe is same, but not zero
    (b) the magnetic field at any point inside the pipe is zero
    (c) the magnetic field is zero only on the axis of the pipe
    (d) the magnetic field is different at different points inside the pipe

17. Two charged particles traverse identical helical paths in a completely opposite sense in a uniform magnetic field $B = B_0 k$.
    (a) They have equal z-components of momenta.
    (b) They must have equal charges.
    (c) They necessarily represent a particle-antiparticle pair.
    (d) The charge to mass ratio satisfy:
$$\left(\frac{e}{m}\right)_1 + \left(\frac{e}{m}\right)_2 = 0$$

18. The magnetism of a magnet is due to:
    (a) earth
    (b) cosmic rays
    (c) due to pressure of big magnet inside the earth
    (d) spin motion of electrons
19. The relation between the magnetic length (L_e) and the geometric length (L_g) is best represented by:
    (a) $L_e > L_g$
    (b) $L_e = L_g$
    (c) $L_e < L_g$
    (d) $L_e = L_g = \infty$
20. Eddy currents can be minimized by using:
    (a) thin wires
    (b) thin sheets of metal
    (c) thick sheets
    (d) laminated sheets
21. A 1.0 m metallic rod is rotated with an angular velocity of 400 rad/s about an axis normal to the rod passing through its one end. The other end of the rod is in contact with a circular metallic ring. A constant and uniform magnetic field of 0.5 T parallel to the axis exists everywhere.
    Calculate the emf developed between the centre and the ring.
    (a) 99 V
    (b) 100 V
    (c) 102 V
    (d) 105 V
22. A square of side L metres lies in the xy-plane in a region, where the magnetic field is given by
    $B = B_0(2\hat{i} + 4\hat{j} + 4\hat{k})\,T$, where B_0 is constant. The magnitude of flux passing through the square is:
    (a) $2B_0L^2\,Wb$
    (b) $3B_0L^2\,Wb$
    (c) $4B_0L^2\,Wb$
    (d) $\sqrt{29}B_0L^2\,Wb$
23. In a series resonant circuit, having L, C and R as its element, the resonance current is i. The power dissipated in circuit at resonance is:
    (a) Zero
    (b) i^2R
    (c) $i^2\omega L$
    (d) $\dfrac{i^2R}{\left(\omega L - \dfrac{1}{\omega C}\right)}$
24. Alternating current is transmitted to distant places:
    (a) at high voltage and low current
    (b) at high voltage and high current
    (c) at low voltage and low current
    (d) at low voltage and high current
25. Alternating current cannot be measured by D.C. ammeter because:
    (a) A.C. cannot pass through D.C. ammeter
    (b) A.C. changes direction
    (c) average value of current for complete cycle is zero
    (d) D.C. ammeter will get damaged

Section - B

This section consists of 24 multiple choice questions with overall choice to attempt any 20 questions. In case more than desirable number of questions are attempted, ONLY first 20 will be considered for evaluation

26. A comb runs through one's dry hair attracts small bits of paper. This happens because:
    (a) comb is a good conductor
    (b) paper is a good conductor
    (c) the atoms in the paper get polarised by the charged comb
    (d) the comb possesses magnetic properties
27. Force (F) between two charges varies with distance (r) between them as:

(a) 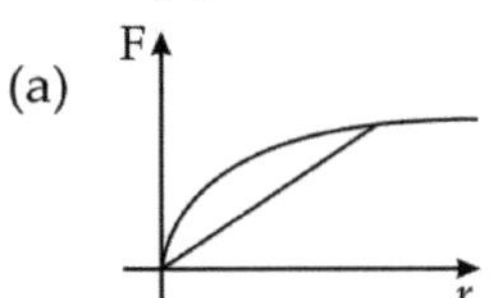
(b) 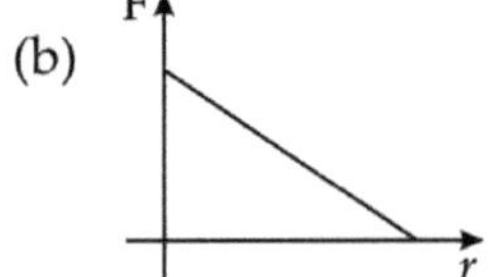
(c) 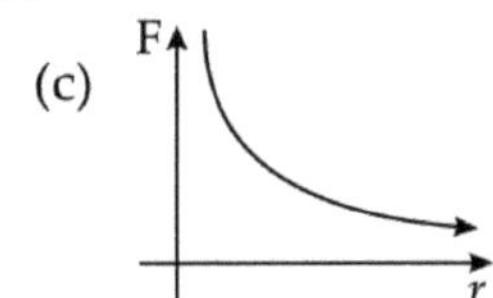
(d) 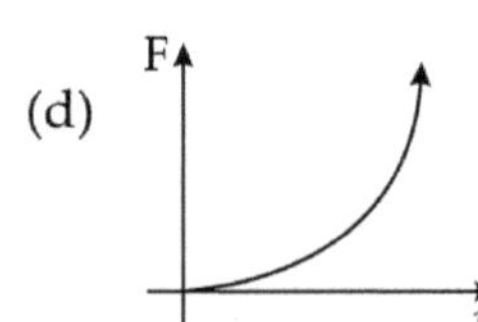

28. The force of interaction between two charges $q_1 = 6\ \mu C$ and $q_2 = 2\ \mu C$ is 12 N. If charge $q = -2\ \mu C$ is added to each of the charges, then the new force of interaction is:
    (a) 2×10^{-7} N
    (b) zero
    (c) 30 N
    (d) 2×10^{-3} N

29. When a person combs his hair, static electricity is sometimes generated by which process ?
    (a) Contact between the comb and hair results in a charge
    (b) Friction between the comb and hair results in the transfer of electrons
    (c) Conduction between the comb and hair
    (d) Induction between the comb and hair
30. A positively charged particle is released from rest in a uniform electric field. The electric potential energy of the charge:
    (a) remains constant because the electric field is uniform
    (b) increases because the charge moves along the electric field
    (c) decreases because the charge moves along the electric field
    (d) decreases because the charge moves opposite to the electric field
31. On what factor does the sharpness of resonance depends in a LCR circuit ?
    (a) It depends on resistance
    (b) It depends on capacitance
    (c) It depends on Inductance
    (d) All of these
32. Can we use capacitors instead of choke coil for reducing current in an A.C. circuit ? Why ?
    (a) Yes
    (b) No
    (c) Maybe
    (d) None of them
33. The electrical resistance of a conductor:
    (a) varies directly to its area of cross-section
    (b) decreases with increase in its temperature
    (c) decreases with increase in its conductivity
    (d) is independent of its shape but depends only on its volume
34. A charge of 60 C passes through an electric lamp in 2 minutes. Then the current in the lamp is:
    (a) 30 A
    (b) 1 A
    (c) 0.5 A
    (d) 5 A
35. Charge through a conductor is given as a function of time t as $q = 4t^2 + 4t + 4$ coulomb. At $2s$ what is the current flowing ?
    (a) 12 A
    (b) 8 A
    (c) 20 A
    (d) 28 A
36. A steady current is flowing through a conductor of non-uniform cross-section. The charge passing through any cross-section of it per unit time is:
    (a) directly proportional to the area of cross-section
    (b) inversely proportional to the area of cross-section
    (c) proportional to square of the area of cross-section
    (d) independent of the area of cross-section
37. The electric resistance of a certain wire of iron is R. If its length and radius are both doubled, then:
    (a) the resistance and the specific resistance will both remain unchanged
    (b) the resistance will be doubled, and the specific resistance will be halved
    (c) the resistance will be halved, and the specific resistance will remain unchanged
    (d) the resistance will be halved, and the specific resistance will be doubled
38. An isosceles right angled current carrying loop PQR is placed in a uniform magnetic field $\vec{B}$ pointing along PR. If the magnetic force acting on the arm PQ is F, then the magnetic force which acts on the arm QR will be:

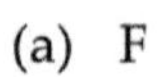

(a) F
(b) 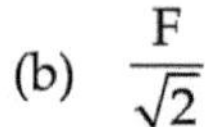 $\dfrac{F}{\sqrt{2}}$
(c) $\sqrt{2}F$
(d) –F

39. In which condition an electron will move undeflected in the presence of crossed electric and magnetic field ?
    (a) When electric and magnetic field in parallel
    (b) When Electric and magnetic field in perpendicular
    (c) Both (a) and (b)
    (d) None of them

40. When a magnetic compass needle is carried nearby to a straight wire carrying current, then:
    (I)   the straight wire cause a noticeable deflection in the compass needle.
    (II) the alignment of the needle is tangential to an imaginary circle with straight wire as its centre and has a plane perpendicular to the wire.
    (a) (I) is correct
    (b) (II) is correct
    (c) Both (I) and (II) are correct
    (d) Neither (I) nor (II) is correct.

41. Which of the following phenomena makes use of electromagnetic induction?
    (a) Magnetising an iron piece with a bar magnet
    (b) Generation of hydroelectricity
    (c) Magnetising a soft iron piece by placing inside a current carrying solenoid
    (d) Charging a storage battery

42. When an AC voltage of 220 V is applied to the capacitor C, then:
    (a) the current is in phase with the applied voltage
    (b) power delivered to the capacitor per cycle is zero
    (c) the maximum voltage between plates is 220 V
    (d) the charge on the plate is not in phase with the applied voltage

43. Which of the following statement is not true ?
    (a) Electrostatic force is a conservative force
    (b) Potential energy of charge q at a point is the work done per unit charge in bringing a charge from any point to infinity
    (c) Spring force and gravitational force are conservative force
    (d) Both (a) and (c)

44. A current carrying solenoid is approaching a conducting loop as shown in the figure. The direction of induced current as observed by an observer on the other side of the loop will be:

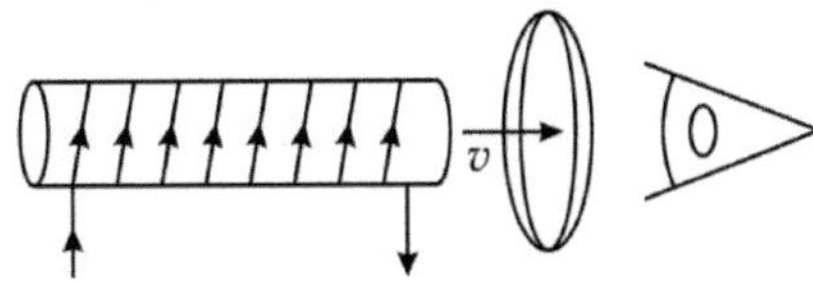

    (a) Clockwise   (b) Anti-clockwise   (c) East   (d) West

45. Given below are two statements labelled as Assertion (A) and Reason (R)

    Assertion (A): The current density $\vec{j}$ at any point in ohmic resistor is in direction of electric field $\vec{E}$ at that point.

    Reason (R): A point charge when released from rest in a region having only electrostatic field always moves along electric lines of force.
    (a) Both A and R are true and R is also the correct explanation of A.
    (b) Both A and R are true but R is not the correct explanation of A.
    (c) A is true but R is false.
    (d) A is false and R is also false.

46. Given below are two statements labelled as Assertion (A) and Reason (R)
    Assertion (A): Work done in moving a charge between any two points in an electric field is dependent of the path followed by the charge, between these points.
    Reason (R): Electrostatic force is a non-conservative force.

(a) Both A and R are true and R is also the correct explanation of A.

(b) Both A and R are true but R is not the correct explanation of A.

(c) A is true but R is false.

(d) A is false and R is also false.

47. Given below are two statements labelled as Assertion (A) and Reason (R)

Assertion (A): Magnetic field on the axial line at a certain distance is twice as compared to that on the equatorial line at the same distance.

Reason (R): Electric field due to a dipole varies inversely as the cube of the distance.

(a) Both A and R are true and R is also the correct explanation of A.

(b) Both A and R are true but R is not the correct explanation of A.

(c) A is true but R is false.

(d) A is false and R is also false.

48. Given below are two statements labelled as Assertion (A) and Reason (R)

Assertion (A): Faraday's laws are consequence of conservation of energy.

Reason (R): In a purely resistive AC circuit, the current lags behind the emf in phase.

(a) Both A and R are true and R is also the correct explanation of A.

(b) Both A and R are true but R is not the correct explanation of A.

(c) A is true but R is false.

(d) A is false and R is also false.

49. Given below are two statements labelled as Assertion (A) and Reason (R)

Assertion (A): The charge on any body can be increased or decreased in terms of e.

Reason (R): Quantization of charge means that the charge on a body is the integral multiple of e.

(a) Both A and R are true and R is also the correct explanation of A.

(b) Both A and R are true but R is not the correct explanation of A.

(c) A is true but R is false.

(d) A is false and R is also false.

Section – C

This section consists of 6 multiple choice questions with an overall choice to attempt any 5. In case more than desirable number of questions are attempted, ONLY first 5 will be considered for evaluation

50. Two identical charged spheres suspended from a common point by two massless strings of lengths l, are initially at a distance d ($d \ll l$) apart because of their mutual repulsion. The charges begin to leak from both the spheres at a constant rate. As a result, the spheres approach each other with a velocity v. Then v varies as a function of the distance x between the spheres, as:

(a) $v \propto x^{\frac{1}{2}}$
(b) $v \propto x$
(c) $v \propto x^{-\frac{1}{2}}$
(d) $v \propto x^{-1}$

51. Figure shows some equipotential lines distributed in space. A charged object is moved from point A to point B.

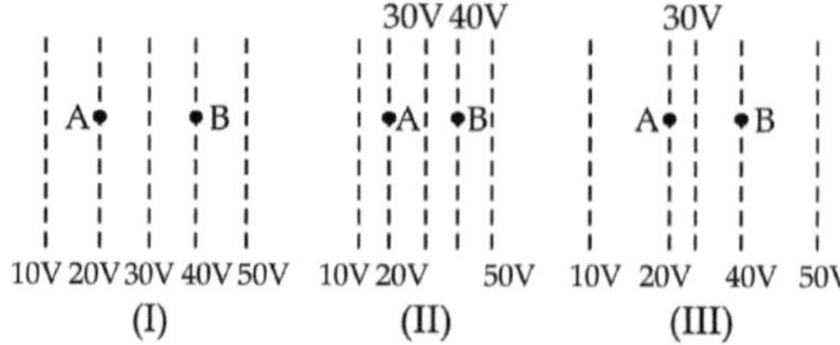

(a) The work done in figure (I) is the greatest.

(b) The work done in figure (II) is the least.

(c) The work done is the same in figure (I), (II) and (III).

(d) The work done in figure (III) is greater than figure (II) but equal to that in figure (I).

Case Study: Read the following paragraph and answer the questions:

A magnetic field can be produced by moving charges or electric currents. The basic equation governing the magnetic field due to a current distribution is the Biot-Savart law.

Finding the magnetic field resulting from a current distribution involves the vector product and is inherently a calculus problem when the distance from the current to the field point is continuously changing.

According to this law, the magnetic field at a point due to a current element of length $\vec{dl}$ carrying current I, at a distance r from the element is $dB = \dfrac{\mu_0}{4\pi} \dfrac{I(d\vec{I} \times \vec{r})}{r^3}$.

Biot-Savart law has certain similarities as well as difference with Coulomb's law for electrostatic field *e.g.,* there is an angle dependence in Biot-Savart law which is not present in electrostatic case.

52. The direction of magnetic field $d\vec{B}$ due to a current element $I\vec{dI}$ at a point of distance $\vec{r}$ from it, when a current I passes through a long conductor is in the direction:

    (a) of position vector $\vec{r}$ of the point

    (b) of current element $d\vec{I}$

    (c) perpendicular to both $d\vec{I}$ and $\vec{r}$

    (d) perpendicular to $\vec{I}$ only

53. The magnetic field due to a current in a straight wire segment of length L at a point on its perpendicular bisector at a distance $r(r \gg L)$:

    (a) decreases as $\dfrac{1}{r}$

    (b) decreases as $\dfrac{1}{r^2}$

    (c) decreases as $\dfrac{1}{r^3}$

    (d) approaches a finite limit as $r \to \infty$

54. Two long straight wires are set parallel to each other. Each carries a current i in the same direction and the separation between them is $2r$. The intensity of the magnetic field midway between them is:

    (a) $\propto_0 \dfrac{i}{r}$

    (b) $4\propto_0 \dfrac{i}{r}$

    (c) zero

    (d) $\propto_0 \dfrac{i}{4r}$

55. A long straight wire carries a current along the z-axis for any two points in the x-y plane. Which of the following is always false?

    (a) The magnetic fields are equal

    (b) The directions of other magnetic fields are the same

    (c) The magnitudes of the magnetic fields are equal

    (d) The field at one point is opposite to that at the other point

❏❏

Sample Paper 2

Physics

Section – A

This section consists of 25 multiple choice questions with overall choice to attempt any 20 questions. In case more than desirable number of questions are attempted, ONLY first 20 will be considered for evaluation.

1. The potential at a point due to a charge of 4×10^{-7} C located 10 cm away is:
   (a) 3.6×10^5 V (b) 3.6×10^4 V (c) 4.5×10^4 V (d) 4.5×10^5 V

2. The work done in taking a charge q one round a circle of radius r having a charge Q at the centre is:
   (a) $\dfrac{qQ}{4\pi\varepsilon_0 r}$ (b) $\dfrac{qQ}{4\pi\varepsilon_0 r^2}$ (c) $\dfrac{qQ}{4\pi\varepsilon_0}(2\pi r)$ (d) zero

3. A point charge $+q$, is placed at a distance from an isolated conducting plane. The field at a point P on the other side of the plane is:
   (a) directed perpendicular to the plane and away from the plane.
   (b) directed perpendicular to the plane but towards the plane
   (c) directed radially away from the point charge.
   (d) directed radially towards the point charge.

4. When the separation between two charges is increased, the electric potential of the charges:
   (a) increases
   (b) decreases
   (c) remains the same
   (d) may increase or decrease

5. Four Capacitors of capacitance 2 μF each are connected in series. What will be the capacitance of the equivalent capacitors ?
   (a) 0.2 μF (b) 0.4 μF (c) 0.5 μF (d) 0.8 μF

6. Two charges of magnitudes $-2Q$ and $+Q$ are located at point $(a, 0)$ and $(4a, 0)$ respectively. What is the electric flux due to these charges through a sphere of radius '$3a$' with its centre at the origin ?
   (a) $\dfrac{Q}{2\varepsilon_0}$ (b) $\dfrac{Q}{\varepsilon_0}$ (c) $-\dfrac{2Q}{\varepsilon_0}$ (d) $\dfrac{2Q}{\varepsilon_0}$

7. If the net electric flux through a closed surface is zero, then we can infer:
   (a) no net charge is enclosed by the surface
   (b) uniform electric field exists within the surface
   (c) electric potential varies from point to point inside the surface
   (d) charge is present inside the surface

8. The filaments of 60 W and 100 W bulbs are of the same length. Then:
   (a) 60 W filament is thicker
   (b) 100 W filament is thicker
   (c) both are of same thickness
   (d) both cannot have same length

9. A resistance R is to be measured using a meter bridge. Student chooses the standard resistances S to be 100 Ω. He finds the null point at $l_1 = 2.9$ cm. He is told to attempt to improve the accuracy. Which of the following is a useful way?
   (a) He should measure l_1 more accurately.
   (b) He should change S to 1000 Ω and repeat the experiment.
   (c) He should change S to 3 Ω and repeat the experiment.
   (d) He should give up hope of a more accurate measurement with a meter bridge.

10. The time rate of flow of charge through any cross section of a conductor is ______.
    (a) electric potential   (b) electric current   (c) electric intensity   (d) electric charge
11. When no current is passed through a conductor:
    (a) the free electrons do not move
    (b) the average speed of a free electron over a large period of time is not zero
    (c) the average velocity of a free electron over a large period of time is zero
    (d) the average of the velocities of all the free electrons at an instant is non-zero
12. Drift velocity of electrons is due to:
    (a) motion of conduction electrons due to random collisions.
    (b) motion of conduction electrons due to electric field E.
    (c) repulsion to the conduction electrons due to inner electrons of ions.
    (d) collision of conduction electrons with each other.
13. The I-V characteristics shown in figure represents:

    (a) ohmic conductors   (b) non-ohmic conductors
    (c) insulators   (d) superconductors
14. If a current of 0.5 A flows in a 60 W lamp, then the total charge passing through it in two hours will be:
    (a) 1800 C   (b) 2400 C   (c) 3000 C   (d) 3600 C
15. If a charged particle enters a magnetic field, then it will:
    (a) always experience a force by the magnetic field
    (b) never experiences any force
    (c) experience a force, if it is moving at right angles to the field
    (d) experience a force, if it is moving parallel to the field
16. A conductor of length 20 cm carries a current of 1 A is kept at an angle with the magnetic field of 4 T. Find
    the angle between the conductor and the magnetic field if it experiences a force of 0.4 N.
    (a) 0°   (b) 30°   (c) 60°   (d) 90°
17. The 'H' quantity (magnetic field intensity) is analogous to which of the following:
    (a) B   (b) D   (c) E   (d) V
18. Which of the following is responsible for the earth's magnetic field?
    (a) Rotational motion of earth   (b) Translational motion of earth
    (c) Convective currents in earth's core (d) Diversive current in earth's core
19. Magnetic field can be produced by:
    (a) a charge at rest.   (b) a changing electric field.
    (c) a moving charge.   (d) both (b) and (c)
20. Lenz's law gives:
    (a) the direction of the induced current
    (b) the magnitude of the induced emf
    (c) the magnitude of the induced current
    (d) both the magnitude and direction of the induced current
21. A moving conductor coil in a magnetic field produces an induced emf. This is in accordance with :
    (a) Lenz's Law   (b) Coulomb's Law
    (c) Faraday's Law   (d) Ampere's Law
22. An induced emf is produced when a magnet is plunged into a coil. The strength of the induced emf is
    independent of:
    (a) number of turns of coil   (b) speed with which the magnet is moved
    (c) the strength of the magnet   (d) the resistivity of the wire of the coil

23. Alternating current cannot be measured by D.C. ammeter because:
    (a) A.C. is virtual
    (b) A.C. changes its direction
    (c) A.C. cannot pass through DC ammeter
    (d) average value of complete cycle is zero

24. The alternating current of equivalent value of $\dfrac{I_0}{\sqrt{2}}$ is:
    (a) rms current
    (b) D.C. current
    (c) peak current
    (d) All of these

25. Quantity that remains unchanged in a transformer is:
    (a) voltage
    (b) current
    (c) frequency
    (d) None of these

Section - B

This section consists of 24 multiple choice questions with overall choice to attempt any 20 questions. In case more than desirable number of questions are attempted, ONLY first 20 will be considered for evaluation

26. What is the electrical force inside a Faraday cage when it is struck by lightning?
    (a) The same as the lightning
    (b) Half that of the lightning
    (c) Zero
    (d) A quarter of the lightning

27. One metallic sphere A is given positive charge whereas another identical metallic sphere B of exactly same mass as of A is given equal amount of negative charge. Then:
    (a) masses of A and B still remain equal
    (b) mass of B increases
    (c) mass of B decreases
    (d) mass of B increases

28. If 10^9 electrons move out of a body to another body every second, then the time required to get a total charge of 1 C on the other body is :
    (a) 250 years
    (b) 100 years
    (c) 198 years
    (d) 150 years

29. Which of the following statements is not true about Gauss's law?
    (a) Gauss's law is not much useful in calculating electrostatic field when the system has some symmetry.
    (b) Gauss's law is based on the inverse square dependence on distance contained in the coulomb's law.
    (c) Gauss's law is true for any closed surface.
    (d) The term q on the right side of Gauss's law includes the sum of all charges enclosed by the surface.

30. The electric potential inside a conducting sphere:
    (a) increases from centre to surface
    (b) decreases from centre to surface
    (c) remains constant from centre to surface
    (d) is zero at every point inside

31. In the given circuit the reading of voltmeter V_1 and V_2 are 300 V each. The reading of the voltmeter V_3 and ammeter A are respectively:

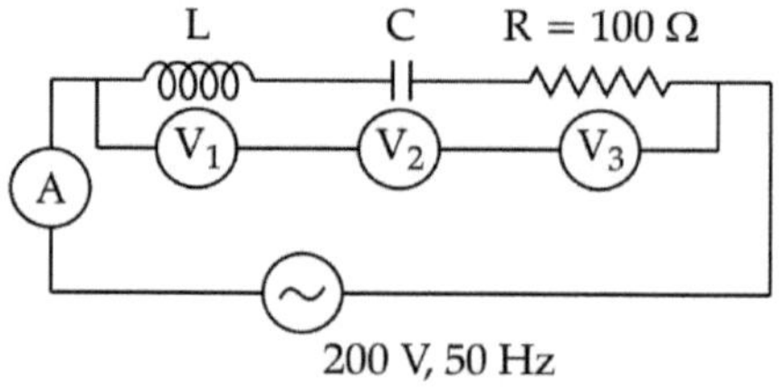

L   C   R = 100 Ω
V_1 V_2 V_3
A
200 V, 50 Hz

    (a) 100 V and 2 A
    (b) 150 V and 2.2 A
    (c) 220 V and 2 A
    (d) 220 V and 2.2 A

32. How does the current in an RC circuit vary when the charge on the capacitor build up?
    (a) It decreases linearly
    (b) It increases linearly
    (c) It decreases exponentially
    (d) It increases exponentially

33. The relaxation time in conductors:
    (a) increases with the increase of temperature
    (b) decreases with the increase of temperature
    (c) it does not depend on temperature
    (d) changes at 400 K

34. The drift velocity of the free electrons in a conducting wire carrying a current i is v. If in a wire of the same metal, but of double the radius, the current be $2i$ then. What will be the drift velocity of the electrons ?
    (a) $\dfrac{1}{2}v$
    (b) $\dfrac{1}{4}v$
    (c) $\dfrac{1}{8}v$
    (d) $\dfrac{2}{3}v$

35. Given a current carrying wire of non-uniform cross-section. Which of the following is constant throughout the length of the wire ?
    (a) Current, electric field and drift speed
    (b) drift speed only
    (c) current and drift speed
    (d) current only
36. A wire has a non-uniform cross-section as shown in the figure. If a steady current is flowing through it, then the drift speed of the electrons:

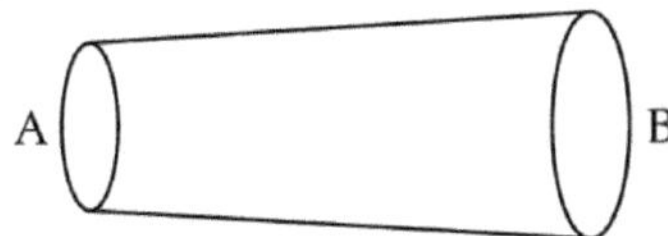

    (a) is constant throughout the wire
    (b) decreases from A to B
    (c) increases from A to B
    (d) varies randomly
37. In a wheat-stone bridge in the battery and galvanometer are interchanged then the deflection in galvanometer will:
    (a) change in previous direction
    (b) not change
    (c) change in opposite direction
    (d) None of these
38. A charged particle moving in a magnetic field experiences a resultant force:
    (a) in the direction perpendicular to both the field and its velocity.
    (b) in the direction of the field.
    (c) in the direction opposite to that of the field.
    (d) None of the above.

39. A charged particle moves with a velocity v in a uniform magnetic field $\vec{B}$. The magnetic force experienced by the particle is:
    (a) never zero.
    (b) always zero.
    (c) zero, if $\vec{B}$ and $\vec{v}$ are parallel.
    (d) zero, if $\vec{B}$ and $\vec{v}$ are perpendicular.
40. If a hole is made at the centre of a bar magnet, then its magnetic moment ______.
    (a) does not change   (b) decreases   (c) increases   (d) vanishes
41. A wire in the form of a tightly wound solenoid is connected to a D.C. source, and carries a current. If the coil is stretched so that there are gaps between successive elements of the spiral coil, will the current increase or decrease ?
    (a) Current will increase
    (b) Current will decrease
    (c) Current remains same
    (d) None of them
42. Find the current passing through battery immediately after key (K) is closed. It is given that initially all the capacitors are uncharged. (Given that: R = 6 Ω and C = 4 μF)

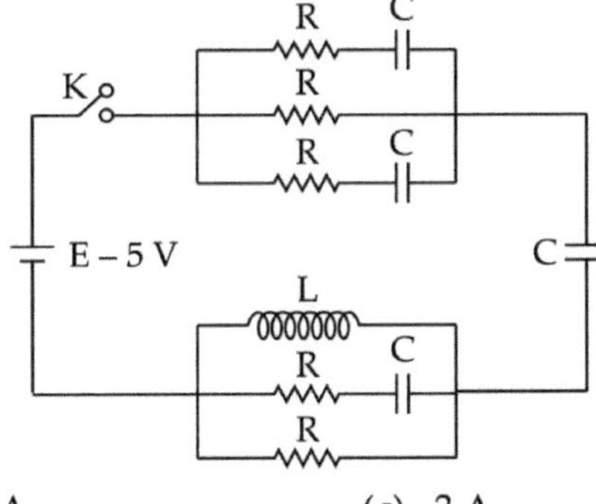

    (a) 1 A   (b) 2 A   (c) 3 A   (d) 5 A
43. A positively charged particle is released from rest in an uniform electric field. The electric potential energy of the charge:
    (a) remains constant because the electric field is uniform
    (b) increases because the charge moves along the electric field
    (c) decreases because the charge moves along the electric field
    (d) decreases because the charge moves opposite to the electric field

44. On cutting a solenoid in half, the field lines remain ______, emerging from one face of the solenoid and entering into the other face.

    (a) alternate   (b) discontinuous   (c) continuous   (d) irregular

45. Given below are two statements labelled as Assertion (A) and Reason (R)

    Assertion (A): In a shunted galvanometer only 10% current passes through the galvanometer. The resistance of the galvanometer is G. Then resistance of the shunt is G/9.

    Reason (R): If S is the resistance of the shunt, then voltage across S and G is same.

    (a) Both A and R are true and R is also the correct explanation of A.

    (b) Both A and R are true but R is not the correct explanation of A.

    (c) A is true but R is false.

    (d) A is false and R is also false.

46. Given below are two statements labelled as Assertion (A) and Reason (R)

    Assertion (A): The properties that the force with which two charges attract or repel each other are not affected by the presence of a third charge.

    Reason (R): Force on any charge due to a number of other charges is the vector sum of all the forces on that charge due to other charges, taken one at a time.

    (a) Both A and R are true and R is also the correct explanation of A.

    (b) Both A and R are true but R is not the correct explanation of A.

    (c) A is true but R is false.

    (d) A is false and R is also false.

47. Given below are two statements labelled as Assertion (A) and Reason (R)

    Assertion (A): Two short magnets are placed on a cork which floats on water. The magnets are placed such that the axis of one produced bisects the axis of other at right angles. Then the cork has neither translational nor rotational motion.

    Reason (R): Net force on the cork is zero.

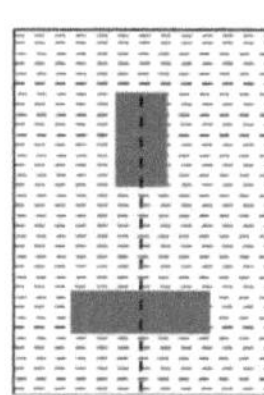

    (a) Both A and R are true and R is also the correct explanation of A.

    (b) Both A and R are true but R is not the correct explanation of A.

    (c) A is true but R is false.

    (d) A is false and R is also false.

48. Given below are two statements labelled as Assertion (A) and Reason (R)

    Assertion (A): Lenz's law is based on the principle of conservation of energy.

    Reason (R): Induced emf always opposes the change in magnetic flux responsible for its production.

    (a) Both A and R are true and R is also the correct explanation of A.

    (b) Both A and R are true but R is not the correct explanation of A.

    (c) A is true but R is false.

    (d) A is false and R is also false.

49. Given below are two statements labelled as Assertion (A) and Reason (R)

    Assertion (A): The electric potential at any point on the equatorial plane of a dipole is non-zero.

    Reason (R): The work done in bringing a unit positive charge from infinity to a point in equatorial plane is not equal for the two charges of the dipole.

    (a) Both A and R are true and R is also the correct explanation of A.

    (b) Both A and R are true but R is not the correct explanation of A.

    (c) A is true but R is false.

    (d) A is false and R is also false.

Section - C

This section consists of 6 multiple choice questions with an overall choice to attempt any 5. In case more than desirable number of questions are attempted, ONLY first 5 will be considered for evaluation

50. Select the correct statements from the following:
(I) inside a charged or neutral conductor, electrostatic field is zero
(II) the electrostatic field at the surface of the charged conductor must be tangential to the surface at any point
(III) there is no net charge at any point inside the conductor
(a) (I) and (II)   (b) (I) and (III)   (c) (II) and (III)   (d) (I), (II) and (III)

51. A parallel plate capacitor having a separation between the plates d, plate area A and material with dielectric constant K has capacitance Co. Now one-third of the material is replaced by another material with dielectric constant 2K, so that effectively there are two capacitors one with area $\frac{1}{3}$ A, dielectric constant 2K and another with area 2.3 A and dielectric constant K. If the capacitance of this new capacitor is C then $\frac{C}{C_0}$ is:

(a) 1   (b) $\frac{4}{3}$ (c) $\frac{2}{3}$ (d) $\frac{1}{3}$

Case Study: Read the following paragraph and answer the questions:

Lenz's Law

This law is mostly used to find the direction current induced in a circuit. According to this law the polarity of e.m.f. induced in the circuit is such that it opposes or checks the variation in magnetic flux responsible for it. If we move North pole of a bar magnet towards coil, then magnetic flux linked with the coil changes (*i.e.*, increases). Due to this current is induced in the coil in anticlockwise direction. The magnetic moment related with the induced current has North polarity towards the North pole. If we move away the bar magnet then magnetic moment has South polarity.

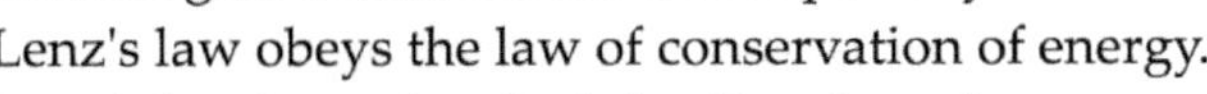

Lenz's law obeys the law of conservation of energy.

52. Lenz's law is used to find the direction of:
(a) Electric field   (b) Force
(c) Induced current   (d) Electrostatic force

53. Lenz's law follows the law of:
(a) Conservation of force   (b) Conservation of mass
(c) Conservation of momentum   (d) Conservation of energy

54. What will be the polarity of magnetic moment towards the magnet if we move the North of magnet towards coil?
(a) North   (b) South
(c) Both (a) and (b)   (d) None of these

55. If we move away the bar magnet from coil then what will be the direction of induced current in coil?
(a) Clockwise   (b) Anticlockwise
(c) Both (a) and (b)   (d) None of these

Sample Paper 3

Physics

Section – A

This section consists of 25 multiple choice questions with overall choice to attempt any 20 questions. In case more than desirable number of questions are attempted, ONLY first 20 will be considered for evaluation.

1. A charge placed at a distance from an electric dipole in the end-on position experiences a force F. If the distance be doubled, the force will become:

   (a) 2 F   (b) $\dfrac{F}{2}$ (c) $\dfrac{F}{4}$ (d) $\dfrac{F}{8}$

2. Electric field is independent of distance of the given surface in which of the case:
   (a) Infinitely long uniformly charged wire
   (b) Infinitely large uniformly charged plane
   (c) Uniformly charged spherical shell
   (d) None of the above

3. Net flux linked to a closed surface around a charge particle is .... times the charge.

   (a) ε_0 (b) $\dfrac{1}{\varepsilon_0}$ (c) ε_0^2 (d) None of these

4. What will the potential difference between the plates if the air between the plates of a capacitor is replaced by a medium of permittivity k.

   (a) It will decreases k times   (b) It will increases k times

   (c) There will be no change   (d) None of them

5. The electric potential at a point in free space due to a charge Q coulomb is $Q \times 10^{11}$ V. The electric field at that point is:

   (a) $12\pi\varepsilon_0 Q \times 10^{22}$ Vm^{-1} (b) $4\pi\varepsilon_0 Q \times 10^{20}$ Vm^{-1}

   (c) $12\pi\varepsilon_0 Q \times 10^{20}$ Vm^{-1} (d) $4\pi\varepsilon_0 Q \times 10^{22}$ Vm^{-1}.

6. Two point charges of $+3\ \mu C$ and $+4\ \mu C$ repel each other with a force of 10 N. If each is given an additional charge of $-6\ \mu C$, the new force is:

   (a) 6 N   (b) 6.5 N   (c) 7.5 N   (d) 7 N

7. Figure shows the field lines of a positive point charge. The work done by the field in moving a small positive charge from Q to P is:

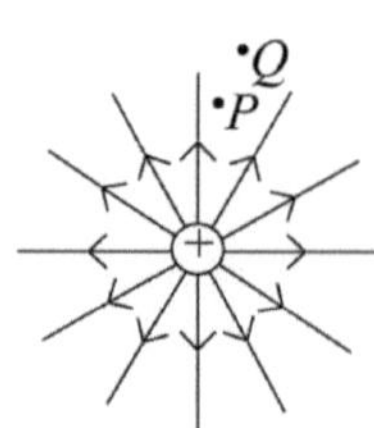

   (a) zero   (b) positive   (c) negative   (d) data insufficient.

8. A steady current flow in a metallic conductor of non-uniform cross-section. The quantity constant along the length of the conductor is:
   (a) Current, electric field and drift speed   (b) Drift speed only
   (c) Current and drift speed   (d) Current only

9. Potential gradient 'k' remains constant until:
   (a) Current in potentiometer wire remains constant
   (b) Potential difference across the potentiometer wire remains constant
   (c) e.m.f. of the testing cell remains constant
   (d) None

10. In current electricity, Ohm's law is obeyed by all:
    (a) Solids   (b) Metals
    (c) Liquids   (d) Gases

11. Consider a current carrying wire (current I) in the shape of a circle. Note that as the current progresses along the wire, the direction of J (current density) changes in an exact manner, while the current I remain unaffected. The agent that is essentially responsible for is:
    (a) source of emf
    (b) electric field produced by charges accumulated on the surface of wire.
    (c) the charges just behind a given segment of wire which push them just the right way by repulsion.
    (d) the charges ahead.

12. A metal wire is subjected to a constant potential difference. When the temperature of the metal wire increases, the drift velocity of the electron in it:
    (a) increases, thermal velocity of electron increases
    (b) decreases, thermal velocity of electron increases
    (c) increases, thermal velocity of electron decreases
    (d) decreases, thermal velocity of electron decreases

13. If N, e, τ and m are representing electron density, charge, relaxation time and mass of an electron respectively, then the resistance of wire of length l and cross-sectional area A is given by:
    (a) $\dfrac{ml}{Ne^2 A\tau}$ (b) $\dfrac{2m\tau A}{Ne^2 l}$ (c) $\dfrac{Ne^2 \tau A}{2ml}$ (d) $\dfrac{Ne^2 A}{2m\tau l}$

14. The direction of drift velocity in a conductor is:
    (a) opposite to that of applied electric field   (b) opposite to the flow of positive charge
    (c) in the direction of the flow of electrons   (d) All of these

15. A galvanometer is said to be sensitive, if it gives a:
    (a) Small deflection for a small current   (b) Small deflection for a large current
    (c) Large deflection for a large current   (d) Large deflection for a small current

16. A current flow along the length of an infinitely long, straight thin-walled pipe. Then:
    (a) the magnetic field at all points inside the pipe is same, but not zero
    (b) the magnetic field at any point inside the pipe is zero
    (c) the magnetic field is zero only on the axis of the pipe
    (d) the magnetic field is different at different points inside the pipe

17. What will be the path of a charged particle moving along the direction of a uniform magnetic field?
    (a) Circular path   (b) Parabolic path
    (c) Straight line path   (d) None of them

18. Angle on the horizontal plane between magnetic North and true North is called:
    (a) Magnetic declination   (b) Electric declination
    (c) Magnetic inclination   (d) Electric inclination

19. The earth's magnetic field varies from point to point in space. Does it also change with time?
    (a) Yes   (b) No   (c) Maybe   (d) None of them

20. An electron is projected with uniform velocity along the axis of a current carrying long solenoid. Which of the following is true?
    (a) The electron will be accelerated along the axis.
    (b) The electron path will be circular about the axis.
    (c) The electron will experience a force at $45°$ to the axis and hence execute a helical path.
    (d) The electron will continue to move with uniform velocity along the axis of the solenoid.

21. The property of coil by which a counter e.m.f. is induced in it when the current through the coil changes is known as :
    (a) Self-induction
    (b) Mutual induction
    (c) Capacitance
    (d) None of these

22. Faraday's laws are consequences of conservation of :
    (a) energy and magnetic field
    (b) energy
    (c) magnetic field
    (d) charge

23. In an AC circuit I = 100 sin 200πt. The time required for the current to achieve its peak value will be:
    (a) $\dfrac{1}{200}$ s
    (b) $\dfrac{1}{400}$ s
    (c) $\dfrac{1}{100}$ s
    (d) $\dfrac{1}{300}$ s

24. The ratio of mean value over half cycle to rms value of AC is:
    (a) $\sqrt{2} : 1$
    (b) $2 : \pi$
    (c) $2\sqrt{2} : \pi$
    (d) $\sqrt{2} : \pi$

25. What is the resistance offered by a capacitor for the steady current?
    (a) one
    (b) zero
    (c) infinity
    (d) depends on the voltage value

Section - B

This section consists of 24 multiple choice questions with overall choice to attempt any 20 questions. In case more than desirable number of questions are attempted, ONLY first 20 will be considered for evaluation

26. What will be the change in electric field, if the charge on an object in halved ?
    (a) Electric field will be doubled
    (b) Electric field will also become half
    (c) Electric field will remain same
    (d) None of them

27. If we increase the charge enclosed by the surface then electric flux will:
    (a) Increases
    (b) Decrease
    (c) Remain same
    (d)   Both (a) and (b)

28. The figure shows a charge +q at point P held in equilibrium in air with the help of four +q charges situated at the vertices of a square. The net electrostatic force on q is given by:

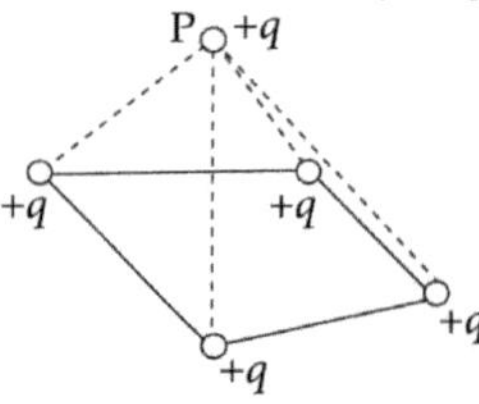

    (a) Newton's law
    (b) Coulomb's law
    (c) Principle of superposition
    (d) Net electric flux out the position of +q

29. As shown in the figure, charges +q and −q are placed at the vertices B and C of an isosceles triangle. The potential at the vertex A is:

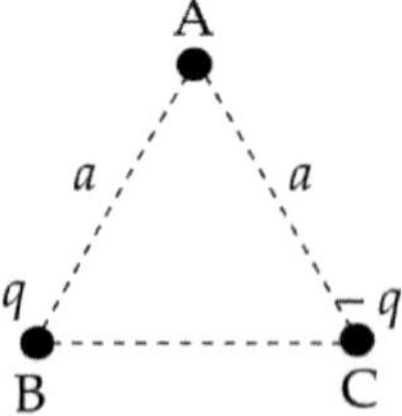

    (a) $\dfrac{1}{4\pi\varepsilon_0} \cdot \dfrac{2q}{\sqrt{a^2}}$
    (b) $\dfrac{1}{4\pi\varepsilon_0} \cdot \dfrac{q}{\sqrt{a^2}}$
    (c) $\dfrac{1}{4\pi\varepsilon_0} \cdot \dfrac{(-q)}{\sqrt{a^2}}$
    (d) zero

30. Four charges each equal to q are placed at the corners of a square of side l. The electric potential at the centre of the square is :
    (a) $\dfrac{1}{4\pi\varepsilon_0} \dfrac{4q}{l}$
    (b) $\dfrac{1}{4\pi\varepsilon_0} \dfrac{4q}{\sqrt{2}l}$
    (c) $\dfrac{1}{\pi\varepsilon_0} \dfrac{\sqrt{2}q}{l}$
    (d) $\dfrac{1}{\pi\varepsilon_0} \dfrac{2q}{l}$

31. At angular frequency 10^3 rad/s, the nature of circuit:

(a) Inductive (b) Capacitive (c) Resistive (d) None of these

32. Same current is flowing in two alternating circuits. The first circuit contains only inductance and the other contains only a capacitor. If the frequency of the emf of AC is increased, the effect on the value of the current will be:

(a) Increases in both the circuits

(b) Decreases in both the circuits

(c) Increases in the first circuit and decreases in the other

(d) Decreases in the first circuit and increases in the other

33. A student connects four cells, each of emf 1.5 V and internal resistance 0.25 Ω in series but one cell has its terminals reversed. This battery sends current in a 2 Ω resistor. What will be the current ?

(a) 2 A (b) 4 A (c) 1 A (d) 3 A

34. A steady current of 1 A is flowing through the conductor. The number of electrons flowing through the cross-section of the conductor in 1 sec is:

(a) 6.25×10^{15} (b) 6.25×10^{17} (c) 6.25×10^{19} (d) 6.25×10^{18}

35. The electric resistance of a certain wire of iron is R. If its length and radius are both doubled, then:

(a) the resistance and the specific resistance both will remain unchanged

(b) the resistance will be doubled, and the specific resistance will be halved

(c) the resistance will be halved, and the specific resistance will remain unchanged

(d) the resistance will be halved, and the specific resistance will be doubled

36. Two wires A and B of the same material, having radii in the ratio 1 : 2 and carry currents in the ratio 4 : 1. The ratio of drift speed of electrons in A and B is:

(a) 16 : 1 (b) 1 : 16 (c) 1 : 4 (d) 4 : 1

37. In a balanced wheatstone network, the resistance in the arms Q and S are interchanged. As a result of this:

(a) network is not balanced

(b) network is still balanced

(c) galvanometer shows zero deflection

(d) galvanometer and the cell must be interchanged to balance.

38. The incorrect statement regarding the lines of force of the magnetic field B is :

(a) Magnetic lines of force form a close curve.

(b) Due to a magnet, magnetic lines of force never cut each other.

(c) Magnetic intensity is a measure of lines of force passing through unit area held normal to it.

(d) Inside a magnet, its magnetic lines of force move from north pole of a magnet toward is south pole.

39. A charged particle of mass m and charge q travels on a circular path of radius r that is perpendicular to a magnetic field B. The time taken by the particle to complete one revolution is:

(a) $\dfrac{2\pi m}{qB}$ (b) $\dfrac{2\pi qB}{m}$ (c) $\dfrac{2\pi mq}{B}$ (d) $\dfrac{2\pi q^2 B}{m}$

40. In the case of bar magnet, lines of magnetic induction:

(a) run continuously through the bar and outside

(b) emerge in circular paths from the middle of the bar

(c) are produced only at the north pole like rays of light from a bulb

(d) start from the north pole and end at the south pole

41. Lenz's law gives:

(a) the direction of the induced current

(b) the magnitude of the induced emf

(c) the magnitude of the induced current

(d) both the magnitude and direction of the induced current

42. In the circuit shown in figure neglecting source resistance the voltmeter and ammeter reading will respectively be:

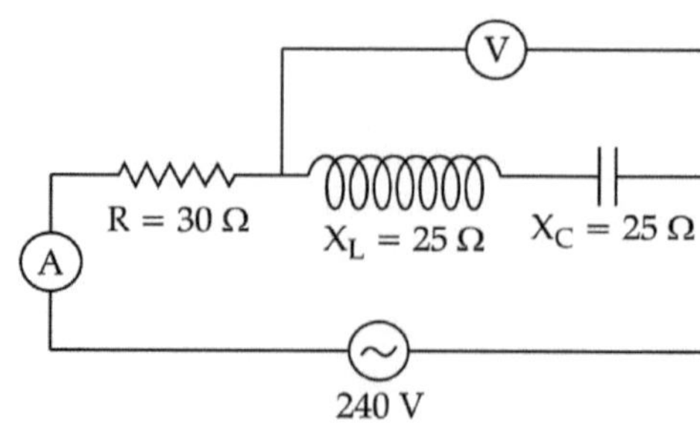

(a) 0 V, 3 A (b) 0 V, 8 A (c) 150 V, 3 A (d) 150 V, 6 A

43. The force of repulsion between two electrons at a certain distance is F. The force between two protons separated by the same distance is: ($m_p = 1836\, m_e$)

(a) 2F (b) F (c) 1836 F (d) $\dfrac{F}{1836}$

44. A conducting rod of length $2l$ is rotating with constant angular speed ω about its perpendicular bisector. A uniform magnetic field $\vec{B}$ exists parallel to the axis of rotation. The emf induced between two ends of the rod is:

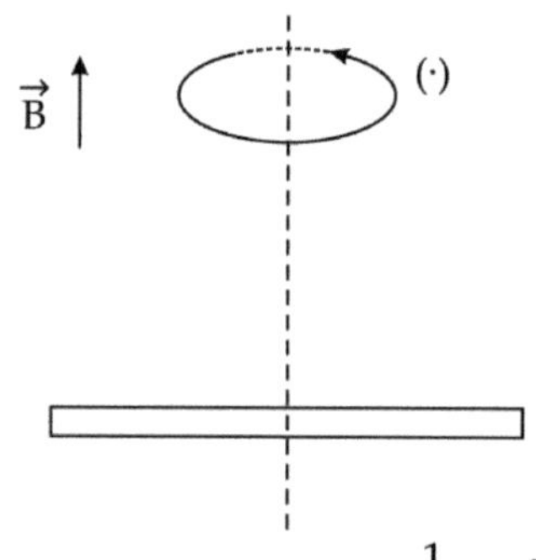

(a) Zero (b) $B\omega l^2$ (c) $\dfrac{1}{2} B\omega l^2$ (d) $\dfrac{1}{8} B\omega l^2$

45. Given below are two statements labelled as Assertion (A) and Reason (R)

Assertion (A): The 200 W bulbs glows with more brightness then 100 W bulbs.

Reason (R): A 100 W bulb has more resistance than a 200 W bulb.

(a) Both A and R are true and R is also the correct explanation of A.

(b) Both A and R are true but R is not the correct explanation of A.

(c) A is true but R is false.

(d) A is false and R is also false.

46. Given below are two statements labelled as Assertion (A) and Reason (R)

Assertion (A): When we rub a glass rod with silk, the rod gets negatively charged and the silk gets positively charged.

Reason (R): On rubbing, electrons from silk cloth move to the glass rod.

(a) Both A and R are true and R is also the correct explanation of A.

(b) Both A and R are true but R is not the correct explanation of A.

(c) A is true but R is false.

(d) A is false and R is also false.

47. Given below are two statements labelled as Assertion (A) and Reason (R)

Assertion (A): Two identical loops, one of copper and another of aluminium are rotated with the same speed in the same magnetic field. The emf induced in both the loop will be same.

Reason (R): The magnitude of induced emf is directly proportional to the rate of change of magnetic flux linked with the circuit.

(a) Both A and R are true and R is also the correct explanation of A.

(b) Both A and R are true but R is not the correct explanation of A.

(c) A is true but R is false.

(d) A is false and R is also false.

48. Given below are two statements labelled as Assertion (A) and Reason (R)

Assertion (A): An alternating current shows magnetic effect.

Reason (R): Alternating current varies with time.

(a) Both A and R are true and R is also the correct explanation of A.

(b) Both A and R are true but R is not the correct explanation of A.

(c) A is true but R is false.

(d) A is false and R is also false.

49. Given below are two statements labelled as Assertion (A) and Reason (R)

Assertion (A): If three capacitors of capacitance $C_1 < C_2 < C_3$ are connected in parallel then their equivalent capacitance $C_p > C_s$.

Reason (R): $\dfrac{1}{C_p} = \dfrac{1}{C_1} + \dfrac{1}{C_2} + \dfrac{1}{C_3}$

(a) Both A and R are true and R is also the correct explanation of A.

(b) Both A and R are true but R is not the correct explanation of A.

(c) A is true but R is false.

(d) A is false and R is also false.

Section – C

This section consists of 6 multiple choice questions with an overall choice to attempt any 5. In case more than desirable number of questions are attempted, ONLY first 5 will be considered for evaluation

50. In figure, two positive charges, q_2 and q_3 fixed along the y-axis, exert a net electric force in the $+x$-direction on a charge fixed along the x-axis. If a positive charge Q is added at $(x, 0)$, the force on q_1:

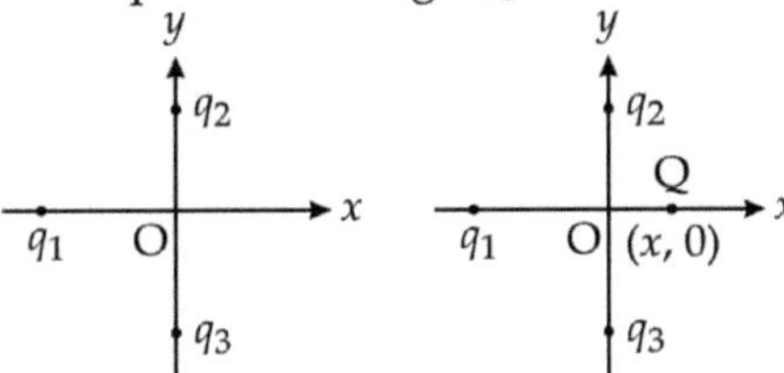

(a) shall increase along the positive x-axis

(b) shall decrease along the positive x-axis

(c) shall point along the negative x-axis

(d) shall increase but the direction changes because of the intersection of Q with q_2 and q_3

51. The energy stored in a parallel plate capacitor is given by $V_E = \dfrac{Q^2}{2C}$. Now which of the following statements is not true ?

(I) The work done in charging a capacitor is stored in the form of electrostatic potential energy given by expression $V_E = \dfrac{Q^2}{2C}$.

(II) The net charge on the capacitor is Q.

(III) The magnitude of the net charge on the plate of a capacitor is Q.

(a) (I) only   (b) (II) only   (c) (I) and (II)   (d) (I), (II) and (III)

Case Study: Read the following paragraph and answer the questions:

The figure shows a series LCR circuit:

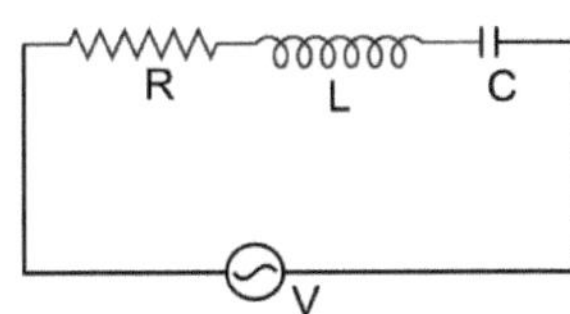

For such a circuit, the impedance $Z = \sqrt{R^2 + (X_L - X_C)^2}$, is given by where X_L and X_C are inductive and capacitive resistances respectively. As the frequency of a.c. is increased, at a particular frequency. X_L become, equal to X_C. For that frequency maximum current occurs. This is because impedance becomes equal is its least value R. Current through the circuit $I = \dfrac{V}{R}$. The circuit behaves like a pure resistive circuit and current and voltage will be in phase. This is called resonance. Frequency of a.c. at which resonance occurs is called resonant frequency. If frequency is less than the resonant frequency, then the capacitive reactance will be more. The circuit will be capacitive in nature and current leads voltage. On the other hand, if frequency is more than the resonant frequency inductive reactance will be more. Circuit is inductive in nature and current lags the voltage.

An LCR circuit with a resistance 50 Ω has a resonant angular frequency 2×10^3 rad/s. At resonance, the voltage across the resistance and inductance are 25 V and 20 V respectively. Then:

52. The value of inductance is:
    (a) 20 mH   (b) 10 mH   (c) 40 mH   (d) 25 mH

53. The value of capacitance is:
    (a) 25 μF   (b) 1 μF   (c) 2 μF   (d) 12.5 μF

54. The impedance at resonance is:
    (a) 50 W   (b) 16 W   (c) 64 W   (d) 25 W

55. Which of the following angular frequency of a.c. will see the circuit as inductive in nature?
    (a) 1.5×10^3 rad/s   (b) 10^3 rad/s   (c) 2×10^3 rad/s   (d) 5×10^3 rad/s

❑❑

Sample Paper 4

Physics

Section – A

This section consists of 25 multiple choice questions with overall choice to attempt any 20 questions. In case more than desirable number of questions are attempted, ONLY first 20 will be considered for evaluation.

1. The capacitance of a capacitor does not depend upon:
   (a) size of the plates
   (b) shape of the plates
   (c) separation between the plates
   (d) charge on the plates

2. A body has a positive charge of 8×10^{-19} C. It has:
   (a) an excess of 5 electrons
   (b) a deficiency of 5 electrons
   (c) an excess of 8 electrons
   (d) a deficiency of 8 electrons

3. If an electron has an initial velocity in a direction different from that of an electric field, the path of the electron is:
   (a) a straight line
   (b) a circle
   (c) an ellipse
   (d) a parabola

4. Can two equipotential surfaces intersect each other?
   (a) Yes
   (b) No
   (c) Sometimes
   (d) Only when surfaces intersect at $90°$

5. If a unit positive charge is taken from one point to another over an equipotential surface, then:
   (a) work is done on the charge
   (b) work is done by the charge
   (c) work done is constant
   (d) no work is done

6. A rectangular frame of area 10 m^2 is placed in a uniform electric field of 20 NC^{-1}, with normal drawn on the surface of the frame making $60°$ angle with the direction of field. What will be the electric flux through the frame ?
   (a) 100 Vm
   (b) 200 Vm
   (c) 50 Vm
   (d) 150 Vm

7. A test charge is moved from lower potential point to a higher potential point. The potential energy of test charge will:
   (a) remains the same
   (b) increase
   (c) decrease
   (d) becomes zero

8. When a current I is set up in a wire of radius r, the drift velocity is v_d. If the same current is set up through a wire of radius $2r$, the drift velocity will be:
   (a) $4v_d$
   (b) $2v_d$
   (c) $\dfrac{v_d}{2}$
   (d) $\dfrac{v_d}{4}$

9. If the resistance of a conductor is 5Ω at $50°$ C and 7Ω at $100°$ C, then mean temperature coefficient of resistance (of material) is:
   (a) 0.013/°C
   (b) 0.004/°C
   (c) 0.006/°C
   (d) 0.008/°C

10. A cylindrical wire has a resistance of $18 \ \Omega$. The resistance of another wire of the same material with the same cross section, but 1.5 times the length is:
    (a) $18 \ \Omega$
    (b) $24 \ \Omega$
    (c) $12 \ \Omega$
    (d) $9 \ \Omega$

11. R is the resistance of a cylindrical wire. If it is stretched to twice of its length, keeping the volume constant, the new resistance will be:
    (a) R
    (b) 2R
    (c) 4R
    (d) $\dfrac{R}{2}$

12. In an experiment, a sample of wire has a resistance $20 \ \Omega$ at $15°$ C. If the experiment is conducted keeping the same wire sample at a temperature of $30°$ C, then the possible value of its resistance can be:
    (a) $20 \ \Omega$
    (b) $10 \ \Omega$
    (c) $15 \ \Omega$
    (d) $22.5 \ \Omega$

13. Conventional current flows from:
    (a) Point of higher potential to lower potential   (b) Point of lower potential to higher potential
    (c) Point of lower potential to lower potential   (d) all of the above

14. In the current against voltage curve in Ohm's law, the slope gives:
    (a) resistance   (b) conductance   (c) resistivity   (d) conductivity

15. A conductor of length 20 cm carries a current of 1 A is kept at an angle with the magnetic field of 4 T. Find the angle between the conductor and the magnetic field if it experiences a force of 0.4 N.
    (a) $0°$ (b) $30°$ (c) $60°$ (d) $90°$

16. A straight wire of diameter 1 mm carries a current of 1 A. It is replaced by another wire of diameter 2 mm, carrying same current. The strength of the magnetic field:
    (a) Twice the former value   (b) One half of the former value
    (c) Same as the former value   (d) One quarter of the former value

17. A charged particle is released from a rest in a region, having steady and uniform electric and magnetic fields. If the two fields are parallel to each other, then the path of the particle will be:
    (a) ellipse   (b) circle   (c) helix   (d) straight line

18. The vertical component of the earth magnetic field is zero at:
    (a) magnetic poles   (b) magnetic equator   (c) Geographic poles   (d) geographic equator

19. What is the relation between angle of dip (δ), B_V and B_H.
    (a) $\sin\delta = \dfrac{B_V}{B_H}$ (b) $\cos\delta = \dfrac{B_V}{B_H}$ (c) $\sec\delta = \dfrac{B_V}{B_H}$ (d) $\tan\delta = \dfrac{B_V}{B_H}$

20. Which of the following phenomena makes use of electromagnetic induction?
    (a) Magnetising an iron piece with a bar magnet
    (b) Generation of hydroelectricity
    (c) Magnetising a soft iron piece by placing inside a current carrying solenoid
    (d) Charging a storage battery

21. The magnetic flux (ϕ) linked with a coil due to its own magnetic field is related to the number (N) of turns of the coil as:
    (a) $\phi \propto N^2$ (b) $\phi \propto N^{-1}$ (c) $\phi \propto N$ (d) $\phi \propto N^{-2}$

22. If the speed of rotation of a dynamo is doubled, then the induced emf will:
    (a) become four times   (b) become half   (c) remain unchanged   (d) become double

23. Quantity that remains unchanged in a transformer is:
    (a) voltage   (b) current   (c) frequency   (d) none of these

24. In an a.c. generator a coil with N turns, each having area A and total resistance R, rotates with frequency ω in a magnetic field B. the maximum value of emf generated in the coil is:
    (a) $NBA\omega$ (b) NAB (c) $NABR\omega$ (d) $NABR$

25. The frequency of an alternating voltage is 50 cps and its amplitude is 120 V. Then the rms value of voltage is:
    (a) 56.5 V   (b) 70.7 V   (c) 101.3 V   (d) 84.8 V

Section – B

This section consists of 24 multiple choice questions with overall choice to attempt any 20 questions. In case more than desirable number of questions are attempted, ONLY first 20 will be considered for evaluation

26. A hollow conducting sphere is placed in an electric field produced by a point charge placed at P as shown in figure. Let V_A, V_B, V_C be the potentials at points A, B and C respectively. Then:

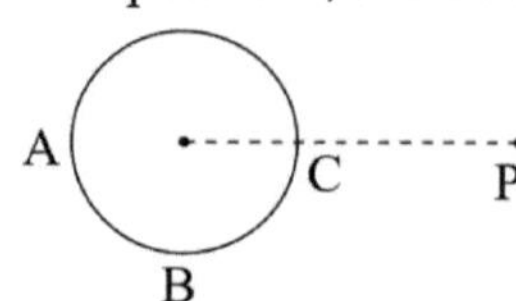

    (a) $V_C > V_B$ (b) $V_B > V_C$ (c) $V_A > V_B$ (d) $V_A = V_C$.

27. Four point charges are placed at the corners of a square ABCD of side 10 cm, as shown in figure. The force on a charge of 1 μC placed at the centre of square is:

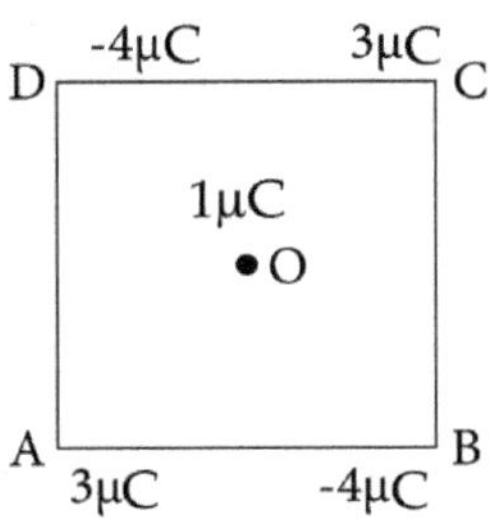

   (a) 7 N   (b) 12 N   (c) 18 N   (d) Zero

28. Three equal charges are placed on the three corners of a square. If the force between q_1 and q_2 is F_{12} and that between q_1 and q_3 is F_{13}, the ratio of magnitudes $\dfrac{F_{12}}{F_{13}}$ is:

   (a) 0.5   (b) 1   (c) 1.5   (d) 2

29. Three charges are placed at the vertices of an equilateral triangle of side 'a' as shown in the following figure. The force experienced by the charge placed at the vertex A in a direction normal to BC is:

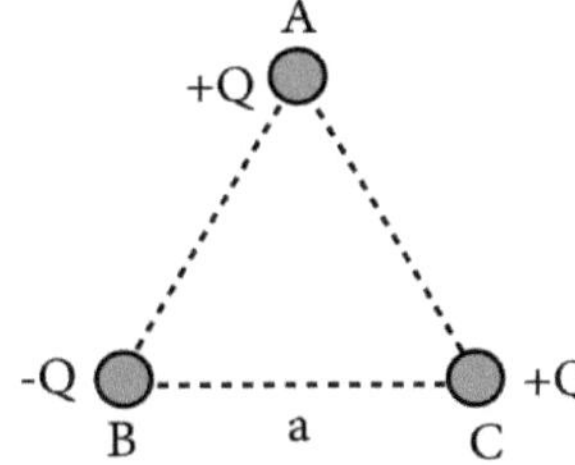

   (a) $\dfrac{Q^2}{(4\pi\varepsilon_0 a^2)}$ (b) $-\dfrac{Q^2}{(4\pi\varepsilon_0 a^2)}$ (c) Zero   (d) 20 N

30. An electric dipole of moment $\vec{p}$ is placed normal to the lines of force of electric field intensity $\bar{E}$, then the work done in deflecting it through an angle of 180° is:

   (a) pE   (b) $2p$E   (c) $-2p$E   (d) zero

31. Can we use capacitors instead of choke coil for reducing current in an a.c. circuit ?

   (a) Yes   (b) No   (c) Maybe   (d) None of them

32. An alternating current of frequency f is flowing in a circuit containing a resistor of resistance R and a choke of inductance L in series. The impedance of this circuit is :

   (a) $R + 2\pi fL$ (b) $\sqrt{R^2 + L^2}$ (c) $\sqrt{R^2 + 2\pi fL}$ (d) $\sqrt{R^2 + 4\pi^2 f^2 L^2}$

33. If a cuboidal conductor is as follows, then its resistance is the most between which pair of points?

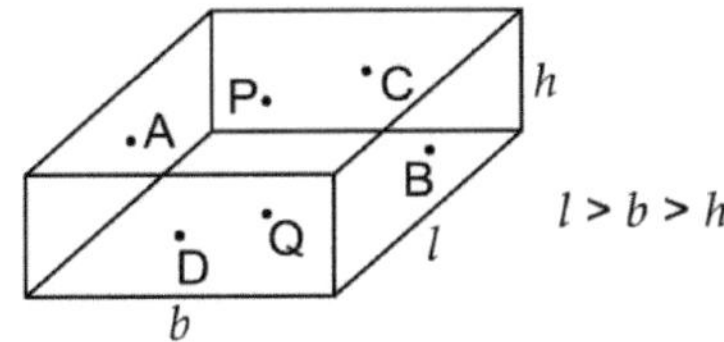

P and Q are the centres of top and bottom surfaces, A and B are those of longer sides and C and D are centres of shorter sides.

   (a) AB   (b) CD

   (c) PQ   (d) All have the same resistance

34. In an experiment, a particular wire sample (A) has a resistance 10 Ω. The person who conducts the experiment has three more sample of wires (B, C and D) of three different materials. All the four samples have the same length and same area of cross section. Resistance of sample B is 15 Ω, that of C is 18 Ω and that of D is 5 Ω.

Choose the incorrect statement from the following:
(a) Resistivity of material of A is less than that of C
(b) Resistivity of material of A twice that of D
(c) Resistivity of B in thrice the resistivity of D
(d) Resistivity of material of C is greater than that of B

35. Drift velocity of a free electron inside a conductor is:
(a) the thermal speed of the free electron
(b) the speed with which a free electron emerges out of the conductor
(c) the average speed acquired by the electron in any direction
(d) the average speed of the electron between successive collisions in the direction opposite to the applied electric field

36. The electric resistance of a certain wire of iron is R. If its length and radius are both doubled, then :
(a) The resistance and the specific resistance will both remain unchanged
(b) The resistance will be doubled, and the specific resistance will be halved
(c) The resistance will be halved, and the specific resistance will remain unchanged
(d) The resistance will be halved, and the specific resistance will be doubled

37. The current-voltage (I-V) graph for a given metallic wire at two different temperatures T_1 and T2 are shown in figure. It follows from the graph that :

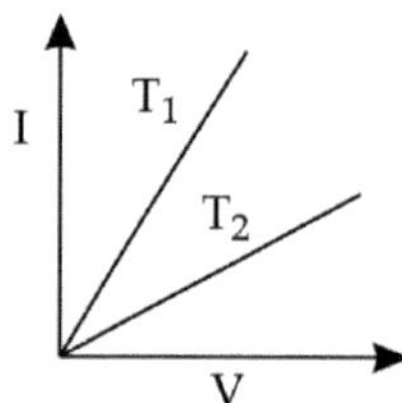

(a) $T_1 > T_2$
(b) $T_1 < T_2$
(c) $T_1 = T_2$
(d) T_1 is greater or less than T_2 depending on whether the resistance R of the wire is greater or less than the ratio $\dfrac{V}{I}$

38. Lorentz force is:
(a) the vector sum of electrostatic and magnetic force acting on a moving charged particle.
(b) the vector sum of gravitational and magnetic force acting on a moving charged particle.
(c) electrostatic force acting on a charged particle
(d) magnetic force acting on a moving charged particle.

39. A copper loop and an aluminium loop are removed from a magnetic field in the same time interval. In which loop will the induced current be greater ?
(a) Copper loop   (b) Aluminium loop   (c) Both (a) and (b)   (d) None of them

40. A north pole of strength 50 Am and south pole of strength 100 Am are separated by a distance of 10 cm in air. Find the force between them.
(a) 20×10^{-6} N   (b) 25×10^{-3} N   (c) 30×10^{-18} N   (d) 50×10^{-3} N

41. The peak value of an alternating emf E given by $E = E_0 \cos \omega t$ is 10 V and its frequency is 50 Hz. At time $t = \dfrac{1}{600}$ s, the instantaneous emf is:
(a) $5\sqrt{3}$ V   (b) 5 V   (c) 10 V   (d) 1 V

42. A series circuit contains a resistor of 20Ω, a capacitor and an ammeter of negligible resistance. It is connected to a source of 220 V – 50 Hz. If the reading of the ammeter is 2.5 A, calculate reactance of the capacitor :
(a) 23.7 Ω   (b) 63.7 Ω   (c) 85.7 Ω   (d) 92.7 Ω

43. A charge q_1 exerts some force on a second charge q_2. If third charge q_3 is brought near, the force of q_1 exerted on q_2:

    (a) decreases

    (b) increases

    (c) remains unchanged

    (d) increases if q_3 is of the same sign as q_1 and decreases if q_3 is of opposite sign

44. A metallic ring is attached with the wall of a room. When the north pole of a magnet is brought near to it, the induced current in the ring will be :

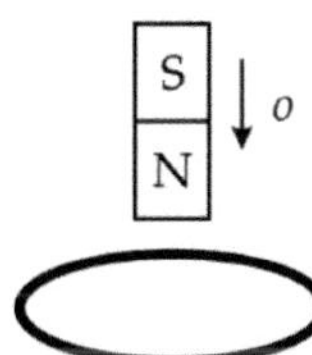

    (a) In clockwise direction   (b) In anticlockwise direction

    (c) First clockwise then anticlockwise   (d) First anticlockwise then clockwise

45. Given below are two statements labelled as Assertion (A) and Reason (R)

Assertion (A): In meter bridge experiment, a high resistance is always connected in series with a galvanometer.

Reason (R): As resistance reads current more accurately then ammeter.

    (a) Both A and R are true and R is also the correct explanation of A.

    (b) Both A and R are true but R is not the correct explanation of A.

    (c) A is true but R is false.

    (d) A is false and R is also false.

46. Given below are two statements labelled as Assertion (A) and Reason (R)

Assertion (A): Free electron always keeps on moving in a conductor even then no magnetic force act on them in magnetic field unless a current is passed through it.

Reason (R): The average velocity of free electron is zero.

    (a) Both A and R are true and R is also the correct explanation of A.

    (b) Both A and R are true but R is not the correct explanation of A.

    (c) A is true but R is false.

    (d) A is false and R is also false.

47. Given below are two statements labelled as Assertion (A) and Reason (R)

Assertion (A): Magnetic moment of helium atom is zero.

Reason (R): All the electron are paired in helium atom orbitals.

    (a) Both A and R are true and R is also the correct explanation of A.

    (b) Both A and R are true but R is not the correct explanation of A.

    (c) A is true but R is false.

    (d) A is false and R is also false.

48. Given below are two statements labelled as Assertion (A) and Reason (R)

Assertion (A): An aircraft flies along the meridian, the potential at the ends of its wings will be the same.

Reason (R): Whenever there is change in the magnetic flux emf induces.

    (a) Both A and R are true and R is also the correct explanation of A.

    (b) Both A and R are true but R is not the correct explanation of A.

    (c) A is true but R is false.

    (d) A is false and R is also false.

49. Given below are two statements labelled as Assertion (A) and Reason (R)

Assertion (A): A current flows in a conductor only when there is an electric field within the conductor.

Reason (R): The drift velocity of electron in presence of electric field decreases.

(a) Both A and R are true and R is also the correct explanation of A.
(b) Both A and R are true but R is not the correct explanation of A.
(c) A is true but R is false.
(d) A is false and R is also false.

Section - C

This section consists of 6 multiple choice questions with an overall choice to attempt any 5. In case more than desirable number of questions are attempted, ONLY first 5 will be considered for evaluation

50. Two spherical conductors B and C having equal radii and carrying equal charges in them repel each other with a force F when kept apart at some distance. A third spherical conductor A having same radius as that of B but uncharged, is brought in contact with B, then brought in contact with C and finally removed away from both. The new force of repulsion between B and C is :

(a) $\dfrac{3F}{4}$ (b) $\dfrac{3F}{8}$ (c) $\dfrac{8F}{3}$ (d) $\dfrac{4F}{3}$

51. A combination of capacitors is set up as shown in the figure. The magnitude of the electric field, due to a point charge Q (having a charge equal to the sum of the charges) on the 4 μF and 9 μF capacitors), at a point distance 30 m from it, would equal :

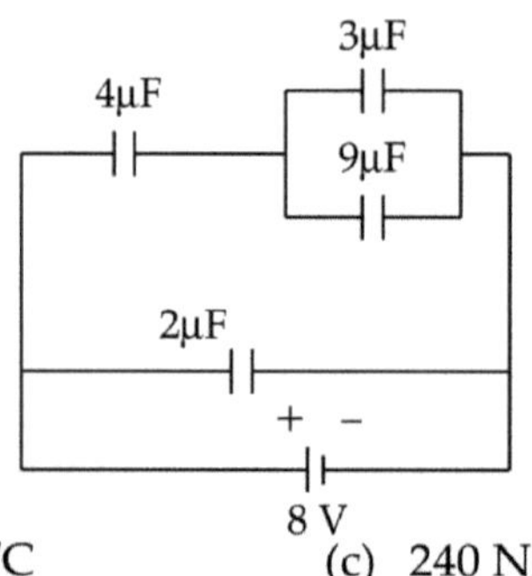

(a) 420 N/C (b) 480 N/C (c) 240 N/C (d) 360 N/C

Case Study: Read the following paragraph and answer the questions:
Biot-Savart's law: Biot Savart law was given by Biot and Savart after doing many experiments. This law is related with the magnetic field induced at a point due to a small current carrying element (conductor). According to the law the magnetic field induced at a point near the current carrying element is directly proportional to the current flowing in conductor, length of the element, sin θ and inversely proportional to the square of the distance of point from the element.

$$dB = \dfrac{\mu_0}{4\pi} \dfrac{idl \sin\theta}{r^2}$$

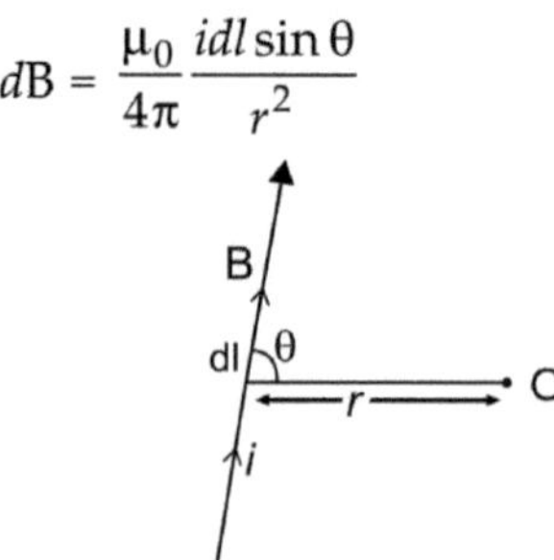

52. Biot Savart law was given by:
    (a) Oersted   (b) Ampere   (c) Biot and Savart   (d) Maxwell
53. Biot Savart law is related with the _________ induced at a point near current carrying element.
    (a) Magnetic field   (b) Gravitational field   (c) Electric field   (d) None of these
54. Induced magnetic field is directly proportional to:
    (a) i (b) dl (c) $\sin\theta$ (d) All of these
55. The magnetic field induced at a point is inversely proportional to:

(a) r^2 (b) r^3 (c) $\dfrac{1}{r}$ (d) $\dfrac{1}{r^2}$

Sample Paper 5

Physics

Section - A

This section consists of 25 multiple choice questions with overall choice to attempt any 20 questions. In case more than desirable number of questions are attempted, ONLY first 20 will be considered for evaluation.

1. In superposition principle, the force acting on the given charge by other charges:
   (a) proportional to the given number charges
   (b) inversely proportional to the given number charges
   (c) unaffected by other charges
   (d) none of the above

2. When the separation between two charges is increased, the electric potential of the charges:
   (a) increases
   (b) Decreases
   (c) remains the same
   (d) may increase or decrease

3. Which of the following has the same charge as the basic unit of charge:
   (a) electron
   (b) proton
   (c) positron
   (d) both (a) and (b)

4. The force per unit charge is known as______.
   (a) electric flux
   (b) electric field
   (c) electric current
   (d) electric potential

5. The electrostatic potential energy of a charge of 5 C at a point in the electrostatic field is 50 J. The potential at that point is:
   (a) 0.1 V
   (b) 5 V
   (c) 10 V
   (d) 250 V

6. Electric lines of force about a negative point charge are______.
   (a) circular anticlockwise
   (b) circular clockwise
   (c) radial, inwards
   (d) radial, outwards

7. When one electron is taken towards the other electron, then the electric potential energy of system :
   (a) decreases
   (b) increases
   (c) remains unchanged
   (d) becomes zero

8. Which of the following characteristics of electrons determine the current in a conductor?
   (a) Drift velocity alone
   (b) thermal velocity alone
   (c) both drift velocity and thermal velocity
   (d) Neither drift nor thermal velocity

9. The basic laws for analyzing an electric circuit are:
   (a) Einstein's theory
   (b) Newton's laws
   (c) Kirchhoff's laws
   (d) Faraday's laws

10. A conductor with a positive charge:
    (a) is always at positive potential
    (b) is always at zero potential
    (c) is always at negative potential
    (d) may be at positive, zero or negative potential

11. There are two metallic spheres of same radii but one is solid and the other is hollow, then
    (a) solid sphere can be given more charge
    (b) hollow sphere can be given more charge
    (c) they can be charged equally (maximum)
    (d) none of the above

12. A potential difference V is applied to a copper wire. If the potential difference is increased to 2V, then the drift velocity of electrons will:
    (a) be double the initial velocity
    (b) remain same
    (c) be $\sqrt{2}$ times the initial velocity
    (d) be half the initial velocity

13. Ohm's law deals with the relation between:

    (a) current and potential difference
    (b) capacity and charge
    (c) capacity and potential
    (d) charge and potential difference

14. Ohm's law is valid when the temperature of the conductor is _____:

    (a) constant
    (b) very high
    (c) very low
    (d) varying

15. A circular loop of magnetic moment M is in an arbitrary orientation in an external magnetic field B. The work done to rotate the loop by 30° about an axis perpendicular to its plane is:

    (a) MB
    (b) $\dfrac{\sqrt{3}}{2}$ MB
    (c) $\dfrac{MB}{2}$
    (d) zero

16. An electron is projected with uniform velocity along the axis of a current carrying long solenoid. Which of the following is true?

    (a) The electron will be accelerated along the axis.
    (b) The electron path will be circular about the axis.
    (c) The electron will experience a force at 45° to the axis and hence execute a helical path.
    (d) The electron will continue to move with uniform velocity along the axis of the solenoid.

17. A charged particle is moving in a circle of radius R with constant speed v, under the influence of a uniform magnetic field. The time period of motion:

    (a) depends on both R and v
    (b) depends on v and not on R
    (c) depends on R and not on v
    (d) is independent of both R and v

18. The 'H' quantity (magnetic field intensity) is analogous to which of the following:

    (a) B
    (b) D
    (c) E
    (d) V

19. Angle on the horizontal plane between magnetic North and true North is called:

    (a) Magnetic declination
    (b) Electric declination
    (c) Magnetic inclination
    (d) Electric inclination

20. Eddy currents are produced when:

    (a) a circular coil is placed in a magnetic field
    (b) a metal is kept in varying magnetic field
    (c) a metal is kept in a steady magnetic field
    (d) current is passes through a circular coil

21. In electromagnetic induction, the induced charge is independent of:

    (a) resistance of the coil
    (b) change of flux
    (c) time
    (d) None of these

22. To induce an emf in a coil, the linking magnetic flux:

    (a) must remain constant
    (b) can either increase or decrease
    (c) must increase
    (d) must decrease

23. When an AC is connected to a resistor what is the phase difference between the current and voltage?

    (a) 90°
    (b) 180°
    (c) 0°
    (d) 60°

24. A resistance of 20 Ω is connected to a source of an alternating potential V = 220 sin (100πt). The time taken by the current to change from its peak value to rms value is:

    (a) 2.5×10^{-3} s
    (b) 25×10^{-3} s
    (c) 0.25 s
    (d) 0.2 s

25. In the case of an inductor:

    (a) Voltage leads the current by $\dfrac{\pi}{4}$
    (b) Voltage leads the current by $\dfrac{\pi}{3}$
    (c) Voltage leads the current by $\dfrac{\pi}{2}$
    (d) Voltage lags the current by $\dfrac{\pi}{2}$

Section - B

This section consists of 24 multiple choice questions with overall choice to attempt any 20 questions. In case more than desirable number of questions are attempted, ONLY first 20 will be considered for evaluation

26. Two charges, each equal to q, are kept at x = –a and x = a on the x-axis. A particle of mass m and charge q0 = q/2 is placed at the origin. If charge q0 is given a small displacement (y << a) along the y-axis, the net force acting on the particle is proportional to:

(a) y
(b) $\dfrac{1}{y}$
(c) $-y$
(d) $-\dfrac{1}{y}$

27. Two insulated charged metallic spheres P and Q have their centres separated by a distance of 50 cm. The radii of P and Q are negligible compared to the distance of separation. The mutual force of electrostatic repulsion if the charge on each is 3.2 × 10⁻² C is:

(a) 3.69×10^{-3} N
(b) 4.69×10^{-3} N
(c) 2.69×10^{-3} N
(d) 3.69×10^{-4} N

28. Among two discs A and B, first have radius 10 cm and charge 10^{-6} C and second have radius 30 cm and charge 10^{-5} C. When they are touched, charge on both q_A and q_B respectively will, be:

(a) $q_A = 2.75$ μC, $q_B = 3.15$ μC
(b) $q_A = 1.09$ μC, $q_B = 1.53$ μC
(c) $q_A = q_B = 5.5$ μC
(d) None of these

29. If one penetrates a uniformly charged spherical cloud, electric field strength:

(a) decreases directly as the distance from the centre
(b) increases directly as the distance from the centre
(c) remains constant
(d) None of these

30. Two charges of equal magnitude 'q' are placed in air at a distance '$2a$' apart and third charge '$-2q$' is placed at midpoint. The potential energy of the system is:
(ε_0 = permittivity of free space) :

(a) $-\dfrac{q^2}{8\pi\varepsilon_0 a}$
(b) $-\dfrac{3q^2}{8\pi\varepsilon_0 a}$
(c) $-\dfrac{5q^2}{8\pi\varepsilon_0 a}$
(d) $-\dfrac{7q^2}{8\pi\varepsilon_0 a}$

31. A 40 Ω electric heater is connected to a 200 V, 50 Hz mains supply. The peak value of electric current flowing in the circuit is approximately:

(a) 10 A
(b) 5 A
(c) 7 A
(d) 2.5 A

32. A current of a 1 A flows through a coil, when a 100 V DC is applied to it. But a current of 0.5 A flows through the same coil, when a 100 V AC of frequency 50 Hz is applied. The resistance and inductance of the coil are given by :

(a) 50 Ω, $\sqrt{0.2}$ H
(b) 50 Ω, $\sqrt{0.3}$ H
(c) 100 Ω, $\sqrt{0.2}$ H
(d) 100 Ω, $\sqrt{0.3}$ H

33. A wire has a non-uniform cross-section as shown in the figure. If a steady current is flowing through it, then the drift speed of the electrons:

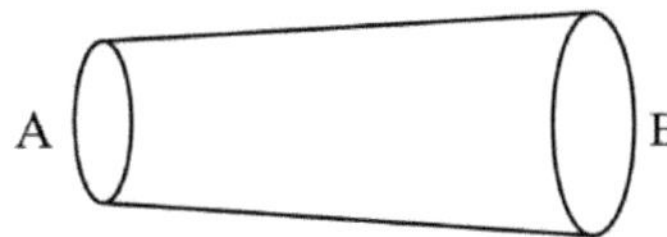

(a) is constant throughout the wire
(b) decreases from A to B
(c) increases from A to B
(d) varies randomly

34. A potential difference of 10 V is applied across a conductor of length 0.1 m. If the drift velocity of electrons is 2 × 10⁻⁴ m/s, the electron mobility is ______ $m^2V^{-1}s^{-1}$.

(a) 1×10^{-6}
(b) 2×10^{-6}
(c) 3×10^{-6}
(d) 4×10^{-6}

35. When the length and area of cross-section both are doubled, then its resistance:

(a) will become half
(b) will be doubled
(c) will remain the same
(d) will become four times

36. For a metallic wire, the ratio V/I (V = the applied potential difference, I = current flowing):
    (a) is independent of temperature
    (b) increases as the temperature rises
    (c) decreases as the temperature rises
    (d) increases or decreases as temperature rises, depending upon the metal

37. If a conductor has a potential zero and there are no charges anywhere else outside, then:
    (a) there must be charges on the surface or inside itself
    (b) there cannot be any charge in the body of the conductor
    (c) there must be charges only on the surface
    (d) both (a) and (b) are correct

38. A charged particle is moving with velocity v in a magnetic field of induction B. The force on the particle will be maximum when:
    (a) v and B are at an angle of 45°
    (b) v and B are perpendicular
    (c) v and B are in the same directions
    (d) v and B are in opposite directions

39. An α-particle enters a magnetic field of 1 T with a velocity 10^6 m/s in a direction perpendicular to the field. The force on α-particle is:
    (a) 1.6×10^{-3} N
    (b) 3.2×10^{-13} N
    (c) 4.8×10^{-13} N
    (d) 7.6×10^{-12} N

40. Which of the following is responsible for the earth's magnetic field?
    (a) Rotational motion of earth
    (b) Translational motion of earth
    (c) Convective currents in earth's core
    (d) Diversive current in earth's core

41. The magnetic flux through a circuit of resistance R changes by an amount $\Delta\phi$ in a time Δt. Then the total quantity of electric charge Q that passes through any point in the circuit during the time Δt is represented by:
    (a) $Q = \dfrac{\Delta\phi}{R}$
    (b) $Q = R\dfrac{\Delta\phi}{\Delta t}$
    (c) $Q = \dfrac{1}{R} \cdot \dfrac{\Delta\phi}{\Delta t}$
    (d) $Q = \dfrac{\Delta\phi}{\Delta t}$

42. A coil has an industance of 0.7 H and is joined in series with a resistance of 220 Ω. When the alternating emf of 220 V at 50 Hz is applied to it then the phase through which current lags behind the applied emf and the wattless component of current in the circuit will be respectively :
    (a) 36°, 1 A
    (b) 30°, 1.5 A
    (c) 45°, 0.5 A
    (d) 60°, 1.5 A

43. Q amount of electric charge is present on the surface of a sphere having radius R. Then electrical potential energy of this system is:
    (a) $\dfrac{kQ}{R}$
    (b) $\dfrac{kQ^2}{R^2}$
    (c) $\dfrac{kQ^2}{2R}$
    (d) $\dfrac{kQ^2}{2R^2}$

44. Two coils have a mutual inductance 0.005 H. The current changes in first coil according to equation $I = I_0 \sin wt$ where $I_0 = 10$ A and $w = 100\pi$ radian/sec. The max value of emf in s coil is :
    (a) π
    (b) 5π
    (c) 4π
    (d) 2π

45. Given below are two statements labelled as Assertion (A) and Reason (R)
    Assertion (A): Fuse wire must have high resistance and low melting point.
    Reason (R): Fuse is used for small current flow only.
    (a) Both A and R are true and R is also the correct explanation of A.
    (b) Both A and R are true but R is not the correct explanation of A.
    (c) A is true but R is false.
    (d) A is false and R is also false.

46. Given below are two statements labelled as Assertion (A) and Reason (R)
    Assertion (A): Coulomb force is the dominating force in the universe.
    Reason (R): Coulomb force is weaker than the gravitational force.
    (a) Both A and R are true and R is also the correct explanation of A.
    (b) Both A and R are true but R is not the correct explanation of A.
    (c) A is true but R is false.
    (d) A is false and R is also false.

47. Given below are two statements labelled as Assertion (A) and Reason (R)

    Assertion (A): Two beams of electrons travelling in the same direction repel each other.

    Reason (R): The electrostatic interaction is less than the magnetic interaction.

    (a) Both A and R are true and R is also the correct explanation of A.

    (b) Both A and R are true but R is not the correct explanation of A.

    (c) A is true but R is false.

    (d) A is false and R is also false.

48. Given below are two statements labelled as Assertion (A) and Reason (R)

    Assertion (A): When charges are shared between any two bodies, no charge is really lost, but some loss of energy does occur.

    Reason (R): Some of the energy is dissipated in the form of heat, sparkling, etc.

    (a) Both A and R are true and R is also the correct explanation of A.

    (b) Both A and R are true but R is not the correct explanation of A.

    (c) A is true but R is false.

    (d) A is false and R is also false.

49. Given below are two statements labelled as Assertion (A) and Reason (R)

    Assertion (A): An induced current will be developed in a conductor, if it is moved in a direction parallel to magnetic field.

    Reason (R): Whenever there is relative motion between loop and magnet an induced current is produced in the loop.

    (a) Both A and R are true and R is also the correct explanation of A.

    (b) Both A and R are true but R is not the correct explanation of A.

    (c) A is true but R is false.

    (d) A is false and R is also false.

Section – C

This section consists of 6 multiple choice questions with an overall choice to attempt any 5. In case more than desirable number of questions are attempted, ONLY first 5 will be considered for evaluation

50. The electric flux through the surface :

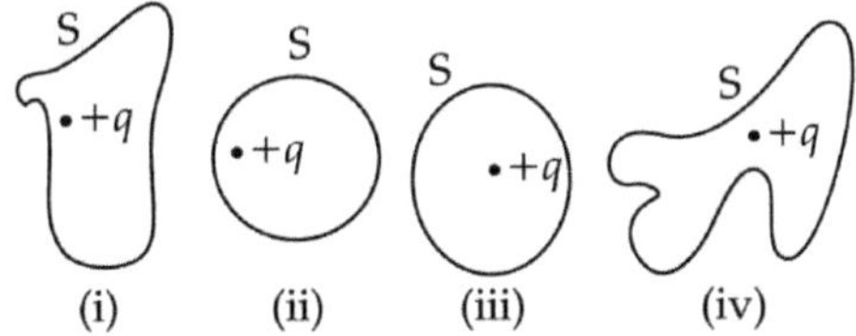

    (a) in figure (iv) is the largest

    (b) in figure (iii) is the least

    (c) in figure (ii) is same as in figure (iii) but is smaller than figure (iv)

    (d) is the same for all the figures

51. In the given circuit diagram, both capacitors are initially uncharged. The capacitance $C_1 = 2$ F and $C_2 = 4$ F emf of battery A and B are 2V and 4V respectively.

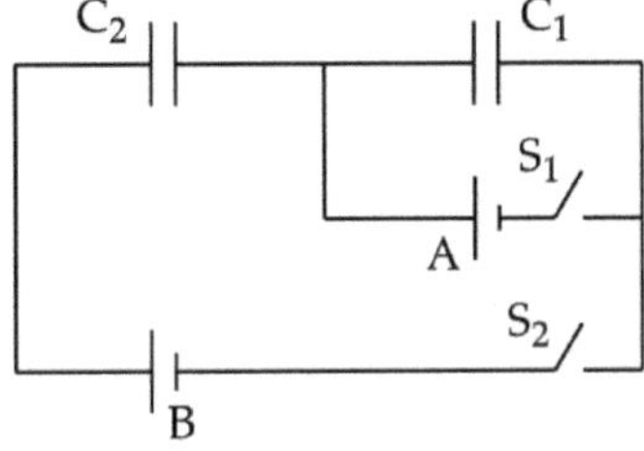

Column I	Column II
A. Switch S_1 is open and S_2 is closed, work done by battery B is	(i) $\dfrac{64}{3}$
B. On closing switch S_1 with S_2 open work done by battery A is	(ii) 4
C. Charge on capacitor C_2 is (after S_1, open and S_2 closed)	(iii) 8
D. Charge on C_1 when both are closed	(iv) $\dfrac{16}{3}$

(a) A (iv), B (i), C (ii), D (iii) (b) A (iii), B (i), C (iv), D (ii)

(c) A (ii), B (iii), C (iv), D (i) (d) A (iv), B (iii), C (i), D (ii)

Case Study: Read the following paragraph and answer the questions:

When an inducator is connected to a source of emf and the switch is closed, initially the indictor offers infinite reactance to the current. As a result, first after closing the switch, the current in the circuit will be zero. But as time passes, the reactance reduces and after a long time the current through the inductor will be maximum.

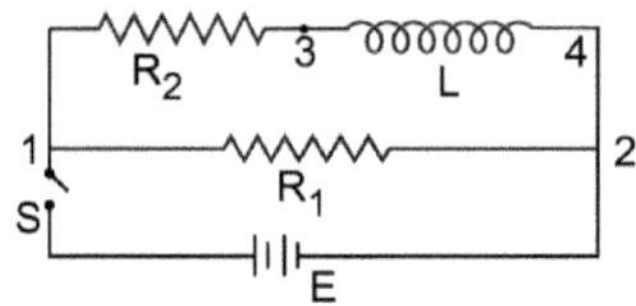

Now consider the following circuit.

$E = 150$ V.

$R_1 = 25\ \Omega$

$R_2 = 50\ \Omega$

$L = 0.15$ H

Switch S is closed at $t = 0$. Just after switch is closed.

52. Which point 1 or 2 is at a higher potential:

(a) 1 (b) 2

(c) Both at same potential (d) None of these

53. The potential difference V_{12} across R_1 is:

(a) 75 V (b) 125 V (c) 150 V (d) 112.5 V

54. The potential difference V_{34} across L is:

(a) 75 V (b) 125 V (c) 150 V (d) 112.5 V

55. Now the switch is open after a long time just after opening the switch, the potential difference across R_1 is:

(a) 37.5 V (b) 75 V (c) 64 V (d) 112.5 V

Sample Paper 

Physics

Section – A

This section consists of 25 multiple choice questions with overall choice to attempt any 20 questions. In case more than desirable number of questions are attempted, ONLY first 20 will be considered for evaluation.

1. Three isolated metal spheres A, B and C have radii R, 2R and 3R respectively, and same charge q. Which of the two spheres will have greater capacitance ?
   (a) A
   (b) B
   (c) C
   (d) None of the above

2. If the radius of the Gaussian surface enclosing a charge q is halved, how does the electric flux through the Gaussian surface change ?
   (a) Reduced to half
   (b) Remains same
   (c) Becomes double
   (d) Increase four times

3. A metal sphere is placed in a uniform electric field. Which path is followed by electric lines ?

   (a) (a)
   (b) (b)
   (c) (c)
   (d) (d)

4. The spherical bobs, one metallic and other of glass, of the same size are allowed to fall freely from the same height above the ground, which of the two would reach the ground earlier?
   (a) Metallic bob
   (b) Glass bob
   (c) Both at the same time
   (d) None of the above

5. The electric field at a point on equatorial line of a dipole and direction of the dipole moment:
   (a) will be parallel
   (b) will be in opposite direction
   (c) will be perpendicular
   (d) are not related

6. An electron is moving towards x-axis. An electric field is along $-x$-axis direction then path of electron is:
   (a) a straight line
   (b) a circle
   (c) an ellipse
   (d) a parabola

7. When air is replaced by a dielectric medium of constant K, the maximum force of attraction between two charges separated by a distance:
   (a) increases K times
   (b) remains unchanged
   (c) decreases K times
   (d) increases K^{-1} times

8. The equation $\rightarrow \Sigma e = \Sigma IR$ is applicable to which law?
   (a) Kirchhoff's third law
   (b) Kirchhoff's junction rule
   (c) Kirchhoff's second law
   (d) Newton's law

9. In a meter bridge experiment the ratio of left gap resistance to right gap resistance is $2 : 3$. The balance point from left is :
   (a) 20 cm
   (b) 40 cm
   (c) 50 cm
   (d) 60 cm

10. The resistivity of a wire:
    (a) increases with the length of the wire
    (b) decreases with the area of cross-section
    (c) decreases with the length and increases with the cross-section of wire
    (d) is unaffected by change in its length and area of cross-section

11. The resistance of a straight conductor does not depend upon its:
    (a) temperature
    (b) length
    (c) material
    (d) shape of cross-section

12. A certain wire has a resistance R. The resistance of another wire identical with the first except having twice its diameter is:
    (a) 2 R
    (b) 0.25 R
    (c) 4 R
    (d) 0.5 R

13. The reciprocal of resistance is:
    (a) conductance
    (b) voltage
    (c) resistivity
    (d) reactance

14. A wire of resistance 4 W is stretched to twice its original length. The resistance of stretched wire would be:
    (a) $2\,\Omega$
    (b) $4\,\Omega$
    (c) $8\,\Omega$
    (d) $16\,\Omega$

15. A moving electron enters a uniform and perpendicular magnetic field. Inside the magnetic field, the electron travels along :
    (a) a straight line
    (b) parabola
    (c) a circle
    (d) a hyperbola

16. A proton of mass m and charge q is moving in a plane with kinetic energy E. If there exists a uniform magnetic field B, perpendicular to the plane of the motion, the proton will move in a circular path of radius:
    (a) $\dfrac{2Em}{qB}$
    (b) $\dfrac{\sqrt{Em}}{2qB}$
    (c) $\dfrac{\sqrt{2Em}}{qB}$
    (d) $\dfrac{\sqrt{2Eq}}{mB}$

17. Two electrons move parallel to each other with equal speed v. The ratio of magnetic and electrical forces between them is:
    (a) $\dfrac{c}{v}$
    (b) $\dfrac{v}{c}$
    (c) $\dfrac{c^2}{v^2}$
    (d) $\dfrac{v^2}{c^2}$

18. Earth's magnetic field inside a closed iron box, as compared to outside is:
    (a) more
    (b) less
    (c) same
    (d) zero

19. An electron moving through a magnetic field does not experience any force. Under what conditions is this possible ?
    (a) $\theta = 0°$ or $\theta = 90°$
    (b) $\theta = 90°$ or $\theta = 180°$
    (c) $\theta = 0°$ or $\theta = 180°$
    (d) $\theta = 180°$

20. An induced emf is produced when a magnet is plunge into a coil. The strength of the induced emf is independent of :
    (a) number of turns of coil
    (b) speed with which the magnet is moved
    (c) the strength of the magnet
    (d) the resistivity of the wire of the coil

21. For two coils with number of turns 500 and 200 each of length 1 m and cross-sectional area 4×10^{-4} m^2, the mutual inductance is :
    (a) 0.5 mμH
    (b) 0.5 H
    (c) 5 mμH
    (d) 0.05 mμH

22. Self induction of a solenoid is :
    (a) inversely proportional to area of cross section
    (b) directly proportional to area of cross section
    (c) directly proportional to its length
    (d) directly proportional to current flowing through the coil

23. At angular frequency 10^3 rad/s, the nature of circuit:
    (a) Inductive
    (b) Capacitive
    (c) Resistive
    (d) None of these

24. Determine the rms value of the emf given by,
$$E \text{ (in V)} = 8 \sin (\omega t) + 6 \sin (2\omega t)$$
    (a) $10\sqrt{2}$ V
    (b) 10 V
    (c) $5\sqrt{2}$ V
    (d) $7\sqrt{2}$ V

25. The rms value of an AC of 50 Hz is 10 A. The time taken by the alternating current in reaching from zero to maximum value and the peak value of current will be:
    (a) 1×10^{-2} s and 7.07 A
    (b) 2×10^{-2} s and 14.14 A
    (c) 5×10^{-3} s and 14.14 A
    (d) 5×10^{-3} s and 7.07 A

Section - B

This section consists of 24 multiple choice questions with overall choice to attempt any 20 questions. In case more than desirable number of questions are attempted, ONLY first 20 will be considered for evaluation

26. A charge Q is enclosed by a Gaussian spherical surface of radius R. If the radius is doubled then what will be the effect on outward electric flux ?
(a) Increases   (b) Decreases   (c) Remain the same   (d) None of them

27. Two metallic spheres of same radii, one solid and the other hollow are charged to the same potential. Which of the two will hold more charge ?
(a) Hollow sphere   (b) Solid Sphere   (c) Both (a) and (b)   (d) None of them

28. Electric lines of force:
(a) exist everywhere
(b) exist only in the immediate vicinity of electric charges
(c) exist only when both positive and negative charges are near one another
(d) are imaginary

29. A force of 2.56 N acts on a charge of 16×10^{-4} C. The intensity of electric field at that point is:
(a) $1600 \ NC^{-1}$ (b) $150 \ NC^{-1}$ (c) $16 \ NC^{-1}$ (d) $1.5 \ NC^{-1}$

30. If in a parallel plate capacitor, which is connected to a battery, we fill dielectrics in whole space of its plates, then which of the following increases?:
(a) Q and V   (b) V and E   (c) E and C   (d) Q and C

31. An alternating voltage given by $V = 140 \sin 314t$ in connected across a pure resistor of $50 \ \Omega$. The rms current through the resistor is:
(a) 2.54 A   (b) 1.98 A   (c) 1.53 A   (d) 2.98A

32. A resistor and a capacitor are connected in series with an AC source. If the potential drop across the capacitor is 5V and that across resistor is 12 V, applied voltage is :
(a) 5 V   (b) 12 V   (c) 13 V   (d) 17 V

33. The decrease in potential across the wire is _________ proportional to the length of the wire.
(a) Directly   (b) Inversely   (c) Both (a) and (b)   (d) None

34. The potentiometer will give accurate result, if the area of cross section of the wire _________.
(a) Increase   (b) Decrease   (c) Remain same   (d) None.

35. The V-I characteristics of four circuit elements are shown. Which of these is ohmic?

(a)   (b)   (c)   (d)

36. A resistance of 5 ohm is connected in the left gap of a meter bridge and 15 ohm in the other gap. The position of the balancing point is :
(a) 10 cm   (b) 20 cm   (c) 25 cm   (d) 75 cm

37. Select the WRONG statement :
(a) A potentiometer is a constant voltage device
(b) A potentiometer is a constant current device
(c) A potentiometer is used to measure emf of a cell
(d) A potentiometer is used to measure potential drop between two points in an electric circuit

38. A proton and a deuterium nucleus having certain kinetic energies enter in a uniform magnetic field with same component of velocity in the direction of magnetic field. Which of the following is correct?
(a) Which particle has greater pitch depends on the fact that which particle has greater component of velocity perpendicular to magnetic field.

   (b) Deuterium nucleus has greater pitch of helical motion.
   (c) Proton has greater pitch of helical motion.
   (d) Both particles have same pitch of helical motion.

39. At neutral point, the horizontal component of the magnetic field due to a magnet is:
   (a) in the opposite direction of the earth's horizontal magnetic field
   (b) equal to earth's horizontal magnetic field
   (c) in the same direction of the earth's horizontal magnetic field
   (d) both (a) and (b)

40. Which of the following is responsible for the earth's magnetic field?
   (a) Rotational motion of earth.
   (b) Translational motion of earth.
   (c) Convective currents in earth's core.
   (d) Diversive current in earth's core

41. What is the direction of induced currents in metal rings 1 and 2 when current I in the wire is increasing steadily.

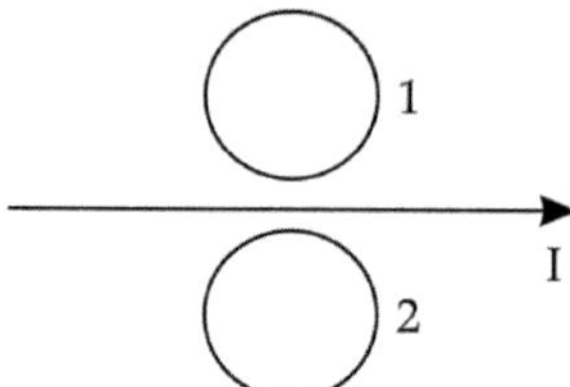

   (a) 1 → Clockwise
       2 → Clockwise
   (b) 1 → Anticlockwise
       2 → Anticlockwise
   (c) 1 → Clockwise
       2 → Anticlockwise
   (d) 1 → Anticlockwise
       2 → Clockwise

42. Which of the following combinations should be selected for better tuning of an LCR circuit used for communication ?
   (a) $R = 20\,\Omega$, $L = 1.5$ H, $C = 35\,\mu$F
   (b) $R = 25\,\Omega$, $L = 2.5$ H, $C = 45\,\mu$F
   (c) $R = 15\,\Omega$, $L = 3.5$ H, $C = 30\,\mu$F
   (d) $R = 25\,\Omega$, $L = 1.5$ H, $C = 45\,\mu$F

43. On decreasing the distance between the plates of a parallel plate capacitor, its capacitance:
   (a) remains unaffected
   (b) decreases
   (c) first increases then decreases
   (d) increases

44. The figure shows a wire sliding on two parallel conducting rails placed at a separation I. A magnetic field B exists in a direction perpendicular to the plane of the rails. The force required to keep the wire moving at a constant velocity v will be :

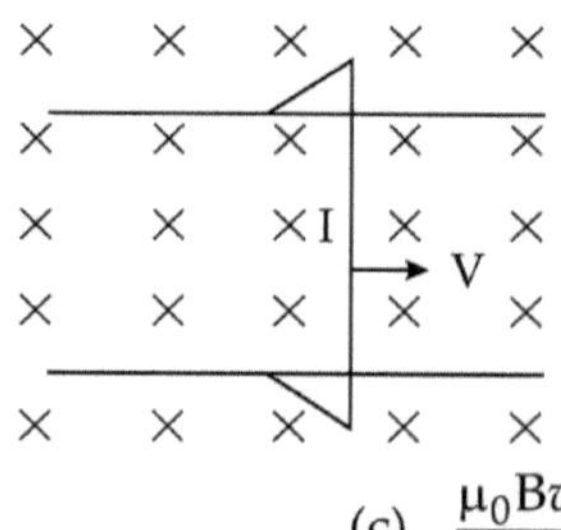

   (a) Zero
   (b) Blv
   (c) $\dfrac{\mu_0 Bv}{4\pi I}$
   (d) evB

45. Given below are two statements labelled as Assertion (A) and Reason (R)

   Assertion (A): Kirchhoff's junction rule can be applied to a junction of several lines or a point in a line.

   Reason (R): When steady current is flowing, there is no accumulation of charges at any junction or at any point in a line.

   (a) Both A and R are true and R is also the correct explanation of A.
   (b) Both A and R are true but R is not the correct explanation of A.
   (c) A is true but R is false.
   (d) A is false and R is also false.

46. Given below are two statements labelled as Assertion (A) and Reason (R)

Assertion (A): Electric potential and electric potential energy are different quantities.

Reason (R): For a system of positive test charge and point charge electric potential energy = electric potential.

(a) Both A and R are true and R is also the correct explanation of A.

(b) Both A and R are true but R is not the correct explanation of A.

(c) A is true but R is false.

(d) A is false and R is also false.

47. Given below are two statements labelled as Assertion (A) and Reason (R)

Assertion (A): In the northern hemisphere the north pole of the dip needle dips downwards.

Reason (R): The north pole of earth as a bar magnet lies in the northern hemisphere.

(a) Both A and R are true and R is also the correct explanation of A.

(b) Both A and R are true but R is not the correct explanation of A.

(c) A is true but R is false.

(d) A is false and R is also false.

48. Given below are two statements labelled as Assertion (A) and Reason (R)

Assertion (A): Eddy currents are produced in any metallic conductor when magnetic flux is changed around it.

Reason (R): Electric potential determines the flow of charge.

(a) Both A and R are true and R is also the correct explanation of A.

(b) Both A and R are true but R is not the correct explanation of A.

(c) A is true but R is false.

(d) A is false and R is also false.

49. Given below are two statements labelled as Assertion (A) and Reason (R)

Assertion (A): Total flux through a closed surface is zero if no charge is enclosed by the surface.

Reason (R): Gauss law is true for any closed surface, no matter what its shape or size is.

(a) Both A and R are true and R is also the correct explanation of A.

(b) Both A and R are true but R is not the correct explanation of A.

(c) A is true but R is false.

(d) A is false and R is also false.

Section – C

This section consists of 6 multiple choice questions with an overall choice to attempt any 5. In case more than desirable number of questions are attempted, ONLY first 5 will be considered for evaluation

50. In the figure, charge q is placed at origin O. When the charge q is displaced from its position the electric field at point P changes :

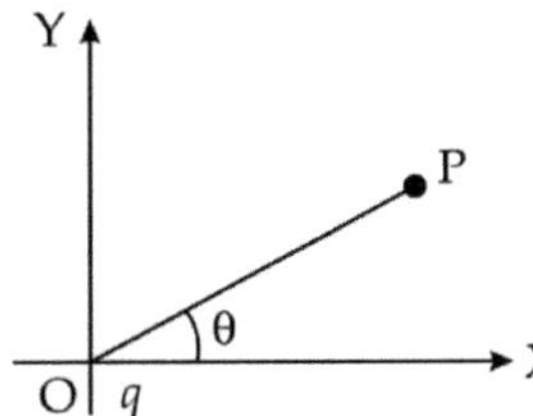

(a) at the same time when q is displaced

(b) at a time after $\dfrac{OP}{c}$ where c is the speed of light

(c) at a time after $\dfrac{OP\cos\theta}{c}$

(d) at a time after $\dfrac{OP\cos\theta}{c}$

51. A parallel plate capacitor is made of two dielectric blocks in series. One of the blocks has thickness d_1 and and dielectric constant K_1, and the other has thickness d_2 and dielectric constant K_2 as shown in figure. This arrangement can be though as a dielectric slab of thickness d $(= d_1 + d_2)$ and effective dielectric constant K. The K is :

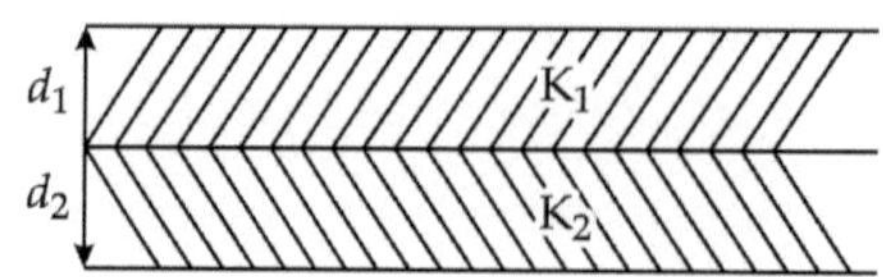

(a) $\dfrac{K_1 d_1 + K_2 d_2}{d_1 + d_2}$
(b) $\dfrac{K_1 d_1 + K_2 d_2}{K_1 + K_2}$
(c) $\dfrac{K_1 K_2 (d_1 + d_2)}{K_2 d_1 + K_1 d_2}$
(d) $\dfrac{2K_1 K_2}{K_1 + K_2}$

The figure shows a series LCR circuit:

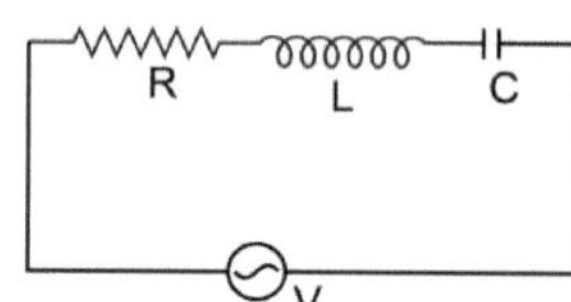

Case Study: Read the following paragraph and answers the questions:

For such a circuit, the inpedance Z is given by. $Z = \sqrt{R^2 + (X_L = X_C)^2}$, where X_L and X_C are inductive and capacitive resistances respectively. As the frequency of a.c. is increased, at a particular frequency. X_L become, equal to X_C. For that frequency maximum current occurs. This is because impedance becomes equal is its least value R. Current through the circuit $I = V/R$. The circuit behaves like a pure resistive circuit and current and voltage will be in phase. This is called resonance. Frequency of a.c. at which resonance occurs is called resonant frequency. If frequency is less than the resonant frequency, then the capacitive reactance will be more. The circuit will be capacitive in nature and current leads voltage. On the other hand, if frequency is more than the resonant frequency inductive reactance will be more. Circuit is inductive in nature and current lags the voltage.

An LCR circuit with a resistance 50 Ω has a resonant angular frequency 2×10^3 rad/s. At resonance, the voltage across the resistance and inductance are 25V and 20V respectively. Than

52. The value of inductance is:
(a) 20 mH
(b) 10 mH
(c) 40 mH
(d) 25 mH

53. The value of capacitance is:
(a) 25 μF
(b) 1 μF
(c) 2 μF
(d) 12.5 μF

54. The impedance at resonance is:
(a) 50 W
(b) 16 W
(c) 64 W
(d) 25 W

55. Which of the following angular frequency of a.c. will see the circuit as inductive in nature?
(a) 1.5×10^3 rad/s
(b) 10^3 rad/s
(c) 2×10^3 rad/s
(d) 5×10^3 rad/s

Sample Paper 7

Physics

Section - A

This section consists of 25 multiple choice questions with overall choice to attempt any 20 questions. In case more than desirable number of questions are attempted, ONLY first 20 will be considered for evaluation.

1. What is the electric potential at a distance of 9 cm from 3 μC ?
   (a) 3 V
   (b) 300 V
   (c) 270 V
   (d) 30 V
2. Relative permitivity of water is 81. If ε_w and ε_0 are permitivity's of water and vacuum respectively, then:
   (a) $\varepsilon_0 = 9\varepsilon_w$
   (b) $\varepsilon_0 = 81\varepsilon_w$
   (c) $\varepsilon_w = 9\varepsilon_0$
   (d) $\varepsilon_w = 81\varepsilon_0$
3. The angle between the dipole moment and electric field at any point on the equatorial plane is:
   (a) 180°
   (b) 0°
   (c) 45°
   (d) 90°
4. Gauss's law should be invalid if:
   (a) the inverse square law was not exactly true
   (b) the velocity of light were not a universal constant
   (c) there were magnetic monopoles
   (d) none of these

5. If a dipole of dipole moment $\vec{p}$ is placed in a uniform electric field $\vec{E}$, then torque acting on it is given by:
   (a) $\vec{\tau} = \vec{p}\,\vec{E}$
   (b) $\vec{\tau} = \vec{p} + \vec{E}$
   (c) $\vec{\tau} = \vec{p} \times \vec{E}$
   (d) $\vec{\tau} = \vec{p} - \vec{E}$

6. A metallic sphere is placed in a uniform electric field. The line of force follows the path(s) shown in the figure as:

   (a) 1
   (b) 2
   (c) 3
   (d) 4
7. If E_a be the electric field strength of a short dipole at a point on its axial line and E_e that on the equatorial line at the same distance, then:
   (a) $E_e = 2E_a$
   (b) $E_e = E_a$
   (c) $E_a = 2E_e$
   (d) $E_e = 4E_a$
8. The variation of potential difference V with length l in case of two potentiometers wires P and Q is as shown. Which one of these will you prefer for comparing emfs of two primary cells ?
   (a) Q
   (b) P
   (c) Both P and Q
   (d) None of the above
9. The drift velocity of the free electrons in a conducting wire carrying a current i is v. If in a wire of the same metal, but of double the radius, the current be $2i$ then the drift velocity of the electrons will be:
   (a) $\dfrac{v}{4}$
   (b) $\dfrac{v}{2}$
   (c) v
   (d) $4v$
10. In a closed circuit, the vector sum of total emf is equal to the sum of the ______:
    (a) currents
    (b) resistances
    (c) products of currents and the resistances
    (d) products of potential differences
11. Kirchhoff's first law i.e., $\Sigma i = 0$ at a junction is based on the law of conservation of:
    (a) charge
    (b) energy
    (c) momentum
    (d) angular momentum
12. According the Kirchhoff's law, in any analytic circuit, if the direction of current is assumed opposite, then the value of current will be:
    (a) i
    (b) $2i$
    (c) $-i$
    (d) 0

13. In a wheatstone bridge in the battery and galvanometer are interchanged then the deflection in galvanometer will:
    (a) change in previous direction
    (b) not change
    (c) change in opposite direction
    (d) None of these

14. A capacitor is connected to a cell of emf E having some internal resistance r. The potential difference across the:
    (a) Cell is < E
    (b) Cell is E
    (c) Capacitor is > E
    (d) Capacitor is < E

15. A moving conductor coil in a magnetic field produces an induced emf. This is in accordance with:
    (a) Lenz's Law
    (b) Coulomb's Law
    (c) Faraday's Law
    (d) Ampere's Law

16. A vertical wire carries a current in upward direction. An electron beam sent horizontally towards the wire will be deflected:
    (a) towards right
    (b) towards left
    (c) upwards
    (d) downwards

17. When will the Lorentz force be zero ?
    (a) $\vec{v}$ and $\vec{B}$ are parallel or antiparallel
    (b) $\vec{v} = 0$
    (c) The particle is neutral
    (d) All of them

18. Under what condition is the force acting on a charge moving through a uniform magnetic field minimum ?
    (a) $\theta = 180°$
    (b) $\theta = 0°$ or $90°$
    (c) $\theta = 90°$
    (d) $\theta = 0°$ or $180°$

19. The magnetic field due to earth has a horizontal component of 26 μT at a place where the dip is 60°. Vertical component of the field at that point is:
    (a) 25 μT
    (b) 30 μT
    (c) 45 μT
    (d) 54 μT

20. Eddy currents may be reduced by using:
    (a) thick piece of cobalt
    (b) thick piece of nickel
    (c) laminated core of steel
    (d) laminated core of iron

21. When current changes from 13 A to 7 A in 0.5 s through a coil, the emf induced is 3×10^{-4} V. The coefficient of self induction is::
    (a) 25×10^{-6} H
    (b) 25×10^{-5} H
    (c) 25×10^{-4} H
    (d) 25×10^{-3} H

22. If a current of 3 A flowing in the primary coil is reduced to zero in 0.01 s then the induced emf in the secondary coil is 1500 V, the mutual inductance between the two coils is:
    (a) 0.5 H
    (b) 1.5 H
    (c) 5 H
    (d) 10 H

23. A pure inductor of 25 mH is connected to a source of 220 V. What will be the inductive reactance and rms current in the circuit, if the frequency of the source is 50Hz.
    (a) 7.85 Ω; 28 A
    (b) 5.54 Ω; 18 A
    (c) 7.85 Ω; 18 A
    (d) 5.54 Ω; 28 A

24. The energy stored in a condenser of capacity C which has been raised to a potential V is given by::
    (a) $\frac{1}{2}CV$
    (b) $\frac{1}{2}CV^2$
    (c) CV
    (d) CV^2

25. An alternating current of frequency f is flowing in a circuit containing a resistor of resistance R and a choke of inductance L in series. The impedance of this circuit is:
    (a) $R + 2\pi f\pi L$
    (b) $\sqrt{R^2 + L^2}$
    (c) $\sqrt{R^2 + 2\pi f L}$
    (d) $\sqrt{R^2 + 4\pi^2 f^2 L^2}$

Section – B

This section consists of 24 multiple choice questions with overall choice to attempt any 20 questions. In case more than desirable number of questions are attempted, ONLY first 20 will be considered for evaluation

26. Which of the following figure represents the electric field lines due to a single positive charge?
    (a)
    (b)
    (c)
    (d)

27. An electric dipole is placed at an angle of 30° to a non-uniform electric field. The dipole will experience:
   (a) a translational force only in the direction of the field
   (b) a translational force only in the direction normal to the direction of the field
   (c) a torque as well as a translational force
   (d) a torque only

28. When an electric dipole $\vec{p}$ is placed in a uniform electric field $\vec{E}$ then at what angle between $\vec{p}$ and $\vec{E}$ the value of torque will be maximum:
   (a) 90°   (b) 0°   (c) 180°   (d) 45°

29. A conducting sphere of radius 10 cm has unknown charge. If the electric field at a distance 20 cm from the centre of the sphere is $1.2 \times 10^3 \, NC^{-1}$ and points radially inwards. The net charge on the sphere is:
   (a) $-4.5 \times 10^{-9} \, C$ (b) $4.5 \times 10^9 \, C$ (c) $-5.3 \times 10^{-9} \, C$ (d) $5.3 \times 10^9 \, C$

30. The capacitor, whose capacitance is 6 µF, 6 µF and 3 µF respectively are connected in series with 20 V line. Find the charge on 3 µF:

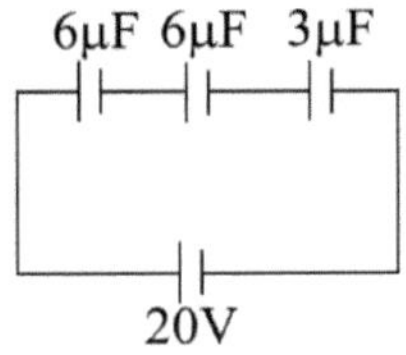

   (a) 30 µC   (b) 48 µC   (c) 60 µC   (d) 120 µC

31. A generator produces a voltage that is given by $V = 240 \sin 120t$ V, where t is in seconds. The frequency and rms voltage are nearly:
   (a) 19 Hz and 120 V   (b) 19 Hz and 170 V   (c) 60 Hz and 240 V   (d) 754 Hz and 170 V

32. The instantaneous voltage through a device of impedance 20 Ω is $e = 80 \sin 100\pi t$. The effective value of the current is:
   (a) 1.732 A   (b) 2.828 A   (c) 3 A   (d) 4 A

33. Between metals and alloys, which has greater value of temperature coefficient of resistance ?
   (a) Metals   (b) Alloys   (c) Both has same   (d) None of them

34. The filament of 60 W and 100 W bulbs are of the same length. Which filament will be thicker ?
   (a) 100 W bulb has thicker filament
   (b) 60 W bulb has thicker filament
   (c) Both filaments are of same thickness
   (d) It is impossible to get different wattage unless lengths are different

35. The figure shows a network of currents. The magnitude of currents is shown here. The current I will be:

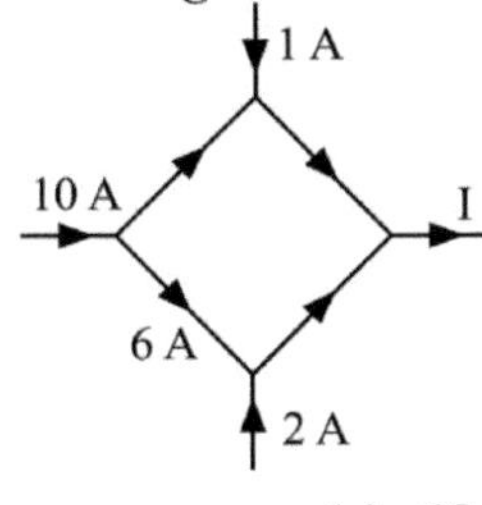

   (a) 3 A   (b) 9 A   (c) 13 A   (d) 19 A

36. If an electron is placed in a non-uniform electric field, then the force experienced by electron is in the direction:
   (a) of the electric field
   (b) opposite to the electric field
   (c) perpendicular to the field
   (d) making some angle to field, which depends on strength of field

37. Which is a wrong statement ?
   (a) The Wheatstone bridge is the most sensitive when all the four resistances are of the same order
   (b) In a balanced Wheatstone bridge, interchanging the positions of galvanometer and cell affects the balance of the bridge

    (c)   Kirchhoff's first law (for currents meeting at a junction in an electric circuit) expresses the conservation of chaise

    (d)   The rheostat can be used as a potential divider

38. Magnetic field due to a ring having n turns at a distance x on its axis is proportional to (if r = radius of ring):

    (a) $\dfrac{r}{(x^2 + r^2)}$ (b) $\dfrac{nr^2}{(x^2 + r^2)^{3/2}}$ (c) $\dfrac{r^2}{(x^2 + r^2)^{3/2}}$ (d) $\dfrac{n^2 r^2}{(x^2 + r^2)^{3/2}}$

39. Biot-Savart law indicates that the moving electron velocity (v) produce a magnetic field B such that:

    (a) $B \perp v$

    (b) $B \parallel v$

    (c) it is along the line joining electron and point of observation

    (d) it obeys inverse cube law

40. The earth's magnetic field at some place on magnetic equator of earth is 0.5×10^{-4} T. Consider the radius of earth at that place as 6400 km. Then, magnetic dipole moment of the earth is Am^2:   ($\mu_0 = 4\pi \times 10^{-7}$ TmA^{-1})

    (a) 1.05×10^{23} (b) 1.15×10^{23}

    (c) 1.31×10^{23} (d) 1.62×10^{23}

41. Lenz's and Faraday's law is expressed by the following formula (here e = induced emf, f = magnetic flux in one turn and N = number of turns) :

    (a) $e = -N\dfrac{d\phi}{dt}$ (b) $e = N\dfrac{d\phi}{dt}$ (c) $e = -\phi\dfrac{dN}{dt}$ (d) $e = -\dfrac{d}{dt}\left(\dfrac{\phi}{N}\right)$

42. A rectangular coil of 100 turns and size 0.1 m × 0.05 m is placed perpendicular to a magnetic field of 0.1 T. If the field drops to 0.05 T in 0.05 s, the magnitude of the emf induced in the coil is :

    (a) 0.5V   (b) 3V   (c) 2V   (d) 6V

43. A parallel plate air capacitor has a capacitance of 100 µF. The plates are at a distance d apart. If a slab of thickness t ($t < d$) and dielectric constant 5 is introduced between the parallel plates, then the capacitance will be:

    (a) 30 µC   (b) 100 µC   (c) 200 µC   (d) 500 µC

44. A step-down transformer has 50 turns on secondary and 1000 turns on primary winding. If a transformer is connected to 220 V, 1A AC source, what is output current of the transformer ?

    (a) 2 A   (b) 20 A   (c) 100 A   (d) $\dfrac{1}{20}$ A

45. Given below are two statements labelled as Assertion (A) and Reason (R)

Assertion (A): In meter bridge experiment, a high resistance is always connected in series with a galvanometer.

Reason (R): As resistance increase current more accurately then ammeter.

    (a) Both A and R are true and R is also the correct explanation of A.

    (b) Both A and R are true but R is not the correct explanation of A.

    (c) A is true but R is false.

    (d) A is false and R is also false.

46. Given below are two statements labelled as Assertion (A) and Reason (R)

Assertion (A): Gauss theorem is not applicable in magnetism.

Reason (R): Mono magnetic pole does not exist.

    (a) Both A and R are true and R is also the correct explanation of A.

    (b) Both A and R are true but R is not the correct explanation of A.

    (c) A is true but R is false.

    (d) A is false and R is also false.

47. Given below are two statements labelled as Assertion (A) and Reason (R)

Assertion (A): Mutual inductance of a pair of coils depends on their separation as well as their relative orientation.

Reason (R): Mutual inductance depends upon the length of the coil only.

(a) Both A and R are true and R is also the correct explanation of A.

(b) Both A and R are true but R is not the correct explanation of A.

(c) A is true but R is false.

(d) A is false and R is also false.

48. Given below are two statements labelled as Assertion (A) and Reason (R)

Assertion (A): Gauss's law shows diversion when inverse square law is not obeyed.

Reason (R): Gauss's law is a consequence of conservation of charges.

(a) Both A and R are true and R is also the correct explanation of A.

(b) Both A and R are true but R is not the correct explanation of A.

(c) A is true but R is false.

(d) A is false and R is also false.

49. Given below are two statements labelled as Assertion (A) and Reason (R)

Assertion (A): The capacity of a given conductor remains same even if charge is varied on it.

Reason (R): Capacitance depends upon nearby medium as well as size and shape of conductor.

(a) Both A and R are true and R is also the correct explanation of A.

(b) Both A and R are true but R is not the correct explanation of A.

(c) A is true but R is false.

(d) A is false and R is also false.

Section – C

This section consists of 6 multiple choice questions with an overall choice to attempt any 5. In case more than desirable number of questions are attempted, ONLY first 5 will be considered for evaluation

50. Figure shows electric field lines in which an electric dipole $\vec{p}$ is placed as shown. Which of the following statements is correct?

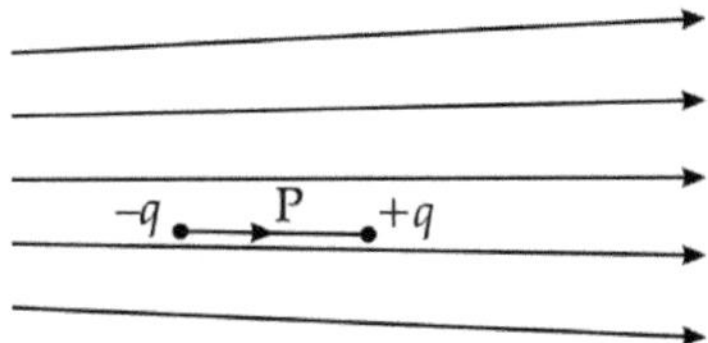

(a) The dipole will not experience any force

(b) The dipole will experience a force towards right

(c) The dipole will experience a force towards left

(d) The dipole will experience a force upwards

51. Find equivalent capacitance between A and B. (Assume each conducting plate is having same dimensions and neglect the thickness of the plate, $\dfrac{\varepsilon_0 A}{d} = 7\ \mu F$, where A is area of plates, A >> d)

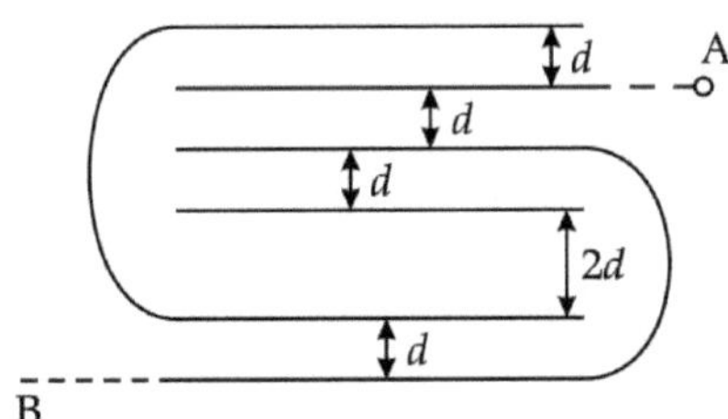

(a) 7 μF   (b) 14 μF

(c) 11 μF   (d) 4 μF

Case Study: Read the following paragraph and answers the questions:

A suspended magnet gets aligned with the earth's magnetic field at that place. Along the equator, a suspended magnet will align horizontally. The orientation of the magnet depends on the dip angle at that place. Angle of dip is the angle between the net magnetic field of earth and the horizontal. At equator, angle of dip is 0 (zero) and at poles its value is 90°. This means, at equator, the earth's magnetic field is completely horizontal and at poles. The earth's magnetic field is verticle.

If S is the angle of dip at a place and B is the Earth's magnetic field, then the horizontal component of Earth's magnetic field $B_H = B \cos \delta$ the vertical component $B_V = B \sin \delta$

$$\Rightarrow \qquad B = \sqrt{B_H{}^2 + B_{V^2}}$$

Also
$$\tan \delta = \frac{B_V}{B_H}$$

52. A magnet stands vertical at a place when suspended that place will be:
    (a) At equator (b) At poles (c) At 30° latitude (d) At 60° latitude

53. The angle of dip of a face where the magnet gets aligned completely horizontal is:
    (a) 0° (b) 90° (c) 30° (d) 45°

54. The horizontal and vertical components of the magnetic field at a place are $\dfrac{\sqrt{3}}{2}R$ and $\dfrac{B}{2}$ respectively. When a magnet is left free at that place, the angle made by its magnetic axis with the horizontal is:
    (a) 45° (b) 30° (c) 60° (d) 15°

55. Earth's magnetic field always has a vertical component except at:
    (a) Poles (b) Equator (c) 30° latitude (d) 75° latitude

❑❑

Answers

Section-A

1. (c) Remains constant from centre to surface

   Explanation: As the electric field inside a conductor is zero so, the potential at any point is constant. Suppose A and B two points inside a conducting sphere. We know that $E = -\dfrac{dV}{dr}$. As $E = 0$, $dV = 0$ or $V_A - V_B = 0$ or $V_A = V_B$.

2. (d) Remains the same.

   Explanation: According to Gauss's law

   $$\phi_E = \frac{Q_{enclosed}}{\varepsilon_0}$$

   If the radius of the Gaussian surface is doubled, the outward electric flux will remain the same. This is because electric flux depends only on the charge enclosed by the surface.

3. (b) a deficiency of 5 electrons

   Explanation: The magnitude of charge on each electron is $q_e = 1.6 \times 10^{-19}$ C
   The body has a positive charge that means it has a deficiency of electrons.
   Total charge on the body is $q = n \times q_e = 8 \times 10^{-19}$ C, Which implies $n = 5$.

4. (a) Perpendicular to the diameter

   Explanation: The electric field is perpendicular to the diameter because component of electric field intensity is parallel to the diameter and cancel out.

5. (a) It will start discharge

   Explanation: The capacitor will be discharged immediately and its energy will be converted into heat energy.

6. (a) It will increase

   Explanation: The radius of the soap bubble will increase.

7. (a) $\dfrac{C_1}{C_2}$

   Explanation: As C_1 and C_2 are connected in parallel, so the potential will be same for both capacitors. Thus, $Q_1 = C_1 V$ and $Q_2 = C_2 V$

   $$\therefore \quad \frac{Q_1}{Q_2} = \frac{C_1 V}{C_2 V} = \frac{C_1}{C_2}$$

8. (d) Conservation of charge, conservation of energy

> **Explanation:** Kirchhoff's first law is based on the conservation of charge because sum of current entering to the junction is equal to sum of current leaving the junction. Kirchhoff's second law states that algebraic sum of potential drops in a closed circuit is zero. So, it is based on the conservation of energy.

9. (b) Electric field produced by charges accumulated on the surface of wire.

> **Explanation:** $\vec{J} = \sigma\vec{E} = \dfrac{\vec{E}}{\rho}$
>
> Where, σ is conductivity and ρ is the resistivity.

10. (a) point of higher potential to lower potential

> **Explanation:** By convention, the direction of motion of positive charges is taken as the direction of electric current.

11. (b) 10 V

> **Explanation:** The potential at the centre of metallic hollow spherical surface is 10 V, because potential at any point inside a hollow metallic sphere is constant. Thus, potential at the centre is equal to the potential at surface of the sphere.

12. (d) decreases and thermal velocity of the electron increases

> **Explanation:** Temperature rise in wire, the thermal velocity of the electron increases due to increase in their thermal energy. As the result, the relaxation time decreases and hence drift velocity of the charge carrier will also decrease because drift velocity is proportional to the relaxation time.

13. (d) $\dfrac{P}{4}$

> **Explanation:** $\qquad\qquad P = \dfrac{V^2}{R}$
>
> Since, resistance remain same for a heater
> $$P \propto V^2$$
> If $\qquad\qquad V' = \dfrac{V}{2}$
>
> $\therefore$ P will become $\dfrac{P}{4}$.

14. (c) $1 : 1 : 1$

> **Explanation:** Since, charge (q) = current (i) × time (t)
> Therefore, charge is equal to area under the curve.
> $\therefore$ Ist rectangle = $q_1 = lb = 2 \times 1 = 2$
> IInd rectangle = $q_2 = lb = 1 \times 2 = 2$
> IIIrd triangle = $q_3 = \dfrac{1}{2}\,lb = \dfrac{1}{2} \times 2 \times 2 = 2$
> Hence, ratio $q_1 : q_2 : q_3 = 1 : 1 : 1$.

15. (a) $B \perp v$

Explanation: According to Biot-savart law, the magnitude of magnetic field is

$$B = \frac{\mu_0}{4\pi} \cdot \frac{|q|\, v \sin\theta}{r^2}$$

Where, $\frac{\mu_0}{4\pi}$ is the proportionality constant and r is the magnitude of position vector from charge to that

point at which we have to find magnetic field and θ is the angle between $\vec{v}$ and $\vec{r}$.

$$B = \frac{\mu_0}{4\pi} \cdot \frac{|q|\,(\vec{v} \times \vec{r})}{r^3}$$

So, we can say that $B \perp v$.

16. (b) The magnetic field at any point inside the pipe is zero

Explanation: Using Ampere's circuital law over a circular loop of any radius less than the radius of the pipe, we can see that net current inside the loop is zero. Hence, magnetic field at every point inside the loop will be zero.

17. (d) The charge to mass ratio satisfy:

$$\left(\frac{e}{m}\right)_1 + \left(\frac{e}{m}\right)_2 = 0$$

Explanation: Charged particles traverse identical helical paths in a completely opposite sense in a uniform magnetic field B, LHS for two particles should be same and of opposite sign. Therefore,

$$\left(\frac{e}{m}\right)_1 + \left(\frac{e}{m}\right)_2 = 0$$

18. (d) spin motion of electrons

Explanation: The spinning electrons possess magnetic dipole moment. This dipole moment is much greater than that due to orbital moment of electrons around the nucleus. So, we can say that magnetism of the magnet is due to the spin motion of electrons.

19. (c) $L_e < L_g$

Explanation: The distance between two poles of a bar magnet is known as the magnetic length (L_e). However, the actual length of a bar magnet is known as the geometric length (L_g).
Since, the relation between them is given by

$$L_e = \left(\frac{5}{6}\right) L_g$$

i.e. $L_e < L_g$

20. (d) laminated sheets

Explanation: The eddy currents can be minimized by using laminated sheets which instead of a single solid mass consists of thin sheets of metal, insulated from each other by the thin layer of varnish. The planes of the sheets are placed perpendicular to the direction of currents that would be set up by the emf induced in the material. The insulation between the sheets then offers high resistance to the induced emf and the eddy currents are reduced.

21. (b) 100 V

Explanation: EMF, $\qquad E = \dfrac{1}{2}B\omega l^2$

Given: B = 0.5 T, ω = 400 rad/s, l = 1 m

$\therefore \qquad\qquad\qquad\qquad E = \dfrac{1}{2}\times 0.5 \times 400 \times (1)^2$

$$= 0.5 \times 200$$
$$= 100 \text{ V}$$

22. (c) $4B_0L^2W\,b$

Explanation: Given, $A = L^2\hat{k}$ and $B = B_0(2\hat{i}+3\hat{j}+4\hat{k})\,T$

$\therefore \qquad\qquad\qquad \phi = B.A = B_0(2\hat{i}+3\hat{j}+4\hat{k}).L^2\hat{k}$

$$= 4B_0L^2\,Wb$$

23. (b) i^2R

Explanation: Given series resonant circuit having L, C and R as its elements. The resonant current is i.

The effective resistance is $\sqrt{R^2 + \left(\omega L - \dfrac{1}{\omega C}\right)^2}$.

But at resonance $\omega = \dfrac{1}{\sqrt{LC}}$.

So, we get effective resistance as R. The power dissipated is i^2R.

24. (a) at high voltage and low current

Explanation: To prevent loss of energy as heat loss = $i^2\,Rt$, current (i) is kept low. Hence, alternating current is transmitted at high voltage and low current.

25. (c) average value of current for complete cycle is zero

Explanation: Average value of AC for complete cycle is zero. Hence, AC cannot be measured by DC ammeter.

Section-B

26. (c) the atoms in the paper get polarised by the charged comb

Explanation: When a comb runs through one's dry hair, then comb gets charged. If then it comes close to the paper, it induces opposite charges on a paper. The field due to the charges on comb, polarises the atoms in the paper. Finally due to the induction of charges, it attracts the paper.

27. (c)

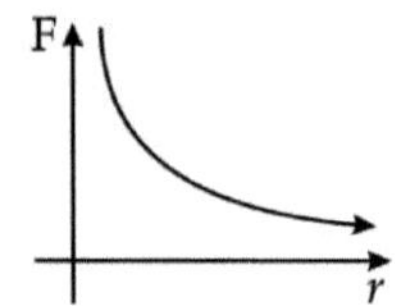

Explanation: According to Coulomb's law, force between two point charges, *i.e.* $F \propto \dfrac{1}{r^2}$. Therefore, the graph between F and r will be as shown in option (c).

28. (b) zero

Explanation: Here,
$$q_1 = (6 - 2)\ \mu C$$
and
$$q_2 = (2 - 2)\ \mu C$$

New force,
$$F = \frac{1}{4\pi\varepsilon_0}\frac{kq_1q_2}{r^2}$$

$$= \frac{1}{4\pi\varepsilon_0}\frac{(6-2)(2-2)}{r^2}\times 10^{-12} = 0$$

29. (b) Friction between the comb and hair results in the transfer of electrons

Explanation: While combing hair, friction between the comb and the hair results in the transfer of electrons.

30. (c) decreases because the charge moves along the electric field

Explanation: Equipotential surface is always perpendicular to the direction of electric field. Positive charge experiences the force in the direction of electric field. When a (+)ve charge is released from uniform electric field, its velocity increases in direction of electric field. So, K.E. increases and P.E. decreases by conservation of law of energy.

31. (d) All of these

Explanation: Resonance in the LCR circuit depends upon resistance, capacitance and inductance.

32. (a) Yes

Explanation: Yes, because the average power dissipated per cycle in an ideal capacitor is also zero.

33. (c) decreases with increase in its conductivity

Explanation: We know that,
$$R = \rho\frac{l}{A}$$
$$R \propto l$$
and
$$R \propto \frac{l}{A}$$

It is directly proportional to the resistivity so, it is inversely proportional to the conductivity. Hence, option (c) is correct.

34. (c) 0.5 A

Explanation: Electric current,
$$l = \frac{q}{t}$$

$$= \frac{60}{2\times 60} = 0.5\ A$$

35. (c) 20 A

Explanation:

$$l = \frac{dq}{dt} = \frac{d}{dt}(4t^2 + 4t + 4)$$

$$= 8t + 4$$

$$l(t = 2\ s) = 8 \times 2 + 4$$

$$= 16 + 4 = 20\ A$$

36. (d) independent of the area of cross-section

Explanation: Since current is constant, charge crossing a given area per unit time is constant and is independent of area of cross-section. However, current density depends on area.

37. (c) the resistance will be halved, and the specific resistance will remain unchanged.

Explanation: According to the given condition,

$$R = \rho\frac{l_1}{A_1}$$

Now,

$$\ell_2 = 2\ell_1$$

$$A_2 = \pi(r_2)^2$$

$$= \pi(2r_1)^2 = 4\pi r_1^2 = 4A_1$$

$\therefore$

$$R_2 = \frac{\rho(2\ell_1)}{4A_1} = \frac{\rho\ell}{2A} = \frac{R}{2}$$

Resistance is halved, but specific resistance remains the same.

38. (d) $-F$

Explanation:

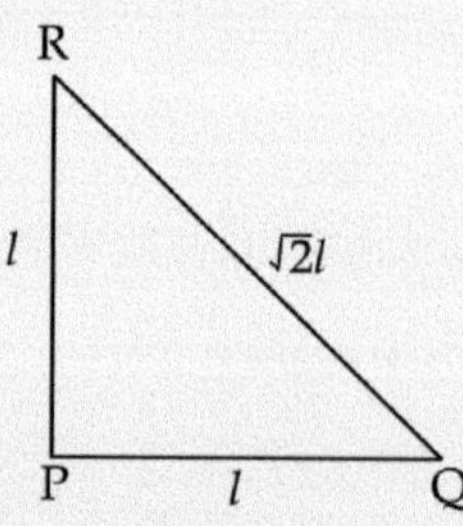

$$F_{PQ} = BIl_{PQ}\sin 90° = F$$
$$BIl = F$$

$$F_{QR} = BIl_{QR}\sin\theta$$

$$= BI(\sqrt{2}\,l)\sin(-45°)$$

$$= -BIl = -F$$

39. (b) When Electric and magnetic field in perpendicular

Explanation: The electron will move undeflected when the electric and magnetic field are in perpendicular direction, such that magnetic force balances the electrostatic force.

$$F_m = F_e$$
$$qvB = qE$$
$$v = \frac{E}{B}$$

40. (c)   Both (I) and (II) are correct

Explanation: When magnetic needle kept in the magnetic field produced by the straight wire, the needle get deflected and it will reach in equilibrium petition in which direction and magnetic field and magnetic moment of the needle direct in same direction. In case magnetic field produced by the straight wire is circular, direction of magnetic needle show the tangent of circle of magnetic field. Hence, both the statements are correct.

41. (b)   Generation of hydroelectricity

Explanation: Hydroelectric plant uses mechanical energy of water to move a magnetic field past coils of wire to generate voltage.

42. (b)   Power delivered to the capacitor per cycle is zero.

Explanation: When an A.C. voltage of 220 V is applied to a capacitor C, the charge on the plates is in phase with the applied voltage.
As the circuit is pure capacitive so, the current developed leads the applied voltage by a phase angle of 90°. Hence, power delivered to the capacitor per cycle is,

$$P = V_{rms}\, I_{rms} \cos 90°$$
$$= 0$$

43. (b)   Potential energy of charge q at a point is the work done per unit charge in bringing a charge from any point to infinity

Explanation: Potential energy of charge q at a point is the work done per unit charge in bringing a charge from infinity to that point.

44. (b)   anti-clockwise

Explanation: The direction of current in the solenoid is clockwise. On displacing it towards the loop a current in the loop will be induced in opposite sense so as to oppose its approach. Therefore, the direction of induced current as observed by the observer will be anti-clockwise.

45. (c)   A is true but R is false.

Explanation: From relation $\vec{j} = \sigma \vec{E}$ the current density $\vec{j}$ at any point in ohmic resistor is in direction of electric field $\vec{E}$ at that point. In space having non-uniform electric field, charges released from rest may not move along electric line of force. Hence, assertion is correct while reason is incorrect.

46. (d)   A is false but R is also false.

Explanation: Electrostatic force is a conservative force.

47. (b)   Both A and R are true but R is not the correct explanation of A.

Explanation: In a short bar magnet the value of magnetic field at a point on the axial line of the magnet is,

$$B_1 = \frac{\mu_0}{4\pi} \cdot \frac{2M}{r^3}$$

and on equatorial line at the same distance is,

$$B_2 = \frac{\mu_0}{4\pi} \cdot \frac{M}{r^3}$$

Therefore, $$B_1 = 2B_2.$$

48. **(b)** Both A and R are true but R is not the correct explanation of A.

Explanation: According to Faraday's laws, the conversion of mechanical energy into electrical energy. This is in accordance with the law of conservation of energy. It is also clearly known that in pure resistance, the emf is in phase with the current.

49. **(a)** Both A and R are true and R is also the correct explanation of A.

Explanation: Protons and electrons are the only basic charges in the universe. All the observable charges have to be integral multiple of e. Thus, if a body contains n_1 electrons and n_2 protons, the total amount of charge on the body is $n_2 e + n_1(- e) = (n_2 - n_1)e$. Since n_1 and n_2 are integers, their difference is also an integer. Thus, the charge on any body is always an integral multiple of e and can be increased or decreased in terms of e.

Section-C

50. **(c)** $v \propto x^{-\frac{1}{2}}$

Explanation: As we know that,

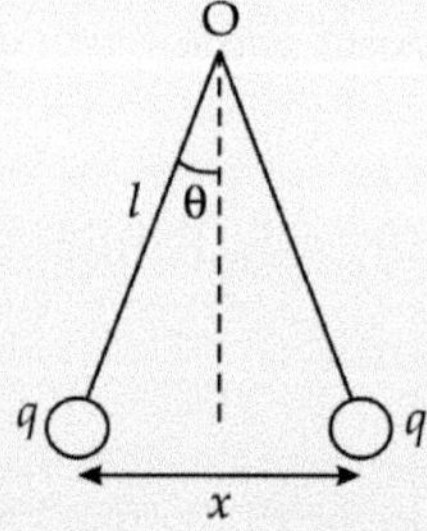

From figure,

$$\tan \theta = \frac{F_e}{mg} = \theta$$

$$\therefore \quad \frac{kq^2}{x^2 mg} = \frac{x}{2l}$$

or, $$x^3 \propto q^2 \qquad \qquad \text{...(i)}$$
or $$x^{3/2} \propto q \qquad \qquad \text{...(ii)}$$

Differentiating (i) w.r.t. time

$3x^2 \dfrac{dx}{dt} \propto 2q \dfrac{dq}{dt}$ but $\dfrac{dq}{dt}$ is constant

so, $x^2 (v) \propto q$ replace q from (ii)

$$x^2 (v) \propto x^{3/2}$$
or, $$v \propto x^{-1/2}$$

51. **(c)** The work done is the same in figure (I), (II) and (III).

Explanation: In all the three figures, $V_A = 20$ V and $V_B = 40$ V.
Work done in carrying a charge q from A to B is $W = q (V_B - V_A)$
Hence, work done is same in all figures.

52. **(c)** perpendicular to both $d\vec{I}$ and $\vec{r}$

Explanation: According to Biot-Savart's law, the magnetic induction due to a current element is given by

$$d\vec{B} = \frac{\mu_0}{4\pi}\,\frac{id\,\vec{I}\times\vec{r}}{r^3}$$

This is perpendicular to both $d\vec{I}$ and $\vec{r}$.

53. (b) decreases as $\dfrac{1}{r^2}$

Explanation: From Biot-savart's law,

$$dB = \frac{\mu_0}{4\pi}\,\frac{I\,\vec{dl}}{r^2}\ \text{i.e.,}\ dB \propto \frac{1}{r^2}$$

54. (c) zero

Explanation:
$$B = \frac{\mu_0}{4\pi}\cdot\frac{i}{r} - \frac{\mu_0}{2\pi}\cdot\frac{i}{r} = 0.$$

55. (a) The magnetic fields are equal.

Explanation: At any two points on z-axis which are at equal distance from the wire, one above the wire and one below the wire, the magnitude of magnetic field will be same and their directions will be opposite to each other. At any two points on z-axis which are at different distances from the wire, one above the wire and other also above the wire, the magnitude of magnetic field will be different and their directions will be same to each other.

Sample Paper 2

Section-A

1. (b) 3.6×10^4 V

Explanation: Given
$$P = \frac{V^2}{R}$$
$$Q = 4 \times 10^{-7}\,\text{C}$$
$$k = 9 \times 10^9$$
$$x = 10\ \text{cm} = \frac{1}{10}\ \text{cm}$$
$$P = \text{Potential} = \frac{kQ}{x}$$
$$P = \frac{9 \times 10^9 \times 4 \times 10^{-7}}{\dfrac{1}{10}}$$
$$= 3.6 \times 10^4\ \text{V}.$$

2. **(d)** Zero

> **Explanation:** $W = 0$
> $\because$ Electrostatic force is conservative force and work done by conservative force depends only upon the initial and final position. Since, final position = initial position, hence work done is zero.

3. **(a)** directed perpendicular to the plane and away from the plane

> **Explanation:** Free electrons are attracted towards the positive charge which results in the development of negative charge towards the positive charge side and an equal charge develops opposite side of the plane.

4. **(d)** may increase or decrease

> **Explanation:** The electric potential is inversely proportional to the distance between the charges. It also depends whether both charges are of same or opposite sign.

5. **(c)** $0.5\ \mu F$

> **Explanation:**
> $$\frac{1}{C} = \frac{1}{C_1} + \frac{1}{C_2} + \frac{1}{C_3} + \frac{1}{C_4}$$
> $$= C_2 = C_3 = C_4 = 2\ \mu F$$
> $$C = 0.5\ \mu F$$

6. **(c)** $-\dfrac{2Q}{\varepsilon_0}$

> **Explanation:** Gauss theorem states that the electric flux through a closed surface enclosing a charge is equal to $\dfrac{1}{\varepsilon_0}$ times the magnitude of the charge enclosed. The sphere encloses a charge of $-2Q$ thus, $\phi = -\dfrac{2Q}{\varepsilon_0}$.
>
> 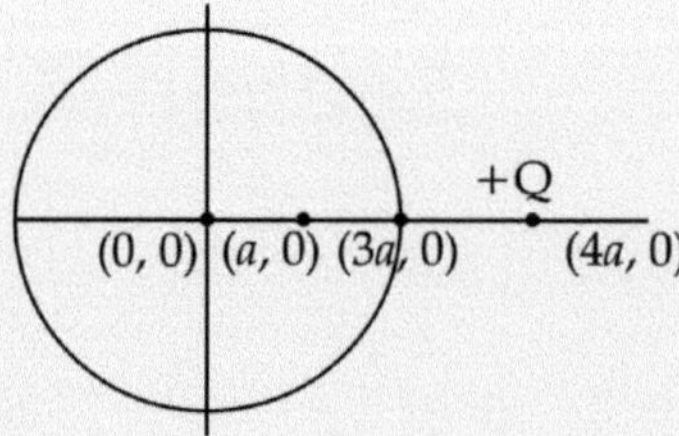
>

7. **(a)** no net charge is enclosed by the surface.

> **Explanation:** According to gauss law, the total electric flux out of a closed surface is equal to the net charge enclosed in the surface divided by the permittivity.

8. **(b)** 100 W filament is thicker

> **Explanation:** We know that, $P = \dfrac{V^2}{R}$ for same mains circuit V is same.
>
> Thus, $\qquad\qquad\qquad\qquad R_{60} > R_{100}$

Also, $R = \dfrac{\rho L}{A}$ where ρ = resistivity, A = area and L = length of wire

Thus, less resistor implies more thicker element. So, the 100 W bulb has thicker filament.

9. (c) He should change S to 3 Ω and repeat the experiment.

Explanation: The percentage error in R can be minimised by adjusting the balance point near the middle of the bridge, *i.e.*, when l_1, is close to 50 cm. This requires a suitable choice of S.

Since,
$$\frac{R}{S} = \frac{l_1}{(100 - l_1)}$$

Here,
$$\frac{R}{S} = \frac{2.9}{97.1} = 2.98 \ \Omega$$

Then the value of S is nearly 33 times to that of R. In order to make this ratio 1 : 1, it is necessary to reduce the value of S nearly $\dfrac{1}{33}$ times, *i.e.*, nearly 3 Ω.

10. (b) electric current

Explanation: The time rate of flow of charge through any cross-section of a conductor is electric current.

11. (d) the average of the velocities of all the free electrons at an instant is non-zero

Explanation: Average of the velocities of all free electrons at an instant is non-zero, if not current is passed through a conductor.

12. (b) motion of conduction electrons due to electric field E.

Explanation: Motion of conduction electrons due to random collisions has no preferred direction and average to zero. Drift velocity is caused due to motion of conduction electrons due to applied electric field.

13. (b) non-ohmic conductors

Explanation: The figure is showing I-V characteristics of non-ohmic or non-linear conductors.

14. (d) 3600 C

Explanation: As we know that,
$$I = \frac{q}{t}$$
$$q = It$$
$$= 0.5 \times 7200$$
$$= 3600 \text{ C.}$$

15. (c) experience a force, if it is moving at right angles to the field

Explanation: Force on charged particle when it enters the magnetic field will be:
$$F = q(v \times B) = qvB \sin \theta$$

If $\theta = 90°$, then $F = qvB$

Thus, a charged particle experiences the maximum force when it moves perpendicular to the magnetic field.

16. (b) $30°$

Explanation: Force $F = Bil \sin \theta$

$$\sin \theta = \frac{F}{Bil} = \frac{0.4}{4 \times 1 \times 0.2} = \frac{1}{2} = 30°.$$

17. (c) E

Explanation: H is magnetic field intensity in a magnetic field which is analogous to the electric field intensity in the electric field.

18. (c) Convective currents in earth's core

Explanation: The earth's core is hot and molten. Hence, convective current in earth's core is responsible for it's magnetic field.

19. (d) both (b) and (c)

Explanation: A magnetic field is produced around a changing electric field or a moving charge.

20. (a) the direction of the induced current

Explanation: The Lenz's law gives the direction of induced current. According to this law, the induced current opposes the cause that produces it.

21. (c) Faraday's Law

Explanation: Faraday's law of induction is a basic law of electromagnetism predicting how a magnetic field will interact with an electric circuit to produce an electromotive force.

22. (d) the resistivity of the wire of the coil

Explanation: When the conductor is moved in a stationary magnetic field to procure a change in the flux linkage, the emf is statically induced.

23. (d) average value of complete cycle is zero

Explanation: In D.C. ammeter, a coil is free to rotate in the magnetic field of a fixed magnet. If an alternating current is passed through such a coil, the torque will reverse its direction each time the current changes direction and the average value of the torque will be zero.

24. (a) rms current

Explanation: We know that,

$$\text{rms current} = \frac{I_0}{\sqrt{2}}$$

25. (c) Frequency

Explanation: The transformer can either increase the output voltage as compared to the input voltage or vice-versa. In all these process, the voltage changes and so does the electric current but the frequency remains unchanged.

Section-B

26. (c) Zero

Explanation: When a faraday cage is struck by lightning, the resulting electric field inside the car is zero.

27. (d) mass of B increases

Explanation: When a body is negatively charged, more electrons are given to it, so its mass increases. So, this is the reason due to which mass of sphere B increases when it is given equal amount of negative charge.

28. (c) 198 years

Explanation: The charge given out in one second
$$= 1.6 \times 10^{-19} \, C \times 10^9 = 1.6 \times 10^{-10} \, C$$
Time required to accumulate a charge of 1 C
$$= \frac{1}{1.6 \times 10^{-10}} = 6.25 \times 10^9 \, s = 198 \text{ years}$$

29. (a) Gauss's law is not much useful in calculating electrostatic field when the system has some symmetry.

Explanation: Gauss's law is often useful towards a much easier calculation of electrostatic field when the system has some symmetry. This is facilitated by the choice of a suitable Gaussian surface.

30. (c) remains constant from centre to surface

Explanation: Electric potential inside a conductor is constant and it is equal to that on the surface of the conductor.

31. (d) 220 V and 2.2 A

Explanation: As $V_L = V_C = 300$ V, resonance will take place.
$$\therefore \qquad VR = 220 \text{ V}$$
Current,
$$I = \frac{220}{100}$$
$$= 2.2 \text{ A}$$
$\therefore$ reading of $\qquad V_3 = 220$ V
and reading of $\qquad A = 2.2$ A

32. (c) It decreases exponentially

Explanation: The current in RC circuit decreases both during charging as well as discharging.

33. (b) decreases with the increases of temperature

> **Explanation:** Because as temperature increases, the resistivity increases and hence the relaxation time decreases for conductors,
>
> $$\tau \propto \frac{1}{\rho}$$

34. (a) $\frac{1}{2}v$

> **Explanation:** The mathematical expression for drift velocity is; $v = \dfrac{1}{n\text{AQ}}$
>
> If radius is doubles, it means area is increased 4 times, and current is doubled that is :
>
> $$v' = \frac{21}{nq \times 4\text{A}}$$
>
> $$v' = \frac{1}{2}v$$
>
> Hence drift velocity is halved.

35. (d) Current only

> **Explanation:** As we know that,
>
> $$\text{I} = \text{constant}$$
>
> $$\text{J} = \frac{\text{I}}{\text{A}}$$
>
> It is clear that, as A changes, current density J changes.
>
> $$\text{E} = \text{J}\rho$$
>
> ρ is constant
>
> As J changes, electric field E changes.
>
> $$\text{I} = ne\text{A}v_d$$
>
> I is constant
>
> So as A changes, drift speed v_d changes.

36. (b) decreases from A to B

> **Explanation:** As area increases, v_d decreases.

37. (b) not change

> **Explanation:** The deflection in galvanometer will not be changed due to interchange of battery and the galvanometer.

38. (a) in the direction perpendicular to both the field and its velocity.

> **Explanation:** Since,
>
> $$\vec{F} = q\left(\vec{v} \times \vec{B}\right)$$

39. (c) zero, if $\vec{B}$ and $\vec{v}$ are parallel.

Explanation: Since,

$$\vec{F} = q\left(\vec{v} \times \vec{B}\right)$$

if, $$\vec{v} \| \vec{B}$$

then, $$\vec{F} = 0$$

40. (a) does not change

Explanation: When a hole is cut in the bar magnet, the pole strength does not change, as the number of free poles at the ends do not change. Length does not change. So, magnetic properties of the magnet should not change.

41. (a) Current will increase

Explanation: If the coil is stretched so that there are gaps between successive elements of the spiral coil, *i.e.*, the wires are pulled apart which lead to the flux leak through the gaps. According to Lenz's law, the emf induced in these spirals must oppose this decrease in magnetic flux, which can be done by an increase in current. So, the current will increase.

42. (a) 1 A

Explanation: According to the question,

$$R_{eq} = \frac{5R}{6}$$

$$\Rightarrow \qquad I = \frac{6E}{5R}$$

$$= 1 \text{ A}$$

43. (c) decreases because the charge move along the electric field

Explanation: The positively charged particle experiences electrostatic force along the direction of electric field, *i.e.* from high electrostatic potential to low electrostatic potential. Thus, the work is done by the electric field on the positive charge, hence electrostatic potential energy of the positive charge decreases.

44. (c) continuous

Explanation: The field lines remain continuous, emerging from one face of the solenoid and entering into the other face.

45. (a) Both A and R are true and R is also the correct explanation of A.

Explanation: Potential drop across galvanometer = Potential drop across the shunt.

i.e., $$I_g G = (I - I_g)S$$

$$\Rightarrow \qquad S = \frac{I_g}{I - I_s} G$$

For $$I_g = \frac{I}{10}$$

$$S = \dfrac{\dfrac{I}{10}}{\left(I - \dfrac{I}{10}\right)} G = \dfrac{G}{9}.$$

46. (b)   Both A and R are true but R is not the correct explanation of A.

Explanation: Force on any charge due to a number of other charges is the vector sum of all the forces on that charge due to the other charges, taken one at a time. The individual force is unaffected due to the presence of other charges. This is the principle of superposition of charges.

47. (a)   Both A and R are true and R is also the correct explanation of A.

Explanation: Since both the magnets exert equal and opposite force or torque on each other. Hence, net force or torque on cork will be zero.

48. (a)   Both A and R are true and R is also the correct explanation of A.

Explanation: Lenz's Law is based on conservation of energy and induced emf opposes the cause of it *i.e.,* change in magnetic flux.

49. (c)   A is true but R is false.

Explanation: Two equipotential surfaces are not necessarily parallel to each other.

Section-C

50. (b)   (I) and (III)

Explanation: (I) Electrostatic field is zero inside a charged conductor or neutral conductor.
(II) electrostatic field at the surface of a charged conductor must be normal to the surface at every point.
(III) There is no net charge at any point inside the conductor and any excess charge must reside at the surface.

51. (b) $\dfrac{4}{3}$

Explanation: As we know that,

$$C_o = \dfrac{k\varepsilon_0 A}{d} \qquad\qquad \text{...(i)}$$

$$C = \dfrac{k\varepsilon_0 2}{3d} + \dfrac{2k\varepsilon_0 A}{3d}$$

$$= \dfrac{4}{3}\dfrac{k\varepsilon_0 A}{d} \qquad\qquad \text{...(ii)}$$

$$\therefore \quad \dfrac{C}{C_o} = \dfrac{\dfrac{4k\varepsilon_0 A}{d}}{\dfrac{k\varepsilon_0 A}{d}}$$

$$= \dfrac{4}{3}$$

52. (c) Induced current

Explanation: Lenz's law is used to determine the directions of induced magnetic fields, currents and emfs.

53. (d) Conservation of energy

Explanation: The Lenz's law is based on the law of conservation of energy. It shows that mechanical energy is spent in doing work against the opposing force experienced by the moving magnet.

54. (a) North

Explanation: As per the lenz's law if we move away the bar magnet from coil then the direction of induced current in coil will be clockwise.

55. (a) Clockwise

Explanation: By lenz's law the polarity of magnetic moment towards the magnet if we move the North of magnet towards coil will be north.

Sample Paper 3

Section-A

1. (d) $\dfrac{F}{8}$

Explanation: The electric field at a distance r from the dipole is $\vec{E} = \dfrac{2P}{r^3}$,

So,
$$E \propto \dfrac{1}{r^3}$$

Force on charge q is $F = qE$ also $F \propto \dfrac{1}{r^3}$

If distance r is doubled, then force will $F' = \dfrac{F}{8}$.

2. (b) Infinitely large uniformly charged plane

Explanation: Electric field due to the infinitely large uniformly charged plane sheet is $\dfrac{\sigma}{2\varepsilon_0}$, which is independent of distance.

3. (b) $\dfrac{1}{\varepsilon_0}$

Explanation:
$$\phi_S = \oint \vec{E}.d\vec{S}$$
$$= \dfrac{q_{enc}}{\varepsilon_0}$$
$$= \dfrac{1}{\varepsilon_0}$$

4. (a) It will decreases k times

> **Explanation:** The potential difference between the plates will decrease k times.

5. (d) $4\pi\varepsilon_0 Q \times 10^{22}$ Vm^{-1}.

> **Explanation:** Given that,
>
> $$V = \frac{Q}{4\pi\varepsilon_0 r} = Q \times 10^{11}\,\text{V}$$
>
> $\therefore \qquad 4\pi\varepsilon_0 r = 10^{-11} \qquad\qquad \text{...(i)}$
>
> Now,
> $$E = \frac{Q \times 4\pi\varepsilon_0}{\left(4\pi\varepsilon_0 r\right)^2}$$
>
> $$= \frac{Q \times 4\pi\varepsilon_0}{\left(10^{-11}\right)^2} \qquad\qquad \text{...[By using (i)]}$$
>
> $$= 4\pi\varepsilon_0 Q \times 10^{22}\,\text{Vm}^{-1}$$

6. (c) 7.5 N

> **Explanation:** Given that,
>
> $q_1 = 3\ \mu C,\ q_2 = +4\ \mu C,\ F = 10\ \text{N}$
>
> $q_1' = +3 - 6 = -3\ \mu C,\ q_2' = +4 - 6 = -2\ \mu C$
>
> $$\therefore \qquad \frac{F'}{F} = \frac{\left(q_1'\right)\left(q_2'\right)}{q_1 q_2}$$
>
> $$= \frac{(-3)\times(-2)}{2\times 4} = \frac{3}{4}$$
>
> $$\therefore \qquad F' = \frac{3}{4} \times F$$
>
> $$= \frac{3}{4} \times 10$$
>
> $$= 7.5\ \text{N}$$

7. (c) negative

> **Explanation:** In moving a small positive charge from Q to P, work has to be done by an external agent against the electric field. Therefore, work done by the field is negative.

8. (d) Current only

> **Explanation:** Current does not depend upon the area of cross-section, hence it remains a constant.

9. (a) Current is potentiometer wire remains constant

> **Explanation:** Potential gradient depends on the strength of the current and resistance per cm of the wire. So, it remains constant till current remains constant.

10. (b) Metals

> **Explanation:** Ohm's law states that the electric current between two points is directly proportional to voltage. The material that follow Ohm's law are ohmic conductors while others are non-ohmic conductors. In current electricity Ohm's law is obeyed by metals.

11. (b) Electric field produced by charges accumulated on the surface of wire.

Explanation:
$$\overrightarrow{J} = \sigma \overrightarrow{E} = \frac{\overrightarrow{E}}{\rho}$$

Where, σ is conductivity and ρ is the resistivity.

12. (b) decreases, thermal velocity of electron increases

Explanation: When the temperature increases, resistance increases. As the emf applied is the same, the current density decreases the drift velocity decreases. But the rms velocity of the electron due to thermal motion is proportional to $\sqrt{T}$. Therefore, the thermal velocity increases.

13. (a) $\dfrac{ml}{Ne^2 A\tau}$

Explanation: If N, e, τ and m are representing electron density, charge, relaxation time and mass of an electron respectively, then the resistance of wire of length l and cross-sectional area A is,

$$\frac{ml}{Ne^2 A\tau}$$

14. (d) All of these

Explanation: The direction of drift velocity in a conductor is opposite to that of applied electric field, opposite to the flow of positive charge, and in the direction of the flow of electrons.

15. (d) Large deflection for a small current

Explanation: A galvanometer is a device to detect current in a circuit. A galvanometer is said to be sensitive if it shows large scale deflection even when a small current is passed through it or a small voltage is applied across it.

16. (b) The magnetic field at any point inside the pipe is zero

Explanation: Using Ampere's circuital law over a circular loop of any radius less than the radius of the pipe, we can see that net current inside the loop is zero. Hence, magnetic field at every point inside the loop will be zero.

17. (c) Straight line path

Explanation: The path of a charged particle will be a straight-line path as no force acts on the particle.

18. (a) Magnetic declination

Explanation: The angle between the geographical meridian and the magnetic meridian at a place is called the magnetic declination.

19. (a) Yes

Explanation: Yes, earth's field undergoes a change with time for example daily change *dl*, annual changes *dl*, secular changes *etc.* Even field reversals have also occurred.

20. (d) The electron will continue to move with uniform velocity along the axis of the solenoid

Explanation: $F = -evB \sin 180° = 0$ (*i.e.*, $0 = 0°$ or $180°$ in both cases F = 0). The electron will continue to move with uniform velocity or will go undeflected along the axis of the solenoid.

21. (a) Self-induction

   Explanation: The property of coil by which a counter e.m.f. is induced in it when the current through the coil changes is known as self-induction.

22. (b) energy

   Explanation: Faraday's laws involve conversion of mechanical energy into electric energy. This is in accordance with the law of conservation of energy.

23. (b) $\dfrac{1}{400}$ s

   Explanation: The current takes $\dfrac{T}{4}$ s to reach the peak value.

   In the given question,

   $$\frac{2\pi}{T} = 200\pi$$

   $$\Rightarrow \qquad T = \frac{1}{100}\ s$$

   $$\therefore \qquad \text{Time to reach the peak value} = \frac{1}{400}\ s.$$

24. (c) $2\sqrt{2} : \pi$

   Explanation: We know that,

   $$I_{rms} = \frac{I_0}{\sqrt{2}}$$

   and $$I_m = \frac{2I_0}{\pi}$$

   $$\therefore \qquad \frac{I_m}{I_{rms}} = \frac{2\sqrt{2}}{\pi}$$

25. (c) Infinity

   Explanation: When the capacitor is connected to the battery and the circuit is closed then the capacitor gets progressively charged until the potential difference across the plates becomes equal to the potential difference across the terminals of the battery. As soon as this happens, the charging of the capacitor stops. Thus, during the capacitor is being charged, an electric current does flow through the rest of the circuit. So, the resistance offered by a capacitor for the steady current is infinity.

Section-B

26. (b) Electric field will also become half

   Explanation: If the charge on the object is halved than the electric field will also become half as electric field is directly proportional to the charge.

27. (a) Increase

   Explanation: $$\text{Total flux} = \frac{\text{Net enclosed charge}}{\varepsilon_0}$$

   Hence, we can say the electric flux depends only on net enclosed charge by surface.

28. (c) Principle of superposition

     Explanation: The weight mg of the charge hold in air is in equilibrium with net electrostatic force exerted by the four charges situated at the corners. The net electrostatic force is given by the vector sum of the individual forces exerted by the charges at the corners. This is principle of superposition.

29. (d) zero

     Explanation: Potential at A = Potential due to $(+q)$ charge + Potential due to $(-q)$ charge

     $$= \frac{1}{4\pi\varepsilon_0}\cdot\frac{q}{\sqrt{a^2}} + \frac{1}{4\pi\varepsilon_0}\frac{(-q)}{\sqrt{a^2}} = 0$$

30. (c) $\dfrac{1}{\pi\varepsilon_0}\dfrac{\sqrt{2q}}{l}$

     Explanation: As we know that,

     $$V = \frac{1}{4\pi\varepsilon_0}\frac{q}{r}$$

     Electric potential due to each charge at the centre of the square is $\dfrac{1}{4\pi\varepsilon_0}\dfrac{\sqrt{2q}}{l}$

     Hence total potential is,

     $$= 4 \times \frac{1}{4\pi\varepsilon_0}\frac{\sqrt{2q}}{l}$$

     $$= \frac{1}{\pi\varepsilon_0}\frac{\sqrt{2q}}{l}$$

31. (b) Capacitive

     Explanation: If $\omega < \omega_r$, the circuit will be capacitive in nature.

32. (d) decreases in the first circuit and increases in the other

     Explanation: For the first circuit,

     $$I = \frac{V}{Z}$$

     $$= \frac{V}{\sqrt{R^2 + \omega^2 L^2}}$$

     $\therefore$ Increase in ω will cause a decrease in I.

     For the second circuit,

     $$I = \frac{V}{\sqrt{R^2 + \dfrac{1}{\omega^2 C^2}}}$$

     $\therefore$ Increase in ω will cause an increase in I.

33. (c) 1 A

Explanation: Equivalent emf in series combination is given by $E_{eq} = E_1 + E_2$ .... In the given question it will be $E_{eq} = 1.5 + 1.5 + 1.5 + 1.5$ $R_{eq} = 0.25 + 0.25 + 0.25 + 0.25 = 2\ \Omega$

Now,
$$1 = \frac{R_{eq}}{E_{eq}}\quad 1 = 1\ A$$

34. (d) 6.25×10^{18}

Explanation: As we know that,
$$q = It$$
$$\Rightarrow \qquad ne = It$$
$$\therefore \qquad n = \frac{It}{e}$$
$$= \frac{1 \times 1}{1.6 \times 10^{-19}}$$
$$= 6.25 \times 10^{18}.$$

35. (c) the resistance will be halved, and the specific resistance will remain unchanged

Explanation: According to the given condition,
$$R = \frac{\rho l_1}{A_1}$$

now,
$$l_2 = 2l_1$$
$$A_2 = \pi (r_2)^2$$
$$= \pi (2r_1)^2 = 4\pi r_1^2 = 4A_1$$
$$\therefore \qquad R_2 = \frac{\rho (2l_1)}{4A_1} = \frac{\rho l}{2A} = \frac{R}{2}$$

Resistance is halved, but specific resistance remains the same.

36. (a) 16:1

Explanation: Current flowing through the conductor, $I = nev_d A$. Hence,
$$\frac{4}{1} = \frac{nev_{d_1} \pi (1)^2}{nev_{d_2} \pi (2)^2}$$

$$\Rightarrow \qquad \frac{v_{d_1}}{v_{d_2}} = \frac{4 \times 1}{1}$$

$$= \frac{16}{1}.$$

37. (a) network is not balanced

Explanation: In a balanced Wheatstone network, the resistances in the arms Q and S are interchanged. As a result of this network is not balanced.

38. (d) Inside a magnet, its magnetic lines of force move from north pole of a magnet towards its south pole.

Explanation: Inside a magnet, magnetic lines of force move from South pole to North pole.

39. (a) $\dfrac{2\pi m}{qB}$

Explanation: Equating magnetic force to centripetal force.

$$\frac{mv^2}{r} = qvB \sin 90°$$

$$r = \frac{mv}{qB} \qquad \qquad ..(i)$$

Time to complete one revolution,

$$T = \frac{2\pi r}{v} = \frac{2\pi m}{qB} \qquad \qquad ...(from\ (i))$$

40. (a) run continuously through the bar and outside

Explanation: In the bar magnet, lines of magnetic induction run continuously through the bar and outside.

41. (a) the direction of the induced current

Explanation: Lenz's law states that an induced electric current flows in a direction such that the current opposes the change that induced it.

42. (b) 0 V, 8 A

Explanation: The voltage V_L and V_C are equal to opposite so voltmeter reading will be zero

Also, $\qquad\qquad R = 30\ \Omega$

$$X_L = X_C = 25\ \Omega$$

So,

$$i = \frac{V}{\sqrt{R^2 + (X_L - X_C)^2}}$$

$$= \frac{V}{R}$$

$$= \frac{240}{30}$$

$$= 8$$

43. (b) F

Explanation: Electrostatic force is given by,

$$F = \frac{1}{4\pi\varepsilon_0} \frac{q_1 q_2}{r^2}$$

Here, charge and distance are same. So, force between two protons will be same.

44. (a) Zero

Explanation: Potential difference between O and A is,

$$V_O - V_A = \frac{1}{2} B l^2 \omega$$

Potential difference between O and B is,

$$V_O - V_B = \frac{1}{2} B l^2 \omega$$

$$\text{So, } V_A - V_B = 0$$

45. (a) Both A and R are true and R is also the correct explanation of A.

Explanation: As we know that,

$$P = \frac{V^2}{R}$$

$$\Rightarrow \qquad R = \frac{V^2}{P}$$

$$\Rightarrow \qquad R \propto \frac{1}{P}$$

That means higher is the wattage of a bulb, lesser is the resistance and so it will glow bright.

46. (d) A is false and R is also false.

Explanation: When we rub a glass rod with silk cloth, electrons from the glass rod are transferred to the silk cloth. Thus the rod gets positively charged and the silk gets negatively charged.

47. (a) Both A and R are true and R is also the correct explanation of A.

Explanation: Since both the loops are identical (same area and number of turns) and moving with a same speed in same magnetic field. Therefore, same emf is induced in both the coils. But the induced current will be more in copper loop as its resistance will be lesser as compared to that of the aluminium loop.

48. (b) Both A and R are true but R is not the correct explanation of A.

Explanation: Like direct current, an alternating current also produces magnetic field. But the magnitude and direction of the field goes on changing continuously with time.

49. (c) A is true but R is false.

Explanation: Equivalent capacitance of parallel combination is $C_p = C_1 + C_2 + C_3$.

Section-C

50. (a) shall increase along the positive x-axis

Explanation: As shown in the figure, since positive charge q_2 and q_3 exert a net force in the +X-direction on the charge q_1 fixed along the x-axis, the charge q_1 is negative. Obviously, due to addition of positive charge Q at $(x, 0)$, the force on $-q$ shall increase along the positive x-axis.

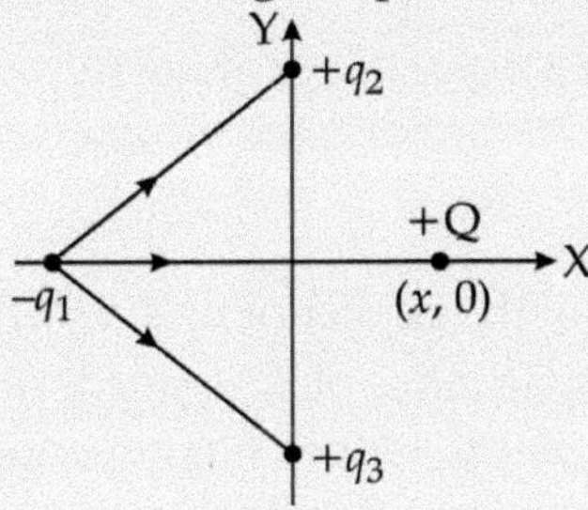

51. (b) (II) only

Explanation: There is equal and opposite charge on the plates of a parallel plate capacitor. Therefore there is no net charge on capacitor.

52. (a) 20 mH

Explanation:

$$X_L = \frac{V_L}{I}$$

$$I = \frac{V_R}{R} = \frac{25}{50} = \frac{1}{2}$$

$$X_L = \frac{20}{\frac{1}{2}} = 20\ \Omega$$

But

$$X_L = \omega L$$

$$L = \frac{X_L}{\omega} = \frac{40}{2 \times 10^3}$$

$$= 20 \times 10^{-3} = 20\ \text{mH}$$

53. (d) 12.5 μF

Explanation:

$$\omega^2 = \frac{1}{L_C}$$

$$\Rightarrow \quad C = \frac{1}{\omega^2 L}$$

$$= \frac{1}{(2 \times 10^3) \times 20 \times 10^{-13}} = 12.5\ \mu\text{F}$$

54. (a) 50 W

Explanation: At resonance, the impedance equal just resistance.

55. (d) 5×10^3 rod/s

Explanation: For inductive nature $\omega > \omega_r$.

Sample Paper 4

Section-A

1. (d) Charge on the plates

> **Explanation:** The capacitance of a capacitor is given by
>
> $$C = \frac{\varepsilon_0 A}{d}$$
>
> Here, A is the area of the plates of the capacitor and d is the distance between the plates.
> So, we can clearly see that the capacitance of a capacitor does depend on the size and shape of the plates and the separation between the plates; it does not depend on the charges on the plates.
>
> 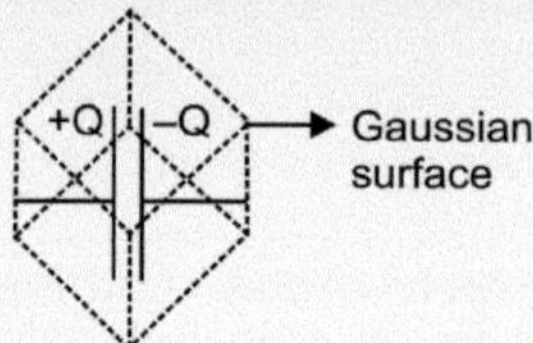
>

2. (b) A deficiency of 5 electrons

> **Explanation:** The magnitude of charge on each electron is $q_e = 1.6 \times 10^{-19}$ C
> The body has a positive charge that means it has a deficiency of electrons.
> Total charge on the body is $q = n \times q_e = 8 \times 10^{-19}$ C, Which implies $n = 5$.

3. (d) A parabola

> **Explanation:** The path is a parabola, because initial velocity can be resolved into two rectangular components, one along $\vec{E}$ and other perpendicular to $\vec{E}$. The former decreases at a constant rate and latter are unaffected. The resultant path is therefore a parabola.

4. (b) No

> **Explanation:** Intersection of two equipotential surfaces at a point will give two directions of electric field intensity at that point, which is not possible.

5. (d) no work is done

> **Explanation:** On the equipotential surface, electric field is normal to the charged surface (where potential exists) So that no work will be done.

6. (a) 100 Vm

> **Explanation:** Electric flux through the frame $\phi = E.A\cos\theta = 20 \times 10 \times \cos 60° = 100$ Vm.

7. (b) increase

> **Explanation:** By using,
>
> $$U = QV$$
> $$\because \qquad Q = +1, U = V$$
>
> At high potential, potential energy will be high and lower potential, low energy it will have.

8. (d) $\dfrac{v_d}{4}$

Explanation: we know that,
$$I = nAev_d$$
or,
$$v_d \propto \dfrac{1}{\pi r^2}$$
If
$$r \to 2r, \text{ then}$$
$$v_d' = \dfrac{1}{\pi(2r)^2}$$
$$v_d' = \dfrac{v_d}{4}.$$

9. (a) 0.013/°C

Explanation: According to the given condition,
$$5\,\Omega = R_0\,(1 + \alpha \times 50) \qquad\qquad \text{...(i)}$$
and
$$7\,\Omega = R_0\,(1 + \alpha \times 100) \qquad\qquad \text{...(ii)}$$
Divide equation (i) by (ii)
$$\dfrac{5}{7} = \dfrac{1 + 50\alpha}{1 + 100\alpha}$$
$$\alpha = \dfrac{2}{150}$$
$$= 0.0133°C.$$

10. (b) 24 Ω

Explanation: $R \propto L$
$$\dfrac{R_1}{R_2} = \dfrac{l_1}{l_2} \Rightarrow \dfrac{18}{R_2} = \dfrac{1}{1.5} \Rightarrow R_2 = 24\Omega$$

11. (c) 4R

Explanation: $R \propto \dfrac{L}{A}$; Length gets doubled and A becomes halved, resistance becomes 4 times.

12. (d) 22.5 Ω

Explanation: As temperature increases, resistivity increases, thereby increasing the resistance.

13. (a) Point of higher potential to lower potential

Explanation: By convention, the direction of motion of positive charges is taken as the direction of electric current.

14. (a) Resistance

Explanation: If voltage is on x-axis and current on y-axis then the slope gives the resistance.

15. (b) 30°

> **Explanation:** Force F = *Bil* sin θ
>
> $$\sin \theta = \frac{F}{Bil} = \frac{0.4}{4 \times 1 \times 0.2} = \frac{1}{2} = 30°.$$

16. (c) Same as the former value

> **Explanation:** Magnetic field $\propto$ I
> Since the current in both the wires is same, there is no change in the strength of the magnetic field.

17. (d) Straight line

> **Explanation:** The positively charged particle will accelerated parallel and negatively charged particle will accelerated anti-parallel to the electric field.
> Therefore, net magnetic force on it will be zero and its path will be straight line.

18. (b) Magnetic equator

> **Explanation:** The angle of dip is 0° at the magnetic equator.

19. (d) What is the relation between angle of dip (δ) , B_V and B_H.

> **Explanation:** $\qquad \tan \theta = \dfrac{B_V}{B_H} \qquad \left[\begin{array}{l} \because B_H = B \cos \theta \\ \text{and } B_V = B \sin \theta \end{array} \right]$

20. (b) Generation of hydroelectricity.

> **Explanation:** Hydroelectric plant uses mechanical energy of water to move a magnetic field passes coils of wire to generate voltage.

21. (c) $\phi \propto N$

> **Explanation:** Since,
>
> $$\phi = N \vec{B}.\vec{A} \text{ and } \phi \propto N.$$

22. (d) Become double

> **Explanation:** Induced emf is directly proportional to the speed of rotation of the dynamo.

23. (c) Frequency

> **Explanation:** The transformer can either increase the output voltage as compared to the input voltage or vice-versa. In all these process, the voltage changes and so does the electric current but the frequency remains unchanged.

24. (a) NBAω

> **Explanation:** The maximum value of emf generated when θ = 90°.

25. (d) 84.8 V

Explanation: We know that,

$$V_{rms} = \frac{V_0}{\sqrt{2}}$$

$$= \frac{120}{1.414}$$

$$= 84.8 \text{ V.}$$

Section-B

26. (d) $V_A = V_C$

Explanation: Conducting surface behaves as equipotential surface.

27. (d) Zero

Explanation: Forces of repulsion on 1 μC charge at O due to 3 μC charge, at A and C are equal and opposite. So they cancel each other. Similarly, forces of attraction of 1 μC charge at O due to −4 μC charges at B and D are also equal and opposite. So they also cancel each other.
Hence the net force on the charge of 1 μC at O is zero.

28. (d) 2

Explanation: By using Coulomb's law

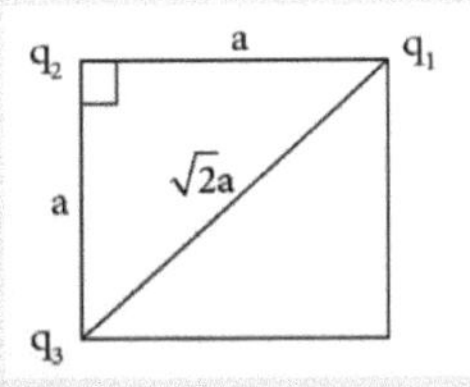

$$F_{12} = \frac{1}{4\pi\varepsilon_0} \times \frac{q^2}{a^2}$$

$$F_{13} = \frac{1}{4\pi\varepsilon_0} \times \frac{q^2}{\left(a\sqrt{2}\right)^2}$$

$$\therefore \quad \frac{F_{12}}{F_{13}} = 2$$

29. (c) Zero

Explanation: As we know that,

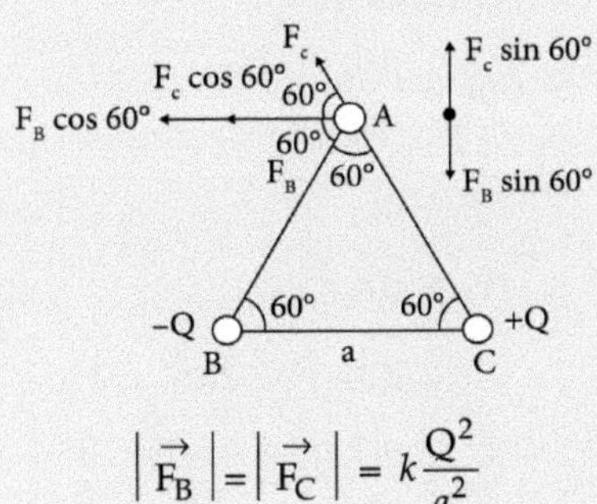

$$\left| \vec{F_B} \right| = \left| \vec{F_C} \right| = k\frac{Q^2}{a^2}$$

30. (d) zero

> **Explanation:** As we know that,
> $$W = p\text{E} (\cos 90° - \cos 270°)$$
> $$= 0$$

31. (a) Yes

> **Explanation:** Yes, because the average power dissipated per cycle in an ideal capacitor is also zero.

32. (d)

> **Explanation:** We know that,
> $$Z = \sqrt{R^2 + X_L^2}$$
> $$X_L = \omega L$$
> $$\omega = 2\pi f$$
> and,
> $$\therefore \quad Z = \sqrt{R^2 + 4\pi^2 f^2 L^2}$$

33. (b) CD

> **Explanation:** $R \propto \dfrac{L}{A}$; L is the most and A is the least between C and D.

34. (c) Resistivity of B is thrice the resistivity of D.

> **Explanation:** $R \propto \rho$
> $$\frac{R_B}{R_D} = \frac{\rho_B}{\rho_D} \Rightarrow \frac{15}{5} = \frac{\rho_B}{\rho_D} \Rightarrow \rho_B = 3\rho_D$$

35. (d) the average speed of the electron between successive collisions in the direction opposite to the applied electric field

> **Explanation:** When no emf is applied, the electrons move randomly inside the conductor. When emf is applied, electrons drift opposite to the applied emf and collide with each other. Between the collisions, average speed in the direction of field is v_d.

36. (c) the resistance will be halved, and the specific resistance will remain unchanged.

> **Explanation:** According to the given condition,
> $$R = \frac{\rho \ell_1}{A_1}$$
> now,
> $$\ell_2 = 2\ell_1$$
> $$A_2 = \pi(r_2)^2$$
> $$= \pi(2r_1)^2 = 2\pi r_1^2 = 4A_1$$
> $$\therefore \quad R_2 = \frac{\rho(2\ell_1)}{4A_1} = \frac{\rho\ell}{2A} = \frac{R}{2}$$
>
> Resistance is halved, but specific resistance remains the same.

37. (b) $T_1 < T_2$

Explanation: It is clear from figure that at a given voltage V_0, the current I_1 in the wire at temperature T_1 is greater than the current I_2 in the wire at temperature T_2. Therefore, the resistance of the wire at temperature T_1 is less than that at temperature T_2. This can happen if T_1 is less than T_2 because the resistance of a wire increases with increase in temperature.

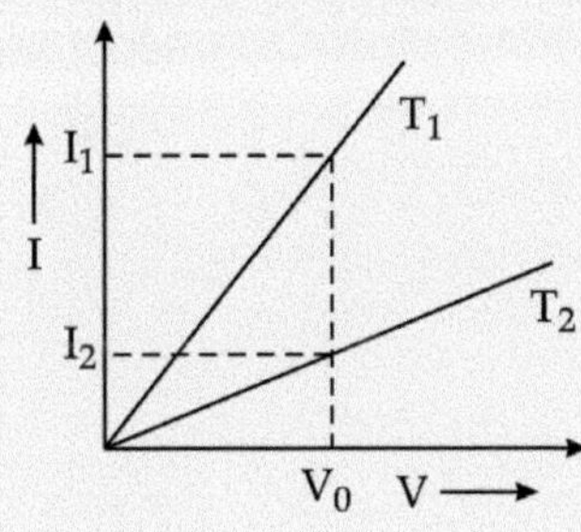

38. (a) the vector sum of electrostatic and magnetic force acting on a moving charged particle.

Explanation: As Lorentz force is given by,

$$\vec{F} = q\left(\vec{E} + \vec{v} \times \vec{B}\right)$$

$$= q\vec{E} + q\left(\vec{v} \times \vec{B}\right)$$

$$\vec{F} = \vec{F_E} + \vec{F_B}$$

39. (a) Copper loop

Explanation: Induced current will be greater in copper loop because its resistance is smaller than that of aluminium loop.

40. (d) 50×10^{-3} N

Explanation: Force between magnetic poles in air is given by,
Given that,

$$F = \frac{u_0}{4\pi} \times \frac{m_1 m_2}{r^2}$$

Given that,

$$m_1 = 50 \text{ Am}$$
$$m_2 = 100 \text{ Am}$$
$$r = 10 \text{ cm} = 0.1 \text{ m}$$
$$\mu_0 = \text{permeability of air}$$
$$= 4\pi \times 10^{-7} \text{ Hm}^{-1}$$

$$\therefore \quad F = \frac{4\pi \times 10^{-7}}{4\pi} \cdot \frac{50 \times 100}{0.1 \times 0.1}$$

$$= 50 \times 10^{-3} \text{ N}$$

41. (a) $5\sqrt{3}$ V

Explanation: We know that,

$$E = E_0 \cos \omega t$$

$$= E_0 \cos \frac{2\pi t}{T}$$

$$= 10 \cos \frac{2\pi \times 50 \times 1}{600}$$

$$= 10 \cos \frac{\pi}{6}$$

$$= 5\sqrt{3} \text{ V.}$$

42. (c) $85.7 \ \Omega$

Explanation: Since,

$$Z = \frac{E_v}{1_v}$$

$$= \frac{220}{2.5}$$

$$= 88 \ \Omega$$

As,
$$R^2 + X_c^2 = Z^2$$

$$X_C = \sqrt{Z^2 - R^2}$$

$$= \sqrt{88^2 - 20^2}$$

$$= 85.7 \ \Omega$$

43. (c)   remains unchanged

Explanation: The force will still remain $\dfrac{q_1 q_2}{4\pi\varepsilon_0 r^2}$ according to the superposition principle.

44. (b) In anticlockwise direction.

Explanation: As it is seen from the magnet side induced current will be anticlockwise.

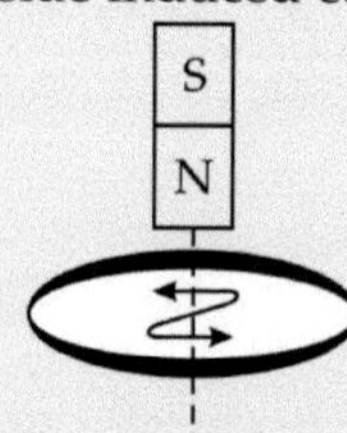

45. (c)   A is true but R is false.

Explanation: The resistance of the galvanometer is fixed. In meter bridge experiments, to protect the galvanometer from a high current, high resistance is connected to the galvanometer in order to protect it from damage.

46. (a) Both A and R are true and R is also the correct explanation of A.

Explanation: In the absence of the electric current, the free electrons in a conductor are in a state of random motion, like molecules in a gas. Their average velocity is zero i.e., they do not have any net velocity in a direction. As a result, there is no net magnetic force on the free electrons in the magnetic field. On passing the current, the free electrons acquire drift velocity in a definite direction, hence magnetic force acts on them, unless the field has no perpendicular component.

47. (a) Both A and R are true and R is also the correct explanation of A.

Explanation: Helium atom has paired electrons so their electron spin are opposite to each other and hence its net magnetic moment is zero.

48. (c) A is true but R is false.

Explanation: As the aircraft flies, magnetic flux changes through its wings due to the vertical component of the earth's magnetic field. Due to this, induced emf is produced across the wings of the aircraft. Therefore, the wings of the aircraft will not be at the same potential.

49. (b) Both A and R are true but R is not the correct explanation of A.

Explanation: Before the presence of electric field, the free electrons move randomly in the conductor, so their drift velocity is zero and therefore there is no current in the conductor. In the presence of electric field, each electron in the conductor experiences a force in a direction opposite to the electric field. Now the free electrons are accelerated from negative and to the positive and of the conductor and hence a current start to flow from the conductor.

Section-C

50. (b) $\dfrac{3F}{8}$

Explanation: Let the spherical conductors B and C have same charge q. The electric force between them is $F = \dfrac{1}{4\pi\varepsilon_0}\dfrac{q^2}{r^2}$, r, being distance between them.

When third uncharged conductor A is brought in contact with B, then charge on each conductor.

$$q_A = q_B$$
$$= \frac{q_A + q_B}{2} = \frac{0+q}{2} = \frac{q}{2}$$

When this conductor a is brought in contact with C, then charge on each conductor,

$$q_A = q_C$$
$$= \frac{q_A + q_C}{2} = \frac{\left(\dfrac{q}{2}\right)+q}{2} = \frac{3q}{4}$$

Hence, electric force acting between B and C is,

$$F' = \frac{1}{4\pi\varepsilon_0}\frac{q_B q_C}{r^2} = \frac{1}{4\pi\varepsilon_0}\frac{\left(\dfrac{q}{2}\right)\left(\dfrac{3q}{4}\right)}{r^2}$$
$$= \frac{3}{8}\left(\frac{1}{4\pi\varepsilon_0}\frac{q^2}{r^2}\right) = \frac{3F}{8}$$

51. (a) 420 N/C

Explanation: As we know that,

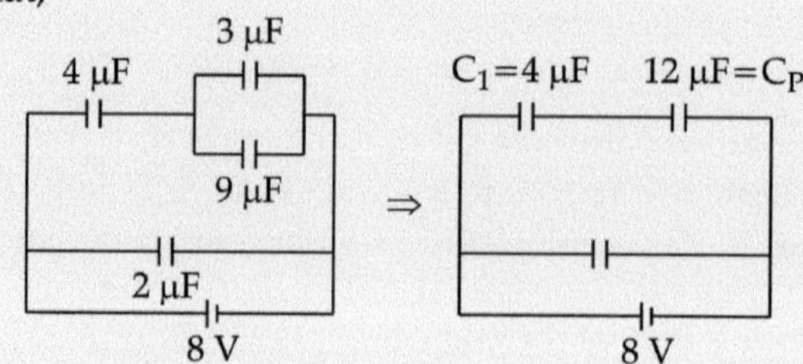

Charge on C_1 is,

$$q_1 = \left[\left(\frac{12}{4+12}\right)\times 8\right]\times 4 = 24 \ \mu C$$

The voltage across C_p is,

$$V_p = \frac{4}{4+12}\times 8 = 2V$$

Therefore, voltage across 9 μF is also 2V
So, total charge on 4 μF and 9 μF = 42 μc

$$E = \frac{KQ}{r^2} = 9\times 10^9 \times \frac{42\times 10^{-6}}{30\times 30} = 420 \ NC^{-1}$$

52. (c) Biot and Savart

Explanation: Biot savart law was given by the Jean-Baptiste Biot and physicist Felix Savart.

53. (a) Magnetic field

Explanation: According to Biot-Savart law, the magnetic field at a point near current carrying element is induced.

$$\text{i.e., } B = k.\frac{i.dl \sin \theta}{r^2}$$

54. (d) All of these

Explanation: $\because \ dB = \frac{\mu_0}{4\pi}\frac{idl \sin \theta}{r^2}$

55. (a) r^2

Explanation: $B \propto \dfrac{1}{r^2}$ or $B \propto r^{-2}$

Sample Paper 5

Section-A

1. (c) Unaffected by other charges

Explanation: According to the superposition theorem the force between two charges is not affected by the presence of other charges.

2. (d) May increase or decrease

> **Explanation:** The electric potential is inversely proportional to the distance between the charges. It also depends whether both charges are of same or opposite sign.

3. (d) Both (a) and (b)

> **Explanation:** Electron and proton has the same magnitude of charge with opposite signs.

4. (b) electric field

> **Explanation:** Force per unit charge is electric field.

5. (c) 10 V

> **Explanation:** As we know that, Potential = potential energy/test charge.

6. (c) radial, inwards

> **Explanation:** Electric lines of force about a negative point charge are radial, inwards.

7. (b) increases

> **Explanation:** Potential energy of the system,
>
> $$U = \frac{1}{4\pi\varepsilon_0} \frac{(-e)\times(-e)}{r}$$

8. (a) Drift velocity time

> **Explanation:** Relation between current and drift velocity is $I = neAv_d$
> Here I is proportional to drift velocity (v_d). So, only drift velocity determines the current in a conductor.

9. (c) Kirchhoff's laws

> **Explanation:** Kirchhoff's extended Ohm's law to complicated circuits and gave two laws, which enable us to determine current in any part of such a circuit.

10. (d) may be at positive, zero or negative potential

> **Explanation:** The conductor may be at positive, zero or negative potential, it is according to the way one defines the zero potential.

11. (c) they can be charged equally (maximum)

> **Explanation:** In case of metallic sphere either solid or hollow, the charge will reside on the surface of the sphere. Since both spheres have same surface area, they can hold equal amount of maximum charge.

12. (a) be double the initial velocity

> **Explanation:** As we know that,
> $$I = nev_d$$
> $$\therefore \quad I \propto v_d$$
> From Ohm's law, $\quad V \propto I \propto v_d$
> If the potential difference is doubled, drift velocity of electrons will also double.

13. (a) current and potential difference

> **Explanation:** Ohm's law deals with the relation between current and potential difference.

14. (a) constant

> **Explanation:** Ohm's law is valid when the temperature of the conductor is constant.

15. (d) Zero

> **Explanation:** The rotation of the loop by 30° about an axis perpendicular to its plane make no change in the angle made by axis of the loop with the direction of magnetic field, therefore, the work done to rotate the loop is zero.

16. (d) The electron will continue to move with uniform velocity along the axis of the solenoid

> **Explanation:** $F = -evB \sin 180° = 0$ (*i.e.*, $0 = 0°$ or $180°$ in both cases $F = 0$). The electron will continue to move with uniform velocity or will go undeflected along the axis of the solenoid.

17. (d) is independent of both R and v

> **Explanation:** The time period of motion $\dfrac{2\pi m}{q\text{B}}$. Time period is independent of terms R and v.

18. (c) E

> **Explanation:** H is magnetic field intensity in a magnetic field which is analogous to the electric field intensity in the electric field.

19. (a) Magnetic declination

> **Explanation:** The angle between the geographical meridian and the magnetic meridian at a place is called the magnetic declination.

20. (b) A metal is kept in varying magnetic field

> **Explanation:** On the surface of the metal plate, we can imagine a loop, which will be associated with a magnetic flux due to magnetic field. As the magnetic field is changing, there is change of magnetic flux through this loop and so an electric current is going to be induced in the loop and known as the eddy currents.

21. (c) time

> **Explanation:** We know that,
>
> $$e = \frac{d\phi}{dt}$$
>
> where
> $$\phi = NBA$$
>
> $$q = \frac{e}{R}\, dt$$
>
> $$= \frac{\Delta\phi}{R}$$

22. (b) can either increase or decrease

> **Explanation:** Emf is induced when there is change in magnetic flux in the coil.

23. (c) $0°$

Explanation: In purely resistive circuit
$$V = V_0 \sin \omega t \text{ and } I = I_0 \sin \omega t$$
From both equations, we observe that V and I are functions of $\sin \omega t$. Hence, the emf and the current are in same phase in a purely resistive circuit.

24. (a) 2.5×10^{-3} s

Explanation: Peak value to *rms* value means, current becomes $\dfrac{1}{\sqrt{2}}$ times.

If peak is at $t = 0$, current is of the form.
$$I = I_0 \cos 100\pi t$$
$$\Rightarrow \quad \frac{1}{\sqrt{2}} \times I_0 = I_0 \cos 100\pi t$$
$$\Rightarrow \quad \cos \frac{\pi}{4} = \cos 100\pi t$$
$$\Rightarrow \quad t = \frac{1}{400} \text{ s}$$
$$= 2.5 \times 10^{-3} \text{ s.}$$

25. (c) Voltage leads the current by $\dfrac{\pi}{2}$

Explanation: In an inductor voltage leads the current by $\dfrac{\pi}{2}$ or current lags the voltage by $\dfrac{\pi}{2}$.

Section-B

26. (a) y

Explanation:

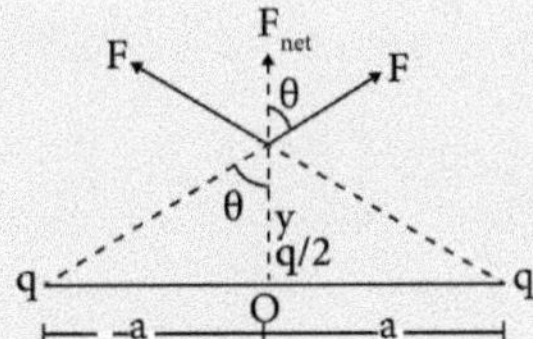

$$F_{net} = 2F \cos \theta$$
$$= \frac{2 \times kq^2}{2(a^2 + y^2)} \times \cos \theta$$
$$= \frac{kq^2}{(a^2 + y^2)} \times \frac{y}{\sqrt{(a^2 + y^2)}}$$

For
$$y \ll a$$
$$F = \frac{kq^2 y}{a^3}$$
$$F \alpha y$$

27. (a) 3.69×10^{-3} N

Explanation: Given that,

$q_1 = q_2 = 3.2 \times 10^{-7}$ C, $r = 50$ cm $= 0.5$ m

$\because$

$$F = \frac{1}{4\pi\varepsilon_0}\frac{q_1 q_2}{r^2}$$

$\therefore$

$$F = \frac{9\times10^9\,(3.2\times10^{-7})^2}{(0.5)^2}$$

$$= 3.69 \times 10^{-3} \text{ N}$$

28. (c) $q_A = q_B = 5.5$ µC

Explanation: The charge on disc A is 10^{-6} C. The charge on disc B is 10×10^{-6} C. The total charge on both $= 11 \times 10^{-6}$ C. When touched, this charge will be distributed equally, i.e., 5.5×10^{-6} C or 5.5 µC on each disc.

29. (a) decreases directly as the distance from the centre

Explanation: Electric Field is directly proportional to the magnitude of charge and inversely proportional to the square of the distance from the charge.

30. (d) $-\dfrac{7q^2}{8\pi\varepsilon_0 a}$

Explanation: As we know that,

$$U = \frac{1}{4\pi\varepsilon_0}\left[\frac{q_1 q_2}{r_{12}} + \frac{q_2 q_3}{r_{23}} + \frac{q_3 q_1}{r_{31}}\right]$$

$$= \frac{1}{4\pi\varepsilon_0}\left[\frac{-2q^2}{a} - \frac{2q^2}{a} + \frac{q^2}{2a}\right]$$

$$= \frac{q^2}{4\pi\varepsilon_0 a}\left[-4 + \frac{1}{2}\right]$$

$$= \frac{-7q^2}{8\pi\varepsilon_0 a}$$

31. (c) 7 A

Explanation: Since,

$$I_{rms} = \frac{E_{rms}}{R}$$

$$= \frac{200}{40}$$

$$= 5 \text{ A}$$

$\therefore$

$$I_a = I_{rms}\sqrt{2}$$

$$= 7.07 \text{ A}.$$

32. (d) $100\ \Omega,\ \sqrt{0.3}\ H$

Explanation: For DC,

$$R = \frac{100}{1}$$

$$= 100\ \Omega$$

$$I = \frac{V}{\sqrt{R^2 + L^2\omega^2}}$$

For AC,

$$\therefore \quad R^2 + L^2\omega^2 = \frac{V^2}{I^2}$$

$$R^2 + L^2\omega^2 = \frac{100 \times 100}{\frac{1}{2} \times \frac{1}{2}}$$

$$= 4 \times 10^4$$

$$\therefore \quad 4 \times 10^4 = (100)^2 + 4\pi^2 L^2 f^2$$

$$\therefore \quad 4 \times 10^4 = 10^4\,(1 + 10L^2)$$

$$\therefore \quad 3 = 10L^2$$

$$\therefore \quad L = \sqrt{0.3}\ H$$

Thus, $\quad R = 100\ \Omega$

and $\quad L = \sqrt{0.3}\ H$

33. (b) decreases from A to B

Explanation: As area increases, v_d decreases.

34. (b) 2×10^{-6}

Explanation: As we know that,

$$E = \frac{V}{l} = \frac{10}{0.1}$$

$$= 100\ V/m$$

$$\therefore \quad \mu = \frac{V_d}{E}$$

$$= \frac{2 \times 10^{-4}}{100}$$

$$= 2 \times 10^{-6}\ m^2 v^{-1} s^{-1}.$$

35. (c) will remain the same

Explanation: As we know that,

$$R_1 \propto \frac{l}{A}$$

$$\Rightarrow \quad R_2 \propto \frac{2l}{2A}$$

$$i.e., \quad R_2 \propto \frac{l}{A}$$

$$\therefore \quad R_1 = R_2.$$

36. (b) increases as the temperature rises

> **Explanation:** As we know that,
> $$\frac{V}{l} = R \text{ and } R \propto \text{temperature.}$$

37. (c) there must be charges only on the surface.

> **Explanation:** If a conductor has a non-zero potential and there are no charges anywhere else outside, then there must be charges on the surface of the conductor or inside the conductor. There cannot be any charge in the body of the conductor.

38. (b) v and B are perpendicular.

> **Explanation:** Since,
> $$F = q(v \times B)$$
> or
> $$|F| = qv\text{Bsin }\theta$$
> F will be maximum when $\theta = 90°$

39. (b) 3.2×10^{-13} M

> **Explanation:** Force acting on a charge q moving with velocity v in magnetic field of intensity B is given by,
> $$F = qv\text{Bsin}\theta$$
> $$= qv\text{B} \qquad ...(\because \theta = 90°, \therefore \sin \theta = 1)$$
> Given that,
> $$q = 2 \times 1.6 \times 10^{-19} \text{ (}\alpha\text{-particle)}$$
> $$v = 10^6 \text{ m/s}$$
> $$B = 1 \text{ T}$$
> Substituting these values, we get
> $$F = 2 \times 1.6 \times 10^{-19} \times 10^6 \times 1$$
> $$= 3.2 \times 10^{-13} \text{ N}$$

40. (c) Convective currents in earth's core.

> **Explanation:** The earth's core is hot and melten. Hence, convective current in earth's core is responsible for its magnetic field.

41. (a) $Q = \dfrac{\Delta\phi}{R}$

> **Explanation:** Since,
> $$\frac{\Delta\phi}{\Delta t} = \varepsilon$$
> $$= IR$$
> $$\Rightarrow \quad \Delta\phi = (I\Delta t)R$$
> $$= QR$$
> $$\Rightarrow \quad Q = \frac{\Delta\phi}{R}$$

42. (c) 45°, 0.5 A

Explanation: According to question,

$$L = 0.7 \text{ H}$$
$$R = 220 \ \Omega$$
$$E_0 = 220 \text{ V}$$
$$v = 50 \text{ Hz}$$

This is an LR circuit.

Phase difference,

$$X_L = 2\pi v L$$
$$= 2 \times \frac{22}{7} \times 50 \times 0.7$$
$$= 220 \ \Omega$$

$$\tan \phi = \frac{X_L}{R}$$
$$= \frac{\omega L}{R}$$
$$= \frac{2\pi v L}{R}$$
$$= \frac{220}{220} = 1$$

or, $$\phi = 45°$$

Wattless component of current,

$$= I_0 \sin \phi$$
$$= \frac{I_0}{\sqrt{2}}$$
$$= \frac{1}{\sqrt{2}} \frac{E_0}{Z}$$
$$= \frac{1}{\sqrt{2}} \frac{220}{\sqrt{X_L^2 + R^2}}$$
$$= \frac{1}{\sqrt{2}} \frac{220}{\sqrt{220^2 + 220^2}}$$
$$= \frac{1}{2} = 0.5 \text{ A}$$

43. (c) $\dfrac{1}{2} \dfrac{kQ^2}{R}$

Explanation: As we know that,

$$U = \int_0^Q V \, dq$$
$$= \int_0^Q \frac{kq}{R} \, dq$$
$$= \frac{1}{2} \frac{kQ^2}{R}$$

44. (b) 5π

Explanation: We know that,

$$\varepsilon = \frac{M}{dt}\,dI$$

$$= 0.005 \times I_0 \cos \omega t \times \omega$$

$$\varepsilon_{max} = 0.005 \times I_0 \times \omega$$

$$= 5\pi$$

45. (c) A is true but R is false.

Explanation: Fuse wire must have high resistance because in series current remains same, therefore according to Joule's law,

$$H = \frac{I^2 R t}{4.2}\ \text{cal}$$

Heat produced is high if R is high. The melting point must be low so that wire may melt with increase in temperature. As the current equal to maximum safe value, flows through the fuse wire, it heats up, melts and break the circuit.

46. (d) A is false and R is also false.

Explanation: Gravitational force is the dominating force in nature and not coulomb's force. Gravitational force is the weakest force. Also,

Coulomb's force $\gg$ gravitational force.

47. (c) A is true but R is false.

Explanation: Two beams of electrons travelling in the same direction repel each other because the electrostatic interaction is more than the magnetic interaction.

48. (a) Both A and A are true and R is also the correct explanation of A.

Explanation: Charges are conserved by the law of conservation of charges. Energy is also conserved, if we take in account of the loss of energy by heat, sparking etc.

49. (d) A is false and R is also false.

Explanation: Induced current will not be developed in a conductor, if it is moved in direction parallel to magnetic field. It is because, in this case, the Lorentz force on free electrons in the conductor is zero. The induced emf is produced only when the magnetic flux linked with the loop changes.

Section-C

50. (d) is the same for all the figures.

Explanation: As per Gauss's theorem in electrostatics, the electric flux through a surface depends only on the amount of charge enclosed by the surface. It does not depend on size and shape of the surface. Therefore, flux through the surface is the same for all figures.

51. (b) A (iii), B (i), C (iv), D (ii)

Explanation: As we know that,
Work done by battery A,

$$W_A = \left(\frac{1}{2}C_1 V_1^2\right)$$

$$= 2 \times 2^2 = 8\ \text{J}$$

Work done by battery B

$$W_B = 2\left(\frac{1}{2}CV_2^2\right)$$

$$= 2\left(\frac{1}{2} \times \frac{4 \times 2}{4+2} \times 4^2\right)$$

$$= \frac{64}{3}$$

$$q_2 = CV$$

$$= \left(\frac{4 \times 2}{4+2}\right) \times 4$$

$$= \frac{16}{3}$$

$$q_1 = C_2V_1$$
$$= 2 \times 2 = 4$$

52. (a) 1

Explanation: Just after the switch is closed, the inductor affers infinite resistance. Current occur cross R_1 only point 1 is at a higher R_1 only.

53. (c) 150 V

Explanation: $V_{12} = E = 150$ V

54. (c) 150 V

Explanation: $V_{34} = V_{12} = 150$ V

55. (b) 75 V

Explanation: Just before opening the switch, the current through the inductor

$$i_0 = \frac{E}{R_2} = \frac{150}{50} = 3A$$

$$V = IR_1 = 3 \times 25 = 75 \text{ V}$$

Sample Paper 6

Section-A

1. (c)   C will have greater resistance.

Explanation: As $\qquad$ $C = 4\pi\varepsilon_0 R$

For sphere A, $\qquad$ $CA = 4\pi\varepsilon_0 R$

For sphere B, $\qquad$ $CB = 4\pi\varepsilon_0 2R = 2CA$

For sphere C, $\qquad$ $CC = 4\pi\varepsilon_0 3R = 3CA$

Clearly $\qquad$ $CC > CB > CA$

2. (b) Remains same

> **Explanation:** Electric flux remains unchanged as $\phi = \dfrac{q_{enclosed}}{\varepsilon_0}$ because the charge enclosed by the Gaussian surface remains same.

3. (d) path will be followed by electric field lines.

> **Explanation:** There will be no electric field inside a metal sphere and field lines are normal to the surface of the sphere.

4. (b) Glass bob

> **Explanation:** Glass bob will reach the ground earlier. In case of metallic bob eddy current will be produced due to it's motion in earth's magnetic field these eddy current will oppose the cause (i.e., the fall) which has produced it, glass bob being a bad conductor will not have eddy current.

5. (b) will be in opposite direction

> **Explanation:** The direction of electric field at equatorial point A or B will be in opposite direction, as that of direction of dipole moment.

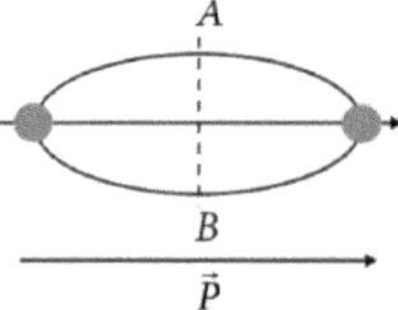

6. (a) a straight line

> **Explanation:** Charged particles move in straight lines and accelerate (or decelerate) if projected into an electric field along the direction of the field.

7. (c) decreases K times

> **Explanation:** As we know that,
>
> $$F_m = \frac{F_o}{K}$$
>
> **So, the maximum force decreases by K times.**

8. (c) Kirchhoff's second law

> **Explanation:** The equation $\rightarrow \sum e = \sum IR$ is applicable to Kirchhoff's second law. This expression tells that in a closed loop, the algebraic sum of emfs is equal to the algebraic sum of the products of the resistance and the current flowing through them.

9. (b) 40 cm

> **Explanation:** Let X is the left gap resistance and R is the right gap resistance l_1 be the balance point from left
>
> From meter Bridge principle:
>
> $$\Rightarrow \qquad \frac{X}{R} = \frac{l_1}{100 - l_1} = \frac{2}{3}$$
>
> $$\Rightarrow \qquad 200 - 2l_1 = 3l_1$$
>
> $$\Rightarrow \qquad 200 = 5l_1$$
>
> $$\Rightarrow \qquad l_1 = 40 \text{ cm}$$

10. (d) is unaffected by change in its length and area of cross-section.

> **Explanation:** Resistivity is the property of the material. It does not depend upon size and shape.

11. (d) shape of cross-section

> **Explanation:** As we know that
>
> $$R = \frac{\rho l}{A}$$
>
> So that, R is independent of shape of cross-section.

12. (b) 0.25 R

> **Explanation:** As we know that,
>
> $$\mathbf{R} \propto \frac{1}{A}$$
>
> $\Rightarrow \qquad \mathbf{R} \propto \dfrac{1}{r^2}$
>
> $$\mathbf{R} \propto \frac{1}{d^2} \qquad\qquad (d = \text{diameter of wire})$$

13. (a) conductance

> **Explanation:** The reciprocal of resistance is called conductance.

14. (d) 16 Ω

> **Explanation:** Let R be the resistance and l be the original length. At constant volume, $R \propto l^2$
> **Resistance of stretched wire is,**
> $$\begin{aligned} \mathbf{R'} &= 4R \\ &= 4(4) \\ &= 16\ \Omega. \end{aligned}$$

15. (c) a circle

> **Explanation:** Electrons in a magnetic field feel a force perpendicular to their velocity. Since their movement is always perpendicular to the force, magnetic forces due no work and the electron's velocity stays constant. Since the force is
>
> $F = qvB$ in a constant magnetic field, an electron feels a force of constant magnitude always directed perpendicular to its motion. The result is a circular orbit.

16. (c) $\dfrac{\sqrt{2Em}}{qB}$

> **Explanation:** Since,
> $$r = \frac{mv}{qB}$$
> $$= \frac{\sqrt{2Em}}{qB}$$

17. (d) $\dfrac{v^2}{c^2}$

Explanation: Electrostatic force,

$$F_e = \frac{1}{4\pi\varepsilon_0} \times \frac{e^2}{r^2}$$

Magnetic force,

$$F_m = \frac{\mu_0}{4\pi}\left(\frac{e^2 v^2}{r^2}\right)$$

$$\therefore \qquad \frac{F_m}{F_e} = \mu_0\mu_0 v^2 = \frac{v^2}{c^2} \qquad \ldots\left(\because \mu_0\varepsilon_0 = \frac{1}{c^2}\right)$$

18. (b) less

Explanation: Earth's magnetic field inside a closed iron box is less compared to outside as lines of forces prefer to concentrate in the iron walls of the box as the magnetic permeability of iron is high.

19. (d) $\theta = 0°$ or $\theta = 180°$

Explanation: This is only possible when the electron is moving either parallel or anti-parallel to the magnetic field. i.e., either $\theta = 0°$ or $\theta = 180°$

20. (d) the resistivity of the wire of the coil

Explanation: When the conductor is moved in a stationary magnetic field to procure a change in the flux linkage, the emf is statically induced.

21. (d) 0.05 mH

Explanation: From the formula,

$$M = \frac{\mu_0 n_2 n_1 A}{l}$$

$$= \frac{4\pi \times 10^{-7} \times 500 \times 200 \times \dfrac{4}{10^4}}{1}$$

$$= 160\pi \times 10^{-7}$$

$$= 0.05 \times 10^{-3}\ \text{H}$$

22. (b) directly proportional to area of cross-section

Explanation: We know that,

$$L = \frac{\mu_0 N^2 A}{l}$$

23. (b) Capacitive

Explanation: If $\omega < \omega_r$, the circuit will be capacitive in nature.

24. (c) $5\sqrt{2}$ V

Explanation: According to questions,

$$E = 8 \sin \omega t + 6 \sin 2\omega t$$

$$\Rightarrow \quad E_0 = \sqrt{8^2 + 6^2}$$

$$= 10 \text{ V}$$

$$E_{rms} = \frac{10}{\sqrt{2}}$$

$$= 5\sqrt{2} \text{ V}.$$

25. (c) 5×10^{-3} s and 14.14 A

Explanation: Time taken by the current to reach the maximum value.

$$t = \frac{T}{4}$$

$$= \frac{1}{4v}$$

$$= \frac{1}{4 \times 50}$$

$$= 5 \times 10^{-3} \text{ s}$$

$$I_0 = I_{rms}\sqrt{2}$$

$$= 10\sqrt{2}$$

$$= 14.14 \text{ A}.$$

Section–B

26. (c) Remain the same

Explanation: If the radius of the Gaussian surface is doubled, the outward electric flux will remain the same. This is because electric flux depends only on the charge enclosed by the surface.

27. (c) Both (a) and (b)

Explanation: Both the spheres will hold the same amount of charge. It is because; the two spheres possess equal capacitance. The capacitance of a sphere depends only of its radius. It does not matter, whether the sphere is hollow or solid.

28. (d) are imaginary

Explanation: An electric line of force is an imaginary continuous line or curve drawn in an electric field.

29. (a) 1600 NC^{-1}

Explanation: As we know that,

$$E = \frac{F}{q}$$

$$\therefore \quad E = \frac{2.56}{16 \times 10^{-4}}$$

$$= 1600 \text{ NC}^{-1}$$

30. (d) Q and C

Explanation: By using,

$$C = \frac{\varepsilon_0 KA}{d} \text{ and } q = CV$$

31. (b) 1.98 A

Explanation: $V_0 = 140$ V, $R = 50\Omega$

$$I_{rms} = \frac{V_{rms}}{R} = \frac{v_0 \times 0.77}{R} = \frac{140 \times 0.707}{50} = 1.98 \text{ A}$$

32. (c) 13 V

Explanation:

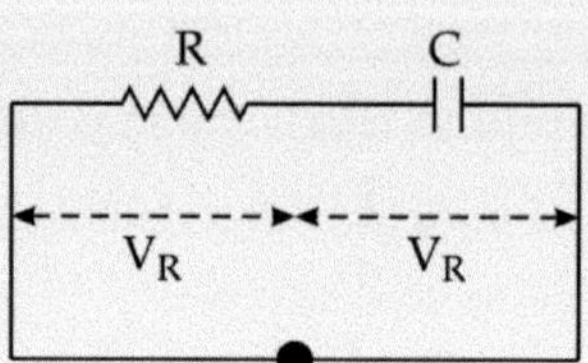

Let the applied voltage be V.
Here,

$$V_E = 12 \text{ V}$$
$$V_C = 5 \text{ V}$$
$$V = \sqrt{V_R^2 + V_C^2}$$
$$= \sqrt{(12)^2 + (5)^2}$$
$$= 13 \text{ V}$$

33. (a) Directly

Explanation: The decrease in potential across the wire is directly proportional to the length of the wire.

34. (c) remain same

Explanation: If the area of cross section of the wire remains same, the potentiometer will give accurate results.

35. (a)

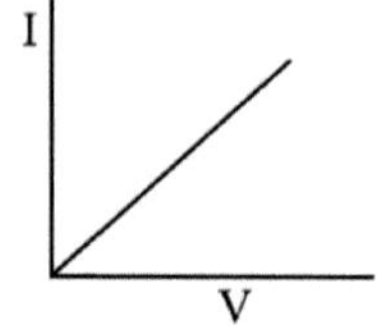

Explanation: For ohmic circuit, $V \propto I$
Graph of such is a straight line through origin with positive slope.

36. (c) 25 cm

Explanation: According to the given condition.

$$\frac{l}{100-l} = \frac{5}{15}$$
$$\frac{l}{100-l} = \frac{1}{3}$$

$$\therefore \quad 3l = 100 - x$$
$$4l = 100$$
$$l = 25 \text{ cm}$$

37. (a) A potentiometer is a constant voltage device.

> **Explanation:** The wrong statement is potentiometer is a constant voltage device.

38. (b) Deuterium nucleus has greater pitch of helical motion.

> **Explanation:** Due to perpendicular component both will execute circular motion for which $T = \dfrac{2\pi m}{qB}$. Since, q is same, therefore $T \propto m$. Hence, deuterium nucleus will travel more distance.

39. (d) both (a) and (b)

> **Explanation:** At neutral point,
> $$B_{eq} = -B_H$$
> $$B_a = -B_H$$

40. (c) Convective currents in earth's core.

> **Explanation:** The earth's core is hot and melten. Hence, convective current in earth's core is responsible for its magnetic field.

41. (c) $1 \rightarrow$ Clockwise
> $2 \rightarrow$ Anticlockwise

> **Explanation:** Using Lenz's law we can predict the direction of induced current in both the rings. Induced current opposes the cause of increasing of magnetic flux.

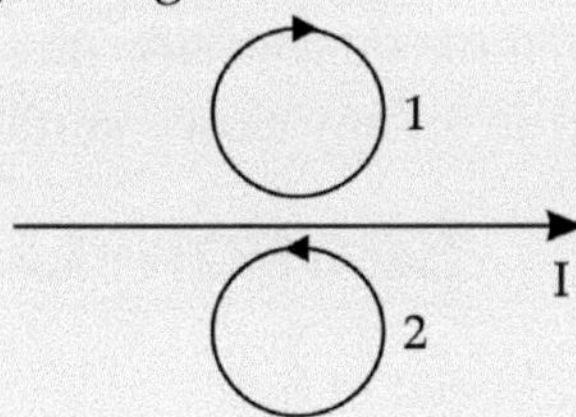

So, induced current will be clockwise in ring 1 and anticlockwise in ring 2.

42. (c) $R = 15\ \Omega$, $L = 3.5$ H, $C = 30\ \mu$F.

> **Explanation:** We know quality factor should be high for better tuning.
> Quality factor (Q) of an LCR circuit is,
> $$Q = \frac{1}{R}\sqrt{\frac{L}{C}}$$
> where R is the resistance, L is the inductance and C is the capacitance of the circuit.
> For high Q factor R should be low, L should be high and C should be low. These conditions are best satisfied by the values given in option (c).

43. (d) increases

> **Explanation:** Since capacitance $C = \dfrac{\varepsilon_0 A}{d}$ as d decreases capacitance increases.

44. (a) zero

> **Explanation:** No change in flux, hence no force required.

45. (a) Both A and R are true and R is also the correct explanation of A.

> **Explanation:** Junction rule or Kirchhoff's first law or Kirchhoff's current law (KCL) states that the algebraic sum of the currents meeting at a junction (point) in an electrical circuit is always zero. Or, the sum of currents flowing towards the junction is equal to sum of currents leaving the junction.
>
> $$\Sigma I = 0$$
> $$I_1 + I_3 = I_2 + I_4$$
>
> 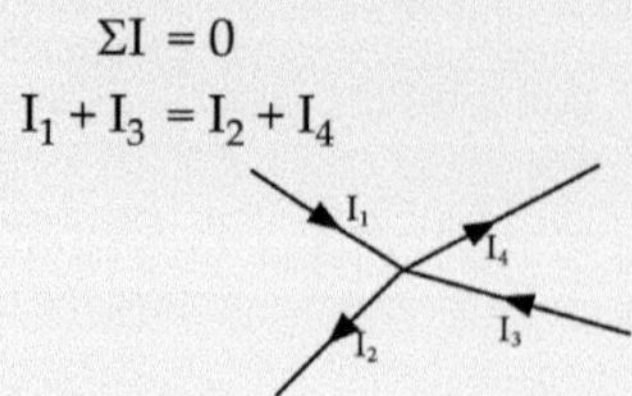

46. (c) A is true but R is false.

> **Explanation:** Potential and potential energy are different quantities and cannot be equated.

47. (c) A is true but R is false.

> **Explanation:** In the northern hemisphere, magnetic needle comes to rest along north-south direction. So that a greater dip angle is expected in northern hemisphere.

48. (b) Both A and R are true but R is not the correct explanation of A.

> **Explanation:** When a metallic conductor is moved in a magnetic field; magnetic flux is varied. It disturbs the free electrons of the metal and set up an induced emf in it. As there are no free ends of the metal i.e., it will be closed in itself so there will be induced current.

49. (b) Both A and R are true but R is not the correct explanation of A.

> **Explanation:** Gauss's law implies that the total electric flux through a closed surface is zero if no charge is enclosed by the surface and it is true for any closed surface, independent of its shape and size.

Section-C

50. (b) at a time after $\dfrac{OP}{c}$ where c is the speed of light

> **Explanation:** The electric field around a charge propagates with the speed of light away from the charge. There fore, the required time $= \dfrac{dis\tan ce}{speed} = \dfrac{OP}{c}$

51. (c) $\dfrac{K_1 K_2 (d_1 + d_2)}{K_2 d_1 + K_1 d_2}$

> **Explanation:** The capacities of two individual condensers are
>
> $$C_1 = \frac{K_1 \varepsilon_0 A}{d_1} \text{ and } C_2 = \frac{K_2 \varepsilon_0 A}{d_2}$$
>
> The arrangement is equivalent to two capacitors joined in series.
> So, equivalent capacitance,
>
> $$\frac{1}{C_{eq}} = \frac{1}{C_1} + \frac{1}{C_2} = \frac{d_1}{K_1 \varepsilon_0 A} + \frac{d_2}{K_2 \varepsilon_0 A}$$
>
> $$= \frac{1}{\varepsilon_a A}\left[\frac{d_1}{K_1} + \frac{d_2}{K_2}\right] = \frac{1}{\varepsilon_a A}\left[\frac{K_2 d_1 + K_1 d_2}{K_1 K_2}\right]$$

or, $$C_{eq} = \varepsilon_a A \left(\frac{K_1 K_2}{K_2 d_1 + K_1 d_2} \right) \qquad \qquad ...(i)$$

Also, $$C_{aq} = \left(\frac{K \varepsilon_0 A}{d_1 + d_2} \right) \qquad \qquad ...(ii)$$

From (i) and (ii)

$$\varepsilon_0 A \left(\frac{K_1 K_2}{d_2 K_1 + d_1 K_2} \right) = \varepsilon_0 A \left(\frac{K}{d_1 + d_2} \right)$$

$$\therefore \qquad K = \frac{K_1 K_2 (d_1 + d_2)}{K_2 d_1 + K_1 d_2}$$

52. (a) 20 mH

Explanation:

$$X_L = \frac{V_L}{I}$$

$$I = \frac{V_R}{R} = \frac{25}{50} = \frac{1}{2}$$

$$X_L = \frac{20}{\frac{1}{2}} = 40 \, \Omega$$

But $$X_L = \omega L$$

$\Rightarrow$ $$L = \frac{X_L}{\omega} = \frac{40}{2 \times 10^3}$$

$$= 20 \times 10^{-3} = 20 \text{ mH}$$

53. (d) 12.5 μF

Explanation:

$$\omega^2 = \frac{1}{L_C} \Rightarrow C = \frac{1}{\omega^2 L}$$

$$= \frac{1}{(2 \times 10^3) \times 20 \times 10^{-13}} = 12.5 \, \mu F$$

54. (a) 50 W

Explanation: At resonance, the impedance equal just resistance.

55. (d) 5×10^3 rad/s

Explanation: For inductive nature $\omega > \omega_r$.

Sample Paper 7

Section-A

1. (b) 300 V

Explanation: Given: $r = 9 \text{ cm} = 0.09 \text{ m}$

Charge $Q = 3 \text{ nC} = 3 \times 10^{-9} \text{ C}$

Potential at a distance 9 cm, $V = rkQ$ where $k = 9 \times 10^9$

$\therefore$ $V = 0.099 \times 10^9 \times 3 \times 10^{-9} = 300 \text{ V}$

2. (d) $\varepsilon_w = 81\varepsilon_0$

> **Explanation:** The relative permeability is defined by:
>
> $$\varepsilon_{rel} = \frac{\varepsilon_w}{\varepsilon_0} = 81$$
>
> Hence, $\qquad\qquad\qquad\qquad \varepsilon_w = 81 \times \varepsilon_0$

3. (a) $180°$

> **Explanation:** The angle between electric dipole moment and electric field on the equatorial line is $180°$ as both of them are in opposite directions.

4. (c) there were magnetic monopoles

> **Explanation:** Gauss's law should be invalid if there were magnetic monopoles.

5. (c) $\vec{\tau} = \vec{p} \times \vec{E}$

> **Explanation:** Given that,
>
> Dipole moment of the dipole = $\vec{p}$ and uniform electric field = $\vec{E}$. We know that dipole moment $(\vec{p})$
>
> $= q.a$ (where q is the charge and a is dipole length). And when a dipole of dipole moment $\vec{p}$ is placed
>
> in uniform electric field $\vec{E}$, then torque (τ) = Electric force × perpendicular distance between the two
>
> forces $= qaE \sin\theta$ or $\vec{\tau} = pE\sin\theta$ or $\vec{\tau} = \vec{p} \times \vec{E}$ (vector form).

6. (d) 4

> **Explanation:** Electric field inside the sphere will be zero.

7. (c) $E_a = 2E_e$

> **Explanation:** As we know that,
>
> $$E_a = \frac{2kp}{r^3}$$
>
> $$E_e = \frac{kp}{r^3}$$
>
> $\therefore \qquad\qquad\qquad E_a = 2E_e$

8. (a) Q

> **Explanation:** For greater accuracy, the potential gradient should be small.
>
> Potential gradient $= \dfrac{v}{l}$ = slope of line.
>
> Slope of line P > slope of line Q. So, potential gradient in case of graph Q is less than the potential gradient of P. So, potentiometer Q will be preferred.

9. (b) $\dfrac{v}{2}$

> **Explanation:** We know that
>
> $$v_d = \frac{i}{ne\pi r^2} = v_d \propto \frac{i}{r^2} = \frac{v}{v'} = \frac{i_1}{i_1} \times \left(\frac{r_2}{r_1}\right)^2 = v' = \frac{v}{2}$$

10. (c) products of currents and the resistances

Explanation: In a closed circuit, the vector sum of total emf is equal to the sum of the products of currents and the resistances.

11. (a) charge

Explanation: Kirchhoff's first law is based on the law of conservation of charge.

12. (c) $-i$

Explanation: According the Kirchhoff's law, in any analytic circuit, if the direction of current is assumed opposite, then the value of current will be $-i$.

13. (b) not change

Explanation: The deflection in galvanometer will not be changed due to interchange of battery and the galvanometer.

14. (b) Cell is E

Explanation: When a capacitor is fully charged, then the current is drawn by it. When no current flows through the circuit, potential difference across the cells emf of cell = potential difference across the capacitor.

15. (c) Faraday's Law

Explanation: Faraday's Law states that when the magnetic flux linking a circuit change, an electromotive force is induced in the circuit proportional to the rate of change of the flux linkage. This results in a moving conductor coil producing EMF.

16. (c) upwards

Explanation: The formula of the force exerted by the magnetic field is given by

$$\vec{F} = q(\vec{v} \times \vec{B})$$

Here, q is the charge on the conductor, v is the velocity of charge and B is the magnetic field.
Explanation: In the given case, cell is in open circuit mode (I = 0). So voltage across the cell is equal to its emf.

17. (d) All of them

Explanation: The Lorentz force on the charge q is `Zero' when,

(i) $\vec{v}$ and $\vec{B}$ are parallel or antiparallel.

     $i.e.,\ \theta = 0°$ or $\theta = 180°$ as $\sin \theta°\ \sin 180° = \theta$

(ii) $\vec{v} = 0$

(iii) The particle is neutral.

18. (d) $\theta = 0°$ or $180°$

Explanation:

Explanation: As $F_m = qvB \sin \theta$; so for minimum force is $\theta = 0°$ or $180°$.
The force will be minimum when charged particle moves parallel to or anti-parallel to the field.

19. (c) 45 μT

Explanation:

$$\tan \delta = \frac{B_V}{B_H}, \ \delta = 60°$$

$$B_V = B_H \tan \delta = 26\ \mu \times \tan 60°$$
$$= 45\ \mu T$$

20. (d) laminated core of soft iron

Explanation: To reduce eddy current, the resistance of the core should be increased.

21. (a) 25×10^{-6} H

Explanation: Coefficient of self induction is given by,

$$e = -L\frac{dI}{dt}$$

$\therefore$
$$L = -\frac{e}{\frac{dI}{dt}}$$

$$= -\frac{300 \times 10^{-6} \times 0.5}{(7-13)}$$

$$= 25 \times 10^{-6}\ H$$

22. (c) 5 H

Explanation: Since,

$$e = -M\frac{dI}{dt}$$

$$1500 = -M\left(\frac{0-3}{0.01}\right)$$

$$M = \frac{1500 \times 0.01}{3}$$

$$= 5\ H$$

23. (a) 7.85 Ω; 28 A

Explanation:

$$L = 25\ mH = 25 \times 10^{-3}H,\ V_{rms} = 220\ V$$
$$\upsilon = 50Hz,\ \omega = 2\pi\upsilon = 100\pi\ rad/s$$
$$X_L = \omega L = 100\pi \times 25 \times 10^{-3} = 7.85\ \Omega$$

$$I_{rms} = \frac{\upsilon_{rms}}{X_L} = \frac{220}{7.85} = 28A$$

24. (b) $\frac{1}{2}CV^2$

Explanation: As we know that,

$$U = \int_0^V CVdV = \frac{1}{2}CV^2$$

25. (d) $\sqrt{R^2 + 4\pi^2 f^2 L^2}$

Explanation: We know that

$$Z = \sqrt{R^2 + X_L^2}$$
$$X_L = \omega L$$

and
$$\omega = 2\pi f$$

$\therefore$
$$Z = \sqrt{R^2 + 4\pi^2 f^2 L^2}$$

Section-B

26. (a) 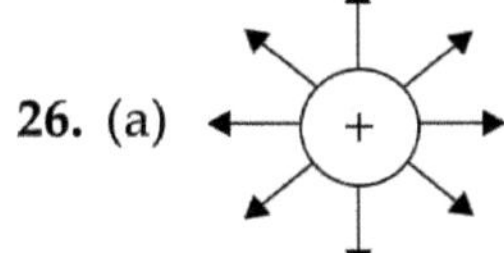

Explanation: The field lines of a single positive charge are radially outward.

27. (c) a torque as well as a translational force

Explanation: As we know that,

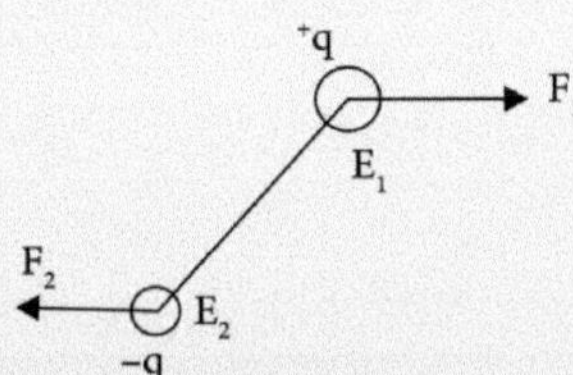

The electric field will be different at the location of force on the two charges. Therefore, the two charges will be unequal. This will result in a force as well as torque.

28. (a) $90°$

Explanation: As we know that,

$$\vec{\tau} = \vec{p} \times \vec{E}$$
$$= pE \sin \theta$$

So, torque will be maximum at $90°$.

29. (c) -5.3×10^{-9} C

Explanation: $r = 20$ cm $= 0.2$ m, $E = -1.2 \times 10^3$ NC^{-1}

$\because$
$$E = \frac{q}{4\pi\varepsilon_0 r^2}$$

$\therefore$
$$q = (4\pi\varepsilon_0 r^2)E$$
$$= \frac{(0.2)^2 \times (-1.2 \times 10^3)}{9 \times 10^9}$$
$$= -5.3 \times 10^{-9} \text{ C}$$

30. (a) $30 \ \mu$F

Explanation: In series $\dfrac{1}{C} = \dfrac{1}{C_1} + \dfrac{1}{C_2} + \dfrac{1}{C_3}$ and charge on each capacitor is same.

$\therefore$
$$\frac{1}{C} = \frac{1}{6} + \frac{1}{6} + \frac{1}{3}$$

$$C = \frac{3}{2} \qquad \text{...(i)}$$

$$\because \quad q = CV$$

$$\because \quad q = 20 \times \frac{3}{2} \qquad \text{[By using (i)]}$$

$$= 30 \ \mu C$$

31. (b) 19 Hz and 170 V

Explanation: Given,

$$V = 240 \sin 120t \ V$$

Comparing with $V = V_0 \sin \omega t$

$$V_0 = 240 \ V$$

$$\omega = 120 \ rad/s$$

$$V_{rms} = \frac{V_0}{\sqrt{2}}$$

$$= \frac{240}{\sqrt{2}} = 169.7$$

$$\approx 170 \ V$$

$$\omega = 2\pi f$$

$$f = \frac{\omega}{2\pi}$$

$$= \frac{120}{2\pi}$$

$$= 19 \ Hz.$$

32. (b) 2.828 A

Explanation: Given,

$$e = 80 \sin 100\pi t \qquad \text{...(i)}$$

Standard equation of instantaneous voltage is given by

$$e = e_m \sin \omega t \qquad \text{...(ii)}$$

Compare (i) and (ii), we get

$$e_m = 80 \ V \text{ where } e_m \text{ is the voltage amplitude.}$$

Current amplitude,

$$I_m = \frac{e_m}{Z}$$

$$= \frac{80}{20} = 4A$$

where Z = impendence.

$$I_{rms} = \frac{4}{\sqrt{2}}$$

$$= \frac{4\sqrt{2}}{2}$$

$$= 2\sqrt{2}$$

$$= 2.828 \ A.$$

33. (a) Metals

> **Explanation:** The value of temperature coefficient of resistance is more for metals than for alloys.

34. (a) 100 W bulb has thicker filament

> **Explanation:** We know that, $P = \dfrac{V^2}{R}$ for same mains circuit V is same. Thus, $R_{60} > R_{100}$, Also $R = \rho \dfrac{L}{A}$
>
> where ρ = resistivity, A = area and L = length of wire. Thus less resistor implies more thicker element. So the 100 W bulb has thicker filament.

35. (c) 13 A

> **Explanation:** On applying Kirchhoff's current law, I = 13 A.

36. (b) opposite to the electric field

> **Explanation:** Electron always moves from negative to positive potential, hence opposite to direction of electric field.

37. (b) In a balanced wheatstone bridge, interchanging the position of galvanometer and cell affects the balance of the bridge.

> **Explanation:** In balanced Wheatstone bridge, the arms of galvanometer and cell can be interchanged without affecting the balance of the bridge.

38. (b) $\dfrac{nr^2}{(x^2 + r^2)^{3/2}}$

> **Explanation:** Magnetic field on the axis of circular coil carrying current,
>
> $$B = \frac{\mu_0}{4\pi} \frac{2\pi n I r^2}{(x^2 + r^2)^{3/2}}$$
>
> $\Rightarrow$
> $$B \propto \frac{nr^2}{(x^2 + r^2)^{3/2}}$$

39. (a) $B \perp v$

> **Explanation:** We know that,
>
> $$d\vec{B} = \frac{\mu_0}{4\pi} \frac{q\left(\vec{v} \times \vec{r}\right)}{r^3}$$
>
> *i.e.,* $\vec{B}$ is perpendicular to $\vec{v}$ and $\vec{r}$ both.

40. (c) 1.31×10^{23}

> **Explanation:** We know that,
>
> $$B_H = \frac{\mu_0 M}{4d^3}$$
>
> $\Rightarrow$
> $$M = \frac{4\pi d^3 B_H}{\mu_0}$$
>
> $$M = \frac{0.5 \times 10^{-4} \times (6.4 \times 10^6)^3}{10^{-7}}$$
>
> $$= 1.31 \times 10^{23} \text{ Am}^2$$

41. (a) $e = -N\dfrac{d\phi}{dt}$

Explanation: Induced emf $e = -N\dfrac{d\phi}{dt}$, where N is the number of turns of the coil.

42. (a) 0.5 V

Explanation: Here, Area of coil,

$$A = 0.1\ \text{m} \times 0.05\ \text{m}$$
$$= 5 \times 10^{-3}\ \text{m}^2$$
$$N = 100$$

Initial flux linked with the coil.

$$\phi_1 = BA \cos \theta$$
$$= 0.1 \times 5 \times 10^{-3} \cos \theta°$$
$$= 5 \times 10^{-4}\ \text{Wb}$$

Final flux linked with the coil,

$$\phi_2 = 0.05 \times 5 \times 10^{-3} \cos \theta°$$
$$= 25 \times 10^{-5}\ \text{Wb}$$
$$= 2.5 \times 10^{-4}\ \text{Wb}$$

The magnitude of induced emf in the coil is,

$$\varepsilon = \frac{N\,|\Delta\phi|}{\Delta t}$$

$$= \frac{N\,|\phi_2 - \phi_1|}{t}$$

$$= \frac{100\,|2.5\times10^{-4} - 5\times10^{-4}|}{0.05}$$

$$= \frac{100 \times 2.5 \times 10^{-4}}{0.05}\ \text{V}$$

$$= 0.5\ \text{V}$$

43. (c) 200 μF

Explanation: Capacitance will increase but not five times (because dielectric is not filled completely). Hence, new capacitance may be 200 μF.

44. (b) 20 A

Explanation: We know that,

$$\frac{N_s}{N_p} = \frac{V_s}{V_p}$$

$$\frac{50}{1000} = \frac{V_s}{220}$$

Now,
$$V_s I_s = V_p I_p$$
$$11 \times I_s = 220 \times 1$$
$$\Rightarrow \qquad I_s = 20\ \text{A}$$

45. (c) A is true but R is false.

Explanation: The resistance of the galvanometer is fixed. In meter bridge experiments, to protect the galvanometer from a high current, high resistance is connected to the galvanometer in order to protect it from damage.

46. (a) Both A and R are true and R is also the correct explanation of A.

Explanation: The magnetic flux through any closed surface is zero.

47. (c) A is true but R is false.

Explanation: The mutual inductance in case of a medium of relative permeability present is,

$$M = \frac{\infty_0 \infty_1 n_1 n_2 r_1^2}{l}$$

48. (b) Both A and R are true but R is not the correct explanation of A.

Explanation: Gauss's theorem is based on inverse square dependence of electric field on distance.

49. (a) Both A and R are true and R is also the correct explanation of A.

Explanation: Capacitance is basically a geometrical quantity.

Section-C

50. (c) the dipole will experience a force towards left.

Explanation: The spacing between electric lines of force increases from left to right. So, E on left is greater than E on right. Force on $+q$ charge of dipole is smaller and to the right. Force on $-q$ charge of dipole is bigger and to the left. Hence the dipole will experience a force towards the left.

51. (c) 11 μF

Explanation: As we know that,

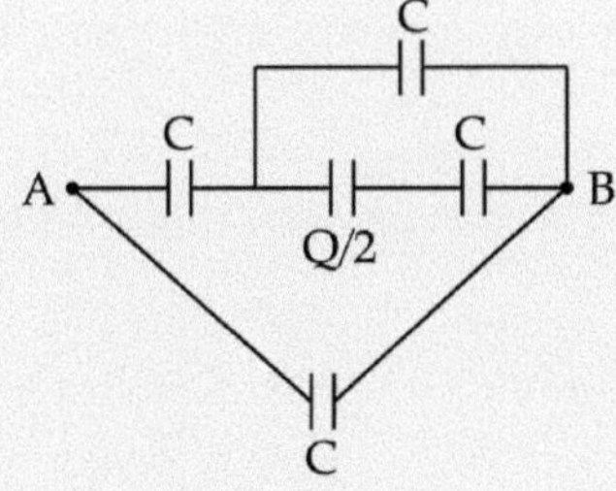

$$C_{eq} = \frac{\dfrac{4C}{3} \times C}{\dfrac{7C}{3} + C}$$

$$= \frac{11C}{7}$$

$\because \quad \dfrac{\varepsilon_0 A}{d} = 7\,\mu F = C \,...(\text{Given})$

$\therefore \quad C_{eq} = 11\,\mu F$

52. (b) At poles

Explanation: Net magnetic field is vertical at poles

53. (a) 0°

> **Explanation:** Earth's magnetic field is completely horizontal at equator. Angle of dip is 0° at equator.

54. (b) 30°

> **Explanation:**
> $$B \cos d = \frac{\sqrt{3}}{2} B$$
> $$\Rightarrow \quad \cos \delta = \frac{\sqrt{3}}{2}$$
> $$\Rightarrow \quad \delta = 30°$$

55. (b) Equator

> **Explanation:** At equator, the magnetic field of earth is completely vertical.

❑❑

Chemistry

Sample Question Paper

Chemistry (043)

Term – I

Time : 90 Minutes   Max. Marks : 35

General Instructions :

1. The Question Paper contains three sections.
2. Section A has 25 questions. Attempt any 20 questions.
3. Section B has 24 questions. Attempt any 20 questions.
4. Section C has 6 questions. Attempt any 5 questions.
5. All questions carry equal marks.
6. There is no negative marking

Section – A

This section consists of 25 multiple choice questions with overall choice to attempt any 20 questions. In case more than desirable number of questions are attempted, ONLY first 20 will be considered for evaluation.

1. Which of the following statements is true:
   (a) Melting point of Phosphorous is less than that of Nitrogen
   (b) N_2 is highly reactive while P_4 is inert
   (c) Nitrogen shows higher tendency of catenation than P
   (d) N-N is weaker than P-P

Ans. (d) N-N is weaker than P-P

> **Explanation:** N-N bond is weaker than the P-P bond, this is because nitrogen has small size and lone pairs on two N atoms repel each other. Phosphorous on the other hand has lager atomic size and the lone pairs on P repel to smaller extent. Thus, the bond strength of P-P bond is greater than the bond strength of N-N bond.

2. Which of the following is a non- stoichiometric defect?
   (a) Frenkel defect   (b) Schottky defect
   (c) metal deficiency defect   (d) interstitial defect

Ans. (c) metal deficiency defect

> **Explanation:** The defects which disturb the stoichiometry of the compounds are called non-stoichiometric defects. These defects are of two types: (i) metal excess defect and (ii) metal deficiency defect.

3. Identify the law which is stated as:
   "For any solution, the partial vapour pressure of each volatile component in the solution is directly proportional to its mole fraction."
   (a) Henry's law   (b) Raoult's law   (c) Dalton's law   (d) Gay-Lussac's Law

Ans. (b) Raoult's law

Explanation: Raoult's law states that, "For any solution, the partial vapour pressure of each volatile component in the solution is directly proportional to its mole fraction."

4. Pink colour of LiCl crystals is due to:
   (a) Schottky defect
   (b) Frenkel defect
   (c) Metal excess defect
   (d) Metal deficiency defect

Ans. (c) Metal excess defect

Explanation: Due to anion vacancies, LiCl crystals has non-stoichiometric metal excess defect. In the LiCl crystal, negatively charged chlorine ions are missing from their lattice sites leaving the holes in which electrons are entrapped to maintain the electrical neutrality. When LiCl is heated, Li atoms gets deposited on the surface of the crystal and Cl^- ions diffuse into the surface and combine with Li atoms to give LiCl. This is so because of loss of electrons by Li atoms to form Li^+. The released electrons diffuse excess into crystal and occupy anionic sites. As a result, there is an excess of Li. The anionic sites occupied by unpaired electrons are F^- centers which imparts a pink color to LiCl crystals. The color is observed as a result of excitation of the electrons trapped in F-centres when they absorb energy from visible light falling on crystals.

5. Which of the following isomer has the highest melting point:
   (a) 1, 2-dicholorbenzene
   (b) 1, 3 -dichlorobenzene
   (c) 1, 4-dicholorbenzene
   (d) all isomers have same melting points

Ans. (c) 1, 4-dicholorbenzene

Explanation:

1, 2-dichlorobenzene (orthodichlorobenzene)

1, 3-dichlorobenzene (metadichlorobenzene)

1, 4-dichlorobenzene (paradichlorobenzene)

Out of the above three isomers of dichlorobenzene, the *p*-isomer is more symmetrical than other two isomers. So, it has more closely packed arrangement of molecules in its crystal lattice. So, *p*-dichlorobenzene has a higher melting point and lower solubility as compared to ortho and meta isomers.

6. Which one of the following reactions is not explained by the open chain Structure of glucose:
   (a) Formation of pentaacetate of glucose with acetic anhydride.
   (b) formation of addition product with 2, 4 DNP reagent
   (c) Silver mirror formation with Tollen's reagent
   (d) existence of alpha and beta forms of glucose.

Ans. (d) existence of alpha and beta forms of glucose

7. Williamson's synthesis of preparing dimethyl ether is an:
   (a) S_N^1 reaction
   (b) Elimination reaction
   (c) S_N^2 reaction
   (d) Nucleophilic addition reaction

Ans. (c) S_N^2 reaction

Explanation: Williamson synthesis is a nucleophilic substitution reaction and follows S_N^2 mechanism. It is an organic reaction, forming an ether from organohalide and alcohol. It involves the reaction of an alkoxide ion with a primary alkyl halide via S_N^2 reaction.

Williamson Ether synthesis: an S_N^2 reaction

alkoxide nucleophile   primary or methyl alkyl halide   ether

8. Chlorine water loses its yellow colour on standing because:

(a) HCl gas is produced, due to the action of sunlight.

(b) a mixture of HOCl and HCl is produced in the presence of light

(c) HOCl and hydrogen gas is produced

(d) a mixture of HCl and ClO_3 is produced, due to the action of sunlight

Ans. (b) a mixture of HOCl and HCl is produced in the presence of light

Explanation: Chlorine is soluble in water and the so the solution is called chlorine water. Chlorine water loses its yellow colour on standing in sunlight because of the formation of a mixture of Hypochlorous acid and Hydrochloric acid.

$$Cl_2(g) + H_2O\,(l) \longrightarrow HCl\,(g) + HOCl(aq)$$

9. During dehydration of alcohols to alkenes by heating with concentrated H_2SO_4, the initiation step is:

(a) protonation of alcohol molecule

(b) formation of carbocation

(c) elimination of water

(d) formation of an ester

Ans. (a) Protonation of alcohol molecule

Explanation: During dehydration of alcohols to alkenes by heating with conc. H_2SO_4, the initiation step is protonation of alcohol molecules. The process of the dehydration of alcohol takes place in three steps:

(1) **Formation of protonated alcohol:** This is the first step in which the protonation of alcohol takes place. Because of the presence of lone pairs of electrons on the oxygen atom, it acts as a lewis base and abstract the hydrogen ion of the protic acid.

Ethanol   Protonated alcohol (Ethyl oxonium ion)

(2) **Carbocation formation:** This is the second step in which the carbon oxygen bond is broken to form a carbocation and water is released.

(3) **Alkene formation:** This is the final step in which the generated proton is removed with the help of a base which results in the formation of alkene.

Ethene

10. Amorphous solids are:

(a) isotropic   (b) anisotropic   (c) isotopic   (d) isomeric

Ans. (a) isotropic

> **Explanation:** Amorphous solids are isotropic in nature which means they have the same physical properties in all the directions due to the irregular arrangement of constituent particles (atoms or ions).

11. Which of the following reactions is used to prepare salicylaldehyde?

(a) Kolbe's reaction   (b) Etard reaction

(c) Reimer- Tiemann reaction   (d) Stephen's reduction.

Ans. (c) Reimer- Tiemann reaction

> **Explanation: Reimer**- Tiemann reaction is used to prepare salicylaldehyde from phenol. When phenol is treated with chloroform in the presence of sodium hydroxide, a –CHO group is introduced at the ortho position of the benzene ring. The intermediate formed during the reaction mechanism is hydrolysed in the presence of an alkali to produce salicylaldehyde. The reaction is as follows:
>
> Kolbe's reaction is used to prepare salicylic acid, Etard reaction for benzaldehyde and Stephen's reduction for aldehyde.

12. Which of the following is an example of a solid solution?

(a) sea water   (b) sugar solution

(c) smoke   (d) 22 carat gold

Ans. (d) 22 carat gold

> **Explanation:** 22 carat gold is an example of solid solution because it is an alloy thus, it is solid in solid solution.

13. The boiling points of alcohols are higher than those of hydrocarbons of comparable masses due to:

(a) Hydrogen bonding   (b) Ion – dipole interaction

(c) Dipole- dipole interaction   (d) Van der Waal's forces.

Ans. (a) Hydrogen bonding

> **Explanation:** The boiling points of alcohols are higher than those of hydrocarbons of comparable masses because of intermolecular hydrogen bonding in alcohols. The molecules of alcohols exist as associated molecules and consequently, a large amount of energy is required to break these bonds and, therefore, their boiling points are higher than that of the corresponding hydrocarbons because hydrogen bonding is absent in hydrocarbons.

14. Which of the following has the lowest boiling point?

(a) H_2O (b) H_2S (c) H_2Se (d) H_2Te

Ans. (b) H_2S

> **Explanation:** Boiling point is defined as the temperature at which the vapour pressure of the liquid becomes equal to the atmospheric pressure. The boiling point of any substance can be determined on the basis of intermolecular forces of attraction between the molecules in a liquid. Greater the forces of attraction more will be the energy required to separate them. In H_2O , there is a strong intermolecular hydrogen bonding between the atoms of oxygen and hydrogen and therefore, more energy will be required to break that bond. Thus, H_2O will have the highest boiling point among the given compounds. On the other hand, among the other options even though sulphur is more electronegative than Se or Te, the size of the molecule plays a bigger role in their interactions. More energy is needed because the size of the hydrides gets bigger on moving down the group. Therefore, the order of boiling point of rest of the compounds is given as:
>
> $$H_2S < H_2Se < H_2Te$$
>
> Thus, H_2S will have the lowest boiling point.

15. Which of the following statement is correct?
    (a) Fibrous proteins are generally soluble in water
    (b) Albumin is an example of fibrous proteins
    (c) In fibrous proteins, the structure is stabilised by hydrogen bonds and disulphide bonds
    (d) pH does not affect the primary structure of protein.

Ans. (d) pH does not affect the primary structure of protein

> **Explanation:** The unfolded protein remains as a single, long chain, but its sequence of amino acids is still intact. Thus, there is no change in primary structure because a highly acidic solution interferes with these interactions, the tertiary level of protein structure is indeed affected by pH changes.

16. Major product obtained on reaction of 3-Phenyl propene with HBr in presence of organic peroxide
    (a) 3- Phenyl 1- bromopropane
    (b) 1 –Phenyl -3- bromopropane
    (c) 1-Phenyl -2-bromopropane
    (d) 3-Phenyl -2- bromopropane

Ans. (a) 3- Phenyl 1- bromopropane

> **Explanation:** The reaction of 3-Phenyl propene with HBr in presence of organic peroxide gives 3- Phenyl 1- bromopropane as a major product. The reaction mechanism follows anti-Markovnikov addition.
>
> $$C_6H_5CH_2CH = CH_2 + HBr \, C_6 \xrightarrow[\text{(Anti--Markovnikov addition)}]{\text{Peroxide effect}} \underset{1-Bromo-3-phenylpropane}{C_6H_5CH_2CH_2CH_2Br}$$

17. Which of the following is a correct statement for C_2H_5Br?
    (a) It reacts with metallic Na to give ethane.
    (b) It gives nitroethane on heating with aqueous solution of $AgNO_2$
    (c) It gives C_2H_5OH on boiling with alcoholic potash.
    (d) It forms diethylthioether on heating with alcoholic KSH.

Ans. (b) It gives nitroethane on heating with aqueous solution of $AgNO_2$

> **Explanation:** The correct statement for C_2H_5Br is that, when it is heated with the aqueous solution of $AgNO_2$, it gives nitroethane.
>
> $$H_3C - CH_2 - Br + AgNO_3 \longrightarrow H_3C - CH_2 - NO_2$$
> ethyl   silver   nitroethane
bromide   nitrite
>
> The other options are incorrect because the reaction of C_2H_5Br with metallic Na gives butane, on boiling with alcoholic potash C_2H_5Br gives ethene and on heating with alcoholic KSH it forms C_2H_5SH (thiol).

18. Covalency of nitrogen is restricted to:

(a) 2 (b) 3 (c) 4 (d) 5

Ans. (c) 4

> **Explanation:** Nitrogen is restricted to a maximum covalency of 4 since only four (one s and three p) orbitals are available for bonding. It cannot exceed its covalency beyond 4 because it does not have vacant d-orbital to exceed its covalency.

19. Solubility of gases in liquids decreases with rise in temperature because dissolution is an:

(a) endothermic and reversible process
(b) exothermic and reversible process
(c) endothermic and irreversible process
(d) exothermic and irreversible process

Ans. (b) exothermic and reversible process

> **Explanation:** According to Le -Chatlier principle, the solubility of gases in liquids decreases with rise in temperature. Therefore, solubility of gases in liquids decreases with rise in temperature because dissolution is an exothermic and reversible process.

20. All elements of Group 15 show allotropy except:

(a) Nitrogen (b) Arsenic (c) Antimony (d) Bismuth

Ans. (a) Nitrogen

> **Explanation:** All elements of Group 15 show allotropy except nitrogen. The small size and high electronegativity of nitrogen atom leads to weak N-N bond in N_2 molecule and this the reason that nitrogen does not show allotropy.

21. Which of the following is a polysaccharide?

(a) glucose (b) maltose (c) glycogen (d) lactose

Ans. (c) Glycogen

> **Explanation:** Glycogen is a polysaccharide because it is a polymer of glucose. Its structure is similar to amylopectin where two polymeric chain of glucose of alpha 1, 4 glucose unit are linked by alpha 1, 6 linkage. It is used as stored reserve in muscles. The glycogen is changed into glucose by glycogenolysis in the muscles and the glucose produces energy in form of ATP to the muscle by the process of glycolysis.

22. Substance having the lowest boiling point:

(a) Hydrogen (b) Oxygen (c) Nitrogen (d) Helium

Ans. (d) Helium

> **Explanation:** Helium has the lowest boiling point because it is monoatomic and has low atomic mass.

23. Lower molecular mass alcohols are:

(a) miscible in limited amount of water
(b) miscible in excess of water
(c) miscible in water in all proportions
(d) immiscible in water

Ans. (c) miscible in water in all proportions

> **Explanation:** Lower molecular mass alcohols are miscible in water in all proportions because they are able to form hydrogen bonds with water.

24. Maximum oxidation state exhibited by Chlorine is:

(a) +1 (b) +3 (c) +5 (d) +7

Ans. (d) +7 ($Cl : 1s^2\, 2s^2\, 2p^6\, 3s^2\, 3p^2$)

Explanation: The maximum oxidation state exhibited by Chlorine is +7. The seven unpaired electrons in the s, p and d orbital of chlorine atoms accounts for its +7 oxidation state.

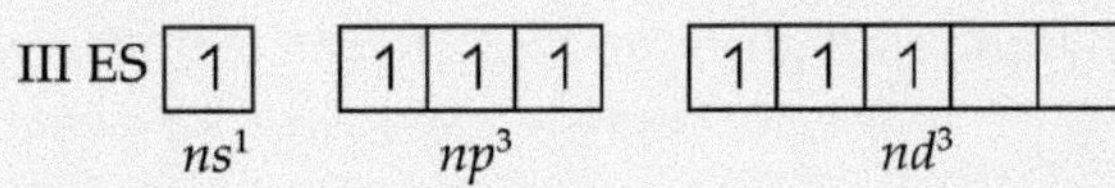

$$ns^1 \qquad np^3 \qquad nd^3$$

(7 unpaired electrons account for +7 oxidation state)

25. In which of the following cases blood cells will shrink:
(a) when placed in water containing more than 0.9% (mass/ volume) NaCl solution.
(b) when placed in water containing less than 0.9% (mass /volume) NaCl solution.
(c) when placed in water containing 0.9% (mass/volume) NaCl solution.
(d) when placed in distilled water.

Ans. (a) When placed in water containing more than 0.9% (mass/ volume) NaCl solution

Explanation: Blood cells will shrink in water containing more than 0.9% (mass/ volume) NaCl solution because fluid inside blood cells is isotonic with 0.9% NaCl solution.

Section-B

This section consists of 24 multiple choice questions with overall choice to attempt any 20 questions. In case more than desirable number of questions are attempted, ONLY first 20 will be considered for evaluation.

26. How much ethyl alcohol must be added to 1 litre of water so that the solution will freeze at– 14°C ? (K_f for water = 1.86°C/mol)
(a) 7.5 mol (b) 8.5 mol (c) 9.5 mol (d) 10.5 mol

Ans. (a) 7.5 mol

Explanation:
$$\Delta T_f = K_f m$$
$$\Delta T_f = K_f \frac{n_2 \times 1000}{w_1}$$
$$14 = 1.86 \times \frac{n_2 \times 1000}{1000}$$
$$n_2 = 7.5 \text{ mol}$$

27. Which reagents are required for one step conversion of chlorobenzene to toluene?
(a) $CH_3Cl / AlCl_3$ (b) CH_3Cl, Na, Dry ether
(c) CH_3Cl/Fe dark (d) $NaNO_2/ HCl /0\text{-}5°C$

Ans. (b) CH_3Cl, Na, Dry ether

Explanation: Chloroform (CH_3Cl), sodium (Na) and dry ether are required for one step conversion of chlorobenzene to toluene. The reaction is as follows:

28. On partial hydrolysis, XeF_6 gives:
(a) $XeO_3 + 4HF$ (b) $XeO_2F + HF$ (c) $XeOF_4 + H_2$ (d) $XeO_2F_2 + 4HF$

Ans. (d) $XeO_2F_2 + 4HF$

Explanation: XeF_6 on partial hydrolysis gives XeO_2F_2 and 4HF. The reaction is as follows:

$$XeF_4 + H_2O \longrightarrow XeO_2F_2 + 4HF$$

Whereas, on complete hydrolysis it gives Xe, XeO_3, F_2 and 6HF. The reaction is as follows:

$$XeF_4 + 3H_2O \longrightarrow Xe + XeO_3 + F_2 + 6HF$$

29. Which one of the following statement is correct about sucrose ?
    (a) It can reduce Tollen's reagent however cannot reduce Fehling's reagent
    (b) It undergoes mutarotation like glucose and fructose
    (c) It undergoes inversion in the configuration on hydrolysis
    (d) It is laevorotatory in nature .

Ans. (c) It undergoes inversion in the configuration on hydrolysis

Explanation: Sucrose undergoes inversion in the configuration on hydrolysis. During the hydrolysis reaction, it breaks down into 1.1 mixture of glucose and fructose. It is also called as invert sugar because the angle of the specific rotation of the plain polarized light is inverted from the positive value for sucrose $(+66.5°)$ to the negative value for the equimolar mixture of fructose and glucose $(-20°)$.

30. Phenol does not undergo nucleophilic substitution reaction easily due to:
    (a) acidic nature of phenol
    (b) partial double bond character of C-OH bond
    (c) partial double bond character of C-C bond
    (d) instability of phenoxide ion

Ans. (b) partial double bond character of C-OH bond

Explanation: Phenol does not undergo nucleophilic substitution reaction easily due to partial double bond character of C-OH bond. Due to Resonance(+R) effect, the oxygen gets attached to the C on the benzene ring and acquires a partial double bond character, making it tough to break.

31. Which of the following has highest ionisation enthalpy?
    (a) Nitrogen   (b) Phosphorus   (c) Oxygen   (d) Sulphur

Ans. (a) Nitrogen

Explanation: Nitrogen has highest ionisation enthalpy. This is because of its smallest size and completely half - filled p subshell. The electronic configuration of nitrogen is $1s^2, 2s^2, 2p_x^1, 2p_y^1, 2p_z^1$. Nitrogen has three electrons in $2p$ subshell which are singly filled. So, by Hund's Rule, half filled and fully filled orbitals are most stable. Therefore, nitrogen is in a most stable state and to release electrons from its outer shell will require lot of energy. Hence, it has highest ionisation enthalpy.

32. Metal M ions form accp structure. Oxide ions occupy ½ octahedral and ½ tetrahedral voids. What is the formula of the oxide?
    (a) MO   (b) MO_2 (c) MO_3 (d) M_2O_3

Ans. (d) M_2O_3

Explanation: Metal M ions form ccp structure.

Let number of ions of M be X

No. of tetrahedral voids $= 2x$

No. of octahedral voids $= x$

Number of oxide ions will be $\dfrac{1}{2}x + \dfrac{1}{2}(2x) = \dfrac{3}{2}x$

Formula of oxide $= MxO\dfrac{3}{2}x = M_2O_3$

33. The reaction of toluene with Cl_2 in presence of $FeCl_3$ gives 'X' while the of toluene with Cl_2 in presence of light gives 'Y'. Thus 'X' and 'Y' are:

(a) X = benzyl chloride Y = o and p – chlorotoluene

(b) X = m – chlorotoluene Y = p – chlorotoluene

(c) X = o and p–chlorotoluene Y = trichloromethylbenzene

(d) X= benzyl chloride, Y = m-chlorotoluene

Ans. (c) X = o and p–chlorotoluene, Y = trichloromethylbenzene

Explanation: The reaction of toluene with Cl_2 in presence of $FeCl_3$ and in dark gives 'X' due to electrophilic substitution reaction on the benzene ring by Cl^+ ion at the ortho and para positions occurs to give o and p–chlorotoluene.

Since methyl group activates the ring at ortho and para positions more than meta positions, the electroscopic substitution occurs mostly at these positions.

$$C_6H_5 - CH_3 + Cl_2 \xrightarrow{FeCl_3} \{o - chlorotoluene + p - chlorotoluene\}$$
$$(X)$$

On the other hand, the reaction of chlorine with toluene in the presence of UV light gives 'Y', due to substitution reaction occurring in the methyl group via free radical mechanism.

$$C_6H_5 - CH_3 + Cl_2 \xrightarrow{UV\ light} C_6H_5 - CCl_3$$
$$(Y)$$

Thus, 'X' and 'Y' are, X = o and p–chlorotoluene.

Y = trichloromethylbenzene

34. Ozone is a/ an ___________________ molecule and the two O-O bond lengths in ozone are (i)_________-and (ii) _____________

(a) linear, 110 pm; 148 pm

(b) angular, 110 pm; 148 pm

(c) linear, 128 pm; 128 pm

(d) angular, 128 pm; 128 pm

Ans. (d) Angular, 128 pm; 128 pm

Explanation: Ozone is a resonance hybrid of two equivalent structures. It is an angular molecule and the two O-O bond lengths in ozone are 128 pm and 128 pm.

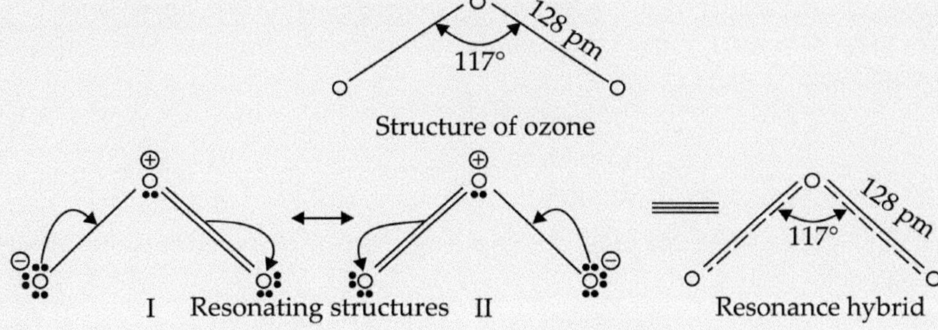

35. Water retention or puffiness due to high salt intake occurs due to:

(a) diffusion

(b) vapour pressure difference

(c) osmosis

(d) reverse osmosis

Ans. (c) osmosis

Explanation: Osmosis is a process by which molecules of a solvent tend to pass through a semipermeable membrane from a less concentrated solution into a more concentrated one. Water retention or puffiness due to high salt intake occurs due to osmosis.

36. In the following reaction, identify A and B:

$$C_6H_{12}O_6 \xrightarrow{\text{Acetic anhydride}} A$$

with Conc. nitric acid → B

(a) A = COOH–$(CH_2)_4$–COOH, B = OHC–$(CHOCOCH_3)_4$–CH_2OCOCH_3

(b) A = COOH–$(CH_2)_4$-CHO , B = OHC–$(CHOCOCH_3)_4$–CH_2OCOCH_3

(c) A = OHC–$(CHOCOCH_3)_3$–CH_2OCOCH_3 B = COOH–$(CH_2)_4$–CHO,

(d) A = OHC–$(CHOCOCH_3)_4$–CH_2OCOCH_3 B = COOH–$(CH_3)_4$–COOH

Ans. (d) A = OHC–$(CHOCOCH_3)_4$ – CH_2OCOCH_3 B = COOH–$(CH_2)_4$ – COOH

Explanation:

$$\underset{\text{glucose}}{\overset{\displaystyle CHO}{\underset{\displaystyle CH_2OH}{\mid (CHOH)_4 \mid}}} + 5(CH_3CH)_2O \longrightarrow \underset{\substack{\text{Glucose penta acetate}\\(A)}}{\overset{\displaystyle CHO}{\underset{\displaystyle CH_2O\text{–}C\text{–}CH_3}{\mid (CHOCOCH_3)_4 \mid}}} + 5CH_3COOH$$

$$\underset{\text{glucose}}{\overset{\displaystyle CHO}{\underset{\displaystyle CH_2OH}{\mid (CHOH)_4 \mid}}} \xrightarrow{HNO_3} \underset{\substack{\text{Saccharic acid}\\(B)}}{\overset{\displaystyle COOH}{\underset{\displaystyle COOH}{\mid (CHOH)_4 \mid}}}$$

37. In lake test for Al^{3+} ions, there is the formation of coloured 'floating lake'. It is due to:

(a) Absorption of litmus by $[Al(OH)_4]^-$

(b) Absorption of litmus by $Al(OH)_3$

(c) Adsorption of litmus by $[Al(OH)_4]^-$

(d) Adsorption of litmus by $Al(OH)_3$

Ans. (d) Adsorption of litmus by $Al(OH)_3$

Explanation: In lake test for Al^{3+} ions, a coloured floating lake is formed as $Al(OH)_3$ which being a solid suspension, adsorbs litmus colour, resulting in coloured floating lake appearance.

$$Al(OH)_3 + 3HCl \longrightarrow AlCl_3 + 3H_2O \ldots\text{dissolution}$$
$$AlCl_3 + 3NH_4OH \longrightarrow 3NH_4Cl + Al(OH)_3\downarrow$$

Blue colour adsorbs on this ppt.

38. A unit cell of NaCl has 4 formula units. Its edge length is 0.50 nm. Calculate the density if molar mass of NaCl = 58.5 g/mol.

(a) 1 g/cm^3 (b) 2 g/cm^3 (c) 3 g/cm^3 (d) 4g/cm^3

Ans. (c) 3 g/cm^3

Explanation: Using formula

$$\text{Density} = \frac{(Z \times m)}{a^3 \times Na}$$

$$D = \frac{4 \times 58.5}{(0.5 \times 10^{-7}) \times 6.023 \times 10^{23}}$$

$$= 3.1 \text{ g/cm}^3$$

39. Which one of the following are correctly arranged on the basis of the property indicated:
   (a) $I_2 < Br_2 < F_2 < Cl_2$ [increasing bond dissociation enthalpy]
   (b) $H_2O > H_2S < H_2Te < H_2Se$ [increasing acidic strength]
   (c) $NH_3 < N_2O < NH_2OH < N_2O_5$ [increasing oxidation state]
   (d) $BiH_3 < SbH_3 < AsH_3 < PH_3 < NH_3$ [increasing bond angle]
Ans. (d) $BiH_3 < SbH_3 < AsH_3 < PH_3 < NH_3$ [increasing bond angle]

Explanation:
(a) $I_2 < Br_2 < F_2 < Cl_2$ [increasing bond dissociation enthalpy]: incorrect order, correct order is $Cl_2 > Br_2 > F_2 > I_2$.
(b) $H_2O > H_2S < H_2Te < H_2Se$ [increasing acidic strength]: incorrect order, correct order is $H_2O < H_2S < H_2Se < H_2Te$
(c) $NH_3 < N_2O < NH_2OH < N_2O_5$ [increasing oxidation state]: incorrect order NH_3 (Oxidation state-2) N_2O (Oxidation state +1) NH_2OH (Oxidation state-1) N_2O_5 (Oxidation state +5)
(d) $BiH_3 < SbH_3 < AsH_3 < PH_3 < NH_3$ [increasing bond angle] : correct order

40. What would be the reactant and reagent used to obtain 2, 4-dimethyl pentan-3-ol?
   (a) Propanal and propyl magnesium bromide
   (b) 3-methylbutanal and 2-methyl magnesium iodide
   (c) 2-dimethylpropanone and methyl magnesium iodide
   (d) 2-methylpropanal and isopropyl magnesium iodide
Ans. (d) 2- methylpropanal and isopropyl magnesium iodide

Explanation:

$$CH_3-\overset{\overset{\displaystyle H}{|}}{CH}-\overset{\overset{\displaystyle H}{|}}{C}=O + (CH_3)_2CHMgI \longrightarrow$$
$$\underset{CH_3}{|} \qquad \text{Isopropyl magnesium iodide}$$

2-Methylpropanal

$$(CH_3)CH-\overset{\overset{\displaystyle H}{|}}{\underset{\underset{\displaystyle CH(CH_3)_2}{|}}{C}}=OMgI \xrightarrow{H_2O} (CH_3)_2CH-\overset{\overset{\displaystyle H}{|}}{\underset{\underset{\displaystyle CH(CH_3)_2}{|}}{C}}=OH$$

2, 4-Dimethylpentan-3-ol

41. o-hydroxy benzyl alcohol when reacted with PCl_3 gives the product as (IUPAC name)
   (a) o- hydroxy benzyl chloride
   (b) 2- chloromethylphenol
   (c) o-chloromethylchlorobenzene
   (d 4-hydroxymethylphenol
Ans. (b) 2- chloromethylphenol

Explanation: o-hydroxy benzyl alcohol when reacted with PCl3 gives the product 2- chloromethylphenol. The reaction is as follows:

CH_2OH / OH + PCl_5 ⟶ CH_2Cl / OH

2- chloromethylphenol

42. Which of the following statements is true?
   (a) Ammonia is the weakest reducing agent and the strongest base among Group 15 hydrides.
   (b) Ammonia is the strongest reducing agent as well as the strongest base among Group 15 hydrides.
   (c) Ammonia is the weakest reducing agent as well as the weakest base among Group 15 hydrides.
   (d) Ammonia is the strongest reducing agent and the weakest base among Group 15 hydrides.

Ans. (a) Ammonia is the weakest reducing agent and the strongest base among Group 15 hydrides.

> **Explanation:** Ammonia is the weakest reducing agent and the strongest base among Group 15 hydrides. This is because the reducing character of hydrides increases down the group due to decrease in bond dissociation enthalpy.

43. Identify the secondary alcohols from the following set:
    (i) $CH_3CH_2CH(OH)CH_3$ (ii) $(C_2H_5)_3COH$

    (iii) [benzene ring with OH substituent]

    (iv) [benzene ring with CH(OH)CH₃ substituent]

    (a) (i) and (iv)   (b) (i) and (iii)   (c) (i) and (ii)   (d) (i), (iii) and (iv)

Ans. (a) (i) and (iv)

> **Explanation:**
> (i) $CH_3CH_2CH(OH)CH_3$ (secondary)
> (ii) $(C_2H_5)_3 COH$ (tertiary)
> (iii) [benzene ring with OH]   Phenol not an alcohol
> (iv) [benzene ring with CH(OH)CH₃] secondary

44. Alkenes decolourise bromine water in presence of CCl₄ due to formation of:
    (a) allyl bromide   (b) vinyl bromide   (c) bromoform   (d) vicinal dibromide

Ans. (d) Vicinal dibromide

> **Explanation:** Alkenes decolourise bromine water in the presence of CCl_4 due to the formation of vicinal dibromide. The reaction is as follows:
> $$CH_2 = CH_2 + Br_2 \longrightarrow BrCH_2 - CH_2Br$$
> $$\text{Vicinal dibromide}$$

45. Given below are two statements labelled as Assertion (A) and Reason (R)
    Assertion (A): Electron gain enthalpy of oxygen is less than that of Flourine but greater than Nitrogen.
    Reason (R): Ionisation enthalpies of the elements follow the order Nitrogen > Oxygen > Fluorine
    Select the most appropriate answer from the options given below:
    (a) Both A and R are true and R is the correct explanation of A
    (b) Both A and R are true but R is not the correct explanation of A.
    (c) A is true but R is false.
    (d) A is false but R is true.

Ans. (c) A is true but R is false

> **Explanation:** Ionisation potential increases across a period from left to right but due to half filled $2p$-orbital, Nitrogen has higher ionisation potential than oxygen but less than flourine and hence ionisation potential order is:
> $$F > N > O$$

Therefore, reason is false. On the other hand,
Electron gain enthalpy increases across a period from left to right and hence the order is:

$$F > O > N$$

Therefore, assertion is true, but reason is false.

46. Given below are two statements labelled as Assertion (A) and Reason (R)

    Assertion (A): Alkyl halides are insoluble in water.

    Reason (R): Alkyl halides have halogen attached to sp^3 hybrid carbon. Select the most appropriate answer from the options given below:

    (a) Both A and R are true and R is the correct explanation of A.

    (b) Both A and R are true but R is not the correct explanation of A.

    (c) A is true but R is false.

    (d) A is false but R is true.

Ans. (b) Both A and R are true but R is not the correct explanation of A.

> **Explanation:** Alkyl halides are insoluble in water and they have halogen attached to sp3 hybrid carbon. They are insoluble in water because they are unable to form hydrogen bonds with water or break pre-existing hydrogen bonds. Hence, both assertion and reason are true but reason is not the correct explanation of assertion.

47. Given below are two statements labelled as Assertion (A) and Reason (R)

    Assertion (A): Molarity of a solution changes with temperature.

    Reason (R): Molarity is a colligative property.

    Select the most appropriate answer from the options given below:

    (a) Both A and R are true and R is the correct explanation of A.

    (b) Both A and R are true but R is not the correct explanation of A.

    (c) A is true but R is false.

    (d) A is false but R is true.

Ans. (c) A is true but R is false.

> **Explanation:** Molarity of a solution is defined as the moles of a solute per liters of a solution. It changes with temperature. Colligative properties are physical properties of solutions, like boiling point elevation and freezing point depression and molarity is not a physical property a colligative property, it is a means to express concentration. Hence, assertion is true but reason is false.

48. Given below are two statements labelled as Assertion (A) and Reason (R).

    Assertion(A): SO_2 is reducing while TeO_2 is an oxidising agent.

    Reason(R): Reducing property of dioxide decreases from SO_2 to TeO_2.

    Select the most appropriate answer from the options given below:

    (a) Both A and R are true and R is the correct explanation of A

    (b) Both A and R are true but R is not the correct explanation of A.

    (c) A is true but R is false.

    (d) A is false but R is true.

Ans. (b) Both A and R are true but R is not the correct explanation of A.

> **Explanation:** Sulphur acts as a reducing agent because of the presence of empty d-orbital, it can expand its oxidation state from the $+4$ to the $+6$ oxidation state. Te is a heavy element and because of the inert pair effect, the lower oxidation state is more stable. Hence, it acts as an oxidising agent. Reducing property of dioxide decreases from SO_2 to TeO_2. Hence, both assertion and reason are true and reason is not the correct explanation of assertion.

49. Given below are two statements labelled as Assertion (A) and Reason (R)

Assertion (A): Cryoscopic constant depends on nature of solvent.

Reason (R): Cryoscopic constant is a universal constant.

Select the most appropriate answer from the options given below:

(a) Both A and R are true and R is the correct explanation of A

(b) Both A and R are true but R is not the correct explanation of A.

(c) A is true but R is false.

(d) A is false but R is true.

Ans. (c) A is true but R is false.

> **Explanation:** Cryoscopic constant depends on nature of solvent but it is not a universal constant as it varies with the type of solvent. Hence, assertion is true but reason is false.

Section-C

This section consists of 6 multiple choice questions with an overall choice to attempt any 5. In case more than desirable number of questions are attempted, ONLY first 5 will be considered for evaluation.

50. Match the following:

I	II
(i) Amino acids	(A) protein
(ii) Thymine	(B) Nucleic acid
(iii) Insulin	(C) DNA
(iv) phosphodiester linkage	(D) Zwitter ion
(v) Uracil	

Which of the following is the best matched options?

(a) i-A, v- D, iii- C, iv-B

(b) i-D, ii-C, iii- A, iv-B

(c) i-D, v- D, iii- A, iv-B

(d) i-A, ii- C, iii- D, iv-B

Ans. (b) i-D, ii-C, iii- A, iv-B

> **Explanation:** Amino acids form proteins and exist as zwitter ion , Thymine is a nitrogenous base in DNA, Insulin is a protein , phosphodiester linkage is found in nucleic acids so also in DNA and Uracil is nitrogenous base found in RNA which is a nucleic acid.

51. Which of the following analogies is correct:

(a) Nitrogen: $1s^2\,2s^2\,2p^3$ :: Argon: $1s^2\,2s^2\,2p^6$

(b) Carbon: maximum compounds :: Xenon: no compounds

(c) XeF_2. Linear :: ClF_3. Trigonal planar

(d) Helium: meteorological observations:: Argon: metallurgical processes

Ans. (d) Helium: meteorological observations :: Argon: metallurgical processes

> **Explanation:** Nitrogen: $1s^2\,2s^2\,2p^3$ :: Argon:$1s^2\,2s^2\,2p^6$ is configuration of Neon not Argon
> Carbon: maximum compounds :: Xenon: no compounds , Xenon forms compounds
> XeF_2. Linear :: ClF_3. Trigonal planar , ClF_3 is T shaped not trigonal planar
> Hence, the correct analogy is Helium: meteorological observations :: Argon: metallurgical processes.

52. Complete the following analogy:

Same molecular formula but different structures: A:: Non superimposable mirror images: B

(a) A: Isomers B: Enantiomer

(b) A: Enantiomers B: Racemic mixture

(c) A: Sterioisomers B: Retention

(d) A: Isomers B: Sterioisomers

Ans. (a) A : Isomers B: Enantiomer

> **Explanation:** Isomers are molecules that have the same molecular formula but different structure. Whereas, enantiomers are the chiral molecules that are mirror images of one another. They have same physical properties. Hence, the correct analogy is A: Isomers B: Enantiomer.

CASE 1. Read the passage given below and answer the following questions 53-55

Early crystallographers had trouble solving the structures of inorganic solids using X-ray diffraction because some of the mathematical tools for analyzing the data had not yet been developed. Once a trial structure was proposed, it was relatively easy to calculate the diffraction pattern, but it was difficult to go the other way (from the diffraction pattern to the structure) if nothing was known a *priori* about the arrangement of atoms in the unit cell. It was important to develop some guidelines for guessing the coordination numbers and bonding geometries of atoms in crystals. The first such rules were proposed by Linus Pauling, who considered how one might pack together oppositely charged spheres of different radii. Pauling proposed from geometric considerations that the quality of the "fit" depended on the **radius ratio** of the anion and the cation.

If the anion is considered as the packing atom in the crystal, then the smaller cation fills interstitial sites ("holes"). Cations will find arrangements in which they can contact the largest number of anions. If the cation can touch all of its nearest neighbour anions then the fit is good. If the cation is too small for a given site, that coordination number will be unstable and it will prefer a lower coordination structure. The table below gives the ranges of cation/anion radius ratios that give the best fit for a given coordination geometry.

Coordination number	Geometry	$\rho = r_{cation}/r_{anion}$
2	linear	0 - 0.155
3	triangular	0.155 - 0.225
4	tetrahedral	0.225 - 0.414
4	square planar	0.414 - 0.732
6	octahedral	0.414 - 0.732
8	cubic	0.732 - 1.0
12	cuboctahedral	1.0

(*Source: Ionic Radii and Radius Ratios. (2021, June 8). Retrieved June 29, 2021, from https://chem.libretexts.org/@go/page/183346*)

53. The radius of Ag^+ ion is 126pm and of I^- ion is 216pm. The coordination number of Ag^+

(a) 2   (b) 3   (c) 6   (d) 8

Ans. (c) 6

> **Explanation:** The radius of Ag+ ion is 126 pm and of I– ion is 216 pm. The coordination number of Ag+ ion is:
>
> $$\rho = r_{cation}/r_{anion} = \frac{126}{216} = 0.58$$
>
> Radius ratio lies in the range 0.414 – 0.732, so has coordination number 6 or 4 according to the table. Since none of the options is 4, so the answer is 6.

54. A solid AB has square planar structure. If the radius of cation A^+ is 120 pm, calculate the maximum possible value of anion B^-

(a) 240 pm   (b) 270 pm   (c) 280 pm   (d) 290 pm

Ans. (d) 290 pm

> **Explanation:** Given: AB has square planar structure
> Radius of cation A^+ = 120 pm

We know that for a square planar structure, ratio is between $0.414 - 0.732$

On calculating the radius of cation/ radius of anion, we get:

radius of cation/radius of anion $= 0.414$; $\dfrac{r_{A^+}}{r_{B^-}} = 0.414$; $r_{B^-} = \dfrac{r_{A^+}}{0.414} = \dfrac{120}{0.414} = 290$ pm

Hence, the maximum possible value of anion B^- is 290 pm.

55. A "good fit" is considered to be one where the cation can touch:
   (a) all of its nearest neighbour anions.
   (b) most of its nearest neighbour anions.
   (c) some of its nearest neighbour anions.
   (d) none of its nearest neighbour anions.

Ans. (a) all of its nearest neighbour anions

Explanation: A "good fit" is considered to be one where the cation can touch all of its nearest neighbour anions.

Sample Paper 1

Chemistry

Section – A

This section consists of 25 multiple choice questions with overall choice to attempt any 20 questions. In case more than desirable number of questions are attempted, ONLY first 20 will be considered for evaluation.

1. Copper has the face centered cubic structure. The coordination number of each ion is:
   (a) 4   (b) 12   (c) 14   (d) 8

2. Which of the following is not a colligative property?
   (a) Depression in freezing point
   (b) Elevation in boiling point
   (c) Osmotic pressure
   (d) Modification of refractive index

3. When acetaldehyde is treated with Grignard reagent, followed by hydrolysis the product formed is:
   (a) Primary alcohol
   (b) Secondary alcohol
   (c) Carboxylic acid
   (d) Tertiary alcohol

4. Which of the following has lowest reducing character?
   (a) H_2O (b) H_2S (c) H_2Te (d) H_2Se

5. Which of the following is an example of fibrous protein?
   (a) Insulin   (b) Haemoglobin   (c) Fibroin   (d) Glycogen

6. When chloroform is heated with aqueous NaOH, it gives :
   (a) Formic acid
   (b) Sodium formate
   (c) Acetic acid
   (d) Sodium acetate

7. α–D(+) glucose and β–D(+) glucose are:
   (a) Geometrical isomers   (b) Enantiomers   (c) Anomers   (d) Optical isomers

8. The geometry of XeF_6 molecule and the hybridization of Xe atom in the molecule is:
   (a) Distorted octahedral and sp^3d^3
   (b) Square planar and sp^3d^2
   (c) Pyramidal and sp^3
   (d) Octahedral and sp^3d^3

9. The action of sodium on alkyl halide to form an alkane is called:
   (a) Grignard reaction
   (b) Wurtz coupling reaction
   (c) Isocyanide reaction
   (d) Halogenation reaction

10. Schottky defect in crystal is observed when:
    (a) An ion leaves its normal site and occupies the interstitial site
    (b) Equal number of cations and anions are missing from the lattice
    (c) Unequal number of cations and anions are missing from the lattice
    (d) Density of the crystal is increased

11. During preparation of XeF_4 from Xenon and Fluorine, these two elements are reacted in which of the following given ratios?
    (a) Xenon (1) Fluorine (Excess)
    (b) Xenon (1) Fluorine (5)
    (c) Xenon (1) Fluorine (20)
    (d) Xenon (1) Fluorine (4)

12. Electrical properties like that of metals are shown by which of the following oxides?
    (a) CrO_2 (b) SiO_2 (c) MgO (d) $SO_2(s)$

13. XeF_2 is hydrolysed to give
    (a) Xe and O_2 (b) Xe, F_2 and O_2 (c) Xe, HF and O_2 (d) Xe and F_2

14. Give the IUPAC name of the following:

$$CH_3CH(Cl)CH(Br)CH_3$$

(a) 3- Bromo -2-Chloro butane (b) 3- Bromo -3-Chloro butane
(c) 2- Bromo -2-Chloro butane (d) 2- Bromo -3-Chloro butane

15. Which of the following carbohydrates does not satisfy the formula $C_x(H_2O)_y$?

(a) Fructose (b) Glucose (c) Deoxyribose (d) Lactose

16. Which of the following is not a volatile substance?

(a) Camphour (b) Petrol (c) Acetone (d) Acetanilide

17. What is the general formula for an aliphatic alcohol? (R=alkyl group)

(a) R-H (b) R-OH (c) R-CHO (d) R-COOH

18. XeF_2 and XeF_4 have

(a) Linear and square planar structures respectively
(b) Square planar and linear structures respectively
(c) Square planar structure
(d) Linear structure

19. Monohalo, dihalo, trihalo and tetrahalo are types of haloalkanes and haloarenes based on the ______

(a) Type of halogen atom
(b) Number of halogen atoms
(c) Nature of carbon atom
(d) Hybridisation of C atom to which halogen is bonded

20. Under which type of solid graphite cannot be classified?

(a) Ionic solid (b) Conducting solid (c) Network solid (d) Covalent solid

21. Which of the following carbohydrates does not have the formula $C_{12}H_{22}O_{11}$?

(a) Galactose (b) Sucrose (c) Allolactose (d) Maltose

22. Complete the following reaction:

$XeF_6 + KF \rightarrow$

(a) $K + XeF_7$ (b) $[XeF_3]^+ [KF_6]^-$ (c) $KXeF_6$ (d) $K^+ [XeF_7]^-$

23. What is the common name of Dichloromethane?

(a) Methylene dichloride (b) Ethyl dichloride
(c) Propane aldehyde (d) None of these

24. Which of the following characteristics is not possessed by an ideal solution?

(a) Obeys Raoult's law.
(b) Volume change on mixing is not equal to zero.
(c) There should be no chemical reaction between solute and solvent.
(d) Only very dilute solutions behave as ideal solutions.

25. What happens to the size of atoms of elements of p-block as we move from left to right in the same period?

(a) Size increases (b) Size decreases
(c) Size does not change (d) Size increases then decreases

Section-B

This section consists of 24 multiple choice questions with overall choice to attempt any 20 questions. In case more than desirable number of questions are attempted, ONLY first 20 will be considered for evaluation.

26. What is the maximum covalency of the nitrogen atom?

(a) One (b) Two (c) Three (d) Four

27. Which one of the following cannot be called as a 'non-stoichiometric defect'?

(a) Metal excess defect due to anion vacancies.
(b) Metal excess defect due to presence of extra cations.

   (c)   Metal deficiency due to absence of cations.
   (d)   Combination of vacancy and interstitial defects.
28. What is the hybridisation of the carbon atom in the allylic halides?
   (a) sp^3 hybridised   (b) sp hybridised   (c) sp^3d^2 hybridised   (d) None of theses
29. In the cubic close packing, the unit cell has _________.
   (a) 4 tetrahedral voids each of which is shared by four adjacent unit cells.
   (b) 4 tetrahedral voids within the unit cell.
   (c) 8 tetrahedral voids each of these is shared by four adjacent unit cells.
   (d) 8 tetrahedral voids within the unit cells.
30. The halide ion easiest to oxidise is:
   (a) F^- (b) Cl^- (c) Br^- (d) I^-
31. Which of the following compounds contain an aryl carbon?
   (a) Ethanol   (b) Benzyl alcohol   (c) Vinyl alcohol   (d) Phenol
32. The phenomenon of lowering of vapour pressure is defined as:
   (a) Decrease in vapour pressure of a solvent on addition of a volatile non electrolyte solute in it.
   (b) Decrease in vapour pressure of a solvent on addition of a non-volatile non electrolyte solute in it.
   (c) Decrease in vapour pressure of a solvent on addition of a volatile electrolyte solute in it.
   (d) Decrease in vapour pressure of a solvent on addition of a non-volatile solute in it.
33. The compound with the formula $C_2(H_2O)_2$ is a _______
   (a) carbohydrate   (b) carboxylic acid   (c) aldehyde   (d) monosaccharide
34. What is the common name of 3-Bromopropene?
   (a) Tert-Butyl bromide   (b) Vinyl bromide
   (c) Allyl bromide   (d) Propylidene bromide
35. In a solid lattice the cation has left a lattice site and is located at an interstitial position, the lattice defect is:
   (a) Interstitial defect   (b) Valency defect
   (c) Frenkel defect   (d) Schottky defect
36. Which of the following class of compounds is not a part of the large group of carbohydrates?
   (a) Polyamino aldehydes   (b) Polyhalo aldehydes
   (c) Polyhydroxy ketones   (d) Polyhydroxy carboxylic acids
37. In the common naming system, the prefix sym- is used for haloarenes with how many halogen atoms?
   (a) 3   (b) 1   (c) 2   (d) 4
38. In which of the following structures coordination number for cations and anions in the packed structure will be same?
   (a) Cl^- ion form fcc lattice and Na^+ ions occupy all octahedral voids of the unit cell.
   (b) Ca^{2+} ions form fcc lattice and F^- ions occupy all the eight tetrahedral voids of the unit cell.
   (c) O_2^- ions form fcc lattice and Na^+ ions occupy all the eight tetrahedral voids of the unit cell.
   (d) S_2^- ions form fcc lattice and Zn^{2+} ions go into alternate tetrahedral voids of the unit cell.
39. What is the common name of Butan-2-ol?
   (a) n-Butyl alcohol   (b) sec-Butyl alcohol   (c) Isobutyl alcohol   (d) tert-Butyl alcohol
40. How many carbon atoms does Isobutyl chloride have in its parent carbon chain?
   (a) 1   (b) 3   (c) 2   (c) 4
41. Vapour pressure decreases with:
   (a) Increase in concentration of the solution.   (b) Decrease in solute particles in the solution.
   (c) Decrease in boiling point.   (d) Increase in freezing point.
42. Which of the following options are not in accordance with the property mentioned against them?
   (a) $F_2 > Cl_2 > Br_2 > I_2$ Oxidising power.
   (b) MI > MBr > MCl > MF Ionic character of metal halide.
   (c) $F_2 > Cl_2 > Br_2 > I_2$ Bond dissociation enthalpy.
   (d) HI < HBr < HCl < HF Hydrogen-halogen bond strength.

43. What is the correct order of reactivity of the following haloacids with a given alcohol?

(a) $HCl > HBr > HI$

(b) $HI > HBr > HCl$

(c) $HBr > HCl > HI$

(d) $HI > HCl > HBr$

44. How many carbon atoms are present in the parent chain of tert-Butyl alcohol?

(a) 2
(b) 3
(c) 4
(d) 5

45. Given below are two statements labelled as Assertion (A) and Reason (R)

Assertion: F_2 has lower bond dissociation enthalpy than Cl_2.

Reason: Fluorine is more electronegative than chlorine.

Select the most appropriate answer from the options given below:

(a) Both A and R are true and R is the correct explanation of A.

(b) Both A and R are true but R is not the correct explanation of A.

(c) A is true but R is false.

(d) A is false but R is true.

46. Given below are two statements labelled as Assertion (A) and Reason (R)

Assertion: Quartz glass is crystalline solid and quartz is an amorphous solid.

Reason: Quartz glass has no long range order.

Select the most appropriate answer from the options given below:

(a) Both A and R are true and R is the correct explanation of A.

(b) Both A and R are true but R is not the correct explanation of A.

(c) A is true but R is false.

(d) A is false but R is true.

47. Given below are two statements labelled as Assertion (A) and Reason (R)

Assertion: Valency of noble gas is 0.

Reason: Noble gases possess complete octet.

Select the most appropriate answer from the options given below:

(a) Both A and R are true and R is the correct explanation of A.

(b) Both A and R are true but R is not the correct explanation of A.

(c) A is true but R is false.

(d) A is false but R is true.

48. Given below are two statements labelled as Assertion (A) and Reason (R)

Assertion: The dissolution of acetone in chloroform is an exothermic process.

Reason: H- bonding occurs between acetone and chloroform molecule on mixing the two.

Select the most appropriate answer from the options given below:

(a) Both A and R are true and R is the correct explanation of A.

(b) Both A and R are true but R is not the correct explanation of A.

(c) A is true but R is false.

(d) A is false but R is true.

49. Given below are two statements labelled as Assertion (A) and Reason (R)

Assertion: Ethanol is a weaker acid than phenol.

Reason: Sodium ethoxide may be prepared by the reaction of ethanol with aqueous NaOH.

Select the most appropriate answer from the options given below:

(a) Both A and R are true and R is the correct explanation of A.

(b) Both A and R are true but R is not the correct explanation of A.

(c) A is true but R is false.

(d) A is false but R is true.

Section-C

This section consists of 6 multiple choice questions with an overall choice to attempt any 5. In case more than desirable number of questions are attempted, ONLY first 5 will be considered for evaluation.

50. Helium is used for filling meteorological balloons and
    (a) In gas cooled-nuclear reactor
    (b) As a cryogenic agent
    (c) Both (a) and (b)
    (d) None of the above

51. Which of the following class of compounds is not a part of the large group of carbohydrates?
    (a) Polyamino aldehydes
    (b) Polyhalo aldehydes
    (c) Polyhydroxy ketones
    (d) Polyhydroxy carboxylic acids

52. Which of the following terms does not describe $CH_2 = CH - CH_2OH$?
    (a) Primary
    (b) Monohydric
    (c) Allylic
    (d) Vinylic

CASE 1: Read the passage given below and answer the following questions 53-55

Point defects play an important part in determining the physical properties of most crystalline substances, most notably those controlling the transport of matter and the properties that stem from it. Even a crystal of high purity under conditions of no irradiation contains point defects in thermal equilibrium. Some lattice sites are vacant, and some atoms are displaced from their normal lattice sites into interstitial positions or onto "wrong" lattice sites. For stoichiometric compounds of high purity, the concentrations of these point defects are very low, even at temperatures up to the melting point. A meaningful model, then, is to consider the crystal as a solvent containing a very dilute solution of simple, individual vacancies and interstitials. Long-range interactions among the defects and with impurity atoms, and short-range interactions that produce pairs or other clusters can be introduced in a first order approximation.

Source: https://www.sciencedirect.com/topics/physics-and-astronomy/point-defects

53. Which one of the given below statements is wrong about Frenkel defect:
    (a) It is a combination of vacancy and interstitial defects.
    (b) Cations leave their actual lattice sites and occupy the interstitial space in the solid.
    (c) Density remains the same.
    (d) Density of the crystal increases.

54. Which one of the following is an 'interstitial void'?
    (a) Octahedral void
    (b) Tetrahedral void
    (c) None of the above
    (d) Both (a) and (b)

55. This type of defect arises due to absence of equal number of cations and anions from lattice sites in the crystalline solid of the type A^+B^- and it lowers the density of the crystal.
    (a) Vacancy defect
    (b) Schottky defect
    (c) Interstitial defect
    (d) Frenkel defect

❑❑

Sample Paper 2

Chemistry

Section – A

This section consists of 25 multiple choice questions with overall choice to attempt any 20 questions. In case more than desirable number of questions are attempted, ONLY first 20 will be considered for evaluation.

1. Relationship between atomic radius (r) and the edge length $'a'$ of a body centred cubic unit cell is.

   (a) $r = \dfrac{a}{2}$ (b) $r = \sqrt{\dfrac{a}{2}}$ (c) $r = \dfrac{\sqrt{3}}{4}a$ (d) $r = \dfrac{3a}{2}$

2. Osmotic pressure of a dilute solution is given by :

   (a) $P = P_0 x$ (b) $pV = nRT$ (c) $p = VRT$ (d) None of these

3. What is the IUPAC name of

$$CH_3-\underset{\underset{CH_3}{|}}{\overset{\overset{CH_3}{|}}{C}}-CH_2Cl$$

   (a) 2-dimethylchloropropane   (b) 1-chloro-2-dimethyl-pentane
   (c) 2, 2-dimethyl-chlorobutane   (d) 1-chloro-2, 2-dimethyl propane

4. Oxygen molecule is :

   (a) Paramagnetic   (b) Diamagnetic   (c) Ferromagnetic   (d) Ferrimagnetic

5. When oxalic acid is heated with glycerol we get:

   (a) Formic acid   (b) Acetic acid   (c) Lactic acid   (d) Tartaric acid

6. The disease albinism is caused by the deficiency of enzyme:

   (a) trypsin   (b) tyrosinase
   (c) phenylalanine hydroxylase   (d) none of these

7. Ethylene chloride and ethylidene chloride are isomers. Identify the correct statements.

   (a) Both the compounds form same product on treatment with alcoholic KOH.
   (b) Both the compounds form same product on treatment with aq.NaOH.
   (c) Both the compounds form same product on reduction.
   (d) Both the compounds are optically active.

8. Which of the following has lowest reducing character?

   (a) H_2O (b) H_2S (c) H_2Te (d) H_2Se

9. An example of intensive property is:

   (a) Number of moles   (b) Mass   (c) Volume   (d) Density

10. Amino acids are:

    (a) acidic   (b) basic   (c) amphoteric   (d) neutral

11. Alkyl halides are prepared from alcohols, which are easily accessible. The hydroxyl group of an alcohol is replaced by halogen on reactions with certain compounds. Which one of the below compounds is inappropriate as a reagent?

    (a) Concentrated halogen acid   (b) Sodium dihalide
    (c) Thionyl chloride   (d) Phosphorus halides

12. In the complex ion $[AuXe_4]^{2+}$, Xe acts as :

    (a) central atom   (b) ligand   (c) chelating agent   (d) electrophile

13. What is the percentage of empty space in a body centred cubic arrangement?
    (a) 74 (b) 68 (c) 26 (d) 32
14. Which of the following is not an Electrophilic substitution reaction of haloarenes?
    (a) Sulphonation (b) Nitration (c) Halogenation (d) Wurtz-Fittig reaction
15. Hybridisation shown by Au in $[AuXe_4]^{2+}$ is :
    (a) sp^3 (b) sp^3d (c) sp^3d^2 (d) sp^2
16. The solutions which obey Raoult's law are known as:
    (a) Ideal solutions (b) Non-ideal solutions (c) Azeotropes (d) Binary solutions
17. Compounds of noble gases except___are known.
    (a) Krypton (b) Radon (c) Helium (d) Xenon
18. The reaction of a primary alcohol with which of the following gives purely a haloalkane?
    (a) Phosphorus trichloride (b) Phosphorus pentachloride
    (c) Thionyl chloride (d) Sulphuryl chloride
19. Xe is a__________ligand:
    (a) ambidentate (b) bidentate (c) unidentate (d) hexadentate
20. What happens when an aldehyde is treated with lithium aluminium hydride?
    (a) Primary alcohol is formed (b) Secondary alcohol is formed
    (c) Tertiary alcohol is formed (d) No reaction
21. Which noble gas was discovered in chromosphere?
    (a) He (b) Ar (c) Xe (d) Rn
22. Why the solutions show deviation from the Raoult's law?
    (a) Interaction in the molecular level (b) Interaction in the atomic level
    (c) Interaction in the ionic level (d) Both (a) and (b)
23. Which of the following carbohydrates is not a sugar?
    (a) Glucose (b) Fructose (c) Lactose (d) Cellulose
24. Which law is followed to increase the solubility of CO_2 in the soft drinks?
    (a) Henry's law (b) Raoult's law
    (c) Le Chatelier's principle (d) Avogadro's law
25. What is the general formula for haloalkanes? (X=halogen atom, n = 1, 2, 3...).
    (a) $C_nH_{2n}X$ (b) $C_nH_{2n+1}X$ (c) $C_nH_{2n-1}X$ (d) $C_nH_{2n-3}X$

Section-B

This section consists of 24 multiple choice questions with overall choice to attempt any 20 questions. In case more than desirable number of questions are attempted, ONLY first 20 will be considered for evaluation.

26. The low bond energy is best explained by:
    (a) The attainment of noble gas configuration
    (b) The low electron affinity of F
    (c) Repulsion by electron pairs on F
    (d) The small size of F
27. What is the correct order of the packing efficiency in different types of unit cells?
    (a) fcc < bcc < simple cubic (b) fcc < bcc > simple cubic
    (c) fcc > bcc > simple cubic (d) bcc < fcc > simple cubic
28. Glucose is prepared commercially from the hydrolysis of ______ by boiling it with dilute H_2SO_4 at 393K under pressure.
    (a) starch (b) sucrose (c) galactose (d) dextrose
29. The oxo-acid of halogen with maximum acidic character is:
    (a) $HClO_4$ (b) $HClO_3$ (c) $HClO_2$ (d) HClO

30. Which of the following point defects are shown by AgBr(s) crystals?
    (A) Schottky defect   (B) Frenkel defect
    (C) Metal excess defect   (D) Metal deficiency defect
    (a) (A) and (B)   (b) (C) and (D)   (c) (A) and (C)   (d) (B) and (D)

31. Which of the following are the most suitable conditions for electrophilic substitution of arenes?
    (a) UV light and heat   (b) Cold and dark
    (c) 40°C temperature and dark   (d) Room temperature and sunlight

32. The maximum amount of a substance that can be dissolved in a specific amount of solvent at a specified temperature is known as:
    (a) Solubility   (b) Liquidity   (c) Fluidity   (d) Viscosity

33. Alcohols have higher boiling point than their corresponding parent alkanes due to:
    (a) Intramolecular hydrogen bonding   (b) Intermolecular hydrogen bonding
    (c) Van der Waals forces   (d) Covalent bonding

34. Which of the following reaction will not occur spontaneously?
    (a) $F_2 + 2Cl^- \longrightarrow 2F^- + Cl_2$ (b) $I_2 + 2Br^- \longrightarrow 2I^- + Br_2$
    (c) $Br_2 + 2I^- \longrightarrow 2Br^- + I_2$ (d) $2I^- + Cl_2^- \longrightarrow 2Cl^- + I_2$

35. Appearance of the violet or lilac in colour on the addition of the excess of potassium ions in the KCl crystal is because of:
    (a) Some of the anionic sites are occupied by an unpaired electron.
    (b) Some of the anionic sites are occupied by a pair of electrons.
    (c) There are vacancies at some anionic sites.
    (d) F-centres are created which impart colour to the crystals.

36. Identify the monosaccharide from the following.
    (a) Deoxyribose   (b) Sucrose   (c) Maltose   (d) Fructose

37. Which of the following is not a colligative property?
    (a) Osmotic pressure   (b) Depression in freezing point
    (c) Lowering of vapour pressure   (d) Depression in boiling point

38. Which entities are formed during the free radical mechanism?
    (a) Carbanion   (b) Carbocation   (c) Free radicals   (d) Atoms

39. The high viscosity and high boiling point of HF is due to:
    (a) Low dissociation energy of F_2 molecule
    (b) Associated nature due to hydrogen bonding
    (c) Ionic character of HF
    (d) High electronegativity of fluorine

40. Which defect is not found in pure alkali metal halides?
    (a) Frenkel defect   (b) Schottky defect   (c) Both (a) and (b)   (d) Point defect

41. Which of the following alcohol is most soluble in water?
    (a) Propanol   (b) Butanol   (c) Pentanol   (d) Hexanol

42. What happens when a non-volatile solute is added to a solution?
    (a) Vapour pressure of the solvent decreases
    (b) Vapour pressure of the solvent increases
    (c) Vapour pressure of the solvent remains constant
    (d) Both (a) and (b)

43. Which of the following disaccharides gives two same monosaccharide units on hydrolysis?
    (a) Maltose   (b) Sucrose   (c) Lactose   (d) Lactulose

44. Why ZnS shows dislocation defect?
    (a) Small size of both the ions   (b) Equal size of both the ions
    (c) Zn^+ ion is larger in size   (d) Zn^+ ion is smaller in size

45. Given below are two statements labelled as Assertion (A) and Reason (R)

    Assertion: The haloalkanes are slightly soluble in water.

    Reason: Energy is required to overcome the attractions between the haloalkanes molecules.

    Select the most appropriate answer from the options given below:

    (a) Both A and R are true and R is the correct explanation of A.

    (b) Both A and R are true but R is not the correct explanation of A.

    (c) A is true but R is false.

    (d) A is false but R is true.

46. Given below are two statements labelled as Assertion (A) and Reason (R)

    Assertion: When NaCl is added to water a depression in freezing point is observed.

    Reason: The lowering of vapour pressure of a solution causes no depression in the freezing point.

    Select the most appropriate answer from the options given below:

    (a) Both A and R are true and R is the correct explanation of A.

    (b) Both A and R are true but R is not the correct explanation of A.

    (c) A is true but R is false.

    (d) A is false but R is true.

47. Given below are two statements labelled as Assertion (A) and Reason (R)

    Assertion: Acidic character of group 16 hydrides increases from H_2O to H_2Te.

    Reason: Thermal stability of hydrides decreases down the group.

    Select the most appropriate answer from the options given below:

    (a) Both A and R are true and R is the correct explanation of A.

    (b) Both A and R are true but R is not the correct explanation of A.

    (c) A is true but R is false.

    (d) A is false but R is true.

48. Given below are two statements labelled as Assertion (A) and Reason (R)

    Assertion: Quartz glass is crystalline solid and quartz is an amorphous solid.

    Reason: Quartz glass has no long range order.

    Select the most appropriate answer from the options given below:

    (a) Both A and R are true and R is the correct explanation of A.

    (b) Both A and R are true but R is not the correct explanation of A.

    (c) A is true but R is false.

    (d) A is false but R is true.

49. Given below are two statements labelled as Assertion (A) and Reason (R)

    Assertion: Interhalogen compounds are more reactive than halogens (except fluorine).

    Reason: They all undergo hydrolysis giving halide ion derived from the smaller halogen and anion derived from larger halogen.

    Select the most appropriate answer from the options given below:

    (a) Both A and R are true and R is the correct explanation of A.

    (b) Both A and R are true but R is not the correct explanation of A.

    (c) A is true but R is false.

    (d) A is false but R is true.

Section-C

This section consists of 6 multiple choice questions with an overall choice to attempt any 5. In case more than desirable number of questions are attempted, ONLY first 5 will be considered for evaluation.

50. In an orthorhombic crystal system axial angles $\alpha = \beta = ¥$ are:

    (a) Equal to 90°   (b) Less than 90°   (c) Greater than 90°   (d) None of these

51. Which of the following is not a solid solution?

    (a) Brass   (b) Bronze   (c) Hydrated salts   (d) Aerated drinks

52. Diamond, silica and silicon carbide are:

    (a) Ionic solid   (b) Covalent solid   (c) Metallic solid   (d) Molecular solid

CASE 1: Read the passage given below and answer the following questions 53-55

Experimental kinetic data on reactions of the chlorine atom with halogenated derivatives of methane and ethane (37 reactions) have been analyzed by the intersecting-parabolas method. The following five factors have an effect on the activation energy of these reactions: the enthalpy of reaction, triplet repulsion, the electronegativities of the reaction center atoms, the dipole–dipole and multidipole interactions between the reaction center and polar groups, and the effect of π electrons in the vicinity of the reaction center. The increments characterizing the contribution from each factor to the activation energy of the reaction have been calculated. The contribution from the polar interaction, $\Delta E\mu$, to the activation energy depends on the dipole moment of the polar group and obeys the following empirical equation: $\ln (\Delta E\mu/\Sigma\mu) = -0.74 + 0.87 (\Delta E\mu/\Sigma\mu) - 0.084 (\Delta E\mu/\Sigma\mu)^2$.

Source: Denisov, E.T., Denisova, T.G. (2017). Reactivity of haloalkanes in their reactions with the chlorine atom. Kinetics and Catalysis, 58, 219–226.

53. Nucleophilic reactions are the most useful classes of organic reactions of alkyl halides in which halogens are bonded to __________ hybridized carbon.

    (a) sp_2 (b) sp^3 (c) sp (d) pp

54. The spatial arrangement of four groups (valences) around a central carbon atom is tetrahedral and if all the substituents attached to that carbon are different, and then such a carbon is called _____

    (a) Achiral   (b) Chiral   (c) Asymmetric   (d) Symmetric

55. In alkyl halides, due to greater polarity as well as higher molecular mass, as compared to the parent hydrocarbon, the intermolecular __________ and __________ of attraction are stronger in the halogen derivatives.

    (a) dipole-dipole and van der Waals forces   (b) Hydrogen bond and dipole-dipole forces

    (c) van der Waals and hydrogen bond forces   (d) dipole-dipole and London forces.

Sample Paper 3

Chemistry

Section – A

This section consists of 25 multiple choice questions with overall choice to attempt any 20 questions. In case more than desirable number of questions are attempted, ONLY first 20 will be considered for evaluation.

1. The most powerful oxidising agent is :
   - (a) Fluorine
   - (b) Chlorine
   - (c) Bromine
   - (d) Iodine

2. The action of sodium on alkyl halide to form an alkane is called:
   - (a) Grignard reaction
   - (b) Wurtz coupling reaction
   - (c) Isocyanide reaction
   - (d) Halogenation reaction

3. Phenol is heated with $CHCl_3$ and alcoholic KOH when salicylaldehyde is produced. This reaction is known as:
   - (a) Rosenmund's reaction
   - (b) Reimer-Tiemann reaction
   - (c) Friedel-Crafts reaction
   - (d) Sommelet reaction

4. Conversion of ethyl bromide to ethylene is an example of:
   - (a) Hydrohalogenation
   - (b) Intramolecular dehydrohalogenation
   - (c) Dehydration
   - (d) Hydration

5. If chlorine gas is passed through hot NaOH solution, two changes are observed in the oxidation number of chlorine during the reaction. These are _________ and _________.
   - (a) 0 to +5
   - (b) 0 to +3
   - (c) 0 to –1
   - (d) 0 to +1

6. Of the following terms are used for denoting concentration of a solution, the one which does not get affected by temperature is:
   - (a) Molarity
   - (b) Molality
   - (c) Normality
   - (d) Formality

7. Lucas test is used for distinction of:
   - (a) Alcohols
   - (b) Phenols
   - (c) Alkyl halides
   - (d) Aldehydes

8. Which of the following is a molecular crystal?
   - (a) Rock salt
   - (b) Quartz
   - (c) Dry ice
   - (d) Diamond

9. When acetaldehyde is treated with Grignard reagent, followed by hydrolysis the product formed is:
   - (a) Primary alcohol
   - (b) Secondary alcohol
   - (c) Carboxylic acid
   - (d) Tertiary alcohol

10. Copper has the face centered cubic structure. The coordination number of each ion is:
   - (a) 4
   - (b) 12
   - (c) 14
   - (d) 8

11. The empty space left in hcp packing is:
   - (a) 26%
   - (b) 74%
   - (c) 52.4%
   - (d) 80 %

12. The most powerful oxidising agent is:
   - (a) Fluorine
   - (b) Chlorine
   - (c) Bromine
   - (d) Iodine

13. Which type of solutions also exists in nature?
   - (a) Liquid solutions
   - (b) Solid solutions
   - (c) Gas solutions
   - (d) None of these

14. The compound C_6H_5F is an example of a _________ halide.
   - (a) Allylic
   - (b) Benzylic
   - (c) Vinylic
   - (d) Aryl

15. Shape of ClF_3 is:
   - (a) Trigonal planar
   - (b) Tetrahedral
   - (c) T-Shaped
   - (d) Distorted octahedral

16. Iodine molecules are held in the crystals lattice by __________.
    (a) London forces
    (b) Dipole-dipole interactions
    (c) Covalent bonds
    (d) Coulombic forces
17. Which of the following aldehydes can produce primary alcohols when treated with Grignard reagent?
    (a) Methanal
    (b) Ethanal
    (c) Propanal
    (d) Butanal
18. Which of the following is a reagent used in the preparation of benzene diazonium chloride from aniline?
    (a) Sodium hydroxide
    (b) Sodium chloride
    (c) Sodium nitrite
    (d) Sodium nitrate
19. What is the molarity of pure water?
    (a) 62.3 M
    (b) 55.55 M
    (c) 21.22 M
    (d) 25.21 M
20. Which of the following types of alcohol contains a bond between sp^2 hybridised carbon and OH group?
    (a) Primary allylic alcohols
    (b) Secondary allylic alcohols
    (c) Tertiary allylic alcohols
    (d) Vinylic alcohols
21. Which of the following statements are correct?
    (a) Among halogens, radius ratio between iodine and fluorine is maximum.
    (b) Leaving F—F bond, all halogens have weaker X—X bond than X—X' bond in interhalogens.
    (c) Among interhalogen compounds maximum number of atoms are present in iodine fluoride.
    (d) Interhalogen compounds are more reactive than halogen compounds.
22. How many isomers does $C_5H_{11}Br$ have?
    (a) 8
    (b) 7
    (c) 6
    (d) 5
23. Which of the following is not a colligative property?
    (a) Osmotic pressure
    (b) Boiling point
    (c) Vapour pressure
    (d) Electrical conductivity
24. Glycerol is a __________ alcohol.
    (a) Monohydric
    (b) Dihydric
    (c) Trihydric
    (d) Tetrahydric
25. The reaction of chlorobenzene with Mg in dry ether leads to the formation of compound X, which on hydrolysis gives
    (a) Benzene
    (b) Phenol
    (c) Methyl benzene
    (d) Benzoic acid

Section-B

This section consists of 24 multiple choice questions with overall choice to attempt any 20 questions. In case more than desirable number of questions are attempted, ONLY first 20 will be considered for evaluation.

26. The minimum excess pressure that has to be applied on the solution to prevent the entry of the solvent into the solution through the semipermeable membrane is called.................
    (a) Osmotic pressure
    (b) Vapour pressure
    (c) Atmospheric pressure
    (d) None of these
27. Which noble gas was discovered in chromosphere?
    (a) He
    (b) Ar
    (c) Xe
    (d) Rn
28. Which of the following is not favourable for the proper dehydration of alcohol to form ether?
    (a) Good temperature control during reaction
    (b) Excess of alcohol
    (c) Presence of protic acids
    (d) Presence of bulky alkyl groups in the alcohol
29. A Grignard reagent may be made by reacting magnesium with
    (a) Methyl amine
    (b) Diethyl ether
    (c) Ethyl iodide
    (d) Ethyl alcohol
30. Which of the following tests does glucose give?
    (a) Tollen's test
    (b) 2, 4-DNP test
    (c) Schiff's test
    (d) Addition product with $NaHSO_3$
31. What is the major product formed when ethanol is dehydrated with concentrated H_2SO_4 at 413K?
    (a) Ethene
    (b) Methoxymethane
    (c) Methoxyethane
    (d) Ethoxyethane

32. Which of the following monosaccharides is a ketohexose?
    (a) Glucose   (b) Galactose   (c) Fructose   (d) Mannose

33. In how many ways non-ideal solutions can occur?
    (a) 2   (b) 1   (c) 4   (d) 9

34. What is the most suitable temperature for the formation of a diazonium salt from aniline?
    (a) 0 K   (b) 273 K   (c) 0°C   (d) 100°C

35. XeF_2 molecule is:
    (a) Trigonal planar   (b) Square planar   (c) Linear   (d) Pyramidal

36. The boiling point of ethers is _______ the boiling point of alcohols of comparable molecular mass.
    (a) lower than   (b) similar to   (c) little higher than   (d) much higher than

37. The α-D-glucose and β-D-glucose isomers of glucose are known as _______
    (a) enantiomers   (b) stereoisomers   (c) anomers   (d) glycomers

38. The noble gas used in the treatment of Cancer is:
    (a) Argon   (b) Xenon   (c) Radon   (d) Helium

39. _________ is the basic repeated structural unit of a crystalline solid.
    (a) Monomer   (b) Molecule   (c) Unit cell   (d) Atom

40. Glucose is prepared commercially from the hydrolysis of _______ by boiling it with dilute H_2SO_4 at 393K under pressure.
    (a) starch   (b) sucrose   (c) galactose   (d) dextrose

41. In XeF_2, Xenon involves the hybridisation:
    (a) sp (b) sp^2 (c) sp^3d (d) sp^3

42. Glucose on Fehling's test gives _______
    (a) no reaction   (b) silver mirror   (c) red precipitate   (d) pungent gas

43. The reaction of glucose with hydrogen cyanide confirms the _______
    (a) straight chain structure of glucose   (b) presence of a carbonyl group in glucose
    (c) presence of an aldehyde group in glucose   (d) presence of a keto group in glucose

44. Which one of the following displaces bromine form an aqueous solution of bromine?
    (a) Cl_2 (b) Cl^- (c) I_2 (d) I_3^-

45. Given below are two statements labelled as Assertion (A) and Reason (R)

    Assertion: Ozone layer serves as the protective layer from UV radiations.

    Reason: Ozone is more oxidising in nature than oxygen.

    Select the most appropriate answer from the options given below:
    (a) Both A and R are true and R is the correct explanation of A.
    (b) Both A and R are true but R is not the correct explanation of A.
    (c) A is true but R is false.
    (d) A is false but R is true.

46. Given below are two statements labelled as Assertion (A) and Reason (R)

    Assertion: Graphite is a good conductor of electricity however diamond belongs to the category of insulators.

    Reason: Graphite is soft in nature on the other hand diamond is very hard and brittle.

    Select the most appropriate answer from the options given below:
    (a) Both A and R are true and R is the correct explanation of A.
    (b) Both A and R are true but R is not the correct explanation of A.
    (c) A is true but R is false.
    (d) A is false but R is true.

47. Given below are two statements labelled as Assertion (A) and Reason (R)

    Assertion: $CH_2 = CH—CH_2—X$ is an example of allyl halides.

    Reason: These are the compounds in which the halogen atom is bonded to an sp^2 hybridised carbon atom.

    Select the most appropriate answer from the options given below:

    (a) Both A and R are true and R is the correct explanation of A.

    (b) Both A and R are true but R is not the correct explanation of A.

    (c) A is true but R is false.

    (d) A is false but R is true.

48. Given below are two statements labelled as Assertion (A) and Reason (R)

    Assertion: The concentration of pollutants in water or atmosphere is often expressed in terms of ppm.

    Reason: Concentration in parts per million can be expressed as mass to mass, volume to volume and mass to volume.

    Select the most appropriate answer from the options given below:

    (a) Both A and R are true and R is the correct explanation of A.

    (b) Both A and R are true but R is not the correct explanation of A.

    (c) A is true but R is false.

    (d) A is false but R is true.

49. Given below are two statements labelled as Assertion (A) and Reason (R)

    Assertion: Acidic character of group 16 hydrides increases from H_2O to H_2Te.

    Reason: Thermal stability of hydrides decreases down the group.

    Select the most appropriate answer from the options given below:

    (a) Both A and R are true and R is the correct explanation of A.

    (b) Both A and R are true but R is not the correct explanation of A.

    (c) A is true but R is false.

    (d) A is false but R is true.

Section-C

This section consists of 6 multiple choice questions with an overall choice to attempt any 5. In case more than desirable number of questions are attempted, ONLY first 5 will be considered for evaluation.

50. Which of the following unit cells has constituent particles occupying the corner positions only?

    (a) Body-centered cell   (b) Primitive cell   (c) Face centered cell   (d) End-centered cell

51. When SO_2 gas is passed through acidified $K_2Cr_2O_7$ solution, the colour of the solution changes to:

    (a) Red   (b) Black   (c) Orange   (d) Green

52. RNA on hydrolysis does not yield which of the following?

    (a) Amino acid   (b) Pentose sugar   (c) Nitrogen base   (d) Phosphoric acid

    CASE 1: Read the passage given below and answer the following questions 53-55

    Ionic solids and melts are compounds in which the interactions are dominated by electrostatic effects. However, the polarization of the ions also plays an important role in many respects as has been clarified in recent years thanks to the development of realistic polarizable interaction potentials. After detailing these models, we illustrate the importance of polarization effects on a series of examples concerning the structural properties, such as the stabilization of particular crystal structures or the formation of highly-coordinated multivalent ions in the melts, as well as the dynamic properties such as the diffusion of ionic species. The effects on the structure of molten salt interfaces (with vacuum and electrified metal) is also described. Although most of the results described here concern inorganic compounds (molten fluorides and chlorides, ionic oxides...), the particular case of the room-temperature ionic liquids, a special class of molten salts in which at least one species is organic, will also be briefly discussed to indicate how the ideas gained from the study of 'simple' molten salts are being transferred to these more complex systems.

Source: https://www.tandfonline.com/doi/abs/10.1080/00268976.2011.617523

53. Which statement is incorrect about crystalline solids?
    (a) They have long range order.
    (b) They have definite melting point
    (c) They are rigid and incompressible
    (d) They break into two pieces with irregular surface

54. Which one of the following is an ionic solid?
    (a) SiO_2
    (b) SiC
    (c) ZnS
    (d) CCl_4

55. 'Atoms are arranged at the corners and at the centre of each faces of the unit cell'. Which one of the following best describes the statement?
    (a) Body centered cubic
    (b) Face centered cubic
    (c) Simple cubic
    (d) Side centered cubic

☐☐

Sample Paper 

Chemistry

Section – A

This section consists of 25 multiple choice questions with overall choice to attempt any 20 questions. In case more than desirable number of questions are attempted, ONLY first 20 will be considered for evaluation.

1. An example of intensive property is:
   (a) Number of moles (b) Mass (c) Volume (d) Density

2. Halogenation of alkane gives:
   (a) Only required alkyl halide
   (b) Alkyl halide and unreacted halogen
   (c) A mixture of mono-, di-, tri- and tetra-halogen derivatives
   (d) Alkyl halide and unreacted alkane

3. Which noble gas was discovered in chromosphere?
   (a) He (b) Ar (c) Xe (d) Rn

4. The number of atoms present in FCC unit cells.
   (a) 1 (b) 2 (c) 3 (d) 4

5. Ethanol on heating with conc. H_2SO_4 at 445 K gives:
   (a) Diethyl sulphate (b) Ethylene, C_2H_4
   (c) Diethyl ether, $(C_2H_5)_2O$ (d) Ethyl hydrogen sulphate, $C_2H_5HSO_4$

6. Amino acids are:
   (a) acidic (b) basic (c) amphoteric (d) neutral

7. Which of the following is most acidic?
   (a) H_2O (b) CH_3OH (c) C_2H_5OH (d) $CH_3CH_2CH_2OH$

8. Which halogen among the following exists only-1 oxidation state ?
   (a) F (b) Cl (c) Br (d) I

9. Oxygen molecule is :
   (a) Paramagnetic (b) Diamagnetic (c) Ferromagnetic (d) Ferrimagnetic

10. Relationship between atomic radius (r) and the edge length $'a'$ of a body centred cubic unit cell is.
    (a) $r = \dfrac{a}{2}$ (b) $r = \sqrt{\dfrac{a}{2}}$ (c) $r = \dfrac{\sqrt{3}}{4}a$ (d) $r = \dfrac{3a}{2}$

11. H_2S is more acidic than H_2O because:
    (a) Oxygen is more electronegative than sulphur.
    (b) Atomic number of sulphur is higher than oxygen.
    (c) H — S bond dissociation energy is less as compared to H — O bond.
    (d) H — O bond dissociation energy is less also compared to H — S bond.

12. Which of the following arrangements of particles does a simple cubic lattice follow?
    (a) ABAB (b) AABB (c) ABCABC (d) AAA

13. Which one of the group 16 elements given below hardly show -2 oxidation state?
    (a) Selenium (b) Tellurium (c) Polonium (d) Oxygen

14. Stainless steel is a/an _______ alloy.
    (a) Vacant (b) Interstitial (c) Substitution (d) Pure

15. Among the following halogens, the one which does not forms an oxyacid is :
    (a) Fluorine (b) Chlorine (c) Bromine (d) Iodine
16. When a non-volatile solid is added to pure water it will:
    (a) boil above 100°C and freeze above 0°C
    (b) boil below 100°C and freeze above 0°C
    (c) boil above 100°C and freeze below 0°C
    (d) boil below 100°C and freeze below 0°C
17. Diamond is an example of ________
    (a) solid with hydrogen bonding
    (b) electrovalent solid
    (c) covalent solid
    (d) glass
18. If 0.1 M solution of glucose and 0.1 M solution of urea are placed on two sides of the semi-permeable membrane to equal heights, then it will be correct to say that:
    (a) Water will flow from urea solution to glucose
    (b) Urea will flow towards glucose solution
    (c) Glucose will flow towards urea solution
    (d) There will be no net movement across the membrane
19. Which one is called oleum?
    (a) Liq. NH_3
    (b) $H_2SO_4 + SO_3$
    (c) Conc. HNO_3
    (d) Dilute solution of H_2O_2
20. Which of the following features are not shown by quartz glass?
    (a) This is a crystalline solid.
    (b) Refractive index is same in all the directions.
    (c) This has definite heat of fusion.
    (d) This is also called super cooled liquid.
21. Colligative properties are:
    (a) dependent only on the concentration of the solute and independent of the solvent's and solute's identity.
    (b) dependent only on the identity of the solute and the concentration of the solute and independent of the solvent's identity.
    (c) dependent on the identity of the solvent and solute and thus on the concentration of the solute.
    (d) dependent only on the identity of the solvent and the concentration of the solute and independent of the solute's identity.
22. Which metal is used to prepare the Grignard's reagent from alkyl halide in ethereal medium?
    (a) Magnesium (b) Calcium (c) Iron (d) Potassium
23. Which of the following reagent does not give O_2 gas on reaction with Ozone?
    (a) $KMnO_4$ (b) $SnCl_2/HCl$ (c) $FeSO_4/H_2SO_4$ (d) PbS
24. Which of the following is not an example of the molecular solid?
    (a) SiC (Silicon carbide) (b) AlN (c) Diamond (d) I_2
25. Assume three samples of juices A, B and C have glucose as the only sugar present in them. The concentration of sample A, B and C are 0.1M, .5M and 0.2 M respectively. Freezing point will be highest for the fruit juice:
    (a) A
    (b) B
    (c) C
    (d) All have same freezing point

Section-B

This section consists of 24 multiple choice questions with overall choice to attempt any 20 questions. In case more than desirable number of questions are attempted, ONLY first 20 will be considered for evaluation.

26. Which metal is present in Haemoglobin?
    (a) Fe (b) Mg (c) Ca (c) Al
27. One molecule of dialkyl ether produces how many molecules of alkyl halides with excess of halogen acid?
    (a) 1 (b) 2 (c) 3 (d) 4
28. Which of the following bases is not present in DNA?
    (a) Adenine (b) Guanine (c) Thymine (d) Uracil

29. Crystalline solids have the different values of
    (a) Refractive index
    (b) Electrical resistance
    (c) Both (a) and (b)
    (d) Short range order

30. Which of the following bases contain two keto groups?
    (a) Adenine
    (b) Guanine
    (c) Thymine
    (d) Cytosine

31. In which mechanism the carbocation intermediate is formed?
    (a) S_N1 reaction mechanism
    (b) S_N2 reaction mechanism
    (c) S_N reaction mechanism
    (d) Both (a) and (b)

32. Which sugar is present in RNA?
    (a) β-D-ribose
    (b) β-D-fructose
    (c) β-D-galactose
    (d) β-D-2-deoxyribose

33. What is the major product of bromination of anisole in ethanoic acid?
    (a) o-Dibromobenzene
    (b) p-Dibromobenzene
    (c) o-Bromoanisole
    (d) p-Bromoanisole

34. Identify which of the following is a colligative property :
    (a) freezing point
    (b) boiling point
    (c) osmotic pressure
    (d) all of these

35. Which step determines the rate of the reaction?
    (a) Slow step of the reaction
    (b) Fast step of the reaction
    (c) Last step of the reaction
    (d) Both (a) and (b)

36. Write the IUPAC name of

    (a) 2-Bromo-2-methylpropan-1-ol
    (b) 3- Bromo- 2 –methylpropanol-1-ol
    (c) Bromo-2-methylpropanol
    (d) None of these

37. Which of the following bases is/are derivative of purines?
    (a) Uracil
    (b) Cytosine
    (c) Adenine
    (d) Thymine

38. Which of the following is not true about the ionic solids?
    (a) Bigger ions form the close packed structure.
    (b) Smaller ions occupy either the tetrahedral or the octahedral voids depending upon their size.
    (c) Occupation of all the voids is not necessary.
    (d) The fraction of octahedral or tetrahedral voids occupied depends upon the radii of the ions occupying the voids.

39. Which of the following is correct about H- bonding in nucleotide?
    (a) A-T, G-C
    (b) A-G, T-C
    (c) G-T,A-C
    (d) A-A, T-T

40. Choose the most suitable classification for the shown compound?
    (a) Secondary alcohol
    (b) Allylic alcohol
    (c) Dihydric alcohol
    (d) Benzylic alcohol

41. Which of the following is not a use of methylene chloride?
    (a) Paint removal
    (b) Propellant in aerosols
    (c) Metal cleaning
    (d) Antiseptic

42. R-O-R, where R represents an alkyl or aryl group is the general formula of which compound?
    (a) Ether
    (b) Ester
    (c) Aldehyde
    (d) Ketone

43. Which of the following is true regarding polyhydric alcohols?
    (a) It should have one or more OH groups
    (b) It should have two or more OH groups
    (c) It should have three or more OH groups
    (d) It should have more than four OH groups

44. When excess chlorine is used in electrophilic substitution of toluene, which of the following dichloroarenes are formed?
    (a) ortho and meta
    (b) ortho and para
    (c) meta and para
    (d) ortho, meta and para

45. Given below are two statements labelled as Assertion (A) and Reason (R)

Assertion: The polypeptide chain in globular protein is folded around itself, giving rise to a spherical structure.

Reason: Some enzymes are globular proteins.

Select the most appropriate answer from the options given below:

(a) Both A and R are true and R is the correct explanation of A.

(b) Both A and R are true but R is not the correct explanation of A.

(c) A is true but R is false.

(d) A is false but R is true.

46. Given below are two statements labelled as Assertion (A) and Reason (R)

Assertion: The solutions which show large positive deviations from Raoult's law form maximum boiling azeotropes.

Reason: 95% aqueous solution of ethanol is maximum boiling azeotrope solution.

Select the most appropriate answer from the options given below:

(a) Both A and R are true and R is the correct explanation of A.

(b) Both A and R are true but R is not the correct explanation of A.

(c) A is true but R is false.

(d) A is false but R is true.

47. Given below are two statements labelled as Assertion (A) and Reason (R)

Assertion: F_2 has low reactivity.

Reason: F-F bond has low $\Delta_{bond} H$

Select the most appropriate answer from the options given below:

(a) Both A and R are true and R is the correct explanation of A.

(b) Both A and R are true but R is not the correct explanation of A.

(c) A is true but R is false.

(d) A is false but R is true.

48. Given below are two statements labelled as Assertion (A) and Reason (R)

Assertion: Ozone layer in the upper region of atmosphere protects earth from UV radiations of sun.

Reason: Ozone is a powerful oxidising agent as compared to oxygen.

Select the most appropriate answer from the options given below:

(a) Both A and R are true and R is the correct explanation of A.

(b) Both A and R are true but R is not the correct explanation of A.

(c) A is true but R is false.

(d) A is false but R is true.

49. Given below are two statements labelled as Assertion (A) and Reason (R)

Assertion: Gases and liquids are called fluids.

Reason: They have the loose intermolecular forces of attraction.

Select the most appropriate answer from the options given below:

(a) Both A and R are true and R is the correct explanation of A.

(b) Both A and R are true but R is not the correct explanation of A.

(c) A is true but R is false.

(d) A is false but R is true.

Section-C

This section consists of 6 multiple choice questions with an overall choice to attempt any 5. In case more than desirable number of questions are attempted, ONLY first 5 will be considered for evaluation.

50. What is the general formula for an aliphatic alcohol? (R=alkyl group)

(a) R-H   (b) R-OH   (c) R-CHO   (d) R-COOH

51. Glucose reacts with HI to form:

(a) n-Hexane   (b) Gluconic acid   (c) Fructose   (d) None of these

52. What happens when a solution of benzene diazonium bromide and an aqueous solution potassium iodide are shaken together?

(a) Iodobenzene is formed   (b) Bromobenzene is formed

(c) A dihaloarene is formed   (d) No reaction

CASE 1: Read the passage given below and answer the following questions 53-55

Current investigations, for example, on antimony(III) and arsenic(III) halogen compounds, have indicated quite similar structural principles as in Te(IV) analogues. In the series of the binary halides of selenium and tellurium, the crystal structure determinations of tellurium tetrafluoride and of tellurium tetrachloride on twinned crystals were the key to understanding the various and partly contradictory spectroscopic and other macroscopic properties, as well as the synthetic potential of the compounds. The chapter discusses the characteristic structural and bonding features of the halogen compounds of the chalcogen(IV) systems, in which the role of the inert pair determines much of the stereochemistry and reactive properties of the whole class of compounds. SCl_4, as the only stable tetrahalide of sulfur besides SF_4, is known to be easily prepared at temperatures below $-34°C$ from the elements or from the reversible reaction of equimolar amounts of SC_{12} and chlorine.

Source: https://www.researchgate.net/publication/277691468_A_Summary_of_Functional_Groups_Containing_ Selenium_and_Tellurium_A_Catalog_of_the_Many_Groups_that_are_Known_and_Some_that_are_Not

53. Bond enthalpy terms in group 16 follow which one of the following trends?

(a) S–S > O–O   (b) Se–Se > S–S   (c) S = S > O = O   (d) S–F < O–F

54. Which statement is incorrect about sulphuric acid?

(a) Crystalline H_2SO_4 possesses a hydrogen-bonded 3-dimensional network.

(b) Pure liquid H_2SO_4 is viscous because of intramolecular hydrogen bonding.

(c) H_2SO_4 is dibasic. In the first and second acid dissociation steps, it behaves as a strong and as a fairly weak acid, respectively.

(d) None of the above

55. The boiling points of hydrides of group 16 are in the order:

(a) $H_2O > H_2Te > H_2S > H_2Se$ (b) $H_2O > H_2S > H_2Se > H_2Te$

(c) $H_2O > H_2Te > H_2Se > H_2S$ (d) None of these

❑❑

Sample Paper 5

Chemistry

Section – A

This section consists of 25 multiple choice questions with overall choice to attempt any 20 questions. In case more than desirable number of questions are attempted, ONLY first 20 will be considered for evaluation.

1. Molecular weight of non-volatile solute can be determined by :
   - (a) Victor-Mayer's method
   - (b) Graham's law of diffusion
   - (c) Gay Lussac's law
   - (d) Raoult's law
2. The action of sodium on alkyl halide to form an alkane is called:
   - (a) Grignard reaction
   - (b) Wurtz coupling reaction
   - (c) Isocyanide reaction
   - (d) Halogenation reaction
3. Alcohols can be obtained from all methods except:
   - (a) Hydroboration-oxidation
   - (b) Oxymercuration-demercuration
   - (c) Reduction of aldehyde/ketones with Zn-Hg/HCl
   - (d) By fermentation of starch
4. The tendency of group 16 elements to form catenated compounds is greatest in case of:
   - (a) Oxygen
   - (b) Sulphur
   - (c) Selenium
   - (d) Tellurium
5. Copper has the face centered cubic structure. The coordination number of each ion is:
   - (a) 4
   - (b) 12
   - (c) 14
   - (d) 8
6. The minimum bond angle in hydrides of group 16 elements is in:
   - (a) H_2O
   - (b) H_2Te
   - (c) H_2Se
   - (d) H_2S
7. Chlorine reacts with ethanol to give:
   - (a) Diethyl chloride
   - (b) Chloroform
   - (c) Acetaldehyde
   - (d) Chloral
8. Conversion of ethyl bromide to ethylene is an example of:
   - (a) Hydrohalogenation
   - (b) Intramolecular dehydrohalogenation
   - (c) Dehydration
   - (d) Hydration
9. The most powerful oxidising agent is :
   - (a) Fluorine
   - (b) Chlorine
   - (c) Bromine
   - (d) Iodine
10. Conversion of ethyl bromide to ethylene is an example of:
    - (a) Hydrohalogenation
    - (b) Intramolecular dehydrohalogenation
    - (c) Dehydration
    - (d) Hydration
11. In a face-centered cubic lattice, a unit cell is shared equally by how many unit cells?
    - (a) 2
    - (b) 4
    - (c) 6
    - (d) 8
12. Which product is obtained in hydroboration oxidation reaction?
    - (a) Propanol
    - (b) Propene
    - (c) Propyne
    - (d) But-1-ene
13. The valence shell electronic configuration of group 15 elements is ns^2np^3. Electronic configuration of Bismuth is:
    - (a) $[He]\,2s^2\,2p^5$
    - (b) $[Xe]\,f^{14}\,5d^{10}\,6s^2\,6p^3$
    - (c) $[Kr]\,4d^{10}\,5s^2\,5p^5$
    - (d) $[Ar]\,3d^{10}\,4s^2\,4p^3$
14. The unit of Cryoscopic constant is:
    - (a) Kelvin kg mol^{-1}
    - (b) Kelvin kg^{-1} mol^{-1}
    - (c) Kelvin kg mol^1
    - (d) Kelvin kg^1 mol^1
15. What other name is given to the amorphous solids?
    - (a) Pseudo solids
    - (b) True solids
    - (c) Super cooled liquids
    - (d) Super cooled solids

16. Identify the correct common name for $CH_3CH_2CH_2CH_2Cl$:
    (a) Isobutyl chloride
    (b) n-Butyl chloride
    (c) sec-Butyl chloride
    (d) tert-Butyl chloride

17. Ionisation enthalpy decreases down the group 15 because:
    (a) atomic size increases gradually
    (b) atomic size decreases gradually
    (c) atomic size does not change going down the group
    (d) atomic size decreases slightly

18. The value of Ebullioscopic constant or boiling point elevation constant does not depends on:
    (a) Amount of solute
    (b) Nature of solute
    (c) Amount of solvent
    (d) Nature of solvent

19. Which of the following types of alcohol contain a bond between sp^2 hybridised carbon and OH group?
    (a) Primary allylic alcohols
    (b) Secondary allylic alcohols
    (c) Tertiary allylic alcohols
    (d) Vinylic alcohols

20. Which one of the following elements have a unique property to form $p\pi$- $p\pi$ multiple bonds with itself?
    (a) Bi
    (b) As
    (c) P
    (d) N

21. Which of the following is formed when glucose is oxidised in the presence of Br_2/H_2O?
    (a) Gluconic acid
    (b) Saccharic acid
    (c) Valeric acid
    (d) Glucaric acid

22. What is the coordination number in a square close packed structure in two dimensions?
    (a) 4
    (b) 3
    (c) 2
    (d) 6

23. Which one of the following best describes the types of oxides formed by nitrogen family elements?
    (a) EO_3 and EO_5
    (b) E_2O_3 and E_2O_5
    (c) E_3O and E_2O
    (d) EO_5 and E_2O_5

24. Which of the following statements are correct:
    (i) Colligative property depends upon number of particles of solute present in the solution.
    (ii) Relative lowering of vapour pressure of a solution is equal to the mole fraction of the non-volatile non-electrolyte solute.
    (a) i
    (b) ii
    (c) Both i and ii
    (d) None of these

25. Phenol can be obtained by _________ of sodium phenoxide :
    (a) acidification
    (b) oxidation
    (c) sulphonation
    (d) hydrolysis

Section-B

This section consists of 24 multiple choice questions with overall choice to attempt any 20 questions. In case more than desirable number of questions are attempted, ONLY first 20 will be considered for evaluation.

26. Which of the following cannot be a catalyst in the electrophilic substitution of arenes?
    (a) $FeCl_3$
    (b) $FeBr_3$
    (c) NH_3
    (d) $AlCl_3$

27. Cumene hydroperoxide on hydrolysis with dilute H_2SO_4 gives _________ :
    (a) alcohol and phenol
    (b) only phenol
    (c) phenol and acetone
    (d) alcohol and acetone

28. In a compound, atoms of element Y form ccp lattice and those of element X occupy 2/3 rd of tetrahedral voids. The formula of the compound will be:
    (a) X_3Y_4
    (b) X_4Y_3
    (c) X_2Y_3
    (d) X_2Y

29. Which type of linkage is a glycosidic linkage?
    (a) Ether linkage
    (b) Ester linkage
    (c) Amide linkage
    (d) Acetyl linkage

30. ....is a water purification process that uses a partially permeable membrane to separate ions, unwanted molecules and larger particles from drinking water:
    (a) Osmosis
    (b) Reverse osmosis
    (c) Osmotic pressure
    (d) None of these

31. How is carbolic acid prepared from benzene diazonium chloride?
    (a) Treating it with nitrous acid at 275K
    (b) Preparing an aqueous solution and warming it
    (c) Treating it with sodium hydroxide
    (d) Freezing it
32. A thermal decomposition method that yields very pure nitrogen uses the following as reactant(s):
    (a) Barium azide
    (b) Sodium nitride
    (c) Ammonium chloride
    (d) Magnesium nitride
33. Which of the following is an example of globular protein?
    (a) Myosin
    (b) Collagen
    (c) Keratin
    (d) Haemoglobin
34. When chloroform is heated with aqueous NaOH, it gives:
    (a) Formic acid
    (b) Sodium formate
    (c) Acetic acid
    (d) Sodium acetate
35. Which of the following is an example of fibrous protein?
    (a) Insulin
    (b) Haemoglobin
    (c) Fibroin
    (d) Glycogen
36. Aqua regia is a mixture of:
    (a) Conc. HNO_3 and conc. H_2SO_4
    (b) Conc. HCl and conc. H_2SO_4 in the ratio of 3: 1
    (c) Conc. HCl and conc. HNO_3 in the ratio of 3: 1
    (d) None of these
37. On how many factors the colligative properties depends?
    (a) 1
    (b) 4
    (c) 2
    (d) 3
38. Which of the following is not a base of RNA?
    (a) Thymine
    (b) Adenine
    (c) Uracil
    (d) Cytosine
39. Which of the following is most reactive towards SN^1 reaction?
    (a) $C_6H_5C(CH_3)C_6H_5Br$
    (b) $C_8H_5CH_2Br$
    (c) $C_6H_5CH(C_6H_5)Br$
    (d) $C_6H_5CH(CH_3)Br$
40. Tailing of mercury is due to the formation of:
    (a) Hg_2O
    (b) HgO
    (c) $Hg(OH)_2$
    (d) $HgCl_2$
41. How are alcohols prepared from haloalkanes?
    (a) By treating with concentrated H_2SO_4
    (b) By heating with aqueous NaOH
    (c) By treating with a strong reducing agent
    (d) By treating with Mg metal
42. Which of the following statements is correct?
    (a) Solutes that dissociate in water experience a decrease in colligative properties
    (b) Colligative properties are independent of the number of particles of the solute in the solution
    (c) Solutes that dissociate in water have molar mass higher than the molar mass of the solute calculated theoretically
    (d) Solutes that associate in water have molar mass higher than the molar mass of the solute calculated theoretically
43. In which of the following reactions the treatment of chlorobenzene with Na in dry ether forms diphenyl?
    (a) Wurtz reaction
    (b) Wurtz-Fittig reaction
    (c) Fittig reaction
    (d) Finkelstein reaction
44. Which of the following process do not yield alcohols?
    (a) Acid catalysed hydration of alkenes
    (b) Hydroboration-oxidation of alkenes
    (c) Reduction of aldehydes
    (d) Free radical halogenation of alkanes
45. Given below are two statements labelled as Assertion (A) and Reason (R)

    Assertion: Tertiary nitroalkanes cannot tautomerise to acid form.

    Reason: Tertiary nitroalkanes do not contain α- hydrogen.

    Select the most appropriate answer from the options given below:
    (a) Both A and R are true and R is the correct explanation of A.
    (b) Both A and R are true but R is not the correct explanation of A.
    (c) A is true but R is false.
    (d) A is false but R is true.

46. Given below are two statements labelled as Assertion (A) and Reason (R)

Assertion: One molar aqueous solution is more concentrated than that of 1 molal aqueous solution.

Reason: Molarity is a function of temperature as volume depends on temperature in the solution.

Select the most appropriate answer from the options given below:
(a) Both A and R are true and R is the correct explanation of A.
(b) Both A and R are true but R is not the correct explanation of A.
(c) A is true but R is false.
(d) A is false but R is true.

47. Given below are two statements labelled as Assertion (A) and Reason (R)

Assertion: S shows paramagnetic nature, when present in vapour state.

Reason: S exists as S_2 in vapour state.

Select the most appropriate answer from the options given below:
(a) Both A and R are true and R is the correct explanation of A.
(b) Both A and R are true but R is not the correct explanation of A.
(c) A is true but R is false.
(d) A is false but R is true.

48. Given below are two statements labelled as Assertion (A) and Reason (R)

Assertion: F_2 is a strong oxidising agent.

Reason: Electron gain enthalpy of fluorine is less negative.

Select the most appropriate answer from the options given below:
(a) Both A and R are true and R is the correct explanation of A.
(b) Both A and R are true but R is not the correct explanation of A.
(c) A is true but R is false.
(d) A is false but R is true.

49. Given below are two statements labelled as Assertion (A) and Reason (R)

Assertion: Osmosis does not take place in two isotonic solutions separated by semipermeable membrane.

Reason: Isotonic solutions have same osmotic pressure.

Select the most appropriate answer from the options given below:
(a) Both A and R are true and R is the correct explanation of A.
(b) Both A and R are true but R is not the correct explanation of A.
(c) A is true but R is false.
(d) A is false but R is true.

Section-C

This section consists of 6 multiple choice questions with an overall choice to attempt any 5. In case more than desirable number of questions are attempted, ONLY first 5 will be considered for evaluation.

50. Which one is called oleum?
(a) Liq. NH_3
(b) $H_2SO_4 + SO_3$
(c) Conc. HNO_3
(d) Dilute solution of H_2O_2

51. Which of the following is an example of aldohexose?
(a) Ribose
(b) Fructose
(c) Sucrose
(d) Glucose

52. Glucose on treatment with NH_2OH undergoes:
(a) Condensation
(b) Reduction
(c) Hydrolysis
(d) Oxidation

CASE 1. Read the passage given below and answer the following questions 53-55

In the simplest cases of monatomic metals such as Cu and α-Fe, mentioned above, the arrangement of metal atoms in the structure is simply the same as the arrangement of lattice points. In more complex structures such as NaCl, the lattice point represents an ion pair. This is still a very simple example, however, and in most inorganic structures the lattice point represents a considerable number of atoms. In crystals of organic molecules such as proteins, the lattice point represents an entire protein molecule. Obviously, the lattice point gives no information whatsoever as to the atoms and their arrangements which it represents; what the lattice does show is how these species are packed together in 3D. The combination of crystal system and lattice type gives the Bravais lattice of a structure. There are 14 possible Bravais lattices.

Source: West, Anthony R. 'Crystal Structures and Crystal Chemistry'. In Solid State Chemistry, 1-81, Wiley, 2014.

53. A mixed oxide has ccp arrangement in which the cations 'X' occupy 1/3rd of octahedral voids and the cations 'Y' occupy 1/3rd of tetrahedral voids. The formula of oxide is:

   (a) $X_2Y_3O_2$ (b) XY_3O (c) X_2YO_3 (d) XY_2O_3

54. AB crystallizes in a body centred cubic lattice with edge length 'a' equal to 387 pm. The distance between two oppositely charged ions in the lattice is:

   (a) 300 pm   (b) 335 pm   (c) 250 pm   (d) 200 pm

55. Percentage of free space in a body centred cubic unit cell is:

   (a) 32%   (b) 34%   (c) 28%   (d) 20%

❑❑

Sample Paper 6

Chemistry

Section – A

This section consists of 25 multiple choice questions with overall choice to attempt any 20 questions. In case more than desirable number of questions are attempted, ONLY first 20 will be considered for evaluation.

1. Which one of the following cannot be called as a 'non-stoichiometric defect'?
   (a) Metal excess defect due to anion vacancies
   (b) Metal excess defect due to presence of extra cations
   (c) Metal deficiency due to absence of cations
   (d) Combination of vacancy and interstitial defects

2. The solubility of a gas varies directly with pressure of the gas is based upon:
   (a) Raoult's law
   (b) Henry's law
   (c) Nernst's distribution law
   (d) None of these

3. Which one absorbs U.V. radiation in stratosphere?
   (a) CO_2
   (b) N_2
   (c) O_3
   (d) H_2

4. Which of the following reagent cannot be used to prepare an alkyl chloride from an alcohol?
   (a) $HCl + ZnCl_2$
   (b) $SOCl_2$
   (c) $NaCl$
   (d) PCl_5

5. Proteins are denatured in the:
   (a) Mouth
   (b) Stomach
   (c) Small intestine
   (d) Large intestine

6. The first step of the acid catalysed hydration of alkenes, involves the protonation of alkene to form a carbocation by electrophilic attack of ________
   (a) H^+
   (b) H_2O
   (c) H_3O^+
   (d) OH^-

7. Glucose and galactose are:
   (a) Anomers
   (b) Optical isomers
   (c) Epimers
   (d) None of these

8. Propene when reacted with water in the presence of H_2SO_4 gives ________
   (a) Propan-1-ol
   (b) Propan-2-ol
   (c) 2-Methylpropan-1-ol
   (d) 2-Methylpropan-2-ol

9. Crystalline solids have the different values of:
   (a) Refractive index
   (b) Electrical resistance
   (c) Both (a) and (b)
   (d) Short range order

10. Which of the following has lowest reducing character?
    (a) H_2O
    (b) H_2S
    (c) H_2Te
    (d) H_2Se

11. Which of the following is a pyrimidine base?
    (a) Adenine
    (b) Guanine
    (c) Uracil
    (d) None of these

12. Chloromethane on treatment with excess of ammonia yields mainly:

    (a) N, N-Dimethylmethanamine $\left(CH_3-N\begin{smallmatrix} CH_3 \\ CH_3 \end{smallmatrix} \right)$

    (b) N–methylmethanamine ($CH_3-NH-CH_3$)
    (c) Methanamine (CH_3NH_2)
    (d) Mixture containing all these in equal proportion

13. Solids do not have:
    (a) Fluidity   (b) Rigidity   (c) Shape   (d) Volume
14. What happens to the size of atoms of elements of p-block as we move from left to right in the same period?
    (a) Size increases   (b) Size decreases
    (c) Size does not change   (d) Size increases then decreases
15. Identify the catalyst in the hydration of alkenes to produce alcohols:
    (a) HCl   (b) $FeCl_3$ (c) Pt   (d) Ni
16. Among the following halogens, the one which does not forms an oxyacid is:
    (a) Fluorine   (b) Chlorine   (c) Bromine   (d) Iodine
17. Carbylamine test involves heating a mixture of:
    (a) Alcoholic KOH, methyl iodide and sodium metal
    (b) Alcoholic KOH, methyl iodide and primary amine
    (c) Alcoholic KOH, chloroform and primary amine
    (d) Alcoholic KOH, methyl alcohol and primary amine
18. Which defect is not found in pure alkali metal halides?
    (a) Frenkel defect   (b) Schottky defect   (c) Both (a) and (b)   (d) Point defect
19. Which of the following is an example of aldohexose?
    (a) Ribose   (b) Fructose   (c) Sucrose   (d) Glucose
20. When chloroform is heated with aqueous NaOH, it gives:
    (a) Formic acid   (b) Sodium formate   (c) Acetic acid   (d) Sodium acetate
21. Only if the calculated molar mass is higher than the actual molar mass of the solute, the calculated molar mass is considered to be abnormal molar mass.
    (a) True   (b) False   (c) Can't say   (d) Both (a) and (b)
22. The linkage which holds various amino acid units in primary structures of proteins is:
    (a) Glycoside linkage   (b) Peptide linkage   (c) Ionic linkage   (d) Hydrogen bond
23. Oxygen molecule is :
    (a) Paramagnetic   (b) Diamagnetic   (c) Ferromagnetic   (d) Ferrimagnetic
24. Positive deviation from Raoult's law is observed when:
    (a) Inter molecular forces of attraction between the two liquids is greater than that between individual liquids.
    (b) Inter molecular forces of attraction between the two liquids is smaller than that between individual liquids.
    (c) Force of attraction between two liquids is greater than that between individual liquids.
    (d) Force of attraction between two liquids is smaller than that between individual liquid.
25. Which of the following class of compounds is not a part of the large group of carbohydrates?
    (a) Polyamino aldehydes   (b) Polyhalo aldehydes
    (c) Polyhydroxy ketones   (d) Polyhydroxy carboxylic acids

Section-B

This section consists of 24 multiple choice questions with overall choice to attempt any 20 questions. In case more than desirable number of questions are attempted, ONLY first 20 will be considered for evaluation.

26. Which of the following has lowest reducing character?
    (a) H_2O (b) H_2S (c) H_2Te (d) H_2Se
27. Which alkyl halides react most readily by nucleophilic substitution?
    (a) CH_3CH_2Cl (b) CH_3CH_2I (c) CH_3CH_2Br (d) CH_3CH_2F
28. Which of the following alcohol is most soluble in water?
    (a) Propanol   (b) Butanol   (c) Pentanol   (d) Hexanol

29. What will be the number of octahedral voids in terms of the number 'N' where N is number of closed packed particles

    (a) 2N   (b) N   (c) 1/2N   (d) 3N

30. Maltose on hydrolysis gives:

    (a) α-D-glucose   (b) α and β-D-glucose   (c) Glucose and fructose   (d) Fructose only

31. Reduction potentials of some ions are given below. Arrange them in decreasing order of oxidising power.

Ion	ClO_4^-	IO_4^-	BrO_4^-
Reduction E^- potential E^-/V	E^- = 1.19V	E^- =1.65V	E^- = 1.74 V

    (a) $ClO_4^- > IO_4^- > BrO_4^-$ (b) $IO_4^- > BrO_4^- > ClO_4^-$

    (c) $BrO_4^- > IO_4^- > ClO_4^-$ (d) $BrO_4^- > ClO_4^- > IO_4^-$

32. The correct IUPAC name of the given compound is:

    (a) Benzene 1,4 –diol   (b) Hydroquinone

    (c) p-Dihydroxy benzene   (d) m-Dihydroxy benzene

33. The solubility of a gas varies directly with pressure of the gas, is based upon:

    (a) Raoult's law   (b) Henry's law

    (c) Nernst's distribution law   (d) None of these

34. What should be the correct IUPAC name for diethylbromomethane?

    (a) 1-Bromo-1,1-diethylmethane

    (b) 3-Bromopentane

    (c) 1-Bromo-1-ethylpropane

    (d) 1-Bromopentane

35. Which of the following carbohydrates is not a sugar?

    (a) Glucose   (b) Fructose   (c) Lactose   (d) Cellulose

36. Packing efficiency of the BCC is:

    (a) 68%   (b) 74%   (c) 52%   (d) 45%

37. Which of the following is true regarding polyhydric alcohols?

    (a) It should have one or more OH groups   (b) It should have two or more OH groups

    (c) It should have three or more OH groups   (d) It should have more than four OH groups

38. Conversion of ethyl bromide to ethylene is an example of:

    (a) Hydrohalogenation

    (b) Intramolecular dehydrohalogenation

    (c) Dehydration

    (d) Hydration

39. The reaction, $3ClO^-$ (aq) $\longrightarrow$ ClO_3^- (aq) + $2Cl^-$ (aq), is an example of:

    (a) Oxidation reaction   (b) Reduction reaction

    (c) Disproportionation reaction   (d) Decomposition reaction

40. Sodium methoxide on heating with bromoethane gives __________

    (a) methoxymethane   (b) methoxyethane

    (c) ethoxyethane   (d) diethyl ether

41. How is osmotic pressure related to the concentration of a solute in a solution?

    (a) $\pi \propto c$ (b) $\pi \propto pv$ (c) $\pi \propto T$ (d) $\pi \propto 1/c$

42. Which of the following is not an interhalogen compound?
    (a) ICl_4^- (b) ClF_5 (c) IPO_4 (d) ClF_3

43. The amino acids are the end products of the digestion of:
    (a) Lipids   (b) Fats   (c) Proteins   (d) Enzymes

44. α-helix refers to:
    (a) Primary structure of proteins   (b) Secondary structure of proteins
    (c) Tertiary structure of proteins   (d) Quaternary structure of proteins

45. Given below are two statements labelled as Assertion (A) and Reason (R)

    Assertion: Crystalline solids melt at the sharp and characteristic temperature.

    Reason: They have definite geometrical shape.

    Select the most appropriate answer from the options given below:
    (a) Both A and R are true and R is the correct explanation of A.
    (b) Both A and R are true but R is not the correct explanation of A.
    (c) A is true but R is false.
    (d) A is false but R is true.

46. Given below are two statements labelled as Assertion (A) and Reason (R)

    Assertion: H_2S is less acidic than H_2Te.

    Reason: It is due to decrease in acidic character down the group.

    Select the most appropriate answer from the options given below:
    (a) Both A and R are true and R is the correct explanation of A.
    (b) Both A and R are true but R is not the correct explanation of A.
    (c) A is true but R is false.
    (d) A is false but R is true.

47. Given below are two statements labelled as Assertion (A) and Reason (R)

    Assertion: The boiling point of *p*-nitrophenol is higher than that of *o*-nitrophenol because

    Reason: *p*-Nitrophenol has intermolecular hydrogen bonding so it has more boiling point and less volatile than *o*-nitrophenol which has intramolecular hydrogen bonding.

    Select the most appropriate answer from the options given below:
    (a) Both A and R are true and R is the correct explanation of A.
    (b) Both A and R are true but R is not the correct explanation of A.
    (c) A is true but R is false.
    (d) A is false but R is true.

48. Given below are two statements labelled as Assertion (A) and Reason (R)

    Assertion: Atomic and ionic radii of group 16 elements increase from top to bottom in the group.

    Reason: The elements of Group16 have six electrons in the outermost shell.

    Select the most appropriate answer from the options given below:
    (a) Both A and R are true and R is the correct explanation of A.
    (b) Both A and R are true but R is not the correct explanation of A.
    (c) A is true but R is false.
    (d) A is false but R is true.

49. Given below are two statements labelled as Assertion (A) and Reason (R)

    Assertion: Molality is a better method to express concentration than molarity.

    Reason: Molality is defined in terms of mass of solvent and not mass of solution.

    Select the most appropriate answer from the options given below:
    (a) Both A and R are true and R is the correct explanation of A.
    (b) Both A and R are true but R is not the correct explanation of A.
    (c) A is true but R is false.
    (d) A is false but R is true.

Section-C

This section consists of 6 multiple choice questions with an overall choice to attempt any 5. In case more than desirable number of questions are attempted, ONLY first 5 will be considered for evaluation.

50. Amino acids are classified as acidic, basic or neutral depending upon the relative number of amino and carboxyl groups in their molecule. Which of the following are acidic?

    (a) $(CH_3)_2CH-CH-COOH$
    $\qquad\qquad\quad\ \ |$
    $\qquad\qquad\quad\ NH_2$

    (b) $HOOC-CH_2-CH_2-CH-COOH$
    $\qquad\qquad\qquad\qquad\ \ |$
    $\qquad\qquad\qquad\qquad\ NH_2$

    (c) $H_2N-CH_2-CH_2-CH_2-COOH$

    (d) $HOOC-CH_2-CH-COOH$
    $\qquad\qquad\qquad\ |$
    $\qquad\qquad\quad\ NH_2$

51. Ozone turns trimethyl paper:

    (a) Green   (b) Violet   (c) Red   (d) Black

52. Which law is followed to increase the solubility of CO_2 in soft drinks and soda water, the bottle is sealed under high pressure.

    (a) Raoult's law   (b) Henry's law   (c) Avogadro's law   (d) Gay Lussac's law

CASE 1: Read the passage given below and answer the following questions 53-55

Point defects play an important part in determining the physical properties of most crystalline substances, most notably those controlling the transport of matter and the properties that stem from it. Even a crystal of high purity under conditions of no irradiation contains point defects in thermal equilibrium. Some lattice sites are vacant, and some atoms are displaced from their normal lattice sites into interstitial positions or onto "wrong" lattice sites. For stochiometric compounds of high purity, the concentrations of these point defects are very low, even at temperatures up to the melting point. A meaningful model, then, is to consider the crystal as a solvent containing a very dilute solution of simple, individual vacancies and interstitials. Long-range interactions among the defects and with impurity atoms, and short-range interactions that produce pairs or other clusters can be introduced in a first order approximation.

Source: Crawford, J.H. & Slifkin, L.M. (2013). Point Defects in Solids: General and Ionic Crystals, Chapter 1, Volume 1, 1-2.

53. Which one of the given below statements is wrong about Frenkel defect -

    (a) It is a combination of vacancy and interstitial defects

    (b) Cations leave their actual lattice sites and occupy the interstitial space in the solid

    (c) Density remains the same

    (d) Density of the crystal increases

54. Which one of the following is an 'interstitial void'?

    (a) Octahedral void   **(b)** Tetrahedral void

    (c) Both (a) and (b)   **(d)** None of the above

55. This type of defect arises due to absence of equal number of cations and anions from lattice sites in the crystalline solid of the type A^+B^- and it lowers the density of the crystal-

    (a) Vacancy defect   **(b)** Schottky defect

    (c) Interstitial defect   **(d)** Frenkel defect

□□

Sample Paper 7

Chemistry

Section – A

This section consists of 25 multiple choice questions with overall choice to attempt any 20 questions. In case more than desirable number of questions are attempted, ONLY first 20 will be considered for evaluation.

1. The elevation in boiling point of a solution of 13.44 g of $CuCl_2$ in 1 kg of H_2O using the following information will be : (Mol. wt. of $CuCl_2$ = 134.4 and K_b = 0.52 K g mol^{-1})
   - (a) 0.16
   - (b) 0.05
   - (c) 0.1
   - (d) 0.2

2. The nucleic acid base having two possible binding sites is:
   - (a) Thymine
   - (b) Cytosine
   - (c) Guanine
   - (d) Adenine

3. What is the valence shell electronic configuration of p-block elements?
   - (a) ns^2
   - (b) $ns^2 np^{1-5}$
   - (c) $ns^2 np^{1-6}$
   - (d) None of these

4. The reaction,

   $$2C_2H_5Br + 2Na \xrightarrow{\text{dry ether}} C_2H_5-C_2H_5 + 2NaBr \text{ is an example of:}$$

   - (a) The Wurtz reaction
   - (b) Sandmeyer's reaction
   - (c) Aldol condensation
   - (d) Williamson's reaction

5. The reaction between tert-Butyl chloride and sodium ethoxide gives _______
   - (a) tert-Butyl ethyl ether
   - (b) tert-Butyl methyl ether
   - (c) 2-Methylprop-1-ene
   - (d) butene

6. A biological catalyst is :
   - (a) An amino acid
   - (b) A carbohydrate
   - (c) The nitrogen molecule
   - (d) An enzyme

7. The incorrect trend regarding group 16 hydrides (H_2E) is:
   - (a) down the group, the H-E-H bond angle increases
   - (b) the acidic character of hydrides increases down the group
   - (c) except water, all hydrides possess reducing properties
   - (d) thermal stability of hydrides decreases down the group

8. For the crystal structures how many numbers of Bravais lattice are there?
   - (a) 3
   - (b) 6
   - (c) 14
   - (d) 24

9. Which concentration measurement is used in Pharmacy?
   - (a) Mass by volume percentage
   - (b) Mole fraction
   - (c) Molarity
   - (d) Molality

10. Grignard's reagent is prepared by the action of magnesium metal on:
    - (a) Alcohol
    - (b) Phenol
    - (c) Alkyl halide
    - (d) Benzene

11. Group 16 elements have lower value of first ionisation enthalpy as compared to group 15 elements because:
    - (a) half-filled p-orbitals in group 15 elements are more stable
    - (b) group 16 elements have smaller size than group 15 elements
    - (c) group 16 elements contain double bond while group 15 elements have triple bond
    - (d) group 16 elements have more number of electrons in p-orbitals

12. Each point in the crystal lattice is known as :
    - (a) Lattice point
    - (b) Lattice dot
    - (c) Lattice shape
    - (d) Lattice origin

13. Which compounds are used to lower the freezing point of the solution?
    (a) Antifreeze   (b) Depressant   (c) Coolant   (d) Fluid

14. Which of the following is halogen exchange reaction?
    (a) $RX + NaI \rightarrow RI + NaX$

    (b) $\rangle C = C \langle \; + HX \; \rightarrow \; \rangle \underset{H}{C} - \underset{H}{C} \langle$

    (c) $R - OH + HX \xrightarrow{ZnCl_2} R - X + H_2O$

    (d) [toluene] $+ X_2 \xrightarrow[\text{dark}]{Fe}$ [o-substituted] $+$ [p-substituted]

15. Solid oxygen has a pale blue colour which is attributed to:
    (a) electronic transitions from the singlet ground state to the triplet excited state
    (b) electronic transitions from antibonding π-molecular orbitals to bonding $\sigma 2p_2$ M.O.s
    (c) electronic transitions from the triplet ground state to anti bonding $\sigma 2p_2$ molecular orbital
    (d) electronic transitions from the triplet ground state to the excited singlet state

16. Which of the following is the least reactive functional group?
    (a) Alcohols   (b) Ethers
    (c) Aldehydes   (d) Ketones

17. The arrangement of the molecules in the crystal lattice is determined through:
    (a) X –ray Diffraction   (b) Gamma rays
    (c) Alpha rays   (d) Radioactive waves

18. Which one of the following will produce a primary alcohol by reacting with CH_3MgI?
    (a) Acetone   (b) Methyl cyanide
    (c) Ethylene oxide   (d) Ethyl acetate

19. At equilibrium the rate of dissolution of a solid solute in a volatile liquid solvent is __________ .
    (a) less than the rate of crystallisation   (b) greater than the rate of crystallisation
    (c) equal to the rate of crystallisation   (d) zero

20. Which of the following is the balanced equation describing the combustion of elemental sulphur?
    (a) $2H_2S + 3O_2 \rightarrow 2SO_2 + 2H_2O$ (b) $H_2S + 2O_2 \rightarrow SO_3 + H_2O$
    (c) $2SO_3 \rightarrow 2S + 3O_2$ (d) $S + O_2 \rightarrow SO_2$

21. How many crystal systems make the 3-D space lattice?
    (a) 7   (b) 6   (c) 5   (d) 4

22. In the sequence $HO-\langle \bigcirc \rangle-SO_3H \xrightarrow[H_2O]{Br_2} X$, is:

    (a) 2-Bromo-4-hydroxybenzene sulphonic acid
    (b) 3, 5-Dibromo-4-hydroxybenzene sulphonic acid
    (c) 2-Bromophenol
    (d) 2, 4, 6-Tribromophenol

23. Of the following terms used for denoting concentration of a solution, the one which does not get affected by temperature is:
    (a) Molarity   (b) Molality   (c) Normality   (d) Formality

24. F centers are also known as:
    (a) Colour centers   (b) Face centers   (c) Line centers   (d) None of these

25. Phenol can be distinguished from ethyl alcohol by all reagents except:
    (a) NaOH   (b) $FeCl_3$ (c) Br_2/H_2O (d) Na

Section-B

This section consists of 24 multiple choice questions with overall choice to attempt any 20 questions. In case more than desirable number of questions are attempted, ONLY first 20 will be considered for evaluation.

26. In which of the following reactions conc. H_2SO_4 is used as an oxidising reagent?

(a) $CaF_2 + H_2SO_4 \rightarrow CaSO_4 + 2HF$

(b) $2HI + H_2SO_4 \rightarrow I_2 + SO_2 + 2H_2O$

(c) $Cu + 2H_2SO_4 \rightarrow CuSO_4 + SO_2 + 2H_2O$

(d) $NaCl + H_2SO_4 \rightarrow NaHSO_4 + HCl$

27. Which of the following species can act as the strongest base?

(a) $^{\ominus}OH$

(b) $^{\ominus}OR$

(c) $^{\ominus}O\,C_6H_5$

(d)

28.

$$\text{Phenol (OH)} + CH_3Cl \xrightarrow{\text{Anhyd. AlCl}_3} \text{o-chlorotoluene} + \text{p-chlorotoluene} + 2HCl$$

The above reaction is known as:

(a) Wurtz-Fittig reaction

(b) Friedel Craft's reaction

(c) Sandmeyer's reaction

(d) Swarts reaction

29. Dry SO_2 does not bleach dry flowers because:

(a) nascent hydrogen responsible for bleaching is produced only in presence of moisture

(b) water is the actual reducing agent responsible for bleaching

(c) water is stronger acid than SO_2

(d) the OH^- ions produced by water cause bleaching

30. Chlorine reacts with ethanol to give:

(a) Diethyl chloride   (b) Chloroform   (c) Acetaldehyde   (d) Chloral

31. Which of the following is a pyrimidine base?

(a) Adenine   (b) Guanine   (c) Uracil   (d) None of these

32. Which reagent will you use for the following reaction?

$$CH_3CH_2CH_2CH_3 \rightarrow CH_3CH_2CH_2CH_2Cl + CH_3CH_2CHClCH_3$$

(a) Cl_2/UV light

(b) $NaCl + H_2SO_4$

(c) Cl_2 gas in dark

(d) Cl_2 gas in the presence of iron in dark

33. An example of intensive property is:

(a) Number of moles   (b) Mass   (c) Volume   (d) Density

34. Identify the monosaccharide from the following.

(a) Deoxyribose   (b) Sucrose   (c) Maltose   (d) Fructose

35. The geometry of XeF_6 molecule and the hybridization of Xe atom in the molecule is:

(a) Distorted octahedral and sp^3d^3

(b) Square planar and sp^3d^2

(c) Pyramidal and sp^3

(d) Octahedral and sp^3d^3

36. Which of the following is an example of aldohexose?

(a) Ribose   (b) Fructose   (c) Sucrose   (d) Glucose

37. The following compound is called:

$$Cl-C_6H_4-CH(CCl_3)-C_6H_4-Cl$$

(a) Chloral   (b) DDT   (c) Lindane   (d) BHC

38. The linkage which holds various amino acid units in primary structures of proteins is:
    (a) Glycoside linkage   (b) Peptide linkage   (c) Ionic linkage   (d) Hydrogen bond

39. If chlorine gas is passed through hot NaOH solution, two changes are observed in the oxidation number of chlorine during the reaction. These are _________ and _________.
    (a) 0 to +5   (b) 0 to +3   (c) 0 to –1   (d) 0 to +1

40. Maltose on hydrolysis gives:
    (a) α-D-glucose   (b) α and β-D-glucose   (c) Glucose and fructose   (d) Fructose only

41. The amino acids are the end products of the digestion of:
    (a) Lipids   (b) Fats   (c) Proteins   (d) Enzymes

42. The tendency of group 16 elements to form catenated compounds is greatest in case of:
    (a) Oxygen   (b) Sulphur   (c) Selenium   (d) Tellurium

43. α-helix refers to:
    (a) primary structure of proteins
    (b) secondary structure of proteins
    (c) tertiary structure of proteins
    (d) quaternary structure of proteins

44. Amino acids are classified as acidic, basic or neutral depending upon the relative number of amino and carboxyl groups in their molecule. Which of the following are acidic?
    (a) $(CH_3)_2CH-CH-COOH$
    $\quad\qquad\qquad |$
    $\qquad\qquad\quad NH_2$
    (b) $HOOC-CH_2-CH_2-CH-COOH$
    $\qquad\qquad\qquad\qquad\quad |$
    $\qquad\qquad\qquad\qquad NH_2$
    (c) $H_2N-CH_2-CH_2-CH_2-COOH$
    (d) $HOOC-CH_2-CH-COOH$
    $\qquad\qquad\qquad |$
    $\qquad\qquad NH_2$

45. Given below are two statements labelled as Assertion (A) and Reason (R)
    Assertion: In crystal lattice, the size of the tetrahedral hole is large than an octahedral hole.
    Reason: The cations occupy less space than anions in crystal packing.
    Select the most appropriate answer from the options given below:
    (a) Both A and R are true and R is the correct explanation of A.
    (b) Both A and R are true but R is not the correct explanation of A.
    (c) A is true but R is false.
    (d) A is false but R is true.

46. Given below are two statements labelled as Assertion (A) and Reason (R)
    Assertion: Hypophosphorous acid is a good reducing agent.
    Reason: The acids which contain P–H bond have strong reducing properties.
    Select the most appropriate answer from the options given below:
    (a) Both A and R are true and R is the correct explanation of A.
    (b) Both A and R are true but R is not the correct explanation of A.
    (c) A is true but R is false.
    (d) A is false but R is true.

47. Given below are two statements labelled as Assertion (A) and Reason (R)
    Assertion: Glucose is dextrose
    Reason: The open chains of glucose have four asymmetrical carbons.
    Select the most appropriate answer from the options given below:
    (a) Both A and R are true and R is the correct explanation of A.
    (b) Both A and R are true but R is not the correct explanation of A.
    (c) A is true but R is false.
    (d) A is false but R is true.

48. Given below are two statements labelled as Assertion (A) and Reason (R)

    Assertion: Valency of noble gas is 0.

    Reason: Noble gases possess complete octet.

    Select the most appropriate answer from the options given below:
    (a) Both A and R are true and R is the correct explanation of A.
    (b) Both A and R are true but R is not the correct explanation of A.
    (c) A is true but R is false.
    (d) A is false but R is true.

49. Given below are two statements labelled as Assertion (A) and Reason (R)

    Assertion: Solutions are the homogenous mixtures of two or more than two components.

    Reason: Since its composition and properties are uniform throughout the mixture.

    Select the most appropriate answer from the options given below:
    (a) Both A and R are true and R is the correct explanation of A.
    (b) Both A and R are true but R is not the correct explanation of A.
    (c) A is true but R is false.
    (d) A is false but R is true.

Section-C

This section consists of 6 multiple choice questions with an overall choice to attempt any 5. In case more than desirable number of questions are attempted, ONLY first 5 will be considered for evaluation.

50. The relation between nucleotide triplets and the amino acids is called:
    (a) transcription   (b) duplication   (c) genetic code   (d) gene

51. Which component determines the physical state of the solution?*
    (a) Solute   (b) Solvent   (c) Water   (d) Protic solvent

52. The minimum bond angle in hydrides of group 16 elements is in:
    (a) H_2O (b) H_2Te (c) H_2Se (d) H_2S

    CASE 1: Read the passage given below and answer the following questions 53-55

    Crystalline solids have regular ordered arrays of components held together by uniform intermolecular forces, whereas the components of amorphous solids are not arranged in regular arrays. The learning objective of this module is to know the characteristic properties of crystalline and amorphous solids. With few exceptions, the particles that compose a solid material, whether ionic, molecular, covalent, or metallic, are held in place by strong attractive forces between them. When we discuss solids, therefore, we consider the positions of the atoms, molecules, or ions, which are essentially fixed in space, rather than their motions (which are more important in liquids and gases).

    Source: https://chem.libretexts.org/Bookshelves/General_Chemistry/Book%3A_Chemistry_(Averill_and_Eldredge)/12%3A_Solids/12.1%3A_Crystalline_and_Amorphous_Solids

53. Solids have the definite
    (a) Shape and volume   (b) Distances   (c) Rigidity   (d) Fluidity

54. Crystalline solids are also known as
    (a) True solids   (b) False solids   (c) Rigid solids   (d) Fluidity solids

55. The best photovoltaic material available for the conversion of the sunlight into electricity is
    (a) Amorphous silica   (b) Glass   (c) Quartz   (d) rubber

❑❑

Answers

Sample Paper 1

Section-A

1. (b) 12

> **Explanation:** The coordination number of a central atom is equal to the number of its surrounding atoms. The face-centered cubic (fcc) has a coordination number of 12 and contains 4 atoms per unit cell.

2. (d) Modification of refractive index

> **Explanation:** Followings are the colligative properties which depends on the number of particles or number of moles.
> (a) Relative Lowering of Vapour Pressure
> (b) Elevation of Boiling Point
> (c) Depression of Freezing Point
> (d) Osmotic Pressure
> Thus modification of the refractive index is not the colligative property, since it is not dependent on number of particles.

3. (b) Secondary alcohol

> **Explanation:** 1.The product formed is secondary alcohol (R-OH) and magnesium hydroxy halide (R-Mg-X). In this reaction in the presence of ether, Grignard reagent and acetaldehyde reacts with each other and produced compound is further proceeded in the presence of H_3O^+ and as a result 2-butanol (secondary alcohol) and magnesium hydroxyl halide is formed.

4. (a) H_2O

> **Explanation:** The reducing nature of an atom or compound depends on how easily it donates or released electrons, thus among the following the H_2O molecule does not lose electrons easily due to the extensive hydrogen bonding in the molecule of the water.

5. (c) Fibroin

> **Explanation:** Silk fibroin is a fibrous protein derived from the Bombyx mori silk worm. It is an amphiphilic block copolymer with a heavy chain composed of 12 repetitive domains predominated by the sequence G-X-G-X-G-X (G = glycine; X = alanine or serine).

6. (b) Sodium formate

> **Explanation:** $$CHCl_3 + 3NaOH \rightarrow CH(OH)_3 \xrightarrow{-H_2O} HCOOH \xrightarrow{NaOH} HCOONa$$
> Chloroform when boiled with aqueous solution of caustic soda, first it forms formic acid which reacts further and forms sodium formate.

7. **(c)** Anomers

Explanation: α–D–(+)-glucose and β–D–(+)-glucose are those diastereomers that differ in configuration at C- 1 atom. Such isomers are referred as anomers. In this case, C-1 carbon atom is the anomeric carbon atom.

α-D-glucopyranose   β-D-glucopyranose

8. **(a)** Distorted octahedral and sp^3d^3

Explanation: The geometry of XeF_6 molecule and the hybridization of Xe atom in the molecule are distorted octahedral and sp^3d^3 respectively. Xe has 6 bond pairs of electrons and one lone pair of electrons. Xe atom possess sp^3d^3 hybridization which results in the electronic geometry of pentagonal bipyramidal and molecular geometry of distorted octahedral.

9. **(b)** Wurtz coupling reaction

Explanation: The Wurtz reaction is a coupling reaction in which two alkyl halides are reacted with sodium metal in dry ether solution to form a higher alkane:
$$2RX + 2Na \; R\!-\!R + 2Na^+X^-$$

10. **(b)** Equal number of cations and anions are missing from the lattice.

Explanation: Schottky defect changes the density as equal number of cations and anions are missing from the lattice.

11. **(b)** Xenon (1) Fluorine (5)

Explanation: Xenon tetrafluoride is prepared by heating a mixture of Xe and F_2 in the molecular ratio 1:5 at 873 K and 7 atm in a sealed nickel tube. In XeF_4, Xenon is in sp^3d^2 hybridised state and has square planar geometry.

$$Xe_{(g)} + 2F_{2(g)} \xrightarrow[\text{7 bar}]{\text{873 K}} XeF_{4(s)}$$

$$(1:5)$$

12. **(a)** CrO_2

Explanation: CrO_2, is a typical metal oxides which show electrical conductivity similar to metal. While SiO_2 and MgO are oxides of metal, semimetal and non-metal which do not show electrical properties.

13. **(c)** Xe, HF and O_2

Explanation: XeF_2 on hydrolysis gives two molecules of Xenon, one molecule of oxygen and one molecule of hydrogen fluoride. The reaction is as follows:
$$2XeF_2 + 2H_2O \xrightarrow{\text{hydrolysis}} 2Xe + 4HF + O_2$$

14. (d) 2- Bromo-3-Chloro butane

> **Explanation:** Alphabetically the Bromo derivative is named first followed by Chloro and word root is Butane as it is a four carbon atom saturated chain.

15. (c) Deoxyribose

> **Explanation:** Initially, most of the carbohydrates had the general formula $C_x(H_2O)_y$. Later on it was found out that few of the compounds either fit into this formula but were not carbohydrates or they did not conform to this formula but were hydrates of carbon.

16. (d) Acetanilide

> **Explanation:** Acetanilide is the non- volatile substance since it does not forms the vapour in the solution while the rest of the three Camphour, petrol and acetone are volatile in nature and are miscible with water.

17. (c) R-CHO

> **Explanation:** Alcohols are compounds having OH group attached to an alkyl group and are hence hydroxy derivatives of hydrocarbons.

18. (a) linear and square planar structures respectively

> **Explanation:** XeF_2 and XeF_4 have Linear and square planar structures respectively.
> In XeF_2, Xe is sp^3d-hybridised but its shape is linear due to the presence of three free pair of electrons, geometry of XeF_2 is distorted from trigonal bi-pyramidal to linear.

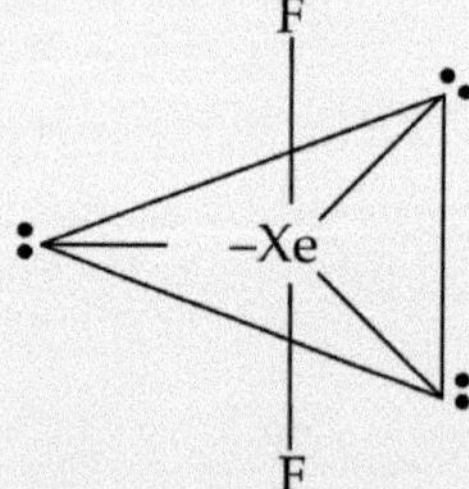

> In XeF_4, Xe is sp^3d^2-hybridised but its shape is square planar due to the presence of two free pair of electrons, geometry of XeF_4 is distorted from octahedral to square planar.

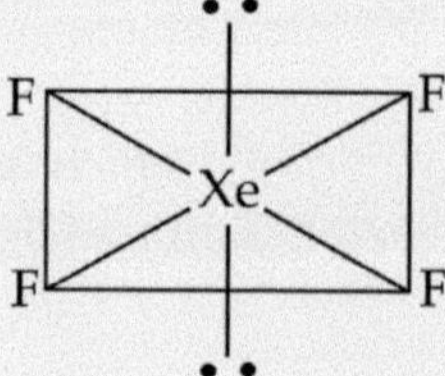

19. (b) Number of halogen atoms

> **Explanation:** Haloalkanes and haloarenes may be classified as mono, di, tri, tetra and so on depending on the number of halogen atoms present in their structure.

20. (a) Ionic solid

> **Explanation:** Graphite cannot be classified as the ionic solid because it is not made up of the opposite ions in the crystal lattice molecule whereas it is the conducting solid, network and the covalent solid in nature.

21. (a) Galactose

> **Explanation:** Galactose is a monosaccharide with the formula $C_6H_{12}O_6$. Sucrose, allolactose and maltose are disaccharides with the same chemical formula $C_{12}H_{22}O_{11}$.

22. (d) $K+[XeF_7]^-$

> **Explanation:** The reaction between XeF_6 and KF leads to the formation of a complex, $K^+[XeF_7]^-$, therefore, it is also known as complex reaction.
> $$XeF_6 + KF \longrightarrow K^+[XeF_7]^-$$

23. (a) Methylene dichloride

> **Explanation:** The common name of dichloromethane is methylene dichloride. It is used as a solvent in wide range of products.

24. (b) Volume change on mixing is not equal to zero.

> **Explanation:** Ideal solutions are the once which obey the Raoult's law over the entire range of concentration. The vapour pressure of such a solution is either higher or lower than that predicted by the Raoult's law and the volume of the solution changes on mixing and is equal to zero.

25. (b) Size decreases

> **Explanation:** The size of the atoms of the elements decrease from left to right in the same period. Considering the row to be the same, the electrons are added to the same shell. However, the increase in atomic number reflects the increase in number of protons i.e. the positive charge. Hence, the overall effective nuclear charge increases. Consequently, the electron cloud is pulled even closer to the nucleus of the atom. Therefore, the size decreases.

Section-B

26. (d) Four

> **Explanation:** Covalency of an atom refers to the number of electrons that atom can share to form chemical bonds. Usually it is the number of bonds formed by the atom. In case of nitrogen, its atom can share up to four electrons, one in the s-subshell and the other three in the p-subshell. In addition to this, absence of d-orbitals restricts its covalency to four only.

27. (d) Combination of vacancy and interstitial defects.

> **Explanation:** Non-stoichiometric defect is the defect that causes the ratio of the number of cations to anions to be different from that indicated by the ideal chemical formula. Such defects are of two types: Metal excess defects and metal deficiency defects. Metal excess defect is caused by anionic vacancies and extra cations in the interstitial sites whereas metal deficiency defect is caused by cationic vacancies and extra anions in the interstitial sites.

28. (a) sp^3 hybridised

> **Explanation:** The compounds with halogen atoms bonded to sp^3 hybridised carbon to carbon-carbon double bond (C = C) i.e. to an allylic carbon. The halogen atom of these compounds is bonded to sp^3-hybridised carbon atom placed next to an aromatic ring.

29. (d) 8 tetrahedral voids within the unit cells.

> **Explanation:** In the cubic close packing, the unit cell has is analogous to face-centered cubic (fcc) structure and number of atoms in a fcc crystal is 4 per unit cell.
> So, number of tetrahedral voids =2×Number of atoms in unit cell = 2 × 4 = 8

30. (d) I^-

> **Explanation:** The order of atomic size or ionic size of the elements in group 17 is as follows: $I^->Br^->Cl^->F^-$. As the size of the atoms increase the distance of the electrons from the nucleus increases and so the attraction of the nucleus over the valence shell electrons decrease and the electrons are easily lost and the atoms are easily oxidized. Hence, the most easily oxidisable ion in the above anions is I^-.

31. (d) Phenol

> **Explanation:** The sp^2 hybridised carbon of an aromatic ring to which the hydroxyl group is attached is called an aryl carbon. In phenol, the OH group is attached to an aryl carbon.

32. (b) Decrease in vapour pressure of a solvent on addition of a non-volatile non electrolyte solute in it.

> **Explanation:** Decrease in vapour pressure of a solvent on addition of a non-volatile non electrolyte solute in it is known as lowering of the vapour pressure.

33. (b) carboxylic acid

> **Explanation:** The compound is acetic acid (CH_3COOH). Even though it has the general formula $C_x(H_2O)_y$ of carbohydrates, it is not one. This is one the flaws of the general formula definition of carbohydrates.

34. (c) Allyl bromide

> **Explanation:** 3-Bromopropene has 3 C atoms in the parent chain with a double bond at C-1 and Br at C-3. This means that Br is attached to the C which is next to the C-C double bond, hence, it is an allylic bromide.

35. (c) Frenkel defect

> **Explanation:** In a solid lattice, the cation has left a lattice site and is located at interstitial position, the lattice defect is Frenkel defect. This defect is observed in compounds having low coordination number and low radius ratio. It is also found in compounds having highly polarizing cation and an easily polarisable anion.

36. (c) Polyhydroxy ketones

> **Explanation:** Polyamino aldehydes and polyhalo aldehydes do not contain an OH group. Polyhydroxy carboxylic acids do not contain a CHO or a keto group. These also do not produce OH substituted compounds on hydrolysis.

37. (a) 3

> **Explanation:** In the common naming system, the prefix sym- is used for haloarenes with 3 halogen atoms. The prefix sym- is used for trihaloarenes with same halogen atom at alternate positions in the benzene ring (1, 3, 5). The prefixes o-, m- and p- are used for dihaloarenes depending on the relative positions of the two identical halogen atoms on the aromatic ring.

38. (a) Cl^- ion form fcc lattice and Na^+ ions occupy all octahedral voids of the unit cell.

> **Explanation:** In NaCl, Cl^- ion form fcc lattice and Na^+ ions occupy all octahedral voids of the unit cell. The coordination number of both cation and anion in this lattice arrangement is 6.

39. (b) sec- Butyl alcohol

> **Explanation:** Butan-2-ol has a parent chain of 4 carbon atoms and the OH group at the second carbon. Such configurations have the prefix sec- in the common name.

40. (b) 3

> **Explanation:** The IUPAC name of Isobutyl chloride is 1-Chloro-2-methylpropane, which means the parent chain consists of 3 carbon atoms with an alkyl group at C-2 and a halogen at C-1.

41. (a) Increase in concentration of the solution.

> **Explanation:** The vapour pressure of the solution decreases with the increase in the concentration of the solution since in the concentrated solution the water (Solution) content is very low as compared to the solute added in the solution, thus less numbers of vapours will be evolved in such case.

42. (b,c) MI > MBr > MCl > MF Ionic character of metal halide.
$F_2 > Cl_2 > Br_2 > I_2$ Bond dissociation enthalpy.

> **Explanation:** Halogens reacts with metals to form metal halides. The ionic character of the halides decreases in the order of MF > MCl > MBr > MI. Bond dissociation enthalpy of halogens decreases to the order of $Cl_2 > F_2 > Br_2 > I_2$. Bond dissociation enthalpy of Cl_2 is greater than F_2 because of large electron-electron repulsion among lone pairs of F_2 molecule.

43. (b) HI > HBr > HCl

> **Explanation:** The bond dissociation enthalpy of the carbon-halogen bond between H and Cl is the highest and that between H and I is the lowest among HI, HBr and HCl.

44. (b) 3

> **Explanation:** The IUPAC name of tert-Butyl alcohol is 2-methylpropan-2-ol, which has two substituent groups at the C-2 position, namely one methyl and one hydroxyl group.

45. (b) Both A and R are true but R is not the correct explanation of A.

> **Explanation:** Flourine has low bond dissociation enthalpy due to small atomic size number of electrons create large repulsion in bonded electron. Thus both assertion and reason are correct but reason is not the correct explanation of assertion.

46. (d)　A is false but R is true.

> **Explanation:** Quartz is a mineral with the chemical formula SiO_2, and like almost all minerals, it is a crystalline solid. Quartz glass is an amorphous solid because it is formed by fusing the crystal and then cooling it rapidly. Crystalline solids have regular ordered arrays of components held together by uniform inter-molecular forces, whereas the components of amorphous solids are not arranged in regular arrays. Crystalline solids have a certain pattern of atoms that is repeated over and over in three dimensions. Thus assertion is false but reason is true.

47. (a)　Both A and R are true and R is the correct explanation of A.

> **Explanation:** Noble gases possess the electronic configuration ns^2np^6 and has 8 electrons in their outer shell, hence there valency is 0. Thus both assertion and reason are true and reason is the correct explanation of the assertion.

48. (a)　Both A and R are true and R is the correct explanation of A.

> **Explanation:** When acetone and chloroform are mixed together a hydrogen bond is formed between them which increases the intermolecular attraction between them and hence decreases the vapour pressure due to the decrease in the vapour pressure the heat is evolved during the reaction. Hence it is an exothermic reaction in nature and thus both assertion and reason are true and reason is the correct explanation of the assertion.

49. (c)　A is true but R is false.

> **Explanation:** EtOH is weaker acid than phenol because it is tough to remove H+ ion from EtOH whereas phenol readily gives H+ to form phenoxide ion (highly stable due to resonance). However, Sodium ethoxide may be prepared by the reaction of EtOH with NaOH not with the aqueous solution of the NaOH. Thus Assertion is true but reason is false statement.

Section-C

50. (c)　Both (a) and (b)

> **Explanation:** Helium is used for filling meteorological balloons, in gas cooled-nuclear reactor and as a cryogenic agent.

51. (c)　Polyhydroxy ketones

> **Explanation:** Polyamino aldehydes and polyhalo aldehydes do not contain an OH group. Polyhydroxy carboxylic acids do not contain a CHO or a keto group. These also do not produce OH substituted compounds on hydrolysis.

52. (d)　Vinylic

> **Explanation:** The given compound contains a sp^3 hybridised C-OH bond and is allylic. Hence it has only one alkyl group attached to the C bonded to the OH group, it is primary alcohol and the presence of only one OH group makes it monohydric.

53. (d)　Density of the crystal increases.

> **Explanation:** Frenkel defect is a combination of vacancy and interstitial defects. In this defect, Cations leave their actual lattice sites and occupy the interstitial space in the ionic crystal. As a result, the density of the crystal remains the same. Thus, in the frenkel defect the density of the ionic crystal remains the same and does not increase.

54. (d) Both (a) and (b)

> **Explanation:** Vacuums in solid states mean empty space in a closed packed system between the constituent particles. Such empty spaces are known as the openings, interstices or interstitial voids. Both tetrahedral and octahedral void are interstitial void.

55. (b) Schottky defect

> **Explanation:** Schottky defect is a stoichiometric defect in which both cations and anions remain missing from their lattice site in equal numbers and hence stoichiometry and electrical neutrality is maintained. This defect lowers the density of the crystal.
>
> Schottky defect in ionic crystal

Sample Paper 2

Section-A

1. (c) $r = \dfrac{\sqrt{3}}{4}a$

> **Explanation:** Usually, the length of the cell edge is represented by a.
> The direction from a corner of a cube to the farthest corner is called body diagonal (say bd).
> $$\text{Face diagonal} = fd$$
> $$bd^2 = fd^2 + a^2$$
> $$= a^2 + a^2 + a^2 = 3a^2$$
> Atoms along the body diagonal (say bd) touch each other. Thus, the body diagonal has a length that is four times the radius of the atom, R.
> $$bd = 4R$$
> The relationship between a and R can be worked out by the Pythagorean theorem.
> $$(4R)^2 = 3a^2$$
> Thus,
> $$4R = \sqrt{3}a$$
> and
> $$r = \dfrac{\sqrt{3}}{4}a$$

2. (b) $pV = nRT.$

> **Explanation:** We know that
> $$\pi v = nRT$$
> $$\pi = \dfrac{n}{v}RT$$

$$\pi = p \text{ and } c = \frac{n}{v}$$

thus
$$pv = nRT$$

3. (d) 1-chloro-2, 2-dimethyl propane

> **Explanation:** As per the IUPAC nomenclature, the numbering of the compound should begin with functional group and then lowest "Locant Rule" should be followed. Hence, the IUPAC name of the compound is 1-Chloro-2, 2-dimethyl propane.

4. (a) Paramagnetic

> **Explanation:** Due to the presence of two unpaired electrons, oxygen molecule is paramagnetic in nature.

5. (a) Formic acid

> **Explanation:** When oxalic acid is heated with glycerol we get Formic acid.

6. (b) Tyrosinase

> **Explanation:** The disease albinism is caused by the deficiency of tyrosinase enzyme. Albinism is an inherited disorder that is characterized by little or no production of the pigment melanin, due to lack of tyrosine enzyme. This enzyme helps the body to change the amino acid tyrosine into melanin pigment. In albinism suffering person, the enzyme is inactive and no melanin is produced, leading to white hair and very light skin colour.

7. (a) Both the compounds form same product on treatment with alcoholic KOH.

> **Explanation:** Ethylene chloride and ethylidene chloride on treatment with alc. KOH show elimination reaction and form ethyne as the product and both these compounds form same products(ethane) on reduction.

8. (a) H_2O

> **Explanation:** Among the following, the hydride which is not a reducing agent is H_2O. Except H_2O all others are reducing agent. The reducing nature of an atom or compound depends on how easily it donates or releases electrons. The reducing nature of hydrides increases so the order is $H_2O < H_2S < H_2Se < H_2Te$.

9. (d) Density

> **Explanation:** Density is an intensive property because there is a narrow range of densities across the samples. No matter what the initial mass was, densities were essentially the same. Since intensive properties do not depend on the amount of material, the data indicate that density is an intensive property of matter.

10. (c) amphoteric

> **Explanation:** Amino acids are amphoteric, which means they have acidic and basic tendencies. The carboxyl group is able to lose a proton and the amine group is able to accept a proton.

11. (b) sodium dihalide

> **Explanation:** Alkyl halides are prepared from alcohols and the hydroxyl group of an alcohol is replaced by halogen on reactions with certain reagents such as concentrated halogen acids, phosphorus halides or thionyl chloride. Thionyl chloride is most preferred because in this reaction alkyl halide is formed along with gases SO_2 and HCl which are escapable, hence, the reaction gives pure alkyl halides. Whereas, the reactions of primary and secondary alcohols with HCl require the presence of a catalyst, $ZnCl_2$. With tertiary alcohols, the reaction is conducted by simply shaking the alcohol with concentrated HCl at room temperature. Phosphorus tribromide and triiodide are usually generated in situ (produced in the reaction mixture) by the reaction of red phosphorus with bromine and iodine respectively. Thus, the reagent which is not used in for replacing the hydroxyl group of an alcohol is sodium dihalide.

12. **(a)** central atom

> **Explanation:** In the complex ion $[AuXe_4]^{2+}$, Xe acts as a central atom and gold acts as a ligand.

13. (d) 32

> **Explanation:** The packing efficiency of the Body centred cubic arrangement is 68% thus the percentage of the empty space available will be:
> The overall packing efficiency of an ideal crystal will be 100%
> Thus percentage of the empty space available will be: 100-68%= 32%

14. (d) Wurtz-Fittig

> **Explanation:** The type of reactions in which an electrophile substitutes another electrophile in any organic compound is known as electrophilic substitution reaction. Out of the given options,nitration, halogenation and sulphonation are examples of electrophilic substitution reaction.Whereas, in Wurtz-Fittig reaction , a mixture of alkyl halide reacts with an aryl halide in the presence of dry ether and sodium to form alkyl arene.
>
> X   R
>
> Na + RX / Ether

15. (b) sp^3d

> **Explanation:** The Au atom in the complex $[AuXe_4]^{2+}$ is sp^3d hybridised.

16. (a) Ideal solutions

> **Explanation:** Ideal solutions are the once which obey the Raoult's law over the entire range of concentration. The vapour pressure of such a solution is either higher or lower than that predicted by the Raoult's law.

17. (c) Helium

> **Explanation:** All noble gases have full s and p outer electron shells, except helium, which has no p sublevel), and so do not form chemical compounds easily. This is because of its inert nature, the atom does not readily accept any extra electrons nor join with anything to make covalent compounds.

18. (c) Thionyl Chloride

> **Explanation:** The reaction of alcohol with $SOCl_2$ gives a chloroalkane along with gases SO_2 and HCl which are easily escapable, leaving behind the pure alkyl chloride.

19. (c) unidentate

> **Explanation:** Xenon is a unidentate ligand.

20. (a) Primary alcohol is formed

> **Explanation:** $LiAlH_4$ acts as a reducing agent which reduces an aldehyde by adding hydrogen atoms to it which result in the formation of a primary alcohol.

21. (a) He

> **Explanation:** The noble gas discovered in the chromosphere of the sun was Helium (He). In 1868, Lockyer discovered a new element looking at the chromosphere of the sun, during a solar eclipse, later that element was found to be noble gas Helium.

22. (a) Interaction in the molecular level

> **Explanation:** The solutions show the deviation from the Raoult's law due to the nature of the interactions at the molecular level.

23. (d) Cellulose

> **Explanation:** Glucose, fructose and lactose are examples of compounds that are sweet in taste and are called sugars. Cellulose is a non-sugar that is tasteless, water insoluble and amorphous.

24. (a) Henry's law

> **Explanation:** Henry's law states that at a constant temperature, the amount of a given gas that dissolves in a given type and volume of liquid is directly proportional to the partial pressure of that gas in equilibrium with that liquid.

25. (b) $C_nH_{2n-1}X$

> **Explanation:** The general formula for haloalkanes is $C_nH_{2n+1}X$ where X is a halogen atom and $n = 1, 2, 3...$ The formulae $C_nH_{2n-1}X$ and $C_nH_{2n-3}X$ are that of haloalkanes and haloalkynes respectively.

Section-B

26. (c) Repulsion by electron pairs on F

> **Explanation:** Due to smaller bond length of fluorine, the lone pairs are nearer and thus the inter electronic repulsions between the lone pairs is more so it has low bond energy.

27. (c) fcc > bcc > simple cubic

> **Explanation:** Packing efficiency is the percentage of total space filled by the constituent particles in the unit cell.
> Packing efficiency = Packing Factor × 100.

The most efficient packing occurs in the hcp and ccp crystal lattice with the efficiency of 74% compared to BCC crystal lattice of 68% and simple cubic structure of 52.4%. Thus the trend will be fcc > bcc > simple cubic.

28. (a) Starch

Explanation: An aqueous solution of corn starch is acidified with dilute H_2SO_4. This is then heated under pressure (2-3 bar) for hydrolysis to take place. After this, the liquid is neutralised with sodium carbonate and the resulting solution is concentrated under reduced pressure to get glucose crystals. This process is also used for obtaining glucose from cellulose.

29. (a) $HClO_4$

Explanation: The acidic strength of oxyacids of chlorine will be in the order $HClO < HClO_2 < HClO_3 < HClO_4$.

30. **(a)** (A) and (B)

Explanation: Schottky defect is a type of point defect or imperfection in solids which is caused by a vacant position that is generated in a crystal lattice due to the atoms or ions moving out from the interior to the surface of the crystal. AgBr shows both Frenkel defect and Schottky defect as in AgBr, Ag^+ ion is small in size than Br^- ion and when removed from lattice point they can occupy interstitial sites and hence shows both Frenkel and Schottky defects.

31. (c) $40°$ C temperature and dark

Explanation: The most suitable conditions for electrophilic substitution of arenes is that such reactions are carried out in the dark at ordinary temperatures of 40°C in the presence of a Lewis acid catalyst.

32. (a) Solubility

Explanation: The maximum amount of a substance that can be dissolved in a specific amount of solvent at a specified temperature is known as its solubility.

33. (b) Intermolecular hydrogen bonding

Explanation: Intermolecular Hydrogen Bonding occurs when the hydrogen bonding is between H-atom of one molecule and an atom of the electronegative element of another molecule.

34. (b) $I_2 + 2Br^- \longrightarrow 2I^- + Br_2$ reaction will not occur spontaneously.

Explanation: A spontaneous reaction is a reaction that favours the formation of products at the conditions under which the reaction is occurring. A roaring bonfire is an example of a spontaneous reaction. Whereas a non spontaneous reaction is a reaction that does not favour the formation of products at the given set of conditions.

35. (a) Some of the anionic sites are occupied by an unpaired electron.
    (d) F-centres are created which impart colour to the crystals.

Explanation: Anionic sites are always occupied by unpaired electrons and never by the paired electrons. Since in the KCl molecule the anionic sites are occupied by an unpaired electron thus there will be no vacant sites in the molecule.

36. (a) Deoxyribose

    Explanation: Monosaccharides are the simplest carbohydrates which cannot be hydrolysed into simpler units. Deoxyribose ($C_5H_{10}O_4$) is a monosaccharide.

37. (c) Lowering of vapour pressure.

    Explanation: Since the lowering in freezing point is not dependent on the number of moles thus it is not a colligative property while the rest of the three options depends on the number of moles thus they all are the colligative properties.

38. (c) Free radicals

    Explanation: Free radicals are generated which contain the lone pair of electrons.

39. (b) Associated nature due to hydrogen bonding

    Explanation: Hydrogen fluoride does not boil until 20°C in contrast to the heavier hydrogen halides, which boil between –85°C (–120°F) and –35°C (–30°F). This hydrogen bonding between HF molecules gives rise to high viscosity in the liquid phase and lowers than expected pressure in the gas phase.

40. (a) Frenkel defect.

    Explanation: The cations of the alkali metals are larger in size due to which they cannot dislocate and occupy an interstitial site within the lattice thus the pure alkali metal halides does not show the Frenkel defect because creation of the vacancy and occupying the interstitial site is essential for the creation of the Frenkel defect.

41. (a) Propanol

    Explanation: Propanol is most soluble in water because the lower alcohols are highly soluble in water due to the presence of –OH group in the alcohols it forms H-bond with itself and molecular association takes place which causes the increase in the boiling point of the corresponding alcohols due to the increase in the number of carbon atoms and thus high temperature is required to break this association of bonds and thus the solubility in water increases. The extent of the hydrogen bonding in alcohols depends on the number of the carbon atoms attached in the chain.

42. (a) Vapour pressure of the solvent decreases

    Explanation: The vapour pressure of a solvent is lowered by the addition of a non-volatile solute to form a solution. This decrease in vapour pressure can be explained by using the entropy differences of the liquid and gas phases along with the position of dissolved particles after the addition of the solute.

43. (a) Maltose

    Explanation: When any carbohydrate undergoes hydrolysis and produces two separate units of monosaccharides, it is a disaccharide. The used units that are produced may be same. Maltose on hydrolysis gives two units of glucose itself.

44. (d) Zn^+ ion is smaller in size

Explanation: ZnS shows the dislocation defect because the size of the cation Zn^{2+} is smaller than the size of the corresponding anion S^{2-} and for the dislocation defect to occur the cation needs to leaves the crystal lattice and creates a vacancy defect at its place in the lattice and interstitial defect within the same crystal and in ZnS the vacancy and interstitial defect are created simultaneously thus it shows the Dislocation defect.

45. (a) Both A and R are true and R is the correct explanation of A.

Explanation: The haloalkanes are slightly soluble in water. Less energy is released when new attractions are set up between the haloalkanes and the water molecules as these are not as strong as the original hydrogen bonds in water. As a result, the solubility of haloalkanes in water is low. Thus both assertion and reason are true and reason is the correct explanation of the assertion.

46. (c) A is true but R is false.

Explanation: On addition of non-volatile solute (viz. NaCl) to water, NaCl solution is formed. Due to relatively lesser number of water molecules at the surface of liquid, the solution exerts a lower vapour pressure as compared to that of pure water. It is because of this lowering of vapour pressure that a depression in freezing point of water is observed. Thus Assertion is true but reason is false statement.

47. (b) Both A and R are true but R is not the correct explanation of A.

Explanation: The acidic character increases down the group and thermal stability of hydrides decreases down the group due to decrease in bond (H—E) dissociation enthalpy down the group. Thus both assertion and reason are true but reason is not the correct explanation of assertion.

48. (d) A is false but R is true.

Explanation: The structure of quartz is crystalline and that of quartz glass is amorphous. The two structures are almost identical yet in case of amorphous quartz glass, there is no long range order. Thus assertion is false but reason is true.

49. (b) Both A and R are true but R is not the correct explanation of A.

Explanation: Interhalogen compounds are more reactive than halogens because X—X′ bond in interhalogens is weaker than X—X bond in halogen (except F—F bond). Thus both assertion and reason are true but reason is not the correct explanation of assertion.

Section-C

50. (a) Equal to 90°

Explanation: For orthorhombic system axial ratios are a = b = c and the axial angles are $\alpha = \beta = \gamma = 90°$. Thus, all the three edge lengths are unequal but all the angles are equal. They are equal to 90°.

51. (d) Aerated drinks

Explanation: A solid solution is a solid-state solution of one or more solutes in a solvent. Brass, bronze, and hydrated salts are examples of solid solutions. Aerated drinks are examples of liquid solutions (gas in liquid).

52. (b) Covalent solid

> **Explanation:** A network solid or covalent network solid is a chemical compound in which the atoms are bonded by covalent bonds in a continuous network extending throughout the material.

53. (b) sp^3

> **Explanation:** As the substitution reaction is initiated by a nucleophile, it is called nucleophilic substitution reaction. It is one of the most useful classes of organic reactions of alkyl halides in which halogen is bonded to sp^3 hybridised carbon atom.

54. (c) Asymmetric

> **Explanation:** The spatial arrangement of four groups (valencies) around a central carbon is tetrahedral and if all the substituents attached to that carbon are different such a carbon is called asymmetric carbon or steriocentre.

55. (a) dipole-dipole and van der Waals forces

> **Explanation:** In alkyl halides, due to greater polarity as well as higher molecular mass, as compared to the parent hydrocarbon, the intermolecular dipole-dipole and van der Waal's forces of attraction are stronger in the halogen derivatives.

Sample Paper 3

Section-A

1. (a) Fluorine.

> **Explanation:** Fluorine is the most powerful oxidizing agent because it is the most electronegative element. Electronegative elements have the property to remove electrons form the elements to which, it is attached.

2. (b) Wurtz coupling reaction

> **Explanation:** The Wurtz reaction is a coupling reaction in which two alkyl halides are reacted with sodium metal in dry ether solution to form a higher alkane:
>
> $$2RX + 2Na \rightarrow R-R + 2Na^+ X^-$$

3. (b) Reimer – Tiemann reaction

> **Explanation:** Phenol reacts with chlorofom and alcoholic KOH to give salicylaldehyde. This reaction is called Reimer-Tiemann reaction.

4. (b) Intramolecular dehydrohalogenation

> **Explanation:** In ethyl alcohol, the attacking species is the ethoxide anion, which is a much stronger base than the hydroxide anion, so it directly extracts the beta hydrogen from ethyl bromide, followed by elimination of the bromide anion from the adjacent carbon atom to form ethene. Thus it is an example of intramolecular dehydrohalogenation.

5. (a,c) 0 to +5, 0 to –1

> **Explanation:** $6NaOH\ (Hot) + 3Cl_2 \rightarrow 5NaCl + NaClO_3$
> Therefore, oxidation number of Chlorine changes from 0 to +5 and 0 to –1.

6. (b) Molality

> **Explanation:** Molality does not get affected by temperature. Molality is the ratio of the number of moles of solute to the mass of solvent (in kg). Molarity, normality and formality contains volume terms and hence are affected by temperature.

7. (a) Alcohols

> **Explanation:** Lucas test is used where alcohol reacts with concentrated hydrochloric acid in presence of anhydrous $ZnCl_2$ to form alkyl halides. The three type of alcohols undergo this reaction at different rates. Order of rate of reaction is: tertiary > secondary > primary.
>
> $$R{-}OH + HCl \xrightarrow{\ ZnCl_2\ } R{-}Cl + H_2O$$
> $$\text{Alkyl chloride}$$

8. (c) Dry ice

> **Explanation:** Although carbon dioxide can be solidified to form 'dry ice', it only does so when squeezed under high pressure or cooled to low temperature. Moreover, dry ice is a molecular crystal, in which the crystal lattice consists of molecules of carbon dioxide rather than of individual carbon or oxygen atoms. Thus it is an example of molecular crystal.

9. (b) Secondary alcohol

> **Explanation:** The product formed is secondary alcohol (R-OH) and magnesium hydroxy halide (R-Mg-X). In this reaction in the presence of ether, Grignard reagent and acetaldehyde reacts with each other and produced compound is further proceeded in the presence of H_3O^+ and as a result 2-butanol (secondary alcohol) and magnesium hydroxyl halide is formed.

10. (b) 12

> **Explanation:** The coordination number of a central atom is equal to the number of its surrounding atoms. The face-centered cubic (fcc) has a coordination number of 12 and contains 4 atoms per unit cell.

11. (a) 26%

> **Explanation:** The space occupied by spheres in the hcp arrangement is 74%.Hence the empty space is 100 – 74 =26 %.

12. (a) Fluorine

> **Explanation:** If a halogen has a high electron affinity, low dissociation energy, and high hydration energy of its ion. It will have high oxidizing power. Although fluorine has a lower electron affinity than chlorine but has low dissociation energy and high hydration energy. Therefore fluorine is the strongest oxidizing agent.

13. (a) Liquid solutions

> **Explanation:** Liquid solutions do exist in nature due to the properties of the solids to dissolve in the liquids due to the solubility effect and oxygen dissolved in water is the example of the liquid solutions.

14. (d) Aryl

> **Explanation:** In C_6H_5F, the F atom is directly attached to the sp^2 hybridised carbon atom of an aromatic ring, i.e., benzene.

15. (c) T-Shaped

> **Explanation:** Chlorine trifluoride has 10 electrons around the central chlorine atom. This means there are five electron pairs arranged in a trigonal bipyramidal shape with a 175° F–Cl–F bond angle. There are two equatorial lone pairs making the final structure T–shaped.

16. (a) London forces

> **Explanation:** Iodine molecules are a form of non-polar constituent particles which form crystals and held together by London force (or induced dipole-dipole interaction) which is a weakly dispersion force.

17. (a) Methanal

> **Explanation:** Methanal on treatment with Grignard reagent forms an adduct which has only one alkyl group attached to the C atom along with two hydrogens and one O-Mg-X (X = halogen) group. This on hydrolysis will form a primary alcohol where the OH group will replace the O-Mg-X group.

18. (c) Sodium nitrite

> **Explanation:** Sodium nitrite reacts with aqueous HCl to form NaCl and HNO_2. The nitrous acid reacts with aniline in cold aqueous solution of HCl to form benzene diazonium chloride.

19. (b) 55.55 M

> **Explanation:** Density of water = 1 g mL^{-1}
> $$\text{Mass of 1000 ml of water} = V \times d$$
> $$= 1000 \text{ mL}^{-1} \times 1 \text{ g}$$
> $$= 1000 \text{ g mL}^{-1}$$
> $$\text{Moles of water} = 55.55 \text{ mol}$$
> Now, mole of H_2O present in 1000 mL or 1 L of water.
> So, molarity = 55.55M

20. (d) Vinylic alcohols

> **Explanation:** Allylic alcohols are those in which OH group is attached to a sp^3 hybridised carbon adjacent to a C-C double bond, i.e., an allylic carbon. Whereas, vinylic alcohols contain OH group attached directly to a C-C double bond.

21. (a,c,d)

Explanation: (i) Among group 17 elements radius ratio of iodine and fluorine is maximum because size of iodine is largest and fluorine is smallest in the group. (ii) The correct statement is inter halogen compounds are more reactive than halogens (except Fluorine). This is because X–X′ bond in interhalogen is weaker than X–X bond in halogens except F–F. (iii) As the ratio between radii of X and X′ increase, the number of atoms per molecule also increases. Thus, iodine (VII) fluoride should have maximum number of atoms as the ratio of radii between I and F will be maximum. (iv) Interhalogen compounds are more reactive than halogens (except fluorine). This is because X–X′ bond in interhalogen is weaker than X–X′ bond in halogens.

22. (a) 8

Explanation: It has a total of 8 isomers, four are primary and two each are secondary and tertiary haloalkanes.

23. (d) Electrical conductivity

Explanation: The osmotic pressure, boiling point and vapour pressure all depends upon the number of moles and mass of the substance, compound taken and the properties which depends upon the number of moles of solute are known as colligative properties whereas in case of electrical conductivity which is the measure of the reciprocal of resistivity is not dependent on the number of moles and is not regarded as the colligative property.

24. (c) Trihydric

Explanation: The IUPAC name of glycerol is Propane-1, 2, 3-triol, signifying that there are three hydroxyl groups attached to three different carbon atoms.

25. (a) Benzene

Explanation: Chlorobenzene reacts with Mg in dry ether to give a compound (A) which further reacts with ethanol to yield benzene as shown by the reaction:

Cl $\xrightarrow{\text{+ Mg, Dry ether}}$ MgCl

Chlorobenzene → Phenyl magnesium chloride

Phenyl magnesium chloride $\xrightarrow{\text{C}_2\text{H}_5\text{OH}}$ Benzene + C₂H₅OMgCl

(C₂H₅OH: Alcohols contains active hydrogen)

Section-B

26. (a) Osmotic pressure

Explanation: The minimum excess pressure that has to be applied on the solution to prevent the entry of the solvent into the solution through the semipermeable membrane is called the osmotic pressure. The osmotic pressure method has the advantage that it uses molarities instead of molarities and it can be measured at room temperature.

27. (a) He

> **Explanation:** Pierre Janssen and Joseph Norman Lockyer had discovered a new element on 18 August, 1868 while looking at the chromosphere of the Sun, and named it helium (He) after the Greek word for the Sun. No chemical analysis was possible at the time, but helium was later found to be a noble gas.

28. (d) Presence of bulky alkyl groups in the alcohol

> **Explanation:** Secondary and tertiary alcohols give alkenes as major products during dehydration, because elimination competes over substitution. Hence, this method is mainly used for primary alcohols.

29. (c) Ethyl iodide

> **Explanation:** $CH_3CH_2I + Mg^- \xrightarrow{\text{Dry ether}} CH_3CH_2MgI$ (Ethyl magnesium iodide)

30. (a) Tollen's test

> **Explanation:** Despite having a CHO group, glucose does not react with $NaHSO_3$ to form an addition product and give either Schiff's test or 2, 4-DNP test like other aldehydes. However, it forms a silver mirror on treatment with Tollen's reagent. These observations indicate the existence of glucose in other forms and gave way to the cyclic structure of glucose.

31. (d) Ethoxyethane

> **Explanation:** Symmetrical ethers are formed when alcohols are dehydrated with H_2SO_4 at controlled temperatures. This is an SN^2 reaction involving the attack of alcohol molecule on a protonated alcohol to give ethers.

32. (c) Fructose

> **Explanation:** Fructose is a monosaccharide that consists of six carbon atoms including a carbonyl carbon of a keto group within its chain. Glucose, galactose and mannose are examples of aldohexoses.

33. (a) 2

> **Explanation:** Non-ideal solutions can occur two ways:
> (a) When intermolecular forces between solute and solvent molecules are *less* strong than between molecules of similar (of the same type) molecules.
> (b) When intermolecular forces between dissimilar molecules are *greater* than those between similar molecules.

34. (c) 0°C

> **Explanation:** Diazonium salts are formed by treating ice-cold solution of aromatic amines in aqueous mineral acid with sodium nitrite at low temperatures of 273-278K.

35. (c) Linear

> **Explanation:** XeF_2 is a linear molecule due to the arrangement of fluorine atoms and the lone pairs of electrons in the symmetric arrangement.

36. (a) lower than

Explanation: The large difference in boiling points of alcohols and ethers is due to the absence of intermolecular bonds in the latter.

37. (c) anomers

Explanation: In the cyclic structure of glucose, the pair of optical isomers that differ in the configuration only around the C_1 carbon (anomeric carbon) are called anomers.

38. (c) Radon

Explanation: Radon due to its radioactive nature is used in treatment of cancer (radiotherapy). Radon is a chemical element with the symbol Rn and atomic number 86. It is a radioactive, colourless, odourless, tasteless noble gas. It occurs naturally in minute quantities as an intermediate step in the normal radioactive decay chains through which thorium and uranium slowly decay into lead and various other short-lived radioactive elements.

39. (c) Unit cell

Explanation: Crystalline solids are composed of many small crystals, each of which is called a unit cell. It is a specific term. Monomer is the basic unit for a polymer, and atoms make up molecules, which can further arrange themselves to form solids, liquids or gases.

40. (a) starch

Explanation: An aqueous solution of corn starch is acidified with dilute H_2SO_4. This is then heated under pressure (2-3 bar) for hydrolysis to take place. After this, the liquid is neutralised with sodium carbonate and the resulting solution is concentrated under reduced pressure to get glucose crystals. This process is also used for obtaining glucose from cellulose.

41. (c) sp^3d

Explanation: The hybridization of XeF_2 (Xenon Difluoride) is a sp^3d type. Hybridization is a concept in which the atomic orbitals of different atoms contribute to form newly hybridized orbitals. The participating atoms in the molecule share their electrons to form new hybrid orbitals. Valence electrons are the maximum number of electrons in which an atom can contribute to the hybridization of a molecule.

42. (c) red precipitate

Explanation: Since glucose is readily oxidised, it acts as a strong reducing agent and reduces Fehling's reagent to form a carboxylate compound (in the place of CHO group which gets oxidised) along with a red precipitate of Cu_2O.

43. (b) presence of a carbonyl group in glucose

Explanation: Glucose reacts with hydrogen cyanide to form glucose cyanohydrin, where the carbonyl double bond gets cleaved to form one C-OH bond and one C-CN bond. This indicates the presence of a carbonyl group but does not confirm whether it is an aldehydic or a keto group.

44. (a) Cl_2

Explanation: Chlorine (Cl_2) displaces bromine from an aqueous solution containing bromide. Reactivity of chlorine is more than that of bromine. So chlorine replaces bromine.

45. (b) Both A and R are true but R is not the correct explanation of A.

> **Explanation:** Ozone is a powerful oxidizing agent compared to oxygen as it is unstable. Ozone layer prevent UV radiations from reaching the earth, hence ozone layer acts as a reactive blanket to earth. Thus both assertion and reason are correct statements but reason is not the correct explanation of the assertion.

46. (b) Both A and R are true but R is not the correct explanation of A.

> **Explanation:** Diamond is bad conductor of electricity because the valence electrons of carbon are involved in bonding. In graphite however three out of four valence electrons are involved in bonding and the fourth electron remains free between adjacent layers which makes it a good conductor. Graphite is soft because parallel layers are held together by weak Vander Waal's force. However, diamond is hard due to compact three-dimensional network of bonding. Thus both assertion and reason are true and reason is not the correct explanation of assertion.

47. (c) A is true but R is false.

> **Explanation:** Allyl halides are the compounds in which the halogen atom is bonded to an sp^3 hybridised carbon atom next to carbon-carbon double bond. Thus assertion is true, but reason is false.

48. (d) A is false but R is true.

> **Explanation:** When a solute is present in trace quantities it is convenient to express concentration in ppm. Thus assertion is false, but reason is true.

49. (b) Both A and R are true but R is not the correct explanation of A.

> **Explanation:** Thermal stability of hydrides decreases down the group in Group VI due to increase in size . But acidic character increases down the group as the M–H bond strength decreases. Thermal stability and acidity are not related.Thus both assertion and reason are true but reason is not the correct explanation of the assertion.

Section-C

50. (b) Primitive cell

> **Explanation:** According to classification of unit cells, a primitive unit cell is one which has all constituent particles located at its corners. BCC has one particle present at the center including the corners. FCC has an individual cell shared between the faces of adjacent cells. End centered cells have cells present at centers of two opposite faces. Thus the primitive unit cell has the particles only at the corners.

51. (d) Green

> **Explanation:** When SO_2 is passed through acidified $K_2Cr_2O_7$ solution, the orange colour of the solution changes to green due to formation of chromic sulphate.
> $$K_2Cr_2O_7 + 3SO_2 + H_2SO_4 \rightarrow K_2SO_4 + Cr_2(SO_4)_2 + 7H_2O + 3S$$

52. (a) Amino acid

> **Explanation:** RNA and DNA are nucleic acids which on complete hydrolysis yield a pentose sugar, phosphoric acid and nitrogen containing heterocyclic compounds called bases.

53. (d) They break into two pieces with irregular surface

> **Explanation:** When the crystalline solids are cut with a sharp edge, the two new halves will have smooth surfaces, whereas for the amorphous solids the two resulting halves will have irregular surfaces.

54. (c) ZnS

> **Explanation:** Ionic solids are composed of cations and anions held together by electrostatic forces. Ionic solids are poor conductors of electricity except when their ions are mobile, such as when a solid is melted or dissolved in solution.

55. (a) Face centered cubic

> **Explanation:** A face-centered cubic unit cell structure consists of atoms arranged in a cube where each corner of the cube has a fraction of an atom with six additional full atoms positioned at the center of each cube face. As such, each corner atom represents one-eighth of an atom.

Sample Paper 4

Section-A

1. (d) Density

> **Explanation:** Density is an intensive property because there is a narrow range of densities across the samples. No matter what the initial mass was, densities were essentially the same. Since intensive properties do not depend on the amount of material, the data indicate that density is an intensive property of matter.

2. (c) A mixture of mono-, di-, tri- and tetra-halogen derivatives.

> **Explanation:** Halogenation of an alkane produces a hydrocarbon derivative in which one or more halogen atoms have been substituted for hydrogen atoms. Alkanes are notoriously unreactive compounds because they are non-polar and lack functional groups at which reactions can take place. Thus they give a mixture of mono, di, tri and tetra halogen derivatives.

3. (a) He

> **Explanation:** The noble gas discovered in the chromosphere of the sun was Helium (He). In 1868, Lockyer discovered a new element looking at the chromosphere of the sun, during a solar eclipse, later that element was found to be noble gas Helium.

4. (d) **4**

> **Explanation:** The number of atoms contained in one face-centred cubic unit cell of monoatomic substance is 4.
>
> 8 atoms are present at 8 corners of a fcc unit cell. Each atom contributes one eight to the unit cell. Total contribution $= 8 \times \dfrac{1}{8} = 1$
>
> 6 atoms are present at 6 corners of a fcc unit cell. Each atom contributes one half to the unit cell. Total contribution $= 6 \times \dfrac{1}{2} = 3$
>
> Total number of atoms in one fcc unit cell $= 1 + 3 = 4$

5. (b) Ethylene, C_2H_4

Explanation: When Ehanol is heated with conc. H_2SO_4 at 445K, by the process of dehydration Ethylene is formed. In this reaction conc. H_2SO_4 acts as a dehydrating agent.

6. (c) amphoteric

Explanation: Amino acids are amphoteric, which means they have acidic and basic tendencies. The carboxyl group is able to lose a proton and the amine group is able to accept a proton.

7. (a) H_2O

Explanation: pKa values of the given compounds are as follows:

$H-OH = 14$

$CH_3-OH = 15.5$

$CH_3CH_2-OH = 16.0$

$CH_3\text{-}CH_2-CH_2-OH = 16.85$

One can observe that pKa value increases as the alkyl chain length attached to the –OH group increases. This is due to the electron donating properties of alkyl groups which, in turn, destabilises the -ve charge on oxygen when the H on the OH ionises.

$$R-OH \longrightarrow RO^- + H^+.$$

8. (a) F

Explanation: Both oxide and fluoride ions are highly electronegative and have a very small size. Due to these properties, they are able to oxidise the metal to its highest oxidation state. Thus the halogen fluorine has the oxidation state of –1 only.

9. (a) Paramagnetic

Explanation: Due to the presence of two unpaired electrons, oxygen molecule is paramagnetic in nature.

10. (c) $r = \dfrac{\sqrt{3}}{4} a$

Explanation: Usually, the length of the cell edge is represented by a.
The direction from a corner of a cube to the farthest corner is called body diagonal (say bd).

$$\text{Face diagonal} = fd$$
$$bd^2 = fd^2 + a^2$$
$$= a^2 + a^2 + a^2 = 3a^2$$

Atoms along the body diagonal (say bd) touch each other. Thus, the body diagonal has a length that is four times the radius of the atom, R.

$$bd = 4R$$

The relationship between a and R can be worked out by the Pythagorean theorem.

$$(4R)^2 = 3a^2$$

Thus,

$$4R = \sqrt{3}a$$

and

$$r = \dfrac{\sqrt{3}}{4} a$$

11. (b) atomic number of sulphur is higher than oxygen.

Explanation: An acid is a species which will donate its proton (H^+ ion). The compound which will donate its proton readily will be stronger or the more acidic compound. Therefore, among hydrogen sulphide (H_2S) and water (H_2O), the more acidic is the one which will release its proton readily. As we know that, oxygen is more electronegative than sulphur thus the H-O bond is stronger than the S-H bond. The energy required to break the S-H bond is lower than that of O-H bond, this energy is the bond dissociation energy which is lower for the S-H bond. Thus, oxygen atoms will not donate the proton readily and this will make it a weaker acid. On the other hand, sulphur atoms will donate the proton readily and this will make it a stronger acid.

12. (d) AAA

Explanation: Simple cubic lattice results from 3D close packing from 2D square-packed layers. When one 2D layer is placed on top of the other, the corresponding spheres of the second layer are exactly on top of the first one. Since both have the same, exact arrangement it is AAA type.

13. (c) Polonium

Explanation: Group 16 elements with their ns^2np^4 electron configurations, are two electrons short of a complete valence shell electronic configuration. Thus, in reactions with metals, they tend to acquire two additional electrons to form compounds in the −2 oxidation state. This tendency is greatest for oxygen, the group 16 element with the highest electronegativity. The heavier, less electronegative chalcogens can lose either four np electrons or four np and two ns electrons to form compounds in the +4 and +6 oxidation state, respectively. Also as in the other groups, the second and third members (Sulphur and selenium) have similar properties because of shielding effects. Only polonium forms ionic compounds in its II and IV oxidation states. The IV oxidation state is the common valence for polonium. Polonium only occasionally occurs in its II and rarely in its VI oxidation states.

14. (b) Interstitial

Explanation: Stainless steel is an interstitial alloy. Carbon atoms are introduced into interstitial spaces of iron lattice as an impurity.

15. (a) Fluorine

Explanation: Among the halogens, fluorine does not form an oxyacid due to high electronegativity and small size. Fluorine forms only one oxyacid, i.e. HOF, hypofluorous acid or fluoric acid.

16. (c) boil above 100°C and freeze below 0°C

Explanation: When a non-volatile solid is added to pure water it will boil above 100°C and freeze below 0°C . This can be explained by elevation in boiling point and depression in freezing point.

17. (c) Covalent solid

Explanation: The solids in which constituent particles are attached to each other by covalent bonds are called covalent solids. Diamond, graphite, silicon, SiC, AIN, quartz are examples of covalent solids.

18. (d) There will be no net movement across the membrane.

Explanation: If 0.1 M solution of glucose and 0.1 M urea solution are placed on two sides of a semipermeable membrane to equal heights, then there is no net movement of the solvent through the semipermeable membrane between two solution of equal concentration.

19. (b) $H_2SO_4 + SO_3$

> **Explanation:** The formula of oleum is $H_2SO_4 + SO_3$ and the structure of oleum is:
>
> $$HO-\overset{\overset{O}{\|}}{\underset{\underset{O}{\|}}{S}}-O-\overset{\overset{O}{\|}}{\underset{\underset{O}{\|}}{S}}-OH$$

20. (a) This is a crystalline solid.
   (c) This has definite heat of fusion

> **Explanation:** Quartz glass is the amorphous solid and thus it does not have the definite heat of fusion like that in the crystalline solids.

21. (d) dependent only on the identity of the solvent and the concentration of the solute and independent of the solute's identity.

> **Explanation:** Colligative properties is dependent only on the identity of the solvent and the concentration of the solute and independent of the solute's identity. Colligative properties include vapour pressure lowering, boiling point elevation, freezing point depression, and osmotic pressure.

22. (a) Magnesium

> **Explanation:** Grignard reagent is prepared with the reaction of alkyl halide with Magnesium in presence of dry ether.
>
> $$\text{RX} \quad + \quad \text{Mg} \qquad\qquad \text{RMgX}$$
> $$\text{Alkyl halide} \quad \text{Magnesium} \longrightarrow \text{Grignard reagent}$$
>
> Grignard is a very important reagent as it is used to form a variety of compounds. On reacting with alkyl halide it forms higher alkanes.

23. (d) PbS

> **Explanation:** PbS reagent does not give O_2 gas on reaction with Ozone.
> $$SnCl_2 + HCl + O_3 \rightarrow SnCl_4 + H_2O$$
> $$FeSO_4 + H_2SO_4 + O_3 \rightarrow Fe_2(SO_4)_3 + H_2O + O_2$$
> $$SO_2 + O_3 \rightarrow SO_3 + O_2$$
> $$Hg + O_3 \rightarrow HgO_2$$

24. (a) SiC (Silicon carbide)
   (b) AlN
   (c) Diamond

> **Explanation:** SiC, Al, N and Diamond are   the covalent or the network solids whereas I_2 is the non-polar molecular solid which is soft in nature while the others are hard in nature.

25. (a) A

> **Explanation:** The depression in freezing point can be given by the formula:
> $$\Delta T_f = T_f - T_f^0$$
> $$\Delta T_f = kfm$$
> $$T_f - T_f^0 = kfm$$
> where kf is the freezing point depression constant

From the above formula, it is clear that change in the freezing point is directly proportional to the net concentration. As the concentration will increase, the change in the freezing point will also increase. Thus, the order of freezing point will be in the order:

Sample A > Sample C > Sample B

Thus, juice in sample A will have the highest freezing point.

Section-B

26. (a) Fe

Explanation: Iron metal is present in haemoglobin. The heme group (a component of the hemoglobin protein) is a metal complex, with iron as the central metal atom, that can bind or release molecular oxygen.

27. (b) 2

Explanation: Dialkyl ethers when treated with excess halogen acid first forms an alkyl halide and alcohol. The alcohol further reacts with the excess acid to form the same alkyl halide and a water molecule. Thus, two alkyl halide molecules are produced in the end.

28. (d) Uracil

Explanation: DNA contains four bases namely adenine (A), guanine (G), cytosine (C) and thymine (T). RNA also contains four bases, A, T, G and uracil (U).

29. (c) Both (a) and (b)

Explanation: Crystalline solids are anisotropic in nature that is they have the different values of the physical properties such as refractive index and the electrical resistance.

30. (c) Thymine

Explanation: Bases are nitrogen containing heterocyclic compounds present in nucleic acids. Adenine has no keto group, guanine and cytosine have one keto group each and thymine and uracil have two keto groups in their rings.

31. (a) S_N1 reaction mechanism

Explanation: S_N1 reaction mechanism involves the formation of a carbocation intermediate. S_N1 reaction mechanism follows a step-by-step process wherein first, the carbocation is formed from the removal of the leaving group. Then the carbocation is attacked by the nucleophile. Finally, the deprotonation of the protonated nucleophile takes place to give the required product. The rate determining step of this reaction depends purely on the electrophilicity of the leaving group.

32. (a) β-D-ribose

Explanation: Nucleic acids are made up of units of pentose sugar, base and phosphoric acid that are linked together to form long chain. The sugar moiety in RNA is β-D-ribose.

33. (d) p-Bromoanisole

Explanation: Phenyl alkyl ethers undergo bromination in the benzene ring with bromine in ethanoic acid. This due to the activation of benzene ring by OCH_3 group and its ortho, para directing effect. The para isomer is obtained in 90% yield.

34. (d) all of the above

   Explanation: Colligative properties are the properties of the solutions which depend upon the number of solute particles present in the solution irrespective of their nature, relative to the total number of particles present in the solution. Examples: Relative lowering of vapour pressure of the solvent, depression of freezing point of the solvent, elevation of boiling point of the solvent, osmotic pressure of the solution.

35. (a) Slow step of the reaction.

   Explanation: Rate determining step is the slowest step within a chemical reaction. The slowest step determines the rate of chemical reaction. The slowest step of a chemical reaction can be determined by setting up a reaction mechanism.

36. (a) 2- Bromo-2-methylpropan-1-ol.

   Explanation: The IUPAC name of the below compound is 2- Bromo-2-methylpropan-1-ol.

37. (c) Adenine

   Explanation: There are two types of bases namely Purines and Pyrimidines. Adenine and Guanine are purine bases present in DNA but the pyrimidine base uracil is present in RNA whereas the base thymine is present in DNA. Thus adenine and Guanine are the derivatives of the purine bases.

38. (d) The fraction of octahedral or tetrahedral voids occupied depends upon the radii of the ions occupying the voids.

   Explanation: In ionic solids anions (which are normally longer in size than cations forms closed pack array. The cation occupies one of the two types of holes remaining between the anions (either tetrahedral void or octahedral void). Depending on the relative sizes of cations and anions, the voids are filled. Occupation of voids depends on the stoichiometry of the compounds. It is not necessary that all voids get filled.

39. (a) A-T, G-C

   Explanation: Adenine pairs with thymine with 2 hydrogen bonds. Guanine pairs with cytosine with 3 hydrogen bonds. Guanine and cytosine bonded base pairs are stronger than thymine and adenine bonded base pairs in DNA.

40. (b) Allylic alcohol

   Explanation: The compound shown is a monohydric, tertiary alcohol in which the OH group is attached to the C next to a C-C double bond, hence make it allylic.

41. (d) Antiseptic

   Explanation: Methylene chloride can harm the human central nervous system and application on the skin may result in intense burning and redness. Therefore, methylene chloride cannot be used as an antiseptic.

42. (a) Ether

> **Explanation:** Ethers are compounds where the hydrogen of a hydrocarbon is replaced by an alkoxy or aryloxy group. It may also be thought of as compounds formed when the hydrogen of the OH group of an alcohol is replaced by an alkyl or aryl group.

43. (b) It should have two or more OH groups

> **Explanation:** Alcohols may be classified as mono-, di- tri- or polyhydric depending on whether it has one, two, three or more OH groups in its structure. Di- and trihydric alcohols are also classified as polyhydric.

44. (b) ortho and para

> **Explanation:** When excess halogen is used, the second halogen also gets incorporated into the aromatic ring at ortho and para positions with respect to the first halogen. This is because the CH_3 group in toluene is ortho and para directing.

45. (c) A is true but R is false.

> **Explanation:** The primary structure of protein is the sequence of amino acids in a chain, *i.e.*, the positional information in a protein. In the secondary structure protein thread is folded in the form of a helix or in the sheet form. The long protein chain is also folded upon itself like a hollow woollen bell, giving rise to the tertiary structure. This gives us a 3-dimensional view of a protein. Tertiary structure is absolutely necessary for many biological activities of proteins. Thus Assertion is true but reason is false statement.

46. (c) A is true but R is false.

> **Explanation:** The solution with large positive deviation from Raoult's law form minimum boiling azeotropes and the boiling point of aqueous solution of ethanol is lower than the water molecules, so it forms minimum boiling azeotrope. Thus Assertion is true but reason is false statement.

47. (d) A is false but R is true.

> **Explanation:** F_2 is more reactive than other halogens because its valence electrons are more closer to nucleus and its more electronegative so, bonded electrons repel each other causing low bond dissociation enthalpy. Thus assertion is false, but reason is true.

48. (b) Both A and R are true but R is not the correct explanation of A.

> **Explanation:** Ozone layer filters the radiation coming from sun, hence serves as the protective layer. Thus both assertion and reason are true but reason is not the correct explanation of assertion.

49. (b) Both A and R are true but R is not the correct explanation of A.

> **Explanation:** Gases and liquids are called fluids because they have the tendency to flow since the particles of the atom are loosely bound to each other in the crystal lattice of the liquids and gases. Thus Assertion and reason both are true but reason is not the correct explanation for assertion.

Section-C

50. (b) R-OH

> **Explanation:** Alcohols are compounds having OH group attached to an alkyl group and are hence hydroxy derivatives of hydrocarbons.

51. (a) *n*-Hexane

> **Explanation:** Glucose on prolonged heating with the HI gives the *n*-hexane and *n*- hexane has 6 carbon atoms connected with each other in the straight chain thus this concludes that all the 6 carbon atoms in the glucose molecule are also connected linearly in the form of a straight chain.

52. (a) Iodobenzene is formed

> **Explanation:** when a solution of benzene diazonium bromide and an aqueous solution potassium iodide are shaken together, iodobenzene is obtained. Diazonium group is replaced withiodo (−I) group.
>
> $$C_6H_5 - N_2^+ \, Cl^- + KI \xrightarrow{\Delta} C_6H_5 - I + N_2\uparrow + KCl$$

53. (a) S–S > O–O

> **Explanation:** Electron gain enthalpy is the amount of energy released when an element accepts an electron. The process is endothermic. Lesser the electronic repulsion faced by an electron to get occupied in the outermost shell higher the amount of energy released. On moving down the group, the electron gain enthalpy decreases from S to Po. Oxygen has an unexpectedly low value of electron gain enthalpy. Since oxygen is smaller in size than S, so incoming electron on oxygen faces more electronic repulsion on oxygen outermost surface due to more electron density as a result electron affinity decreases.The increasing order of electron gain enthalpy with negative sign is
>
> O(−141.4kJ/mol) < Po(−174kJ/mol) < Te(−190.0kJ/mol) < Se(−195.5kJ/mol) < S(−208.8kJ/mol)
>
> Thus, the bond enthalpy terms in group 16 follows the following trend:
> S–S > O–O

54. (b) Pure liquid H_2SO_4 is viscous because of intramolecular hydrogen bonding.

> **Explanation:** Pure liquid H_2SO_4 is a clear liquid like oil and has high viscosity because of extensive hydrogen bonding. It is an unsymmetrical molecule and so, has a permanent dipole and the hydrogens attached to oxygen has hydrogen bonding. Hence, the incorrect statement about sulphuric acid is that Pure liquid H_2SO_4 is viscous because of intramolecular hydrogen bonding.

55. (c) $H_2O > H_2Te > H_2Se > H_2S$

> **Explanation:** Among hydrides of group 16 elements, with the increase in molecular weight, van der Waal's forces increase so boiling point also increases. However, H_2O unexpectedly has highest boiling point due to presence of hydrogen bonding. Hence, the correct order of boiling point among hydrides of group 16 elements is:
> $$H_2O > H_2Te > H_2Se > H_2S$$

Sample Paper 5

Section-A

1. (d) Raoult's law.

> **Explanation:** According to Raoult's law, when a non-volatile solid is added to the solvent its vapour pressure decreases and it would become equal to that of solid solvent at lower temperature. Thus, the freezing point of the solvent decreases. Let T_f° be freezing point of pure solvent.
> T_f be freezing point of solution. Then, increase in freezing point
> $$\Delta T_f = T_f - T_f^{\circ}$$

ΔT_f know as depression of freezing point. By experiments we know

$$\Rightarrow \qquad \Delta T_f = K_f m$$
$$T_f - T_f^\circ = K_f m$$

Where, $\qquad\qquad K_f$ = freezing point depression constant.

2. (b) Wurtz coupling reaction

Explanation: The Wurtz reaction is a coupling reaction in which two alkyl halides are reacted with sodium metal in dry ether solution to form a higher alkane:

$$2RX + 2Na \; R - R + 2Na^+ X^-$$

3. (c) Reduction of aldehyde/ketones with Zn-Hg/HCl

Explanation: Reduction of aldehydes and ketones with Zn(Hg)/HCl yields alkanes – (Clemmensen reduction). Clemmensen reduction is a chemical reaction described as a reduction of ketones (or aldehydes) to alkanes using zinc amalgam and concentrated hydrochloric acid. The substrate must be tolerant of the strongly acidic conditions of the Clemmensen reduction (37% HCl).

4. (b) Sulphur

Explanation: Catenation is the property of forming bond with a maximum number of atoms. In group sixteen elements, sulphur has maximum catenation property because of high bonding energy of sulphur atoms. Its electronegativity is close to that of carbon, which helps easy bonding with many atoms.

5. (b) 12

Explanation: The number of spheres which are touching a given sphere is said to be coordination number. As copper has face-centered cubic structure, any atom present in this lattice touches 12 other atoms. Hence the co-ordination number of each ion is 12.

6. (b) H_2Te

Explanation: All these are the hydrides of 16th group elements in which the central atom undergo sp^3 hybridization and should possess the bond angle 109° but the bond angle distorts due to the repulsion between lone pair and lone pair. But this repulsion is minimum in H_2Te as the tellurium has large size which makes the repulsion minimum.

7. (d) Chloral

Explanation: When chlorine reacts with ethanol in the presence of NaOH, Chloral is obtained as a final product.

$$3Cl + C_2H_5OH \xrightarrow{\text{NaOH}} C_2HCl_3O$$
$$\text{(Chloral)}$$

8. (b) Intramolecular dehydrohalogenation

Explanation: In ethyl alcohol, the attacking species is the ethoxide anion, which is a much stronger base than the hydroxide anion, so it directly extracts the beta hydrogen from ethyl bromide, followed by elimination of the bromide anion from the adjacent carbon atom to form ethene. Thus it is an example of intramolecular dehydrohalogenation.

9. (a) Fluorine.

Explanation: Fluorine is the most powerful oxidising agent because it is the most electronegative element. Electronegative elements have the property to remove electrons form the elements to which, it is attached.

10. (b) Intramolecular dehydrohalogenation

Explanation: In ethyl alcohol, the attacking species is the ethoxide anion, which is a much stronger base than the hydroxide anion, so it directly extracts the beta hydrogen from ethyl bromide, followed by elimination of the bromide anion from the adjacent carbon atom to form ethene. Thus it is an example of intramolecular dehydrohalogenation.

11. (c) 6

Explanation: A cubic unit cell has six faces. Therefore, in a cubic lattice irrespective of its nature, a cubic unit cell is shared equally by 6 unit cells.

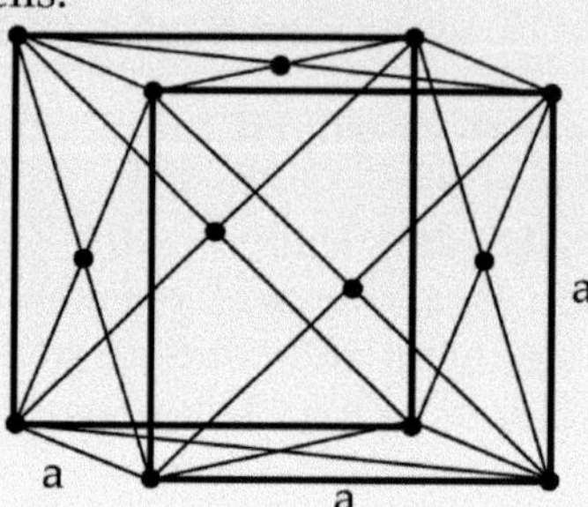

12. (a) Propanol

Explanation: The hydroboration oxidation reaction is shown.

$$CH_3-CH=CH_2 + (H-BH_2)_2 \longrightarrow CH_3-\underset{\underset{H}{|}}{CH}-\underset{\underset{BH_2}{|}}{CH_2}$$

Propene   Diborane

$$\downarrow CH_3-CH=CH_2$$

$$(CH_3-CH_2-CH_2)_3B \xleftarrow{CH_3-CH=CH_2} (CH_3-CH_2-CH_2)_2BH$$

$$\underset{H_2O}{\Big|}\ 3H_2O_2,OH \downarrow$$

$$3CH_3-CH_2-CH_2-OH + B(OH)_3$$

Propan–1–ol

13. (b) $[Xe]4f^{14}\,5d^{10}\,6s^2\,6p^5$

Explanation: The electronic configuration of Bismuth is $[Xe]4f^{14}\,5d^{10}\,6s^2\,6p^5$

14. (a) Kelvin kg mol^{-1}

Explanation: The constant which is involved in relating the molality with the freezing point of depression is called as cryoscopic constant. It is the ratio of freezing point of depression to that of molality. It is used to determine the freezing point depression which occur while addition of appropriate amount of non-volatile solute to appropriate amount of solvent. It is expressed in unit called K. Kg. mol^{-1}.

15. (a, c) (a) Pseudo solids and (c) Super cooled liquids

Explanation: Amorphous solids are called pseudo solids because they are not true solids and they are called as super cooled liquids because the amorphous solids have the tendency to flow due to this property of fluidity they are called pseudo solids and super cooled liquids.

16. (b) n-butyl chloride

Explanation: The compound $CH_3CH_2CH_2CH_2Cl$ is 1-Chlorobutane, it has 4 C atoms in the parent chain and the only halogen compound present at the end of the chain. This type of structure has the prefix n- in the common name. Thus, the common name of the given compound is *n*-butyl chloride.

17. (a) atomic size increases gradually

> **Explanation:** On moving down the group 15, ionization enthalpy decreases due to gradual increase in atomic size. As the atomic size increases, the outermost electron get increasingly farther from the nucleus and there is an increased shielding of the nuclear charge by the electrons in the inner levels. As a result, ionisation enthalpy decreases down the group.

18. (d) Nature of solvent

> **Explanation:** Molal elevation constant or ebullioscopic constant is defined as the elevation in boiling point when one mole of non-volatile solute is added to one kilogram of solvent. Ebullioscopic constant (Eb) is the constant that expresses the amount by which the boiling point T_b of a solvent is raised by a non-dissociating solute. Its units are K Kg mol^{-1}.
>
> $$\Delta T_b = E_b b$$
>
> b = molality of the solute.
>
> The value of ebullioscopic constant or boiling point elevation constant does not depend on nature of solvent.

19. (d) Vinylic alcohols

> **Explanation:** Allylic alcohols are those in which OH group is attached to a sp^3 hybridised carbon adjacent to a C-C double bond, i.e., an allylic carbon. Whereas, vinylic alcohols contain OH group attached directly to a C-C double bond.

20. (d) N

> **Explanation:** Element nitrogen have a unique property to form $p\pi$-$p\pi$ multiple bonds with itself. In diatomic: $N \equiv N$:, 1 bond is sigma and the remaining 2 bonds are $P\pi$–$P\pi$ bonds.
>
> Other elements of group 15 do not form $P\pi$–$P\pi$ multiple bonds due to repulsion between non bonded electrons of the inner core and size. There is no such repulsion in case of smaller nitrogen atoms as they have only $1s$ 2 electrons in their inner core and hence, their p orbitals easily overlap to form $P\pi$–$P\pi$ multiple bonds.

21. (a) Gluconic acid

> **Explanation:** Glucose gets oxidised to six carbon carboxylic acid on reaction with a mild oxidising agent like bromine water. This indicates that the carbonyl group is present as an aldehydic group.

22. (a) 4

> **Explanation:** In square close-packed layer, a molecule is in contact with four of its neighbours. Therefore, the two-dimensional coordination number of a molecule in square close-packed layer is 4 as it is occupied by 4 neighbouring atoms.

23. (b) E_2O_3 and E_2O_5

> **Explanation:** The types of oxides formed by nitrogen family elements are E_2O_3 and E_2O_5. The oxide in the higher oxidation state (+5) of the element is more acidic than that of lower oxidation state (+3) which means N_2O_5 is more acidic than N_2O_3.

24. (c) Both i and ii

> **Explanation:** Colligative property depends upon number of particles of solute present in the solution which in turn depends on the number of the moles and the relative lowering of vapour pressure of a solution is equal to the mole fraction of the non-volatile and non-electrolyte solute present in the solution.

25. (a) acidification

> **Explanation:** When halobenzene is fused with NaOH at 623 K and 320 atm with a copper salt as catalyst, sodium phenoxide is produced which on treatment with dilute HCl yields phenol. This is also known as Dow's process.

Section-B

26. (c) NH_3

> **Explanation:** The electrophilic substitution of arenes requires the presence of a Lewis acid catalyst which acts as a halogen carrier. NH_3 is a Lewis base.

27. (c) phenol and acetone

> **Explanation:** When cumene hydroperoxide is hydrolysed with a solution of dilute acid, it results in the formation of phenol and acetone, of which the latter is obtained in large quantities.

28. (b) X_4Y_3

> **Explanation:** Y occupies CCP lattice, hence the effective number of atoms of Y in CCP is 4
> X occupies 2/3 of tetrahedral voids. Number of tetrahedral voids generated in any unit cell is $= 2Z$ (twice of an effective number of atoms in unit cell) $= 2 \times 4 = 8$
>
> Since X occupies 2/3 of tetrahedra voids, so effective number of $X = \dfrac{2}{3} \times 8 = \dfrac{16}{3}$
>
> So $X = \dfrac{16}{3}$ and $Y = 4$.
>
> Hence simplest formula is X_4Y_3.

29. (a) Ether linkage

> **Explanation:** A glycosidic linkage is a type of covalent bond that joins a carbohydrate (sugar) molecule to another group, which may or may not be another carbohydrate. In other words, the linkage between two monosaccharide units through oxygen atom is called glycosidic linkage and the ether bond is when more than two hydrocarbons are linked by a single bond to an oxygen. Hence, glycosidic bond is an ether bond.

30. (b) Reverse osmosis

> **Explanation:** Reverse osmosis (RO) is a water purification process that uses a partially permeable membrane to remove ions, unwanted molecules and larger particles from drinking water. In the process of reverse osmosis, an applied pressure is used to overcome osmotic pressure, that is driven by chemical potential differences of the solvent, a thermodynamic parameter. Reverse osmosis can remove many types of dissolved and suspended chemical species as well as biological ones such as bacteria from water, and is used in both industrial processes and the production of potable water.

31. (b) Preparing an aqueous solution and warming it

> **Explanation:** Carbolic acid is another name for phenol. Simply warming an aqueous solution of benzene diazonium chloride salt or treating it with a dilute acid, will result in the formation of phenol.

32. (a) barium azide

> **Explanation:** Very pure nitrogen can be obtained by thermal decomposition of sodium barium azide. The reaction is as follows:
>
> $$Ba(N_3)_2 \longrightarrow Ba + 3N_2$$
>
> Barium azide $\qquad\qquad$ Nitrogen

33. (d) Haemoglobin

> **Explanation:** Haemoglobin is the complex globular protein made up of globules structure of 4 sub units.

34. (b) Sodium formate

> **Explanation:** The reaction of chloroform with aqueous NaOH solution to form the sodium formate is shown below:
>
> $$CHCl_3 + 2NaOH \rightarrow CH(OH)_3 \xrightarrow{-H_2O} HCOOH \xrightarrow{NaOH} HCOONa$$

35. (c) Fibroin

> **Explanation:** Fibroin has the sheet like structure made up of long chain of polypeptide chains thus it is a fibrous protein.

36. (c) Conc. HCl and conc. HNO_3 in the ratio of $3:1$

> **Explanation:** Aqua regia is a mixture of nitric acid and hydrochloric acid, optimally in a molar ratio of 1:3. Aqua regia is a yellow-orange (sometimes red) fuming liquid, so named by all chemists because it can dissolve the noble metals gold and platinum, though not all metals.

37. (b) 4

> **Explanation:** The factors on which the colligative properties depend are:
> 1. Concentration of the solute
> 2. Temperature
> 3. Number of the particles of the solute
> 4. Association or dissociation of the electrolytic solute.

38. (a) Thymine

> **Explanation:** There are two types of bases namely Purines and Pyrimidines. Adenine and Guanine are the purine bases present in DNA but the pyrimidine base uracil is present in RNA whereas the base thymine is present in DNA.

39. (a) $C_6H_5C(CH_3)C_6H_5Br$

> **Explanation:** The tertiary carbocation intermediate obtained from $C_6H_5C(CH_3)C_6H_5Br$ is the most stable that is obtained from because it is stablised by two phenyl group due to resonance and an electron donating methyl group.

40. (a) Hg_2O

> **Explanation:** The tailing of mercury is the reaction of mercury with ozone due to which mercury loses its meniscus and it starts sticking to the walls of the thermometer due to the formation of the mercurous oxide. The meniscus can be restored by shaking with water. The tailing of mercury on exposure to air shows a change in oxidation number by one. The reaction is as follows:
>
> $$2Hg + O_3 \rightarrow Hg_2O + O_2$$

41. (b) By heating with aqueous NaOH

> **Explanation:** Haloalkanes when heated with aqueous NaOH or KOH gives respective alcohols. This is a nucleophilic substitution reaction where the halide group is replaced by the OH nucleophile.

42. (d) Solutes that associate in water have molar mass higher than the molar mass of the solute calculated theoretically.

> **Explanation:** The molecular mass of the solute is inversely proportional to its colligative properties. Therefore, the solutes that associate in water have molar mass higher than the molar mass of the solute calculated theoretically.

43. (b) Wurtz-Fittig reaction

> **Explanation:** In the Wurtz-Fittig reaction chlorobenzene is treated with Na in dry ether to form diphenyl.
>
> 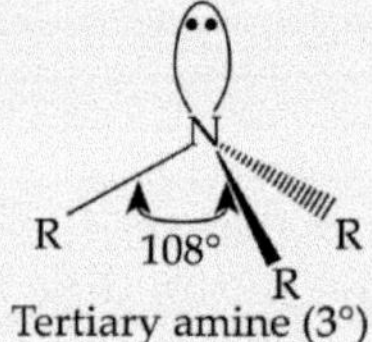
>
> $$2Na + R\text{–}I + Br\text{–}\langle\bigcirc\rangle \longrightarrow R\text{–}\langle\bigcirc\rangle + NaBr + NaI$$
>
> Where R is the alkyl group.

44. (d) Free radical halogenation of alkanes

> **Explanation:** Alkanes on free radical halogenation produce a mixture of haloalkanes and not alcohols. Alcohols can be prepared from alkenes by acid catalysed hydration and hydroboration-oxidation or from reduction of aldehydes.

45. (a) Both A and R are true and R is the correct explanation of A.

> **Explanation:** Tertiary nitro alkanes cannot tautomerize because they do not have a labile hydrogen atom, which is a necessary condition for tautomerization. Thus both assertion and reason are true and reason is the correct explanation of the assertion.
>
> R   108°   R
> R
> Tertiary amine (3°)

46. (b) Both A and R are true but R is not the correct explanation of A.

> **Explanation:**
>
> $$M = \frac{\text{Moles of solute}}{\text{Volume of solution (litres)}}$$
>
> $$\text{Molality} = \frac{\text{Moles of solute}}{\text{Mass of solvent (kg)}}$$
>
> 1 molar aqueous solution is more concentrated than 1 molal aqueous solution because 1 molar solution contain 1 mole solute in 1 litre solution which include both solute and solvent. So, the mass of the solvent is less than 1000g. Therefore, 1 molar aqueous solution contain 1 mole of solute in less than 1000 g of solvent while. 1 molal solution has 1 mole of solute in 1000 gram of solvent. Hence concentration will be more in 1 molar solution.
>
> Also, molarity is a functon of temperature as volume depends upon temperature.
>
> Ex. Osmotic pressure equation $\pi = CRT$
>
> $C \propto \dfrac{1}{T}$ where C is concentration
>
> Thus both assertion and reason are true but reason is not the correct explanation of the assertion.

47. **(a)** Both A and R are true and R is the correct explanation of A.

Explanation: In vapour state S exists as S_2 and it behaves like O_2. It has 2 unpaired electrons in antibonding pi orbitals. Presence of these unpaired electrons make S paramagnetic. Thus both assertion and reason are true and reason is the correct explanation of assertion.

48. **(b)** Both A and R are true but R is not the correct explanation of A.

Explanation: As F_2 has low bond dissociation energy and high hydration energy than Cl_2 but less electron gain enthalpy due to its smaller size. Due to these factors F_2 wins in getting reduced fastly. Thus both assertion and reason are true and reason is not the correct explanation of assertion.

49. **(a)** Both A and R are true and R is the correct explanation of A.

Explanation: It could be the movement of water (osmosis), or other (diffusion). If a cell is placed in an isotonic solution, which means the amount of stuff inside the cell and outside the cell is equal. There will be some movement of water and salt across the cell membrane, but there will be no net concentration change. Thus both assertion and reason are true and reason is the correct explanation of the assertion.

Section-C

50. **(b)** $H_2SO_4 + SO_3$

Explanation: Oleum is produced in the contact process, where sulphur is oxidised to sulphur trioxide which is subsequently dissolved in concentrated sulphuric acid. Sulphuric acid itself is regenerated by dilution of part of the oleum. Sulphur trioxide produced by the contact process is absorbed in concentrated sulphuric acid.

51. **(d)** Glucose

Explanation: Glucose is aldohexose since it contains 6 carbon atoms.

52. **(a)** Condensation

Explanation: Glucose on treatment with NH_2OH undergoes condensation reaction as it leads to the formation of an oxime with the release of water molecule. During the reaction, the aldehyde group of glucose reacts with hydroxylamine to form $CH = NOH$ group known as the oxime group.

$$
\begin{array}{ccc}
\begin{array}{l}
CH{=}NOH \\
\mid \\
H{-}C{-}OH \\
\mid \\
HO{-}C{-}H \\
\mid \\
H{-}C{-}OH \\
\mid \\
H{-}C{-}OH \\
\mid \\
CH_2OH \\
D(+)\ glucose
\end{array}
& + NH_2OH \longrightarrow &
\begin{array}{l}
CH{=}NOH \\
\mid \\
H{-}C{-}OH \\
\mid \\
HO{-}C{-}H \\
\mid \\
H{-}C{-}OH \\
\mid \\
H{-}C{-}OH \\
\mid \\
CH_2OH \\
Oxime
\end{array}
\quad + H_2O
\end{array}
$$

53. **(c)** X_2YO_3

Explanation: The cations 'X' occupy 1/3rd of octahedral voids and the cations 'Y' occupy 1/3rd of tetrahedral voids.

The effective number of oxide ions = 4

Using formula to calculate the effective number of cations X

Effective number of cations $X = \dfrac{1}{3} \times$ Number of octahedral voids

Effective number of cations $X = \dfrac{1}{3} \times 8$

Effective number of cations $X = \dfrac{8}{3}$

Using formula of calculate the effective number of cations Y

Effective number of cations $Y = \dfrac{1}{3} \times$ Number of tetrahedral voids

Effective number of cations $Y = \dfrac{1}{3} \times 4$

Effective number of cations $Y = \dfrac{4}{3}$

Hence, the formula of the compound will be X_2YO_3.

54. (b) 335 pm

Explanation: The distance between them would be:

$$2r = \sqrt{(3)} \times \dfrac{a}{2}$$

$$2r = 387 \times \dfrac{\sqrt{3}}{2} = 335 \text{ pm approximately}$$

Hence, the distance between the two opposite charges would be 335 pm.

55. (a) 32%

Explanation: Packing fraction = $\dfrac{\text{volume occupied by atoms in a unit cell}}{\text{volume of the unit cell}}$

For bcc,

$$\text{Packing fraction} = \dfrac{2 \times \dfrac{4}{3}\pi r^3}{\left(\dfrac{4r}{\sqrt{3}}\right)^3} = \dfrac{\sqrt{3}\neq}{8} = 0.68$$

Volume occupied = 68%
Volume vacant = 100 − 68 = 32%
Hence, the percentrage of free space in a body centred cubic unit cell is 32%.

Sample Paper 6

Section-A

1. (d) Combination of vacancy and interstitial defects

Explabtion: Non-stoichiometric defect is the defect that causes the ratio of the number of cations to anions to be different from that indicated by the ideal chemical formula. Such defects are of two types: Metal excess defects and metal deficiency defects. Metal excess defect is caused by anionic vacancies and extra cations in the interstitial sites whereas metal deficiency defect is caused by cationic vacancies and extra anions in the interstitial sites. Thus, Combination of vacancy and interstitial defects cannot be called as non-stoichiometric defect.

2. (b) Henry's law.

> **Explanation:** Henry's law states that at a constant temperature, the solubility of a gas is directly proportional to the pressure of the gas. In other words, the partial pressure of the gas in vapour phase (p) is proportional to the mole fraction of the gas (x) in the solution.
>
> $$p = K_H \, x$$
>
> Where K_H is the Henry's law constant.
> Hence, the given statement is Henry's law.

3. (c) O_3

> **Explanation:** The ozone layer or ozone shield is a region of Earth's stratosphere that absorbs most of the sun's ultraviolet radiation. It contains a high concentration of ozone (O_3) in relation to other parts of the atmosphere, although still small in relation to other gases in the stratosphere.

4. (c) NaCl

> **Explanation:** Alkyl Chloride is an ionic compound which cannot displace –OH group by Cl. Rest all other reagents (HCl + $ZnCl_2$, $SOCl_2$, PCl_5) displaces –OH from alcohol and provide Cl.

5. (b) Stomach

> **Explanation:** Denaturation involves the breaking of many of the weak linkages, or bonds (e.g., hydrogen bonds), within a protein molecule that are responsible for the highly ordered structure of the protein in its natural (native) state. Denatured proteins have a looser, more random structure and are insoluble in nature the denaturation of proteins takes place in the stomach.

6. (c) H_3O^+

> **Explanation:** The water reacts with the H^+ ion of the mineral acid to form a hydronium ion (H_3O^+). This ion attacks the carbon double bond to form a carbocation and give a water molecule.

7. (b) Optical isomers

> **Explanation:** An optically active compounds exists in two isomeric forms that rotate the plane polarized light in opposite directions. They are called optical isomers and the phenomena is called optical isomerism. Optical isomers have the same physical properties such as Melting point, boiling point, density etc.

8. (b) Propan-2-ol

> **Explanation:** Since propene is an unsymmetrical alkene, the given hydration reaction takes place in accordance to Markovnikov's rule, to form propan-2-ol. The double bond is broken and the OH group attaches at the second carbon.

9. (c) Both (a) and (b)

> **Explanation:** Crystalline solids are anisotropic in nature, that is, some of their physical properties like electrical resistance or refractive index show different values when measured along different directions in the same crystals. This arises from different arrangement of particles in different directions. Since the arrangement of particles is different along different directions, the value of the same physical property is found to be different along each direction.

10. (a) H_2O

> **Explanation:** H_2S is the effective reducing agent. Reducing agent is the one which reduce the oxidizing agent. It becomes H_2SO_4 after receiving oxygen atoms.

11. (c) Uracil

> **Explanation:** DNA contains the deoxyribose sugar whereas RNA contains the Ribose sugar. All the purine bases Adenine and Guanine are same in both DNA and RNA while the pyrimidine base cytosine and thymine are present in DNA and uracil is present in RNA instead of the thymine as a pyrimidine base.

12. (c) Methanamine (CH_3NH_2)

> **Explanation:** Primary amine is obtained as a major product by taking large excess of ammonia.
> $$CH_3Cl + NH_3 \rightarrow CH_3NH_2 + HCl$$

13. (a) Fluidity

> **Explanation:** Solids do not have the property to flow that is they do not flow since the intermolecular forces between the solids are strong and the particles of the constituent are tightly packed.

14. (b) Size decreases

> **Explanation:** The size of the atoms of the elements decrease from left to right in the same period. Considering the row to be the same, the electrons are added to the same shell. However, the increase in atomic number reflects the increase in number of protons i.e. the positive charge. Hence, the overall effective nuclear charge increases. Consequently, the electron cloud is pulled even closer to the nucleus of the atom. Therefore, the size decreases.

15. (a) HCl

> **Explanation:** Alkenes react with water in the presence of a mineral acid as a catalyst to form alcohols. The H^+ ion from the acid helps to form a carbocation for nucleophilic attack.

16. (a) Fluorine

> **Explanation:** Fluorine does not form any oxy-acid. An oxyacid, oxoacid, or ternary acid is an acid that contains oxygen. Specifically, it is a compound that contains hydrogen, oxygen and at least one other element, with at least one hydrogen atom bonded to oxygen that can dissociate to produce the H^+ cation and the anion of the acid.

17. (c) Alcoholic KOH, chloroform and primary amine

> **Explanation:** Aliphatic and aromatic primary amines on heating with CCl_4 and alcoholic potassium hydroxide (alc. KOH) gives alkyl isocyanides or carbylamines. So, Carbylamine test is performed in alcoholic KOH by heating a mixture of chloroform and primary amine.

18. (a) Frenkel defect.

> **Explanation:** Frenkel defect is not found in the pure alkali metal halides because this defect is due to vacancy of ion, which is shifted in interstitial spaces and because the ions are too large and cannot get into interstitial sites.

19. (d) Glucose

> **Explanation:** Aldohexoses have four chiral centers because of that there are 16 possible stereoisomers. Examples of aldohexoses are glucose, mannose, galactose, etc. Glucose is a one of the products of photosynthesis in plants and other photosynthetic organisms. It also serves as an important metabolic intermediate of cellular respiration.

20. (b) Sodium formate

> **Explanation:** Chloroform when heated with aqueous solution of caustic soda, first it produces formic acid which reacts further and forms sodium formate.
>
> $$CHCl_3 + 3NaOH \rightarrow CH(OH)_3 \xrightarrow{-H_2O} HCOOH \xrightarrow{NaOH} HCOONa$$

21. (b) False

> **Explanation:** When we correlate molar mass with osmotic pressure as a colligative property, we sometimes encounter a situation where the calculated molar mass of the solute is either higher or lower than the actual molar mass. This is called the abnormal molar mass. Abnormal molar mass occurs as a result of dissociation or association of molecules. Thus, the statement "Only if the calculated molar mass is higher than the actual molar mass of the solute, the calculated molar mass is considered to be abnormal molar mass."

22. (b) Peptide linkage

> **Explanation:** Peptide linkage is the peptide bond formed between the amino acids. It is a covalent bond formed between amino group of one molecule and carboxylic acid group of another molecule. The primary structure of a peptide or protein is the linear sequence of its amino acid structural units. The primary structure of a protein is reported starting from the amino-terminal (N) end to the carboxyl-terminal (C) end.

23. (a) Paramagnetic

> **Explanation:** According to molecular orbital Theory (MOT), there is 1 unpaired electron in the $\pi^2 px$ anti-bonding orbital and another unpaired electron in $\pi^2 py$ anti-bonding orbital. As molecules containing unpaired electrons are strongly attracted by magnetic field, hence oxygen has paramagnetic nature. Unpaired electrons spin in the same direction of each other which increases magnetic field effect.

24. (c) Force of attraction between two liquids is smaller than that between individual liquid.

> **Explanation:** The solutions that follow Raoult's law are known as ideal solutions. The enthalpy and volume of mixing are zero. The solutions undergoing mixing do not show any kind of interactions. But those solutions that show deviations from Raoult's law have weaker intermolecular forces of attraction between the two liquids than between individual liquids. Such liquid solutions have weaker bonds and solutions exhibit higher vapour pressure than the vapour pressure of individual liquids. Such kinds of solutions absorb heat while getting mixed and the enthalpy of the mixing is endothermic. They have low boiling points. An example of such a solution is acetone and benzene. Thus, positive deviation from Raoult's law is observed when force of attraction between two liquids is smaller than that between individual liquid.

25. (c) Polyhydroxy ketones

> **Explanation:** Polyamino aldehydes and polyhalo aldehydes do not contain an OH group. Polyhydroxy carboxylic acids do not contain a CHO or a keto group. These also do not produce OH substituted compounds on hydrolysis.

Section-B

26. (a) H_2O

> **Explanation:** H_2O has lowest reducing character. Water is an inorganic, transparent tasteless, odourless and nearly colourless chemical substance, which is the main constituent of Earth's hydrosphere and the fluids of all known living organisms in which it acts as a solvent. It is vital for all known forms of life, even though it provides no calories or organic nutrients. It's chemical formula is H_2O.

27. (b) CH_3CH_2I

> **Explanation:** The melting and boiling points of molecular compounds are generally quite low compared to those of ionic compounds. Ionic solids typically melt at high temperatures and boil at even higher temperatures. For example, sodium chloride melts at 801°C and boils at 1413°C. So in this case CH_3CH_2I will react most readily by nucleophilic substitution

28. (a) Propanol

> **Explanation:** Propanol is most soluble in water because the lower alcohols are highly soluble in water due to the presence of –OH group in the alcohols it forms H-bond with itself and molecular association takes place which causes the increase in the boiling point of the corresponding alcohols due to the increase in the number of carbon atoms and therefore high temperature is required to break this association of bonds and thus the solubility in water increases.

29. (b) N

> **Explanation:** The atom in octahedral void is in contact with 6 neighbouring atom. If the number of close packed sphere be N, then the number of octahedral void generated will be N.

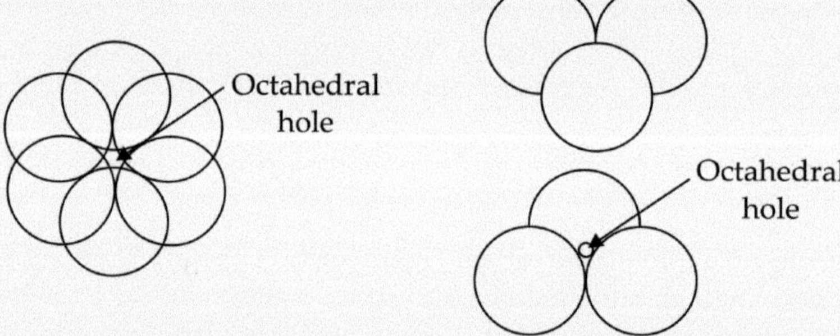

30. (a) α-D-glucose

> **Explanation:** Maltose is also known as malt sugar. It is a disaccharide, made up of two D - glucose units. The two units of glucose are linked with an alpha 1,4 glycosidic bond. Maltose dissociates it into its monosaccharide after hydrolysis. Using the hydrolysis reaction of maltose we can determine the products.

31. (c) $BrO_4^- > IO_4^- > ClO_4^-$

> **Explanation:** The reduction potential of the substance is the ability of the substance to be reduced. So as the reduction potential increases reducing ability of the substance increases. It means oxidizing power of the substance (The ability of the substance to make the other substance to lose the electrons increases which noting but oxidizing power) increases. So the decreasing order of oxidizing power is $BrO_4^- > IO_4^- > ClO_4^-$.

32. (a) Benzene 1, 4 –diol

> **Explanation:** The International Union of Pure and Applied Chemistry (IUPAC) have given certain rules to name the organic compounds known as the nomenclature system. It is a set of logical rules devised to circumvent problems caused by arbitrary nomenclature.

33. (b) Henry's law

> **Explanation:** Henry's law states that at a constant temperature, the solubility of a gas is directly proportional to the pressure of the gas. In other words, the partial pressure of the gas in vapour phase (p) is proportional to the mole fraction of the gas (x) in the solution.

$$p = K_H x$$

Here, K_H is the Henry's law constant.

Hence, the given statement is Henry's law.

34. (b) 3-Bromopentane

Explanation:

$$\overset{5}{H_3C}H_2\overset{4}{C}-\overset{3}{\underset{|}{C}}H-\overset{2}{C}H_2\overset{1}{C}H_3$$

with Br attached to carbon 3.

35. (d) Cellulose

Explanation: Glucose, fructose and lactose are examples of compounds that are sweet in taste and are called sugars. Cellulose is a non-sugar that is tasteless, water insoluble and amorphous.

36. (a) 68%

Explanation: The packing efficiency of the BCC crystal lattice is 68% with the empty space of 32% in the crystal lattice.

37. (b) It should have two or more OH groups

Explanation: Alcohols may be classified as mono-, di- tri- or polyhydric depending on whether it has one, two, three or more OH groups in its structure. Di- and trihydric alcohols are also classified as polyhydric.

38. (b) Intramolecular dehydrohalogenation

Explanation: In ethyl alcohol, the attacking species is the ethoxide anion, which is a much stronger base than the hydroxide anion, so it directly extracts the beta hydrogen from ethyl bromide, followed by elimination of the bromide anion from the adjacent carbon atom to form ethene. So, it is an example of Intramolecular dehydrohalogenation.

39. (c) Disproportionation reaction

Explanation: The reaction $3ClO^- (aq) \rightarrow ClO_3^- (aq) + 2Cl^- (aq.)$ is an example of disproportionation reaction. In this reaction, chlorine is oxidized as well as reduced. The oxidation states of chlorine in ClO^- (aq), ClO_3^- (aq.) and Cl^- (aq.) are +1, +5 and −1 respectively.

40. (b) methoxymethane

Explanation: This is an example of Williamson synthesis of unsymmetrical ether, where CH_3ONa is reacted with CH_3CH_2Br to form $CH_3CH_2OCH_3$, which is ethyl methyl ether.

41. (a) $\pi \propto c$

Explanation: The osmotic pressure of a solution is proportional to the molar concentration of the solute particles in solution. Mathematically it can be represented as:

$$\pi \propto C$$
$$\pi = C\,R\,T \text{ (For Electrolytic solution)}$$
$$\pi = i\,C\,RT \text{ (For Non-electrolytic solution)}$$

42. (c) IPO_4

> **Explanation:** Interhalogen compounds are formed when halogen group elements react with each other. In other words, it is a molecule which consists of two or more different elements of group 17. These are four types of interhalogen compounds: Diatomic interhalogens (AX), Tetratomic interhalogens (AX_3), Hexatomic interhalogens (AX_5) and Octatomic interhalogens (AX_7). ICl_4^-, ClF_5, ClF_3 are the examples of Interhalogen compounds.

43. (c) Protein

> **Explanation:** The amino acids are the end products of the digestion of proteins. The hydrolysis of proteins to amino acids is carried out in presence of base or proteolytic enzymes. The amino acids obtained can be separated by various physical techniques such as electrophoresis, paper chromatography and ion exchange chromatography.

44. (b) Secondary structure of proteins

> **Explanation:** α-helices, β-sheets and random coils are the most common elements of secondary structure in proteins. α-helices are formed and maintained by backbone interactions parallel to the primary axis of the helix.

45. (a) Both A and R are true and R is the correct explanation of A.

> **Explanation:** Crystalline solids melt at the sharp and characteristic temperature. They have definite geometrical shape. Thus both assertion and reason are true and reason is the correct explanation for assertion.

46. (c) A is true but R is false.

> **Explanation:** Due to the decrease in bond (E–H) dissociation enthalpy down the group, acidic character increases. Thus assertion is true but reason is false.

47. (a) Both A and R are true and R is the correct explanation of A.

> **Explanation:** The boiling point of p-nitrophenol is higher than that of o-nitrophenol because p-Nitrophenol has intermolecular hydrogen bonding so it has more boiling point and less volatile than o-nitrophenol which has intramolecular hydrogen bonding. Thus both assertion and reason are true and reason is the correct explanation for assertion.

48. (b) Both A and R are true and R is not the correct explanation of A.

> **Explanation:** Due to increase in the number of shells, atomic and ionic radii of group 16 elements increase from top to bottom in the group. Thus both assertion and reason are true but reason is not the correct explanation of the assertion.

49. (a) Both A and R are true and R is the correct explanation of A.

> **Explanation:** Molality is a better method to express concentration than molarity because molality is defined in terms of mass of solvent and not mass of solution. Thus both assertion and reason are true and reason is the correct explanation for assertion.

Section-C

50. (b, d)

Explanation:

(b) $HOOC-CH_2-CH_2-\underset{\underset{\displaystyle NH_2}{|}}{CH}-COOH$

Number of COOH group = 2

Number of NH_2 group = 1

Since number of COOH groups (2) > number of NH_2 group (1). Therefore this amino acid is an acidic amine acid.

(d) $HOOC-CH_2-CH_2-\underset{\underset{\displaystyle NH_2}{|}}{CH}-COOH$

Number of COOH group = 2

Number of NH_3 groups = 1

Since, Number of COOH group (2) > Number of NH_2 group (1). Therefore amino acid is acidic. Write other two are neutral amino acid as number of NH_2 group is equal to number of COOH group in then.

51. (b) Violet

Explanation: Ozone turns trimethyl paper to violet colour.

52. (b) Henry's law

Explanation: Henry's law states that "The partial pressure of the gas in vapour phase is proportional to the mole fraction of the gas in the solution."

53. (d) density of the crystal increases

Explanation: In frenkel defect, there is no effect on the density of the crystalline solid because no anion or cation leaves the lattice site. Hence, the statement which is incorrect about frenkel defect is that density of the crystal increases.

54. (c) both (a) and (b)

Explanation: Vacuums in solid states mean empty space in a closed packed system between the constituent particles. Such empty spaces are known as the openings, interstices or interstitial voids. Interstitial voids are of two types, tetrahedral void and octahedral void.

55. (b) Schottky defect

Explanation: This type of defect arises due to absence of equal number of cations and anions from lattice sites in the crystalline solid of the type A^+B^- and it lowers the density of the crystal.

Sample Paper 7

Section-A

1. (b) 0.05.

   Explanation: The elevation in boiling point of a solution is 0.16

$$\Delta T_b = iK_f m$$

$$\Delta T_b = \frac{1000 \times 0.52 \times 13.44}{134.4 \times 1000}(1+2\alpha)$$

$$\therefore \qquad \Delta T_b = 0.156 \qquad\qquad (\because \alpha = 1)$$

2. (a) Thymine.

   Explanation: Two possible binding sites in guanine.

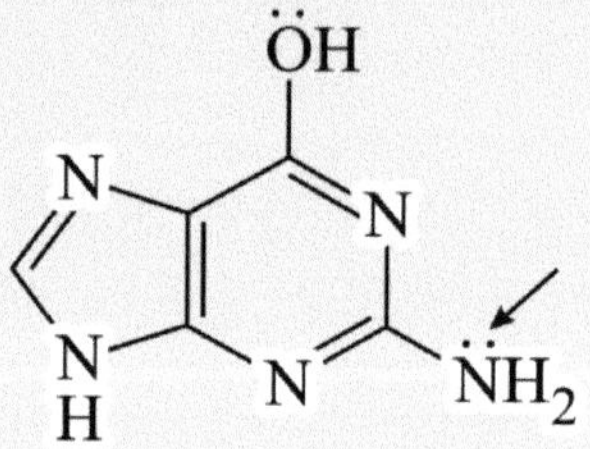

Structure of Guanine

3. (c) The valence shell electronic configuration of p-block element is $ns^2np^{1\text{-}6}$.

   Explanation: The valence shell electronic configuration of p-block element is $ns^2np^{1\text{-}6}$. The general electronic outer configuration for p block components is $ns^2np^{(1\text{-}6)}$. The general electronic outer configuration of f-block element configuration is $(n-2)f^{(0\text{-}14)}(n-1)d^{(0\text{-}1)}ns^2$.

4. (a) The Wurtz reaction

   Explanation: The reaction, $C_2H_5Br + 2Na + C_2H_5Br \rightarrow C_4H_{10} + 2NaBr$ is known as Wurtz reaction.

5. (c) 2-Methylprop-1-ene

   Explanation: The reactant sodium ethoxide is a strong nucleophile as well as a strong base, and hence elimination predominates over SN_2 to form alkene as a major product.

6. (d) An enzyme.

   Explanation: Enzymes are macromolecular biological catalysts. These are highly selective catalysts greatly accelerating both the rate and specificity of metabolic reactions. All enzymes are insoluble since they exist in the colloidal state.

7. (a) down the group, the H-E-H bond angle increases

   Explanation: The acidic character of hydrides increases down the group. Except water, all hydrides possess reducing properties and thermal stability of hydrides decreases down the group.

8. (c) 14

   Explanation: A lattice system is a class of lattices with the same set of lattice point groups, which are subgroups of the arithmetic crystal classes. The 14 Bravais lattices are grouped into seven lattice systems: triclinic, monoclinic, orthorhombic, tetragonal, Rhombohedral, hexagonal, and cubic.

9. (a) Mass by volume percentage

Explanation: Mass by volume percentage is used in the pharmacy due to the small size of the medicines in which the mass by volume measure of the concentration is used to get the most appropriate size of the medicine.

10. (c) Alkyl halide

Explanation: Grignard reagents is prepared by the reaction of an alkyl or aryl halide with magnesium metal.

11. (a) half-filled p-orbitals in group 15 elements are more stable

Explanation: Group 16 elements have a lower value of first ionisation enthalpy as compared to group 15 elements. As group 15 elements have half filled p-orbital due to which group 15 elements have extra stability.

12. (a) Lattice Point

Explanation: Each point in the crystal lattice is determined by the lattice point also known as the lattice site to determine the position of the spheres in the crystal lattice.

13. (a) Antifreeze

Explanation: Antifreeze compounds are the once which lowers the freezing point of the solution by lowering the vapour pressure of the solution.

14. (a) $RX + NaI \rightarrow RI + NaX$

Explanation: Exchange of halogen between RX and NaI.

15. (d) electronic transitions from the triplet ground state to the excited singlet state

Explanation: Solid oxygen has a pale blue colour which is attributed to electronic transition from the singlet ground state to the triplet ground state electronic transitions from antibonding r^* molecular orbitals (triplet state) to bonding (doublet) molecular orbitals electronic transitions from the antibonding orbital to molecular orbitals (triplet state) to excited anti bonding O_2 molecular orbital (singlet state) electronic transitions from the triplet ground state to the singlet ground state.

16. (b) Ethers

Explanation: This is because the (–O–) group in ethers does not contain any active site as compared to for example, hydroxyl group (OH) in alcohols. However, they undergo C–O bond cleavage in drastic conditions.

17. (a) X –ray Diffraction

Explanation: X-ray Diffraction consists of an X-ray beam being fired at a solid, and from the diffraction of the beams calculated by Bragg's Law the configuration can be determined through the X-ray diffraction of the crystal lattice.

18. (c) Ethylene oxide

Explanation: The product will be Ethylene oxide.

$$CH_2-CH_2 + CH_3MgI \rightarrow \begin{array}{c} CH_2-CH_2 \\ | \\ CH_3-OMgI \end{array} \rightarrow$$

$$CH_3-CH_2-CH_2-OH + Mg\begin{array}{c} I \\ OH \end{array}$$

Ethylene oxide

19. (c) equal to the rate of crystallisation

Explanation: Crystallisation is the process of the formation of solid crystals precipitating from a solution. In an unsaturated solution, the rate of dissolution of a solute in a volatile liquid solvent is greater than the rate of crystallisation. In a supersaturated solution, the rate of dissolution of a solute in a volatile liquid solvent is less than the rate of crystallisation. At equilibrium, the rate of dissolution of a solute in a volatile liquid solvent is equal to the rate of crystallisation.

20. (d) $S + O_2 \rightarrow SO_2$

Explanation: In the given combination reaction $S + O_2 \rightarrow SO_2$, we have S and O_2 combining to form SO_2. Carefully count the atoms up on each side of the equation and then make sure are equal. The number of S atoms on each side of the equation is equal. The number of O atoms on each side of the equation is equal.

21. (a) 7

Explanation: There are seven crystal systems that atoms can pack together to produce 3D space lattice. In which the arrangement of the ions can be determined through the different techniques these systems are Cubic, Tetragonal, Orthorhombic, hexagonal, Rhombohedral, Monoclinic and triclinic respectively.

22. (b) 3, 5-Dibromo-4-hydroxybenzene sulphonic acid

Explanation: The compound 'X' will be 3, 5-Dibromo-4-hydroxybenzene sulphonic acid.

23. (b) Molality

Explanation: Molarity of a given solution is defined as the total number of moles of solute per litre of solution.

$$M = n/V$$

Here, M is the molarity of the solution that is to be calculated, n is the number of moles of the solute and V is the volume of solution given in terms of litres which depends on the temperature and changes with the temperature.

24. (a) Colour centres

Explanation: F centers are also known as colour centers because they impart colour to the crystal due to the electronic transitions between the molecules.

25. (d) Na

Explanation: As Sodium (Na) reacts with both phenol and ethyl alcohol, thus it can not be used to distinguish phenol from ethyl alcohol. Rest all can be used to distinguish phenol from ethyl alcohol.

Section-B

26. (b,c)

> **Explanation:** Among the given four options (b) and (c) represent the oxidising behaviour of H_2SO_4. In (b) reaction it oxidises HI and itself reduces to SO_2 oxidation state of central atom Sulphur decreases from +6 to +4. In option (c) it oxidises copper and itself gets reduced to SO_2.

27. (b) $^{\ominus}OR$

> **Explanation:** Weakest acid forms the strongest conjugate base. Since, ROH is the weakest acid, so RO⁻ is the strongest base.

28. (d) Swarts reaction

> **Explanation:** Swarts' reaction generally produces alkyl fluorides from alkyl chlorides or alkyl bromides. This reaction is conducted by heating of the alkyl chloride/bromide in the presence of the fluoride of some heavy meals such as silver fluoride.

29. (a) nascent hydrogen responsible for bleaching is produced only in presence of moisture.

> **Explanation:** Dry SO_2 does not bleach dry flowers because nascent hydrogen responsible for bleaching is produced only in presence of moisture. In bleaching by SO_2, H_2O is important in order to produce nascent hydrogen which is responsible for the bleaching action.
>
> $$SO_2 + 2H_2O \rightarrow H_2SO_4 + 2\,[H]$$

30. (d) Chloral

> **Explanation:** When chlorine reacts with ethanol, Chloral is formed.
>
> $$C_2H_5OH \xrightarrow[-2HCl]{Cl_2} CH_3CHO \xrightarrow[-3HCl]{3Cl_2} CCl_3CHO \text{ (Chloral)}$$

31. (c) Uracil

> **Explanation:** DNA contains the Deoxyribose sugar whereas RNA contains the Ribose sugar. All the purine bases Adenine and Guanine are same in both DNA and RNA while the pyrimidine base cytosine and thymine are present in DNA and uracil is present in RNA instead of the thymine as a pyrimidine base.

32. (a) Cl_2/UV light

> **Explanation:** Direct chlorination of alkanes takes place in presence of sunlight (UV light).

33. (d) Density

> **Explanation:** An intensive property is a property of matter that does not change as the amount of matter changes, thus density of the solution does not changes with the change in the amount of the matter.

34. (a) Deoxyribose

> **Explanation:** Monosaccharides are the simplest carbohydrates which cannot be hydrolysed into simpler units. Deoxyribose ($C_5H_{10}O_4$) is a monosaccharide.

35. (a) Distorted octahedral and sp^3d^3

> **Explanation:** The geometry of XeF_6 molecule and the hybridization of Xe atom in the molecule are distorted octahedral and sp^3d^3 respectively. Xe has 6 bond pairs of electrons and one lone pair of electrons. Xe atom possess sp^3d^3 hybridization which results in the electronic geometry of pentagonal bipyramidal and molecular geometry of distorted octahedral.

36. (d) Glucose

> **Explanation:** Aldohexoses have four chiral centers because of that there are 16 possible stereoisomers. Examples of aldohexoses are glucose, mannose, galactose, etc. Glucose is a one of the products of photosynthesis in plants and other photosynthetic organisms. It also serves as an important metabolic intermediate of cellular respiration.

37. (b) DDT

> **Explanation:** Common name of the given compound is DDT (Dichloro-Diphenyl Trichloroethane).

38. (b) Peptide linkage

> **Explanation:** Peptide linkage is the peptide bond formed between the amino acids. It is a covalent bond formed between amino group of one molecule and carboxylic acid group of another molecule. The primary structure of a peptide or protein is the linear sequence of its amino acid structural units. The primary structure of a protein is reported starting from the amino-terminal (N) end to the carboxyl-terminal (C) end.

39. (a,c) 0 to +5, 0 to –1

> **Explanation:** $6NaOH$ (Hot) $+ 3Cl_2 \rightarrow 5NaCl + NaClO_3$
> Therefore, oxidation number of Chlorine changes from 0 to +5 and 0 to –1.

40. (a) α-D-glucose

> **Explanation:** Maltose is also known as malt sugar. It is a disaccharide, made up of two D - glucose units. The two units of glucose are linked with an alpha 1,4 glycosidic bond. Maltose dissociates it into its monosaccharide after hydrolysis. Using the hydrolysis reaction of maltose we can determine the products.

41. (c) Proteins

> **Explanation:** The amino acids are the end products of the digestion of proteins. The hydrolysis of proteins to amino acids is carried out in presence of base or proteolytic enzymes. The amino acids obtained can be separated by various physical techniques such as electrophoresis, paper chromatography and ion exchange chromatography.

42. (b) Sulphur

> **Explanation:** Catenation is the property of forming bond with a maximum number of atoms. In group sixteen elements, sulphur has maximum catenation property because of high bonding energy of sulphur atoms. Its electronegativity is close to that of carbon, which helps easy bonding with many atoms.

43. (b) Secondary structure of proteins

> **Explanation:** α-helices, β-sheets and random coils are the most common elements of secondary structure in proteins. α-helices are formed and maintained by backbone interactions parallel to the primary axis of the helix.

44. (b,d)

> **Explanation:**
> (b) $HOOC-CH_2-CH_2-\underset{\underset{NH_2}{|}}{CH}-COOH$
>
> Number of COOH group = 2
> Number of NH_2 group = 1

Since number of COOH groups (2) > number of NH_2 group (1). Therefore this amino acid a acidic amine acid.

(d) $HOOC-CH_2-CH_2-\underset{\underset{\displaystyle NH_2}{|}}{CH}-COOH$

Number of COOH group = 2

Number of NH_3 groups = 1

Since, Number of COOH group (2) > Number of NH_2 group (1). Therefore amino acid is acidic. Write other two are neutral amino acid as number of NH_2 group is equal to number of COOH group in then.

45. (d) A is false but R is true.

Explanation: Tetrahedral holes are smaller in size than octahedral holes. Cations usually occupy less space than anions. Thus assertion is false but reason is true.

46. (a) Both A and R are true and R is correct explanation for A.

Explanation: Hypophosphorous acid is a good reducing agent as it contains two P–H bonds. Thus both assertion and reason are true and reason is the correct explanation for assertion.

47. (b) Both A and R are true but R is not the correct explanation for A.

Explanation: Glucose is also known as dextrose, because it is dextrorotatory (meaning that as an optical isomer rotates the plane polarized light to the right and also an origin for the D designation and the open chains of glucose have four asymmetrical carbons. Thus both assertion and reason are true but reason is not the correct explanation for assertion.

48. (a) Both A and R are true and R is the correct explanation of A.

Explanation: Noble gases possess the electronic configuration ns^2np^6 and has 8 electrons in their outer shell, hence there valency is 0. Thus Assertion and reason both are true and reason is the correct explanation for assertion.

49. (a) Both A and R are true and R is the correct explanation of A.

Explanation: Solutions are the homogenous mixtures of two or more than two components and their composition and properties are uniform. Thus both assertion and reason are true and reason is the correct explanation for assertion.

Section-C

50. (c) Genetic code

Explanation: The relationship between the nucleotide triplets and the amino acids is called a genetic code. This determines the sequence of amino acids in the proteins that are synthesized.

51. (b) Solvent

Explanation: The component that is having more number of moles is known as solvent and the solvent component of the solution determines the physical state of the solution.

52. (b) H_2Te

Explanation: All these are the hydrides of 16th group elements in which the central atom undergo sp^3 hybridization and should possess the bond angle 109° but the bond angle distorts due to the repulsion between lone pair and lone pair. But this repulsion is minimum in H_2Te as the tellurium has large size which makes the repulsion minimum.

53. (a) Shape and volume

> **Explanation:** Solids have definite shape and volume due to the strong force of attraction between the constituent molecules or atoms in the crystal.

54. (a) True solids

> **Explanation:** Crystalline solids have a long-range order which means that there is a regular pattern of arrangement of particles which repeats itself periodically over the entire crystal. It has a definite regular geometry. Thus they are called true solids.

55. (a) Amorphous silica

> **Explanation:** Amorphous silica is the best photovoltaic material available for the conversion of the sunlight into electricity.

□□

53. (a) Shape and volume

    Explanation: Solids have definite shape and volume due to the strong force of attraction between the constituent molecules or atoms in the crystal.

54. (a) True solids

    Explanation: Crystalline solids have a long-range order which means that there is a regular pattern of arrangement of particles which repeats itself periodically over the entire crystal. It has a definite regular geometry. Thus they are called true solids.

55. (a) Amorphous silica

    Explanation: Amorphous silica is the best photovoltaic material available for the conversion of the sunlight into electricity.

□□

Biology

Sample Question Paper

Biology

Term – I

Time : 90 Minutes   Max. Marks : 35

General Instructions :
1. The Question Paper contains three sections.
2. Section A has 24 questions. Attempt any 20 questions.
3. Section B has 24 questions. Attempt any 20 questions.
4. Section C has 12 questions. Attempt any 10 questions.
5. All questions carry equal marks.
6. There is no negative marking.

SECTION – A

Section – A consists of 24 questions. Attempt any 20 questions from this section.

<u>The first attempted 20 questions would be evaluated.</u>

1. The structure of bilobed anther consists of:
   - (A) 2 thecae, 2 sporangia
   - (B) 4 thecae, 4 sporangia
   - (C) 4 thecae, 2 sporangia
   - (D) 2 thecae, 4 sporangia

Ans. (D) 2 thecae, 4 sporangia

> **Explanation:** A typical angiospermic anther is bilobed with each lobe having two theca, *i.e.*, they are dithecous. A dithecous anther is tetrasporangiate having four microsporangia. Each lobe has two microsporangia separated by a strip of sterile tissue.

2. In the figure of anatropous ovule given below, choose the correct option for the characteristic distribution of cells within the typical embryo sac.

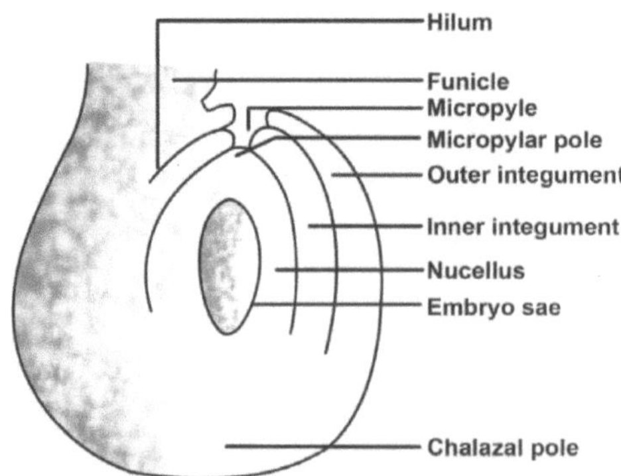

	Number of cells at chalazal end	Number of cells at micropylar end	Number of nuclei left in central cell
(A)	3	2	3
(B)	3	3	2
(C)	2	3	3
(D)	2	2	4

Ans. (B) 3, 3, 2

> **Explanation:** A characteristic distribution of the cells is seen within the embryo sac. Three cells are grouped together at the micropylar end and constitute the egg apparatus. The egg apparatus, in turn, consists of two synergids and one egg cell. Three cells are at the chalazal end and are called the antipodals. The large central cell has two polar nuclei.

3. The coconut water from tender coconut is:

(A) cellular endosperm.

(B) free nuclear endosperm.

(C) both cellular and nuclear endosperm.

(D) free nuclear embryo.

Ans. (B) Free nuclear endosperm

> **Explanation:** Tender coconut water is a clear liquid found inside the young tender coconut. During the nuclear phase of the development, it provides a termination for the endosperm of the coconut. In the nuclear endosperm formation, free-nuclear divisions are repeatedly done; if a cell wall is developed it will form after free-nuclear divisions, commonly referred to as liquid endosperm. Coconut water from a tender coconut is an example of this process i.e, free nuclear endosperm.

4. Pollen grains are well preserved as fossils because of presence of:

(A) sporopollenin   (B) cellulose   (C) lignocellulose   (D) pectocellulose

Ans. (A) sporopollenin

> **Explanation:** Pollen grains are made up of three components:
>
> During fossilisation, the inside of the cell, which is filled with living cytoplasm, deteriorates rapidly.
>
> The inner layer of the cell wall, intine, is made up of cellulose and pectin. The intine, like the cytoplasm, destroys fast during fossilisation.
>
> Exine, the cell wall's outer layer, is mostly made up of sporopollenin. It is one of the most durable materials. It's a N-free polymeric molecule that belongs to the terpene family of chemical compounds.
>
> One of the most chemically inert biological polymers is sporopollenin. It is a key component of plant spores and pollen grains' robust outer (exine) walls. It has a chemical stability that allows it to survive in soils and sediments. Because of the presence of sporopollenin, pollen grains are highly preserved as fossils.

5. Which of the following statements are true related to Seed X and Y?

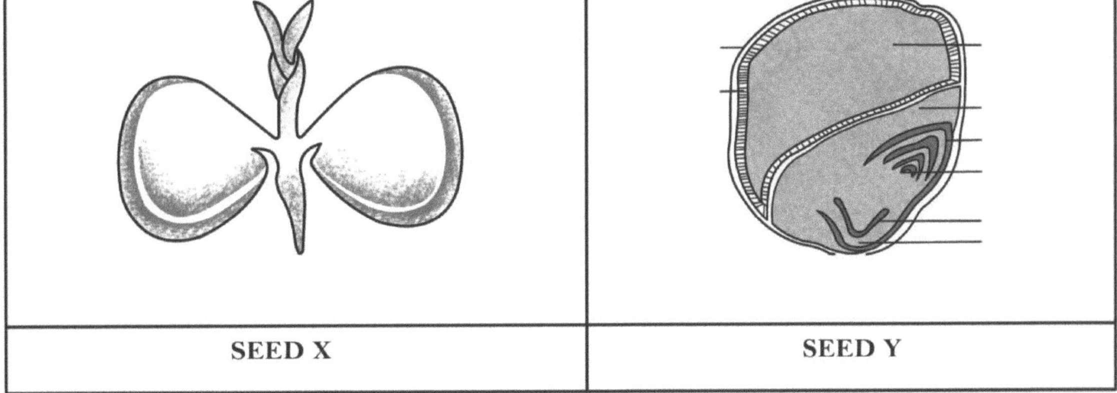

(i)   Seed X is dicot and endospermic or albuminous.

(ii)   Seed X is dicot and non-endospermic or non-albuminous.

(iii) Seed Y is monocot and endospermic or albuminous.

(iv) Seed Y is monocot and non-endospermic or non-albuminous.

Choose the correct option with the respect to the nature of the seed

(A) (i) and (iii)   (B) (ii) and (iii)   (C) (i) and (iv)   (D) (ii) and (iv)

Ans. (B) (ii) and (iii)

> **Explanation:** Endosperm is a food-laden tissue, surrounding the embryo on all sides or either present on one side of the embryo. Depending on its presence or absence, seeds are of two types:
>
> (i) Non-endospermic or exalbuminous seeds:
>
> In these seeds like gram, pea, groundnut, the endosperm is completely consumed by the embryo.
>
> Seed X is dicot and non-endospermic or non-albuminous
>
> (ii) Endospermic or albuminous seeds:
>
> In monocots and castor bean (dicots) embryo does not consume all endosperm. So, it persists in the mature seed. Such seeds are called as endospermic or albuminous seeds. In these seeds, food is stored in endosperm. In monocot seeds, the membranous covering present around radicle is called as coleorrhiza and around plumule is called as coleoptile.
>
> Seed Y is monocot and endospermic or albuminous.

6. Which of the following statements are correct with respect to hormones secreted by placenta?
   (i)   Placenta secretes relaxin during later stage of pregnancy.
   (ii) Placenta secretes high amount of FSH during pregnancy.
   (iii) Placenta secretes relaxin during initial stage of pregnancy.
   (iv) Placenta secretes hCG and hPL during pregnancy.
   (A) (i) and (iv)   (B) (i), (ii) and (iv)
   (C) (iii) and (iv)   (D) (ii), (iii) and (iv)

Ans. (A) (i) and (iv)

> **Explanation:** Hormones emitted by the placenta are Estrogen, Progesterone, hCS, hPL and hCG. The placenta is an endocrine gland that is solitary present at the time of pregnancy. hCG or the human chorionic gonadotropin is liberated in a superfluous amount in early pregnancy. Its presence in urine is utilized for the pregnancy test. Relaxin is a hormone produced by the ovary and the placenta with important effects in the female reproductive system and during pregnancy. In preparation for childbirth, it relaxes the ligaments in the pelvis and softens and widens the cervix.

7. Figure A shows the front view of the human female reproductive system and Figure B shows the development of a fertilized human egg cell.

Figure A

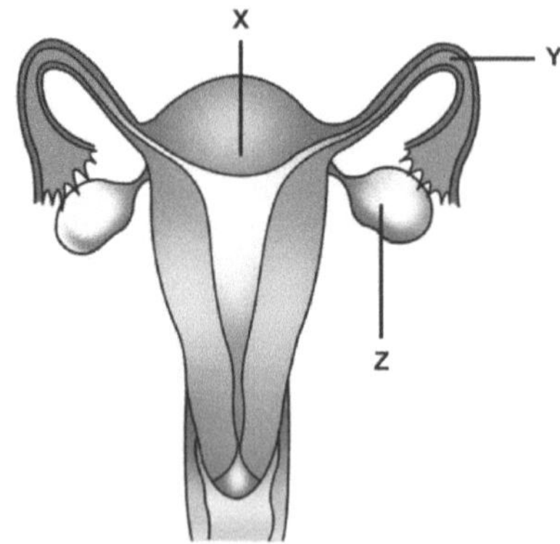

Figure B

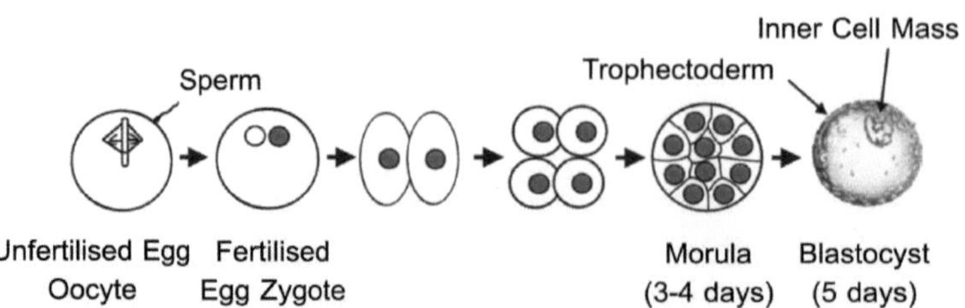

Identify the correct stage of development of human embryo (Figure B) that takes place at the site X, Y and Z respectively in the human female reproductive system (Figure A).

Choose the correct option from the table below:

	X	Y	Z
(A)	Morula	Fertilized egg	Blastocyst
(B)	Unfertilised egg	Fertilized egg	Morula
(C)	Blastocyst	Fertilized egg	Unfertilized egg
(D)	Fertilised egg	Morula	Blastocyst

Ans. (C) Blastocyst, Fertilized egg, Unfertilized egg

Explanation: The process of fertilization occurs in several steps. The sperm and the egg cell, which has been released from one of the female's two ovaries (Z) unite in one of the two fallopian tubes. After fertilization zygote is formed inside the fallopian tube (Y). The zygote then divides repeatedly to form a spherical mass of cells known as 'Morula'. The morula then develops into a hollow sphere of cells with a surrounding cellular layer and an inner cell mass projecting from it centrally. This stage is known as the 'blastocyst'. It implants itself into the uterine wall (X).

8. Penetration of the sperm in the ovum is followed by:
   - (A) formation of first polar body.
   - (B) completion of meiosis II.
   - (C) first meiosis.
   - (D) dissolution of zona pellucida.

Ans. (B) completion of meiosis II

Explanation: In human beings, the secondary oocyte is released from the mature Graafian follicle of an ovary (ovulation). The oocyte is received by the nearby Fallopian funnel and sent into the Fallopian tube by movements of fimbriae and their cilia. The secondary oocyte can be fertilized only within 24 hours after its release from the ovary.

The secondary oocyte is surrounded by numerous sperms but only one sperm succeeds in fertilizing the oocyte. Since, the second meiotic division is in progress, so the sperm enters the secondary oocyte. Second meiotic division is completed by the entry of the sperm into the secondary oocyte (fallopian tube). After this secondary oocyte is called ovum (egg).

9. The correct sequence of hormone secretion from beginning of menstruation is:
   - (A) FSH, progesterone, estrogen.
   - (B) estrogen, FSH, progesterone.
   - (C) FSH, estrogen, progesterone.
   - (D) estrogen, progesterone, FSH.

Ans. (C) FSH, estrogen, progesterone

Explanation: Before the start of the menstrual cycle, the estrogen and progesterone levels are low. Low levels of estrogen and progesterone signal the pituitary gland to produce Follicle Stimulating Hormone (FSH). FSH begins the process of maturing. The follicle produces more estrogen. Increased estrogen levels trigger a sharp rise in Luteinizing Hormone (LH) from the pituitary gland, causing release of the egg from the follicle. The ruptured follicle called the corpus luteum now secretes more progesterone and estrogen to continue to prepare the uterus for pregnancy. If the egg is not fertilized, estrogen and progesterone levels drop and the menses begin.

10. In the dioecious aquatic plant shown, identify the characteristics of the male flowers that reach the female flowers for pollination:

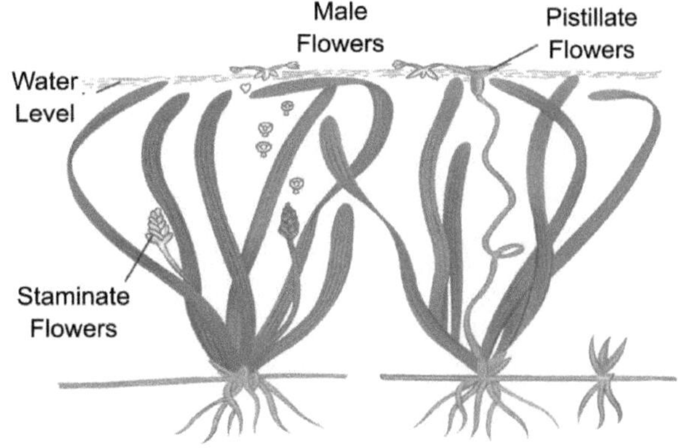

	Size of the flower	Colour of flower	Characteristic feature of pollen grain
(A)	small	brightly coloured	light weight and non-sticky
(B)	large	colourless	large and sticky
(C)	small	white	small, covered with mucilage
(D)	large	colourless	non sticky

Ans. (C) small, white, small, covered with mucilage

Explanation: Vallisneria are dioecious, meaning individual plants produce either male or female flowers. The female flowers are borne on long stalks that reach up to the water surface. Because of their positioning, water tension causes a slight depression around the flowers at the surface. The depression resembles a little dimple with a tiny white flower in the center. Both wind and water pollinated flowers are not very colourful and do not produce nectar.

Male flowers are very different, much smaller than the female flowers, a single inflorescence can contain thousands of individual male organs. As they mature underwater, the male flowers break off from the inflorescence and float to the surface. Similar to wind pollinated terrestrial plants, Vallisneria use water currents to disperse their pollen.

Pollen grains of water pollinated flowers are long ribbon like protected by mucilaginous covering and are produced in large number.

11. The thalamus contributes to the fruit formation in:
    (A) banana (B) orange (C) strawberry (D) guava

Ans. (C) strawberry

Explanation: Thalamus is the globular part of the stem from where the parts of the flower grow. This thalamus may sometimes contribute to the formation of fruit other than the ovary. They are also called false or pseudocarp fruits.

In some fruits like apple, cashew the thalamus also contributes to fruit formation, hence it is a false fruit. In strawberry, the whole soft, edible part of which is represented by an overgrown receptacle. Hence, it is a false fruit.

12. How many types of gametes would be produced if the genotype of a parent is AaBB?
    (A) 1 (B) 2 (C) 3 (D) 4

Ans. (B) 2

Explanation: There are two possible combinations of gametes for the AaBB parent.

Half of the gametes get a dominant A and a dominant B allele; the other half of the gametes get a recessive a and a dominant B allele.

13. Which of the following statements indicates parallelism in genes and chromosomes?
    (i)   They occur in pairs.
    (ii) They segregate during gamete formation.
    (iii) They show linkage.
    (iv) Independent pairs segregate independently.
    (A) (i) and (iii) (B) (ii) and (iii) (C) (i), (ii) and (iii) (D) (i), (ii) and (iv)

Ans. (D) (i), (ii) and (iv)

Explanation: Sutton and Boveri recognised close parallelism between the Mendelian factor and behaviour of chromosomes during sexual reproduction, like:

Chromosomes occur in homologous pairs. Therefore, Mendel also assumed that factors exist in pairs.

Synapsed chromosomes segregate during gametogenesis, precisely, meiosis-I. Mendel also suggested the segregation of paired factors during gametogenesis. This is Mendel's law of segregation.

The chromosomes of the various homologous pairs are assorted at random, and chromosomes of each pair segregate independently. This is the same behaviour of factors, as Mendel suggested. This is Mendel's law of Independent assortment.

The homologous chromosomes from two parents fuse during fertilisation, and thus, the zygote has one homologous chromosome from each parent. Mendel held the opinion that paternal and maternal characters mix up in the progeny. The chromosomes retain their structures and individuality throughout the life cycle of an individual. Mendel also suggested that the characters are not lost, even if they are not expressed.

14. Which of the following amino acid substitution is responsible for causing sickle cell anemia?
    (A) Valine is substituted by Glutamic acid in the α globin chain at the sixth position
    (B) Valine is substituted by Glutamic acid in the β globin chain at seventh position
    (C) Glutamic acid is substituted by Valine in the α globin chain at the sixth position
    (D) Glutamic acid is substituted by Valine in the β globin chain at the sixth position

Ans. (D) Glutamic acid is substituted by Valine in the β globin chain at the sixth position

Explanation: Sickle-cell anemia is caused by a point mutation in the β-globin chain of hemoglobin, replacing the amino acid glutamic acid with the less polar amino acid valine at the sixth position of the β chain. The mutation occurs in exon 1 and changes the nucleic acid sequence from GAG to GTG.

15. In human beings, where genotype AABBCC represents dark skin colour, aabbcc represents light skin colour and AaBbCc represents intermediate skin colour; the pattern of genetic inheritance can be termed as:
    (A) Pleiotropy and codominance
    (B) Pleiotropy and incomplete dominance
    (C) Polygenic and qualitative inheritance
    (D) Polygenic and quantitative inheritance

Ans. (D) Polygenic and quantitative inheritance

Explanation: Human skin colour is a polygenic inheritance that produces melanin pigment in three pairs of polygenes A, B and C, which induces human skin colour. Skin colour is regulated in humans by more than 1 gene.

Dark pigmentation is dominated by three "dominant" capital letter genes (A, B and C) so more melanin is made. Since lower levels of melanin are formed, the "recessive" alleles of these three genes (a, b and c) regulate light pigmentation.

There would be the darkest skin colour out of the 64 offspring, followed by a number of middle shades from dark to bright, as there is a self-cross between AaBbCc. The highest volume of melanin and very dark skin has a genotype of all "dominant" AABBCC capital genes. A genotype has the lowest level of melanin and very light skin for all "recessive" aabbcc genes. The darkest of all will be AABBCC, followed by AAbbCC, then AAbbcc and Aabbcc.

Aabbcc has the lowest level of melanin in the human genotype and has very light skin. If the human skin colour genotype is AAbbcc and AaBbcc respectively, light brown and dark brown are the phenotypes of these genotypes. Just one dominant allele A is found in genotype AAbbcc. Two alleles, A and B, are dominant in the AaBbcc genotype.

16. Which of the following combination of chromosome numbers represents the correct sex determination pattern in honey bees?
    (A) Male 32, Female 16
    (B) Male 16, Female 32
    (C) Male 31, Female 32
    (D) Female 32, Male 31

Ans. (B) Male 16, Female 32

Explanation: A male honey bee or drone is haploid because its somatic cells only contain maternal chromosomes from the queen bee, while the female is diploid. Male insects are haploid because they develop parthenogenetically from unfertilized eggs. The phenomenon is called arehenotoky. Meiosis does not occur during the formation of sperms. Females grow from fertilized eggs and are hence diploid.

17. Rajesh and Mahesh have defective haemoglobin due to genetic disorders. Rajesh has too few globin molecules while Mahesh has incorrectly functioning globin molecules. Identify the disorder they are suffering from.

	Rajesh	Mahesh
(A)	Sickle cell anaemia–an autosome linked recessive trait.	Thalassemia–an autosome linked dominant trait.
(B)	Thalassemia–an autosome linked recessive blood disorder.	Sickle cell anaemia–an autosome linked recessive trait.
(C)	Sickle cell anaemia–an autosome linked recessive trait.	Thalassemia–an autosome linked recessive blood disorder.
(D)	Thalassemia–an autosome linked recessive blood disorder.	Sickle cell anaemia–an autosome linked dominant trait.

Ans. **(B)**

	Rajesh	Mahesh
	Thalassemia–an autosome linked recessive blood disorder.	Sickle cell anaemia–an autosome linked recessive trait.

Explanation: Thalassemia and sickle cell anaemia are genetic disorders in which hemoglobin synthesis is affected. In thalassemia, there is a defect in the α or β globin chain. This leads to the synthesis of abnormal red blood cells due to the decreased synthesis of globin molecules. Whereas in sickle-cell anaemia there is a mutation in β globin gene resulting in sickle like shape of red blood cells.

Thalassemia is a quantitative problem of too few globins synthesized, whereas sickle-cell anaemia (a hemoglobinopathy) is a qualitative problem of synthesis of an incorrectly functioning globin. Thalassemia usually result in underproduction of normal globin proteins, often through mutations in regulatory genes.

18. Which of the following criteria must a molecule fulfil to act as a genetic material?
    (i)   It should not be able to generate its replica.
    (ii) It should chemically and structurally be stable.
    (iii) It should not allow slow mutation.
    (iv) It should be able to express itself in the form of Mendelian Characters.
    (A) (i) and (ii)　　　(B) (ii) and (iii)　　　(C) (iii) and (iv)　　　(D) (ii) and (iv)

Ans. (D) (ii) and (iv)

Explanation: A genetic material should be chemically and structurally stable so as to maintain its integrity with age, cell cycle and different physiology of individuals. At the same time, it should be prone to random changes that impart genetic variations and serve as raw material for evolution. Inheritance of genetic material requires its replication with each cell division to ensure its transmission to progeny. It should carry the information required for regulation of whole cell functioning and the information should be expressed as functional proteins. Mendel proposed the set of genes or characters were present as a pair of dominant or recessive alleles having expression based on their occurrence.

19. The promoter site and the terminator site for transcription are located at:
    (A) 3′ (downstream) end and 5′ (upstream) end, respectively of the transcription unit
    (B) 5′ (upstream) end and 3′ (downstream) end, respectively of the transcription unit
    (C) the 5′ (upstream) end of the transcription unit
    (D) the 3′ (downstream) end of the transcription unit

Ans. (B) 5′ (upstream) end and 3′ (downstream) end, respectively of the transcription unit

Explanation: The promoter is the binding site for RNA polymerase of transcription. The promoter is located towards 5′-end (upstream) of the structural gene of coding strands and provides the binding site for RNA polymerase. The promoter sequence needs to lie in front of the start site or upstream to it in the 5′ end and the terminator should lie in the 3′ end downstream as transcription proceeds in the 5′ to 3′ direction.

20. Which of the following is correct about mature RNA in eukaryotes?
   (A) Exons and introns do not appear in the mature RNA.
   (B) Exons appear, but introns do not appear in the mature RNA.
   (C) Introns appear, but exons do not appear in the mature RNA.
   (D) Both exons and introns appear in the mature RNA.

Ans. (B) Exons appear, but introns do not appear in the mature RNA.

> **Explanation:** The coding sequences or expressed sequences are defined as exons. These sequences (exons) appear in mature or processed RNA, Eukaryotic transcripts possess extra segments called introns or intervening sequences or noncoding sequences. The exons are interrupted by introns or intervening sequences which do not appear in mature or processed RNA. Exons are the functional coding sequences. Splicing is removal of introns and fusion of exons to form functional RNAs.

21. In *E. coli*, the lac operon gets switched on when:
   (A) lactose is present and it binds to the repressor.
   (B) repressor binds to operator.
   (C) RNA polymerase binds to the operator.
   (D) lactose is present and it binds to RNA polymerase.

Ans. (A) lactose is present and it binds to the repressor.

> **Explanation:** Lac operon of *Escherichia coli* is an inducible operon system which was discovered by Jacob and Monod (1961). The repressor of the operon is synthesized (all-the-time-constitutively) from the i gene. The repressor protein binds to the operator region of the operon and prevents RNA polymerase from transcribing the operon. In the presence of an inducer, such as lactose or allolactose, the repressor is rendered inactive so that it cannot attach on operator gene and synthesis of mRNA takes place.

22. Oswald Avery, Colin MacLeod and Maclyn McCarty used enzymes to purify biochemicals such as proteins, DNA and RNA from the heat-killed S cells to see which ones could transform live R cells into S cells in Griffith's experiment. They observed that:
   (A) Proteases and RNases affected transformation.
   (B) DNase inhibited transformation.
   (C) Proteases and Lipases affected transformation.
   (D) RNases inhibited transformation.

Ans. (B) DNase inhibited transformation.

> **Explanation:** Oswald Avery, Colin MacLeod, and Maclyn McCarty showed that DNA (not proteins) can transform the properties of cells, clarifying the chemical nature of genes. They identified DNA as the "transforming principle" while studying *Streptococcus pneumoniae*, bacteria that can cause pneumonia. Avery and McCarty observed that proteases - enzymes that degrade proteins - did not destroy the transforming principle. Neither did lipases - enzymes that digest lipids. They found that the transforming substance was rich in nucleic acids, but ribonuclease, which digests RNA, did not inactivate the substance. They also found that the transforming principle had a high molecular weight. They had isolated DNA. This was the agent that could produce an enduring, heritable change in an organism. Only in the culture treated with DNase did the S strain bacteria failed to grow.

23.

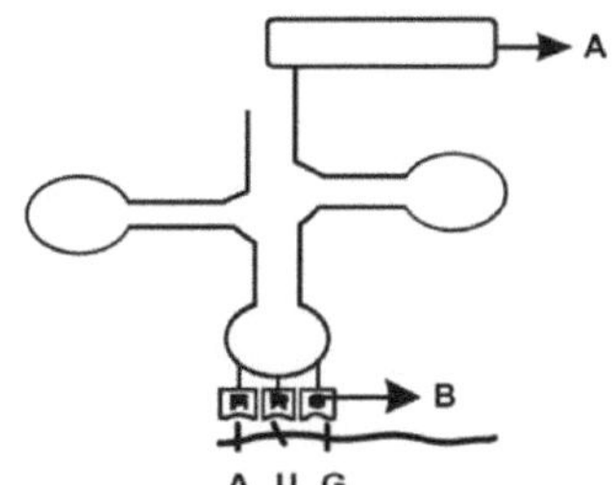

AUG on the mRNA will result in the activation of which of the following RNA having correct combination of amino acids:

	Site A	Site B
(A)	UAC	Methionine
(B)	Methionine	UAC
(C)	Methionine	AUG
(D)	AUG	Methionine

Ans. **(B)**

	Site A	Site B
	Methionine	UAC

> **Explanation:** AUG codes for the amino acid methionine. The amino acid formyl-methionine (methionine in eukaryotes) initiates the process. It is carried by tRNA having UAC anticodon which bonds to AUG initiator codon of mRNA by hydrogen bonds.

24. Short stretches of DNA used to identify complementary sequence in a sample are called:
    (A) Probes   (B) Markers   (C) VNTRs   (D) Primers

Ans. (A) Probes

> **Explanation:** A probe is a single-stranded sequence of DNA or RNA used to search for its complementary sequence in a sample genome. The probe is placed into contact with the sample under conditions that allow the probe sequence to hybridize with its complementary sequence.

SECTION - B

Section – B consists of 24 questions (Sl. No. 25 to 48). Attempt any 20 questions from this section. <u>The first attempted 20 questions would be evaluated.</u>

> **Question No. 25 to 28** consist of two statements – Assertion (A) and Reason (R). Answer these questions selecting the appropriate option given below:
> A. Both A and R are true and R is the correct explanation of A.
> B. Both A and R are true and R is not the correct explanation of A.
> C. A is true, but R is false.
> D. A is False, but R is true.

25. **Assertion:** Lactational amenorrhea is the natural method of contraception.
    Reason: It increases the phagocytosis of sperm.

Ans. (C) A is true but R is false.

> **Explanation:** Lactational amenorrhea (absence of menstruation) method is based on the fact that ovulation and therefore the cycle do not occur during the period of intense lactation following parturition. Therefore, as long as the mother breastfeeds the child fully, chances of conception are almost nil. Lactational amenorrhea do not increase the phagocytosis of sperm.

26. **Assertion:** Saheli, an oral contraceptive for females, contains a steroidal preparation.
    Reason: It is a "once a week" pill with very few side effects.

Ans. (D) A is False but R is true.

> **Explanation:** Saheli - the new oral contraceptive for the females contains a non-steroidal preparation. It is a once a week pill with very few side effects and high contraceptive value.

27. **Assertion:** Parturition is induced by a complex neuro endocrine mechanism.
    Reason: At the end of gestation period, the maternal pituitary releases prolactin which causes uterine contractions.

Ans. (C)   A is true but R is False.

> **Explanation:** Parturition is induced by a complex neuroendocrine mechanism which is triggered by fully formed foetus and the placenta called foetal ejection complex. A developing foetus secretes hormones from its adrenal glands. These hormones diffuse into the maternal blood and accumulate to stimulate the release of oxytocin (birth hormone) from the mother's posterior pituitary. Oxytocin acts on the uterine muscle and causes stringer uterine contractions, which in turn stimulates further secretion of oxytocin. The stimulatory reflex between the uterine contraction and oxytocin secretion continues resulting in stronger and stronger contractions. This leads to expulsion of the baby out of the uterus through the birth canal.

28. **Assertion:** When the two genes in a dihybrid cross are situated on the same chromosome, the proportion of parental gene combinations is much higher than non-parental type.

    Reason: Higher parental gene combinations can be attributed to crossing over between two genes.

Ans. (C)   A is true but R is false.

> **Explanation:** Morgan and his group observed in *Drosophila* that when the two genes in a dihybrid cross were situated on the same chromosome, the proportion of parental gene combinations were much higher than the non-parental type or new combinations (also called recombination) of genes.
>
> They also found that the proportion of recombinants varies, even if the two genes are present on the same chromosome. They attributed this due to physical association of the two genes and coined the term 'linkage'

29. Concentration of which of the following substances will decrease in the maternal blood as it flows from embryo to placenta through the umbilical cord?

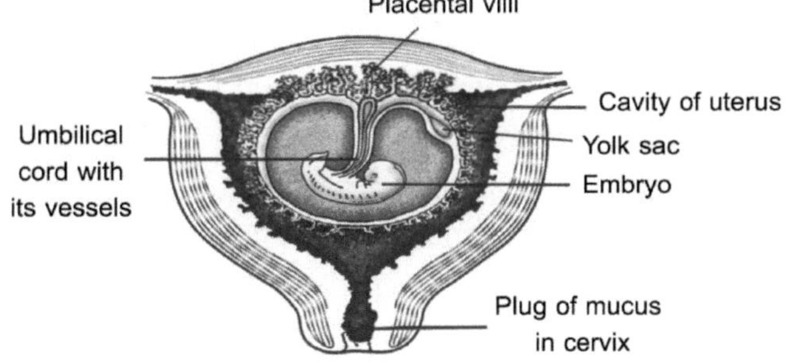

(i) Oxygen	(ii) Amino Acids	(iii) Carbon dioxide	(iv) Urea
(A) (i) and (ii)	(B) (ii) and (iv)	(C) (iii) and (iv)	(D) (i) and (iv)

Ans. (A) (i) and (ii)

> **Explanation:** Placenta is a structure that establishes firm connection between the foetus and the mother. By means of placenta the developing embryo obtains nutrients and oxygen from the mother and gives off carbon dioxide and nitrogenous waste.
>
> In the placenta, the foetal blood comes very close to the maternal blood, and this permits the exchange of materials between the two. Food (glucose, amino acids, lipids), water, mineral salts, vitamins, hormones, antibodies and oxygen pass from the maternal blood into the foetal blood, and foetal metabolic wastes, such as carbon dioxide, urea pass into the maternal blood.

30. In a fertilized ovule, n, $2n$ and $3n$ conditions occur respectively in:
    - (A) antipodal, zygote and endosperm
    - (B) zygote, nucellus and endosperm
    - (C) endosperm, nucellus and zygote
    - (D) antipodals, synergids and integusments

Ans. (A) antipodal, zygote and endosperm

> **Explanation:** In embryo sac, n, $2n$, $3n$ conditions are found respectively in antipodal, zygote, and endosperm. In a majority of flowering plants, one of the megaspores remains functional while the other three degenerate. Only the functional megaspore then develops into the female gametophyte or 'embryo sac'.

On observing the distribution of cells inside the embryo sac, we come to know that:

There is a large central cell. At the micropylar end, 3 cells are grouped together to form an egg apparatus. The egg apparatus, in turn, consists of two synergids and one 'egg cell'. Whereas, three cells at the chalazal end are together called 'antipodals'. They are haploid. Now, during double fertilization one of the male gametes moves towards the egg cell and fuses with its nucleus thus completing the 'syngamy'. This results in the formation of a diploid cell, which is named as 'zygote' While the other male gamete moves towards the two polar nuclei located in the central cell. Here, a fusion occurs among them to form a triploid 'primary endosperm nucleus' (PEN). As this process involves the fusion of three haploid nuclei, it is called 'triple fusion'.

31. A botanist studying *Viola* (common pansy) noticed that one of the two flower types withered and developed no further due to some unfavorable condition, but the other flower type on the same plant survived and it resulted in an assured seed set. Which of the following will be correct?

    (A) The flower type which survived is Cleistogamous and it always exhibits autogamy.

    (B) The flower type which survived is Chasmogamous and it always exhibits geitonogamy.

    (C) The flower type which survived is Cleistogamous and it exhibits both autogamy and geitonogamy.

    (D) The flower type which survived is Chasmogamous and it never exhibits autogamy.

Ans. (A) The flower type which survived is Cleistogamous and it will always exhibit autogamy

Explanation: Cleistogamy is a type of automatic self-pollination of certain plants that can propagate by using non-opening, self-pollinating flowers. The principal advantage of cleistogamy is that it requires fewer plant resources to produce seeds than does chasmogamy, because development of petals, nectar and large amounts of pollen is not required. This efficiency makes cleistogamy particularly useful for seed production on unfavorable sites or adverse conditions. Cleistogamous flowers are those which do not open at all and pollen from other plants cannot land on the stigma of these flowers. Thus, in such plants cross pollination cannot occur and only autogamy occurs. Therefore, cleistogamy ensures autogamy.

32. During parturition, a pregnant woman is having prolonged labour pains and child birth has to be fastened. It is advisable to administer a hormone that can:

    (A) increase the metabolic rate.

    (B) release glucose in the blood.

    (C) stimulate the ovary.

    (D) activate smooth muscles.

Ans. (D) activate smooth muscles.

Explanation: Parturition results from the establishment of phasic regular uterine contractions. Contractility in myometrial smooth muscle is stimulated to fasten the process.

33. A female undergoing IVF treatment has blocked fallopian tubes. The technique by which the embryo with more than 8 blastomeres will be transferred into the female for further development is:

    (A) ZIFT   (B) GIFT   (C) IUT   (D) AI

Ans. (C) IUT

Explanation: Despite unprotected sex lives, a variety of couples are unable to have children. Assisted reproductive technologies (ART) are recommended for such people. This includes IVF, in which the ova and the sperm are collected and induced to produce a zygote in the laboratory under simulated conditions. ZIFT, or zygote intrafallopian transfer, is the process of transferring an embryo with about 8 blastomeres into the fallopian tubes.

IUT, or intrauterine transfer, is when the zygote is transferred to the uterus.

Another specialised method of embryo formation in the laboratory is ICSI, or intracytoplasmic sperm injection, in which a sperm is directly inserted into the ovum.

GIFT, or gamete intrafallopian transfer, is a procedure in which eggs from the same mother or another female are mixed with sperm and delivered into the recipient mother's fallopian tubes to provide a fertile environment.

34. The mode of action of the copper ions in an IUD is to:
(A) increase the movement of sperms
(B) decrease the movement of the sperms
(C) make the uterus unsuitable for implantation
(D) make the cervix hostile to the sperms

Ans. (B) decrease the movement of the sperms

> **Explanation:** The mode of action of copper IUDs is to prevent fertilization. Copper acts as a spermicide within the uterus that increases the levels of copper ions, prostaglandins, and white blood cells within the uterine and also tubal fluids. Copper IUDs have added contraceptive effects due to the presence of copper ions. Copper ions are associated with an inflammatory response in the uterus, meaning sperm cannot reach the egg to fertilize it and create an embryo. Copper ions decrease the sperm's ability to move and prevent the sperm from passing through the cervical mucus and going on to fertilize the egg.

35. To produce 400 seeds, the number of meiotic divisions required will be:
(A) 400
(B) 200
(C) 500
(D) 800

Ans. (C) 500

> **Explanation:** The seed is a ripened ovule (megasporangium). In young megasporangium, only one cell functions as megaspore mother cell that undergoes meiosis to form 4 haploid cells. Out of these only one cell is functional and develops into megaspore. Megaspore develops into female gametophyte (embryo sac), that is retained permanently in the megasporangium (ovule) as it is indehiscent. One of the cells of embryo-sac functions as oosphere or egg. Thus, one meiotic division is required for the formation of one oosphere (female gamete or egg).
>
> Pollen grains (microspores) are produced in the anther. The anther has 4 lobes, each representing a micro-sporangium. Cells of sporogenous tissue in micro-sporangium function as microspore mother cells. Each microspore mother cell undergoes meiosis to form 4 haploid micropores. Each microspore (pollen grain) develops into male gametophyte that produces male gamete. Thus, one meiotic division produces 4 micropores and consequently 4 male gametes. The oosphere is fertilized by male gamete to form diploid oospore that develops into embryo. The latter is enclosed permanently inside ovule, that ripens into seed. Four oospheres and four male gametes are required for the formation of four seeds. Four meiotic divisions are required for the formation of four oospheres and only one meiotic division for the formation of four male gametes. Thus, 5 meiotic divisions are needed for the formation of 4 seeds and 500 meiotic divisions are required for the formation of 400 seeds.

36. A cross is made between tall pea plants having green pods and dwarf pea plants having yellow pods. In the F_2 generation, out of 80 plants how many are likely to be tall plants?
(A) 15
(B) 20
(C) 45
(D) 60

Ans. (D) 60

> **Explanation:** A dihybrid cross is a cross between two plants that are identical hybrids for two traits. The two plants are heterozygous for two traits. A pure pea plant with green pods is homozygous for dominant traits and a pure short plant with yellow pods is homozygous for recessive traits. In the F_1 generation, all heterozygous plants are produced and in the F_2 generation, plants with the ratio of $9:3:3:1$ are produced. When the cross is made between a pure tall pea plant and a pure short pea plant, all tall green plants are produced in the F_1 generation and 16 plants are produced in the F_2 generation. Out of 16 plants, 9 are tall green, 3 are tall yellow, 3 are dwarf green and 1 is dwarf yellow. Tall and green pods are the dominant traits and small and yellow are the recessive traits. Observing the ratio of dihybrid cross *i.e.,* $9:3:3:1$ ratio, 9 plants have both dominant features, 3 have first dominant and second recessive features, 3 have first recessive and second dominant feature and 1 have both recessive features. Out of 16 plants produced in the F_1 generation, 12 are tall plants and 4 are short plants.
>
> Therefore, $(12/16) \times 80 = 60$.

37. In *Antirrhinum*, RR is phenotypically red flowers, rr is white and Rr is pink. Select the correct phenotypic ratio in F_1 generation when a cross is performed between RR × Rr:
(A) 1 red : 2 Pink : 1 white
(B) 2 Pink : 1 white
(C) 2 Red : 2 Pink
(D) All Pink

Ans. (C) 2 Red : 2 Pink

> **Explanation:** The inheritance of flower colour in the *Antirrhinum majus* (snapdragon or dog flower) is an example of incomplete or partial dominance. Incomplete dominance is the phenomenon in which neither of the two alleles of a gene is completely dominant over the other. In a cross between true-breeding red-flowered (RR) and Rr the F_1 plants obtained will be 2 (RR) Red: 2 (Rr) Pink. As R is not completely dominant over r and this made it possible to distinguish Rr (pink) from RR (red) and rr (white).

38. What would be the genotype of the parents if the offspring have the phenotypes in 1 : 1 proportion?
(A) Aa × Aa   (B) AA × AA   (C) Aa × AA   (D) Aa × aa

Ans. (D) Aa × aa

> **Explanation:**

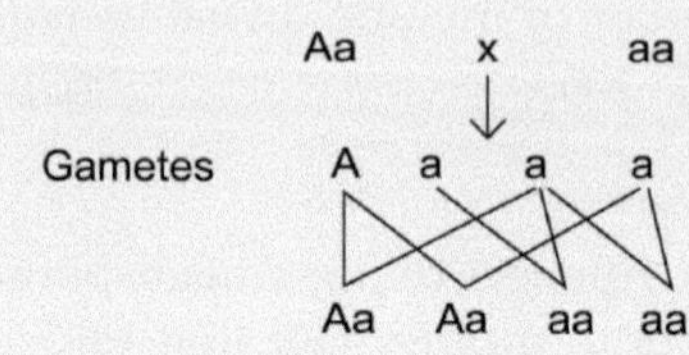

39.

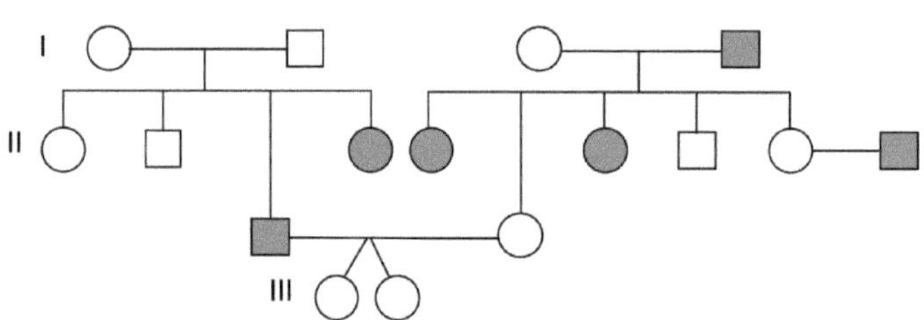

What is the pattern of inheritance in the above pedigree chart?
(A) Autosomal dominant (B) Autosomal recessive (C) Sex -linked dominant (D) Sex -linked recessive

Ans. (B) Autosomal recessive

> **Explanation:** Males and females are showing the same chance of expressing the trait. The trait is expressed only in homozygous condition. The trait is also showing skip in generation (III).

40. A couple has two daughters. What is the probability that the third child will also be a female?
(A) 25%   (B) 50%   (C) 75%   (D) 100%

Ans. (B) 50%

> **Explanation:** There are two sex chromosomes X and Y. Humans are diploid having two sex chromosomes, in females a pair of the X chromosome is found while in males an X and Y chromosome is present. There is 50% chance that the subsequent child is going to be a boy because it entirely depends upon the chromosome of the sperm which fertilizes the ovum. Each pregnancy features a 50% chance of leading to a boy or girl and this doesn't include the likelihood of multiples. Having 2 daughters previously doesn't affect the probabilities of any resulting pregnancy. The prospect of getting a boy remains at 50%.

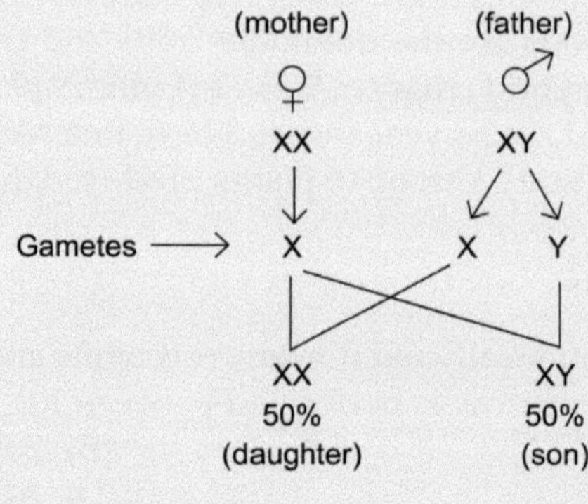

41. Genotypic ratio of 1 : 2 : 1 is obtained in a cross between:

(A) AB × AB   (B) Ab × Ab   (C) Ab × ab   (D) ab × ab

Ans. (B) Ab × Ab

> **Explanation:** The genotypic ratio represents the pattern of offspring distribution according to genotype, which is the genetic constitution determining the phenotype of an organism. It describes the number of times a genotype would appear in the offspring. For example, a test cross between two organisms with the same genotype, Ab, for a heterozygous dominant trait will result in offspring with genotypes: AA, Ab, and bb. In this example, the predicted genotypic ratio is 1:2:1.

42. Total number of nucleotide sequences of DNA that codes for a hormone is 1530. The proportion of different bases in the sequence is found to be Adenine = 34%, Guanine = 19%, Cytosine = 23%, Thymine = 19%.

Applying Chargaff's rule, what conclusion can be drawn?

(A) It is a double stranded circular DNA.

(B) It is a single stranded DNA.

(C) It is a double stranded linear DNA.

(D) It is a single stranded DNA coiled on Histones.

Ans. (B) It is a single stranded DNA.

> **Explanation:** The rules of base pairing explain the phenomenon that whatever the amount of adenine (A) in the DNA of an organism, the amount of thymine (T) is the same (Chargaff's rule). Similarly, whatever the amount of guanine (G), the amount of cytosine (C) is the same.
>
> The amount of adenine = 34% and thymine = 19% is only in single stranded DNA molecule.

43. A stretch of an euchromatin has 200 nucleosomes. How many bp will there be in the stretch and what would be the length of the typical euchromatin?

(A) 20,000 bp and $13,000 \times 10^{-9}$ m   (B) 10,000 bp and $10,000 \times 10^{-9}$ m

(C) 40,000 bp and $13,600 \times 10^{-9}$ m   (D) 40,000 bp and $13,900 \times 10^{-9}$ m

Ans. (C) 40,000 bp and $13,600 \times 10^{-9}$ m

> **Explanation:** Nucleosomes appear as a "beads-on-a-string" arrangement. Here beads represent complexes of histones and DNA. Each bead contains eight histone molecules: two copies each of H_2A, H_2B, H_3, and H_4; out of 200 bp DNA, 146 bp DNA is bound tightly around the histone core and the remainder serve as linker DNA between nucleosomal beads. The H_1 histone associated with the linker DNA to pack adjacent nucleosomes together. Each nucleosome has total of 9 histones and 200 bp DNA. So, stretch of an euchromatin with 200 nucleosomes will have 40,000 bp. The distance between two consecutive base pairs is 0.34 nm (0.34×10^{-9} m), the length of DNA double is calculated simply by multiplying the total number of bp with distance between two consecutive bp, that is 0.34×10^{-9} m $\times 40,000 = 13,600 \times 10^{-9}$ m.

44. Observe structures A and B given below. Which of the following statements are correct?

5'
HOCH2
OH
4' C
C 1'
H
H
H
3' 2'
H
C
C
OH
OH
A

5'
HOCH2
OH
4' C
C 1'
H
H
H
3' 2'
H
C
C
OH
H
B

(A) A is having 2'–OH group which makes it less reactive and structurally stable, whereas B is having 2'–H group which makes it more reactive and unstable.

(B) A is having 2′–OH group which makes it more reactive and structurally unstable, whereas B is having 2′–H group which makes it less reactive and structurally stable.

(C) A and B both have –OH groups which make it more reactive and structurally stable.

(D) A and B both are having –OH groups which make it less reactive and structurally stable

Ans. (B) A is having 2′–OH group which makes it more reactive and structurally unstable, whereas B is having 2′–H group which makes it less reactive and structurally stable.

> **Explanation:** DNA contains deoxyribose whereas RNA contains ribose. Due to its deoxyribose sugar, which contains one less oxygen-containing hydroxyl group, DNA is a more stable molecule than RNA, which is characterised by the presence of the 2′-hydroxyl group on the pentose ring. This hydroxyl group make RNA less stable than DNA because it is more susceptible to hydrolysis.

45. If Meselson and Stahl's experiment is continued for sixth generations in bacteria, the ratio of Heavy strands $^{15}N/^{15}N$: Hybrid $^{15}N/^{14}N$: light $^{14}N/^{14}N$ containing DNA in the sixth generation would be:

(A) $1:1:1$ (B) $0:1:7$ (C) $0:1:15$ (D) $0:1:31$

Ans. (D) $0:1:31$

> **Explanation:** Meselson and Stahl's experiment is based on the semi-conservative replication of the DNA. It means that when a parental DNA undergoes replication, each strand of the parental DNA serves as a template and the new daughter strand is synthesized on the template strand. Keeping the semi-conservative replication in view, and starting with DNA strands having N^{15} and thereafter N^{14}, the number of heavy, hybrid, and light chains are as follows-
>
> In the sixth generation, n = 6,
>
> The number of heavy chains is zero and the number of Hybrid chains are always two.
>
> By using $2^n - 2$, we can find out the light chains.
>
> Thus, there are total 62 light chains, *i.e.*, $N^{15}N^{14}$.
>
> Therefore, $0:2:62$ or $0:1:31$

46. Two important RNA processing events lead to specialized end sequences in most human mRNAs: __(i)__ at the 5′ end, and __(ii)__ at the 3′ end. At the 5′ end the most distinctive specialized end nucleotide, __(iii)__ is added and a sequence of about 200 __(iv)__ is added to the 3′ end.

(A) (i) Initiator codon (ii) Promotor (iii) Terminator codon (iv) Release factors

(B) (i) Promotor (ii) Elongation (iii) Regulation (iv) Termination.

(C) (i) Capping (ii) Polyadenylation (iii) $^{m}G_{ppp}$ (iv) Poly(A).

(D) (i) Repressor (ii) Co repressor (iii) Operon (iv) Release factors

Ans. (C) (i) Capping (ii) Polyadenylation (iii) $^{m}G_{ppp}$ (iv) Poly(A).

> **Explanation:** The primary mRNA transcript is longer and localized into the nucleus, where it is also called heterogeneous nuclear RNA (hnRNA) or pre-mRNA. At the 5 end of hnRNA, a cap (consisting of 7-methyl guanosine triphosphate or 7 ^{m}G) and a tail of poly A (Adenylate residues) at the 3 end are added. These processes are respectively called as capping and tailing. The cap is a chemically modified molecule of guanosine triphosphate (GTP). The primary mRNAs are made up of two types of segments; non-coding introns and the coding exons. The introns are removed by a process called RNA splicing and the exons are joined in a defined order.

47. What are minisatellites?

(A) 10-40 bp sized small sequences within the genes

(B) Short coding repetitive region on the eukaryotic genome

(C) Short non-coding repetitive sequence forming large portion of eukaryotic genome

(D) Regions of coding strands of the DNA

Ans. (C) Short non-coding repetitive sequence forming large portion of eukaryotic genome

Explanation: A minisatellite is a tract of repetitive DNA in which certain DNA motifs (ranging in length from 10–60 base pairs) are typically repeated 5-50 times. A variable number tandem repeat (or VNTR) is a location in a genome where a short nucleotide sequence is organized as a tandem repeat. These can be found on many chromosomes especially in minisatellites.

Minisatellite analysis, like RFLPs, also involves digestion of genomic DNA with restriction endonucleases, but minisatellites are a conceptually very different class of marker. They consist of chromosomal regions containing tandem repeat units of a 10-50 base motif, flanked by conserved DNA restriction sites

48. There was a mix-up at the hospital after a fire accident in the nursery division. Which of these children belong to the parents?

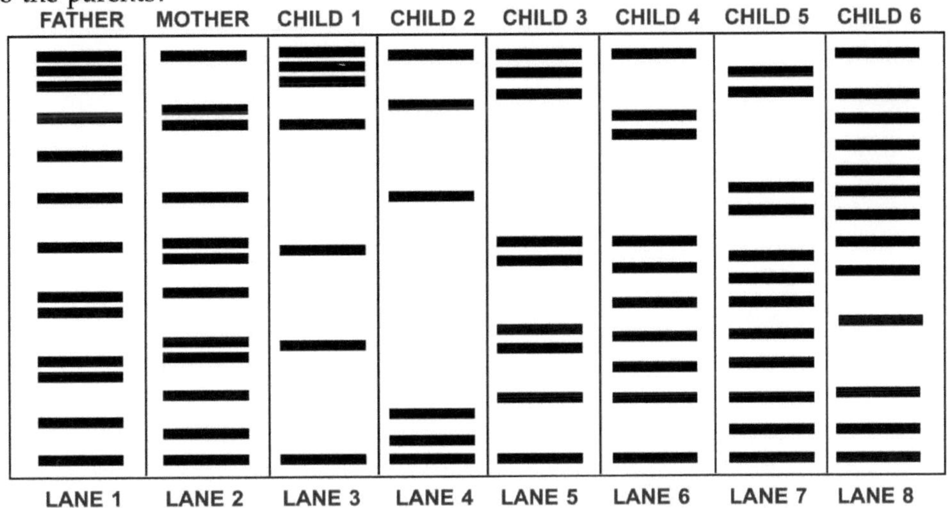

(A) All of the children

(B) Children 2, 3 and 6

(C) Children 1 and 3

(D) Children 2 and 4

Ans. (C) Children 1 and 3

Explanation: DNA profiling can be used to help confirm whether two people are related to one another and is commonly used to provide evidence that someone is, or is not, the biological parent of a child. By comparing the DNA profiles of two parents and children. We can see STRs in the children 1 and 3 have been inherited from parents.

SECTION - C

Section-C consists of one case followed by 6 questions linked to this case

(Q.No. 49 to 54). Besides this, 6 more questions are given. Attempt any 10 questions in this section. <u>The first attempted 10 questions would be evaluated.</u>

Case : To answer the questions, study the graphs below for Subject 1 and 2 showing different levels of certain hormones.

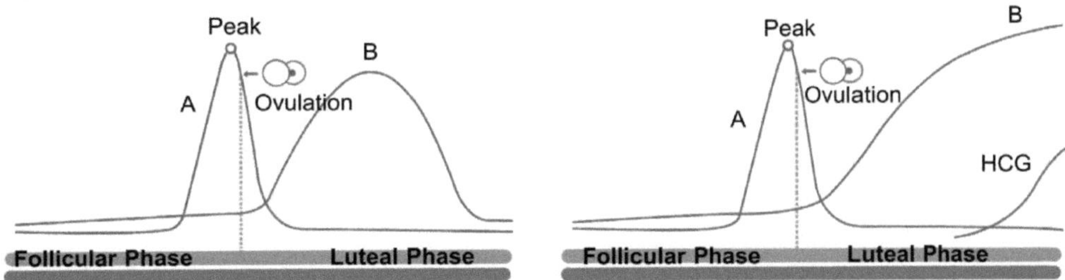

49. The peak observed in Subject 1 and 2 is due to:

(A) estrogen

(B) progesterone

(C) luteinizing hormone

(D) follicle stimulating hormone

Ans. (C) luteinizing hormone

> **Explanation:** Ovulation is an important reproductive process in females which is highly coordinated and controlled by hormones. Hormones produced by hypothalamus, pituitary gland and ovaries play an important role in the maintenance of the female reproductive system. Hypothalamus produces gonadotropin-releasing hormone (GnRH) which influences the production of follicle-stimulating hormone (FSH) and luteinizing hormone (LH) which in turn stimulates the ovaries to produce ovarian hormones. LH and FSH are gonadotropins produced by the pituitary gland. Both LH and FSH reach a peak level in the middle of the menstrual cycle. LH secretion rapidly increases to its maximum level called LH surge which ruptures the Graafian follicle and releases the ovum. Therefore, LH is the main hormone which induces ovulation.

50. Subject 2 has higher level of hormone B, which is:
    (A) estrogen
    (B) progesterone
    (C) luteinizing hormone
    (D) follicle stimulating hormone

Ans. (B) progesterone

> **Explanation:** After ovulation, graafian follicle rupture into corpus luteum which secretes the amount of progesterone hormone for the maintenance of endometrium. Progesterone hormone is also known as the pregnancy hormone. It prepares the uterus for implantation of the blastocyst to the uterine walls and helps in the formation of the placenta.

51. If the peak of Hormone A does not appear in the study for Subject 1, which of the following statement is true?
    (A) Peak of Hormone B will be observed at a higher point in the graph
    (B) Peak of Hormone B will be observed at a point lower than what is given in the graph
    (C) There will be no observed data for Hormone B
    (D) The graph for Hormone B will be a sharp rise followed by a plateau

Ans. (C) There will be no observed data for Hormone B

> **Explanation:** Luteinising hormone stimulates the corpus luteum to produce progesterone, which is required to support the early stages of pregnancy, if fertilisation occurs. LH is the main hormone which induces ovulation. In case of deficiency of LH, there will be no observed data for Progesterone.

52. Which structure in the ovary will remain functional in subject 2?
    (A) Corpus Luteum
    (B) Tertiary follicle
    (C) Graafian follicle
    (D) Primary follicle

Ans. (A) Corpus Luteum

> **Explanation:** Corpus luteum is a structure that is formed by the remains of the graafian follicle after ovulation. It is responsible for the production and secretion of the ovarian hormone progesterone. This hormone is responsible for not letting the endometrial lining of the uterus to break.
>
> HCG (human chorionic gonadotropin) is released from the placental tissue during pregnancy in a woman. The main function of this hormone is to prevent the corpus luteum from degenerating so that progesterone production will be continued for the maintenance of the uterus lining. This will allow the placenta to be intact which is essential for the growth of the fetus.

53. For subject 2 it is observed that the peak for hormone B has reached the plateau stage. After approximately how much time will the curve for hormone B descend?
    (A) 28 days
    (B) 42 days
    (C) 180 days
    (D) 280 days

Ans. (D) 280 days

> **Explanation:** Progesterone is also necessary for implantation of the fertilized egg in the uterus and for maintaining pregnancy. Levels of progesterone remain elevated throughout pregnancy for 280 days. These elevated levels also prevent the body from producing additional eggs during the pregnancy.

54. Which of the following statements is true about the subjects?

   (A) Subject 1 is pregnant   (B) Subject 2 is pregnant

   (C) Both subject 1 and 2 are pregnant   (D) Both subject 1 and 2 are not pregnant

Ans. (B) Subject 2 is pregnant

> **Explanation:** Subject 2 shows elevated progesterone and HCG levels which infers that Subject 2 is pregnant.

55. The gene that controls the ABO blood group system in human beings has three alleles – I^A, I^B and i. A child has blood group O. His father has blood group A and mother has blood group B. Genotypes of other offsprings can be:

   (i) $I^B I^B$ (ii) $I^A i$ (iii) $I^B i$ (iv) $I^A I^B$

   (v) ii

   (A) (i), (ii), (iii), (v)   (B) (ii), (iii), (iv), (v)

   (C) (iii), (iv), (v)   (D) (iv), (iii), (i)

Ans. (B) (ii), (iii), (iv), (v)

> **Explanation:** The genotype of parents of a child having blood group. 'O' will be $I^A i$ (male) and $I^B i$ (female). The possible genotypes of the other offsprings will be.
>
> If parents are heterozygous *i.e.*, father $I^A i$ and mother $I^B i$ then offspring will be.

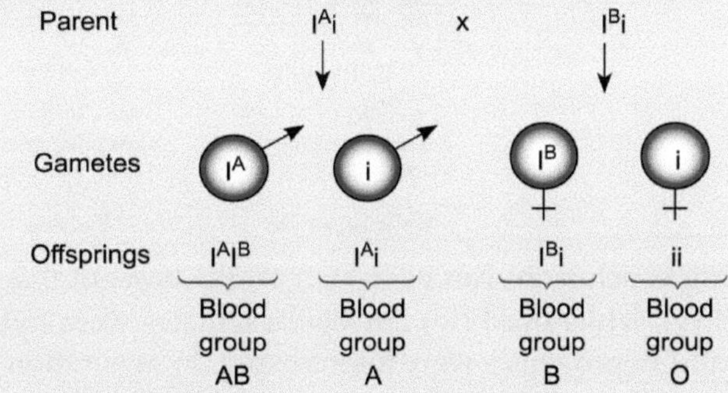

Parental genotypes $I^A i$ and $I^B i$ give progeny with 1 ($I^A I^B$) : 1 ($I^B i$) : 1 ($I^A i$) : 1 (ii) genotypic ratio.

56. Placed below is a karyotype of a human being.

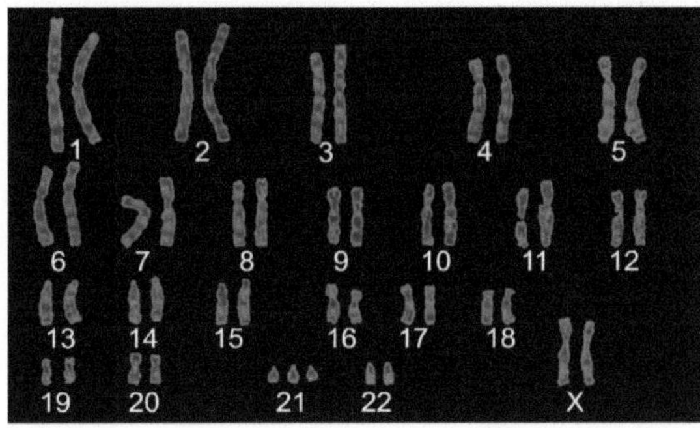

On the basis of this karyotype, which of the following conclusions can be drawn:

   (A) Normal human female

   (B) Person is suffering from Colour Blindness

   (C) Affected individual is a female with Down's syndrome

   (D) Affected individual is a female with Turner's syndrome

Ans. (C) Affected individual is a female with Down's syndrome

> **Explanation:** The trisomy 21 karyotype figure shows the chromosomal arrangement, with the prominent extra chromosome 21. Since the figure shows two X chromosomes, this karyotype is from a typical female.

57. Given below is a dihybrid cross performed on *Drosophila*.

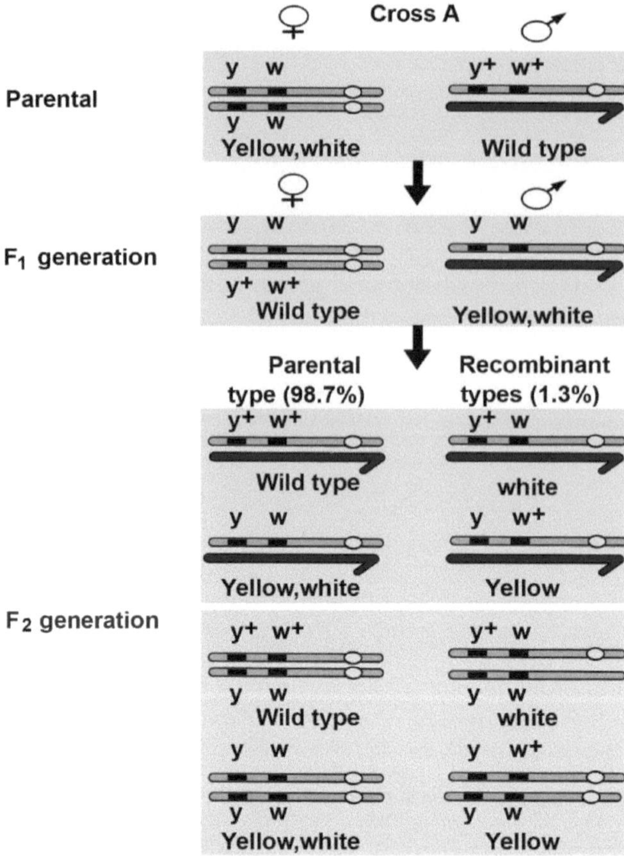

Which of the following conclusions can be drawn on the basis of this cross?

When yellow bodied (y), white eyed (w) *Drosophila* females were hybridized with brown bodied (y$^+$), red eyed males (w$^+$) and F$_1$ progenies were intercrossed, F$_2$ generation would have shown the following ratio:

(A) 1 : 2 : 1 because of linkage of genes

(B) 9 : 3 : 3 : 1 because of recombination of genes

(C) Deviation from 9:3:3:1 ratio because of segregation of genes

(D) Deviation from 9:3:3:1 ratio because of linkage of genes

Ans. (D) Deviation from 9:3:3:1 ratio because of linkage of genes

> **Explanation:** In *Drosophila*, the genes for body and eye colour are located on X chromosome. When two genes in a dihybrid cross are situated on the same chromosome, the proportion of parental gene combination are higher than non-parental type. This occurs due to physical association or linkage of the two genes while non-parental gene combinations due to recombination between genes. Thus, linkage and recombination deviate the ratio from Mendelian ratio of a dihybrid cross (9:3:3:1).

58. Which cellular process is shown below?

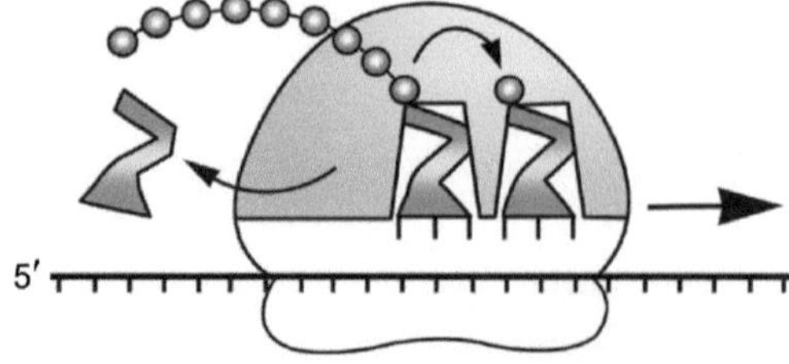

(A) DNA Replication

(B) Translation - Initiation

(C) Translation - Elongation

(D) Translation – Termination

Ans. (C) Translation- Elongation

Explanation: Translation is the process of translating the sequence of mRNA (messenger RNA) into a sequence of amino acids. This translation takes place during protein synthesis. During elongation the first codon mRNA binds with the anticodon of the methionyl tRNA complex in the P site. The other aminoacyl tRNA complex with the appropriate amino acids thus enters the ribosome and attaches to A site. The peptide bond is formed between the first and second amino acids when the anticodon binds to the second codon in the mRNA in the presence of an enzyme, peptidyl transferase.

Then, the translocation takes place *i.e.,* when the first amino acids and the tRNA are broken, this tRNA is removed from the P site and the second tRNA from the A site is pulled to the P site along with the mRNA.

59. Origin of replication of DNA in *E. coli* is shown below, Identify the labelled parts (i), (ii), (iii) and (iv).

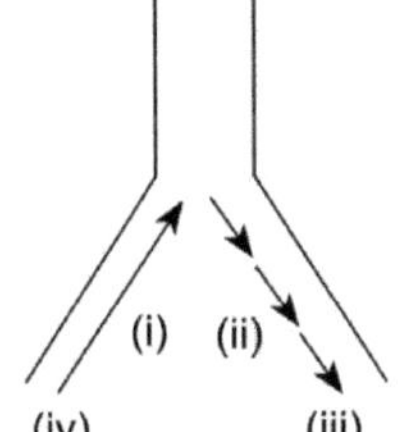

(A) (i)- discontinuous synthesis, (ii)- continuous synthesis, (iii)- 3′ end, (iv)- 5′end

(B) (i)- continuous synthesis, (ii)- discontinuous synthesis, (iii)- 5′ end, (iv)- 3′end

(C) (i)- discontinuous synthesis, (ii)- continuous synthesis, (iii)- 5′ end, (iv)- 3′end

(D) (i)- continuous synthesis, (ii)- discontinuous synthesis, (iii)- 3′ end, (iv)- 5′end

Ans. (D) (i)- continuous synthesis, (ii)- discontinuous synthesis, (iii)- 3′ end, (iv)- 5′end

Explanation: The synthesis of a new strand of a replicating DNA molecule as a series of short fragments that are subsequently joined together. Only one of the new strands, the so-called lagging strand, is synthesized in this way. The other strand (leading strand) is synthesized by continuous addition of nucleotides to the growing end, *i.e.,* continuous replication. The difference arises because of the different orientations of the parent template strands. The template of the leading strand is oriented in the 3′ → 5′ direction (according to the numbering of atoms in the sugar residues), which means that the leading strand itself is oriented in the opposite 5′ → 3′ direction, providing an –OH group at the 3′ end for the continual addition of nucleotides by DNA polymerase, which moves forwards as the template strands unwind at the replication fork. However, the template of the lagging strand is oriented in a 5′ → 3′ direction, so the lagging strand itself is oriented in the 3′ → 5′ direction, and hence the DNA polymerase complex must move backwards away from the replication fork.

60. Transcription unit is represented in the diagram given below.

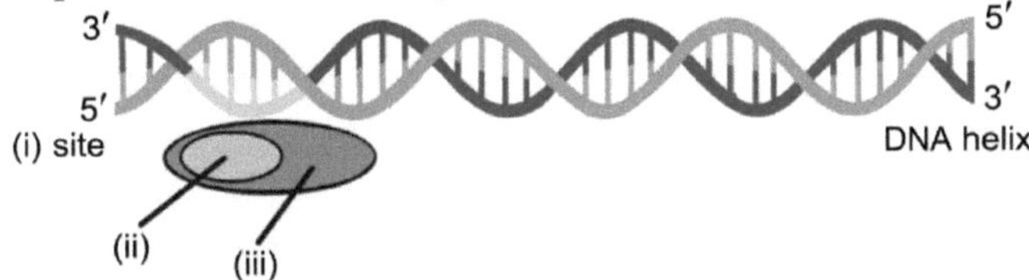

Identify site (i), factor (ii) and Enzyme (iii) responsible for carrying out the process.
(A) (i) Promoter Site, (ii) Rho factor, (iii) RNA polymerase
(B) (i) Terminator Site, (ii) Sigma factor, (iii) RNA polymerase
(C) (i) Promoter Site, (ii) Sigma factor, (iii) RNA polymerase
(D) (i) Promoter Site, (ii) Sigma factor, (iii) DNA polymerase

Ans. (C) (i) Promoter Site, (ii) Sigma factor, (iii) RNA polymerase

Explanation: The process of copying genetic information from antisense or template strand of the DNA into RNA is called transcription. The segment of DNA that takes part in transcription is called transcription unit. It has three components - a promoter, the structural gene and a terminator. A promoter is a region of DNA that initiates transcription of a particular gene. Promoters are located near the transcription start sites of genes on the same strand and upstream on the DNA. RNA polymerase is the main transcription enzyme. Transcription begins when RNA polymerase binds to a promoter sequence near the beginning of a gene (directly or through helper proteins). A sigma factor (σ factor or specificity factor) is a protein needed for initiation of transcription in bacteria.

❑❑

Sample Paper 1

Biology

SECTION – A

Section – A consists of 24 questions. Attempt any 20 questions from this section. The first attempted 20 questions would be evaluated.

1. Which one of the following is the most widely accepted method of contraception in India at present?
 (a) Cervical caps
 (b) Tubectomy
 (c) Diaphragms
 (d) IUDs (Intra Uterine Devices)

2. Parthenogenesis is common in:
 (a) Grapes
 (b) Mango
 (c) Citrus
 (d) Litchi

3. A strand is shown below. What will be the polarity of it's complementary strand?

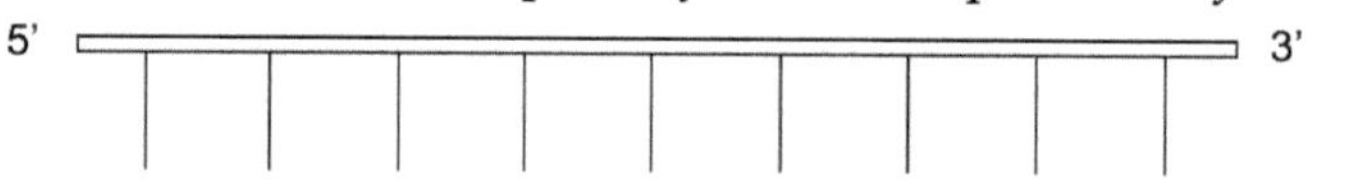

 (a) Parallel, $3' \to 5'$
 (b) Antiparallel, $3' \to 5'$
 (c) Parallel, $5' \to 3'$
 (d) Antiparallel, $5' \to 3'$

4. The F_2 genotypic ratio of monohybrid cross is:
 (a) $1:1$
 (b) $1:2:1$
 (c) $2:1:2$
 (d) $9:3:3:1$

5. Which of the following is the actual structure of the tRNA?

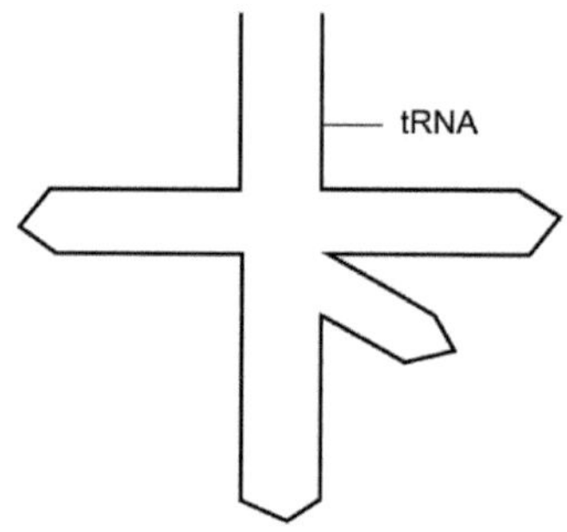

 (a) Clover leaf like structure
 (b) Football like structure
 (c) An inverted L shaped structure
 (d) An inverted T shaped structure

6. Endosperm cell of an angiosperm has 36 chromosomes. The number of chromosomes in the gametes would be:
 (a) 11
 (b) 12
 (c) 8
 (d) 9

7. Label the part marked as 2.

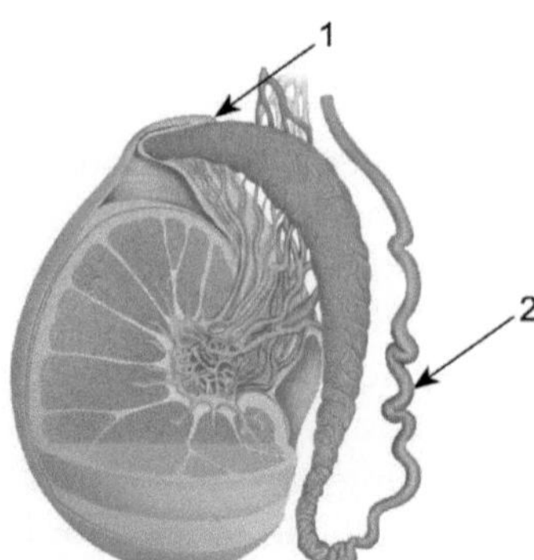

 (a) Epididymis
 (b) Corpus epididymis
 (c) Vas deferens
 (d) Vasa efferentia

8. Khorana was awarded nobel prize for:
   (a) discovering DNA
   (b) discovering RNA
   (c) chemical synthesis of gene
   (d) discovering DNA polymerase

9. Which of the following does not belong to STDs?
   (a) Gonorrhea
   (b) Syphilis
   (c) AIDS
   (d) Dengue

10. What process does the image show?

   (a) Fertilisation
   (b) Parthenogenesis
   (c) Torrulation
   (d) Sporulation

11. A cross between two tall plants resulted in offspring having few dwarf plants. What would be the genotypes of both the parents?
   (a) TT and Tt
   (b) Tt and Tt
   (c) TT and TT
   (d) Tt and tt

12. The chromosomal theory of inheritance violates which of the following laws?
   (a) Law of dominance
   (b) Law of segregation
   (c) Law of independent assortment
   (d) None of these

13. Location and secretion of leydig cells are:
   (a) Liver-cholesterol
   (b) Ovary-estrogen
   (c) Testis-testosterone
   (d) Pancreas-glucagon

14. In rice genome project large insert genomic libraries used as the primary sequencing templates are constructed in:
   (a) Bacterial temporary chromosomes (BTCs)
   (b) Yeast artificial chromosomes (YACs)
   (c) Bacterial artificial chromosomes (BACs)
   (d) Yeast mechanical chromosomes (YMCs)

15. Name the specific component(s) that form deoxyadenosine.
   (a) A phosphate group
   (b) Adenine
   (c) Both (a) and (b)
   (d) Thymine

16. What is chemical name for thymine known as?
   (a) 3-methoxy uracil
   (b) 3-methyl uracil
   (c) 5-methyl uracil
   (d) 5-methoxy uracil

17. Name the gland(s) that contribute to human seminal plasma.
   (a) Prostate gland
   (b) Bulbourethral gland
   (c) Seminal vesicle
   (d) All of these

18. Name one dioecious plant.
   (a) Cucurbits
   (b) Coconuts
   (c) Marchantia
   (d) Chara

19. In DNA tertiary structure, what is a histone octamer?
   (a) A complex consisting of eight positively charged histone proteins (two of each H_2A, H_2B, H_3 and H_4) that aid in the packaging of DNA
   (b) A complex consisting of eight negatively charged histone proteins (two of each H_2A, H_2B, H_3 and H_4) that aid in the packaging of DNA
   (c) A complex consisting of nine positively charged histone proteins (H_1 and two of each H_2A, H_2B, H_3 and H_4) that aid in the packaging of DNA.
   (d) A complex consisting of nine negatively charged histone proteins (H_1 and two of each H_2A, H_2B, H_3 and H_4) that aid in the packaging of DNA.

20. How many stop codons are there in the genetic code?
   (a) 1
   (b) 2
   (c) 3
   (d) 4

21. The main function of tRNA with regards to protein synthesis is:
   (a) Proofreading
   (b) Identifies amino acids and transports them to ribosomes
   (c) Inhibits protein synthesis
   (d) All of these

22. The following DNA strand is used as a template for transcription 3' CGTAAGCGGCT 5'. Which of the following RNA strand will be produced?

(a) 5' AGCCGCUUACG 3'

(b) 5' GCAUUCGCCGA 3'

(c) 5' CGUAAGCGGCU 3'

(d) 5' UCGGCGAAUGC 3'

23. The given figure represents the inheritance pattern of a certain type of traits in humans.

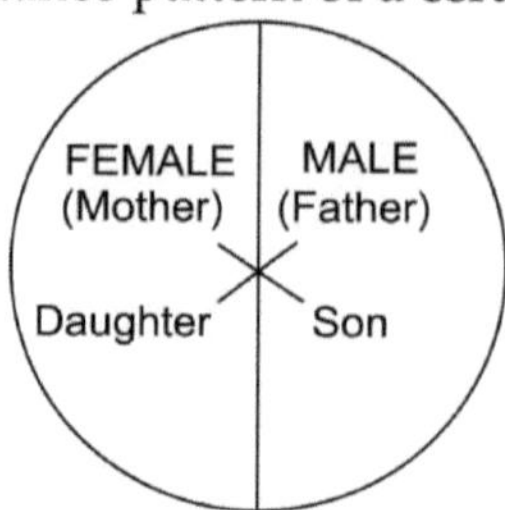

Which one of the following conditions could be an example of this pattern?

(a) Thalassemia   (b) Haemophilia   (c) Phenylketonuria   (d) Turner's syndrome

24. What is the role of topoisomerases in eukaryotic DNA replication?

(a) Topoisomerase enzymes cut, uncoil and reseal the double stranded DNA.

(b) Topoisomerase enzymes bind to the origin of replication sites within double stranded DNA.

(c) Topoisomerase enzymes open up the double stranded DNA at the replication fork.

(d) Topoisomerase enzymes join the Okazaki fragments together with phosphodiester bonds.

SECTION – B

Section – B consists of 24 questions (Sl. No.25 to 48). Attempt any 20 questions from this section. The first attempted 20 questions would be evaluated.

25. Assertion: Double fertilisation is a characteristic feature of angiosperms.

Reason: Double fertilisation involves triple fusion.

(a) Assertion and reason both are correct statements and reason is the correct explanation of the assertion.

(b) Assertion and reason both are correct statements, but reason is not the correct explanation of the assertion

(c) Assertion is true, but reason is false statement.

(d) Assertion is false, but reason is true statement.

26. Assertion: Repetitive sequences make up very large portion of human genome.

Reason: Repetitive sequences do not have direct coding functions in the genome.

(a) Assertion and reason both are correct statements and reason is the correct explanation of the assertion.

(b) Assertion and reason both are correct statements, but reason is not the correct explanation of the assertion

(c) Assertion is true, but reason is false statement.

(d) Assertion is false, but reason is true statement.

27. Assertion: Breast-feeding during initial period of infant growth is recommended.

Reason: Colostrum contains several antibodies, essential to render immunity in new-borns.

(a) Assertion and reason both are correct statements and reason is the correct explanation of the assertion.

(b) Assertion and reason both are correct statements, but reason is not the correct explanation of the assertion

(c) Assertion is true, but reason is false statement.

(d) Assertion is false, but reason is true statement.

28. Assertion: Hepatitis-B is a sexually transmitted disease.

Reason: Hepatitis-B is completely curable if detected early and treated properly.

(a) Assertion and reason both are correct statements and reason is the correct explanation of the assertion.

(b) Assertion and reason both are correct statements, but reason is not the correct explanation of the assertion

(c) Assertion is true, but reason is false statement.

(d) Assertion is false, but reason is true statement.

29. Inhetitance of which of the following traits is shown in the given cross?

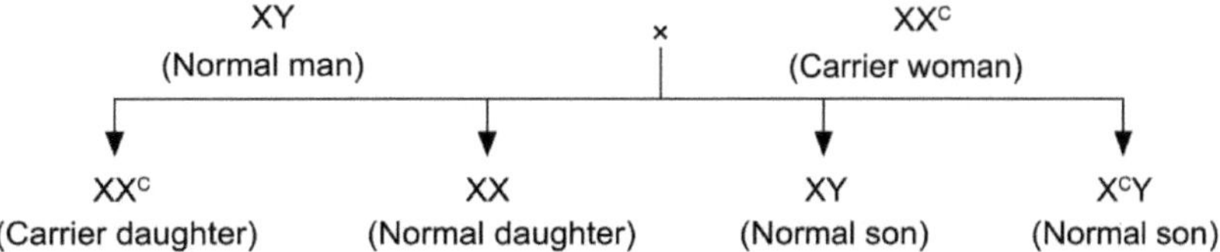

(a) X-linked dominant trait

(b) X-linked recessive trait

(c) Autosomal recessive trait

(d) Autosomal dominant trait

30. What is the ratio of homozygous plants for both dominant characters in F_2 of a dihybrid cross?

(a) 1/16
(b) 3/16
(c) 4/16
(d) 9/16

31. Finger-like structure above the urethral opening is called:

(a) vulva
(b) clitoris
(c) vagina
(d) labia minora

32. What does the failure of cell division after DNA replication result in?

(a) Polyploidy
(b) Aneuploidy
(c) Apoptosis
(d) Migration of cells

33. What determines the differences between the progeny and parents?

(a) Inheritance
(b) Heritage
(c) Genetics
(d) Variation

34. Surgical methods are also called as:

(a) fertilisation
(b) sterilisation
(c) ejaculation
(d) emission

35. Which of the following statements is correct regarding DNA and RNA?

(a) DNA is highly reactive.

(b) RNA is not catalytic.

(c) RNA cannot be easily degraded.

(d) DNA is a better genetic material than RNA.

36. RTI is an acronym for:

(a) Reproductive Tract Infarctions

(b) Reproductive Tract Infections

(c) Respiratory Tract Infarctions

(d) Respiratory Tract Infections

37. Which of the following is not the function of a placenta?

(a) Supply of nutrients to the fetus

(b) Removal of excretory products from the fetus

(c) Supply of carbon dioxide to the fetus

(d) Supply of oxygen to the fetus

38. Which of the following is a recessive trait in pea plants?

(a) Dwarf stem height
(b) Violet flowers
(c) Axial flowers
(d) Inflated pods

39. Which of the following principles of Mendel is shown by the following figure?

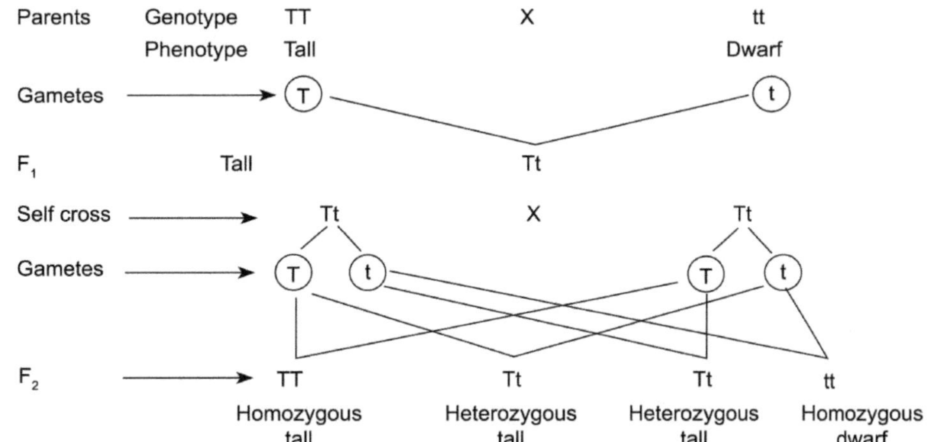

(a) Law of segregation

(b) Law of independent assortment

(c) Law of dominancy

(d) None of these

40. What happens when the small subunit of the ribosome encounters mRNA?

(a) Separation of the small and the larger subunit of the ribosome

(b) Translation of the central dogma of DNA

    (c) Joining of the small and the larger subunit of the ribosome

    (d) Transcription of the central dogma of DNA

41. What is the generation of plants produced by the crossing of true-breeding plants called?

    (a) F_1 (b) F_0 (c) F_2 (d) F_3

42. Where are the untranslated regions (UTRs) present?

    (a) At both the 5′ and the 3′ end   (b) At only the 5′ end

    (c) At only the 3′ end   (d) Outer to the 5′ and the 3′ end

43. What is the genotype of a plant showing a dominant phenotype of violet flowers if it is test crossed and produces only violet-flowered plants?

    (a) VV   (b) Vv   (c) vv   (d) v

44. Label 1.

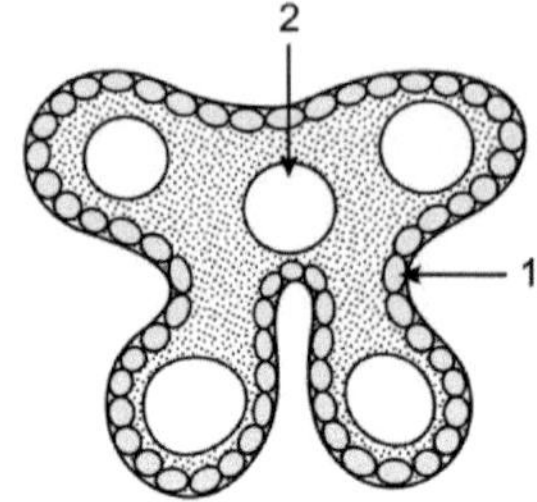

    (a) Edge   (b) Filament   (c) Stomium   (d) Tapetum

45. The part of embryonal axis above the level of cotyledons is called:

    (a) hypocotyl   (b) haustorium   (c) hypophysis   (d) epicotyl

46. What is the process of activation of amino acids in the presence of ATP and its linkage to their cognate tRNA known as?

    (a) Charging of tRNA   (b) Charging of ATP

    (c) Aminoacetylation of tRNA   (d) Aminoacetylation of ATP

47. ____________ is the process formation of zygote to an embryo.

    (a) Fertilisation   (b) Syngamy   (c) Embryogenesis   (d) Blastocyst

48. What happens when S-strain and the biomolecule (Lipid) are together, when testing the transformation with regards to the R-strain?

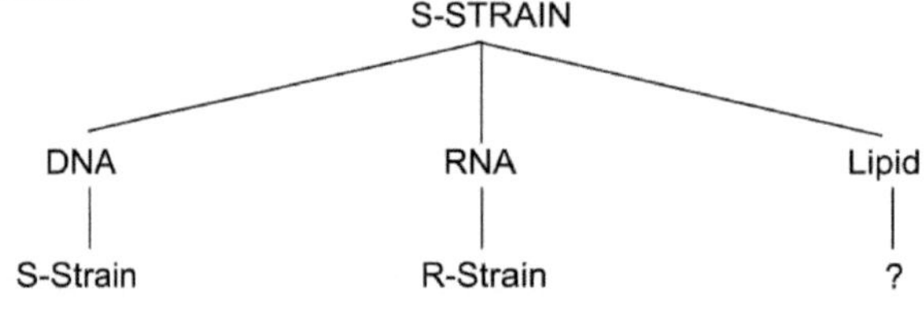

    (a) R-strain   (b) S-strain

    (c) R-strain and S-strain   (d) Dead R-strain

SECTION – C

Section–C consists of one case followed by 6 questions linked to this case (Q.No. 49 to 54). Besides this, 6 more questions are given. Attempt any 10 questions in this section. <u>The first attempted 10 questions would be evaluated.</u>

Case : Study the given figure of embryo sac in angiosperms and answer the questions that follows:

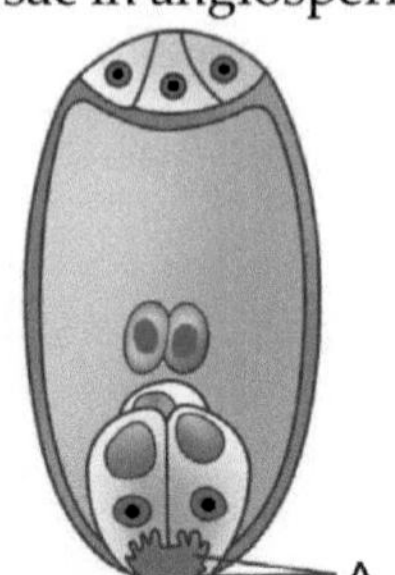

49. Embryo sac is also called:
    (a) female gamete
    (b) synergids
    (c) female gametophyte
    (d) egg of angiosperm

50. The arrangement of the nuclei in a normal embryo sac in the dicot:
    (a) $3+2+3$
    (b) $2+3+3$
    (c) $3+3+2$
    (d) $2+4+2$

51. Antipodal nuclei in a typical angiospermic embryo sac are found towards:
    (a) micropylar end
    (b) in the middle (polar) region
    (c) chalazal end
    (d) on the lateral sides

52. What does the labelled part A do at the entrance into ovule?
    (a) It brings about opening of the pollen tube.
    (b) It guides pollen tube from a synergid to egg.
    (c) It helps in the entry of pollen tube into a synergid.
    (d) It prevents entry of more than one pollen tube into the embryo sac.

53. _____________ is a mass of finger like projections on the synergid wall.
    (a) Egg
    (b) Chalaza
    (c) Micropylar
    (d) Filiform apparatus

54. What are 3 chalazal cells called?
    (a) Synergids
    (b) Antipodal cells
    (c) Polar nuclei
    (d) Chalaza

55. Which of the following Mendel's law is shown by the following figure?

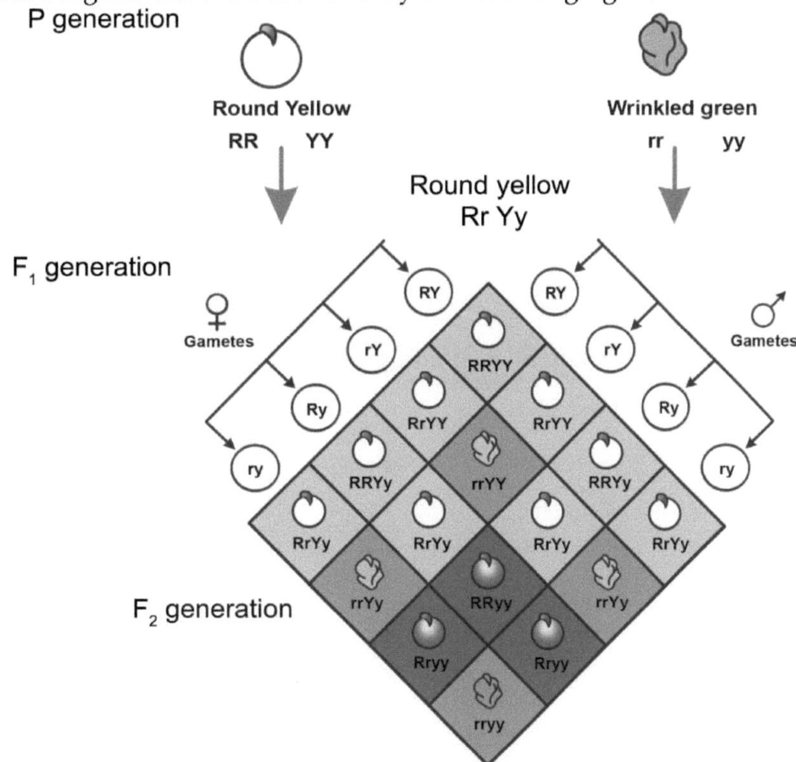

    (a) Monohybrid cross and law of independent assortment
    (b) Dihybrid cross and law of independent assortment
    (c) Dihybrid cross and law of dominance
    (d) Monohybrid cross and law of dominance

56. Name the following structures.

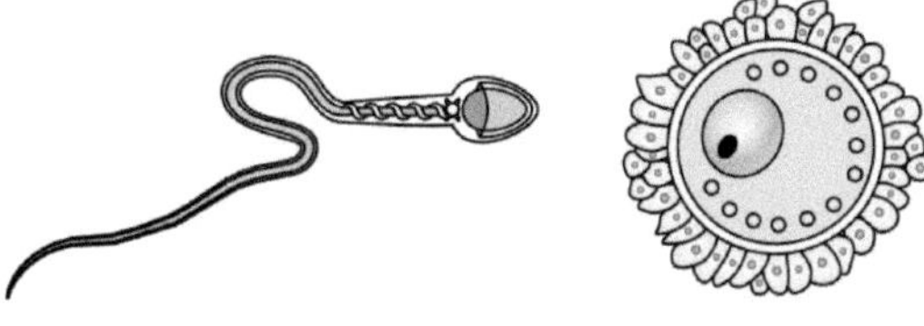

(a) (X) is male gamete and (Y) is female gamete
(b) (X) is female gamete and (Y) is male gamete
(c) Both (X) and (Y) are male gametes
(d) Both (X) and (Y) are female gametes

57. The DNA helical structure is linked to which type of histone protein in the following diagram'?' ?

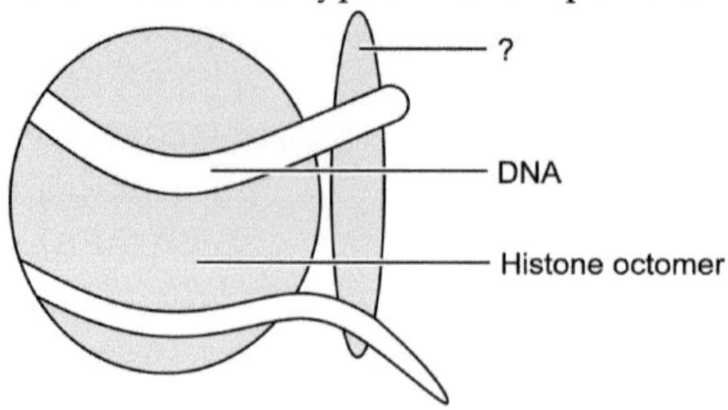

(a) H_2A histones
(b) H_1 histones
(c) H_2B histones
(d) H_3 histones

58. Label the part marked with arrow.

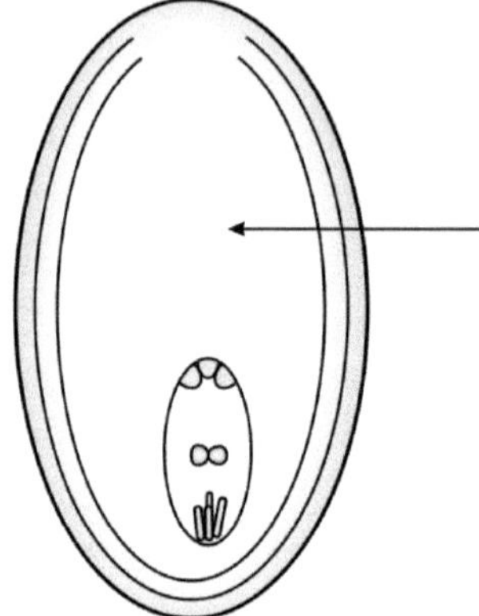

(a) Chalaza
(b) Micropyle
(c) Egg
(d) Nucellus

59. In the following human pedigree, the filled symbols represent the affected individuals. Identify the type of given pedigree.

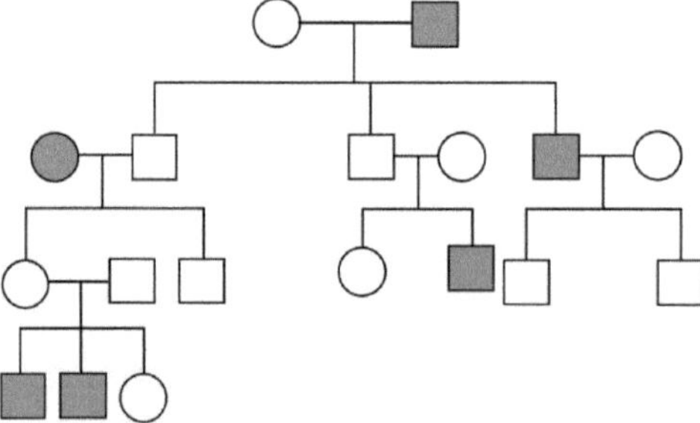

(a) X-linked recessive
(b) Autosomal recessive
(c) X-linked dominant
(d) Autosomal dominant

60. What is the structure present inside the nucleus known as'?' ?

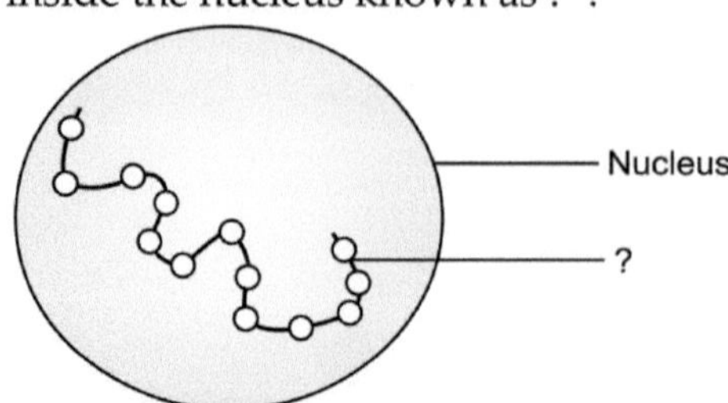

(a) Chromosome
(b) Chromatid
(c) Ribosome
(d) Lysosome

Sample Paper 2

Biology

SECTION – A

Section – A consists of 24 questions. Attempt any 20 questions from this section.
The first attempted 20 questions would be evaluated.

1. Mating of an organism to a double recessive in order to determine whether it is homozygous or heterozygous for a character under consideration is called:
   (a) Reciprocal cross (b) Test cross (c) Dihybrid cross (d) Back cross

2. Which of the following enzymes remove supercoiling in replicating DNA ahead of the replication fork?
   (a) DNA polymerases (b) Helicases (c) Primases (d) Topoisomerases

3. Name the part 3.

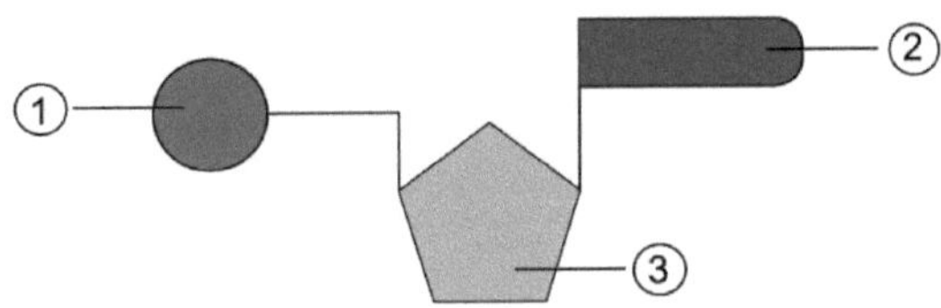

   (a) nitrogenous base (b) phosphate group
   (c) deoxyribose sugar (d) none of these

4. In angiosperms _______ lead to the formation of a mature male gametophyte from a pollen mother cell.
   (a) two meiotic divisions (b) three mitotic division
   (c) two mitotic and one meiotic division (d) a single mitotic division

5. In the following pedigree chart, the mutant trait is shaded.

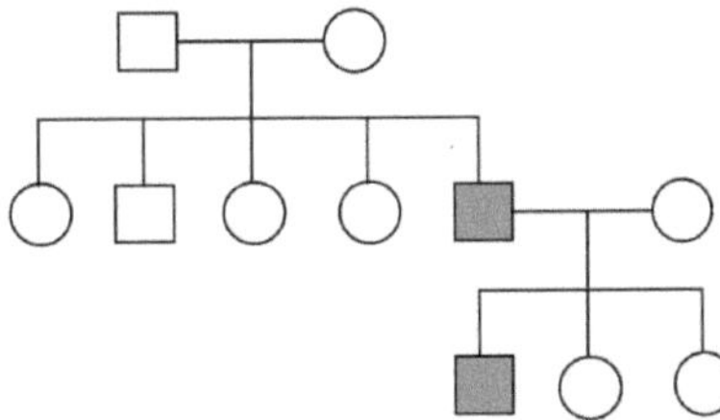

   The gene responsible for the trait is:
   (a) dominant and sex-linked (b) dominant and autosomal
   (c) recessive and sex-linked (d) recessive and autosomal

6. Which of the following genotypes show the heterozygous condition?
   (a) Rr (b) RR (c) rr (d) None of these

7. What does the given diagram represent?

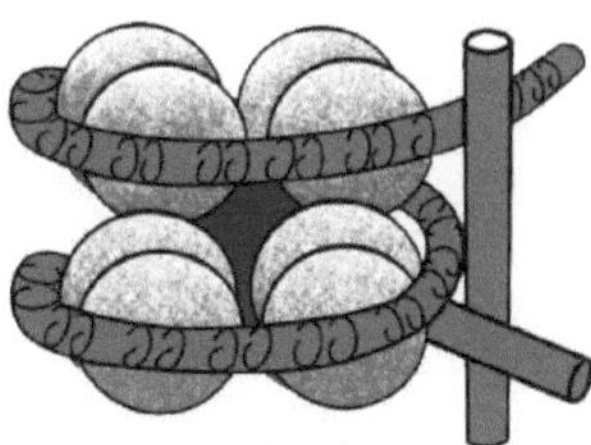

   (a) Nucleosome (b) Spliceosome
   (c) Histone complex (d) Both (a) and (b)

8. Usually pollen grains are shed at:
   (a) one-celled stage   (b) two-celled stage   (c) four-celled stage   (d) five-celled stage
9. The promoter site and terminator site for transcription are located at:
   (a) 3′ (downstream) end and 5′ (upstream) end respectively of transcription unit
   (b) 5′ (upstream) end and 3′ (downstream) end respectively of transcription unit
   (c) 5′ (upstream) end
   (d) 3′ (downstream) end
10. Refer to the given figure:

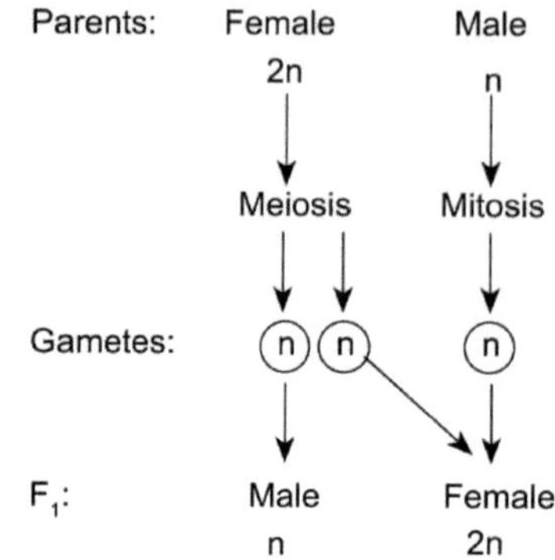

   This type of sex-determination is found in:
   (a) grasshoppers and cockroaches   (b) birds and reptiles
   (c) butterflies and moths   (d) honeybees, ants and wasps
11. Clitoris in females is:
   (a) homologous to penis   (b) analogous to penis
   (c) functional penis in female   (d) non-functional
12. During what phase of menstrual cycle are primary follicles converted to Graafian follicles?
   (a) Menstrual phase   (b) Follicular phase   (c) Luteal phase   (d) Secretory phase
13. Which of the following are the functions of RNA?
   (a) It is carrier of genetic information from DNA to ribosome synthesizing polypeptides
   (b) It carries amino acids to ribosomes
   (c) It is constituent component of ribosomes
   (d) All of these
14. The permissible use of the technique amniocentesis is for:
   (a) detecting any genetic abnormality
   (b) detecting sex of the unborn foetus
   (c) artificial insemination
   (d) transfer of embryo into the uterus of a surrogate mother
15. Where the formation of Embryo sac occurs?
   (a) Stigma   (b) Ovule   (c) Ovary   (d) None of these
16. Filiform apparatus is:
   (a) thick layer at micropylar end   (b) thin layer at micropylar end
   (c) thick layer at chalazal end   (d) thin layer at chalazal end
17. Microsporogenesis is defined as:
   (a) development of microspores outside microsporangia
   (b) development of megaspores inside microsporangia
   (c) development of microspores inside microsporangia
   (d) development of megaspore outside microsporangia
18. What are the basic components of a nucleotide?
   (a) A nitrogenous base   (b) A pentose sugar   (c) A phosphate group   (d) All of these

19. The location of the Sertoli cells in humans:

(a) ovaries   (b) testes   (c) germ cells   (d) none of these

20. What does the Mendel's law of dominance say about the 'factor'?

(a) Occur in pairs   (b) One member of the pair dominates the other

(c) Both (a) and (b)   (d) Do not occur in pairs

21. Aneuploidy leads to:

(a) gain of a chromosome   (b) loss of a chromosome

(c) gain or loss of a chromosome   (d) none of these

22. Example of polygenic inheritance:

(a) Flower colour in *Mirabilis jalapa*   (b) Skin colour in dogs

(c) Skin colour in humans   (d) None of these

23. Given figure represents the DNA double helix model as proposed by Watson and Crick (1953). Select the option that shows correct measurement of A, B and C.

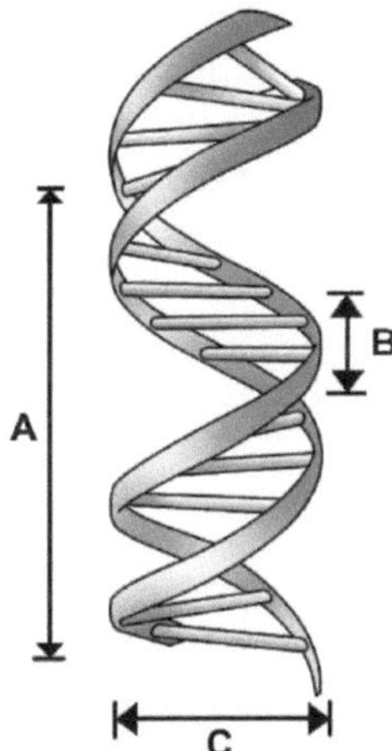

(a) A – 3.4 nm, B – 0.34 nm, C – 2 nm   (b) A – 34 nm, B – 0.3.4 nm, C – 20 nm

(c) A – 3.4 Å, B – 0.34 Å, C – 20 Å   (d) A – 34 Å, B – 3.4 Å, C – 2 Å

24. What, according to Mendel, was responsible for the inheritance of specific traits?

(a) Genes   (b) Chromosomes   (c) Factors   (d) DNA

SECTION - B

Section – B consists of 24 questions (Sl. No.25 to 48). Attempt any 20 questions from this section. <u>The first attempted 20 questions would be evaluated.</u>

25. Assertion: MTP is carried out to get rid of unwanted pregnancies either due to casual unprotected intercourse or failure of the contraceptive used during coitus or rapes.

Reason: MTP is also essential in certain cases where continuation of the pregnancy could be harmful or even fatal either to the mother or to the foetus or both.

(a) Assertion and reason both are correct statements and reason is the correct explanation of the assertion.

(b) Assertion and reason both are correct statements, but reason is not the correct explanation of the assertion

(c) Assertion is true, but reason is false statement.

(d) Assertion is false, but reason is true statement.

26. Assertion: Progesterone is essential for maintenance of the endometrium.

Reason: Endometrium is essential for implantation of embryo.

(a) Assertion and reason both are correct statements and reason is the correct explanation of the assertion.

(b) Assertion and reason both are correct statements, but reason is not the correct explanation of the assertion

(c) Assertion is true, but reason is false statement.

(d) Assertion is false, but reason is true statement.

27. **Assertion:** Behaviour of chromosome is parallel to gene.

   Reason: Genes are located on the chromosome.

   (a) Assertion and reason both are correct statements and reason is the correct explanation of the assertion.

   (b) Assertion and reason both are correct statements, but reason is not the correct explanation of the assertion

   (c) Assertion is true, but reason is false statement.

   (d) Assertion is false, but reason is true statement.

28. **Assertion:** Pollen grain of angiosperm is considered as a male gametophyte.

   Reason: Pollen grain consists of stigma, style and ovary.

   (a) Assertion and reason both are correct statements and reason is the correct explanation of the assertion.

   (b) Assertion and reason both are correct statements, but reason is not the correct explanation of the assertion

   (c) Assertion is true, but reason is false statement.

   (d) Assertion is false, but reason is true statement.

29. The following statements are drawn as conclusions from the given graph:

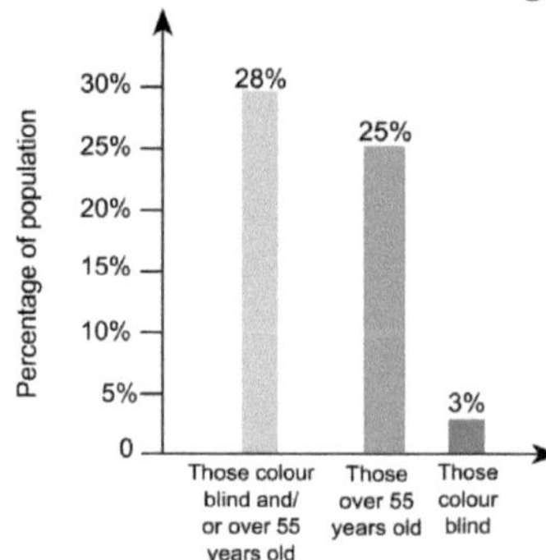

   I.   Those colourblind who are over 55 years's old are more than overall colourblind people.

   II. The percentage of colourblind people is 3% of total population.

   III. The percentage of people who are 55 years's old is 28% of the total population

   (a) Only II is true   (b) I and III are true

   (c) Only I is true   (d) I, II and III are true

30. What are the steps involved during the process of transcription in bacterial species?

   (a) Initiation   (b) Elongation   (c) Termination   (d) All of these

31. The pedigree analysis is a method of studying:

   (a) genetic disorders   (b) brain disorders   (c) linkage   (d) none of these

32. Which of the following will not cause variations among siblings?

   (a) Independent assortment of genes   (b) Crossing over

   (c) Linkage   (d) Mutation

33. The first amino acid added by the tRNA is added to the anticodon:

   (a) AUG   (b) UAC   (c) ACG   (d) UGC

34. __________ stores sperm prior to ejaculation.

   (a) Epididymis   (b) Vas deferens

   (c) Leydig cells   (d) Seminiferous tubules

35. _________ should be consulted to discuss the pros and cons of a contraceptive.

   (a) Politicians   (b) Lawyers   (c) Astrologists   (d) Doctors

36. How many types of nucleic acids are present in the living systems?

   (a) One   (b) Two   (c) Three   (d) Four

37. In ____________, female gametophytes stop their growth at 8 nucleate stage.

   (a) cleistogamous   (b) chasmogamous

   (c) gymnosperms   (d) angiosperms

38. All genes located on the same chromosome:
  (a) form different groups depending upon their relative distance
  (b) form one linkage group
  (c) will not form any linkage groups
  (d) form interactive groups that affect the phenotype.

39. What is the figure given below showing in particular?

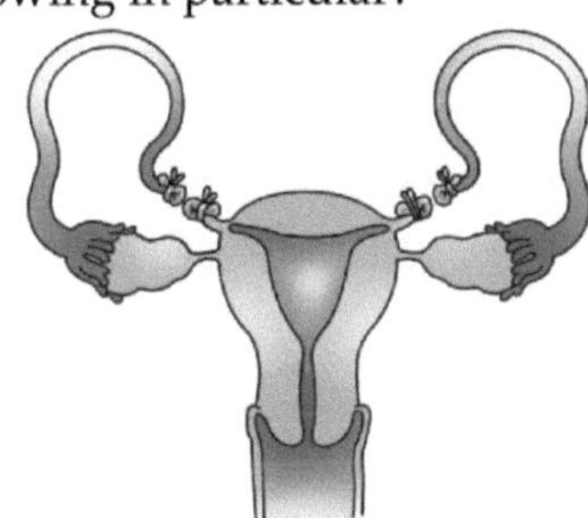

  (a) Ovarian cancer   (b) Uterine cancer
  (c) Tubectomy   (d) Vasectomy

40. In *Mirabilis jalapa*, red and white-coloured flowers are seen. When they are crossed, all flowers are pink coloured in:
  (a) F_1 generation   (b) F_2 generation   (c) Both (a) and (b)   (d) Gametes

41. Aneuploidy arises due to:
  (a) non-disjunction of homologous chromosome.   (b) disjunction of homologous chromosome
  (c) non-disjunction of alleles   (d) none of these

42. What is the nature of the strands of the DNA duplex?
  (a) Anti-parallel and complementary   (b) Identical and complementary
  (c) Anti-parallel and non-complementary   (d) Dissimilar and non-complementary

43. Which of the following is a sex-linked recessive disease?
  (a) Hemophilia   (b) Colour blindness
  (c) Both (a) and (b)   (d) Down's syndrome

44. Identify the incorrect labelled part.

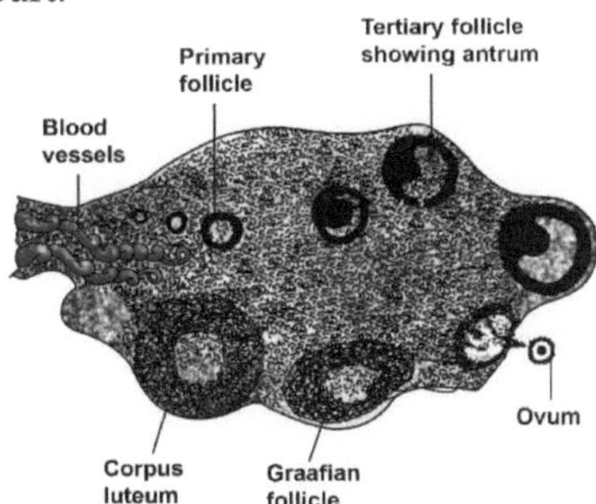

  (a) Primary follicle   (b) Ovum
  (c) Graafian follicle   (d) Corpus luteum

45. When _______ pairs of traits are combined in a hybrid, _______ of one pair of characters is independent of the other pair of characters.
  (a) one. linkage   (b) two, segregation
  (c) one, segregation   (d) None of these

46. Hershey and Chase's experiment was based on the principle of:
  (a) Transformation   (b) Translation   (c) Transduction   (d) Transcription

47. The codon is a ____________.
  (a) singlet   (b) duplet   (c) triplet   (d) quadruplet

48. Choose the correct option.

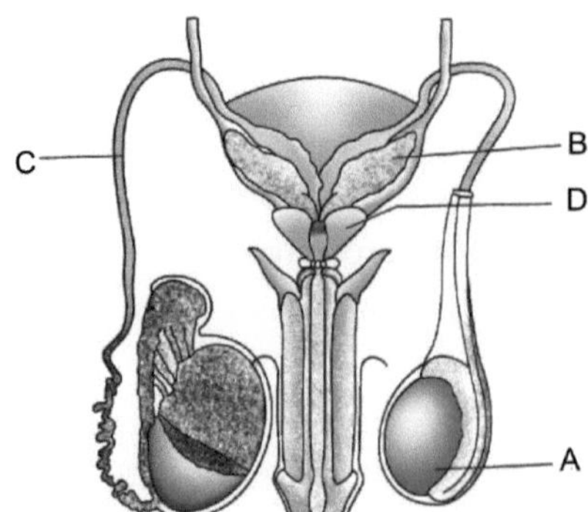

(a) A—Testes-possesses 3-4 testicular lobules

(b) B—Seminal vesicle-storage of sperm

(c) C—Vas deferens-helps in sperm transfer

(d) D—Prostate gland-secretes seminal fluid

SECTION - C

Section-C consists of one case followed by 6 questions linked to this case

(Q.No. 49 to 54). Besides this, 6 more questions are given. Attempt any 10 questions in this section. <u>The first attempted 10 questions would be evaluated.</u>

Case: To answer the questions, study the figure given below:

Physical features

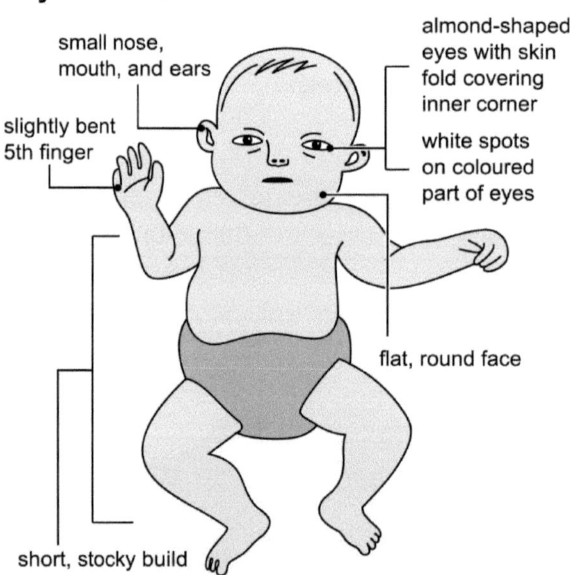

Intellectual disabilities and developmental delays vary in individual.

49. Person with the disease shown in the image usually have __________ copies of chromosome 21.

    (a) no   (b) one   (c) two   (d) three

50. Characteristics of disease shown in the image is/are:

    (a) short stature   (b) round head   (c) mental retardation   (d) All of these

51. Disease shown in the image may be detected by:

    (a) A karyotype from chorionic villi testing   (b) A karyotype from amniocentesis

    (c) A test to detect substances in the maternal blood   (d) All of these

52. Another name for the disease shown in the image is:

    (a) Trisomy 21   (b) Trisomy 13   (c) Diploid 21   (d) Trisomy 8

53. The disease shown in the image is caused because of:

    (a) Bacterial infection

    (b) A chromosomal abnormality

    (c) Viral infection

    (d) Lack of oxygen supply to the brain during birth

54. The graph below shows the relation between maternal age and occurrence of risk factors for disease in image. The following statements are drawn as conclusions from the graph given below:

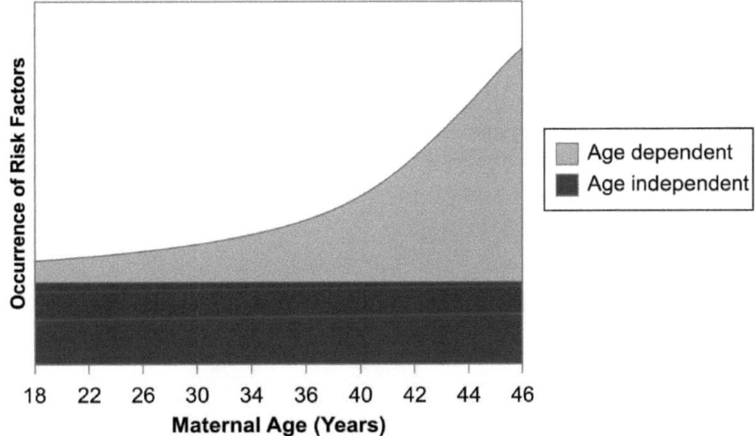

    I. Age-dependent risk factors usually intensify with advancing age and so one would expect highest frequency of such factors among older age group.

    II. Advanced maternal age is a risk for birth with the disease.

    III. There is no relation between maternal age and disease.

    IV. Nothing can be concluded with the graph about the maternal age and disease.

    Choose from below the correct alternative.

    (a) Both I and II are correct

    (b) All are true

    (c) Only III is correct

    (d) Only I is correct

55. What is A, B and C in the given figure of an embryo sac?

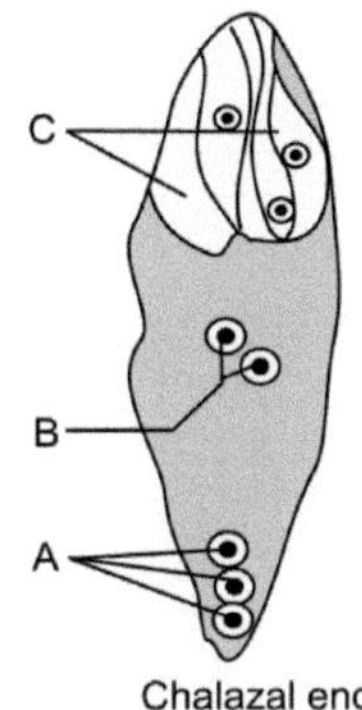

    (a) A–Antipodals, B–Polar nuclei, C–Synergids

    (b) A–Antipodals, B–Central cells, C–Egg cells

    (c) A–Synergids, B–Polar nuclei, C–Egg cells

    (d) A–Synergids, B–Egg cells, C–Filiform apparatus

56. The diagram given below shows an important concept (proposed by D) in the genetic implication of DNA. The process occurring in that concept are marked as A and B. Identify A, B, C, and D.

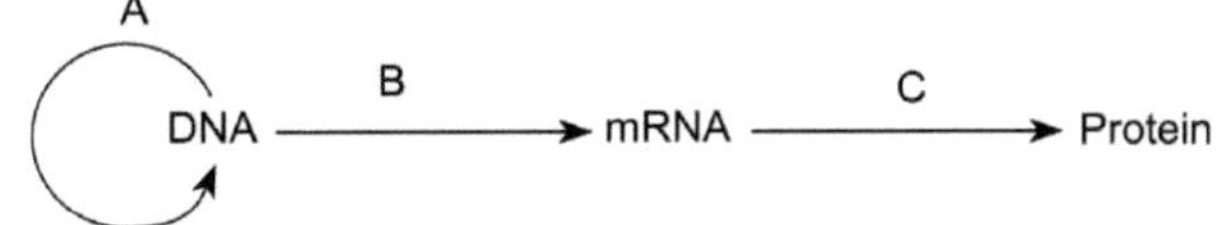

    (a) A–Translation, B–Transcription, C–Replication, D–Erwin Chargaff

    (b) A–Replication B–Transcription C–Translation D–Francis Crick

    (c) A–Transcription, B–Replication, C–Transcription, D–James Watson

    (d) A–Replication, B–Translation, C–Transcription, D–Francis Crick

57. The inheritance of flower colour in *Antirrhinum* (dog flower) is an example of:

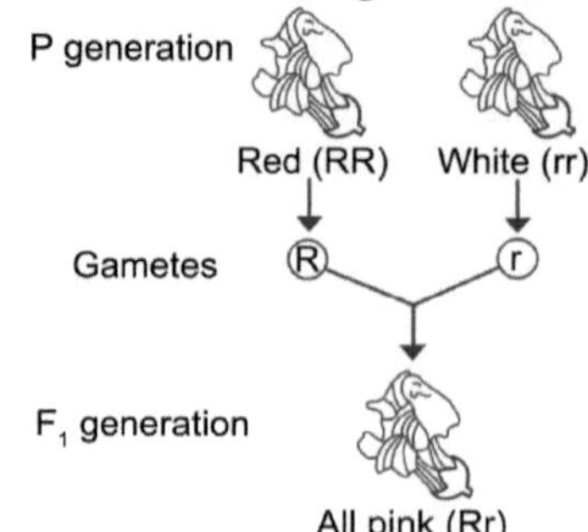

(a) incomplete dorminance   (b) co-dominance   (c) multiple alletes   (d) linkage

58. Refer to the given figure.

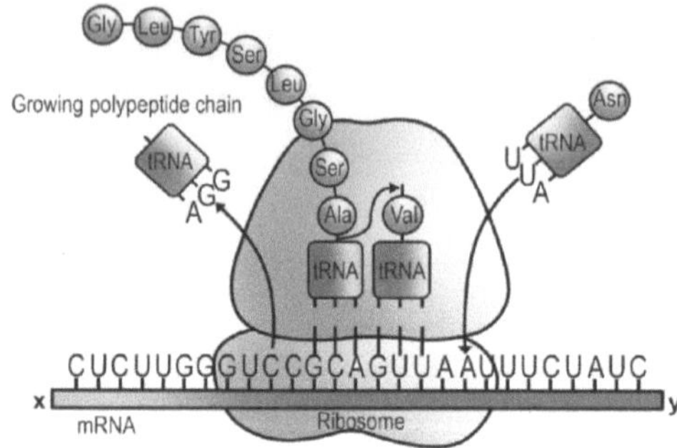

Select the option which identifies polarity X and Y and DNA sequence coding for serine (P) and the anticodon for the same amino acid (Q).

	X	Y	P	Q
(a)	3′	5′	TCA	UCA
(b)	5′	3′	UUG	TCA
(c)	3′	5′	UCA	TCA
(d)	5′	3′	TCA	UCA

59. Identify A to D in the following diagram:

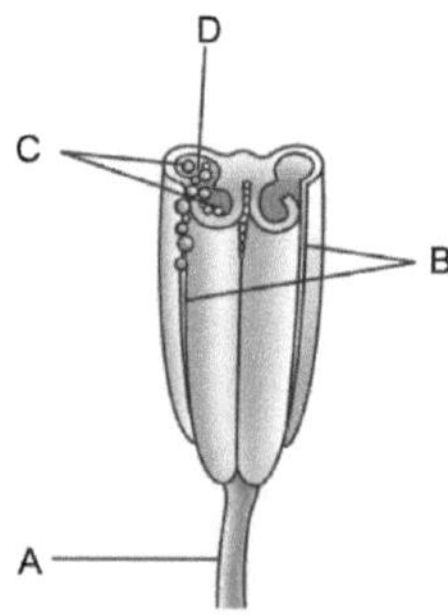

(a) A–Filament (stalk), B–Pollen sac, C–Pollen grain, D–Line of dehiscence
(b) A–Filament (stalk), B–Pollen sac, C–Line of dehiscence, D–Pollen grain
(c) A–Line of dehiscence, B–Filament (stalk), C–Pollen sac, D–Pollen grains
(d) A–Filament (stalk), B–Line of dehiscence, C–Pollen sac, D–Pollen grains

60. Following pedigree chart show.

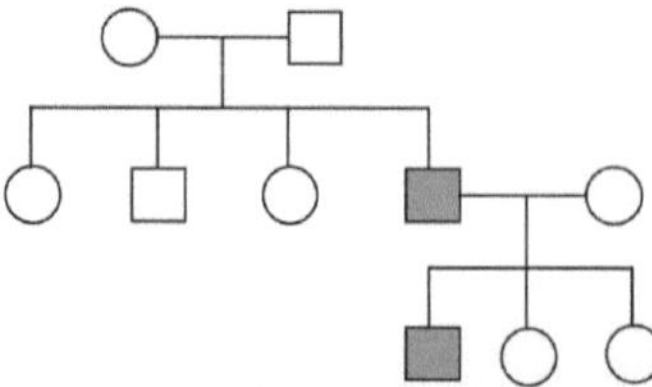

(a) Recessive and autosomal   (b) Recessive and sex-linked
(c) Dominant and sex-linked   (d) Dominant and autosomal

Sample Paper 3

Biology

SECTION - A

Section – A consists of 24 questions. Attempt any 20 questions from this section.

<u>The first attempted 20 questions would be evaluated.</u>

1. Which of the following is primary sex organ?
   (a) Scrotum   (b) Penis   (c) Testes   (d) Prostate

2. The method of directly injecting a sperm into ovum in assisted reproductive technology is called:
   (a) GIFT   (b) ZIFT   (c) ICSI   (d) ET

3. In the given diagram, identify A, B and C.

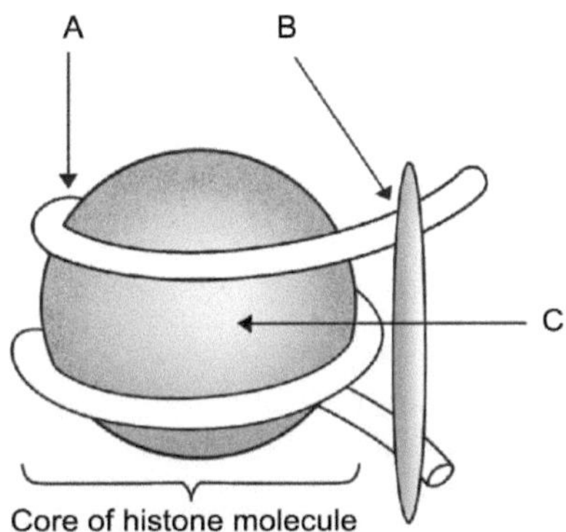

   (a) A–DNA, B–H_1 histone, C–Histone octamer
   (b) A–RNA, B–Cistron, C–DNA
   (c) A–DNA, B–H_3 histone, C–Histone tetramer
   (d) A–RNA, B–H_1 histone, C–Histone octamer

4. With regard to mature mRNA in eukaryotes, which of the following is true?
   (a) Exons and introns do not appear in the mature RNA
   (b) Exons appear but introns do not appear in the mature mRNA
   (c) Introns appear but exons do not appear in the mature mRNA
   (d) Both exons and introns appear in the mature mRNA

5. Study the pedigree chart of a family showing the inheritance of myotonic dystrophy.

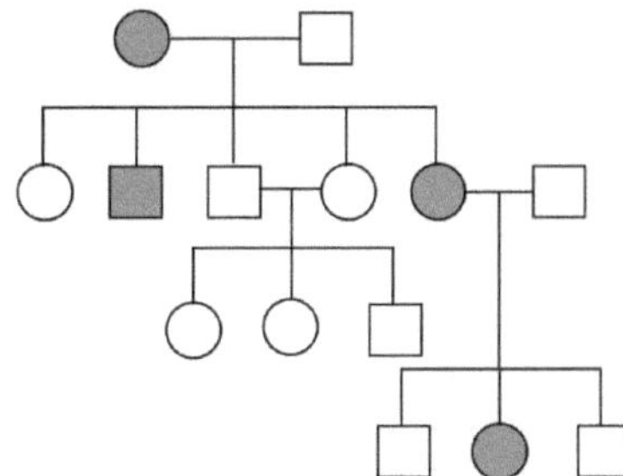

   The trait under study is:
   (a) dominant X-linked
   (b) recessive X-linked
   (c) autosomal dominant
   (d) recessive Y-linked

6. In 28 days of human ovarian cycle, ovulation occurs on:
   (a) Day 1
   (b) Day 5
   (c) Day 14/15
   (d) Day 28

7. What will be the outcome when R-strain is injected into the mice?

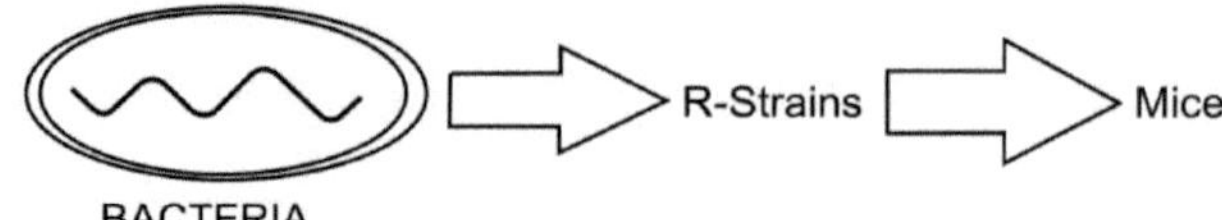

   (a) Mice dies as soon as it is injected
   (b) Mice lives with the bacteria and dies suddenly
   (c) Mice dies after ejecting out the bacteria
   (d) Mice lives even after injecting the R-strain of the bacterium

8. Tt × tt is :
   (a) Reciprocal cross   (b) Hybridisation   (c) Test cross   (d) Back cross

9. Oral contraceptive pills help in the birth control by:
   (a) Killing sperms   (b) Killing ova
   (c) Preventing ovulation   (d) Forming barrier between sperm and ova

10. Identify A, B, C and D.

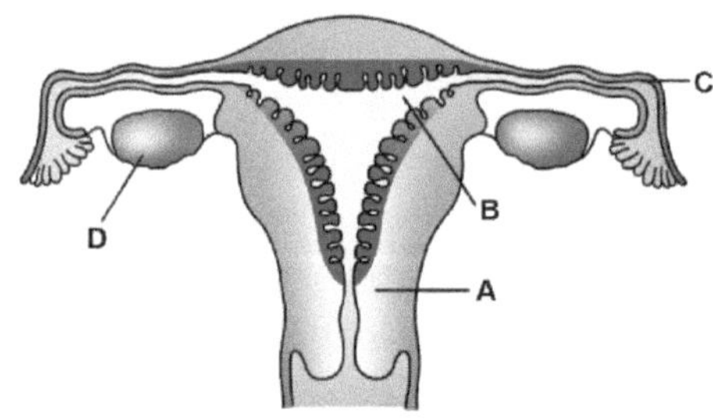

   (a) A–Oviduct, B–Uterus, C–Cervix, D–Ovary
   (b) A–Cervix, B–Uterus, C–Ovary, D–Tumour
   (c) A–Uterus, B–Uterine cavity, C–Oviductal funnel, D–Ovary
   (d) A–Cervix, B–Uterine cavity, C–Fallopian tube, D–Ovary

11. Common test to find genotype of hybrid is by:
    (a) Studying sexual behaviour of F_1 progeny
    (b) Crossing F_1 individuals with recessive parents
    (c) Crossing one F_2 progeny with male parent
    (d) Crossing one F_2 progeny with female parent

12. In case of codominance product is _______________.
    (a) produced from both the alleles   (b) produced from one allele
    (c) incompletely produced from both alleles   (d) none are functional

13. Meiosis occurs in:
    (a) endosperm cells   (b) intercalary meristems
    (c) apical meristems   (d) spore mother cells

14. RNA polymerase II is responsible for the transcription of:
    (a) tRNA   (b) rRNA   (c) hnRNA   (d) snRNA

15. Which of the following is not an accessory duct of male reproductive system?
    (a) Rete testis   (b) Vasa efferentia
    (c) Fallopian tube   (d) Epididymis

16. Mother and father of a person with 'O' blood group have 'A' and 'B' blood group respectively. What would be the genotype of both mother and father?
    (a) Mother will be heterozygous for 'A' blood group, father will be homozygous for 'B' blood group.
    (b) Mother will be homozygous for 'A' blood group, father will be heterozygous for 'B' blood group.
    (c) Both mother and father will be homozygous for 'A' and 'B' blood group.
    (d) Both mother and father will be heterozygous for 'A' and 'B' blood group.

17. Why the discontinuous synthesis of DNA occurs on one strand only?
    (a) DNA dependent DNA polymerase catalysis polymerisation only in one direction ($3' \to 5'$)
    (b) DNA dependent DNA polymerase catalysis polymerisation only in one direction ($5' \to 3'$)
    (c) DNA dependent RNA polymerase catalysis polymerisation only in one direction ($5' \to 3'$)
    (d) DNA dependent DNA polymerase catalysis polymerisation only in one direction ($3' \to 5'$)

18. At what stage the pollen grains shed?
    (a) 2-3 celled   (b) one celled   (c) four celled   (d) five celled

19. Which of the following statement/statements signify test cross?
    (a) It determines the genetic constitution of an organism.
    (b) It helps in verifying the laws of inheritance
    (c) It is very useful to breeders and geneticists as well.
    (d) All of these

20. A male honeybee has 16 chromosomes whereas its female has 32 chromosomes. This is due to:
    (a) Polyploidy   (b) Aneuloploidy   (c) Haplodiploidy   (d) Diplohaploidy

21. Name the parts of an angiosperm flower in which development of male and female gametophyte takes place respectively.
    (a) anther, ovule   (b) ovule, anther   (c) ovule, ovule   (d) anther, anther

22. _______________ is based on the study of patterns of inheritance.
    (a) Genetics   (b) Immunology
    (c) Evolution   (d) Ecology

23. What does the diagram represent?

 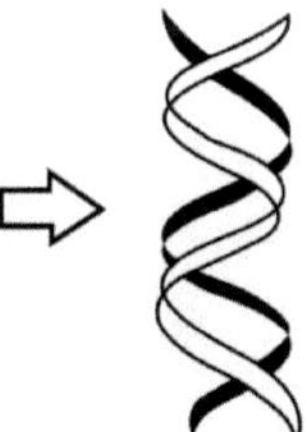 

    (a) Semiconservative nature of DNA   (b) Conservative nature of DNA
    (c) Semiconservative nature of RNA   (d) None of these

24. Sexual reproduction produces _____________ than asexual reproduction.
    (a) more variations   (b) large number of offsprings
    (c) less variations   (d) none of these

SECTION - B

Section – B consists of 24 questions (Sl. No.25 to 48). Attempt any 20 questions from this section. <u>The first attempted 20 questions would be evaluated.</u>

25. **Assertion:** Gynoecium consists of pistil.
    Reason: It represents the male reproductive part in flowering plants.
    (a) Assertion and reason both are correct statements and reason is the correct explanation of the assertion.
    (b) Assertion and reason both are correct statements, but reason is not the correct explanation of the assertion
    (c) Assertion is true, but reason is false statement.
    (d) Assertion is false, but reason is true statement.

26. **Assertion:** HIV infection can be avoided by use of condoms.
    Reason: Condoms secrete anti-viral interferons.
    (a) Assertion and reason both are correct statements and reason is the correct explanation of the assertion.
    (b) Assertion and reason both are correct statements, but reason is not the correct explanation of the assertion

(c) Assertion is true, but reason is false statement.

(d) Assertion is false, but reason is true statement.

27. Assertion: When yellow bodied, white-eyed *Drosophila* females were hybridised with brown bodied, red-eyed males; the two genes segregate independently of each other.

   Reason: The two genes are on the different chromosomes and the proportion of non-parental gene combinations is much higher than the parental type.

   (a) Assertion and reason both are correct statements and reason is the correct explanation of the assertion.

   (b) Assertion and reason both are correct statements, but reason is not the correct explanation of the assertion

   (c) Assertion is true, but reason is false statement.

   (d) Assertion is false, but reason is true statement.

28. Assertion: Parthenocarpy involves formation of seedless fruit.

   Reason: Apomixis occurs without fertilisation.

   (a) Assertion and reason both are correct statements and reason is the correct explanation of the assertion.

   (b) Assertion and reason both are correct statements, but reason is not the correct explanation of the assertion

   (c) Assertion is true, but reason is false statement.

   (d) Assertion is false, but reason is true statement.

29. The following statements are drawn as conclusions from the given below graph:

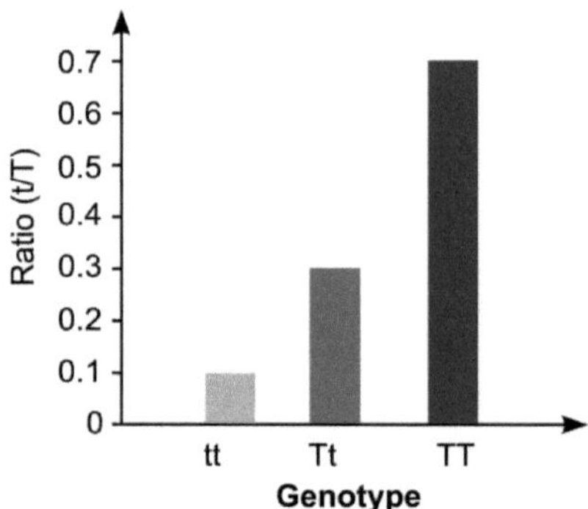

   I.   t/T ratio for the genotype TT is 0.5

   II. Combined ratio for homozygous trait is 0.8

   III. Ratio of homozygous to heterozygous trait is less than 1

   IV. Genotype Tt has the ratio of 0.3

   Choose from below the correct alternative:

   (a) Only II is true

   (b) II and IV are true

   (c) I, II and III are true

   (d) Only IV is true

30. Which of the following is the initial "start site" for the process of transcription?

   (a) Promoter   (b) Terminator   (c) Organiser   (d) Structural gene

31. Vigorous contractions of the uterus during parturition are induced by:

   (a) neuroendocrine mechanism   (b) embryo pushing out

   (c) endocrine mechanism   (d) uterine fluids

32. ____________ in plant biology was used by Gregor Mendel to derive the patterns of inheritance.

   (a) Hybridization   (b) Mutagenesis

   (c) Embryogenesis   (d) None of these

33. Consanguineous mating is the mating between _________ individuals which are ___________.

   (a) two different, same species   (b) two different, unrelated

   (c) two closely related, same species   (d) two closely related, different species

34. Which of the following is not a transcription unit of the DNA?

   (a) Terminator   (b) Promoter   (c) Organiser   (d) Structural gene

35. The average duration of the gestation for humans is:
    (a) 6 months
    (b) 9 months
    (c) 8 months
    (d) None of these
36. What is determined by Pollen–pistil interaction?
    (a) Compatibility of the pollen
    (b) Colour of the pollen
    (c) Nature of the pollen
    (d) Maturation of the pollen
37. What is the inability to conceive a baby even after unprotected intercourse called?
    (a) Sterility
    (b) Infertility
    (c) Fertility
    (d) Reproductivity
38. Translation is the ___________ stage during the central dogma of DNA.
    (a) first
    (b) secon
    (c) third
    (d) fourth
39. Inheritance of which of the following traits is shown in the given cross?

$$X$$

	XY (Normal man)		XX^c (Carrier woman)	
XX^c (Carrier daughter)	XX (Normal daughter)		XY (Normal son)	X^{c}Y (Diseased son)

    (a) X-linked dominant trait
    (b) X-linked recessive trait
    (c) Autosomal recessive trait
    (d) Autosomal dominant trait
40. Size of rice genome is:
    (a) 430 Gb
    (b) 300 Mb
    (c) 430 Mb
    (d) None of these
41. ___________ incompatibility promotes cross pollination.
    (a) Inbreeding
    (b) Intraspecific
    (c) Outbreeding
    (d) Interspecific
42. During transcription, adenosine forms a base pair with ________ instead of thymine.
    (a) cytosine
    (b) uracil
    (c) any nitrogen base
    (d) none of these
43. Which of the following is correct with respect to aneuploidy?
    (a) Arises due to the non-disjunction of homologous pair of chromosomes
    (b) One gamete comes to have an extra chromosome
    (c) Another gamete becomes deficient in one chromosome
    (d) All of these
44. Identify P-V in the given figure and select the correct option.

    (a) P–Petal, Q–Sepal, R–Filament, S–Anther, T–Style, U–Stigma, V–Ovary
    (b) P–Petal, Q–Sepal, R–Anther, S–Filament, T–Stigma, U–Style, V–Ovary
    (c) P–Sepal, Q–Petal, R–Anther, S–Filament, T–Stigma, U–Style, V–Ovary
    (d) P–Ovary, Q–Petal, R–Anther, S–Filament, T–Stigma, U–Style, V–Sepal

45. Beadle and Tatum showed that each kind of mutant bread mould they studied lacked a specific enzyme. Their experiments demonstrated that:
    (a) Cells need specific enzymes in order to function   (b) Genes are made of DNA
    (c) Gene carry information for making proteins   (d) Enzymes are required to repair damage

46. Which of the following is/are example of aneuploidy?
    (a) Turner's syndrome   (b) Down's syndrome
    (c) Klinefelter's syndrome   (d) All of these

47. What technique involves fertilization outside the body of the female?
    (a) Intrauterine fertilization   (b) In vitro fertilization
    (c) In vivo fertilization   (d) Ex vivo fertilization

48. Which of the following figures depict an offspring whose sex is unspecified?

(a) 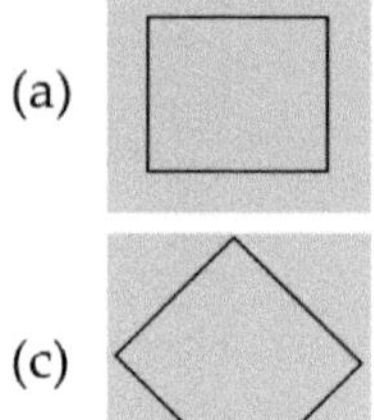   (b) 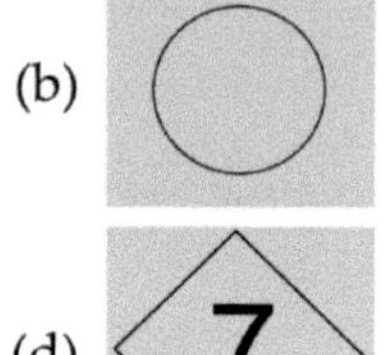

(c)   (d) 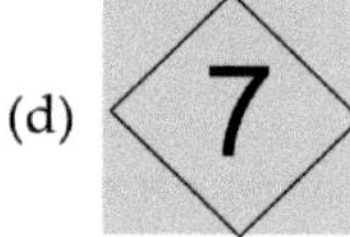

SECTION - C

Section-C consists of one case followed by 6 questions linked to this case (Q.No. 49 to 54). Besides this, 6 more questions are given. Attempt any 10 questions in this section. <u>The first attempted 10 questions would be evaluated.</u>

Case: To answer the questions, study the figure given below.

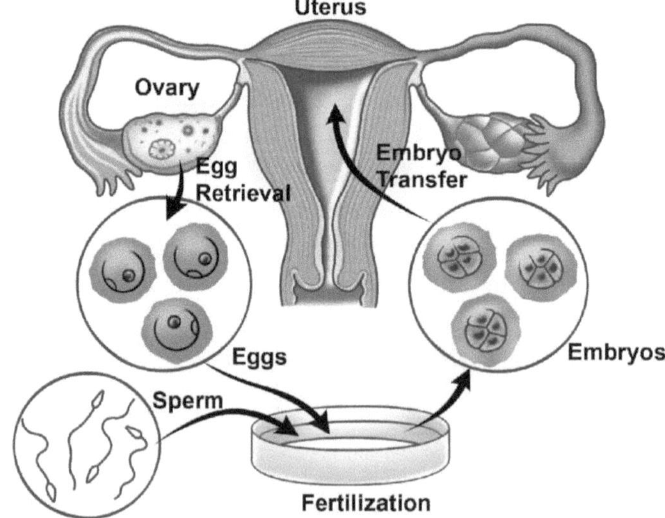

49. Which process is represented in the following image?
    (a) ZIFT   (b) IVF
    (c) ICSI   (d) None of these

50. ZIFT is transfer of:
    (a) Zygote into fallopian tube.
    (b) A mixture of sperms and ova into the fallopian tube.
    (c) A mixture of sperms and ova into the uterus.
    (d) Embryo into the uterus.

51. Embryo with more than 16 blastomeres formed due to In Vitro Fertilisation is transferred into:

(a) Cervix (b) Uterus (c) Fallopian tube (d) Fimbriae

52. In case of a couple, where the male is having a very low sperm count, which technique will be suitable for fertilisation?

(a) Intrauterine transfer

(b) Gamete intracytoplasmic fallopian transfer

(c) Artificial Insemination

(d) Intra cytoplasmic sperm injection

53. Artificial insemination means:

(a) Artificial introduction of sperms of a healthy donor into the vagina

(b) Introduction of sperms of a healthy donor directly into the ovary

(c) Transfer of sperms of a healthy donor to a test tube containing ova

(d) Transfer of sperms of husband to a test containing ova

54. What follows IVF?

(a) Coitus

(b) Embryo transfer

(c) Embryo sacrifice

(d) Embryo delivery

55. Who performed the experiment shown below and what was proved by this experiment?

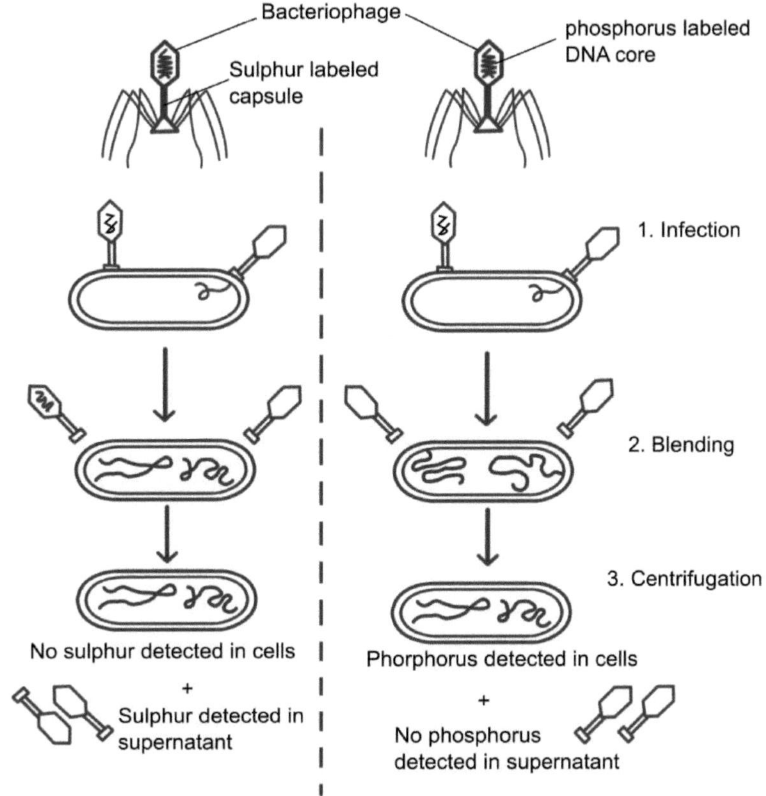

(a) Hershey and Chase, DNA is the genetic material

(b) Beadle and Tatum, DNA is the genetic material

(c) Hershey and Chase, RNA is the genetic material

(d) None of these

56. Given diagram depicts the experiment of Meselson and Stahl.

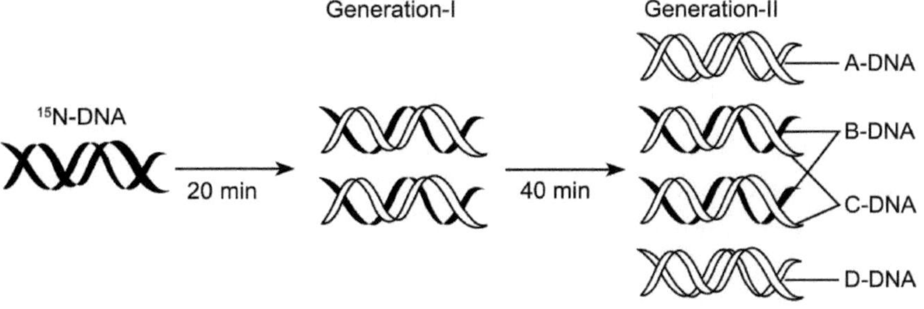

Which of the following is correctly depicted from the above diagram?

I.   Equal amount of light DNA and hybrid DNA was observed in *E. coli* culture after two generations.

II. The generation time of *E. coli* culture was 40 minutes.

III. Equal amount of light DNA and hybrid DNA was observed in *E. coli* culture after two generations.

(a) I and II

(b) Only III

(c) I and III

(d) II and III

57. Which of the following figures represent parents with a male child affected with a disease?

(a) 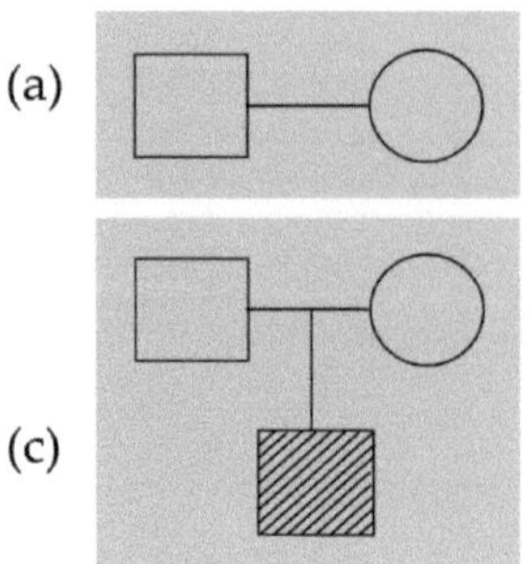

(b) 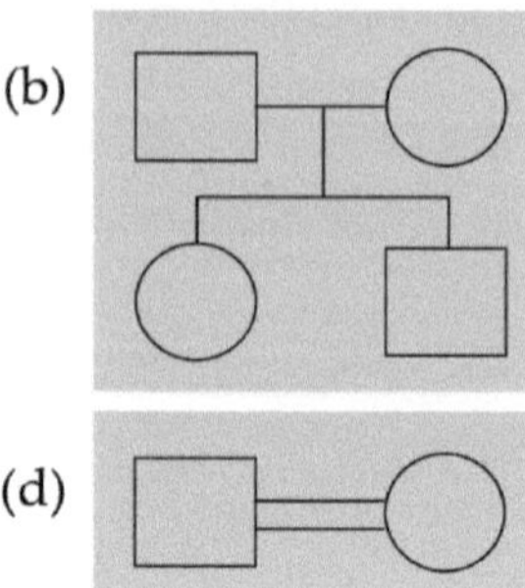

(c)

(d)

58. The below diagram describes the changes that occur in the endometrium during a normal menstruation. Choose the option with correct description for points A, B, C and D.

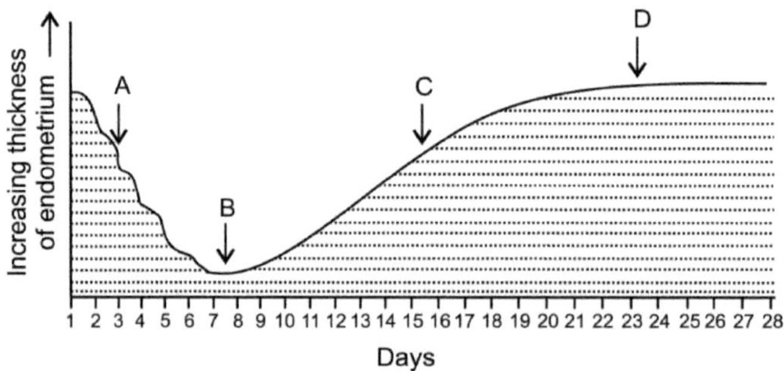

(a) A–Ovulation, B–Menstruation

(b) A–Ovulation, C–Menstruation

(c) A–Menstruation, C–Ovulation

(d) B–Ovulation, D–Menstruation

59. Identify the various parts A to C in the given diagram of an ovule.

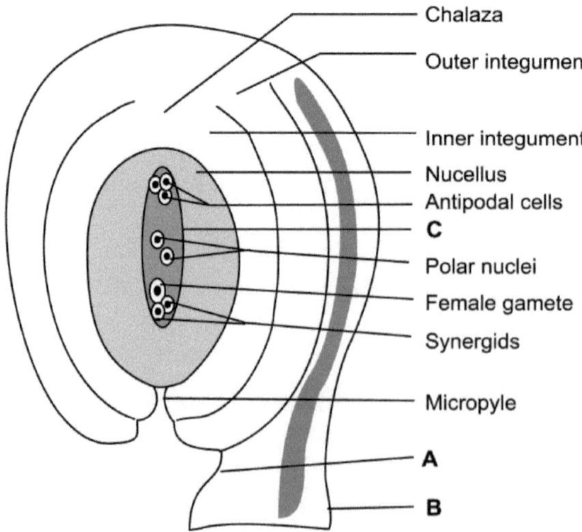

(a) A–Embryo sac, B–Inner integuments, C–Outer integuments

(b) A–Inner integuments, B–Nucellus, C–Chalazal

(c) A–Hilum, B–Funicle, C–Embryo sac

(d) A–Micropylar end, B–Hilum, C–Inner integuments

60. The diagram shows the uterine tubes of four woman (P, Q, R and S).

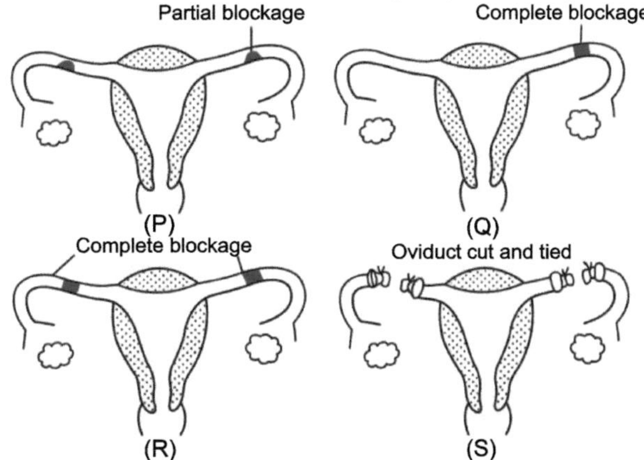

In which two woman is fertilisation impossible at present?

(a) P and Q

(b) Q and R

(c) R and S

(d) S and P

Sample Paper 4

Biology

SECTION – A

Section – A consists of 24 questions. Attempt any 20 questions from this section.
The first attempted 20 questions would be evaluated.

1. The international rice genome sequencing project begin in:

   (a) September 2006   (b) July 1997   (c) May 2006   (d) September 1997

2. Another name for Down syndrome is:

   (a) Trisomy 21   (b) Trisomy 13   (c) Diploid 21   (d) Trisomy 8

3. What will be the genotype of the following Punnett square?

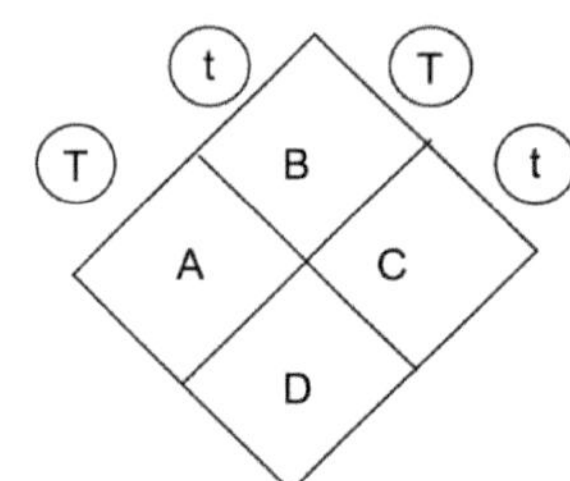

   (a) A-TT; B-tt ;C-tt; D-Tt   (b) A-tt ; B-Tt ;C-tt; D-Tt
   (c) A-TT; B-Tt ;C-tt; D-Tt   (d) A-TT; B-Tt ;C-tt; D-tt

4. Which among the following exhibit Anemophily?

   (a) *Salvia*   (b) *Vallisneria*   (c) Coconut   (d) Bottle brush

5. Select the dominant and recessive traits.

  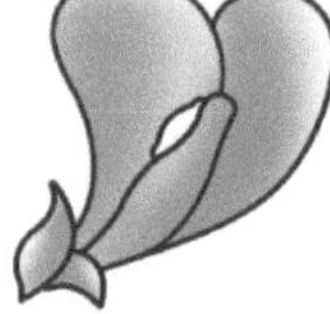 

Round	Wrinkled	Violet	White
(A)	(B)	(C)	(D)

   (a) (A) and (B) are dominant and (C) and (D) are recessive
   (b) (A) and (C) are dominant and (B) and (D) are recessive
   (c) (A) and (D) are dominant and (B) and (C) are recessive
   (d) (B) and (C) are dominant and (A) and (D) are recessive

6. The genetic ratio of 9 : 3 : 3 : 1 is due to:

   (a) Segregation of characters   (b) Crossing over of character
   (c) Independent assortment of genes   (d) Homologous pairing between chromosomes

7. What are X & Y in the following figure?

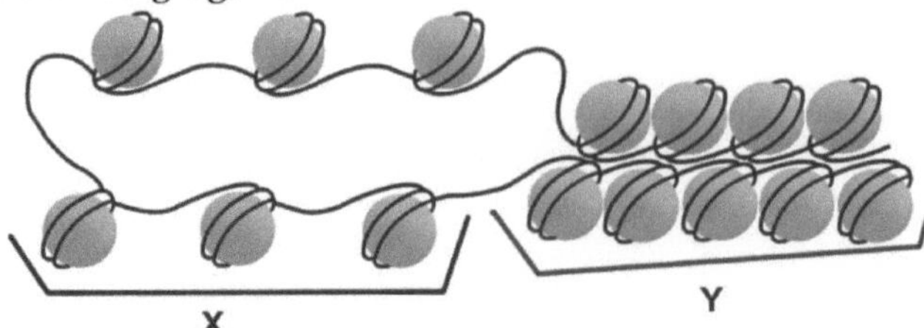

   (a) (X)-Euchromatin; (Y)-Heterochromatin   (b) (X)- Heterochromatin; (Y)- Euchromatin
   (c) Both (X) and (Y) are Euchromatin   (d) Both (X) and (Y) are Heterochromatin

8. Marchantia is a:
   (a) Monoecious plant   (b) Homothallic plant   (c) Dioecious plant   (d) Bisexual plant

9. Peptide synthesis in a cell takes place in:
   (a) Chloroplast   (b) Ribosome   (c) Mitochondria   (d) Golgi body

10. Study the given pedigree chart showing the inheritance of an X-linked trait controlled by gene 'r'

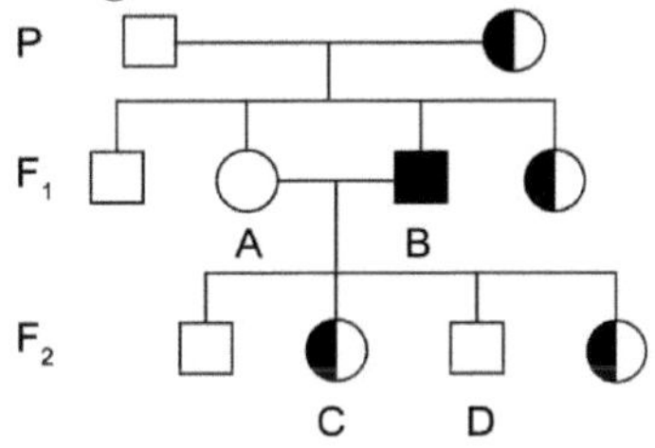

What will be genotypes of individuals A, B, C and D respectively?
   (a) XX, X^rY, X^rX, XY   (b) X^rX^r, XY, XX, XY
   (c) X^rX, X^rX^r, X^rX^r, X^rY (d) XX, X^rX^r, XX, XY

11. Egg is liberated from ovary in:
   (a) secondary oocyte stage   (b) primary oocyte stage
   (c) oogonial stage   (d) mature ovum stage

12. The secretions of the accessory glands are rich in :
   (a) magnesium   (b) glucose   (c) potassium   (d) fructose

13. In eukaryotic cell, transcription, RNA splicing and RNA capping take place in:
   (a) Nucleus   (b) Cytoplasm   (c) Ribosomes   (d) Golgi body

14. Diaphragms are contraceptive device used by females. Choose the correct option from the statement given below:
   (i) They are introduced into the uterus.   (ii) They are placed to cover the cervical region.
   (iii) They act as physical barrier for sperm entry.   (iv) They act as spermicidal agents
   (a) (i) and (ii)   (b) (i) and (iii)
   (c) (ii) and (iii)   (d) (iii) and (iv)

15. The genetic ratio of $9 : 3 : 3 : 1$ is due to which phenomenon of genetics?
   (a) Chromosomal theory of inheritance   (b) Law of segregation
   (c) Independent assortment of genes   (d) None of these

16. What are the basic components of a nucleotide?
   (a) A nitrogenous base   (b) A pentose sugar
   (c) A phosphate group   (d) All of these

17. In a DNA strand, the nucleotides are linked together by what kind of bonds?
   (a) phosphodiester bond   (b) phosphoester bond
   (c) hydrogen bond   (d) None of these

18. Name the cells which secrete androgens in human testes.
   (a) Interstitial cells   (b) Leydig cells
   (c) Sertoli cells   (d) None of these

19. State the role of deoxyribonucleoside triphosphates during DNA replication.
   (a) They are the building blocks for the DNA-strand.
   (b) They serve as energy source in the form of ATP.
   (c) They serve as energy source in the form of GTP.
   (d) All of these

20. What is an anther?
   (a) bilobed structure   (b) a unit of female reproductive system
   (c) trilobed structure   (d) none of these

21. The parallelism between Mendelian factors and chromosomes led to the discovery of:
    (a) law of independent assortment
    (b) chromosomal theory of inheritance
    (c) law of segregation
    (d) none of these
22. Which of the following is/are the function of codon AUG?
    (a) It acts as an initiation codon
    (b) It acts as a termination codon
    (c) The AUG codes for valine
    (d) None of these
23. What type of cross is this?

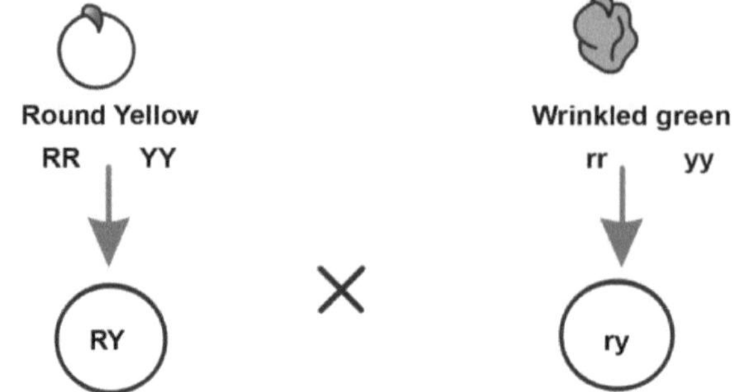

    (a) Monohybrid cross
    (b) Dihybrid cross
    (c) Trihybrid cross
    (d) Tetrahybrid cross
24. A woman has an X-linked condition on one of her X-chromosomes. This chromosome can be inherited by:
    (a) Only grand children
    (b) Only sons
    (c) Only daughters
    (d) Both (b) and (c)

SECTION – B

Section – B consists of 24 questions (Sl. No.25 to 48). Attempt any 20 questions from this section. The first attempted 20 questions would be evaluated.

25. **Assertion:** A wide range of contraceptive methods are available for family planning.

    Reason: Natural method includes condoms, diaphragms, etc., while barrier methods use of included methods like periodic abstinence, lactational amenorrhea, etc.

    (a) Assertion and reason both are correct statements and reason is the correct explanation of the assertion.
    (b) Assertion and reason both are correct statements, but reason is not the correct explanation of the assertion
    (c) Assertion is true, but reason is false statement.
    (d) Assertion is false, but reason is true statement.

26. **Assertion:** All copulations do not lead to fertilisation and pregnancy.

    Reason: Fertilisation can only occur if the ovum and sperms are transported simultaneously to the ampullary isthmic junction.

    (a) Assertion and reason both are correct statements and reason is the correct explanation of the assertion.
    (b) Assertion and reason both are correct statements, but reason is not the correct explanation of the assertion
    (c) Assertion is true, but reason is false statement.
    (d) Assertion is false, but reason is true statement.

27. **Assertion:** An additional copy of chromosome number 21 causes Down's syndrome.

    Reason: Aneuploidy occurs from an extra copy of chromosome.

    (a) Assertion and reason both are correct statements and reason is the correct explanation of the assertion.
    (b) Assertion and reason both are correct statements, but reason is not the correct explanation of the assertion
    (c) Assertion is true, but reason is false statement.
    (d) Assertion is false, but reason is true statement.

28. **Assertion:** In a microsporangium, the tapetal cells possess little cytoplasm and generally have a single prominent nucleus.

    Reason: During microsporogenesis, the microspore mother cells undergo meiotic divisions to produce haploid microspore tetrads.

    (a) Assertion and reason both are correct statements and reason is the correct explanation of the assertion.

    (b) Assertion and reason both are correct statements, but reason is not the correct explanation of the assertion

    (c) Assertion is true, but reason is false statement.

    (d) Assertion is false, but reason is true statement.

29. Which of the following information is correct about the following figure?

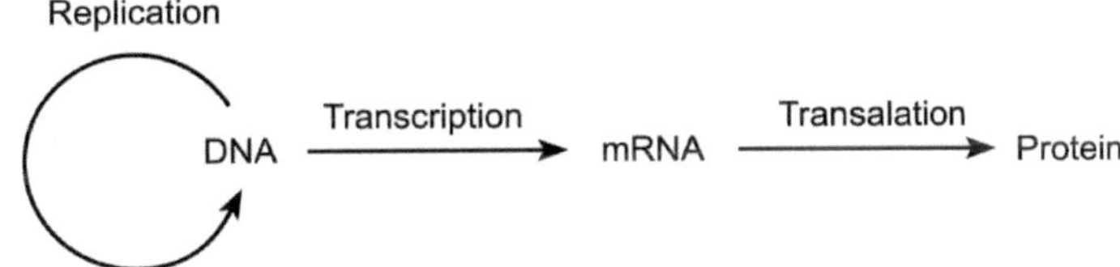

    (a) This figure shows that genetic information flows from DNA to RNA and RNA to protein.

    (b) This figure shows that genetic information flows from DNA to DNA and then protein.

    (c) This figure shows that genetic information flows from RNA to DNA and then protein.

    (d) This figure shows that genetic information flows from protein to RNA and RNA to DNA.

30. All of the following are part of an operon except:

    (a) an operator

    (b) a promoter

    (c) an enhancer

    (d) structural genes

31. The outermost and innermost wall layers of microsporangium in an anther are respectively:

    (a) Endothecium and tapetum

    (b) Epidermis and endodermis

    (c) Epidermis and middle layer

    (d) Epidermis and tapetum

32. Aminoacylation of tRNA is essential for:

    (a) replication of RNA

    (b) formation of peptide bond

    (c) splicing

    (d) initiation of transcription

33. In hemophilia, the affected protein is a part of a cascade of protein which is involved in the:

    (a) formation of RBCs

    (b) formation of WBCs and platelets

    (c) coagulation of blood

    (d) anticoagulation

34. S-type strain of *Streptococcus pneumoniae* is:

    (a) capsulated, virulent, smooth

    (b) non-capsulated, avirulent, rought

    (c) capsulated, avirulent, rough

    (d) non-capsulated, virulent, smooth

35. Progesterone or progestogen-oestrogen combination injections and implants are used by the females under the:

    (a) skin of the inner arm above elbow

    (b) vagina

    (c) stomach's upper skin

    (d) cervix

36. Which of the following cells have haploid number of chromosomes?

    (a) 1° spermatocytes

    (b) 2° spermatocytes

    (c) Spermatid

    (d) Both (b) and (c)

37. Tapetal cells are characterised by the presence of dense cytoplasm and many nuclei. This statement is:

    (a) True

    (b) False

    (c) Cannot say

    (d) Partially true or false

38. Nucleosome consists of:

    (a) nucleolus

    (b) genes

    (c) microfilaments

    (d) histones

39. If map distance between genes P and Q is 4 units, between P and R is 11 units, and between Q and R is 7 units, the order of genes on the linkage map can be traced as follows:

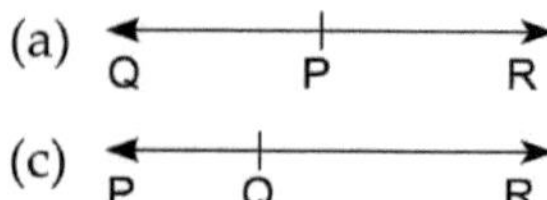

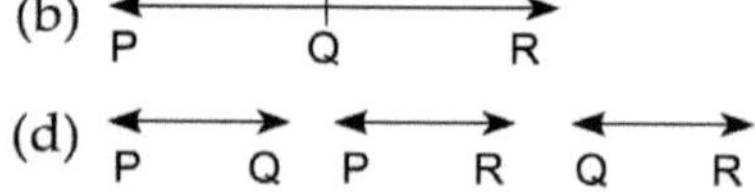

40. The number of contrasting characters studied by Mendel for his experiments was:

(a) 14   (b) 4   (c) 2   (d) 7

41. VNTRs are the key factor in DNA profiling because:

(a) the length of the regions having VNTRs is different in each individual

(b) the length of the regions having VNTRs is same in each individual

(c) they have nucleotide

(d) short pieces of nucleotides are same in all persons

42. All genes located on the same chromosome.

(a) form different groups depending upon their relative distance

(b) form one linkage group

(c) will not form any linkage group

(d) form interactive groups that affect the phenotype

43. The main function of fimbriae of fallopian tube is to:

(a) help in development of ovary

(b) help in collection of the ovum after ovulation

(c) help in development of ova

(d) help in fertilisation

44. In the given fertilised embryo sac, identify A to E.

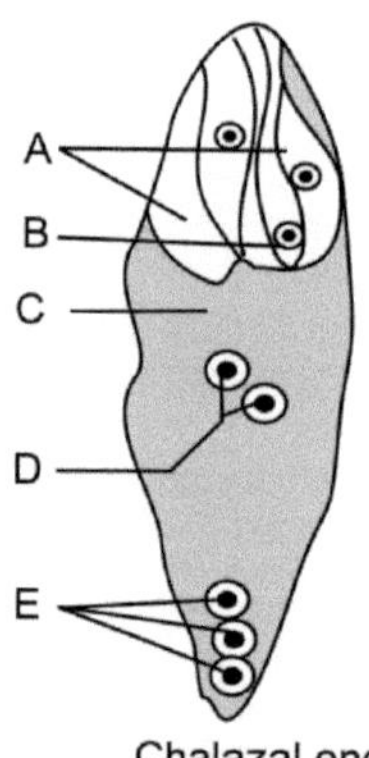

(a) A–Degenerating antipodal cell, B–Primary endosperm nucleus, C–Primary endosperm cell, D–Synergid cell, E–Zygote

(b) A–Synergid cell, B–Antipodal cell, C–Zygote, D–Endosperm cell, E–Chalazal cell

(c) A–Degenerating synergids, B–Zygote, C–Primary endosperm cell, D–Primary endosperm nucleus, E–Degenerating antipodal cell

(d) A–Zygote, B–Synergid, C–Primary endosperm cell, D–Primary endosperm nucleus, E–Degenerating antipodal cell

45. The terminator codons are:

(a) UAA, UAG, UGA   (b) AUG, UAG, UGA

(c) UAC, AUG, UAG   (d) UCC, UAA, CAC

46. Which of the following characteristics represents 'Inheritance of blood groups' in humans?

I.   Dominance   II. Codominance

III. Multiple allele   IV. Incomplete dominance

V.   Polygenic inheritance

(a) I, IV and V   (b) I, II and III

(c) II, III and V   (d) I, III and V

47. Among the following characters, which one was not considered by Mendel in his experiments on pea?
    (a) Stem–Tall or Dwarf
    (b) Trichomes–Glandular or Non-glandular
    (c) Seed–Green or Yellow
    (d) Pod–Inflated or Constricted
48. Given diagram depicts the experiment of Meselson and Stahl. Identify the type of isotopic DNA formed after 40 minutes (A, B, C and D)

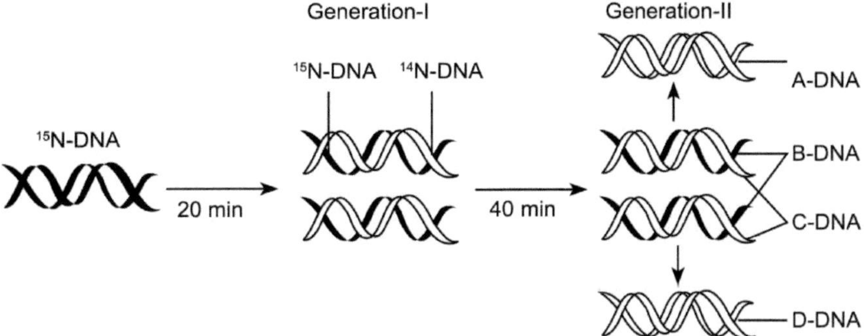

    (a) A–^{14}N-DNA, B–^{15}N-DNA, C–^{14}N-DNA, D–^{15}N-DNA
    (b) A–^{14}N-DNA, B–^{15}N-DNA, C–^{14}N-DNA, D–^{14}N-DNA
    (c) A–^{14}N-DNA, B–^{15}N-DNA, C–^{15}N-DNA, D–^{15}N-DNA
    (d) A–^{14}N-DNA, B–^{15}N-DNA, C–^{15}N-DNA, D–^{15}N-DNA

SECTION – C

Section-C consists of one case followed by 6 questions linked to this case

(Q.No. 49 to 54). Besides this, 6 more questions are given. Attempt any 10 questions in this section. The first attempted 10 questions would be evaluated.

Case: To answer the questions, study the figure given below.

Females of reproductive age experience cycles of hormonal activity that repeat at about one-month intervals. The average menstrual cycle takes about 28 days and occurs in phases: the follicular phase, the ovulatory phase (ovulation), and the luteal phase.

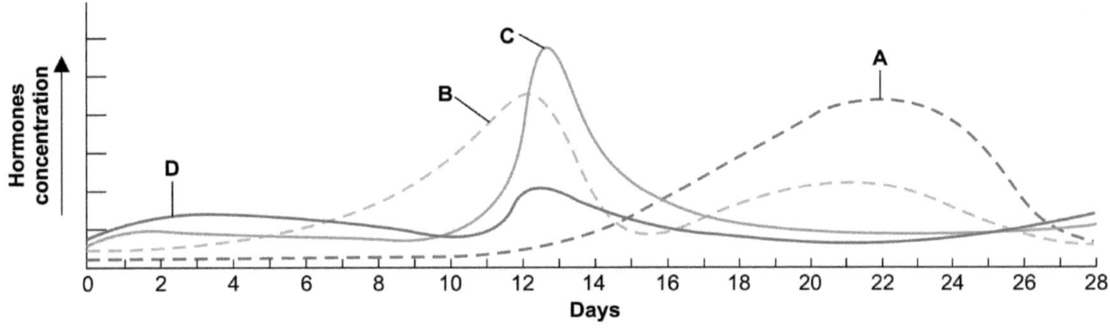

49. What layer of the uterus is shredded during menstruation?
    (a) Perimetrium
    (b) Myometrium
    (c) Epimetrium
    (d) Endometrium
50. The follicular phase is also known as ___________.
    (a) menstrual phase
    (b) luteal phase
    (c) proliferative phase
    (d) secretory phase
51. During what phase of menstrual cycle are primary follicles converted to Graafian follicles?
    (a) Menstrual phase
    (b) Follicular phase
    (c) Luteal phase
    (d) Secretory phase
52. What pituitary hormones are at peak during the proliferative phase?
    (a) LH only
    (b) FSH only
    (c) Neither LH or FSH
    (d) LH and FSH
53. The graph above shows different phases of menstruation cycle's hormones. Select the option giving correct identification together with it's source of secretion and function.
    (a) A → Progesterone; Graafian follicle; Proliferation of endometrium
    (b) B → Estrogen; developing follicle; Proliferation of endometrium

    (c) C → LH; Corpus Luteum; Ovulation

    (d) D → FSH; Hypothalamus; Spermatogenesis

54. Which of the following hormone is not involved in menstrual cycle?

    (a) luteinizing hormone   (b) estrogen

    (c) progesterone   (d) thyroid stimulating hormone

55. Find out A, B and C in the diagram given below

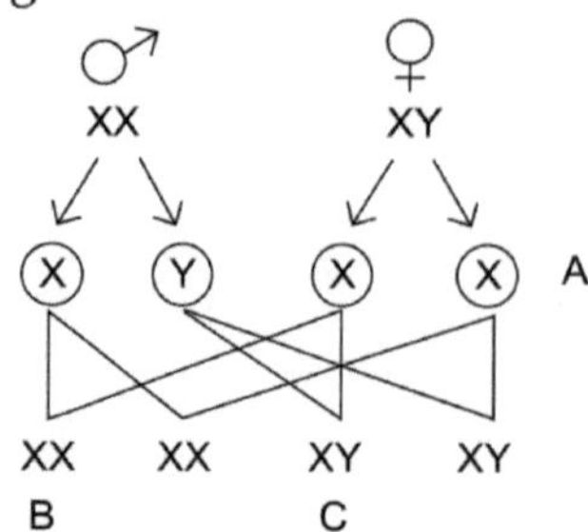

    (a) A–Male gamete, B–Female, C–Gametes   (b) A–Male, B–Female, C–Sperm

    (c) A–Female, B–Male, C–Gametes   (d) A–Gametes, B–Female, C–Male

56. In given diagram, find out A-E

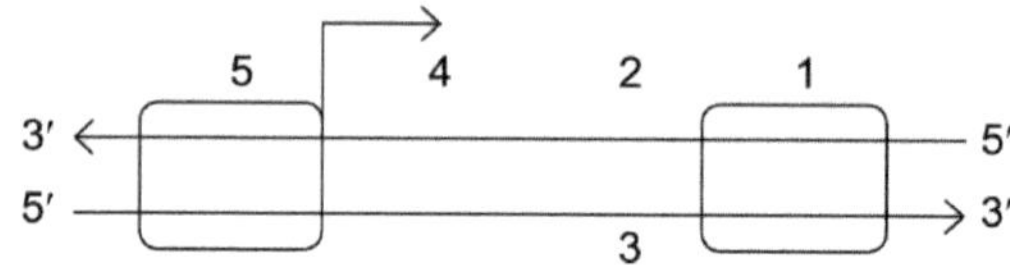

    A. Promoter site   B. Structural gene   C. Terminator site

    D. Template strand   E. Coding strand

    Codes:

	A	B	C	D	E
(a)	5	1	4	2	3
(b)	5	1	4	3	2
(c)	5	4	1	2	3
(d)	1	4	5	2	3

57. Identify A, B and C in the diagram below:

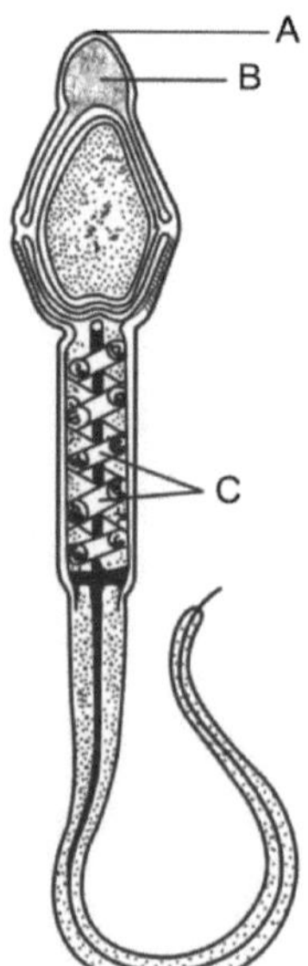

    (a) A–Acrosome, B–Tail, C–Mitochondria

    (b) A–Plasma membrane, B–Acrosome, C–Mitochondria

    (c) A–Mitochondria, B–Acrosome, C–Plasma membrane

    (d) A–Mitochondria, B–Plasma membrane, C–Tail

58. Choose the correct option from A, B and C.

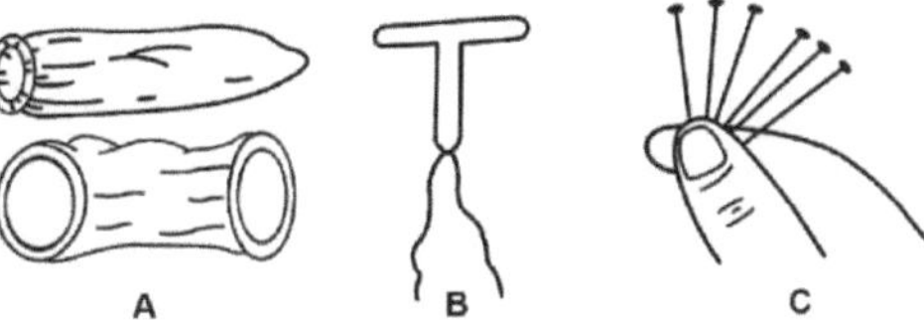

(a) A–Condoms, B–Copper-T, C–Implants

(b) A–Tubectomy, B–Implants, C–Copper-T

(c) A–Vasectomy, B–Condoms, C–Copper-T

(d) A–Copper-T, B–Condoms, C–Implants

59. Given below diagram refers to the TS of testes showing few seminiferous tubules.

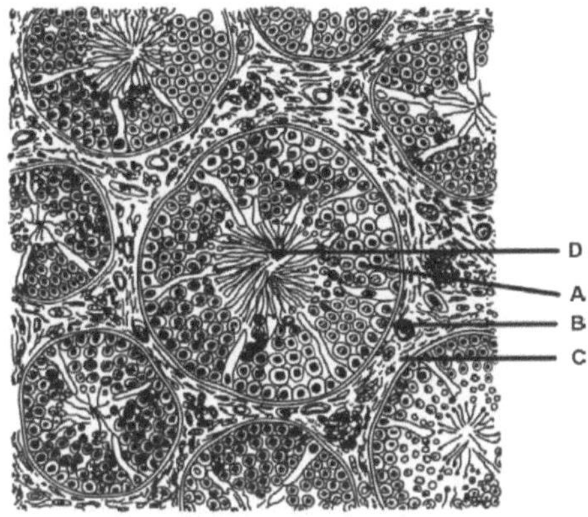

A, B, C and D in the above figure represent.

(a) A–Sertoli cells, B–Secondary spermatocyte, C–Interstitial cells, D–Sperms

(b) A–Interstitial cells, B–Spermatogonia, C–Sertoli cells, D–Sperms

(c) A–Sertoli cells, B–Spermatozoa, C–Interstitial cells, D–Sperms

(d) A–Sertoli cells, B–Spermatogonia, C–Interstitial cells, D–Sperms

60. Identify A to G in following figure and answer accordingly.

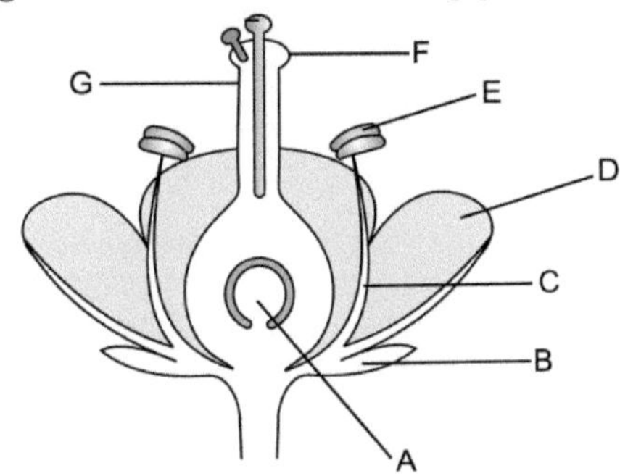

(a) A–Ovary, B–Filament, C–Sepal, D-Petal, E–Style, F–Stigma, G–Anther

(b) A–Sepal, B–Ovary, C–Petal, D–Filament, E–Anther, F–Stigma, G–Style

(c) A–Ovary, B–Sepal, C–Filament, D–Petal, E–anther, F–Stigma, G–Style

(d) A–Petal, B–Anther, C–Stigma, D–Style, E–Filament, F–Sepal, G–Ovary

Sample Paper 5

Biology

SECTION – A

Section – A consists of 24 questions. Attempt any 20 questions from this section.
<u>The first attempted 20 questions would be evaluated.</u>

1. G. J. Mendel was a:

(a) British monk   (b) Australian monk   (c) Austrian monk   (d) German scientist

2. What is the role of RNA polymerase III?

(a) Transcription of rRNAs   (b) Transcription of mRNAs

(c) Transcription of tRNAs   (d) Transcription of hnRNA

3. Which of the following figures correctly represents the replication fork formed during DNA replication?

(a) 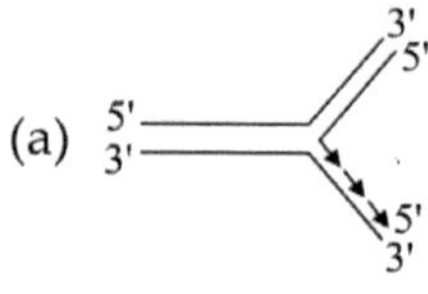   (b) 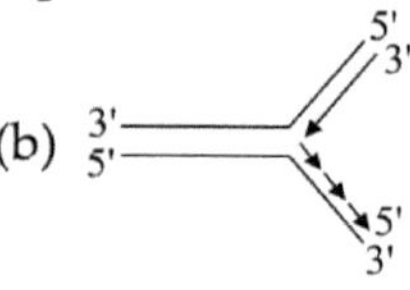

(c) 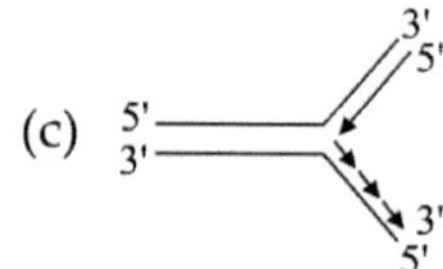   (d) 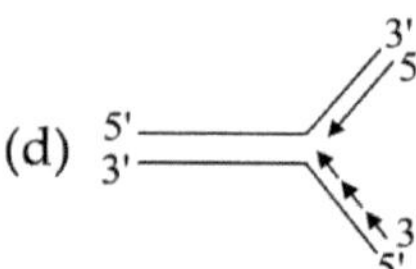

4. Embryo sac is also called:

(a) microspore   (b) megaspore   (c) megagametophyte   (d) microgametophyte

5. What does A and B represent in the given representation?

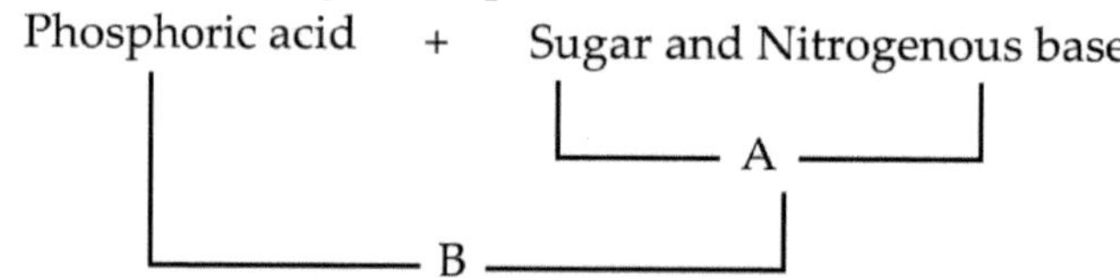

	A	B
(a)	Nucleoside	Nucleotide
(b)	Ribonucleoside	Deoxyribonucleoside
(c)	Riboncleotide	Deoxyribonucleotide
(d)	Nucleotide	Nucleoside

6. Which one of the following is an example of polygenic inheritance?

(a) Flower colour in *Mirabilis jalapa*   (b) Production of male honeybee

(c) Pod-shape in garden pea   (d) Skin colour in humans

7. Study the given monohybrid cross :

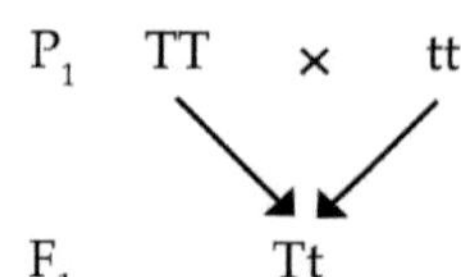

(a) Tt × TT   (b) Tt × tt   (c) Tt × Tt   (d) TT × tt

8. Site of fertilisation in human beings is:

(a) ovary   (b) uterus   (c) vagina   (d) fallopian tube

9. In a DNA strand, the nucleotides are linked together by:
   (a) glycosidic bonds
   (b) phosphodiester bonds
   (c) peptide bonds
   (d) hydrogen bonds
10. The given image represents:

Meiosis I-anaphase

Meiosis II-anaphase

Germ cells

   (a) chromosomes assorting independently.
   (b) segregation of incompletely linked genes.
   (c) crossing over between factors carried on the chromosomes.
   (d) Both (a) and (c)
11. Cu-T prevents pregnancy by preventing:
   (a) Fertilisation
   (b) Ovulation
   (c) Implantation of fertilised egg
   (d) None of these
12. Continuous use of alcohol causes:
   (a) Gastritis
   (b) Neuritis
   (c) Swelling of liver
   (d) All of these
13. The first genetic material is:
   (a) Protein
   (b) Carbohydrates
   (c) DNA
   (d) RNA
14. Sporopollenin occurs in:
   (a) female gametophyte
   (b) male gametophyte
   (c) vegetative cells of pollen grain
   (d) exine of pollen wall
15. How the genetic defect Adenosine Deaminase (ADA) deficiency may be curbed permanently by introducing bone marrow cells producing ADA into cells at:
   (a) early embryonic stages
   (b) late embryonic stages
   (c) any stage
   (d) None of these
16. What is Parthenocarpy?
   (a) development of fruits without fertilisation of the ovary
   (b) development of vegetables without fertilisation of the ovary
   (c) development of fruits with fertilisation of the ovary
   (d) None of these
17. The hybrids containing alleles expressing two contrasting traits are termed as:
   (a) alleles
   (b) genes
   (c) homologous chromosome
   (d) None of these
18. Assisted reproductive technologies are:
   (a) Artificial Insemination
   (b) Gamete Intra Fallopian Transfer
   (c) Zygote Intra Fallopian Transfer
   (d) All of these
19. At what level the control of gene expression takes place?
   (a) Transcription
   (b) Translation
   (c) Replication
   (d) None of these

20. What is splicing?

(a) Removal of introns in a transcription unit

(b) Removal of exons in a transcription unit

(c) Removal of introns in a translation unit

(d) Removal of exons in a translation unit

21. In a lac operon, what is an inducer?

(a) glucose   (b) galactose   (c) lactose   (d) None of these

22. Name the post-fertilization event in flowering plants.

(a) Development of pistil

(b) Development of anther

(c) Embryo development

(d) None of these

23. Given below is a pedigree chart of a family with five children. It shows the inheritance of attached ear lobes as opposed to the free ones. The squares represent the male individuals and circles the female individuals. Which one of the following conclusions drawn is correct?

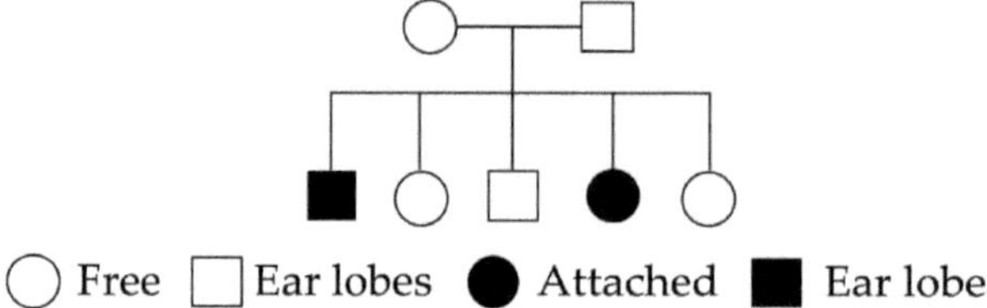

(a) The parents are homozygous recessive.

(b) The parents are homozygous dominant.

(c) The trait is Y-linked.

(d) The parents are heterozygous.

24. A DNA molecule consists of:

(a) two polynucleotide chains composed of four types of nucleotide subunits

(b) one polynucleotide chain composed of four types of nucleotide subunits

(c) two polynucleotide chains composed of two types of nucleotide subunits

(d) one polynucleotide chain composed of four types of nucleotide subunits

SECTION - B

Section – B consists of 24 questions (Sl. No.25 to 48). Attempt any 20 questions from this section. The first attempted 20 questions would be evaluated.

25. Assertion: The bulbourethral gland is a male accessory gland.

Reason: The secretions of bulbourethral glands helps in the lubrication of the penis.

(a) Assertion and reason both are correct statements and reason is the correct explanation of the assertion.

(b) Assertion and reason both are correct statements, but reason is not the correct explanation of the assertion

(c) Assertion is true, but reason is false statement.

(d) Assertion is false, but reason is true statement.

26. Assertion: Megaspore mother cell undergoes meiosis to produce four megaspores.

Reason: Megaspore mother cell and megaspore both are haploid.

(a) Assertion and reason both are correct statements and reason is the correct explanation of the assertion.

(b) Assertion and reason both are correct statements, but reason is not the correct explanation of the assertion

(c) Assertion is true, but reason is false statement.

(d) Assertion is false, but reason is true statement.

27. Assertion: The maximum frequency of recombination that can result from crossing over between linked genes is 50%.

Reason: Linked genes show higher frequency of crossing over if the distance between them is longer.

(a) Assertion and reason both are correct statements and reason is the correct explanation of the assertion.

(b) Assertion and reason both are correct statements, but reason is not the correct explanation of the assertion.

(c) Assertion is true, but reason is false statement.

(d) Assertion is false, but reason is true statement.

28. **Assertion:** Chlamydiosis is most common bacterial sexually transmitted disease.
    Reason: It can be easily differentiated from gonococcal urethritis.
    (a) Assertion and reason both are correct statements and reason is the correct explanation of the assertion.
    (b) Assertion and reason both are correct statements, but reason is not the correct explanation of the assertion
    (c) Assertion is true, but reason is false statement.
    (d) Assertion is false, but reason is true statement.

29. Select the option with correct combination of pedigree symbol and its representation.

    (a) Unaffected female—▢
    (b) Affected male—●
    (c) Mating between relatives—▢—◯ 
    (d) Unaffected male—▢

30. Which of the following is the carrier of genetic information?
    (a) Proteins   (b) Amino acids   (c) DNA   (d) Carbohydrates

31. Which of the following is not a characteristic feature of Down's syndrome?
    (a) Small round head   (b) Very tall
    (c) Furrowed tongue   (d) Partially open mouth

32. In which of the following levels can gene expression not be exerted?
    (a) Transitional level   (b) Reverse transcriptional level
    (c) Transcriptional level   (d) Processing level

33. What are polygenic traits?
    (a) Traits controlled by a single gene   (b) Traits not controlled by any genes
    (c) Traits controlled by two genes   (d) Traits controlled by three or more genes

34. The four whorls of the flower arranged on:
    (a) Ovaries   (b) Petals
    (c) Stem   (d) Thalamus

35. The number of primary follicles at birth and puberty is not equal.
    (a) True   (b) False
    (c) Partially true or false   (d) Cannot say

36. Which of the following is not the role of Reproductive and Child Health Care (RCH) programs?
    (a) Awareness about reproductive health
    (b) Providing support to reproductively sick people
    (c) Providing facilities to build a reproductively healthy society
    (d) Promote abortion

37. Which part of the flower consists of anthers and filaments?
    (a) gynoecium   (b) androecium
    (c) calyx   (d) corolla

38. Chromosomal disorders are based on:
    (a) Mutant allele and their defective products
    (b) Mutant allele and chromosome arrangement
    (c) Mutant allele and imbalance in chromosome number
    (d) Imbalance in chromosome number and chromosome arrangement

39. Given diagram represents the schematic structure of a transcription unit with some parts labelled as A, B, C, and D. Select the option which shows its correct labelling.

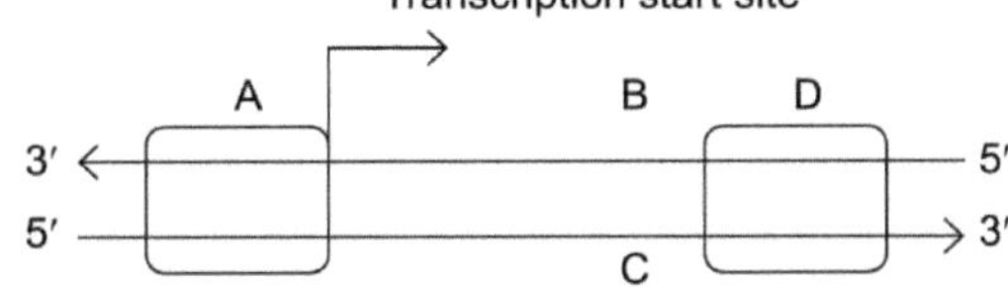

	A	B	C	D
(a)	Termination	Template strand	Coding strand	Promoter
(b)	Promoter	Coding strand	Template strand	Terminator
(c)	Terminator	Coding strand	Template strand	Promoter
(d)	Promoter	Template strand	Coding strand	Terminator

40. Regulatory protein can act as:

(a) an activator (b) a repressor (c) Both (a) and (b) (d) an inducer

41. The genotype of the person suffering from Klinefelter's syndrome is:

(a) 44 + XXX (b) 44 + XXY (c) 42 + XXY (d) 42 + XXX

42. The process of activation of amino acids in the presence of ATP and its linkage to their cognate tRNA is known as:

(a) Charging of ATP (b) Aminoacetylation of tRNA

(c) Charging of tRNA (d) Aminoacetylation of ATP

43. Traits described by Mendel were:

(a) Alternative forms (b) Contrasting traits

(c) Mixed forms (d) Opposite and recessive forms

44. Label the part marked 1.

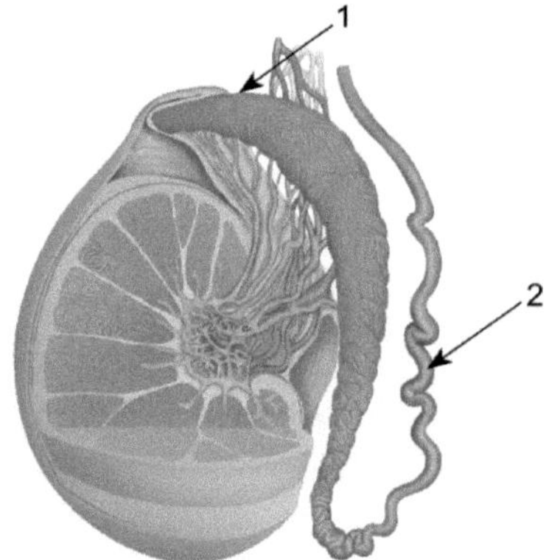

(a) Rete testes (b) Vas deferens (c) Epididymis (d) Vasa efferentia

45. The cell organelle responsible for the synthesis of proteins:

(a) Lysosomes (b) Nucleus (c) Mitochondria (d) Ribosomes

46. The set of positively charged basic proteins is known as:

(a) Histidine (b) DNA (c) RNA (d) Histones

47. The first round of meiosis of oogonium is completed in:

(a) Graafian follicle (b) Secondary follicle

(c) Primary follicle (d) Tertiary follicle

48. What does the part B stand for?

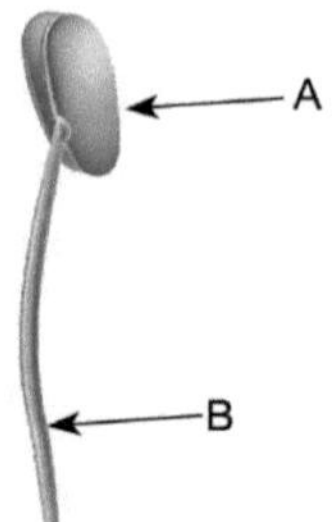

(a) Ovaries (b) Anther

(c) Filament (d) Thalamus

SECTION – C

Section-C consists of one case followed by 6 questions linked to this case (Q.No. 49 to 54). Besides this, 6 more questions are given. Attempt any 10 questions in this section. <u>The first attempted 10 questions would be evaluated.</u>

Case: To answer the questions, study the figure given below.

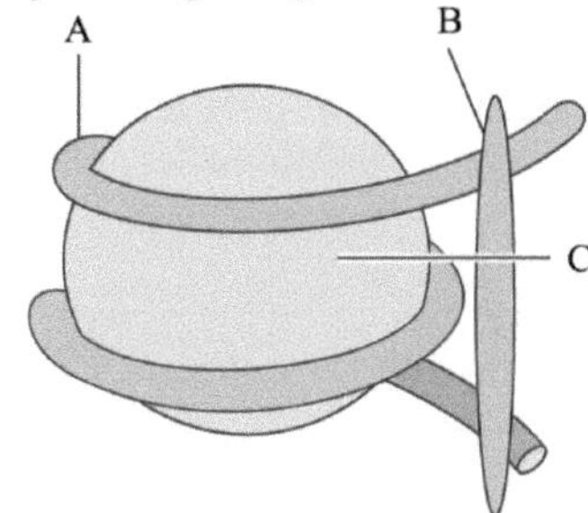

49. What does the given structure represent?
  (a) nucleotide   (b) nucleoside   (c) nucleosome   (d) none of these

50. Name the part A.
  (a) RNA   (b) DNA   (c) mRNA   (d) None of these

51. What is the role of part B?
  (a) binds to linker DNA between nucleosomes forming the macromolecular structure
  (b) Separates linker DNA between nucleosomes
  (c) Provides rigidity to histone octamer
  (d) None of these

52. Histones are:
  (a) a set of negatively charged, acidic proteins   (b) a set of positively charged, acidic proteins
  (c) a set of negatively charged, basic proteins   (d) a set of positively charged, basic proteins

53. The _______ charged DNA is wrapped around the positively charged histone octamer to form_____________.
  (a) positively, nucleosome   (b) negatively, nucleosome
  (c) positively, nucleotide   (d) negatively, nucleotide

54. The types of histone protein are:
  (a) H_2A, H_2B, H_3, and H_4 (b) H_3A, H_2B, H_3, and H_4
  (c) H_2A, H_3B, H_3, and H_4 (d) H_2A, H_2B, H_3, and H_5

55. The following is the diagram of TS of anther. Identify the parts labelled A, B and C.

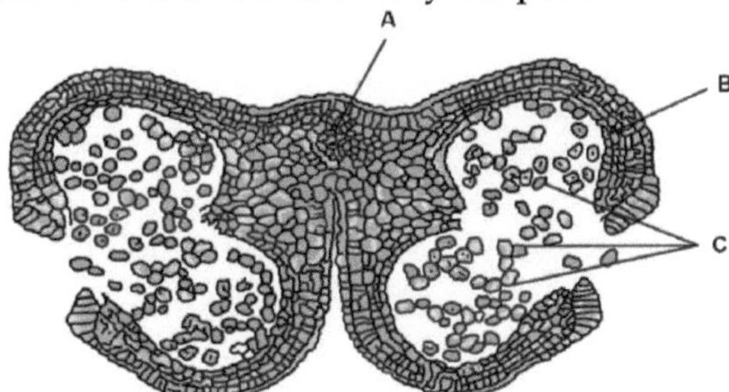

  (a) A—Connective tissue, B—Endothecium, C—Pollen grain
  (b) A—Endothecium, B—Connective tissue, C—Endothecium
  (c) A—Pollen grain, B—Connective tissue, C—Endothecium
  (d) A—Endothecium, B—Pollen grain, C—Connective tissue

56. The given figure represents one of the steps in the process of transcription in bacteria. Identify the step and label A and B marked in the figure.

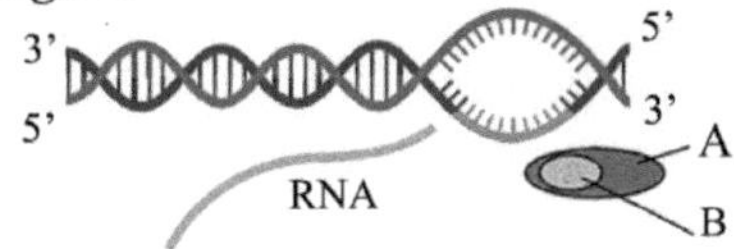

	Steps	A	B
(a)	Termination	RNA polymerase	Sigma factor
(b)	Initiation	DNA polymerase	Rho factor
(c)	Elongation	RNA polymerase	Sigma factor
(d)	Termination	RNA polymerase	Rho factor

57. Which of the following products are produced when lactose is hydrolysed?

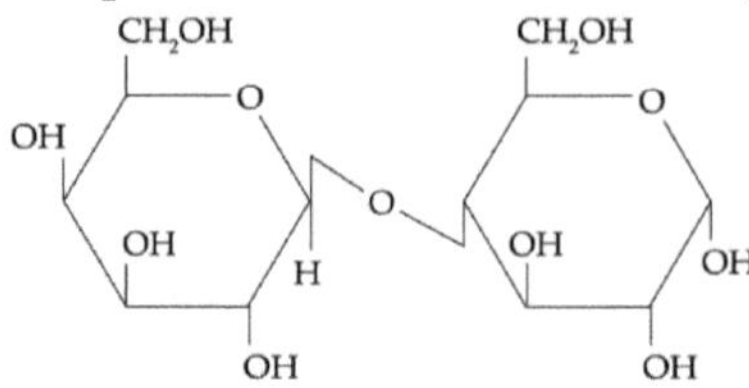

  (a) Glucose and Fructose   (b) Two molecules of glucose

  (c) Glucose and Galactose   (d) Fructose and Galactose

58. Identify the part labelled as A.

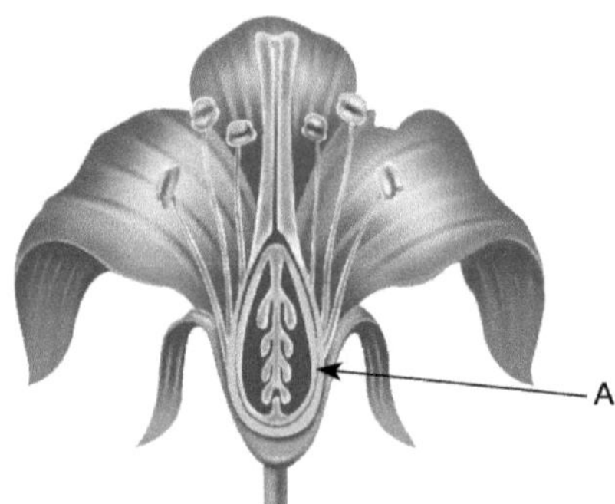

  (a) Gynoecium   (b) Androecium   (c) Self-pollination   (d) Cross-pollination

59. Find out spermatid and sertoli cell in diagram given below.

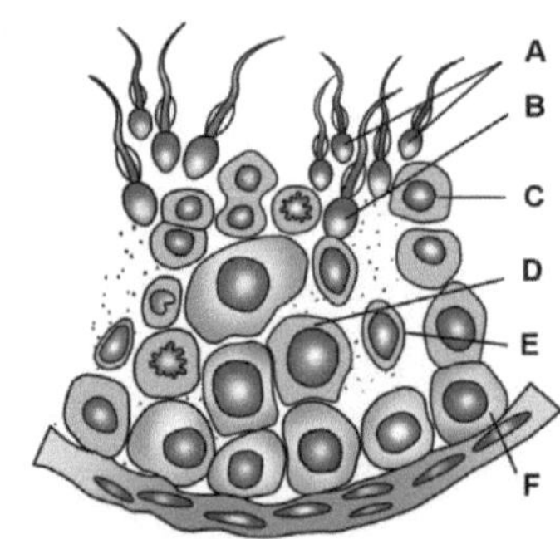

  (a) D and E   (b) E and F   (c) A and C   (d) B and E

60. Identify A, B, C and D in the given diagram of a *lac* operon.

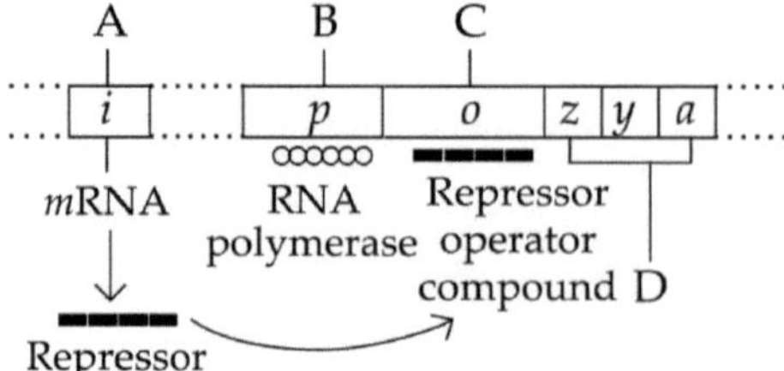

  (a) A—Regulatory gene, B—Promoter, C—Operator, D—Structural gene

  (b) A—Regulatory gene, B—Promoter, C—Structural gene, D—Operator

  (c) A—Regulatory gene, B—Structural gene, C—Promoter, D—Operator

  (d) A—Regulatory gene, B—Structural gene, C—Operator gene, D—Promoter gene

Sample Paper 6

Biology

SECTION – A

Section – A consists of 24 questions. Attempt any 20 questions from this section.
The first attempted 20 questions would be evaluated.

1. The autosomal disorder/disease in humans is:
   - (a) Colour blindness
   - (b) Thalassemia
   - (c) Hemophilia
   - (d) Turner's Syndrome

2. A dicotyledonous plant bears flowers but never produces fruits and seeds. The most probable cause for the above situation is:
   - (a) Plant is dioecious and bears only pistillate flowers.
   - (b) Plant is dioecious and bears both pistillate and staminate flowers.
   - (c) Plant is monoecious.
   - (d) Plant is dioecious and bears only staminate flowers.

3. The following pedigree shows a particular trait which is absent in the parents but found in the subsequent generation irrespective of the sexes. The pedigree shows:

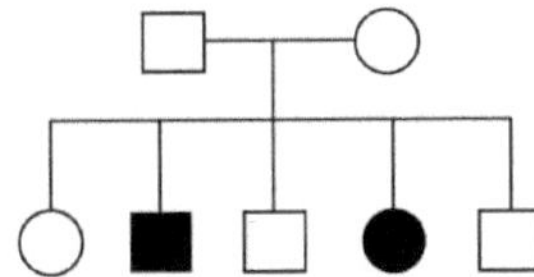

   - (a) Autosomal recessive disorder
   - (b) Autosomal dominant disorder
   - (c) X linked disorder
   - (d) Y linked disorder

4. Removal of introns in a transcription unit is:
   - (a) Transformation
   - (b) Splicing
   - (c) Tailing
   - (d) Capping

5. Read the following statements about the following diagram and select the correct option.

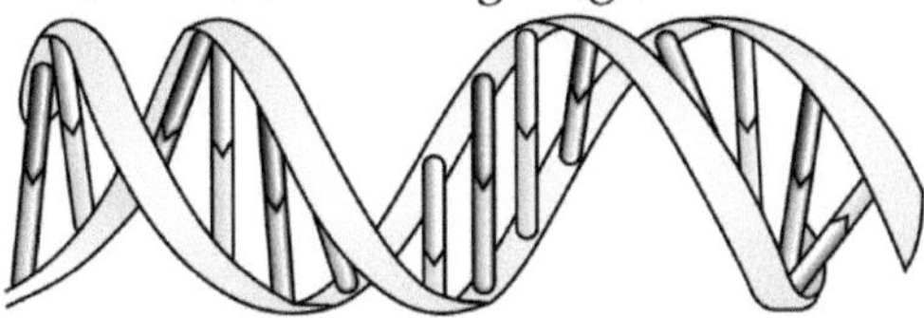

   Statement-(A): This structure is of double stranded DNA.
   Statement-(B): The base pairs of DNA are Adenine, Guanine, Thymine and Cytosine.
   Statement-(C): Adenine pair with Thymine, Guanine pair with Cytosine.
   Statement-(D): Both the chains are coiled in a right hand fashion.
   - (a) Statements (A) and (B) are correct but (C) and (D) are incorrect.
   - (b) Statements (C) and (D) are correct but (A) and (B) are incorrect.
   - (c) Statements (A) and (C) are correct but (B) and (D) are incorrect.
   - (d) All the statements (A), (B), (C) and (D) are correct.

6. Urethral meatus refers to the:
   - (a) Urinogenital duct
   - (b) Opening of vas deferens into urethra
   - (c) External opening of the urinogenital duct
   - (d) Muscles surrounding the urinogenital duct

7. This process is known as:

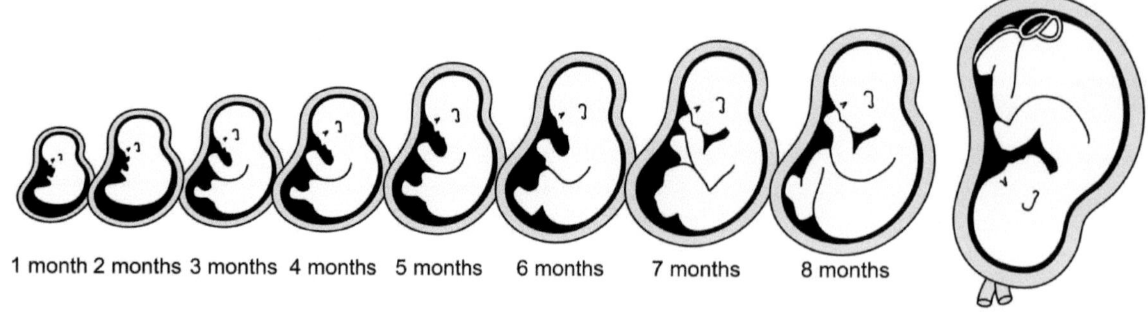

   (a) Fertilisation   (b) Parthenocarpy   (c) Embryogenesis   (d) Fusion of gametes

8. Common test to find genotype of hybrid is by:
   (a) Studying sexual behaviour of F_1 progeny
   (b) Crossing F_1 individuals with recessive parents
   (c) Crossing one F_2 progeny with male parent
   (d) Crossing one F_2 progeny with female parent

9. From the sexually transmitted diseases mentioned below, identify the one which does not specifically affect the sex organs:
   (a) Syphilis   (b) AIDS   (c) Gonorrhea   (d) Genital warts

10. The process shown in the figure is known as:

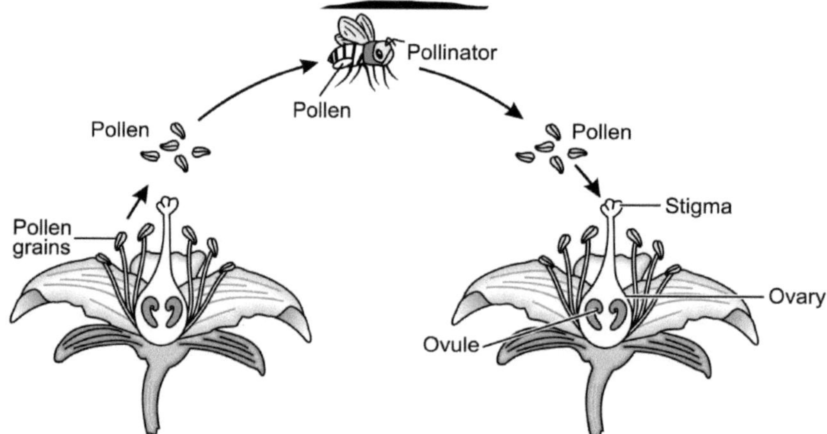

   (a) Fertilisation   (b) Pollination   (c) Parthenogenesis   (d) None of these

11. In eukaryotic cell, transcription, RNA splicing and RNA capping take place in:
   (a) Nucleus   (b) Cytoplasm   (c) Ribosomes   (d) Golgi body

12. A national level approach to build up a reproductively healthy society was taken up in our country in:
   (a) 1950s   (b) 1960s   (c) 1980s   (d) 1990s

13. How many haploid cells are present in a mature female gametophyte of a flowering plant ?
   (a) six   (b) eight   (c) seven   (d) five

14. Name the enzyme that joins the small fragments of DNA of a lagging strand during DNA replication.
   (a) RNA polymerase   (b) DNA polymerase   (c) DNA ligase   (d) None of these

15. Both deoxyribose and ribose belong to a class of sugars called:
   (a) Trioses   (b) hexoses   (c) Pentoses   (d) Polysaccharides

16. Experimental verification of the chromosomal theory of inheritance was done by:
   (a) Sutton   (b) Boveri   (c) Morgan   (d) Mendel

17. Progestogens in the contraceptive pill:
   (a) prevents ovulation   (b) inhibits estrogen
   (c) checks attachment of zygote endometrium   (d) All of these

18. Pollen tube is covered by:
    (a) pectocellulose
    (b) sporopollenin
    (c) cellulose
    (d) lingnocellulose
19. Nucleoside differs from a nucleotide. It lacks the:
    (a) base
    (b) sugar
    (c) phosphate group
    (d) hydroxyl group
20. Which of the following most appropriately describes hemophilia?
    (a) Recessive gene disorder
    (b) X-linked recessive gene disorder
    (c) Chromosomal disorder
    (d) Dominant gene disorder
21. Condoms are barriers that cover:
    (a) Penis in male and ovary in female
    (b) Penis in male and cervix and vagina in female
    (c) Scrotum in male and cervix and vagina in female
    (d) Cervix in male and vagina in female
22. The genes controlling the seven pea characters studied by Mendel are now known to be located on _____ different chromosomes.
    (a) four
    (b) seven
    (c) six
    (d) five
23. Which of the following figure is used for mating between relatives?
    (a)
    (b)
    (c)
    (d)
24. The primary function of DNA polymerase is to:
    (a) add nucleotides to the growing daughter strand
    (b) seal nicks along the sugar-phosphate backbone of the daughter strand
    (c) unwind the parent DNA double helix
    (d) prevent reassociation of the denatured parent DNA strands

SECTION - B

Section – B consists of 24 questions (Sl. No.25 to 48). Attempt any 20 questions from this section. The first attempted 20 questions would be evaluated.

25. **Assertion:** In barrier methods, ovum and sperms are prevented from physical meeting.
    Reason: Barrier methods are used during coitus, to prevent the entry of ejaculated semen into the female reproductive tract.
    (a) Assertion and reason both are correct statements and reason is the correct explanation of the assertion.
    (b) Assertion and reason both are correct statements, but reason is not the correct explanation of the assertion
    (c) Assertion is true, but reason is false statement.
    (d) Assertion is false, but reason is true statement.
26. **Assertion:** Cells of the tapetum posses dense cytoplasm and generally have more than one nucleus.
    Reason: The anther and the filament are attached together with the help of connective.
    (a) Assertion and reason both are correct statements and reason is the correct explanation of the assertion.
    (b) Assertion and reason both are correct statements, but reason is not the correct explanation of the assertion.
    (c) Assertion is true, but reason is false statement.
    (d) Assertion is false, but reason is true statement.
27. **Assertion:** The male reproductive system is located in the pelvis region and it includes a pair of testes along with accessory ducts, glands and external genitalia.
    Reason: The testes of human males are situated inside the abdominal cavity within a pouch called rectum.
    (a) Assertion and reason both are correct statements and reason is the correct explanation of the assertion.
    (b) Assertion and reason both are correct statements, but reason is not the correct explanation of the assertion.
    (c) Assertion is true, but reason is false statement.
    (d) Assertion is false, but reason is true statement.

28. **Assertion:** Pleiotropy should not be confused with polygenic traits.

    Reason: In polygenic traits, multiple genes result in single phenotype.
    (a) Assertion and reason both are correct statements and reason is the correct explanation of the assertion.
    (b) Assertion and reason both are correct statements, but reason is not the correct explanation of the assertion.
    (c) Assertion is true, but reason is false statement.
    (d) Assertion is false, but reason is true statement.

29. What is the probability of male child in this fertilisation?

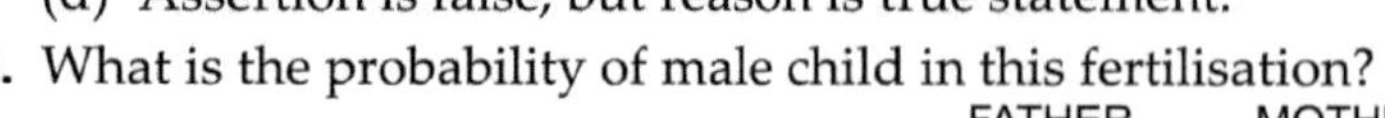
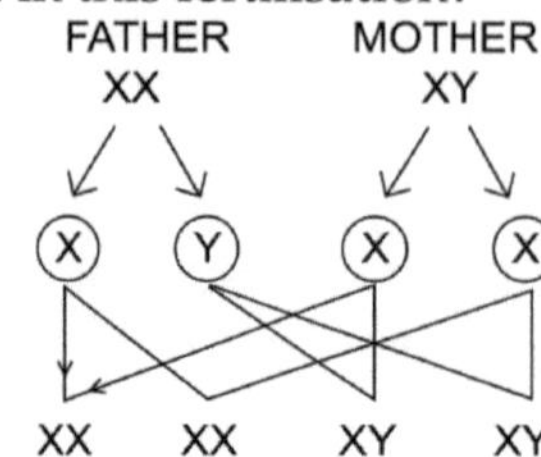

    (a) 100%   (b) 75%   (c) 50%   (d) 0%

30. A red-flowered plant crossed with a white-flowered plant of the same species, produced F_1 plants which all had pink flowers. Self-pollination of the F_1 plants produced and F_2 generation in which 39 plants had red flowers, 83 had pink flowers and 40 had white flowers. What does this experiment demonstrate?
    (a) Co-dominance   (b) Continuous variation
    (c) A dihybrid cross   (d) Linkage

31. Level of which hormones are at their highest during the luteal phase (second half of the cycle) of the menstrual cycle?
    (a) Estrogen   (b) Progesterone
    (c) Luteinizing hormone   (d) Follicular stimulating hormone

32. Which of the following is a suitable vector for the process of cloning in Human Genome Project (HGP)?
    (a) PAC (Protozoa Artificial Chromosomes)   (b) FAC (Fungal Artificial Chromosomes)
    (c) VAC (Viral Artificial Chromosomes)   (d) YAC (Yeast Artificial Chromosomes)

33. What is the pattern of inheritance for a sex-linked allele?
    (a) Every affected person has an affected parent.
    (b) Unaffected parents can produce children who are affected.
    (c) Unaffected mothers have affected sons and daughters who are carriers.
    (d) None of these

34. Amniocentesis is the withdrawal of amniotic fluid during:
    (a) Menopause   (b) Lactation   (c) Gestation   (d) Pregnancy

35. Eukaryotic chromosomes:
    (a) are circular and contain origin and terminator sequences
    (b) are linear and have origins and telomeres
    (c) contain coding and non-coding sequences
    (d) Both (b) and (c)

36. Sex determination in grasshoppers, humans, and *Drosophila* is similar because:
    (a) females are hemizygous
    (b) males have one X-chromosome and females have two X-chromosomes
    (c) all males always have one Y-chromosome in all three species
    (d) the ratio of autosomes to sex chromosomes is the same in all three organisms

37. The major part of the semen is the secretion of:
    (a) Cowper's gland   (b) Pineal gland
    (c) Prostate gland   (d) Seminal vesicle

38. The following ratio is generally constant for a given species:
    (a) $\dfrac{A+G}{C+T}$ (b) $\dfrac{T+C}{G+A}$ (c) $\dfrac{G+C}{A+T}$ (d) $\dfrac{A+C}{T+G}$

39. The experiment in the image below was done by which of the following scientists?

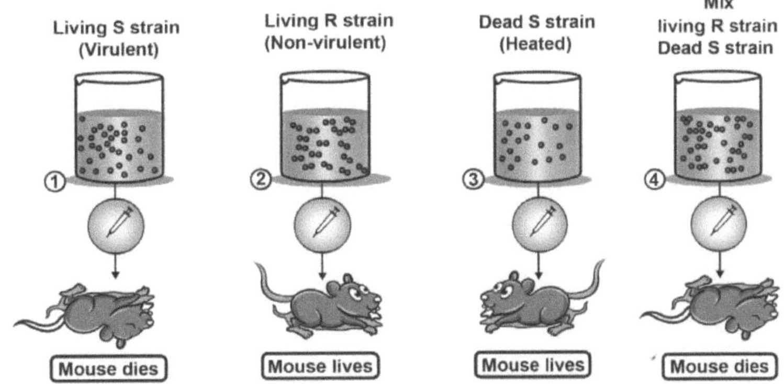

   (a) Johannsen   (b) Frederick Griffith

   (c) Gregor Mendel   (d) T.H. Morgan

40. True-breeding plants:

   (a) produce the same offspring when crossed for many generations

   (b) result from a monohybrid cross

   (c) result from a dihybrid cross

   (d) result from crossing over during prophase I of meiosis

41. A DNA strand with the sequence AACGTAACG is transcribed. What is the sequence of the mRNA molecule synthesized?

   (a) AACGTAACG   (b) UUGCAUUGC   (c) AACGUAACG   (d) TTGCATTGC

42. Which one of the following traits of garden pea studied by Mendel was a recessive feature?

   (a) Round seed shape   (b) Axial flower position

   (c) Green seed colour   (d) Green pod colour

43. Genetic code is:

   (a) triplet, universal, ambiguous and degenerate

   (b) triplet, universal, non-ambiguous and non-degenerate

   (c) triplet, universal, non-ambiguous and degenerate

   (d) triplet, universal, ambiguous and non-degenerate

44. In which of the following parts of female reproductive system, fertilisation takes place?

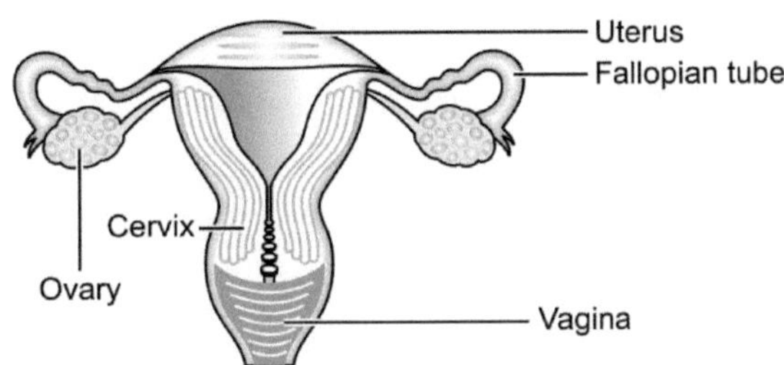

   (a) Uterus   (b) Cervix   (c) Fallopian tube   (d) Vagina

45. Which one of following is not an example of parthenocarpic fruit?

   (a) Apple   (b) Persimmon   (c) Grapefruit   (d) Watermelon

46. A gene showing co-dominance has:

   (a) alleles tightly linked on the same chromosome

   (b) alleles that are recessive to each other

   (c) both alleles independently expressed in the heterozygote

   (d) one allele dominant on the other

47. Information flow or central dogma of modern biology is:

   (a) RNA $\rightarrow$ Proteins $\rightarrow$ DNA   (b) DNA $\rightarrow$ RNA $\rightarrow$ RNA

   (c) RNA $\rightarrow$ DNA $\rightarrow$ Proteins   (d) DNA $\rightarrow$ RNA $\rightarrow$ Proteins

48. Which of the following chromatins is transcriptionally more active?

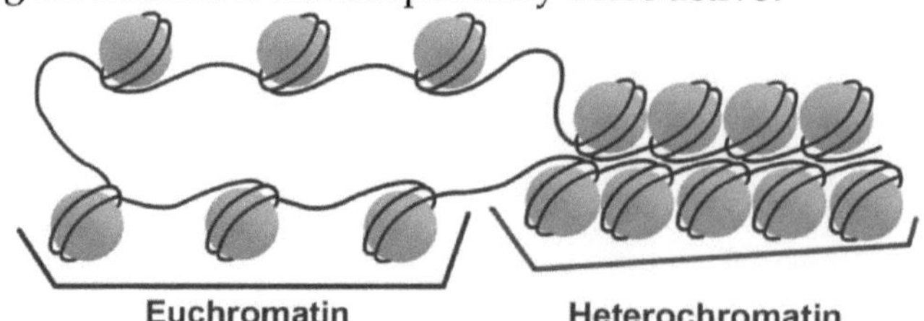

(a) Euchromatin is more active than heterochromatin.

(b) Heterochromatin is more active than euchromatin.

(c) Activity of both chromatins are same.

(d) Sometimes euchromatin is more active and vice-versa.

SECTION - C

Section-C consists of one case followed by 6 questions linked to this case (Q.No. 49 to 54). Besides this, 6 more questions are given. Attempt any 10 questions in this section. <u>The first attempted 10 questions would be evaluated.</u>

Case: Observe the following schematic representation of determination of sex (XX-XY type mechanism) and answer the question that follows:

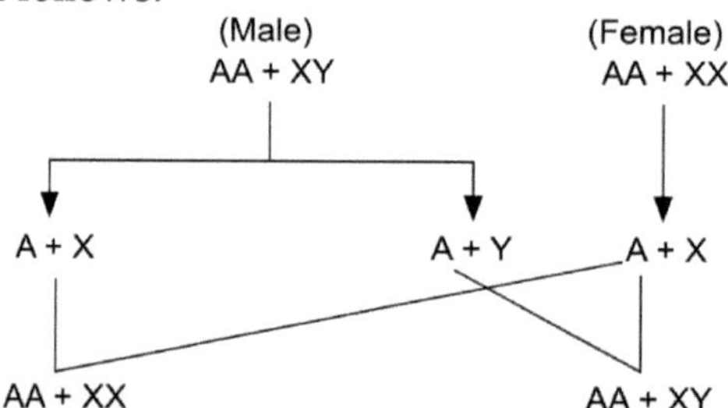

49. In an entity with genetic composition AA + XXY such as *Drosophila* will be a normal female. In the case of mammals, it will be:

(a) Turner's syndrome

(b) Klinefelter's syndrome

(c) Normal female

(d) Normal male

50. ___________ discovered XY sex chromosome.

(a) MJD White

(b) R. Brown

(c) Nettie Stevens

(d) Mendel

51. This number of Barr bodies are found in a female with XXXXY chromosomes.

(a) four

(b) three

(c) two

(d) one

52. If a boy has sexual characters of that of a girl, its genotype would be:

(a) XXY

(b) XYY

(c) XO

(d) XY

53. The chromosomes accounted for sex determination are referred to as:

(a) Heterosis

(b) Multiple alleles

(c) Allosomes

(d) Autosome

54. The chromosomal basis of sex determination was discovered by which of the following scientists?

(a) Stevens

(b) Grey

(c) Henking

(d) Wilson

55. This structure is:

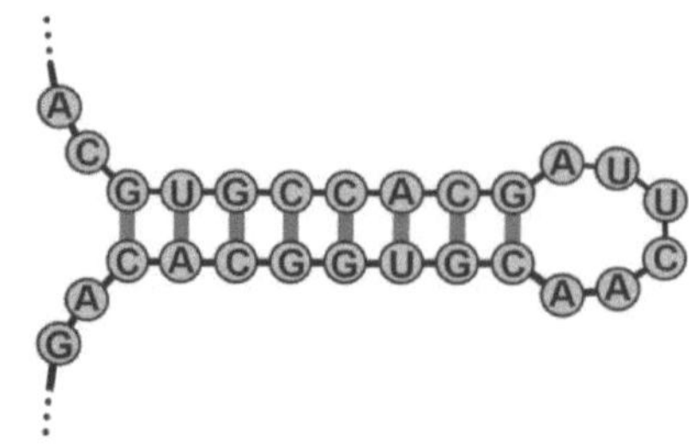

(a) DNA

(b) RNA

(c) Protein

(d) Both (a) and (b)

56. What is the process shown in the following figure?

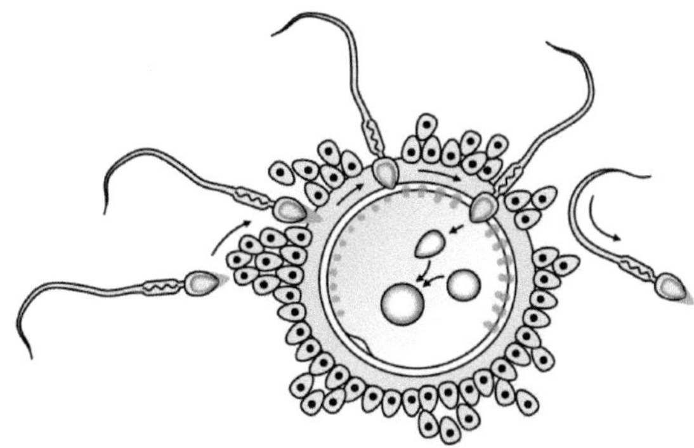

(a) Syngamy

(b) Fertilisation

(c) Parthenogenesis

(d) Both (a) and (b)

57. Why this fly is suitable for laboratory experiments?

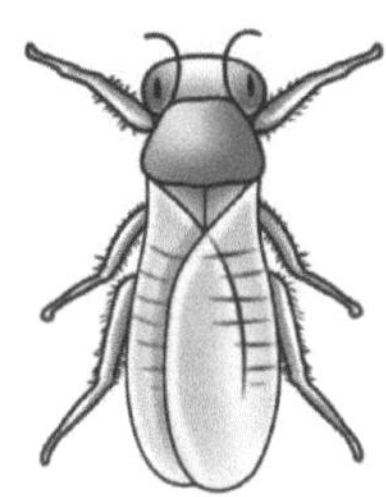

(a) It's life span is too short

(b) It can reproduce on synthetic medium

(c) A single mating can produce a large number of flies

(d) All of these

58. What are A and B in the following figure?

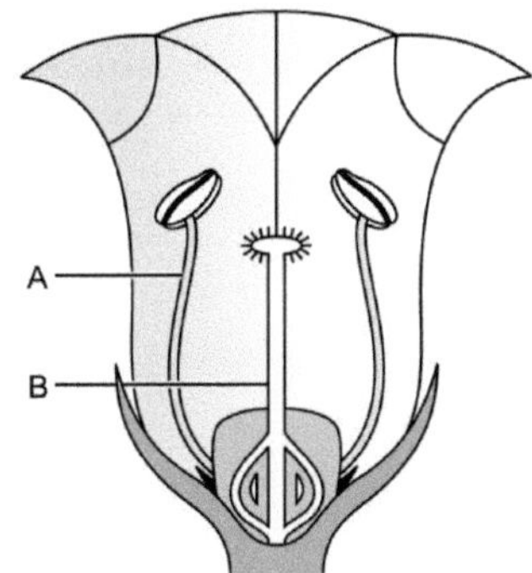

(a) A– Carpel; B– Stamen

(b) A– Stamen; B– Carpel

(c) Both A and B are carpel

(d) Both A and B are stamen

59. Give the genotypes of the parents shown in generation I.

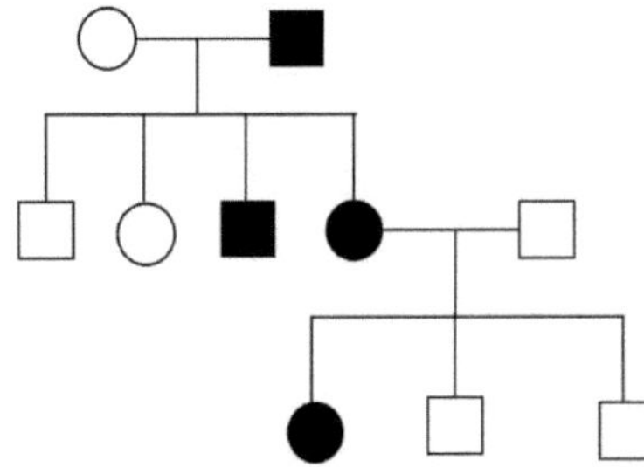

(a) Female: aa and Male: Aa

(b) Female: Aa and Male: aa

(c) Female: Aa and Male: Aa

(d) Female: aa and Male: aa

60. Which of the following scientist performed the experiment shown below?

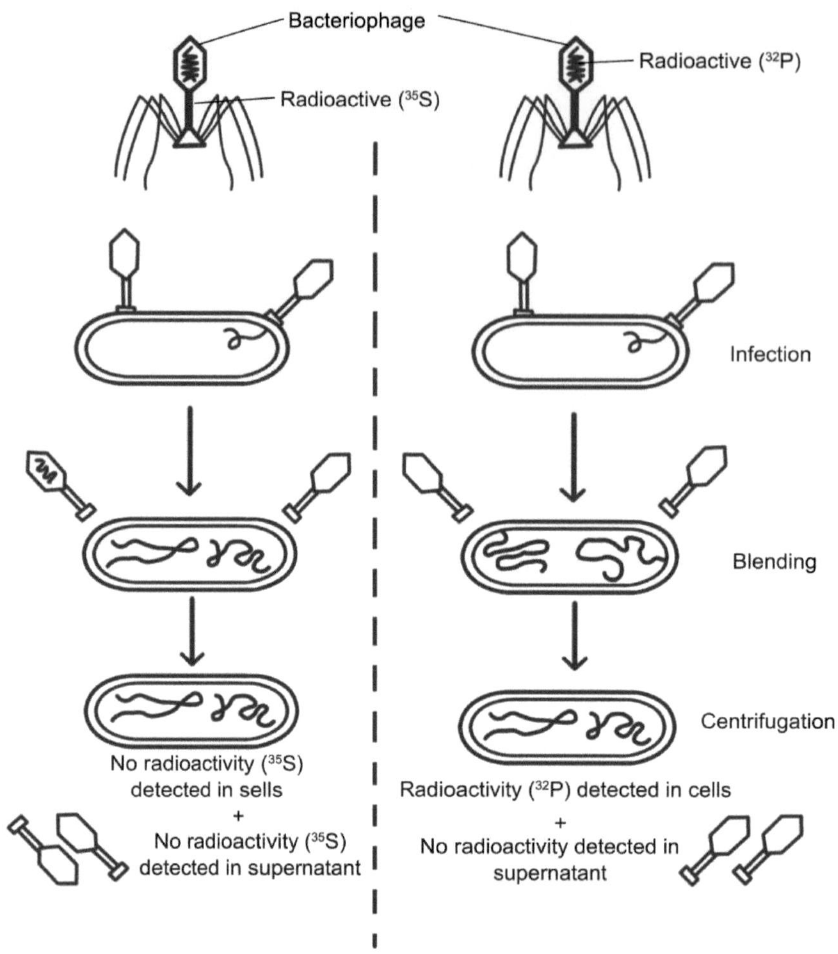

(a) Watson and Crick

(b) Sutton and Morgan

(c) F. Griffith and Chase

(d) Hershey and Chase

❑❑

Sample Paper 7

Biology

SECTION - A

Section – A consists of 24 questions. Attempt any 20 questions from this section.

The first attempted 20 questions would be evaluated.

1. Conditions of a karyotype 2n + 1, 2n – 1 and 2n + 2, 2n – 2 are called:

   (a) Aneuploidy   (b) Polyploidy   (c) Allopolyploidy   (d) Monosomy

2. Match the following and choose the correct options:

COLUMN A	COLUMN B
(A) Trophoblast	(i) Embedding of blastocyst in the endometrium
(B) Cleavage	(ii) Group of cells that would differentiate as embryo
(C) Inner cell mass	(iii) Outer layer of blastocyst attached to the endometrium
(D) Implantation	(iv) Mitotic division of zygote

   (a) A–(i), B–(iii), C–(ii), D–(iv)   (b) A–(iii), B–(iv), C–(ii), D–(i)
   (c) A–(iii), B–(ii), C–(iv), D–(i)   (d) A–(i), B–(ii), C–(iii), D–(iv)

3. Which of the following processes is shown by the following figure?

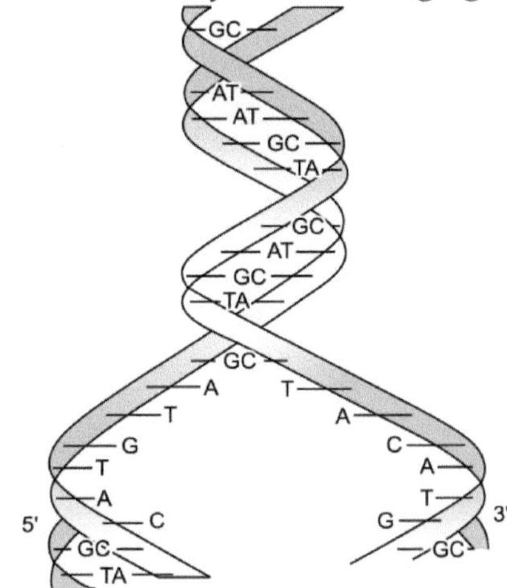

   (a) Semiconservative replication of DNA   (b) Replication of RNA
   (c) Cannot determine either DNA or RNA   (d) Replication of DNA as well as RNA

4. The Okazaki fragments in DNA chain:
   (a) polymerise in the 5'→ 3' direction and explain 3'→ 5' DNA replication.
   (b) prove semi-conservative nature of DNA replication.
   (c) result in transcription.
   (d) polymerise in the 3'→ 5' direction and form replication fork.

5. Diagram given below is called:

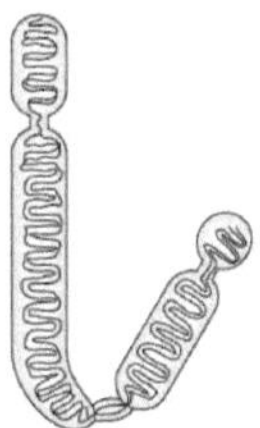

   (a) Chromosomes means coloured body
   (b) Chromosomes which carry forward characters
   (c) DNA which carry forward genetic characters
   (d) Both (a) and (b)

6. Condoms are one of the most popular contraceptives because of the following reasons:
   (a) These are effective barriers for insemination
   (b) They do not interfere with coital act
   (c) These help in reducing the risk of STDs
   (d) All of these

7. Identify the type of inheritance shown in the given pedigree:

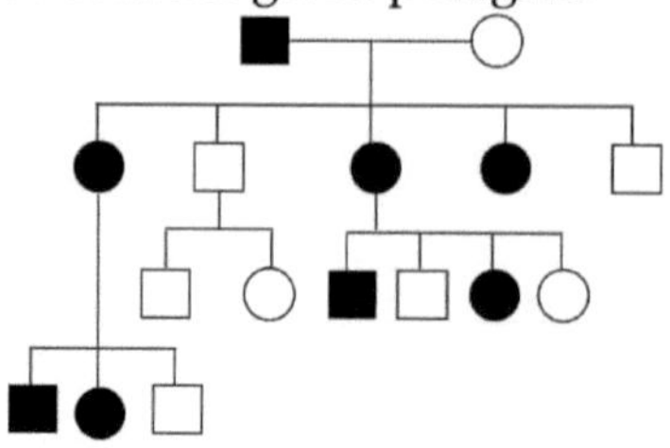

   (a) Dominant X-linked
   (b) Recessive X-linked
   (c) Dominant Y-linked
   (d) Recessive Y-linked

8. A specific nucleotide sequence to which RNA polymerase attaches to initiate transcription of mRNA from a gene called:
   (a) promoter gene
   (b) structural gene
   (c) operon
   (d) regulation gene

9. Autogamy can occur in a chasmogamous flower if:
   (a) Pollen matures before maturity of ovule
   (b) Ovules mature before maturity of pollen
   (c) Both pollen and ovules mature simultaneously
   (d) Both anther and stigma are of equal lengths.

10. In the following lac operon model, read the following statements and select the correct options:

P	i	P	o	z	y	a

    Statement-1: z gene codes for beta-galactosidase
    Statement-2: y gene codes for permeases
    Statement-3: a gene codes of transacetylase
    Statement-4: i gene codes for repressor of lac operon
    (a) Statement 1 and 2 are correct and 3 and 4 are incorrect
    (b) Statement 3 and 4 are correct and 1 and 2 are incorrect
    (c) Statement 1 and 3 are correct and 2 and 4 are incorrect
    (d) All the statements are correct

11. Persons with Down syndrome usually have __________ copies of chromosome 21.
    (a) no
    (b) one
    (c) two
    (d) three

12. Which of the following is a post-fertilisation event in flowering plants?
    (a) Transfer of pollen grains
    (b) Embryo development
    (c) Formation of flower
    (d) Formation of pollen grains

13. F_1 generation means:
    (a) first flowering generation
    (b) first fertile generation
    (c) first filial generation
    (d) first seed generation

14. A typical angiospermic embryo sac is:
    (a) 7-celled and 7-nucleate.
    (b) 8-celled and 7-nucleate.
    (c) 7-celled and 8-nucleate.
    (d) None of these

15. What is the full form of DNA?
    (a) Degenerative acid
    (b) Deoxyribonucleic acid
    (c) Deadly nucleic acid
    (d) Disoriented acid

16. The part that determines the compatible nature of pollen grains is:
    (a) stigma
    (b) style
    (c) ovary
    (d) ovule

17. If one parent belongs to 'A' blood group and the other to 'O' blood group, their children possibly represent:
    (a) A and B groups
    (b) AB only
    (c) A and O groups
    (d) All four groups
18. Given below are the statements regarding embryonic development in humans.
    (i) Cleavage divisions bring about considerable increase in the mass of protoplasm.
    (ii) With more cleavage divisions, the resultant blastomeres become smaller and smaller.
    (iii) The blastomeres in the blastocyst are arranged into two layers, trophoblast and endometrium.
    (iv) Cleavage divisions result in a solid ball of cells called morula.
    Select the option with incorrect statements.
    (a) (i), (ii), and (iv)
    (b) (i) and (iii)
    (c) (i) and (iv)
    (d) (ii) and (iv)
19. Which of the following is not a function of RNA?
    (a) Messenger
    (b) Catalysis
    (c) Adapter
    (d) Modifier
20. The distance between the genes is measured by:
    (a) Angstrom
    (b) Map unit
    (c) Dobson unit
    (d) Millimetre
21. Who considered DNA as a "Nuclein"?
    (a) James Watson
    (b) Friedrich Meischer
    (c) Francis Crick
    (d) Rosalind Franklin
22. The flowers of water hyacinth and water lily are pollinated by:
    (a) water
    (b) birds
    (c) bats
    (d) insects or wind
23. Read the statements about (X), (Y) and (Z).

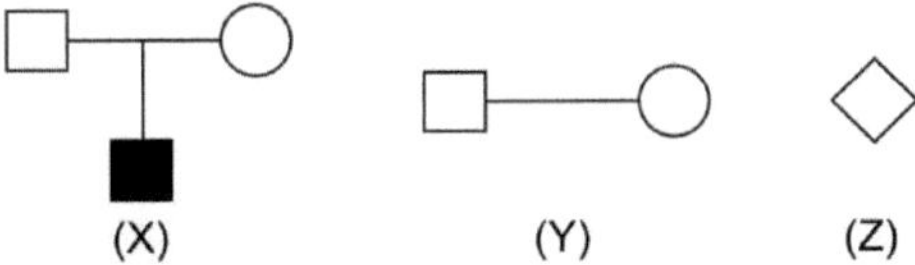

    (A) Symbol (X) is used for affected male child
    (B) Symbol (Y) is used for mating
    (C) Symbol (Y) is used for unspecified sex
    (a) Statement (A) is correct while (B) and (C) are incorrect
    (b) Statement (B) is correct while (A) and (C) are incorrect
    (c) All the statements are correct
    (d) All the statements are incorrect
24. Identify the incorrect statement for sex-determination in humans.
    (a) Humans contain 23 pairs of autosomes.
    (b) Females produce only one type of ovum.
    (c) Genetic makeup of sperm determines the sex of the child.
    (d) In males, two types of gametes are produced.

SECTION - B

Section – B consists of 24 questions (Sl. No.25 to 48). Attempt any 20 questions from this section. <u>The first attempted 20 questions would be evaluated.</u>

25. **Assertion:** The megasporangia, commonly called ovules arise from placenta.
    Reason: The number of ovules in an ovary may be one as in wheat, mango etc., to many as in papaya, watermelon and orchids.
    (a) Assertion and reason both are correct statements and reason is the correct explanation of the assertion.
    (b) Assertion and reason both are correct statements, but reason is not the correct explanation of the assertion.
    (c) Assertion is true, but reason is false statement.
    (d) Assertion is false, but reason is true statement.

26. **Assertion:** Male urethra is also called urinogenital duct.
    Reason: The male urethra carries both urine and sperms.
    (a) Assertion and reason both are correct statements and reason is the correct explanation of the assertion.
    (b) Assertion and reason both are correct statements, but reason is not the correct explanation of the assertion.
    (c) Assertion is true, but reason is false statement.
    (d) Assertion is false, but reason is true statement.

27. **Assertion:** Saheli is a new oral contraceptive for the females contains a non-steroidal preparation.
    Reason: Saheli is a daily pill with many side effects and low contraceptive value.
    (a) Assertion and reason both are correct statements and reason is the correct explanation of the assertion.
    (b) Assertion and reason both are correct statements, but reason is not the correct explanation of the assertion.
    (c) Assertion is true, but reason is false statement.
    (d) Assertion is false, but reason is true statement.

28. **Assertion:** Grasshopper is an example of XO type of sex determination in which the males have only one X-chromosome besides the autosomes, whereas females have a pair of X-chromosomes.
    Reason: In a number of insects and mammals including man XY types of sex determination is seen where both male and female have same number of chromosome.
    (a) Assertion and reason both are correct statements and reason is the correct explanation of the assertion.
    (b) Assertion and reason both are correct statements, but reason is not the correct explanation of the assertion.
    (c) Assertion is true, but reason is false statement.
    (d) Assertion is false, but reason is true statement.

29. Name the types of synthesis 'a' and 'b' occurring in the replicating fork of DNA as shown below:

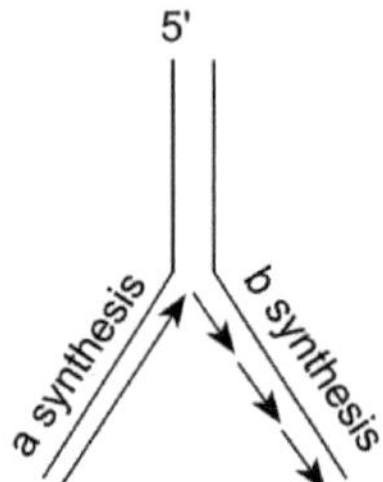

    (a) leading strand, lagging strand
    (b) lagging strand, leading strand
    (c) leading strand, leading strand
    (d) lagging strand, lagging strand

30. Which of the following occurs in the process of central dogma reverse?
    (a) Conversion of a strand of mRNA to DNA
    (b) Changes in the chromosomal karyotype
    (c) Gene replication process
    (d) Protein production process

31. The gene disorder phenylketonuria is an example of:
    (a) multiple allelism
    (b) polygenic inheritance
    (c) multiple factor
    (d) pleiotropy

32. Which of the following is responsible for the transmission of genetic information?
    (a) DNA
    (b) RNA
    (c) Proteins
    (d) Mitochondria

33. Starch synthesis gene in pea plant in heterozygous condition produces starch grain of intermediate size. This shows:
    (a) Complete dominance
    (b) Incomplete dominance
    (c) Codominance
    (d) None of these

34. A rapid decline in which of the following is not associated with a rise in population?
    (a) Death rate
    (b) Maternal mortality rate (MMR)
    (c) Infant mortality rate (IMR)
    (d) Fertility

35. Megaspore mother cell differentiates in the:
    (a) nucellus near chalazal region
    (b) integuments
    (c) hilum
    (d) nucellus near the micropylar region

36. Select the unpaired structure in male.
    (a) Epididymis   (b) Ejaculatory duct   (c) Urethra   (d) Vas deferens

37. What are oral contraceptives called?
    (a) Alcohols   (b) Pills   (c) Injections   (d) Salines

38. Which was considered to be as the genetic material prior to the works done by Oswald Avery, Colin MacLeod and Maclyn McCarty?
    (a) Nucleoids   (b) Nucleons   (c) Protein   (d) Chromosome

39. Which of the following statements is correct for A and B?

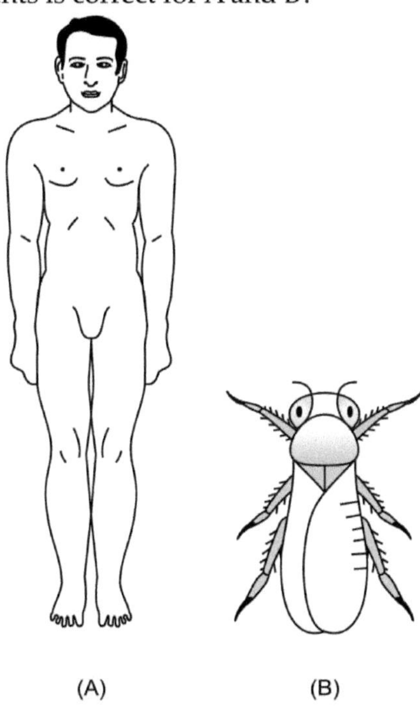

(A)   (B)

    (a) A has XX and XY type of chromosomes   (b) B has XX and XY type of chromosomes
    (c) A has ZW and ZX type of chromosomes   (d) Both (a) and (b) are correct

40. Down's syndrome is caused by an extra copy of chromosome number 21. What percentage of offspring produced by an affected mother and a normal father would be affected by this disorder?
    (a) 100%   (b) 75%   (c) 50%   (d) 25%

41. Which of the following bacterium is responsible for causing urinary tract infections?
    (a) *Staphylococcus saprophyticus*   (b) *Streptococcus pyogenes*
    (c) *Staphylococcus aureus*   (d) *Streptococcus pneumoniae*

42. Which of the following is suitable for experiment on linkage?
    (a) aaBB × aaBB   (b) AABB × aabb   (c) AaBb × AaBb   (d) AAbb × AaBB

43. What will be the next product in the process shown below?
    DNA → RNA → ?
    (a) mRNA   (b) tRNA   (c) rRNA   (d) Protein

44. Label part 2 in the image given below.

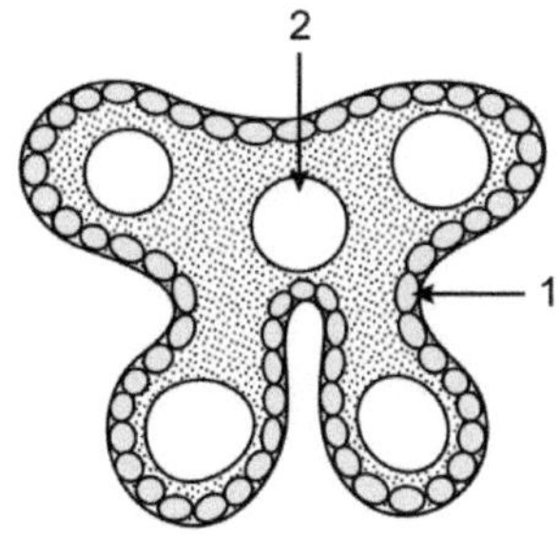

    (a) Vascular strands   (b) Pollen sacs   (c) Pollen grains   (d) Meristematic cells

45. Choose the correct pair.

(a) Gynecomastia–Development of breasts

(b) Turner's syndrome – Loss of an X-chromosome in females

(c) Syndrome–A group of symptoms

(d) All of these

46. What does the structural gene (y) of a lac operon code for?

(a) β-galactosidase   (b) Transacetylase   (c) Permease   (d) Glucagon

47. Sertoli cells are found in:

(a) between the seminiferous tubules

(b) the germinal epithelium of seminiferous tubules

(c) the cortical zone of stroma of ovary

(d) the medulla zone of stroma of ovary

48. The figure given below shows the various events occurring during a menstrual cycle with few events marked as 1, 2, 3, 4 and 5. Which of the following options shows the correct events?

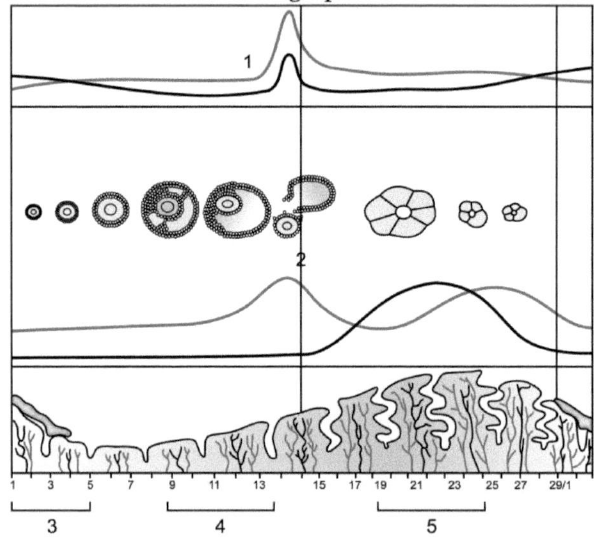

(a) 1 - LH, 2 - Ovulation, 3 - Menstruation, 4 - Proliferative phase, 5 - Luteal phase

(b) 1 - FSH, 2 - Implantation, 3 - Follicular phase, 4 - Menstruation phase, 5 - Luteal phase

(c) 1 - Estrogen, 2 - Parturition, 3 - Luteal phase, 4 - Follicular phase, 5 - Secretory phase

(d) 1 - Progesterone, 2 - Fertilisation, 3 - Menstruation phase, 4 - Secretory phase, 5 - Follicular phase.

SECTION - C

Section-C consists of one case followed by 6 questions linked to this case

(Q.No. 49 to 54). Besides this, 6 more questions are given. Attempt any 10 questions in this section. <u>The first attempted 10 questions would be evaluated.</u>

Case: Observe the diagram of various contraceptive methods used for birth control and answer the questions that follows:

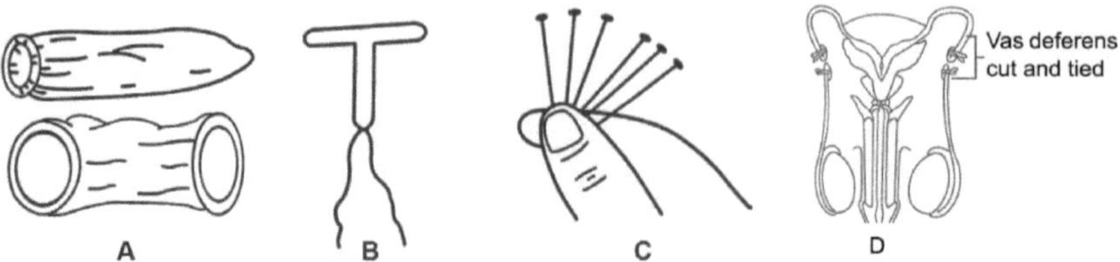

49. Which of the following is a mechanical barrier used in birth control?

(a) A   (b) B   (c) C   (d) D

50. B prevents pregnancy by preventing:

(a) fertilisation

(b) ovulation

(c) implantation of fertilised egg

(d) none of these

51. The difference between oral contraceptives and hormonal implants:
    (a) Differ in sites of implantation
    (b) Differ in duration of action
    (c) Both (a) and (b)
    (d) Differ in constituents

52. If the vasa deferentia of man is surgically removed then:
    (a) semen will be without sperms
    (b) spermatogenesis will not take place
    (c) sperms in semen will be non-motile
    (d) sperms will be enucleated

53. Intrauterine methods exist _______________.
    (a) only for females
    (b) only for males
    (c) both male and female
    (d) cannot say

54. LNG-20 is an IUD, hence releases ____________ to terminate pregnancy.
    (a) Cu^{2+} ions
    (b) progestin
    (c) LH
    (d) none of these

55. The given figure shows one of the elements releasing intrauterine device. Select the option which shows the correct identification of the device and its feature.

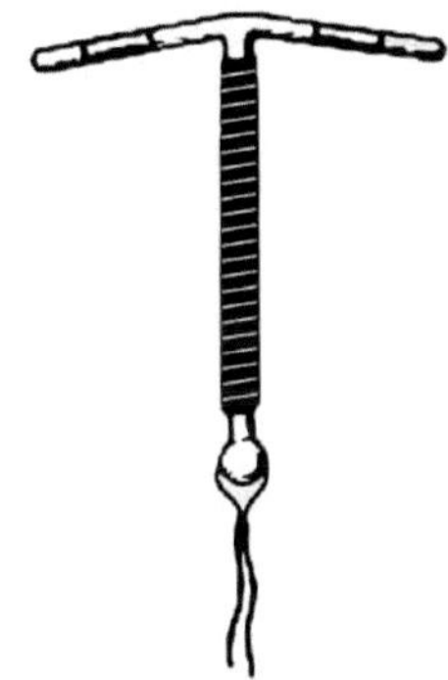

    (a) Cu-T: Suppress sperm motility and its fertilizing capacity.
    (b) Cu-T: Make uterus unsuitable for the attachment of blastocysts.
    (c) Lippes loop: Protect the users from contracting AIDS and STDs.
    (d) LNG-20: Acts as spermicidal means and decrease the contraceptive efficiency.

56. The given figure represent one of the step in the process of transcription in bacteria. Identify the step and label A, B and C marked in the figure.

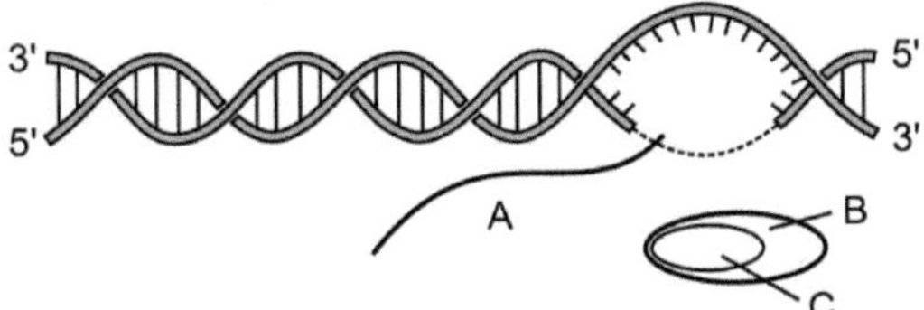

    (a) Initiation; A - DNA, B - RNA, C - Promoter
    (b) Termination; A - RNA, B - RNA polymerase, C - Rho factor
    (c) Elongation; A - RNA, B - RNA polymerase, C - Sigma factor
    (d) Elongation; A-DNA, B - DNA polymerase, C - RNA

57. What will be the genotype of the following Punnet square?

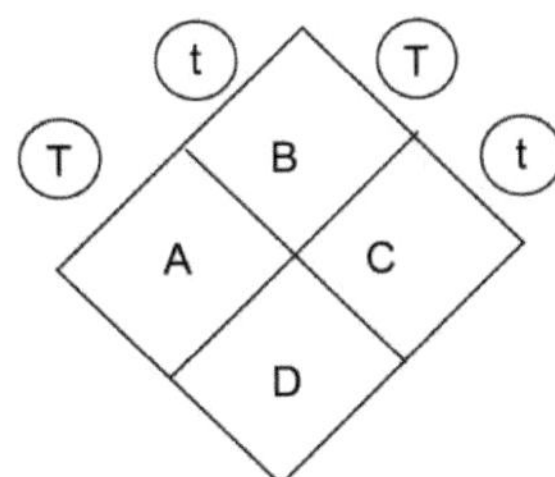

    (a) A-TT; B-tt ;C-tt; D-Tt
    (b) A-tt ; B-Tt ;C-tt; D-Tt
    (c) A-TT; B-Tt ;C-tt; D-Tt
    (d) A-TT; B-Tt ;C-tt; D-tt

58. What are the spots in the picture?

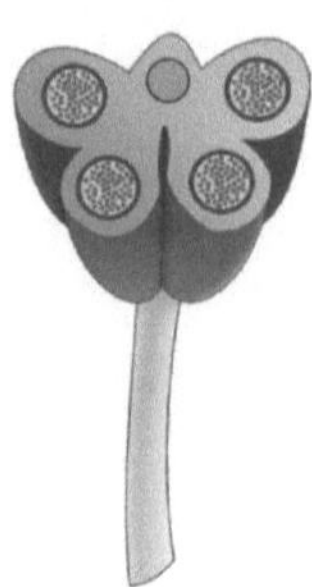

(a) Pollen sac   (b) Pollen grains   (c) Eggs   (d) Dirt

59. Which of the following human development stage becomes embedded in the uterine endometrium by a process called implantation and leads to pregnancy?

(a) 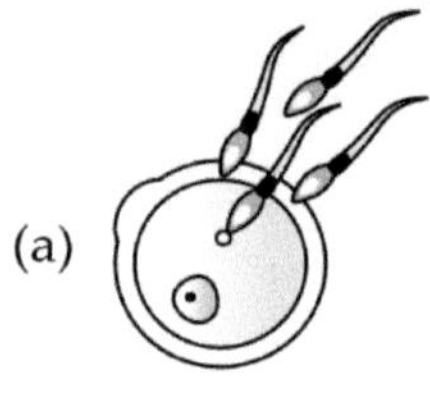

(b) 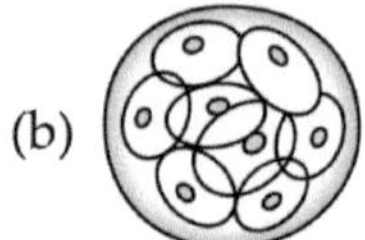

(c) 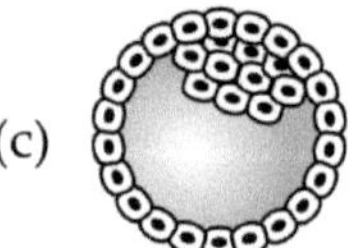

(d) 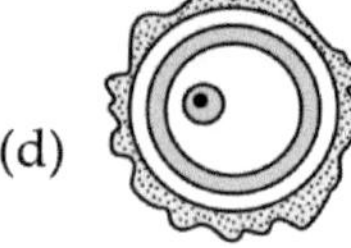

60. This child is affected by which of the following genetic disease?

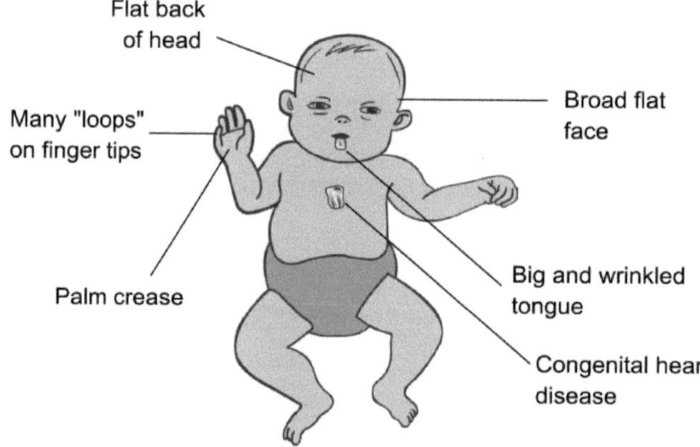

(a) Down's syndrome   (b) Turner's syndrome

(c) Phenylketonuria   (d) Klinefeller's syndrome

Answers

Sample Paper 1

SECTION – A

1. (d) IUDs (Intra Uterine Devices)

> **Explanation:** Intrauterine Devices (IUDs) are a popular and efficient means of contraception (IUDs). Doctors or expert nurses place these devices in the uterus through the vaginal canal. Non-medicated IUDs (*e.g.*, Lippes loop), copper-releasing IUDs (CuT, Cu7, Multiload 375), and hormone-releasing IUDs (CuT, Cu7, Multiload 375) are currently available (Progestasert, LNG-20).

2. (a) Grapes

> **Explanation:** Parthenocarpic fruits are seedless fruits that develop asexually without ovule fertilisation. Parthenocarpy refers to the natural occurrence of banana, grape, and orange. Mango can also be classified as a parthenocarpic fruit, as new seedless kinds are being developed. Mango seeds are also used to cultivate the fruit.

3. (b) Antiparallel, $3' \rightarrow 5'$

> **Explanation:** The two strands of DNA run antiparallel to each other for the effective bonding. The two chains will be having an anti-parallel polarity. If the polarity of one chain is from $3' \rightarrow 5'$, then the polarity of other chain will be $5' \rightarrow 3'$ and vice versa.

4. (b) $1 : 2 : 1$

> **Explanation:** We can see two types of plants in the F_2 generation, tall and dwarf, that emerge phenotypically in a $3 : 1$ ratio. However, because tall plants are divided into two types, homozygous tall (TT) and heterozygous tall (Tt), the genotypic ratio is $1 : 2 : 1$.

5. (c) An inverted L shaped structure

> **Explanation:** The actual structure of the tRNA is actually a compact molecule which appears to be like an inverted L shaped molecule. But, the secondary structure of the tRNA appears to look like a clover leaf shaped structure.

6. (b) 12

> **Explanation:** Endosperm of angiospermic plants is a triploid ($3n$) structure and gametes are haploid (n). As $3n = 36$, therefore, $n = 12$. Hence, the number of chromosomes in the gamete is 12.

7. (c) Vas deferens

> **Explanation:** A 40 cm long vas deferens emerges from the cauda epididymis on each side and leaves the scrotal sac and enters the abdominal cavity through the inguinal canal.

8. (c) chemical synthesis of gene

> **Explanation:** In vitro synthesis of polypeptides utilising artificially synthesised mRNA was awarded the Nobel Prize to M. Nirenberg, Khorana, and Holley.

9. (d) Dengue

Explanation: Dengue is a mosquito-borne viral infection, found in tropical and sub-tropical climates worldwide, mostly in urban and semi-urban areas. The virus responsible for causing dengue is called dengue virus.

10. (a) Fertilisation

Explanation: Fertilisation is the process of fusion of the male and female gamete to form zygote. It is a type of sexual reproduction.

11. (b) Tt and Tt

Explanation: In the case of TT and Tt; all offspring would be tall (TT, Tt). In the case of option 'c' no gene for a dwarf is present, so all offspring will be tall. In the case of option 'd', one of the parent plants is dwarf, so it is incorrect. In the case of option 'b', most of the offspring will be tall and a few will be a dwarf (TT, Tt, tt).

12. (d) None of these

Explanation: The chromosomal theory of heredity did not violated any of Mendel's principles because the only difference was the presence of genes in the chromosome; otherwise, the laws remained same.

13. (c) Testes-testosterone

Explanation: The Leydig cells are the interstitial cells which are located adjacent to the seminiferous tubules in the testes. The important function known of the leydig cells is to produce the androgen and testosterone.

14. (c) Bacterial artificial chromosomes (BACs)

Explanation: Large insert genomic libraries which are used as the primary sequencing templates are constructed in bacterial artificial chromosomes (BACs).

15. (c) Both (a) and (b)

Explanation: The components will be a phosphate group and adenine. They are linked with the help of hydrogen bonds.

16. (c) 5-methyl uracil

Explanation: In RNA structure, Uracil is present in the case of Thymine. Thymine is a nitrogenous base which is achieved, when the Uracil is being methylated at the 5th carbon. Hence, the name 5-methyl uracil.

17. (d) All of these

Explanation: The glands that contribute to human seminal plasma are prostate gland, bulbourethral gland and seminal vesicle.

18. (c) Marchantia

Explanation: Marchantia is one of the dioecious plants. It develops separate male and female organs. The plant having the male reproductive part is called antheridiophore and the plant having female reproductive part is known as archegoniophore.

19. (a) A complex consisting of eight positively charged histone proteins (two of each H_2A, H_2B, H_3 and H_4) that aid in the packaging of DNA.

Explanation: A histone octamer is the eight protein complex present at the center of a nucleosome central particle. It is composed of two copies of each of the four core histone proteins (H_2A, H_2B, H_3, and H_4). The octamer joins when a tetramer, involving two copies of both H_3 and H_4, complexes with two H_2A/H_2B dimers.

20. (c) 3

> **Explanation:** There are 3 STOP codons in the genetic code - UAG, UAA, and UGA. These codons signal the end of the polypeptide chain during translation. These codons are also known as nonsense codons or termination codons as they do not code for an amino acid.

21. (b) Identifies amino acids and transports them to ribosomes.

> **Explanation:** The main function of the tRNA in protein synthesis is to carry the correct amino acid to the site of protein synthesis in the ribosome.

22. (b) 5′ GCAUUCGCCGA 3′

> **Explanation:** The RNA product is complementary to the template strand and is almost identical to the other DNA strand, called the non template (or coding) strand. Three of the four nitrogenous bases that make up RNA — adenine (A), cytosine (C), and guanine (G) — are also found in DNA. In RNA, however, a base called uracil (U) replaces thymine (T) as the complementary nucleotide to adenine.

23. (b) Hemophilia

> **Explanation:** Hemophilia is inherited in an X-linked recessive pattern. The genes associated with these conditions are located on the X chromosome, which is one of the two sex chromosomes. In males (who have only one X chromosome), one altered copy of the gene in each cell is sufficient to cause the condition.

24. (a) Topoisomerase enzymes cut, uncoil and reseal the double stranded DNA.

> **Explanation:** Type II topoisomerases change DNA topology by breaking and rejoining double-stranded DNA. These enzymes can introduce or remove supercoils and can separate two DNA duplexes that are interwined.

SECTION - B

25. (a) Assertion and reason both are correct statements and reason is the correct explanation of the assertion.

> **Explanation:** Angiosperms are known for their ability to fertilise themselves twice. It entails two fusions: one female gamete combines with an egg cell to make a zygote, while the other male gamete fuses with a diploid secondary nucleus to form a triploid primary endosperm nucleus. Thus, both assertion and reason are true and reason is the correct explanation of assertion.

26. (b) Assertion and reason both are correct statements, but reason is not the correct explanation of the assertion

> **Explanation:** Repeated or repetitive sequences make up a large portion of human genome. These sequences are nucleotide sequences that are repeated many times, sometimes hundred to thousand times. They have no direct coding function but provide information as to chromosome structure, dynamics, and evolution. Thus, both assertion and reason are true but reason is not the correct explanation of assertion.

27. (a) Assertion and reason both are correct statements and reason is the correct explanation of the assertion.

> **Explanation:** Colostrum is the milk produced during the first few days of lactation, and it contains many antibodies that are critical for the development of resistance in newborn babies. Breast-feeding throughout the first six months of an infant's life is suggested by doctors for a healthy child's development. Thus, both assertion and reason are true and reason is the correct explanation of assertion.

28. (c) Assertion is true, but reason is false statement.

Explanation: Sexually transmitted illnesses are diseases or infections that are spread through sexual contact (STDs). Sexually transmitted diseases such as AIDS and hepatitis B are sexually transmitted diseases. Hepatitis B can also be spread through the sharing of contaminated syringes, surgical tools, blood transfusions, and other methods. Hepatitis B does not have a permanent cure. Thus, assertion is true but reason is false.

29. (b) X-linked recessive trait

Explanation: In the given cross, disease is passed from carrier female to male progeny, this is known as criss-cross inheritance. The trait which shows criss-cross inheritance is located on the sex chromosome. In XX^C, single recessive gene X^C is present, that does not cause the disease.

30. (a) 1/16

Explanation: The probability of homozygous plants for both dominant characters in F_2 generation of a dihybrid cross is 1/16.

31. (c) clitoris

Explanation: The clitoris is a tiny finger-like structure which lies at the upper junction of the two labia minora above the urethral opening. It is erectile and highly sensitive and is equivalent to the male penis.

32. (a) Polyploidy

Explanation: The failure of the cell cycle process results in polyploidy. Polyploidy is a chromosomal abnormality in which two paired sets of chromosomes are present in the cells.

33. (d) Variation

Explanation: Variation is the difference between individuals within a population. These arise between the progeny and parents/ancestors and form a backbone for natural selection to act on.

34. (b) sterilization

Explanation: Surgical methods are non-reversible. Hence, these render the person sterile. These methods are therefore called sterilization.

35. (d) DNA is a better genetic material than RNA.

Explanation: DNA is comparatively less reactive than RNA. The 2'–OH group which is present at the nucleotide of the RNA is the reactive group. This makes the RNA highly reactive in comparison to the DNA. RNA is also catalytic and liable. It cannot be easily degraded. Due to these reasons, the conclusion is that DNA is the better genetic material than the RNA.

36. (b) Reproductive Tract Infections

Explanation: RTI stands for Reproductive Tract Infections. This class of diseases or infections spread through sexual intercourse. The major mode of transmission is the mixing of body fluids like semen, vaginal fluids, and blood. Since semen and vaginal fluids undergo mixing during intercourse, these diseases are often transmitted during unprotected intercourse.

37. (c) Supply of carbon dioxide to the fetus

Explanation: Placenta connects the maternal system to the fetal system. It provides nutrients for the fetus. It also removes the excretory products that would be harmful to it. It also provides a gaseous exchange by providing oxygen and removing carbon dioxide.

38. (a) Dwarf stem height

Explanation: Recessive traits are the ones that require both alleles to be present to result in the expression of the gene product. Of the mentioned traits, only dwarf stem height is a recessive trait.

39. (a) Law of segregation

> **Explanation:** In this figure F_1 generation is same like his parents but in F_2 generation different characters are segregated. So, this is called law of segregation.

40. (b) Translation of the central dogma of DNA

> **Explanation:** The central dogma of DNA occurs in its 2 stages. They are transcription and translation. When the small subunit of the ribosome encounters an mRNA, the process of translation commences. The process of translation from the mRNA to the proteins occur.

41. (a) F_1

> **Explanation:** : True-breeding plants are taken as parental plants in crosses. Hence offsprings produced by the crossing of these true-breeding plants are F_1 progeny.

42. (a) At both the 5' and the 3' ends

> **Explanation:** : The untranslated regions (UTRs) are the additional sequences of the mRNA which aren't translated during the process of translation into proteins. This region is present at both the 5' and the 3' end. They are required so that an efficient process of translation occurs.

43. (a) VV

> **Explanation:** Test cross involves a cross between the plant whose genotype is to be determined with the homozygous recessive plants. If a violet-flowered plant is crossed with white-flowered plant, the offsprings will have one v allele. Thus, to exhibit a phenotype of violet-flowering, the genotype will be Vv. Hence the parent will have a genotype of VV.

44. (c) Stomium

> **Explanation:** When the pollen grains mature, the anther breaks open to release the pollen grains. This phenomenon is known as dehiscence. Stomium is the region of the anther where this phenomenon occurs.

45. (d) epicotyl

> **Explanation:** A typical dicotyledonous embryo consists of an embryonal axis and two cotyledons. The part of embryonal axis above the level of cotyledons is called epicotyl.

46. (a) Charging of tRNA

> **Explanation:** : In order to form a peptide bond, a certain quantity of energy is required. The first phase in this process is known as charging of tRNA. It is also known as Aminoacylation of tRNA. In this process, the amino acids are activated in the presence of ATP and are linked to their cognate tRNA.

47. (c) Embryogenesis

> **Explanation:** Embryogeny is a process that follows fertilization. It is the process of development of a mature embryo from a zygote through cell division.

48. (a) R-strain

> **Explanation:** Only DNase has the ability to inhibit transformation. The other enzymes like RNase and lipase do not possess that ability. The process of transformation is not seen when the biochemical DNase is with S-strain. Lipase is an enzyme that catalyzes the hydrolysis (H_2O addition) of lipids and fats. The process of transformation will occur in lipids. As a result, R-strains will be produced in lipids.

SECTION - C

49. (c) female gametophyte

> **Explanation:** Embryo sac is also called the female gametophyte. In flowering plants, it is formed by the division of the haploid megaspore nucleus and acts as the site of fertilisation and development of the embryo.

50. (a) $3 + 2 + 3$

> **Explanation:** The arrangement of nuclei in normal embryo sac in dicot plant is $3 + 2 + 3$. Three at micropylar and [2 synergids, one egg cell], two in central region [2 polar nuclei] and three at chalazal end [3 antipodals].

51. (c) chalazal end

> **Explanation:** Antipodal cells are haploid in nature. These three haploid cells in the embryo sac of flowering plants are situated at the chalazal region (end).

52. (c) It helps in the entry of pollen tube into a synergid

> **Explanation:** The synergids have special cellular thickenings at the micropylar tip called filiform apparatus. The function of the filiform apparatus is that it helps the pollen tubes to enter the ovule through synergids. This is an important process during fertilisation in the angiosperms.

53. (d) Filiform apparatus

> **Explanation:** : Filiform apparatus is a mass of finger like projections of the wall of the synergid cells into the cytoplasm. It may or may not be present. It guides the male gametophytes during fertilisation.

54. (b) Antipodal cells

> **Explanation:** The 3 chalazal cells are called antipodal cells. These are vegetative cells that provide nourishment to the embryo sac. After fertilization these cells degenerate. Internally they are connected to the central cell by plasmodesmata.

55. (b) Dihybrid cross and law of independent assortment

> **Explanation:** This is dihybrid cross. Mendel's law of independent assortment states that when two pairs of traits are combined in a hybrid, segregation of one pair of characters is independent of the other pair of characters.

56. (a) (X) is male gamete and (Y) is female gamete

> **Explanation:** Both of these are gametes *i.e.*, (X) is male gamete (sperm) and (Y) is female gamete *i.e.*, ovum.

57. (b) H_1 histones

> **Explanation:** H_1 histones are commonly known as the linker histones. These histones can be located at the passage ways of the DNA, namely the entry and the exit sites. It is mostly found in protists and bacteria. It is also commonly known as nucleoproteins

58. (d) Nucellus

> **Explanation:** : It's the nucellus. Nucellus is the place where the embryo sac rests. It is made up of cushion like cells called parenchymatous cells. Nucellus helps in the nourishment of the embryo sac.

59. (b) Autosomal recessive

> **Explanation:** Autosomal recessive is a type of disorder in which two copies of an abnormal gene must be found for the disease in the affected person.

60. (b) Chromatid

> **Explanation:** The structure present inside the nucleus is known as the chromatid. The small circular structures which are present on it are called as the nucleosomes. Chromosomes are the condensed form of the chromatids. Ribosome are the components which help in the synthesis of proteins. Lysosome are the cell components which are also known are the suicidal bags of the cells.

Sample Paper 2

SECTION - A

1. (b) Test cross

> **Explanation:** A test cross is defined as the crossing of an organism with a double (homozygous) recessive in order to ascertain if it is homozygous or heterozygous for a given feature.

2. (d) Topoisomerases

> **Explanation:** Strand separation causes topological stress in the helical DNA structure, which topoisomerases can alleviate.

3. (d) deoxyribose sugar

> **Explanation:** The basic building blocks of DNA are nucleotides, which are composed of a sugar group, a phosphate group, and a nitrogen base. The sugar and phosphate groups link the nucleotides together to form each strand of DNA. Among the three components of DNA structure, sugar is the one which forms the backbone of the DNA molecule. It is also called deoxyribose.

4. (c) two mitotic division and one meiotic division

> **Explanation:** Pollen grains are produced during meiosis. Its cell divides mitotically to make generative (and tube cell) cells, which then divide by mitosis again to produce two male gametes.

5. (d) recessive and autosomal

> **Explanation:** The given trait cannot be sex-linked as sex-linked traits follow criss-cross inheritance and in the given pedigree, no criss-cross inheritance is being followed. The trait exhibited in pedigree chart is autosomal recessive and appears in case of marriage between two heterozygous individuals (AA × Aa = 3Aa + 1aa), a recessive individual with hybrid (Aa × aa = 2Aa + 2aa) and two recessive (aa × aa = aa). It expresses its effect only in pure or homozygous state. If the trait had been controlled by dominant gene, then one of the parent must have possessed the dominant gene and hence the disease.

6. (a) Rr

> **Explanation:** Heterozygous refers to when there are two different alleles, whereas homozygous refers to when there are two similar alleles. The remaining individuals are homozygous.

7. (a) Nucleosome

> **Explanation:** Nucleosomes are the basic packing unit of DNA built from histone proteins around which DNA is coiled. They serve as a scaffold for formation of higher order chromatin structure as well as for a layer of regulatory control of gene expression.

8. (b) two-celled stage

> **Explanation:** Pollen grain is uninucleate (1-celled) in the beginning but at the time of liberation, it becomes 2-3 celled. Actually, pollen grain nucleus grows in size and shifts to one side near the wall. The protoplast then divides to form two unequal cells - generative cells (small) and tube or vegetative cell (large).

9. (b) 5' (upstream) end and 3' (downstream) end respectively of transcription unit

> **Explanation:** The promoter and terminator sites for transcription are positioned at the transcription unit's 5' (upstream) and 3' (downstream) ends, respectively.

10. (d) honeybees, ants and wasps

> **Explanation:** Haploid-diploid mechanism or haplodiploidy is a unique phenomenon in which an unfertilised egg develops into a male and fertilised egg develop into a female. Therefore, the female is diploid and the male is haploid (n). Eggs are formed by meiosis and sperms by mitosis. Fertilisation restores the diploid number of chromosomes in the zygote which gives rise to the female. If the egg is not fertilised, it will still develop but into a male (arrhenotoky). It is seen in hymenopterous insects, such as bees, wasps, saw flies and ants.

11. (a) homologous to penis

> **Explanation:** The clitoris is structurally and functionally homologous to the penis of the male reproductive system, except that the clitoris does not contain the urethra and plays no role in urination.

12. (b) Follicular phase

> **Explanation:** The follicular phase begins on the first day of your period and ends when you ovulate (there is some overlap with the menstrual phase). The brain sends a signal to your pituitary gland to release follicle-stimulating hormone, which initiates the process (FSH). Your ovaries are stimulated to create follicles by this hormone.

13. (d) All of these

> **Explanation:** The three types of RNA involved in gene expression are rRNA, mRNA, and tRNA. rRNAs bind protein molecules to form ribosomes. mRNA carries coded information from DNA for translation into polypeptide formation. tRNA is called soluble or adapter molecule.

14. (a) detecting any genetic abnormality

> **Explanation:** The permissible use of amniocentesis is for genetic testing, fetal lung testing, diagnosis of fetal infection, and paternity testing. It can also be used to determine the gender or sex of the unborn fetus. But it is legally banned in countries like India in order to prevent female foeticides.

15. (b) Ovule

> **Explanation:** Embryo sac is produced in ovule by the megasporogenesis process and by the process of megagametogenesis. During the megasporogenesis, a megaspore mother cell that is diploid in nature goes through meiosis and as a result it forms four spores that are haploid. These are also called megaspores.

16. (a) thick layer at micropylar end

> **Explanation:** Cellular thickening present at the micropylar tip called filiform apparatus, plays an important role in guiding the pollen tube into the synergids.

17. (c) development of microspores inside microsporangia

> **Explanation:** The development of microspores inside microsporangia (pollen sacs) in angiosperms is known as microsporogenesis. A microsporocyte or pollen mother cell, a diploid cell in the microsporangium, conducts meiosis and produces four haploid microspores.

18. (d) All of these

> **Explanation:** The three basic components of a nucleotide are:
> (i)   A nitrogenous base–purines and pyrimidines.
> (ii) A pentose sugar–ribose in RNA and deoxyribose in DNA.
> (iii) A phosphate group.

19. (b) testes

> **Explanation:** Sertoli cells reside in the seminiferous epithelium in seminiferous tubules of the testes. They nourish and shape the germ cells and spermatozoa as they mature.

20. (c) Both (a) and (b)

> **Explanation:** Factors are discrete units occurring in pairs and when dissimilar, one member of the pair dominates the other.

21. (c) gain or loss of a chromosome

> **Explanation:** Aneuploidy occurs when chromatid segregation fails during the cell division cycle, resulting in the gain or loss of a chromosome. It has the potential to cause genetic abnormalities such as Down's syndrome and Turner's syndrome.

22. (c) Skin colour in humans

> **Explanation:** Some examples of polygenic inheritance are: human skin and eye colour; height, weight and intelligence in people; and kernel colour of wheat.

23. (a) A – 3.4 nm, B – 0.34 nm, C – 2 nm

> **Explanation:** The DNA helix makes one complete spiral turn every 3.4 nm has a diameter of 2 nm. The distance between adjacent stacks is 0.34 nm.

24. (c) Factors

> **Explanation:** Mendel discovered the laws of inheritance. He attributed these traits being encoded by factors. Later studies showed that these factors are genes.

SECTION - B

25. (b) Assertion and reason both are correct statements, but reason is not the correct explanation of the assertion

> **Explanation:** MTP is used to prevent undesired pregnancies that occur as a result of unprotected intercourse, contraceptive failure during coitus, or rapes. MTPs are also necessary in some situations where the mother or the foetus could be harmed or even killed if the pregnancy is continued. Thus, both assertion and reason are true but reason is not the correct explanation of assertion.

26. (b) Assertion and reason both are correct statements, but reason is not the correct explanation of the assertion

Explanation: The hormone progesterone released by the corpus luteum in the ovary plays important role in the menstrual cycle and in maintaining the early stages of pregnancy. After fertilisation, progesterone stimulates the growth of blood vessels that supply the lining of the endometrium and stimulates its glands to secrete nutrients that nourish the early embryo. Thus, both assertion and reason are true but reason is not the correct explanation of assertion.

27. (a) Assertion and reason both are correct statements and reason is the correct explanation of the assertion.

Explanation: During Anaphase of meiosis I, the two chromosome pairs can align at the metaphase plate independently of each other. Sutton and Boveri argued that the pairing and separation of a pair of chromosomes would lead to the segregation of a pair of factors they carried. Thus, both assertion and reason are true and reason is the correct explanation of assertion.

28. (c) Assertion is true, but reason is false statement.

Explanation: The pollen grains represent the male gametophytes. The pistil or gynoecium represents the female reproductive part of flower. Each pistil has three parts- the stigma, style, and ovary. The stigma serves as a landing platform for pollen grains. The style is the elongated slender part beneath the stigma. The basal bulged part of the pistil is the ovary. Thus, assertion is true but reason is false.

29. (a) Only II is true

Explanation: It is clear from the given graph that the percentage of clourblind people is 3% of the total population.

30. (d) All of these

Explanation: The steps involved during the process of transcription in bacterial species are initiation, elongation and termination.

31. (a) genetic disorders

Explanation: The pattern of inheritance of Mendelian disorders which are transmitted to offspring as per Mendelian principles, can be traced in a family by using the pedigree analysis which is a method of studying human genetic disorders.

32. (c) Linkage

Explanation: Linkage does not cause variations among siblings.
A sibling is one of two or more individuals having one or both parents in common. The emotional bond between siblings is often complicated and is influenced by factors such as parental treatment, birth order, personality, and personal experiences outside the family. Identical twins share 100% of their DNA. Full siblings are first-degree relatives and, on average, share 50% of their genes out of those that vary among humans. Half-siblings are second-degree relatives and have, on average, a 25% overlap in their human genetic variation.

33. (b) UAC

Explanation: The first amino acid added is methionine which is coded by the codon AUG. Thus, the anticodon for this codon in the tRNA is UAC.

34. (a) Epididymis

Explanation: Epididymis stores sperm prior to ejaculation. Storage in the epididymis makes the sperm motile and mature. If not ejaculated they are reabsorbed. Spermatozoa are produced continuously whether ejaculation takes place or not.

35. (d) Doctors

Explanation: Contraceptive methods are difficult to select from. Based on the needs of the couple/person, a particular class of contraceptives would serve the best. To receive help in choosing the right contraceptive, they should consult a qualified doctor.

36. (b) Two

Explanation: The two main types of nucleic acids are deoxyribonucleic acid (DNA) and ribonucleic acid (RNA). DNA is the genetic material found in all living organisms, ranging from single-celled bacteria to multicellular mammals.

37. (d) angiosperms

Explanation: Double fertilization occurs only in angiosperms. The female gametophyte in angiosperms abruptly stop their growth at 8 nucleate stage.

38. (b) form one linkage group

Explanation: A linkage group is a group of linked gene (on the same chromosome) and corresponds to the genome of organism, like human has 23 linkage groups, pea and *Neurospora* has 7 linkage groups, *Drosophila* has 4 linkage groups.

39. (c) Tubectomy

Explanation: Tubectomy, also known as tubal sterilization, is a permanent method of contraception in women. It is a surgical process that blocks the fallopian tubes, thereby preventing the egg released by the ovary from reaching the uterus.

40. (a) F_1 generation

Explanation: In *Mirabilis jalapa*, red and white-coloured flowers are seen. When they are crossed, in the F_1 generation, all flowers are pink coloured. This is because of the incomplete dominance of red-coloured flowers.

41. (a) non-disjunction of homologous chromosome.

Explanation: Failure of segregation of chromatids during cell division cycle results in the gain or loss of a chromosome(s), called aneuploidy. Aneuploidy arises due to non-disjunction of homologous chromosome.

42. (a) Anti-parallel and complementary

Explanation: The two strands of DNA run in opposite directions. These strands are held together by the hydrogen bond that is present between the two complementary bases. The strands are helically twisted, where each strand forms a right-handed coil and ten nucleotides make up a single turn.

43. (c) Both (a) and (b)

Explanation: Sex-linked recessive disease is a genetic disease which is transferred from a phenotypically normal but carrier female to only some of the male progeny. For example, Haemophilia/Bleeder's disease, Colour-blindness.

44. (c) Graafian follicle

Explanation: When the tertiary follicle containing the oocyte matures, the Graafian follicle is formed and under the influence of the luteinising hormone, the ovum is released from the Graafian follicle which then changes into the corpus luteum. In the figure, the cell after the release of ovum would be corpus luteum.

45. (b) two, segregation

Explanation: Based upon such observations on dihybrid crosses (crosses between plants differing in two traits) Mendel proposed a second set of generalisations that we call Mendel's Law of Independent Assortment. The law states that "When two pairs of traits are combined in a hybrid, segregation of one pair of characters is independent of the other pair of characters".

46. (c) Transduction

Explanation: Hershey and Chase showed that when bacteriophages, which are composed of DNA and protein, infect bacteria, their DNA enters the host bacterial cell through the process of transduction, but most of their protein does not. Hershey and Chase and subsequent discoveries all served to prove that DNA is the hereditary material.

47. (c) triplet

Explanation: Codons are made up of any triplet combination of the four nitrogenous bases.

48. (c) C–Vas deferens-helps in sperm transfer

Explanation: The vas deferens is a long, muscular tube that travels from the epididymis into the pelvic cavity, to just behind the bladder. The vas deferens transports mature sperm to the urethra in preparation for ejaculation.

SECTION - C

49. (d) Three

Explanation: Babies with Down's syndrome however, end up with three chromosomes at position 21, instead of the usual pair.

50. (d) All of these

Explanation: A few of the common physical traits of Down's syndrome are low muscle tone, small stature, an upward slant to the eyes, and a single deep crease across the center of the palm – although each person with Down's syndrome is a unique individual and may possess these characteristics to different degrees, or not at all.

51. (d) All of these

Explanation: Amniocentesis, chorionic villus sampling (CVS) and ultrasound are the three primary procedures for diagnostic testing. Amniocentesis is used most commonly to identify chromosomal problems such as Down's syndrome.

52. (a) Trisomy 21

Explanation: Down's syndrome is also referred to as Trisomy 21. This extra copy changes how the baby's body and brain develop, which can cause both mental and physical challenges for the baby.

53. (b) A chromosomal abnormality

Explanation: Down syndrome is a genetic disorder caused when abnormal cell division results in an extra full or partial copy of chromosome 21. This extra genetic material causes the developmental changes and physical features of Down's syndrome.

54. (a) Both I and II are correct.

Explanation: The following conclusions are drawn from the graph given in the question:
I.   Age-dependent risk factors usually intensify with advancing age and so one would expect highest frequency of such factors among older age group.
II. Advanced maternal age is a risk for birth with the disease.

55. (a) A–Antipodals, B–Polar nuclei, C–Synergids

> **Explanation:**
>
> 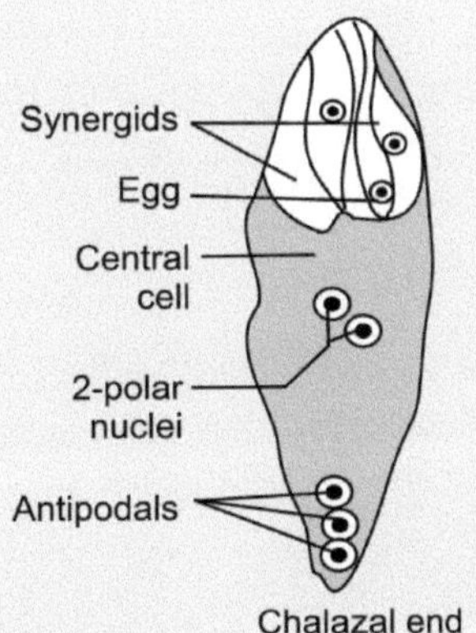
>

56. (b) A–Replication B–Transcription C–Translation D–Francis Crick

> **Explanation:** Francis Crick proposed the central dogma in molecular biology, which states that the genetic information flows from DNA → RNA → Protein.

57. (a) incomplete dominance

> **Explanation:** Snapdragon shows incomplete dominance by producing pink-coloured snapdragon flowers. The cross-pollination between red and white snapdragons leads to pink colour flowers because none of the alleles (white and red) is dominant.

58. (d)

X	Y	P	Q
5'	3'	TCA	UCA

> **Explanation:** X and Y represents the 5' end and 3' end of mRNA respectively. The DNA sequence coding for serine is TCA and anticodon for the same amino acid is UCA.

59. (d) A–Filament (stalk), B–Line of dehiscence, C–Pollen sac, D–Pollen grains

> **Explanation:** A respresents the filament to which anther is attached. B is the line of dehiscence. C represents the pollen sac in which pollen grain (D) are found.

60. (b) Recessive and sex-linked

> **Explanation:** Given pedigree analysis indicates the transmission of recessive sex-linked trait from parents to their offspring because only 25% male progeneis are affected.

Sample Paper 3

SECTION - A

1. (c) Testes

> **Explanation:** The testes are the primary male reproductive organ and are responsible for testosterone and sperm production.

2. (c) ICSI

Explanation: Intracytoplasmic sperm injection (ICSI) is one of the Assisted Reproductive Technology (ART) procedures that assists couples in overcoming infertility. In ICSI, sperm is directly injected into an ovum in vitro, resulting in the formation of a zygote. The resulting embryo is then transplanted into a woman using ZIFT.

3. (a) A–DNA, B–H_1 histone, C–Histone octamer

Explanation:

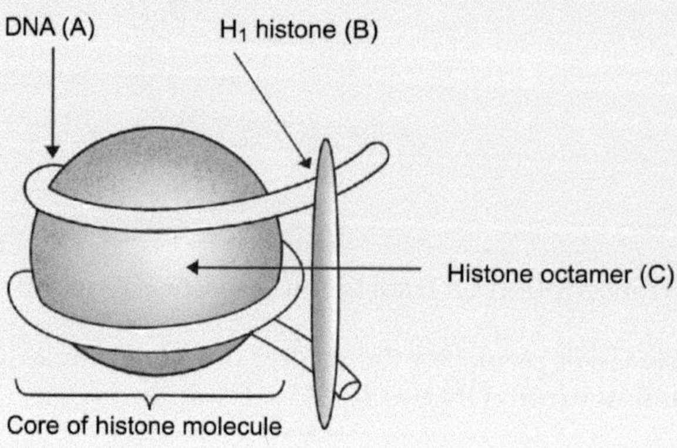

4. (b) Exons appear but introns do not appear in the mature mRNA.

Explanation: Introns are removed by RNA splicing as RNA matures therefore a mature RNA has exons but not introns.

5. (c) autosomal dominant

Explanation: Autosomal dominant trait can express its effect in homozygous as well as heterozygous condition.

6. (c) Day 14/15

Explanation: FSH secreted by anterior pituitary during the follicular phase (day 0 to 10) stimulates the development of follicle. LH surge at day 14/15 causes rupture of Graafian follicle and release of the ovum.

7. (d) Mice lives even after injecting the R-strain of the bacterium

Explanation: : R-strains are the non-virulent strains. So, when they are injected into the mice, they won't cause any damage to it. As a result, the mice will be able to live without complications. The bacteria contain both the S and R strains, but, only the R-strain is being injected in this scenario.

8. (c) Test cross

Explanation: Testcross is a cross of any genotype showing dominant phenotype with a recessive homozygote to determine the genotype of a dominant parent if it is a heterozygous or homozygous dominant. Being a hybrid Tt shows dominant phenotype and tt is the recessive parent; it is a test cross.

9. (c) Preventing ovulation

Explanation: Oral contraceptives (birth-control pills) are used to prevent pregnancy. Estrogen and progesterone are two female sex hormones. Combinations of estrogen and progesterone work by preventing ovulation (the release of eggs from the ovaries).

10. (d) A–Cervix, B–Uterine cavity, C–Fallopian tube, D–Ovary

> **Explanation:** The ovaries are a pair of small glands located on the left and right sides of the pelvic body cavity, lateral to the superior portion of the uterus.
>
> The fallopian tubes are a pair of muscular tubes, that extend from the left and right superior corners of the uterus to the edge of ovaries.
>
> The uterus is a hollow, muscular, pear-shaped organ located posterior and superior to the urinary bladder. It is connected to the two fallopian tubes on its superior end and to the vagina via cervix on the inferior end.
>
> The vagina is an elastic, muscular tube that connects the cervix of the uterus to the exterior of the body.

11. (b) Crossing F_1 individuals with recessive parents.

> **Explanation:** To find the genotype of a hybrid, test cross is performed in which an organism showing dominant phenotype is crossed with the recessive parent instead of selfing. The progenies of such cross can easily be analysed to predict the genotype of the test organism.

12. (a) produced from both the alleles

> **Explanation:** In the instance of codominance, the product is made up of both alleles and expressed in its whole. There is no one allele that is more dominant than the others. The ABO blood group, for example, is characterised by the expression of both alleles A and B. Individuals with blood type AB inherit allele A from their mother and allele B from their father.

13. (d) spore mother cells

> **Explanation:** The spore mother cells of spores are diploid. They go through meiosis and produce four haploid spores. Sporogenesis is the process of producing haploid spores from a diploid spore mother cell via meiosis. Microspores and megaspores are two types of spores.

14. (c) hnRNA

> **Explanation:** The RNA polymerase II enzyme is responsible for transcription of hnRNA. This enzyme reads the DNA sequence and adds the corresponding nucleotides to make new RNA molecules. The RNA polymerase III and RNA polymerase II enzymes are in charge of tRNA and hnRNA transcription from template DNA strands.

15. (b) Vasa efferentia

> **Explanation:** Rete testis, vasa efferentia, epididymis, vasa deferens are the accessory ducts of male reproductive system. The fallopian tubes are muscular tubes, found in the female reproductive tract.

16. (b) Both mother and father will be heterozygous for 'A' and 'B' blood group.

> **Explanation:** If any of the two parents have homozygous blood group, it will be inherited in their offsprings. So, if the parents have heterozygous blood groups 'A' and 'B' respectively, then the offsprings can have 'O' blood group.

17. (b) DNA dependent DNA polymerase catalysis polymerisation only in one direction ($5' \rightarrow 3'$)

> **Explanation:** The discontinuous synthesis of DNA occurs on one strand only because DNA dependent DNA polymerase catalysis polymerisation only in one direction ($5' \rightarrow 3'$). At the replicating fork, this adds a layer of complexity. As a result, replication is continuous on one strand (the template with polarity $3' \rightarrow 5'$) but discontinuous on the other (the template with polarity $5' \rightarrow 3'$). The enzyme DNA ligase joins the fragments that are synthesising discontinuously.

18. (a) 2-3 celled

> **Explanation:** Pollen grain protoplast is uninucleate or 1-celled in the beginning but at the time of shedding, it becomes 2-3 celled.

19. (d) All of these

> **Explanation:** Test cross is significant due to following reasons:
> (i) It determines the genetic constitution of an organism.
> (ii) The test cross helps in verifying the laws of inheritance and is very useful to breeders and geneticists as well.

20. (c) Haplodiploidy

> **Explanation:** It is because of Haplodiploidy, sex determination in which males develops parthenogenetically from unfertilised eggs and are haploid, and females develop from fertilized eggs and are diploid.

21. (a) anther, ovule

> **Explanation:** The male gametophyte or the pollen grains develop inside the pollen chamber of an anther, whereas the female gametophyte develops inside the nucleus of an ovule from the functional megaspore.

22. (a) Genetics

> **Explanation:** : Genetics is the branch of biology that deals with questions of inheritance. It uses techniques from various disciplines like molecular biology, cell biology, and many more to understand the basis of inheritance.

23. (a) Semiconservative nature of DNA

> **Explanation:** Semiconservative replication describes the mechanism of DNA replication in all known cells. This process is known as semi-conservative replication because two copies of the original DNA molecule are produced. Each copy contains one original strand and one newly-synthesized strand.

24. (a) more variations

> **Explanation:** Sexual reproduction involves two parents and the exchange of genetic material. Thus producing higher variations. Asexual reproduction is simply the replication of DNA and involves very low to almost no variation.

SECTION – B

25. (c) Assertion is true, but reason is false statement.

> **Explanation:** The gynoecium represents the female reproductive part of the flower consisting of pistil. Thus, assertion is true but reason is false.

26. (c) Assertion is true, but reason is false statement.

> **Explanation:** When used the right way every time, condoms are highly effective in preventing HIV and other sexually transmitted diseases (STDs). If condoms are paired with other option like ART, they provide even more protection. Thus, assertion is true but reason is false.

27. (d) Assertion is false, but reason is true statement.

Explanation: When the genes for certain features (like yellow/white bodied or white/red eyed *Drosophila*) are located very close to each other on a chromosome, there are little chances of crossing over, giving higher parental combination. When the genes are on different loci on a chromosome, the distance between them considerable, there are higher chances of recombination, giving rise to mixed or non-parental features, for autosomes. However, since genes for body colour and eye colour are present on X chromosomes, the deviation will be in relation to the gender in addition to recombination, which will not occur in males as they are homozygous for the trait they carry. Thus, assertion is false but reason is true.

28. (b) Assertion and reason both are correct statements, but reason is not the correct explanation of the assertion

Explanation: Production and development of seedless fruits is called parthenocarpy. It is of two types, vegetative and stimulative. Apomixis is a mode of reproduction which does not involve formation of zygote through gametic fusion. It is, therefore, similar to asexual reproduction. In plants apomixis commonly mimics sexual reproduction but produce seeds without fertilisation, e.g., some species of Asteraceae and grasses. Thus, both assertion and reason are true but reason is not the correct explanation of the assertion.

29. (b) II and IV are true

Explanation: Homozygous traits are tt and TT *i.e.*, $0.1 + 0.7 = 0.8$ and genotype Tt has the ratio of 0.3. So, option (b) is true.

30. (a) Promoter

Explanation: The promoter region which is present towards the 5' end of the coding strand is the start site for transcription to occur. These are regions on the DNA where the RNA polymerase enzyme will bind. This leads to the process of transcription.

31. (a) neuroendocrine mechanism

Explanation: : Two major processes induce the contractions of the uterine wall during parturition. The hormones secreted from the pituitary and placenta alongside the reflexes induced by the oxytocin function to stimulate the muscle continuously. Thus, this is a neuroendocrine process

32. (a) Hybridization

Explanation: Gregor Mendel carried out the hybridization of pea plants with specific characters and used manual counting to carry out estimates of factors over generations. This gave rise to the laws of inheritance, as we know today.

33. (b) two different, different species

Explanation: Consanguineous mating is the mating between two different individuals which are unrelated.

34. (c) Organiser

Explanation: The transcription unit of a DNA molecule consists of a promoter region, the structural gene and a terminator. A transcription unit consists of a sequential arrangement of nucleotides which are used to code for the RNA molecule during the process of transcription

35. (b) 9 months

Explanation: The period from conception to birth of a viviparous organism is its gestation period. It varies for different organisms. It is 40 weeks approximately or 9 months for humans.

36. (a) compatibility of the pollen

Explanation: Pollen-pistil interaction determines the suitability of pollen for carrying out the process of sexual reproduction. If it is not compatible, fertilization process will not begin.

37. (b) Infertility

Explanation: : Infertility is the inability of an individual or a couple to achieve pregnancy even if unprotected sexual intercourse is carried out. Sterility is an inability to produce and release gametes. Sterility leads to infertility. However, all infertile individuals are not sterile.

38. (b) second

Explanation: : Translation is the second stage during the central dogma of DNA. Only a single strand of DNA is copied into the RNA for the synthesis of protein.

39. (b) X-linked recessive trait

Explanation: In the given cross, passing of disease is from carrier female to male progeny (criss-cross inheritance). Any trait that shows criss-cross inheritance is located on the sex chromosome. Presence of a single recessive gene, *i.e.,* X^C in carrier individuals (XX^C) does not cause the disease, thus the trait is recessive.

40. (c) 430 Mb

Explanation: A genome size of 430 Mb nonetheless represents a daunting task for whole genome sequencing. The rice genome is 3.5 times the size of the *Arabidopsis* genome and the third largest public genome project undertaken, behind the human and mouse genomes.

41. (b) Intraspecific

Explanation: Intraspecific incompatibility promotes cross pollination and ensures heterozygosity which helps in evolution. It is achieved by self-sterility. It is also called self-incompatibility.

42. (b) uracil

Explanation: : In DNA, the double hydrogen base pairing is seen between adenine and thymine. Likewise, the triple hydrogen base pairing is seen between guanine and cytosine. But uracil is present in the place of thymine in the single stranded structure of RNA. So, adenosine forms a base pair with uracil instead of thymine.

43. (d) All of these

Explanation: Aneuploidy arises due to the non-disjunction of the homologous pair of chromosomes. It results in the formation of gamete with an extra chromosome and the other gamete deficient in one chromosome.

44. (c) P–Sepal, Q–Petal, R–Anther, S–Filament, T–Stigma, U–Style, V–Ovary

Explanation:

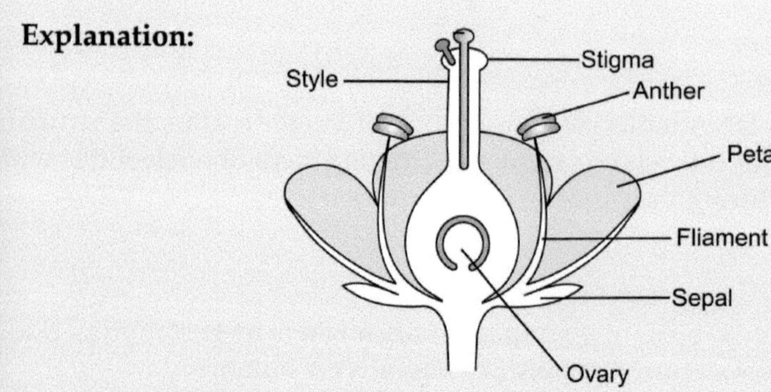

45. (c) Gene carry information for making proteins

> **Explanation:** Beadle and Tatum carried out experiment on mutant bread mould that lacked specific enzymes. They demonstrated that gene carry information for making proteins.

46. (d) All of these

> **Explanation:** The examples of aneuploidy are Down's syndrome, Klinefelter's syndrome, and Turner's syndrome where Down's and Klinefelter's syndrome show trisomy condition while Turner's syndrome show monosomic condition.

47. (b) In vitro fertilization

> **Explanation:** In vitro fertilization is also popularly known as IVF. It is an ART used to carry out fertilization outside the body of the female.

48. (c) 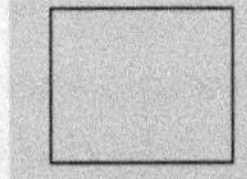

> **Explanation:** Pedigree analysis is done with the help of a pedigree which is also known as a family tree. Some of the symbols used in the pedigree analysis are:
>
> (i) Unaffected male 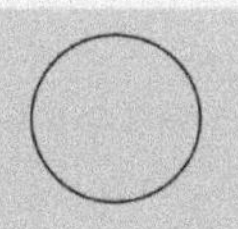   (ii) Unaffected female 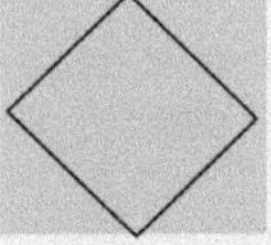
>
> (iii) Sex unspecified    (iv) Seven unaffected offspring

SECTION - C

49. (b) IVF

> **Explanation:** In vitro fertilization (IVF) is a complex series of procedures used to help with fertility or prevent genetic problems and assist with the conception of a child. During IVF, mature eggs are collected (retrieved) from ovaries and fertilized by sperm in a lab. Then the fertilized egg (embryo) or eggs (embryos) are transferred to a uterus.

50. (a) Zygote into fallopian tube.

> **Explanation:** Zygote intrafallopian transfer (ZIFT) is a technique in which a woman's egg is fertilized outside the body, then implanted in one of her fallopian tubes. This technique is one of the methods used to overcome infertility, the inability of couples to produce offspring on their own.

51. (b) Uterus

> **Explanation:** Embryo with more than 16 blastomeres formed is transferred to the female uterus. Two or three embryos are transferred into the female Uterus. After 14 days, the gravida test is performed to confirm pregnancy.

52. (c) Artificial Insemination

Explanation: In case of a couple where a man is having a very low sperm count, the sperms cannot travel the female genital tract to get fertilized due to its low count. So artificial insemination technique is used to get sperm fertilized inside the female. In this technique, the sperm is introduced into a female's cervix and the uterine cavity for the purpose of achieving a pregnancy through in vivo fertilization by means other than sexual intercourse.

53. (a) Artificial introduction of sperms of a healthy donor into the vagina

Explanation: : In artificial insemination, a doctor inserts sperm directly into a woman's cervix, fallopian tubes, or uterus. The most common method is called "intrauterine insemination (IUI)," when a doctor places the sperm in the uterus.

54. (b) Embryo transfer

Explanation: During IVF , mature eggs are collected (retrieved) from ovaries and fertilized by sperm in a lab. Then the fertilized egg (embryo) or eggs (embryos) are transferred to a uterus. One full cycle of IVF takes about three weeks. Sometimes these steps are split into different parts and the process can take longer.

55. (a) Hershey and Chase, DNA is the genetic material

Explanation: Hershey-Chase experiment was performed in 1952 to further confirm that DNA was the genetic material. They experimented with Bacteriophages. Bacteriophages are the viruses that infect & replicate within bacteria. It was concluded that it was not the proteins, rather DNA which entered into the bacteria. Therefore, DNA causes the replication of viruses inside the bacteria. DNA was thus proved to be the genetic material.

56. (b) Only III

Explanation: Only observation III is depicted in the figure is correct. Equal amount of light DNA and hybrid DNA was observed in *E. coli* culture after two generations.

57. (c) 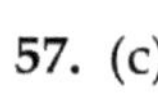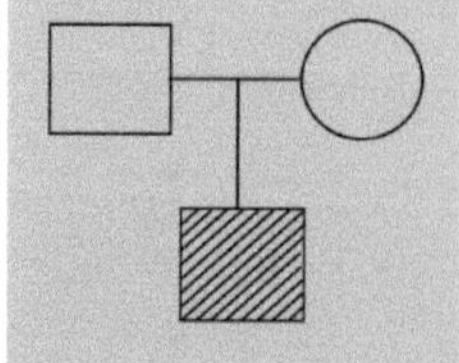

Explanation: Pedigree analysis is useful for genetic counsellors to advise couples (who are going to marry) about the possibility of having children with genetic defects. Some of the matings between males and females are shown. C option represents the mating between parents with a male child who is affected by a disease.

58. (c) A–Menstruation, C–Ovulation

Explanation: There are four phases in the menstrual cycle-
(i) Menstruation: During this phase, a menstrual fluid consisting of blood, mucus, and the cells of the uterine lining is eliminated through the vaginal opening. This is your period. It can last anywhere between 2 to 7 days.
(ii) The Follicular Phase: The follicular phase of your menstrual cycle begins from the first day of your period and lasts up until ovulation. In the course of this phase, oestrogen levels rise, and the ovaries prepare for the release of an egg for possible fertilization. The follicular phase also stimulates the phase where the uterine lining begins to build again.

(iii) Ovulation: In this phase, ovaries release the egg. It travels through the fallopian tubes and implants itself into the lining along the walls of your uterus. This phase usually occurs around two weeks prior to periods. During this process, the oestrogen level peaks and drops just shortly after.

(iv) The Luteal Phase: The phase that occurs between ovulation and the first day of your period is called the luteal phase. This phase sees a rise in the level of progesterone, required to maintain the thickness of the uterine lining to nurture the fertilised egg. Now, if during that time, pregnancy does not occur, progesterone levels drop. This causes the uterine lining to break down and shed away, along with other menstrual fluid.

59. (c) A–Hilum, B–Funicle, C–Embryo sac

Explanation:

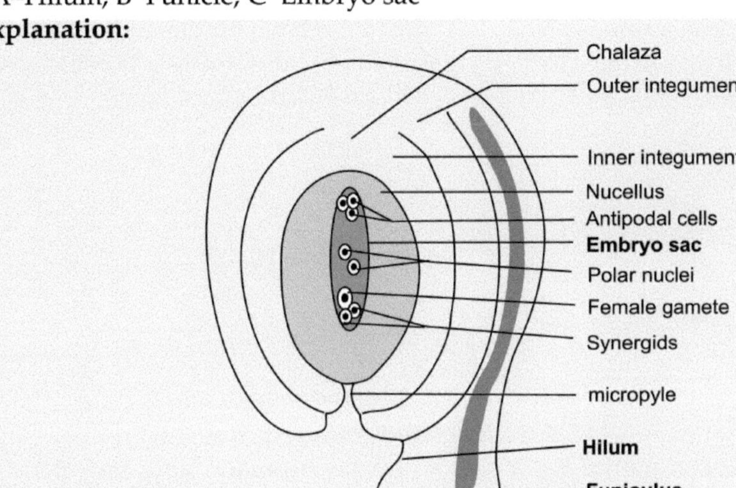

60. (c) R and S

Explanation: Figure R is showing complete blockage of fallopian tubes and figure S is showing tubectomy which is a surgical method of contraception in females. When both the fallopian tubes are blocked or cut and tied, there will be no transport of gamete and thus no fertilisation will occur.

Sample Paper 4

SECTION - A

1. (d) September 1997

Explanation: The International Rice Genome Sequencing Project begin in September 1997 and established in 1998, pooled the resources of sequencing groups in ten nations to obtain a complete finished quality sequence of the rice genome.

2. (a) Trisomy 21

Explanation: Down syndrome, also known as trisomy 21, is a genetic disease characterised by the presence of a third copy of chromosome 21 in all or part of a person. Physical growth delays, mild to moderate intellectual handicap, and distinctive facial traits are all common symptoms.

3. (c) A-TT; B-Tt ;C-tt; D-Tt

Explanation: Punnett square is a graphical representation of the possibility of genotype of all the plants.

4. (c) Coconut

> **Explanation:** Anemophily is also called as wind pollination in which pollen grains are transported through wind from male flower of one plant to female flower of another plant. For example, coconut.

5. (b) (A) and (C) are dominant and (B) and (D) are recessive

> **Explanation:** Round seeds and violet colour are dominant traits while wrinkled seeds and white colour are recessive traits.

6. (c) Independent assortment of genes

> **Explanation:** Among all laws the given ratio $9:3:3:1$ is due to the law of independent assortment. In order to explain this, an example will be given, a cross is made between two parents with two different contrasting characters, and this type of cross is called a dihybrid cross.

7. (a) (X)-Euchromatin; (Y)-Heterochromatin

> **Explanation:**

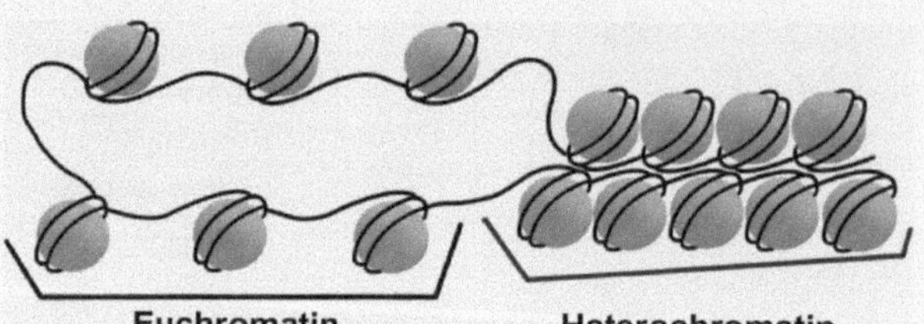

> In nucleus, some region of chromatin are loosely packed that is referred to as Euchromatin and that is more packed are called Heterochromatin. So, X and Y are Euchromatin and Heterochromatin respectively.

8. (c) Dioecious plant

> **Explanation:** Marchantia is dioecious, therefore it is heterothallic. Marchantia can reproduce sexually or asexually. In sexual reproduction, sperm from the antheridia fertilizes an egg in the archegonia. These antheridia and archegonia are the special gametophyte stalks which are present on the separate thalli.

9. (b) Ribosome

> **Explanation:** Peptide synthesis occurs in ribosomes which are considered as protein factory of the cell. Ribosomes are present in all cells and are involved in protein synthesis.

10. (a) XX, X^rY, X^rX, XY

> **Explanation:** Genotypes of different individuals in the given pedigree chart can be illustrated as:

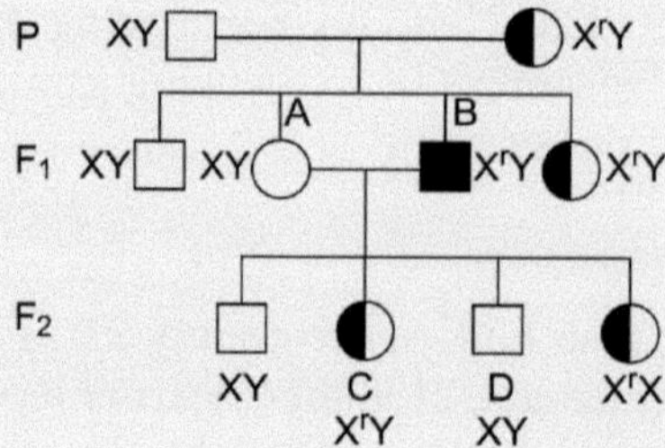

11. (a) secondary oocyte stage

> **Explanation:** During the process of ovulation, the release of the egg occurs at the secondary oocyte stage in which meiosis-I have been completed.

12. (d) fructose

> **Explanation:** Secretions of the accessory glands constitute the seminal plasma which is rich in fructose, calcium and certain enzymes (acid phosphatase, amylase, pepsinogen).

13. (a) Nucleus

> **Explanation:** Inside the nucleus, RNA splicing and RNA capping occur during eukaryotic cell transcription. The mature mRNA (processed mRNA) is subsequently transferred to the cytoplasm, where it can be translated by the ribosome.

14. (c) (ii) and (iii)

> **Explanation:** Diaphragms are used to cover the cervical region and act as a physical barrier to sperm entrance. They do not act as spermicidal agents.

15. (c) Independent assortment of genes

> **Explanation:** $9 : 3 : 3 : 1$ phenotypic ratio is the classic Mendelian ratio for a dihybrid cross in which the alleles of two different genes assort independently into gametes. If both parents are heterozygous for both traits the ratio of phenotypes is the ratio of 9:3:3:1. One trait is dominant and the other trait is recessive. Of the 16 possible offsprings only 1 will have both recessive genes. Only with double recessives will the phenotype show both recessives.

16. (d) All of these

> **Explanation:** The three basic components of nucleotide are:
> (i)　A nitrogenous base–purines and pyrimidines.
> (ii)　A pentose sugar–ribose in RNA and deoxyribose in DNA.
> (iii)　A phosphate group.

17. (a) phosphodiester bond

> **Explanation:** The nucleotides in a DNA strand are joined together by $3' \rightarrow 5'$ phosphodiester linkage (bonds) to form a dinucleotide. A polynucleotide chain can be extended by joining more nucleotides in a successful manner.

18. (b) Leydig cells

> **Explanation:** The Leydig cells in the testes secrete androgens and act on the sertoli cells in the testes to produce the sperms.

19. (d) All of these

> **Explanation:** The role of deoxyribonucleoside triphosphates during DNA replication are:
> (i)　They are the building blocks for the DNA-strand.
> (ii)　They serve as energy source in the form of ATP and GTP.

20. (a) bilobed structure

> **Explanation:** It is a unit of male reproductive system, terminally situated at the stamen having bilobed structure and produces male reproductive unit called pollen grain.

21. (b) chromosomal theory of inheritance

> **Explanation:** The chromosomal theory of inheritance was not the work of a single scientist, but rather the collaborative result of multiple researchers working over multiple decades. The seeds of this theory were first planted in the 1860s, when Gregor Mendel and Charles Darwin each proposed possible systems of heredity.

22. (a) It acts as an initiation codon.

Explanation: : Two functions of codon AUG are

(i)   The AUG codes for methionine.

(ii) It acts as an initiation codon.

23. (b) Dihybrid cross

Explanation: In the figure, we see that there are two character (shape and colour of the pod) in the cross. So, it is a dihybrid cross.

24. (d) Both (b) and (c)

Explanation: In the given problem, the woman has an X-linked condition and she can transmit the carrier allele to both her son and daughter. The resulting son will be affected because X-linked disorder always affect males as males contain a single X-chromosome. The daughter offspring will be a carrier, but not diseased because females are affected by X-linked disorder in homozygous recessive condition only, *i.e.*, two recessive alleles are required.

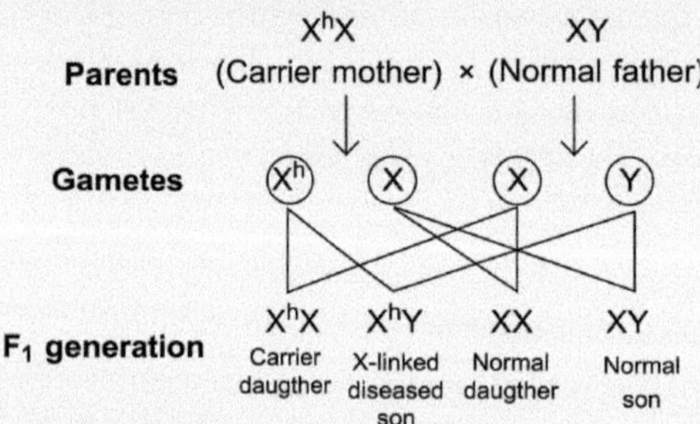

Hence, out of the 4 offspring 25% of sons are diseased and 25% are normal. Similarly, 50% daughters are normal out of which half are carriers.

SECTION - B

25. (c) Assertion is true, but reason is false statement.

Explanation: Natural methods work on the principle of avoiding chances of meeting of ovum and sperm, *e.g.*, periodic abstinence, lactational amenorrhea. In barrier methods, ovum and sperm are prevented from physically meeting with help of a barrier, *e.g.*, condoms, cervical caps, etc. Thus, assertion is true but reason is false.

26. (a) Assertion and reason both are correct statements and reason is the correct explanation of the assertion.

Explanation: Fertilisation can only occur if the ovum and sperms are transported simultaneously to the ampullary-isthmic junction and ovum is released only once a month. This is one of the reasons why all copulations do not lead to fertilisation and pregnancy. Thus, both assertion and reason are true and reason is the correct explanation of assertion.

27. (a) Assertion and reason both are correct statements and reason is the correct explanation of the assertion.

Explanation: Aneuploidy is the presence of an aberrant number of chromosomes in a cell, such as 45 or 47 instead of the usual 46 in a human cell. Aneuploidy occurs when a cell divides incorrectly, resulting in the improper number of chromosomes in the "daughter" cells. Trisomy 21, often known as Down syndrome, is a genetic disease caused by the presence of all or part of chromosome 21. Thus, both assertion and reason are true and reason is the correct explanation of assertion.

28. (d) Assertion is false, but reason is true statement.

Explanation: Tapetum is the innermost wall layer of a microsporangium. It nourishes the developing pollen grains. The tapetal cells enlarge radically and become filled with dense protoplasmic contents as well as nutrients. Microsporogenesis refers to the process of formation of haploid microspores mother cell or pollen mother cell through meiosis. Thus, assertion is false but reason is true.

29. (a) This figure shows that genetic information flows from DNA to RNA and RNA to protein.

   Explanation: This is central dogma model proposed by F.Crick. According to this model, genetic information flows from DNA to RNA and from RNA to protein.

30. (c) an enhancer

   Explanation: Enhancer sequences are DNA sequences that act as regulators. Specific proteins known as transcription factors bind to these sequences. These proteins' interaction will boost the transcription of a related gene. They don't belong in the operon structure.

31. (d) Epidermis and tapetum

   Explanation: Epidermis, endothecium, middle layers, and tapetum are the wall layers of a microsporangium, from outermost to innermost. The first three layers usually give protection and aid with anther dehiscence. Tapetum serves as a source of nutrition for pollen grains.

32. (b) formation of peptide bond

   Explanation: Charging or Aminoacylation of *t*RNA is esential for protein synthesis, *i.e.*, polypeptide formation through formation of peptide bonds between amino acids.

33. (c) coagulation of blood

   Explanation: Hemophilia is a sex-linked recessive disease. In this disease, a single protein that is a part of the cascade of proteins involved in the clotting of blood is affected. Due to this, in an affected individual, a simple cut will result in non-stop bleeding.

34. (a) capsulated, virulent, smooth

   Explanation: Avery, MacLeod and McCarty identified DNA as the "transforming principle" while studying *Streptococcus pneumoniae*, bacteria that can cause pneumonia. The bacteriologists were interested in the difference between two strains of Streptococci that Frederick Griffith had identified in 1923: one, the S (smooth) strain, has a polysaccharide coat and produces smooth, shiny colonies on a lab plate; the other, the R (rough) strain, lacks the coat and produces colonies that look rough and irregular. The relatively harmless R strain lacks an enzyme needed to make the capsule found in the virulent S strain.

35. (a) skin of the inner arm above elbow

   Explanation: To achieve contraception, six matchstick-sized capsules containing steroids are inserted under the skin of female's inner arm above the elbow. These steroid capsules slowly release the synthetic progesterone for about five years.

36. (d) Both (b) and (c)

   Explanation: Primary (1°) spermatocytes are diploid in number. Secondary (2°) spermatocytes and spermatids are haploid in number.

37. (a) True

   Explanation: The tapetal layer is the innermost layer of anther wall. It is composed of a single layer of cells characterised by the presence of dense cytoplasm and generally have more than one nucleus.

38. (d) histones

> **Explanation:** Histones are main structural proteins found in eukaryotic cells. The nucleosome core is made up of four types of histone proteins, *i.e.*, H_2A, H_2B, H_3 and H_4 occurring in pairs. 200 bp of DNA helix wraps around the nucleosome by turns, plugged by H_1 histone protein. So, nucleosome consists of histones.

39. (c) 

> **Explanation:**
>
> 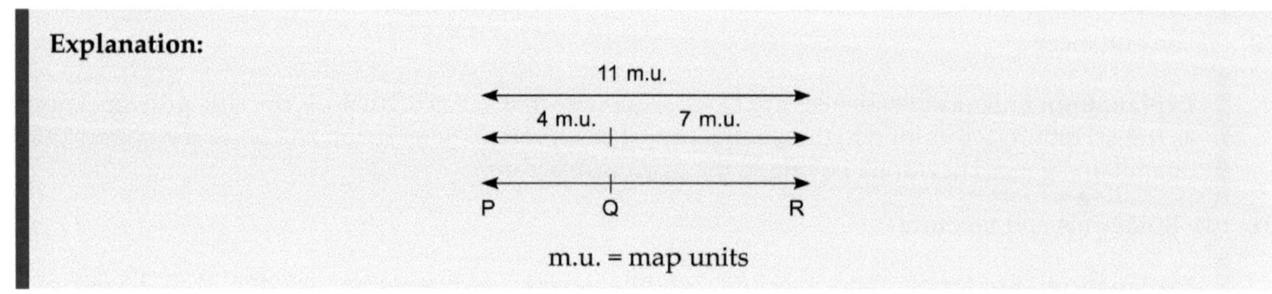
>

40. (a) 14

> **Explanation:** Mendel selected 7 pairs or 14 characters of true breeding pea plant varieties for his experiment.

41. (a) the length of the regions having VNTRs is different in each individual

> **Explanation:** VNTRs are key factors in DNA profiling because their length differ in each individual. These include satellite DNA, minisatellites or microsatellites.

42. (b) form one linkage group

> **Explanation:** All the genes, present on a particular chromosome form a linkage group. The number of linkage group of a species corresponds to the total number of different chromosomes of that species.

43. (b) help in collection of the ovum after ovulation

> **Explanation:** A small fringe of finger-like cellular projections and located at the end of the fallopian tube is known as fimbria. Its main function is to collect the egg released from the ovary after ovulation and draw it into the fallopian tube.

44. (c) A–Degenerating synergids, B–Zygote, C–Primary endosperm cell, D–Primary endosperm nucleus, E–degenerating antipodal cell

> **Explanation:**
>
> 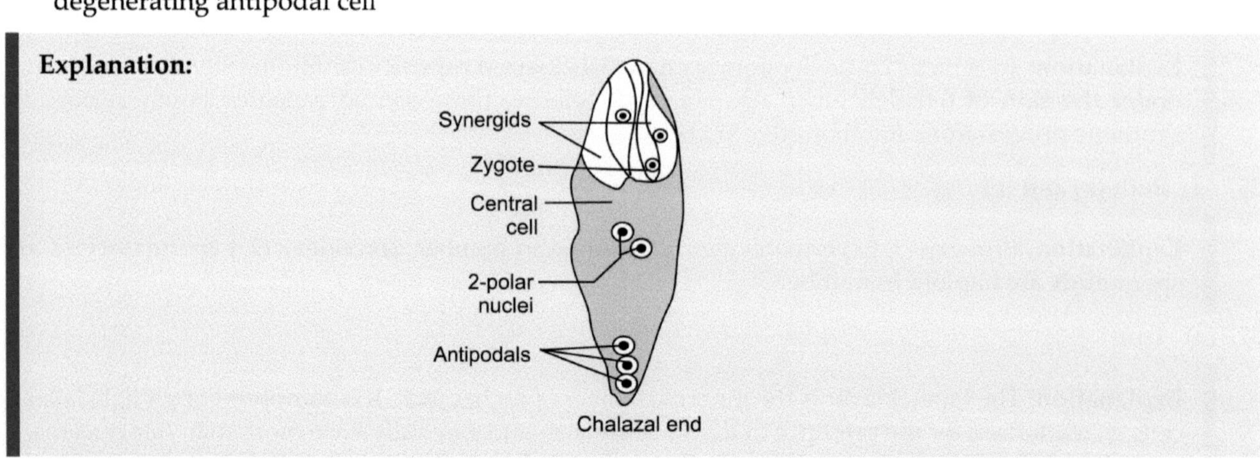
>

45. (a) UAA, UAG, UGA

> **Explanation:** UAA (ochre), UAG (amber) and UGA (opal) are the three condons, which bring about termination of polypeptide chain and thus, called terminator codons.

46. (b) I, II and III

> **Explanation:** Dominance, codominance and multiple alleles are the chracteristics that represent 'inheritance of blood groups' in humans. ABO blood group are determined by the gene I.
>
> There are multiple (three) alleles, I^A, I^B and i of the gene. Alleles I^A and I^B are dominant over i. However, when I^A and I^B alleles are present together, they show codominance. Therefore, option (b) is correct.

47. (b) Trichomes-Glandular or Non-glandular

> **Explanation:** Trichomes are the epidermal tissues structure. These are formed when epidermal cells become glandular and hair like, called as trichomes. This character was not amongst the seven pairs of characters of the pea plant.

48. (b) A–^{14}N-DNA, B–^{15}N-DNA, C–^{14}N-DNA, D–^{14}N-DNA

> **Explanation:** A–^{14}N-DNA, B–^{15}N-DNA, C–^{14}N-DNA, D–^{14}N-DNA

SECTION - C

49. (d) endometrium

> **Explanation:** Endometrium is the inner lining which is shed during your period.

50. (c) proliferative phase

> **Explanation:** The follicular phase of the female menstrual cycle includes the maturation of ovarian follicles to prepare one of them for release during ovulation. During the same period, there are concurrent changes in the endometrium, which is why the follicular phase is also known as the proliferative phase.

51. (b) Follicular phase

> **Explanation:** Primary follicles converted to graafian follicle during follicular phase of menstrual cycle.

52. (d) LH and FSH

> **Explanation:** LH and FSH hormones are at peak during proliferative phase of menstrual cycle.

53. (a) A → Progesterone; Graafian follicle; Proliferation of endometrium

> **Explanation:** A represents progesterone. It is secreted by graafian follicle whose function is proliferation of endometrium.

54. (d) thyroid stimulating hormone

> **Explanation:** There are four major hormones involved in the menstrual cycle: follicle-stimulating hormone, luteinizing hormone, estrogen, and progesterone.

55. (d) A–Gametes, B–Female, C–Male

> **Explanation:** A represent gametes which are haploid. B represent females with XX choromosomes while C represents male with XY chromosomes.

56. (c)   A   B   C   D   E

           5   4   1   2   3

Explanation: A–Promoter site-5 (binding of RNA polymerase)

B–Structural gene–4 (formation of functional protein)

C–Terminator site–1 (stopping of transcription)

D–Template strand–2 (part of DNA through which RNA is transcribed)

E–Coding strand–3 (complementary strand of DNA to RNA)

57. (b) A–Plasma membrane, B–Acrosome, C–Mitochondria

Explanation:

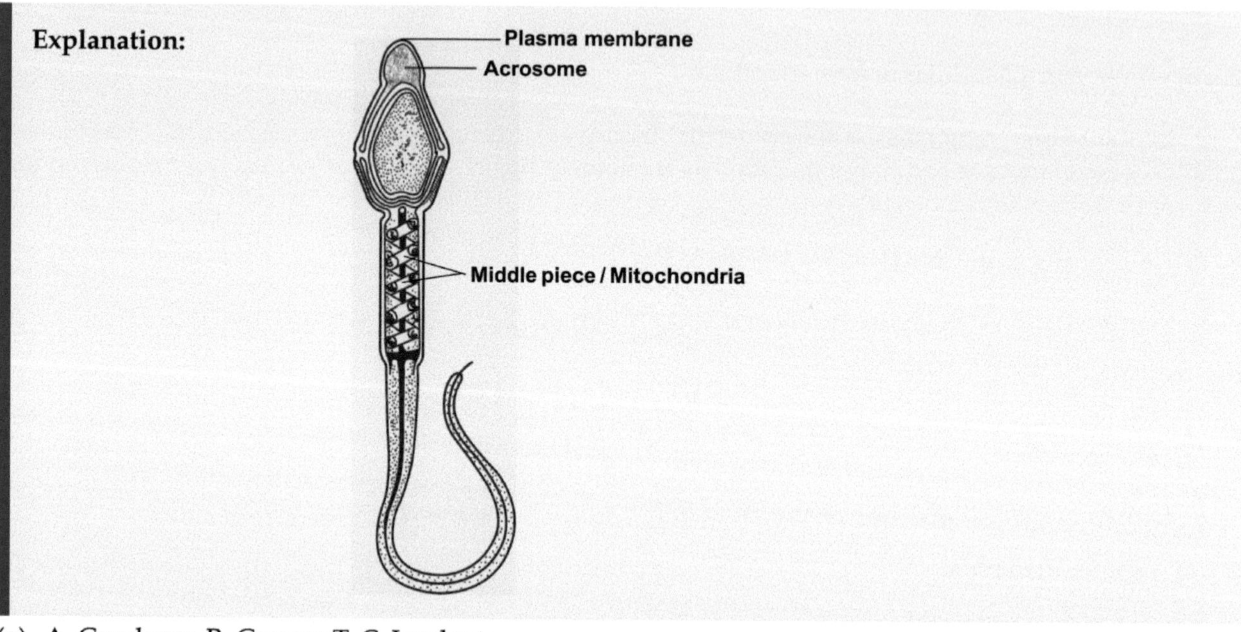

58. (a) A–Condoms, B–Copper-T, C–Implants

Explanation: Condom (represented by A) is a barrier method of contraception and protection from sexually-transmitted diseases. It is a barrier that covers the penis (male condom) or goes inside the vagina (female condom). It is used during sexual activity to prevent pregnancy. It is a sheath of latex rubber. Copper-T (represented by B) is sterilisation which is used to prevent unwanted pregnancy i.e. Generally Sexual activity without the use of any effective contraception through choice is the only main cause of unintended or unwanted pregnancy. Implantable contraception often called the birth control implant (represented by C) is a small, flexible plastic tube that doctors put under the skin of a girl's upper arm.

59. (d) A–Sertoli cells, B–Spermatogonia, C–Interstitial cells, D–Sperms

Explanation:

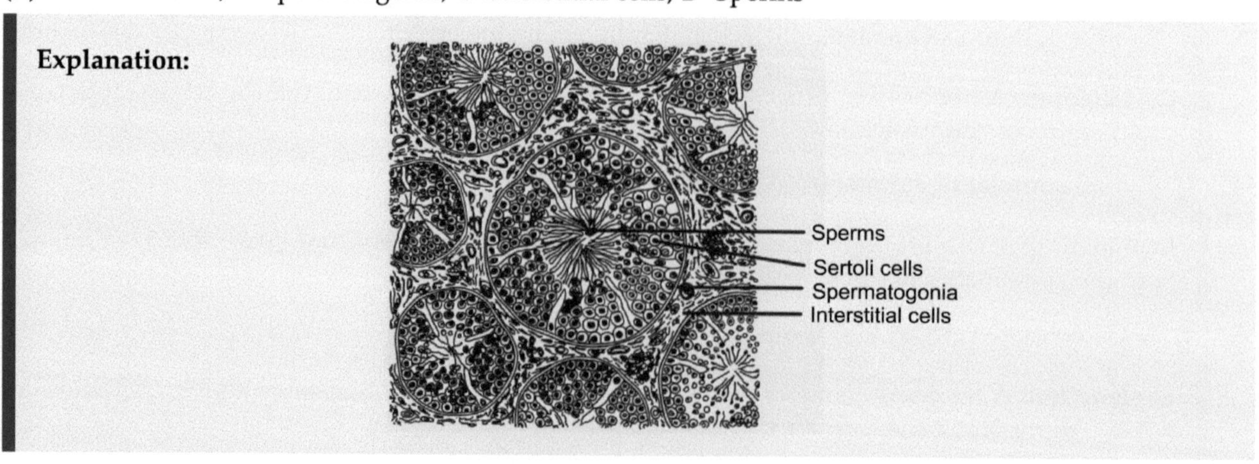

60. (c) A–Ovary, B–Sepal, C–Fillament, D–Petal, E–anther, F–Stigma, G–Style

Explanation:

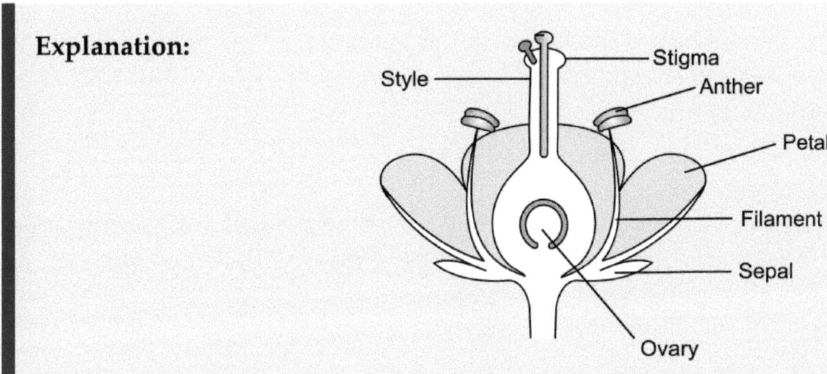

Sample Paper 5

SECTION - A

1. (c) Austrian monk

> **Explanation:** Gregor Mendel was an Austrian monk, teacher, and Augustinian prelate who lived in the 1800s. He experimented on garden pea hybrids while living at a monastery and is known as the father of modern genetics.

2. (c) Transcription of tRNAs

> **Explanation:** rRNAs are transcribed with the help of RNA polymerase I. RNA polymerase II is responsible for the transcription of mRNA, which is the heterogeneous nuclear RNA (hnRNA). RNA polymerase III transcribes the tRNAs, 5s rRNAs and snRNAs.

3. (c)

> **Explanation:** Synthesis of DNA by DNA polymerases occurs only in $5' \rightarrow 3'$ direction. Consequently, on one strand (the template with polarity $3' \rightarrow 5'$), the replication is continuous, while on the other (the template with polarity $5' \rightarrow 3'$), it is discontinuous. These short segments are called Okazaki fragments which are joined together by the action of DNA ligase.

4. (c) megagametophyte

> **Explanation:** Megaspores are produced by meiosis in megaspore mother cell. Megaspore then develops into female gametophyte or embryo sac. Megagametophyte or the female gametophyte is the embryo sac that develops from the megaspore through megagametogenesis.

5.

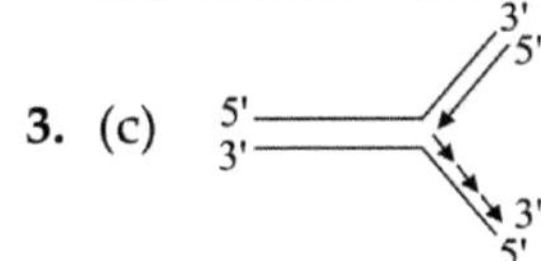

	A	B
(a)	Nucleoside	Nucleotide

> **Explanation:** A nucleotide has three components—a nitrogenous base, a pentose sugar, and a phosphate group. A nitrogenous base is linked to the pentose sugar through N-glycosidic linkage to form a nucleoside, such as adenosine or deoxyadenosine, guanosine or deoxyguanosine, cytidine or deoxycytidine and uridine or deoxythymidine. When a phosphate group is linked to $5'$–OH of a nucleoside through phosphoester linkage, a corresponding nucleotide (or deoxynucleotide depending upon the type of sugar present) is formed.

6. (d) Skin colour in humans

> **Explanation:** When two or more genes control the same trait, it is known as polygenic inheritance. Genes are frequently large in number but little in effect. Height, skin colour, eye colour, and weight are examples of polygenic inheritance in humans

7. (b) Tt × tt

> **Explanation:** Test cross is performed always between the F_1 heterozygous plant and pure recessive parent plant.

8. (d) fallopian tube

> **Explanation:** Fertilization occurs in the fallopian tube, which connects an ovary to the uterus. An embryo begins to grow if the fertilised egg successfully travels down the fallopian tube and implants in the uterus.

9. (b) phosphodiester bonds

> **Explanation:** In DNA molecule the nucleotides are linked by phosphodiester bonds whereas the nitrogen bases are held by hydrogen bonds.

10. (a) chromosomes assorting independently.

> **Explanation:** The given image represents that during anaphase of meiosis I, the two chromosome pairs can align at the metaphase plate independently of each other followed by their separation into different gametes. So, it shows the independent assortment of chromosomes.

11. (a) Fertilisation

> **Explanation:** Copper IUDs work by interfering with the process of fertilisation, which occurs when male sperm and female eggs combine to form a fertilised embryo.

12. (d) All of these

> **Explanation:** Excessive use of alcohol use can lead to the development of chronic diseases and other major issues such as high blood pressure, heart disease, stroke, liver disease, neuritis and digestive issues over time.

13. (d) RNA

> **Explanation:** As RNA can both store genetic information and catalyse chemical reactions, it is the first genetic material in cells. Metabolic, translational, and splicing mechanisms have all developed around RNA.

14. (d) exine of pollen wall

> **Explanation:** One of the most chemically inert biological polymers is sporopollenin. It's a key component of plant spores and pollen grains' robust outer (exine) walls. It has a chemical stability that allows it to survive in soils and sediments

15. (a) early embryonic stages

> **Explanation:** The genetic defect Adenosine Deaminase (ADA) deficiency may be curbed permanently by introducing bone marrow cells producing ADA into cells at early embryonic stages.

16. (a) development of fruits without fertilisation of the ovary

> **Explanation:** The development of fruits without the act of the fertilisation of the ovary is called parthenocarpy.

17. (a) alleles

> **Explanation:** The hybrids containing alleles expressing two contrasting traits are known as alleles. Alleles are alternate form of genes.

18. (d) All of these

> **Explanation:** Assisted reproductive techniques are positively useful for those couples who are having problem of inactive sperms or ovum's. Some of the ART techniques that are boon for such couples are listed below:
>
> (i) Artificial Insemination
>
> (ii) Test Tube Baby
>
> (iii) Gamete Intra Fallopian Transfer
>
> (iv) Zygote Intra Fallopian Transfer
>
> (v) Intra Uterine Transfer

19. (a) Transcription

> **Explanation:** By gene expression we mean the transcription of a gene into mRNA and its subsequent translation into protein. Gene expression is primarily controlled at the level of transcription, largely as a result of binding of proteins to specific sites on DNA.

20. (a) Removal of introns in a transcription unit

> **Explanation:** Splicing is the process by which introns, the noncoding regions of genes, are excised out of the primary messenger RNA transcript, and the exons (i.e., coding regions) are joined together to generate mature messenger RNA.

21. (c) lactose

> **Explanation:** In the case of the lac operon, lactose is the inducer. If lactose is present, it binds to and inactivates the repressor by causing it to fall off the operator.

22. (c) Embryo development

> **Explanation:** Embryo development is the post-fertilization event in flowering plants. The major events in post-fertilisation of a flower include development of endosperm and embryo, maturation of ovules into seeds and ovary into fruit.

23. (d) The parents are heterozygous

> **Explanation:** The given pedigree represents the appearance of trait attached ear lobes in the progeny of the parents (which do not represent this trait) so they must be heterozygous.

24. (a) two polynucleotide chains composed of four types of nucleotide subunits

> **Explanation:** Two long polynucleotide chains made up of four different nucleotide subunits make up a DNA molecule. A DNA chain, sometimes known as a DNA strand, is one of these chains. The two chains are held together by hydrogen bonds between the base regions of the nucleotides

SECTION - B

25. (b) Assertion and reason both are correct statements, but reason is not the correct explanation of the assertion

> **Explanation:** The accessory glands of the male reproductive system are the seminal vesicles, prostate gland, and the bulbourethral glands. Bulbourethral glands also known as Cowper glands, provide mucus that lubricate the urethra and counteract the acidity of any urine leftover in the urethra. Thus, both assertion and reason are correct statements but reason is not the true of assertion.

26. (c) Assertion is true, but reason is false statement.

> **Explanation:** The megaspore mother cell is diploid and has a large nucleus and dense cytoplasm. This cell undergoes meiosis (reduction division) to produce a group of four haploid cells called megaspore. One of these develops into the functional rnegaspore that develops into female gametophyte. Thus, assertion is true but reason is false.

27. (b) Assertion and reason both are correct statements, but reason is not the correct explanation of the assertion.

> **Explanation:** Genetic markers located on the same chromosome tend to remain together during sexual reproduction, a phenomenon called linkage. If two genes are completely linked, all gametes would carry the parental combinations and no recombinants would be produced. This in sharp contrast to the 50% recombinant gametes a characteristic of independent assortment. Hence, frequency that can result from crossing over between linked genes is between 0-50 percent. Linked genes show higher frequency of crossing over if the distance between them is higher and lower frequency if the distance is small. Thus, both assertion and reason are true, but the reason is not the correct explanation of the assertion.

28. (b) Assertion and reason both are correct statements, but reason is not the correct explanation of the assertion.

> **Explanation:** Chlamydiosis, often known as Chlamydia infection, is a sexually transmitted disease that affects the genital organs. Chlamydia trachomatis is the bacteria that cause this. Gonorrhea, also known as gonococcal urethritis, is a sexually transmitted infection that affects men and is caused by the bacterium *Neisseria gonorrhoeae*. This infection is similar to *Chlamydia trachomatis*. Thus, both assertion and reason are true, but the reason is not the correct explanation of the assertion.

29. (d) Unaffected male—▨

> **Explanation:** ● represents the affected female and ▨—◯ represents mating.

30. (c) DNA

> **Explanation:** DNA is the carrier of genetic information. Genes located on the DNA present in the chromosome controls each and every feature of an organism.

31. (b) Very tall

> **Explanation:** Tallness is not a characteristic feature of Down's syndrome. Some characteristic features of Down's syndrome include- short stature, small round head, partially open mouth, furrowed tongue, etc.

32. (b) Reverse transcriptional level

> **Explanation:** Gene expression regulation happens at many levels in eukaryotes. There are four levels: transcription, processing, transport of mRNA from the nucleus to the cytoplasm, and translation.

33. (d) Traits controlled by three or more genes

> **Explanation:** Traits are characteristics that allow us to recognise organisms. Polygenic traits are defined as features that are regulated by three or more genes

34. (d) Thalamus

> **Explanation:** The four whorls of the flower are arranged successively on a swollen end of a stalk or pedicel known as the thalamus or the receptacle. The receptacle gives rise to edible parts of the fruit.

35. (a) True

Explanation: Primary follicles are formed as a result of enveloping of primary oocytes by a layer of granulosa cells. These are formed during embryonic development and undergo a process of degeneration as the female matures to puberty. Hence the number of primary follicles that survive to puberty is far less, reaching only about 60,000-80,000 in each ovary.

36. (d) Promote abortion

Explanation: RCH (Reproductive and Child Health Care) programmes were created to address a wide range of reproduction-related concerns. There was no mention of abortion in any of these.

37. (b) androecium

Explanation: Androecium consists of the anthers and filaments. They are the male reproductive structures. Male gametes that are in pollen grains are on the anthers. Depending on the species, the stamens (anthers and filaments) may or may not protrude out of the flower.

38. (d) Imbalance in chromosome number and chromosome arrangement

Explanation: The chromosomal disorders are the disorders that are based on the imbalance in chromosome number and chromosomal arrangement. The disorders which are due to the mutant allele and their defective products are known as Mendelian disorders.

39. (d)

A	B	C	D
Promoter	Template strand	Coding strand	Terminator

Explanation: The segment of DNA that takes part in transcription is called transcription unit. It has three components (i) a promoter, (ii) the structural gene, and (iii) a terminator. Promoter is located upstream of structural gene. It is called 5′ end of coding strand which is 3′ end of template strand. Terminator region is present downstream of structural gene at the 3′ end of coding strand which is actually 5′ end of the template strand.

40. (c) Both (a) and (b)

Explanation: The regulatory proteins have the ability to act both as an activator and a repressor. They will be positive when they are activators. They will be negative when they are repressors

41. (b) 44 + XXY

Explanation: The genotype of the person suffering from Klinefelter's syndrome is 44 + XXY. This deviation from a normal person's genotype is due to the additional copy of the X-chromosome.

42. (c) Charging of tRNA

Explanation: In order to form a peptide bond, a certain quantity of energy is required. The first phase in this process is known as charging of tRNA. It is also known as Aminoacylation of tRNA. In this process, the amino acids are activated in the presence of ATP and are linked to their cognate tRNA.

43. (b) Contrasting traits

Explanation: Through the experiments of pea conducted by Mendel, he described distinct contrasting traits such as flower colour which are either purple or white.

44. (c) Epididymis

Explanation: The epididymis is a comma shaped mass of 6m long narrow closely coiled tubule which lies along the upper, lower and inner side of each testis. The epididymis by its peristaltic and segmenting contractions pushes the sperms into the vas deferens.

45. (d) Ribosomes

> **Explanation:** Lysosomes help in the break down and digestion of the worn out or dead cell components. Mitochondria is known as the power house of the cell for the production of ATP molecules. Nucleus helps in carrying the information from one generation to the next generation. Ribosomes help in the synthesis of proteins.

46. (d) Histones

> **Explanation:** Histones are rich in basic amino acid (AA) residues such as lysine and arginine. These two amino acids carry a positive charge at their side chains. Due to this reason, histones are called as the set of positively charged basic proteins.

47. (d) Tertiary follicle

> **Explanation:** The oogonium starts meiosis but is arrested at Prophase I, thereby forming primary oocyte. This oocyte then forms a primary, then secondary, and finally a tertiary follicle with the addition of granulosa cells, theca and antrum. This stage of follicle promotes further division of primary oocyte. Thus, the first division of meiosis is completed in the tertiary follicle.

48. (c) Filament

> **Explanation:** The whole image is a stamen. The part-A depicts the anther that carries the male gametes and the part-B is the filament. The anther is fused with the filament.

SECTION – C

49. (c) nucleosome

> **Explanation:** A nucleosome is a section of DNA that is wrapped around a core of proteins. Inside the nucleus, DNA forms a complex with proteins called chromatin, which allows the DNA to be condensed into a smaller volume.

50. (b) DNA

> **Explanation:** Each nucleosome is composed of a little less than two turns of DNA wrapped around a set of eight proteins called histones, which are known as a histone octamer.

51. (b) Separates linker DNA between nucleosomes

> **Explanation:** DNA connecting two adjacent nucleosomes is called linker DNA which bears histone proteins.

52. (d) a set of positively charged, basic proteins

> **Explanation:** There is a set of positively charged, basic proteins called histones. Histones are rich in the basic amino acid residues, lysine and arginine.

53. (b) negatively, nucleosome

> **Explanation:** The negatively charged DNA is wrapped around the positively charged histone octamer to form nucleosome.

54. (a) H_2A, H_2B, H_3, and H_4

> **Explanation:** There are five types of histone proteins – H_1, H_2A, H_2B, H_3 and H_4. Four of them (H_2A, H_2B, H_3 and H_4) produce histone octamer called nu body or core of nucleosome.

55. (a) A—Connective tissue, B—Endothecium, C—Pollen grain

> **Explanation:** A strand of connective tissue extends from the filament to the anther. It is present between the two lobes and thus maintains their connectivity. In the diagram, it is labeled as 'A'.
>
> The anther is bilobed with two pollen sacs each called microsporangia. In the wall of a mature anther, the epidermis is the outermost layer, followed by a single layer of endothelium (labelled as B), then one to the three-layered thick middle layer, and innermost single-layered tapetum.
>
> Stomium is a layer of thin-walled epidermal cells that are present at the line of dehiscence. Thus, when the time comes for the dispersal of pollen grains (labelled as C), and anther breaks and splits at this line of dehiscence only.

56. (d)

Steps	A	B
Termination	RNA polymerase	Rho factor

> **Explanation:** : In the given figure, the step shown is termination of transcription in bacteria. The labels A and B are RNA polymerase and rho factor, respectively. RNA polymerase is an enzyme that synthesises the formation of RNA from a DNA template during transcription. Rho factor is a termination factor which releases RNA from the DNA template.

57. (c) Glucose and Galactose

> **Explanation:** Lactose is a carbohydrate molecule that is made up of two disaccharide molecules. When a disaccharide is hydrolyzed, two monosaccharide molecules are produced. We acquire one molecule of glucose and galactose when we hydrolyze a single molecule of lactose. Sucrose hydrolysis produces glucose and fructose. Maltose hydrolysis yields two molecules of glucose.

58. (a) Gynoecium

> **Explanation:** Gynoecium is the labelled part A. It is female reproductive components. It is made up of three parts: style, stigma, and ovary.

59. (d) B and E

> **Explanation:**
>
> 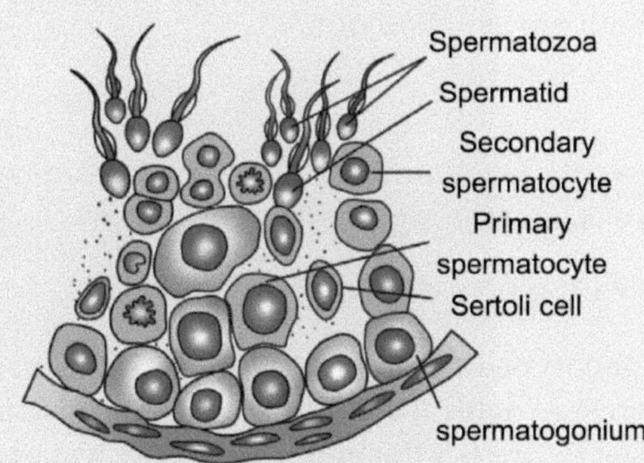
>

The spermatid (labelled as B), is the haploid male gamete that results from division of secondary spermatocytes. As a result of meiosis, each spermatid contains only half of the genetic material present in the original primary spermatocyte. Sertoli cells (labelled as E), facilitate the progression of germ cells to spermatozoa via direct contact and by controlling the environment within the seminiferous tubules.

60. (a) A—Regulatory gene, B—Promoter, C—Operator, D—Structural gene

> **Explanation:** A represents the regulatory gene, B represents the promoter, C represents the operator and D represents the structural genes.

❑❑

Sample Paper 6

SECTION – A

1. (b) Thalassemia

> **Explanation:** Thalassemia is inherited in an autosomal recessive manner; however, the inheritance can be quite complex as multiple genes can influence the production of hemoglobin.

2. (d) Plant is dioecious and bears only staminate flowers.

> **Explanation:** In dioecious plants, the unisexual male flower is staminate, *i.e.*, bearing stamens only, while the female is pistillate or bearing pistils only. For the production of fruits and seeds, a flower must be pistillate.

3. (a) Autosomal recessive disorder

> **Explanation:** : The pedigree shows an autosomal recessive disorder. The parents are the carrier of the disease so the disease will be visible in only a few offsprings. The other offsprings will be either a carrier or non-carrier.

4. (b) Splicing

> **Explanation:** : Introns and exons both are present in the primary transcript. Splicing is the process by which the cell removes the introns from the mature mRNA.

5. (d) All the statements (A), (B), (C) and (D) are correct.

> **Explanation:** This is double stranded structure of DNA. In DNA A,T,G,C base pairs are present. A (Adenine) pair with T (Thymine) and G (Guanine) pair with C (Cytosine).

6. (c) External opening of the urinogenital duct

> **Explanation:** Urethral meatus refers to the external opening of urinogenital duct, through which, in males, urine and semen both are expelled out.

7. (c) Embryogenesis

> **Explanation:** The process of development of embryo from zygote to young one is known as embryogenesis. The figure is of embryogenesis.

8. (b) Crossing F_1 individuals with recessive parents

> **Explanation:** To find the genotype of a hybrid, test cross is performed in which an organism showing dominant phenotype is crossed with the recessive parent instead of selfing. The progenies of such cross can easily be analysed to predict the genotype of the test organism.

9. (b) AIDS

> **Explanation:** HIV (Human Immunodeficiency Virus, a retrovirus) causes AIDS (Acquired Immune Deficiency Syndrome). By infecting T-helper cells, it mostly affects them. In most cases, there is a significant delay between infection and onset of symptoms. The person becomes sensitive to pathogenic germs that would not otherwise cause disease due to a decrease in TH cell count.

10. (d) None of these

> **Explanation:** The process shown in the figure is known as pollination. In this process transfer of pollen grains occurs from one plant to the stigma of other plant. Due to this process fertilisation occurs.

11. (a) Nucleus

Explanation: Inside the nucleus, RNA splicing and RNA capping occur during eukaryotic cell transcription. The mature mRNA (processed mRNA) is subsequently transferred to the cytoplasm, where it can be translated by the ribosome. The signal recognition particle may direct translation to the endoplasmic reticulum or to the cytoplasm of ribosomes.

12. (a) 1950s

Explanation: A national level approach to build up a reproductively healthy society was taken up in our country in 1950s.

13. (a) six

Explanation: Six haploid cells are present in a mature female gametophyte of a flowering plant. They are three antipodal cells, one egg cell, two synergids.

14. (c) DNA ligase

Explanation: The enzyme is DNA ligase that joins the small fragments of DNA of a lagging strand during DNA replication.

15. (c) Pentoses

Explanation: Both deoxyribose and ribose belong to the class pentoses as it contains '5' carbon atoms.

16. (c) Morgan

Explanation: Experimental verification of the chromosomal theory of inheritance was done by Morgan. Sutton and and Boveri proposed chromosomal theory of inheritance but it was experimentally verified by T.H. Morgan.

17. (a) prevents ovulation

Explanation: Birth control pills (oral contraceptives) check ovulation in female by inhibiting the secretion of follicle stimulating hormone and luteinizing hormone that are important for ovulation.

18. (a) pectocellulose

Explanation: Pollen has two membranes:
(i)   inner intine – It is composed of callose.
(ii) outer exine – It is composed of pectin with cellulose.

19. (c) Phosphate group

Explanation: A nitrogenous base is attached to the pentose sugar by N-glycosidic linkage to form a nucleoside, *i.e.*, Nucleoside = Nitrogen base + Pentose sugar. When a phosphate group is attached to the 5' –OH of a nucleoside through phosphodiester linkage, a nucleotide is formed, *i.e.*, Nucleotide = Nitrogen base + Pentose sugar + Phosphate group (PO_4). So, a nucleoside differs from a nucleotide as it lacks the phosphate group.

20. (b) X-linked recessive gene disorder

Explanation: Hemophilia A and hemophilia B are inherited in an X-linked recessive pattern. The genes associated with these conditions are located on the X-chromosome, which is one of the two sex chromosomes. In males (who have only one X-chromosome), one altered copy of the gene in each cell is sufficient to cause the condition. In females (who have two X-chromosomes), a mutation would have to occur in both copies of the gene to cause the disorder. Because it is unlikely that females will have two altered copies of this gene, it is very rare for females to have hemophilia. A characteristic of X-linked inheritance is that fathers cannot pass X-linked traits to their sons.

21. (b) Penis in male and cervix and vagina in female

> **Explanation:** Condoms are barriers made of thin rubber/latex sheath that are used to cover the penis in the male or vagina and cervix in the female, just before coitus so that the ejaculated semen would not enter into the female reproductive tract. This can prevent conception.

22. (a) four

> **Explanation:** The seven traits are known to be present on four different chromosomes. But they do not show linkage because of large distances between them on the chromosome.

23. (a)

> **Explanation:** These symbols are used for pedigree analysis for human being. First symbol is used for mating between relatives (consanguineous mating).

24. (a) add nucleotides to the growing daughter strand

> **Explanation:** DNA polymerase add nucleotides to an existing nucleotide strand. The DNA polymerase synthesize DNA from deoxyribonucleotides, the building blocks of DNA. The DNA copies are created by the pairing of nucleotides to bases present on each strand of the original DNA molecule.

SECTION - B

25. (a) Assertion and reason both are correct statements and reason is the correct explanation of the assertion.

> **Explanation:** In barrier methods, ovum and sperms are prevented from physically meeting with the help of barriers. Such methods are available for both males and females. Condoms are barriers made of thin rubber/latex sheath that are used to cover the penis, in the male or vagina and cervix in the female, just before coitus so that the ejaculated semen would not enter into the female reproductive tract. This can prevent conception. Thus, both assertion and reason are true and reason is the correct explanation of the assertion.

26. (b) Assertion and reason both are correct statements, but reason is not the correct explanation of the assertion.

> **Explanation:** In tapetum, cells are generally polyploid, multinucleate and possess dense cytoplasm. In tapetal cells, the nucleus divides but cytokinesis does not take place, so same cell contains two or more nuclei connective consist of vascular strand which is made up of vascular tissues. Thus both assertion and reason are true but reason is not the correct explanation of the assertion.

27. (c) Assertion is true, but reason is false statement.

> **Explanation:** The testes of human males are situated outside the abdominal cabity within a pouch called scrotum. It is connected to the abdomen via inguinal canal. Thus, assertion is true but reason is false.

28. (a) Assertion and reason both are correct statements and reason is the correct explanation of the assertion.

> **Explanation:** When a gene control number of phenotypes that are mostly unrelated, it is said to exhibit pleiotropy. Thus, both assertion and reason are true and reason is the correct explanation of the assertion.

29. (c) 50%

> **Explanation:** There is always 50% possibility of male and female child.

30. (a) Co-dominance

Explanation: The alleles for red and white flowers are co-dominant, resulting in pink flowers when both are present in the genotype.

31. (b) Progesterone

Explanation: The ovulation (ovulatory phase) is followed by the luteal phase (latter phase of the menstrual cycle) during which the remaining parts of the Graafian follicle transform as the corpus luteum, which produces progesterone. So, progesterone is highest at luteal phase.

32. (d) YAC (Yeast Artificial Chromosomes)

Explanation: Both BAC (Bacterial Artificial Chromosomes) and YAC (Yeast Artificial Chromosomes) act as a suitable vector for the process of cloning in HGP whereas bacteria and yeast act as the host for cloning in HGP.

33. (c) Unaffected mothers have affected sons and daughters who are carriers

Explanation: The most common sex-linked alleles are X-linked and are passed from a mother to her son (since the mother always donates one of her X-chromosome to her son and the father always donates his Y-chromosome to his son). Daughters can also receive the X-linked allele from their mothers, but the father donates the other X-chromosome, so daughter can be carriers.

34. (d) Pregnancy

Explanation: Amniotic fluid is secreted by amnion of foetus during pregnancy.

35. (d) Both (b) and (c)

Explanation: Prokaryotic chromosome are circular and contain termination sequences.

36. (b) males have one X-chromosome and females have two X-chromosomes

Explanation: In these three species, females have two X-chromosomes and males have one X-chromosome. The ratio of X-chromosomes to autosomes is important (and different in each organism) in *Drosophila* and grasshoppers, but not in humans. In all three species, males have one Y-chromosome, but the Y is required for male fertility, not for *Drosophila* to be male (in *Drosophila*, male files can be XO).

37. (d) Seminal vesicle

Explanation: Seminal fluid, often known as semen, is a slightly alkaline mixture of sperm cells and accessory gland secretions. The seminal vesicles secrete around 60% of the volume of the semen, with the prostate gland producing the majority of the rest.

38. (c) $\dfrac{G + C}{A + T}$

Explanation: According to Chargaff purines and pyrimidines are in equal amounts. Purine (adenine) is equimolar with pyrimidine (thymine) and purine (guanine) is equimolar with pyrimidine (cytosine).

39. (b) Frederick Griffith

Explanation: This experiment was done by Frederick Griffith. *Streptococcus pneumonia* has two strains- R and S. Mice infected with R strain die from pneumonia while mice infected with S strain does not get infected with pneumonia.

40. (a) produce the same offspring when crossed for many generations

> **Explanation:** Monohybrid and dihybrid crosses produce heterozygous individuals; true-breeding individuals are always homozygous.

41. (b) UUGCAUUGC

> **Explanation:** When a DNA strand with the sequence AACGTAACG is transcribed, the resultant sequence of the mRNA molecule synthesized is UUGCAUUGC. This is based on the paring of nitrogen bases-adenine pairs with thymine (in DNA) and uracil (in RNA) and guanine with cytosine.

42. (c) Green seed colour

> **Explanation:** Yellow seed colour is dominant over green seed colour.

43. (c) triplet, universal, non-ambiguous and degenerate

> **Explanation:** Genetic code is the depiction of codon by which the information in RNA is decoded in a polypeptide chain. The information is transferred in the form of triplet of bases coding for one amino acid. It is triplet, universal, non-ambiguous and degenerate in nature.

44. (c) Fallopian tube

> **Explanation:** : Fertilisation occurs when a male gamete fuse with female gamete. In human beings this process occurs in fallopian tube.

45. (a) Apple

> **Explanation:** Fruit formation without fertilisation is known as parthenocarpy. The fruit looks like a normal fruit but has no seeds. Natural parthenocarpy can be found in pineapple, banana, cucumber, grape, orange, watermelon, grapefruit, persimmon, and breadfruit varieties. False fruits, on the other hand, are those that originate from any floral component other than the ovary (*e.g.*, apple).

46. (c) both alleles independently expressed in the heterozygote

> **Explanation:** In co-dominance, both alleles are independently expressed in the heterozygote.

47. (d) DNA → RNA → Proteins

> **Explanation:** Central dogma was proposed by Crick (1958). It proposes unidirectional or one way flow of information from DNA to RNA and then to protein (polypeptide).
>
> 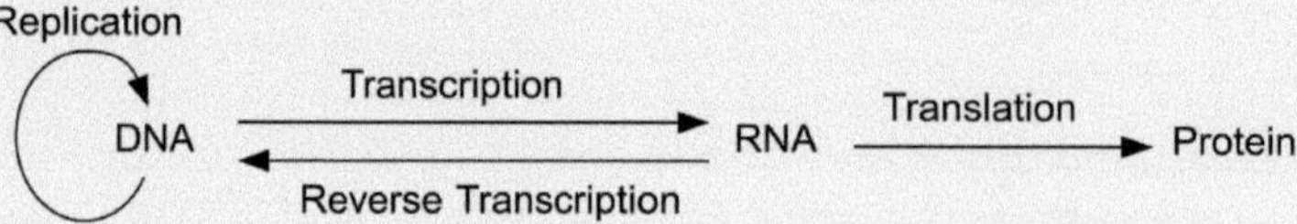
>

48. (a) Euchromatin is more active than heterochromatin.

> **Explanation:** Two types of chromatin are present- euchromatin and heterochromatin. Euchromatin is said to be transcriptionally active.

SECTION – C

49. (b) Klinefelter's syndrome

> **Explanation:** Klinefelter's syndrome affects boys and men who have the normal X and Y chromosomes plus one extra X chromosome, for a total of 47 chromosomes (47, XXY). On the X chromosome, boys and men with Klinefelter's syndrome have an extra copy of numerous genes.

50. (c) Nettie Stevens

Explanation: The chromosomal XY sex-determination system, *i.e.,* the fact that males have XY sex chromosomes and females have XX sex chromosomes, was separately discovered by Nettie Stevens and Edmund Beecher Wilson in 1905.

51. (b) three

Explanation: The process of inactivation of one X chromosome happens so as to avoid passing of unnecessary information to the next generation. Lynon had made a hypothesis, and following are its postulates,

(i) The inactivation of X chromosome happens in random.

(ii) The inactivation of X chromosome occurs during the development.

(iii) The inactive X chromosome is always inactivated across all generation of cells.

(iv) In female, only one of two X-chromosomes in the somatic cell is inactive.

As we know, only one X is always active, thus, in XXXXY, three X are degenerated. Therefore, there are three Barr bodies present in XXXXY.

52. (a) XXY

Explanation: The presence of an additional X chromosome causes a boy to have sexual traits similar to a girl, resulting in a 47, XXY karyotype. Some children with this genetic disorder appear to have no symptoms at all, while others may experience a variety of cognitive, social, psychological, and learning difficulties.

53. (c) Allosomes

Explanation: Unlike the rest of the chromosomes (autosomes), the X and Y sex chromosomes differ in form and size, and are sometimes referred to as allosomes.

54. (c) Henking

Explanation: The foundation of the chromosomal basis of sex determination was laid down by Henking in 1891. He studied a specific nuclear structure though spermatogenesis in a few insects.

55. (b) RNA

Explanation: This structure is of RNA because we can see that in place of thymine, uracil is present.

56. (d) Both (a) and (b)

Explanation: The figure shows both syngamy and fertilisation. The difference between syngamy and fertilisation is that syngamy is the process of fusing two gametes to form a zygote, whereas fertilisation is the act or process of rendering fertile.

57. (d) All of these

Explanation: The fly is *Drosophila melanogaster*. This fly is suitable for laboratory experiment because it can be reproduce on a synthetic medium and single mating can produce a large number of flies. Its lifespan is also too short (two weeks).

58. (b) A– Stamen; B– Carpel

Explanation: It is the structure of a bisexual plant in which both male and female reproductive organs are present on same plant. A represents the stamen (male reproductive organ) and B represents pistil/carpel (female reproductive organ).

59. (a) Female: aa and Male: Aa

> **Explanation:** The genotype of parents in generation I – Female: aa and Male: Aa

60. (d) Hershey and Chase

> **Explanation:** This experiment was done by Hershey and Chase on the bacteriophage. They proved that DNA is the genetic material.

Sample Paper 7

SECTION - A

1. (a) Aneuploidy

> **Explanation:** The chromosomal disorders are caused due to lack or additions or abnormal arrangement of one or more chromosomes. Failure of segregation of chromatids during cell division cycle results in the gain or loss of chromosome(s) is called aneuploidy. For example, Down's syndrome results due to gain of extra copy of chromosome 21. Similarly, Turner's syndrome results due to loss of an X chromosome in human females.

2. (b) A–(iii), B–(iv), C–(ii), D–(i)

> **Explanation:** A. The blastomeres in the blastocyst are arranged into an outer layer called trophoblast and an inner group of cells attached to trophoblast called the inner cell mass. The trophoblast layer gets attached to the endometrium.
> B. Cleavage is the repeated mitotic division of cells in the early embryo.
> C. Inner cell mass gets differentiated as the embryo.
> D. Implantation is the process of attachment and invasion of the uterus endometrium by the blastocyst and it leads to pregnancy.

3. (a) Semiconservative replication of DNA

> **Explanation:** The figure shows the semiconservative replication of DNA. From the base pairs of strands we can identify that it's a DNA.

4. (a) polymerise in the $5' \to 3'$ direction and explain $3' \to 5'$ DNA replication.

> **Explanation:** On DNA template strand with $5' \to 3'$ orientation, DNA polymerase synthesises short pairs on new DNA (about 1000 nucleotides long) in $5' \to 3'$ direction and then joins these pieces together. These small fragments are called Okazaki fragments and new DNA strand made in this discontinuous manner is called lagging strand. Okazaki fragments are joined by means of DNA ligase.

5. (d) Both (a) and (b)

> **Explanation:** This structure shown in the figure is called chromosome means coloured body . This structure carries forward characters from one generation to another.

6. (d) All of these

> **Explanation:** : Condoms are the physical barrier methods. These are user-friendly, safe and effective. These are convenient to find and cost-effective. They do not affect with coitus and help prevent STDs.

7. (a) Dominant X-linked

> **Explanation:** Families with an X-linked recessive disorder often have affected males, but rarely affected females, in each generation. For X-linked dominant diseases, however, a mutation in one copy of an X-linked gene will result in disease for both males and females.

8. (a) promoter gene

> **Explanation:** A promoter is a DNA region that stimulates the transcription of a specific gene in genetics. Promoters are found on the same strand and upstream on the DNA (towards the 5′ region of the sense strand), near the transcription start sites of genes.

9. (c) Both pollen and ovules mature simultaneously

> **Explanation:** Autogamy is pollination within a flower. Chasmogamous flowers are those in which anthers and stigma are exposed. For autogamy, in such a flower to take place, pollen and ovule should mature simultaneously and anther and stigma should lie close to each other.

10. (d) All the statements are correct

> **Explanation:** : It is lac operon model. It consists of one regulatory gene (i) and three structural genes (z, y and a)

11. (d) Three

> **Explanation:** Trisomy 21 is a condition in which a person has three copies of chromosome 21 in all cells, rather than the usual two copies. This is caused by aberrant cell division during the sperm or egg cell's development.

12. (b) Embryo development

> **Explanation:** Events in sexual reproduction after the fertilization are called post-fertilization events. After fertilization, a diploid zygote is formed in all sexually reproducing organisms. Zygote divides by mitosis and gives rise to the proembryo and subsequently to the globular, heart shaped mature embryo. The process of development of an embryo from the zygote is called embryogenesis.

13. (c) first filial generation

> **Explanation:** The first generation obtained by crossing two parents is called as first filial generation or F_1 generation.

14. (c) 7-celled and 8-nucleate

> **Explanation:** : A typical embryo sac contains 8 nuclei but 7 cells which are 3 micropylar, 3 chalazal, and 1 central. The three micropylar cells are collectively known as egg apparatus. The three chalazal cells of the embryo sac are called antipodal cells.

15. (b) Deoxyribonucleic acid

> **Explanation:** DNA stands for deoxyribonucleic acid. It is a genetic material known for the majority of organisms living on this planet. This substance is responsible for controlling the inheritance of traits.

16. (a) stigma

> **Explanation:** Compatible nature of pollen grain is determined by the stigma of carpel or pistil.

17. (c) A and O groups

Explanation: A parent with A blood group can have two possible genotypes: $I^A I^A$ and $I^A I^O$; similarly parent with O blood group can have one possible genotype: $I^O I^O$. Thus, they have two alleles: I^A and I^O, which can make total three genotypes, *i.e.*, $I^A I^A$, $I^O I^O$ and $I^A I^O$.

18. (b) (i) and (iii)

Explanation: Cleavage is a series of rapid mitotic divisions of the zygote, characterised by absence of growth in daughter cells. The blastomeres in the blastocyst get arranged into outer layer called trophoblast and an inner group of cells attached to trophoblast called the inner cell mass.

19. (d) Modifier

Explanation: RNA does not behave as a modifier. Instead, it functions as a messenger that carries genetic information. It also acts as an adapter for picking up amino acids and in some cases behaves as a catalytic molecule.

20. (b) map unit

Explanation: The distance between genes is measured by map unit. 1% crossing over between two linked genes is known as 1 map unit or centi Morgan (cM). 100% crossing over is termed as Morgan (M) and 10% crossing over as deci Morgan (dM).

21. (b) Friedrich Meischer

Explanation: Friedrich Meischer had originally called the DNA to be as the "Nuclein". He observed DNA to be as an acidic substance found in the nucleus. Since technology hadn't been developed much in the 1860s, he wasn't able to fully study about the structure of the DNA and isolate such a long polymer. Later in the 1950s, Rosalind Franklin did an X-Ray diffraction study on the DNA using the X-Ray crystallography method. James Watson and Francis Crick on observing the X-Ray pattern of the DNA molecule, gave the molecular structure of the DNA.

22. (d) insects or wind

Explanation: In a majority of aquatic plants such as water hyacinth and water lily, the flowers emerge above the level of water and are pollinated by insects or wind like most of the land plants.

23. (c) All the statements are correct

Explanation: These symbols are used in human pedigree analysis

24. (a) Humans contain 23 pairs of autosomes.

Explanation: Statement in option (a) is incorrect and can be corrected as :
Humans contain 22 pairs of autosomes (XX) and one pair of sex chromosome (XY).

SECTION - B

25. (b) Assertion and reason both are correct statements, but reason is not the correct explanation of the assertion.

Explanation: The placenta is located inside the ovarian cavity. The development of ovule is the first stage in female gametogenesis. Thus, both assertion and reason are true but reason is not the correct explanation of assertion.

26. (a) Assertion and reason both are correct statements and reason is the correct explanation of the assertion.

Explanation: The male urethra is lined by pseudostratified epithelium. Thus, both assertion and reason are true and reason is the correct explanation of assertion.

27. (c) Assertion is true, but reason is false statement.

> **Explanation:** Saheli is a non-steroidal contraceptive pill that is taken once a week. It has high contraceptive value and is well accepted as it has very few side effects. Thus, assertion is true but reason is false.

28. (b) Assertion and reason both are correct statements, but reason is not the correct explanation of the assertion.

> **Explanation:** In both grasshopper and humans male heterogamety is found and in the both cases female homogamety is present. Thus, both assertion and reason are true but reason is not the correct explanation of assertion.

29. (a) leading strand, lagging strand

> **Explanation:** 'a' – synthesis of leading / continuous strand.
> 'b' – synthesis of lagging / discontinuous strand.

30. (a) Conversion of a strand of mRNA to DNA

> **Explanation:** Central dogma is the process of conversion of DNA → mRNA → protein. On the contrary, central dogma reverse is the conversion of RNA → DNA. The formed DNA in the process of central dogma reverse or reverse transcription, can undergo the processes of transcription and translation after that.

31. (d) pleiotropy

> **Explanation:** An example of pleiotropy is phenylketonuria, an inherited disorder that affects the level of phenylalanine, an amino acid that can be obtained from food, in the human body. Phenylketonuria causes this amino acid to increase in amount in the body, which can be very dangerous.

32. (b) RNA

> **Explanation:** The storage of the genetic information takes place in the DNA. It carries all the necessary information needed for heredity. The stability of the DNA is more too, this helps in carrying information. During the central dogma, DNA in transcripted to RNA after which RNA will be responsible for the transmission of the genetic information.

33. (b) incomplete dominance

> **Explanation:** In starch synthesis gene, following conditions to seen.
> BB–rounded (due to more starch synthesis)
> bb–wrinkled (due to less starch synthesis)
> Bb–in between round and wrinkled size. It produces starch of intermediate quantity between BB to bb homozygous condition. So, it is incomplete dominance.

34. (d) Fertility

> **Explanation:** Highly developed medications, treatment options, quick transports, increased number of hospitals have all resulted in a decrease in death rate, MMR, IMR, and infertility. This has resulted in a longer lifespan of humans and also a rise in population.

35. (d) nucellus near the micropylar region

> **Explanation:** Ovules generally differentiate a single megaspore mother cell (MMC) in the micropylar region of the nucellus.

36. (c) Urethra

> **Explanation:** Urethra is a tube that travels through the penis and carries urine and semen from urinary bladder and ejaculatory ducts, respectively to the urinary meatus.

37. (b) Pills

> **Explanation:** Oral contraceptives are delivered in the form of tablets. Hence, these are called oral pills. They come in the form of capsules since the drug has to pass through the digestive tract which has an extremely low pH. The capsule is designed so that the drug is released only in the small intestine, where it is absorbed into the blood.

38. (c) Protein

> **Explanation:** Prior to the works done by Oswald Avery, Colin MacLeod and Maclyn McCarty, the genetic material was thought to be as the protein. Nucleoids are the irregular shaped structures in the prokaryotic cell. They contain nearly all of the genetic material of the prokaryotes. Nucleons are present inside the nucleus of an atom, alongside with the protons. Chromosome carries the genetic information of the genes.

39. (d) Both (a) and (b) are correct

> **Explanation:** A and B are human being and *Drosophila* respectively. In both of these organisms female has XX type of chromosomes and male has XY type of chromosomes.

40. (c) 50%

> **Explanation:** Down's syndrome is the example of autosomal aneuploidy. Here, an extra copy of chromosome 21 occurs. As it is an autosomal disease, the offspring produced from affected mother and normal father should be 50%.

41. (a) *Streptococcus saprophyticus*

> **Explanation:** *Streptococcus pyogenes* causes tonsillitis and rheumatic fever. *Staphylococcus aureus* causes abscesses. *Streptococcus pneumoniae* causes pneumonia. *Staphylococcus saprophyticus* causes urinary tract infections.

42. (b) AABB × aabb

> **Explanation:** AABB × aabb is suitable for experiment on linkage. Linkage is the tendency for certain genes to be inherited together, because they are on the same chromosome. Thus, parental combinations of characters are found more frequently in offspring than non-parental characters.

43. (d) Protein

> **Explanation:** The codons present in the mRNA will code for the respective amino acid or protein depending on the bases that are present on the strand. mRNA, tRNA and rRNA are the types of RNA. They won't be formed in the translation process of the central dogma.

44. (a) Vascular strands

> **Explanation:** Vascular bundles constitute the xylem and phloem. Xylem transfers water and phloem transfers the nutrients from the root. It is important for the development of the anther and male gametes.

45. (d) All of these

> **Explanation:** (i) Gynecomastia is the development of breasts in males.
> (ii) Turner's syndrome is a genetic disorder caused due to a complete or partial missing of X chromosome in females.
> (iii) A syndrome is a group of medical signs and symptoms which are related with each other.

46. (c) Permease

> **Explanation:** The structural gene (z) of the lac operon codes for β-galactosidase. It is responsible for the hydrolysis of polysaccharides. The 'y' genes code for permease. It increases the permeability of a cell to β-galactosidase. The 'a' genes code for transacetylase.

47. (b) the germinal epithelium of seminiferous tubules.

> **Explanation:** Each seminiferous tubule is lined on its inside by two types of cells called male germ cells(spermatogonia) and sertoli cells.

48. (a) 1 - LH, 2 - Ovulation, 3 - Menstruation, 4 - Proliferative phase, 5 - Luteal phase

> **Explanation:**

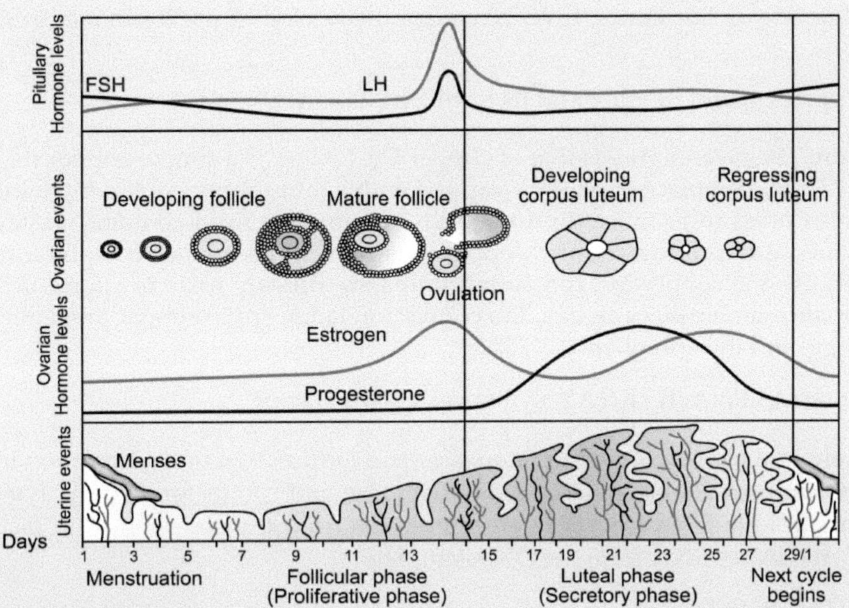

LH is luteinising hormone secreted from the anterior pituitary gland. In females, an acute rise of LH (called LH surge) triggers ovulation and development of the corpus luteum. Ovulation is the process when a mature egg is released from the ovary, pushed down the fallopian tube, and is available for fertilisation. Menstruation is a woman's monthly bleeding. Menstrual blood flows from the uterus through the small opening in the cervix and passes out of the body through the vagina. Proliferative and luteal are phases of the menstrual cycle.

SECTION - C

49. (a) A

> **Explanation:** Mechanical barriers are devices that provide a physical barrier between the sperm and the egg. Example of mechanical barriers include the male condom, female condom, diaphragm, cervical cap and sponge. The condom is the only contraceptive method that helps to prevent Sexually Transmitted Infections (STIs).

50. (a) fertilisation

> **Explanation:** Cu-T (B) is an intrauterine copper releasing IUD. This device is inserted by doctors in the uterus through vagina. Cu^{2+} ions that are released in the uterus suppress, sperm motility and the fertilising capacity of the sperms. Thus, it prevents pregnancy by preventing fertilisation.

51. (c) Both (a) and (b)

> **Explanation:** Hormonal implants and oral contraceptives contain the combination of oestrogen and progestogen hormones. Their mode of working is same but the site of implantation and the duration of action is different.

52. (a) semen will be without sperms

> **Explanation:** Function of vasa deferentia is the conduction of sperms from testes to external genitalia. If it is disconnected, semen will be without sperms.

53. (a) only for females

> **Explanation:** Intrauterine methods are designed to be inserted into uterus through vagina. These exist only for females. There is no similar counterpart for males because the act of fertilization occurs in the female genital tract.

54. (b) progestin

> **Explanation:** LNG-20 is an IUD. However, not all IUDs release Cu^{2+} ions. LNG-20 belongs to the class of IUDs that release hormones. LNG-20 causes the release of the hormone progestin in the uterine cavity.

55. (a) Cu-T: Suppress sperm motility and its fertilizing capacity.

> **Explanation:** The given figure is that of copper Cu-T. Cu-T is a simple copper releasing IUD made of a flexible, "T" shaped piece of plastic wrapped with a thin copper containing wire. It helps the uterus and fallopian tubes to produce fluid that kills sperm. This fluid contains white blood cells, copper ions, enzymes, and prostaglandins. Copper ions prevent pregnancy by inhibiting the movement of sperm, because the copper-ion containing fluids are directly toxic to sperm. Even if an aggressive little spermatozoan fertilizes an egg, the copper ion laden environment prevents implantation of the fertilised egg, and thus pregnancy.

56. (b) Termination; A - RNA, B - RNA polymerase, C - Rho factor

> **Explanation:** In the given figure, the step shown is termination of transcription in bacteria. The label A, B and C are respectively RNA, RNA polymerase and rho factor. RNA polymerase is an enzyme that synthesizes the RNA from a DNA template during transcription. Rho factor is a termination factor which releases RNA from the DNA template.

57. (c) A-TT; B-Tt ; C-tt; D-Tt

> **Explanation:** Punnet square is a graphical representation of the possibility of genotype of all the plants.

58. (b) Pollen grains

> **Explanation:** The image is a cross section of an anther. The spots are the pollen grains. They are present within the pollen sacs. The stem like portion is called the filament. All of this constitute a stamen.

59. (c) 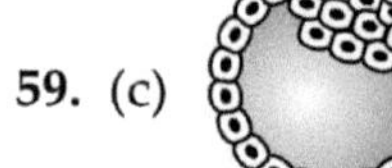

> **Explanation:** Figure [c] refers to blastocysts stage. Blastocyst is embedded in the uterine endometrium by a process called implantation and leads to pregnancy. It possesses an inner cell mass (ICM) which subsequently forms the embryo. The outer layer of the blastocyst consists of cells collectively called the trophoblast. This layer surrounds the inner cell mass and a fluid-filled cavity known as the blastocoel. The trophoblast gives rise to the placenta.

60. (a) Down's syndrome

> **Explanation:** The child is affected by Down's syndrome which is a genetic disease. This disease is caused due to trisomy of 21 chromosome.

Name of Exam : _______________________________

2021-22

OMR Response Sheet

Roll No.

1 ○ ○ ○ ○ ○ ○ ○
2 ○ ○ ○ ○ ○ ○ ○
3 ○ ○ ○ ○ ○ ○ ○
4 ○ ○ ○ ○ ○ ○ ○
5 ○ ○ ○ ○ ○ ○ ○
6 ○ ○ ○ ○ ○ ○ ○
7 ○ ○ ○ ○ ○ ○ ○
8 ○ ○ ○ ○ ○ ○ ○
9 ○ ○ ○ ○ ○ ○ ○
0 ○ ○ ○ ○ ○ ○ ○

Name _______________________________

Class & Section _______________________________

Subject _______________________________

Subject Code : ☐ ☐ ☐

Date of Exam : D D M M YYYY
☐☐/☐☐/☐☐ ☐☐

Candidate's Sign.

Invigilator's Sign.

Instructions for filling the OMR sheet :

1. Use only black blue ballpoint pen to fill the circle
2. Use of pencil is strictly prohibited
3. Circle should be designed completely and properly
4. Cutting and erasing on this sheet is not allowed

Q. No.	A	B	C	D
1.	○	○	○	○
2.	○	○	○	○
3.	○	○	○	○
4.	○	○	○	○
5.	○	○	○	○
6.	○	○	○	○
7.	○	○	○	○
8.	○	○	○	○
9.	○	○	○	○
10.	○	○	○	○
11.	○	○	○	○
12.	○	○	○	○
13.	○	○	○	○
14.	○	○	○	○
15.	○	○	○	○
16.	○	○	○	○
17.	○	○	○	○
18.	○	○	○	○
19.	○	○	○	○
20.	○	○	○	○

Q. No.	A	B	C	D
21.	○	○	○	○
22.	○	○	○	○
23.	○	○	○	○
24.	○	○	○	○
25.	○	○	○	○
26.	○	○	○	○
27.	○	○	○	○
28.	○	○	○	○
29.	○	○	○	○
30.	○	○	○	○
31.	○	○	○	○
32.	○	○	○	○
33.	○	○	○	○
34.	○	○	○	○
35.	○	○	○	○
36.	○	○	○	○
37.	○	○	○	○
38.	○	○	○	○
39.	○	○	○	○
40.	○	○	○	○

Q. No.	A	B	C	D
41.	○	○	○	○
42.	○	○	○	○
43.	○	○	○	○
44.	○	○	○	○
45.	○	○	○	○
46.	○	○	○	○
47.	○	○	○	○
48.	○	○	○	○
49.	○	○	○	○
50.	○	○	○	○
51.	○	○	○	○
52.	○	○	○	○
53.	○	○	○	○
54.	○	○	○	○
55.	○	○	○	○
56.	○	○	○	○
57.	○	○	○	○
58.	○	○	○	○
59.	○	○	○	○
60.	○	○	○	○

Name of Exam : ___________________________

2021-22

OMR Response Sheet

Roll No.

1 ○ ○ ○ ○ ○ ○ ○
2 ○ ○ ○ ○ ○ ○ ○
3 ○ ○ ○ ○ ○ ○ ○
4 ○ ○ ○ ○ ○ ○ ○
5 ○ ○ ○ ○ ○ ○ ○
6 ○ ○ ○ ○ ○ ○ ○
7 ○ ○ ○ ○ ○ ○ ○
8 ○ ○ ○ ○ ○ ○ ○
9 ○ ○ ○ ○ ○ ○ ○
0 ○ ○ ○ ○ ○ ○ ○

Name ___________________________

Class & Section ___________________________

Subject ___________________________

Subject Code : | | | |

Date of Exam : D D M M   YYYY
□□/□□/□□□□

Candidate's Sign.

Invigilator's Sign.

Instructions for filling the OMR sheet :

1. Use only black blue ballpoint pen to fill the circle
2. Use of pencil is strictly prohibited
3. Circle should be designed completely and properly
4. Cutting and erasing on this sheet is not allowed

Q. No.	A	B	C	D
1.	○	○	○	○
2.	○	○	○	○
3.	○	○	○	○
4.	○	○	○	○
5.	○	○	○	○
6.	○	○	○	○
7.	○	○	○	○
8.	○	○	○	○
9.	○	○	○	○
10.	○	○	○	○
11.	○	○	○	○
12.	○	○	○	○
13.	○	○	○	○
14.	○	○	○	○
15.	○	○	○	○
16.	○	○	○	○
17.	○	○	○	○
18.	○	○	○	○
19.	○	○	○	○
20.	○	○	○	○

Q. No.	A	B	C	D
21.	○	○	○	○
22.	○	○	○	○
23.	○	○	○	○
24.	○	○	○	○
25.	○	○	○	○
26.	○	○	○	○
27.	○	○	○	○
28.	○	○	○	○
29.	○	○	○	○
30.	○	○	○	○
31.	○	○	○	○
32.	○	○	○	○
33.	○	○	○	○
34.	○	○	○	○
35.	○	○	○	○
36.	○	○	○	○
37.	○	○	○	○
38.	○	○	○	○
39.	○	○	○	○
40.	○	○	○	○

Q. No.	A	B	C	D
41.	○	○	○	○
42.	○	○	○	○
43.	○	○	○	○
44.	○	○	○	○
45.	○	○	○	○
46.	○	○	○	○
47.	○	○	○	○
48.	○	○	○	○
49.	○	○	○	○
50.	○	○	○	○
51.	○	○	○	○
52.	○	○	○	○
53.	○	○	○	○
54.	○	○	○	○
55.	○	○	○	○
56.	○	○	○	○
57.	○	○	○	○
58.	○	○	○	○
59.	○	○	○	○
60.	○	○	○	○

Name of Exam : _______________________

2021-22

OMR Response Sheet

Roll No.

| Name _______________________ |

Class & Section _______________________

Subject _______________________

Subject Code :

Date of Exam : D D   M M   YYYY
□□ / □□ / □□ □□

Candidate's Sign.

Invigilator's Sign.

Instructions for filling the OMR sheet :

1. Use only black blue ballpoint pen to fill the circle
2. Use of pencil is strictly prohibited
3. Circle should be designed completely and properly
4. Cutting and erasing on this sheet is not allowed

Q. No.	A	B	C	D
1.	○	○	○	○
2.	○	○	○	○
3.	○	○	○	○
4.	○	○	○	○
5.	○	○	○	○
6.	○	○	○	○
7.	○	○	○	○
8.	○	○	○	○
9.	○	○	○	○
10.	○	○	○	○
11.	○	○	○	○
12.	○	○	○	○
13.	○	○	○	○
14.	○	○	○	○
15.	○	○	○	○
16.	○	○	○	○
17.	○	○	○	○
18.	○	○	○	○
19.	○	○	○	○
20.	○	○	○	○

Q. No.	A	B	C	D
21.	○	○	○	○
22.	○	○	○	○
23.	○	○	○	○
24.	○	○	○	○
25.	○	○	○	○
26.	○	○	○	○
27.	○	○	○	○
28.	○	○	○	○
29.	○	○	○	○
30.	○	○	○	○
31.	○	○	○	○
32.	○	○	○	○
33.	○	○	○	○
34.	○	○	○	○
35.	○	○	○	○
36.	○	○	○	○
37.	○	○	○	○
38.	○	○	○	○
39.	○	○	○	○
40.	○	○	○	○

Q. No.	A	B	C	D
41.	○	○	○	○
42.	○	○	○	○
43.	○	○	○	○
44.	○	○	○	○
45.	○	○	○	○
46.	○	○	○	○
47.	○	○	○	○
48.	○	○	○	○
49.	○	○	○	○
50.	○	○	○	○
51.	○	○	○	○
52.	○	○	○	○
53.	○	○	○	○
54.	○	○	○	○
55.	○	○	○	○
56.	○	○	○	○
57.	○	○	○	○
58.	○	○	○	○
59.	○	○	○	○
60.	○	○	○	○

Printed by Libri Plureos GmbH in Hamburg,
Germany